T&T CLARK HANDBOOK OF PUBLIC THEOLOGY

Forthcoming titles in this series include

T&T Clark Handbook of Christology, *edited by Darren O. Sumner and Chris Tilling*
T&T Clark Handbook of Election, *edited by Edwin Chr. van Driel*
T&T Clark Handbook of Modern Theology, *edited by Philip G. Ziegler and R. David Nelson*
T&T Clark Handbook of the Doctrine of Creation, *edited by Jason Goroncy*
T&T Clark Introduction to Asian American Christian Ethics, *edited by Grace Yia-Hei Kao*
T&T Clark Handbook of Theology and the Arts, *edited by Imogen Adkins and Stephen M. Garrett*
T&T Clark Handbook of Intercultural Theology and Mission Studies, *edited by John G. Flett and Dorottya Nagy*
T&T Clark Handbook of Biblical Thomism, *edited by Matthew Levering, Piotr Roszak and Jörgen Vijgen*

Titles already published include

T&T Clark Handbook of Christian Theology and Climate Change, *edited by Ernst M. Conradie and Hilda P. Koster*
T&T Clark Handbook of Political Theology, *edited by Rubén Rosario Rodríguez*
T&T Clark Handbook of Pneumatology, *edited by Daniel Castelo and Kenneth M. Loyer*
T&T Clark Handbook of Ecclesiology, *edited by Kimlyn J. Bender and D. Stephen Long*
T&T Clark Handbook of Christian Theology and the Modern Sciences, *edited by John P. Slattery*
T&T Clark Handbook of Christian Ethics, *edited by Tobias Winright*
T&T Clark Handbook of John Owen, *edited by Crawford Gribben and John W. Tweeddale*
T&T Clark Handbook of Theological Anthropology, *edited by Mary Ann Hinsdale and Stephen Okey*

T&T CLARK HANDBOOK OF PUBLIC THEOLOGY

Edited by
Christoph Hübenthal and Christiane Alpers

LONDON • NEW YORK • OXFORD • NEW DELHI • SYDNEY

T&T CLARK
Bloomsbury Publishing Plc
50 Bedford Square, London, WC1B 3DP, UK
1385 Broadway, New York, NY 10018, USA
29 Earlsfort Terrace, Dublin 2, Ireland

BLOOMSBURY, T&T CLARK and the T&T Clark logo are trademarks of
Bloomsbury Publishing Plc

First published in Great Britain 2022
Paperback edition published 2024

Copyright © Christoph Hübenthal, Christiane Alpers and contributors, 2022

Christoph Hübenthal and Christiane Alpers have asserted their right under the Copyright,
Designs and Patents Act, 1988, to be identified as Editors of this work.

Cover image: EyeEm / Alamy Stock Photo

All rights reserved. No part of this publication may be reproduced or transmitted in
any form or by any means, electronic or mechanical, including photocopying,
recording, or any information storage or retrieval system, without prior
permission in writing from the publishers.

Bloomsbury Publishing Plc does not have any control over, or responsibility for, any
third-party websites referred to or in this book. All internet addresses given in this book
were correct at the time of going to press. The author and publisher regret any
inconvenience caused if addresses have changed or sites have ceased to
exist, but can accept no responsibility for any such changes.

A catalogue record for this book is available from the British Library.

Library of Congress Cataloging-in-Publication Data
Names: Hübenthal, Christoph, editor. | Alpers, Christiane, editor.
Title: T&T Clark handbook of public theology / edited by Christoph Hübenthal and
Christiane Alpers.
Description: London ; New York : T&T Clark, 2022. | Series: T&T Clark handbooks |
Includes bibliographical references and index. |
Identifiers: LCCN 2021056295 (print) | LCCN 2021056296 (ebook) | ISBN 9780567692153
(hardback) | ISBN 9780567707048 (paperback) | ISBN 9780567692160 (pdf) |
ISBN 9780567692177 (epub)
Subjects: LCSH: Public theology.
Classification: LCC BT83.63 .T155 2022 (print) | LCC BT83.63 (ebook) |
DDC 230–dc23/eng/20220207
LC record available at https://lccn.loc.gov/2021056295
LC ebook record available at https://lccn.loc.gov/2021056296

ISBN: HB: 978-0-5676-9215-3
PB: 978-0-5677-0704-8
ePDF: 978-0-5676-9216-0
eBook: 978-0-5676-9217-7

Series: T&T Clark Handbooks

Typeset by Deanta Global Publishing Services, Chennai, India

To find out more about our authors and books visit www.bloomsbury.com and
sign up for our newsletters.

CONTENTS

LIST OF CONTRIBUTORS — ix

Introduction — 1
Christoph Hübenthal and Christiane Alpers

Part I Conditions and self-positioning

1. The public sphere — 13
   Maureen Junker-Kenny

2. Liberal democracy — 33
   Hans-Martien ten Napel

3. The secular — 48
   Christoph Hübenthal

4. Post-secularity and the pluralization of public theology — 69
   William Barbieri

5. The distinction of public theology from political and liberation theologies — 86
   Gaspar Martinez

6. Public theology as apologetics — 107
   Elaine Graham

Part II The ecumenical scope of public theology

7 The legacy of theological liberalism: A ghost in public theology 127
   Ulrich Schmiedel

8 Public theology in the Catholic tradition 147
   Katie Dunne

9 A public Orthodox theology 164
   Aristotle Papanikolaou

10 Post-liberal positions in public theology 179
    Ben Fulford

11 Ecumenical collaboration in public theology 200
    Florian Höhne

12 Relations to other religions 221
    Manfred L. Pirner

Part III Theological tenets in public theology

13 Public theology and social ethics 247
    Hak Joon Lee

14 Public theology and the doctrine of God 265
    Anne Siebesma

15 A Black soteriological dialogue with public theology 283
    Reggie Nel

16 Public theology and ecclesiology 301
    Al Barrett

17 Liturgy and public theology 320
    Catherine Pickstock

18 Public eschatology: Seeking hope in a world of despair 339
    Mary Doak

Part IV Challenges for public theology

19 Politics 359
    Amy Daughton

20	Race, gender and public theology *Brian Bantum*	380
21	Public theology and culture *Graeme Smith*	396
22	Economics *Devin Singh*	414
23	Ecological theology as a public theology *Hilda P. Koster*	432
24	Challenges for public theology: Sports *Dries Vanysacker*	448

Part V The international scope of public theology

25	Africa *Dion A. Forster*	469
26	Public theology in Asia *Alexander Chow*	489
27	Public theology in Australia *Robert Gascoigne*	503
28	Public theology in Europe: Towards a performative-political approach *Martin Kirschner*	521
29	Public theology in North America: Commonality amid plurality *Nicholas Hayes-Mota*	538
30	Public theology in Latin America *Eneida Jacobsen*	556

INDEX   571

CONTRIBUTORS

Christiane Alpers works in a home for people with psychiatric illnesses in Berlin. Before, she was a research and teaching fellow at the Catholic University of Eichstätt-Ingolstadt's faculty of theology. Her research focuses on twentieth-century Catholic theology and contemporary public and political theologies. In 2017, she earned her PhD on Edward Schillebeeckx's Christology and public theology from Radboud University Nijmegen and KU Leuven, a version of which has been published as *A Politics of Grace: Hope for Redemption in a Post-Christendom Context* (2018). She more recently published 'Christ and Grace', in *T&T Clark Handbook of Edward Schillebeeckx* (2019): 299–311; 'The End of Kenotic Suffering: The Centrality of God's Love of Sinners in Schillebeeckx's and Balthasar's Soteriologies', *Studies in Spirituality* 29 (2019): 333–53; 'Gott und Mensch in der Öffentlichkeit. Zur Sakramentalität des Säkularen', *Ethik und Gesellschaft* (2019); 'De zichtbare heiligheid van de kerk: Een onvolmaakt teken van onzichtbare genadegaven', *Tijdschrift voor Theologie* 59 (2019): 356–71; 'Bekehrende Begegnung von Kirche und Welt: De Lubac und Schillebeeckx im Gespräch', *Geist und Leben: Zeitschrift für christliche Spiritualität* 92 (2019): 152–61; and with Martin Kirschner, 'Zur Relevanz asketischer Theologie: Sarah Coakley und Erich Przywara SJ', *Geist und Leben* 93 (2020): 226–35.

Brian Bantum (PhD, Duke University) holds the Neil F. and Ila A. Fisher Chair of Theology at Garrett-Evangelical Theological Seminary in Evanston (Illinois). His research interests comprise Christology, theological anthropology, identity, race, mixed-race, art and theological method, critical theory, cultural studies and baptism. Among his publications are *The Death of Race: Building a New Christianity in a Racial World* (2016) and *Redeeming Mulatto: A Theology of Race and Christian Hybridity* (2010).

William Barbieri is Professor of theology and religious studies at the Catholic University of America, where he teaches in the religion and culture and moral theology/ethics academic areas. There he also directs the McLean Center for the Study of Culture and Values and the Peace and Justice Studies Programme. In addition to his monographs *Ethics of Citizenship: Immigration and Group Rights in Germany* (1998) and *Constitutive Justice* (2015), he has edited *From Just War to Modern Peace Ethics* (with Heinz-Gerhard Justenhoven; 2012) and *At the Limits of the Secular: Reflections on Faith and Public Life* (2014). His research includes publications in the areas of human rights, comparative ethics, peace studies, Catholic social teaching and German studies. Current projects of his concern the historicity of morals and ecological ethics. He holds a doctorate in religious studies from Yale University.

Al Barrett is a priest in the Church of England and Rector of Hodge Hill Church in Birmingham, UK. Al has been an honorary research fellow with the Queen's Foundation for Ecumenical Theological Education since 2017, when he completed his doctorate in political theology with the VU University of Amsterdam. He has published articles and book chapters in practical, political and liturgical theology, with particular attention to issues of gender, class and race. He is the author of two books: *Interrupting the Church's Flow: A Radically Receptive Political Theology in the Urban Margins* (2020) and – co-authored with Ruth Harley – *Being Interrupted: Re-imagining the Church's Mission from the Outside, In* (2020).

Alexander Chow is a Chinese American, born and raised in Southern California. He is Senior Lecturer in theology and world christianity in the School of Divinity, University of Edinburgh, and is co-director of the Centre for the Study of World Christianity. Before Edinburgh, he completed his PhD in theology at the University of Birmingham and worked as a postdoctoral fellow at the Renmin University of China. He is co-editor of the journal *Studies in World Christianity* and editor of the Liu Institute Series in Chinese Christianities. He is the author or editor of a number of books, including *Chinese Public Theology: Generational Shifts and Confucian Imagination in Chinese Christianity* (2018) and *Ecclesial Diversity in Chinese Christianity* (co-edited with Easten Law; 2021).

Amy Daughton is Lecturer in practical theology at the Department of Theology and Religion at the University of Birmingham, where she is also currently the Head of Department and Director of the doctoral programme in practical theology. Her research is situated at intersections of theology, politics and practice and is ultimately concerned with questions of the moral life and the contributions of theology in a plural society. A particular emphasis is on the philosophy of Paul Ricoeur, especially the centrality of the ethical relationships between self, other and institutions. Significant recent publications include extensive work on Paul Ricoeur and intercultural hermeneutics in conversation with Thomas Aquinas in her book *With and for Others: Developing Ricoeur's Ethics of Self Using Aquinas's Language of Analogy* (2016), and she co-edited the *T&T Clark Reader in Political Theology* (2021).

Mary Doak (PhD, the University of Chicago) is Professor of theology at the University of San Diego, where she has taught since 2007. Her recent publications include *A Prophetic Public Church: Witness to Hope Amid the Global Crises of the 21st Century* (2020) and *Divine Harmony: Seeking Community in a Broken World* (2017), along with other books and articles on public theology, ecclesiology and eschatology. She had the honour of serving as president of the College Theology Society from 2019 to 2021 and as president of the American Theological Society (Midwest) from 2007 to 2008.

Katie Dunne is a lecturer in religious education in St Angela's College, a college of the National University of Ireland, Galway. She holds a PhD in Theology alongside MTh and BATh degrees from St Patrick's Pontifical University, Maynooth. Prior to joining the faculty at St Angela's College, she was Assistant Professor in theology in the school or religion, Trinity College, Dublin. Her research interests include development ethics, feminist theologies, Catholic social teaching, narrative theology and post-holocaust political theologies. She has published articles on the capability approach to human development and on narrative theology. Her current research examines gender inequality in Catholic social teaching and can be found in *The Promotion of Integral Human Development: Catholic Social Teaching and the Capability Approach* (2022).

Dion A. Forster is a professor in systematic theology and ethics, focusing on public theology. He serves as the director of the Beyers Naudé Centre for Public Theology and the chair of the Department of Systematic Theology and Ecclesiology at the University of Stellenbosch. He holds a PhD in systematic theology (2006) and a PhD in New Testament (2017). His most recent books are *African Public Theology* (edited with Sunday Agang and H Jurgens Hendriks; 2020) and *The (Im)possibility of Forgiveness?* (2019). He is a research fellow at Wesley House, University of Cambridge, and the Allan Gray Centre for Values Based Leadership, Graduate School of Business, University of Cape Town. He serves as a member of the World Economic Forum's Expert Network and a member of the G20's Interfaith anti-racism policy team.

Ben Fulford is Senior Lecturer in systematic theology in the Department of Theology and Religious Studies at the University of Chester. He did his doctoral studies at the University of Cambridge. His research interests include early Christian and modern theology, Gregory of Nazianzus and the Cappadocians, Hans Frei and postliberal theologies, the theological interpretation of Scripture, theological anthropology and political theology. He is the author of *Divine Eloquence and Human Transformation: Rethinking Scripture and History Through Gregory of Nazianzus and Hans Frei* (2013) and *God's Patience and Our Work: Hans Frei, Generous Orthodoxy and the Ethics of Hope* (forthcoming).

Robert Gascoigne is an emeritus professor of the School of Theology of Australian Catholic University. He is a past president of the Australian Catholic Theological

Association and was an Australian representative on the Asian regional committee of the Catholic Theological Ethics in the World Church network (2012–18). He is the author of a number of publications on Christian faith and contemporary society including *The Public Forum and Christian Ethics* (2001) and *The Church and Secularity: Two Stories of Liberal Society* (2009), as well as of *Freedom and Purpose: An Introduction to Christian Ethics* (2004).

Elaine Graham was Grosvenor Research Professor of Practical Theology at the University of Chester from 2009 until her retirement in July 2021. She now holds the title of Professor Emerita. She was educated at the Universities of Bristol and Manchester. Between 1998 and 2009 she was Samuel Ferguson Professor of Social and Pastoral Theology at the University of Manchester. She is the author of several major books, including *Transforming Practice: Pastoral Theology in a Time of Uncertainty* (1996), *Representations of the Post-Human* (2002) and *Words Made Flesh: Writings in Pastoral and Practical Theology* (2009); with Heather Walton and Frances Ward, *Theological Reflection: Methods*, second edition (2019); and with Zoe Bennett, Stephen Pattison and Heather Walton, *Invitation to Practical Theology Research* (2018). Her most recent work considers public theology as a form of Christian apologetics: *Between a Rock and a Hard Place: Public Theology in a Post-Secular Age* (2013) and *Apologetics without Apology: Speaking of God in a World Troubled by Religion* (2017). Her current research interests include an examination of the life, thought and legacy of the Cambridge philosopher and theologian Don Cupitt, as well as continued interest in public theology and post-secularity. In July 2021 she was elected a fellow of the British Academy.

Nicholas Hayes-Mota is a PhD candidate and teaching fellow in theological ethics at Boston College. His dissertation examines the possibility of a 'politics of the common good' within a pluralistic and divided society and draws on faith-based community organizing and Catholic social thought to propose a constructive way forward. More broadly, his research explores the connection between moral and political agency; the public role of religion in contemporary liberal democracies; and the relationship between public, political and liberation theologies. His work has been published in *Ecumenical Trends* and *Syndicate*. In addition to his research and teaching, Nicholas serves as a trainer in public narrative and community organizing with the Leading Change Network (LCN). He received his AB from Harvard College and his MDiv from Harvard Divinity School.

Florian Höhne is a 'Wissenschaftlicher Mitarbeiter' (research associate/assistant lecturer) at the chair for systematic theology (ethics and hermeneutics) and the Berlin Institute for Public Theology (BIPT) at Humboldt-Universität zu Berlin. He worked as a journalist and is an ordained minister in the Lutheran Church of Bavaria. His research focuses on public theology, ethics of digitization, media ethics and ethics of responsibilty. His publications include *Öffentliche Theologie: Begriffsgeschichte und Grundfragen* (Öffentliche Theologie 31) (2015) or 'On Doing Public Theology: Reflections Towards a More Public Praxis', in Matthew

Ryan Robinson and Inja Inderst (eds), *What Does Theology Do, Actually? Observing Theology and the Transcultural* (2020), 195–210. Together with Torsten Meireis, he edited the volume: *Religion and Neo-Nationalism in Europe* (ethik und gesellschaft 7), (2020).

Christoph Hübenthal is Professor of systematic theology at Radboud University Nijmegen and Director of the Center for Catholic Studies there. He received his PhD from the University of Tübingen (1996), where he also habilitated in 2006. Among his publications are *Substanz, System, Struktur: Zur theologisch-ethischen Relevanz der Strukturphänomenologie Heinrich Rombachs* (1997) and *Grundlegung der Christlichen Sozialethik: Versuch eines freiheitsanalytisch-handlungsreflexiven Ansatzes* (2006). He also co-edited *Lexikon der Ethik* (2005), *Handbuch Ethik* (2012, third edition) and *Sport & Christianity: A Sign of the Time in the Light of Faith* (2012). His continuing interest in public theology is documented not only by the present volume but also by noumerous journal articles and book chapters on the subject.

Eneida Jacobsen holds doctoral and master's degrees in theology from Faculdades EST (former Escola Superior de Teología), Brazil, and a master's degree in philosophy from Villanova University, United States. At Villanova University, Jacobsen is currently pursuing a doctoral degree in philosophy while teaching philosophy as an adjunct professor. She authored *Theologie und politische Theorie: Kritische Annäherungen zwischen zeitgenössischen theologischen Strömungen und dem politischen Denken von Jürgen Habermas* (2018) and co-edited *Public Theology in Brazil: Social and Cultural Challenges* (2013).

Maureen Junker-Kenny has recently retired as Professor in theology and Fellow of Trinity College Dublin. Having studied at the Universities of Tübingen, Trinity College Dublin, the Milltown Institute of Philosophy and Theology, and Münster, she did MAs (Staatsexamen) in English, Catholic theology and philosophy. Her doctoral thesis (1989) treated F. Schleiermacher's Christology and theory of religion, her Habilitation (1996) the reception and critique of J. Habermas's discourse ethics. She was a lecturer in Tübingen (1985–93) before coming to Trinity College Dublin (1993–2021), where she served as Head of Department (1997–2000; 2012–18) and as Head of the Confederal School of Religions, Theology and Ecumenics (2011–13). Her publications include *Religion and Public Reason: A Comparison of the Positions of J. Rawls, J. Habermas and P. Ricoeur* (2014); *Approaches to Theological Ethics. Sources, Traditions, Visions* (2019); (co-edited with K. Viertbauer) *European Journal of Philosophy of Religion*, Special Issue 2019, 'Habermas on Religion'; *Self, Christ and God in Schleiermacher's Dogmatics. A Theology Reconceived for Modernity* (2020); *'The Bold Arcs of Salvation History'. Faith and Reason in Jürgen Habermas's Reconstruction of the Roots of European Thinking* (2022). Her research interests are religion and public reason; philosophy of religion, hermeneutics and theology in modernity; and biomedical ethics.

Martin Kirschner holds the chair for Theology in Transformational Processes and is Director of the KU Center for Religion, Church and Society in Transformation (ZRKG) at the Catholic University of Eichstätt-Ingolstadt. After studying Catholic theology and political sciences in Trier and Tübingen, he received his doctorate in 2005 in Tübingen. He was a research assistant of Peter Hünermann (2001–6), then assistant (2006–12) and private lecturer (2012–16) at the chair of dogmatics at the University of Tübingen. His Habilitation in 2011 was on theological rationality in Anselm of Canterbury. In 2016 he established the new Chair for Theology in Transformational Processes founded by the Heisenberg-Programme of the 'Deutsche Forschungsgemeinschaft' (DFG). His main research interests include the doctrine of God and ecclesiology, theological rationality and epistemology, political and public theology, transformation and liberation theologies, Second Vatican Council. Among his publications are: *Gotteszeugnis in der Spätmoderne: Theologische und sozialwissenschaftliche Reflexionen zur Sozialgestalt der katholischen Kirche* (2006); *Gott – größer als gedacht. Die Transformation der Vernunft aus der Begegnung mit Gott bei Anselm von Canterbury* (2013); (editor with K. Ruhstorfer) *Die gegenwärtige Krise Europas. Theologische Antwortversuche* (2018); (editor with R. Nate) *Europa - Krisen, Vergewisserungen, Visionen. Interdisziplinäre Annäherungen* (transcript 2019) 9–32; (editor) *Subversiver Messianismus. Interdisziplinäre Agamben-Lektüren* (2020).

Hilda P. Koster is the Sisters of St Joseph Associate Professor of Ecological Theology and the director of the Elliott Allen Institute for Theology and Ecology at the University of St. Michael's College in the University of Toronto. A native of the Netherlands, she received a BA and MDiv from the University of Groningen, a ThM from Princeton Theological Seminary and earned her doctorate from the Divinity School of the University of Chicago. Dr Koster's research focuses on eco-feminist theology, climate justice and resource extraction. Her publications have appeared in *Theology Today, Modern Theology, The Journal of Religion, The Anglican Theological Review* and *Scriptura*. She co-edited/authored *The Gift of Theology: The Contribution of Kathryn Tanner* (2015) with Rosemary Carbine; *Planetary Solidarity: Global Women's Voices on Christian Doctrine and Climate Justice* (2017) with Grace Ji-Sun Kim; *The T&T Clark Handbook of Christian Theology and Climate Change* (2019) with Ernst M. Conradie and *Solidarity with Earth: A Multi-Disciplinary Theological Engagement with Gender and Resource Extraction* (forthcoming in 2022). Dr Koster is also the co-editor of the T&T Clark book series *Explorations in Theology, Gender and Ecology*.

Hak Joon Lee is Lewis B. Smedes Professor of Christian Ethics at Fuller Theological Seminary. Lee's research focuses on covenant ethics, public theology, global ethics, and Asian American theology and ethics. He has also centred much of his attention on the ethics and spirituality of Martin Luther King Jr. and has been invited to be the keynote speaker for Martin Luther King Jr. Day celebrations in several cities. Lee has published several monographs, including *God and Community Organizing: A Covenantal Approach* (2020), *The Great World House: Martin Luther King Jr.*

and Global Ethics (2011), *We Will Get to the Promised Land: Martin Luther King Jr.'s Communal-Political Spirituality* (2006) and *Covenant and Communication: A Christian Moral Conversation with Jürgen Habermas* (2006). Most recently, *Christian Ethics: A New Covenant Model* (2021), an innovative methodology of Christian ethics based on the New Covenant of Jesus, was published. With his passion for church renewal, Lee has edited several culturally engaging curricula for youth, parents and pastors. He enjoys hiking, travelling and fellowship over meals with his friends and students.

Gaspar Martinez is a Catholic priest of the Diocese of Bilbao. After getting his Licenciate in economics and business management from the University of Basque Country (1974) and completing further managerial studies at London Business School (Sloan Fellow 1988), he earned a PhD in theology from the Divinity School of the University of Chicago (1997). He is currently Fellow of the Instituto Diocesano de Teología y Pastoral (Bilbao) and Professor Emeritus of Dogmatics and Spiritual Theology of the Facultad de Teología de Vitoria. His research interests include contextual theology, religion and culture, church and society, and spirituality. He is the author of the book *Confronting the Mystery of God: Political, Liberation, and Public Theologies* (2001) and of the article 'Liberation and Political Theologies', in *The Cambridge Companion to Karl Rahner* (2005). He has published several articles in different reviews and periodicals.

Hans-Martien ten Napel, PhD, is an associate professor of constitutional and administrative law at Leiden University. During the 2014–15 academic year, he served as a research fellow in legal studies at the Center of Theological Inquiry in Princeton, NJ. As a fruit of the fellowship, in 2017, he published the monograph *Constitutionalism, Democracy and Religious Freedom. To Be Fully Human* (2017). Most recently, he also co-edited and co-authored the volumes *The Powers That Be: Rethinking the Separation of Powers* (2016), *Een nieuwe politieke formule. Ideeën voor staat en samenleving geïnspireerd door Alexis de Tocqueville* (A new political formula. Ideas for state and society inspired by Alexis de Tocqueville) (2021) and *Het radicale midden overzee. Verkenningen van het postliberalisme* (The radical middle overseas. Explorations of postliberalism) (2021). Since 2015 he has been part of the editorial board of the *Tijdschrift voor Religie, Recht en Beleid* (*The Journal for Religion, Law and Policy*). Since 2021, he has also been a senior fellow at the Center for Religion, Culture and Democracy in Plano, TX. He serves on the Executive Editorial Council of the *Journal of Religion, Culture & Democracy*.

Reggie Nel is Dean at the Faculty of Theology at Stellenbosch University and Professor in the Department of Practical Theology and Missiology, with a special interest in the interplay between missiology, anti-racism, postcolonial theories and youth movements. He also serves on the Executive Committee of the International Association for Mission Studies (IAMS) and previously on the Executive Committee of the International Association for the study of Youth Ministry. He was formerly the editor of *Missionalia: The Journal of the Southern African Missiological Society* until his move to Stellenbosch University in 2017. He completed his doctorate in 2013, under the supervision of Professor Klippies Kritzinger with the title, 'Discerning an African Missional Ecclesiology in Dialogue with Two Uniting Youth Movements'. His most recent chapter is entitled, 'Keep Yourself Busy: Young People, Faith-Based Organisations and Social Cohesion in Riverlea', in the book *Stuck in the Margins? Young People and Faith-based Organisations in South Africa and Nordic Localities*, Ignatius Swart et al. (2022). He also ministers at the Vlottenburg congregation of the Uniting Reformed Church in Southern Africa (URCSA) and serves on the Congregational Ministries Taskteam of the Regional Synod.

Aristotle Papanikolaou is Professor of theology, the archbishop Demetrios Chair of Orthodox Theology and Culture and the co-director of the Orthodox Christian Studies Center at Fordham University. He is also Senior Fellow at the Emory University Center for the Study of Law and Religion. In 2012, he received the Award for Excellence in Undergraduate Teaching in the Humanities. Among his numerous publications, he is the author of *Being with God: Trinity, Apophaticism, and Divine-Human Communion* (2006) and *The Mystical as Political: Democracy and Non-Radical Orthodoxy* (2012). He is also co-editor of *Political Theologies in Orthodox Christianity* (2017), *Fundamentalism or Tradition: Christianity after Secularism* (2020), *Christianity, Democracy and the Shadow of Constantine* (2017) (Winner of 2017 Alpha Sigma Nu Award in Theology), *Orthodox Constructions of the West, Orthodox Readings of Augustine* (2008) and *Thinking Through Faith: New Perspectives from Orthodox Christian Scholars* (2004). He enjoys Russian literature, Byzantine and Greek music and is a bit of a foodie.

Catherine Pickstock (PhD, University of Cambridge) is the Norris-Hulse Professor of divinity at the University of Cambridge. She is one of the founding figures of the radical orthodox movement. Her research is concerned with the relationship between theology and philosophy and of both to language, poetics and the history of ideas. Among her many publications are *After Writing: On the Liturgical Consummation of Philosophy* (1997), *Repetition and Identity: The Literary Agenda* (2013) and *Aspects of Truth: A New Religious Metaphysics* (2020).

Manfred L. Pirner is Ordinary Professor of religious education at Friedrich-Alexander-University Erlangen-Nürnberg, Germany; Director of the Research Unit for Public Religion and Education (RUPRE); Co-director of the Competence Centre for School Development and Evaluation (KSE); founding member of the Centre for Human Rights Erlangen-Nürnberg (CHREN); associated member of the Bavarian Research Center for Interreligious Discourses (BaFID). Pirner's main research fields are public theology and public education; human rights, education and religion; refugees and religion; religiosity and professionalism of teachers; popular culture, digital media and religious education; faith-based schools; and content- and language-integrated learning (CLIL) in religious education. His recent publications are M. L. Pirner et al. (eds.), *Public Theology Perspectives on Religion and Education* (2019); M. L. Pirner et al. (eds.), *Public Theology, Religious*

Diversity, and Interreligious Learning: Contributing to the Common Good through Religious Education (2018); M. L. Pirner, J. Lähnemann & H. Bielefeldt (eds.), *Human Rights and Religion in Educational Contexts* (2016).

Ulrich Schmiedel is Lecturer in theology, politics and ethics in the School of Divinity, University of Edinburgh. The deputy director of Edinburgh's Centre for Theology and Public Issues, he has published widely on public and political theology. He is the author of *Elasticized Ecclesiology: The Concept of Community after Ernst Troeltsch* (2017) and *Terror und Theologie: Der religionstheoretische Diskurs der 9/11-Dekade* (2021), as well as the co-author of *The Claim to Christianity: Responding to the Far Right* (2020), written with Hanna Strømmen. Currently, he leads the international and interdisciplinary project 'Public Theology in the Post-Migrant Society: The Role of Religion in Multi-Faith Refugee Relief' in cooperation with A World of Neighbours, Europe's largest multi-faith refugee relief network.

Anne Siebesma is a PhD candidate in theology at Radboud University Nijmegen. She studied theology at Radboud University Nijmegen and KU Leuven. She has published in *Tijdschrift voor Theologie*, presented at various international conferences, and is co-editor of *Zoals de Vader mij gezonden heeft, zo zend ik u. Apostelen: De kerk in beweging* (2019). She has also been secretary of the Edward Schillebeeckx Foundation. Her research interests are in sacramental theology, ecclesiology and political theology.

Devin Singh (PhD, Yale) is Associate Professor of religion at Dartmouth College and faculty associate in Dartmouth's Consortium of Studies in Race, Migration and Sexuality. He teaches courses on modern religious thought in the West, social ethics, philosophy of religion and the relations among religion, economics and politics. Singh is the author of *Divine Currency: The Theological Power of Money in the West* (2018), co-editor of *Reimagining Leadership on the Commons* (2021) and author of articles in *Journal of Religious Ethics, Harvard Theological Review, Scottish Journal of Theology, Implicit Religion, Political Theology, Religions* and *Telos*. He is currently completing a book on the relation of Christian thought to economy and a book on religion and debt.

Graeme Smith is Professor of Public Theology at the University of Chichester. He has published two books, *Oxford 1937: The Universal Christian Council for Life and Work Conference* (2004) and *A Short History of Secularism* (2008). He has edited volumes on Christian Mission in Western society and the European refugee crisis. He has written numerous articles on issues and questions in social, political and cultural theology, in particular exploring the Christian commitment of UK political leaders such as Margaret Thatcher and Tony Blair. He founded the journal *Political Theology* and was its editor for fifteen years. He is currently completing a major project on port chaplaincy and beginning a new project examining the work of the philosopher and theologian Don Cupitt. This examines questions of radical theology in a postmodern age.

Dries Vanysacker obtained his PhD in the arts and philosophy at the KU Leuven in 1992, with a dissertation on Cardinal Giuseppe Garampi (1725–92). Since October 2011, he has been Professor at the Faculty of Theology and Religious Studies, KU Leuven, and member of the Research Unit History of Church and Theology. Since January 2021 he has been the academic secretary of the *Revue d'histoire ecclésiastique. Louvain Journal of Church History*. As an associate professor he teaches on 'History of Mission and Evangelization', 'General History of Church and Theology (all time-periods)' and several methodology courses within the Faculty of Theology and Religious Studies and on 'Religions in Europe: Structures and Cultures' at the Faculty of Arts (History). He has published on the history of witchcraft and magic during the early modern period, on the church history of the eighteenth century and on the contemporary history of missions and on sport. For the moment he especially concentrates on the relationship between Christianity and sport. His latest publication *Katholicisme en sport in de Lage Landen (19de eeuw – heden): een moeilijk evenwicht* (2021) studies the history of Catholicism and sport in the Low Countries from the nineteenth century until today in an European context.

Introduction

CHRISTOPH HÜBENTHAL AND CHRISTIANE ALPERS

Usually, the appearance of survey works on a particular academic discipline as handbooks, manuals or companions indicates that the field in question has reached a certain level of repletion. The involved experts know what the discipline is about, the topics, research methods and standards for the production of novel insights have been established and a common body of knowledge has been developed. The essential content of the discipline can be communicated to a wider public through the aforementioned media. The publication of a handbook normally witnesses to a high level of disciplinary *consolidation*. Cynics, however, hold that such consolidation often goes along with an unhealthy *saturation*. As soon as a common body of knowledge can be seized in a handbook, they assert, a discipline has already lost its inner momentum and vitality. The exiting years of discovering unknown challenges, generating fresh vocabularies, inventing new research perspectives or sampling competing approaches are over, and the professionals have moved on to business as usual. A handbook, so the malicious commentary goes, serves more as a mausoleum than as a stimulus to initiate further developments.

Now, such observations may be true for other academic fields, but not for public theology. Since the coining of the term by Martin Marty in 1974, the discipline has experienced a tremendous proliferation, and it seems very unlikely that this will end in the near future. If there is a centre of public theology, its evolution over the past five decades exhibits rather a centrifugal than a centripetal direction. The discipline expands, reaches out into undiscovered territories and explores new nomenclatures, methods and forms of thought. Sure, with the foundation of the Global Network for Public Theology and the launching of the *International Journal of Public Theology* in 2007, the discipline has gained a firm institutional platform and a highly esteemed medium of publication. Fortunately, these devices were never meant to pretend unity, let alone to confine the discourse. On the contrary, already a quick survey of the journal's articles, as well as of the network's three annual meetings, shows how diverse and varied the debates are. The countless books, anthologies, papers and conference proceedings that engage with public theology, too, give evidence to this variety. Moreover, 'public theology' denotes a wide range of activities, initiatives and enterprises that not only reflect upon public issues but seek to put the theory into practice. Current public theology, therefore, is concerned with an expanding variety of issues, methodologies, approaches, contexts, key figures, projects, ventures and activities. This accelerating dynamic is anything but surprising because the main reference point of public theology is, after all, the *public*. Not only since David Tracy do we know that the public cannot be spoken of in the singular. There are many publics, all of them in a permanent process of self-preservation, renovation, contextualization and re-contextualization. Almost necessary, the shape of public theology reflects such dynamic because the discipline does not stand over against the multiple expressions of public life, but rather – according to its explicit self-understanding – constitutes an integral part of them. The vitality of the publics explains the vitality of public theology itself. Accordingly, the discipline has not yet reached a state of consolidation or even saturation and will probably – or hopefully – never do.

But why then a handbook? At first glance, the topical, discursive, contextual or practical diversity of public theology seems not to allow for an adequate inventory summary of the field. Merely viewed in this light, a handbook of public theology would indeed, if at all, hardly be more than an insufficient snapshot of the status quo. But in spite of the centrifugal tendencies which result from the internal dynamics of public life, public theology still has a centre from which it never departed. In effect, public theology is not only a theoretical and practical preoccupation with public matters but first and foremost it is *theology*. This means that it speaks about God, however diverse the modes and contexts of this talk may be. If we, moreover, qualify the term 'theology' by the predicate 'Christian', it turns out that the centre of public theology is none other than Jesus of Nazareth, who was soon confessed as the 'Christ'. In light of this, the centrifugal evolution of public theology must not be taken as a removal from the centre but rather as an attempt to understand the relations of this centre to the 'margins', to the multiple challenges all possible publics are confronted with, and to communicate this relation to these publics in their respective languages. Public theology bespeaks *Christ's relevance to all conceivable publics*. Precisely this conviction forms the unifying core of the present handbook. Of course, other public theologies are possible and do actually exist. Jews, Muslims, Hindus, Buddhists and many others are also concerned with public issues and have engendered a great deal of theoretical and practical insights that are more than worth to be heard. Accordingly, it would be a terrible misconception if a public theology of the Christian provenance were to ignore these voices or refused to enter into a constructive dialogue with them. But since this handbook wishes to provide a deliberately Christian view on public theology, its centre is Christ. The volume can thus be read as an attempt – albeit limited and selective – to make Christ's relevance to all possible publics visible.

That there is a unifying core which justifies the venture of a handbook, however, is not to say that this core exists in a pure form. Just as there are multiple publics, so there are many interpretations of Christ and his relevance to public life. Of course, the doctrinal developments within, say, the first five centuries of Christianity have generated a widely shared consensus in terms of creedal or dogmatic language so that most public theologians would agree, for example, that it was in Jesus Christ that the triune God revealed Godself in human shape. But what that means for life in general and for public life in particular remains fairly contested. It makes a huge difference, after all, whether you see Christ primarily as the educator of the human race, as an exemplar of what it means to be truly human, as the redeemer from our sinful condition, as the head of a communal body or as the liberator from oppressive structures. Such and countless other images have been cultivated throughout the history of Christianity; and though they are not necessarily compatible with each other, one cannot say from the outset that any of them is completely mistaken. The centre itself, therefore, appears in various facets. Relating a multifaceted centre to the margins of different publics, narratives and discursive formations, then, creates an almost unmanageable multiplicity of mediations which, once more, explains the prolific character and diversity of current public theology. Yet, the flip side of this dynamic seems to be that the centre tends to become invisible and public theology gets more and more – to borrow a film title from Sofia Coppola – 'lost in translation'.

Perhaps it is this tendency that gave rise to a growing suspicion about the current shape of the discipline. Indeed, there are more than a few critics who doubt that public theology does justice at all to its Christian centre. First of all, they bemoan that public theologians have adopted an accommodationist stance towards the surrounding culture. In their view, it is the wider society which sets the discursive agenda, while public theologians only react. In trying to counter the privatization of religion, so the argument goes, public theologians unqualifiedly commit themselves to public opinions and their appraisement of significance and importance. They participate in debates on diverse issues and occasionally decorate their contributions with theological ornaments, but, in fact, they do not conduct theology. Even worse, by employing a generally accessible language and by trusting in the persuasive power of universal reason, they voluntarily subject to a logic which is neither neutral nor compatible with Christianity. Public discourses, despite their alleged neutrality and reasonableness, are in fact expressions of an ideology that tries to domesticate religion and to stabilize the power of states, markets, sciences or the secular culture. Such forces create a narrative which is decidedly hostile to Christianity. When public theologians thus willingly comply with the rules of the game of these discourses, they effectively serve idolatrous purposes and eventually give up their Christian identity. On this account, the critics prefer an *alternative model* of public theology, that is, a model which regards the Christian church as a body politic on its own, as a counter-public that is able to accomplish true community over against the false and power-dominated sects of the secular society. The church's policy, then, consists in the effectuation of a liturgical, virtuous and aesthetic practice that does not as much convince by good reasons as by its performative beauty.

No doubt, this alternative model has its merits. It can legitimately claim to have Christ as its centre. Likewise, it points to a problem that not all public theologians sufficiently are aware of, for it is true that an all too uncritical engagement with other – particularly secular – publics bears the danger of being absorbed by false gods. And finally, this model rightly emphasizes that public theology not only has to care for the common good of the wider society but must primarily be concerned with the Christian community and its credible self-expression. However, the question is whether the Christian/non-Christian dichotomy on which this model rests is tenable. In the footmark of Augustine's distinction between the *civitas Dei* and the *civitas terrena* and supported by an arguable genealogy of modernity, this model tends to draw a sharp distinction between the Christian narrative and its secular counterparts. It does so by building on the metaphysical assumption that the entirety of created reality participates in God's being. At the same time, however, it claims that at a certain point in history people began to see themselves as autonomous and thus construed the world *etsi Deus non daretur*, as if God did not exist. Though the paradox of how such a mental exodus from divine being was even possible remains unresolved in this model, its representatives are nonetheless convinced that the (post)modern mindset and its corresponding publics, discourses and narratives cannot provide any access to the divine. In this way, an unbridgeable chasm is set between the ecclesial public, on the one hand, which accomplishes true peace and community and secular publics, on the other, which pretend to do the same, but in fact promote nihilism, war and hostility.

Though the present handbook will, due to their valuable critical observations and their undeniable merits, give sufficient room to these alternative voices, it likewise fosters the view that the relevance of Christ is indeed translatable into whatever public setting. If Christ proves to be 'the way, and the truth, and the life' (Jn 14.6 ESV), then this *is* not only communicable to everyone; it also *must* be communicated to everyone since no one may be deprived of the true way of living. Moreover, it becomes evident that such communication cannot suffice with merely performing the Christian practice in a liturgically authentic or aesthetically appealing manner. Admittedly, in the wake of a derailed postmodernism, intellectuals have come to believe that truth is always depending on narrative presuppositions, which is why it cannot be expressed in universal terms. But – apart from the question of whether this statement itself claims to be universally true (which would amount to a self-contradiction) or whether it claims to have an only limited validity (which would entail to saying nothing) – Christian theology can simply not accept that the truth of Christ should not be communicable by a generally intelligible language. If this were the case, the notion of truth would have completely lost its meaning. No doubt, the truth of the Logos is not reducible to reason alone, but neither can it be conceived without it. So if Christ's truth is relevant to all, then it must be reasonably communicable in all possible publics, discourses and narratives. Public theology is convinced that *mutual understanding is possible*. This conviction is far from supporting some sort of ecclesial or theological triumphalism. Any articulation of truth is fallible and must expose itself to the critical investigation of others. Precisely this is one of the reasons why public theology seeks to enter into every possible public, not only in a *proclaiming* but also in *learning* mode. By dialogically mediating the Christian truth with other forms of thought – be they political or economic, ecological or scientific, cultural or social, contextual or global, religious or secular – public theology helps others to better understand what Christians believe in. At the same time, though, it helps Christians to better understand themselves.

Public theology makes an indispensable contribution to the *self-elucidation of Christian faith*. But it is more than that. As the present handbook will show, theological engagement with other publics and discursive formations also seeks to foster the improvement of individual and social life. This was already the intention of great public theologians *avant la lettre* as Abraham Kuyper, Dietrich Bonhoeffer, H. Richard Niebuhr, John Courtney Murray or Martin Luther King Jr., and it still holds true for all strands of current public theology. Starting from the observation that there are damaged, deprived, oppressed and distorted forms of human life, public theology raises questions about the personal, structural or cultural conditions that make such deformations possible and real. It tries to uncover why so many people – individually, collectively and globally – are prevented from living a good and fulfilled life. In recent years, public theologians have indeed identified and analysed countless forms of poverty, deprivation and social injustices, they have addressed the outgrowths of an uncontrolled capitalism, they have dealt with postcolonial challenges and the traumatizing effects of sexism and racism, they have pointed to the dangers of populism or consumerism, they have examined the ecological crisis and the climate change and many other issues. But, of course, public theology is not only concerned with analysing such challenges, it also works out local, national or global solutions to the violations of human dignity and the destruction of the environment. By so employing a *social ethics* that offers innovative answers to urgent problems, public theology makes important contributions to the achievement of justice, human flourishing and the common good.

Yet, others do this as well. Political philosophers, social ethicists, NGOs, trade unions, political parties, social movements, intellectual circles, critical journalists and even alert artists provide similar analyses or pursue the same solutions. And oftentimes, to be honest, they do this much better than public theologians. So it goes without saying that public theology is in need of an *interdisciplinary collaboration* with competent allies. Only in cooperation with others it is capable of appropriately addressing the ethical challenges of our time. And still, there is one thing that none of the partners can offer. Public theology's centre is Christ, and Christ is the centre of and hope for all creation. Accordingly, public theology not only strives for the betterment of specific situations or the solution of concrete problems but virtually aspires to the *salvation* of creation as a whole. Each particular effort to uncover, to understand or to alleviate human and non-human suffering must thus be taken as an attempt to place the unredeemed within the all-encompassing context of eschatological redemption. This does not mean that public theology itself can promote the salvation of the world, let alone accomplish it. Redeeming the world is exclusively the work of God. But by fulfilling its ethical tasks and pursuing justice, human flourishing and the common good public theology *foreshadows* and *depicts* the universal salvation as it was already accomplished in Jesus Christ and is yet to come in its fullness. Placing the unredeemed within the context of eschatological redemption thus means expressing the *hope* that the moral striving of humans – Christians and non-Christians alike – is not in vain. It points at an ultimate *telos* whose realization has been promised in Christ and will definitely be consummated by the triune God. In many respects public theology, therefore, is engaged in the same social-ethical projects as other agents, but this engagement witnesses to the hope for something which humankind can ever make real.

Now to the structure of the present handbook: in the opening section, the 'Conditions and Self-Positioning' of public theology will be dealt with. Here, first of all, notions like the *public sphere* and *liberal democracy* have to be clarified. It goes without saying, however, that public theology cannot contend itself with merely descriptive accounts of such concepts, since only an evaluative approach proves capable of revealing their theological relevance. Accordingly, next to the discussion of sociological, political or juridical issues, a decidedly normative stance will be employed to elucidate these notions. In a similar vein, it needs no mentioning that the contemporary situation within which public theology finds itself is the outcome of countless historical processes. Hence, positioning oneself on the basis of a sheer inventory of the present does not suffice. For this reason, most of the chapters will provide a historical account of how the current state of affairs has come about. Only on that condition it is possible to recognize, for instance, that there is no contradiction in portraying the present age as secular and post-secular at the same time. Whereas *the secular* signifies a particular historical project that resulted in our contemporary self-understanding, *post-secularity* can be seen as the pluralizing effects of this project. Moreover, the self-positioning of public theology requires some reflections on what it is and what it is not. For that purpose, the similarities and dissimilarities with *political and liberation theologies* have to be investigated. Here, it will turn out that all those theologies deal with public issues but relate to different contexts, address specific problems and build on distinct theological approaches. Last but not least, the first part introduces a strong plea for an apologetic mode of doing public theology. For bringing the centre to the margins requires, as we have already seen, some sort of communication that is basically accessible to all. It includes all sorts of expressive means, from liturgy to reason. Such communication, so it will be argued, can best be called *apologetics*.

Christ is the centre of Christian public theology, but the centre proves to be multifaceted. Particularly, the existence and the shape of the major confessional traditions give witness to the many facets of Christ. While some, for instance, emphasize Christ's sacramental presence in the church, others see Christ primarily as God becoming human so that humans might become God. Still others focus on Christ's redemptive work through which the justification of the sinner was made possible. Today, as a result of an intensified ecumenical dialogue, we can also observe lots of hybrid forms and crosslinks between confessional theologies. This proves to be a positive development – not at least because it helps to come to a more comprehensive picture of Christ. Against this backdrop, it is clear that the handbook has to contain a section on 'The Ecumenical Scope of Public Theology'. The discipline, as is well known, first emerged from *liberal Protestantism* in North America and Germany. This came as no surprise since liberal Protestantism was built not only on a long history of societal engagement but was also one of the driving forces of the cultural development in these countries. The *Roman Catholic* tradition, being very influential in other parts of the world, could easily join in those debates because it had already developed a social doctrine which addressed similar issues as early public theology. To a greater or lesser extent, this applies also to *Orthodox* traditions. In former communist societies, however, their cultural influence blossomed only after the breakdown of the Eastern Bloc when civil societies began to emerge and a social doctrine was developed. *Post-liberal theologies*, on their part, can be seen as an ecumenical reaction to the multiple distortions of a liberal modernity. While liberal Protestantism and also some strands of post-Vatican II Catholicism seem to exhibit a great affinity with modern culture, post-liberals with diverse denominational backgrounds seek to promote an alternative, more ecclesiocentric model of public theology. Yet, ecumenism is by no means confined to post-liberal positions. In a sense, public theology can virtually be seen as an epitome of ecumenism. Perhaps, it is also this ecumenical spirit which recently enabled public theologians to advance their *relations to other religions*. In a time of global challenges, after all, no religious tradition alone can claim to have the right solutions.

As mentioned earlier, public theology is not primarily a theoretical or practical preoccupation with public matters, but first of all it is theology. So there are reasons enough to include a section on 'Theological Tenets in Public Theology' in this handbook. To zoom in on the field, first the similarities and the differences between *social ethics* and *public theology* have to be clarified. The universal scope of public theology is not so much related to the concrete issues both disciplines are dealing with, but rather to the doctrinal beliefs on which public theology relies and which, therefore, locate these issues in an eschatological context. After having touched upon the dogmatic core of public theology, it can be investigated in which way some of the central Christian doctrines impact the shape of the discipline. Particularly, the *doctrine of God* is of importance here. Depending on how one conceives of God's engagement with the world, for instance, the role of human activities will significantly differ. If one – to point out one side of the spectrum – completely reduces every creaturely potency, including human agency, to divine causation, then the human concurrence in God's salvific work will tend to zero. If one, by contrast, takes God's presence in the world as an invitation to respond to God's grace, then this leaves much more room for the theological significance of human engagement, in the public sphere and elsewhere. More or less the same applies to *soteriology*. Here, too, Christ's redemptive activity can either be seen as a totally new creation of the fallen nature or as a release of the human faculty to resonate with God's call. Apparently, understanding salvation in one or the other way makes an enormous difference for the conceptualization of public theology. When it comes to *ecclesiology*, the spectrum of possibilities stretches from a self-assured church which forms the one and only true body politic to a humble church which enters into the various publics in order to determine dialogically the best way to justice, human flourishing or the common good. At first sight, the church's *liturgy* seems to have little impact on public life since it is performed solely by the assembly of believers. Yet, if one recognizes the community-building effect of the liturgical practice and, moreover, expects this community to operate within the public realm in affectionate, peaceful and charitable ways, then liturgy turns out to be an extraordinarily significant political and cultural factor. This becomes all the more true as soon as one realizes that particularly the liturgical practice designates and anticipates ultimate redemption given by God. Therefore, as has already been indicated, it is primarily the eschatological frame that distinguishes public theology from other social-ethical enterprises. *Eschatology*, as it were, articulates and reflects upon just that hope that public theology seeks to communicate by means of its social-ethical engagement.

All too often, public theology has been charged with not being theologically enough. For this reason the handbook puts so much emphasis on the theological tenets and hopefully shows that there can be no question of a theological lacuna at all. But, of course, the discipline is primarily known for its commitment to public issues. Accordingly, attention must be paid to the major 'Challenges for Public Theology'. The first topic to be treated here is *politics*. Some post-liberal theologians construe a sharp divide between the church and the political sphere which then compels them to present ecclesial performances as an alternative policy. The challenge for public theology is to develop a more comprehensive conception which conceives of politics not so much in terms of competition and conflict but rather as a common endeavour to create a world liveable for all. *Race and gender*, too, are artificial distinctions meant to justify existing power relations and to maintain oppressive structures. Public theology faces the challenge of dismantling the underlying logics of such ideological constructs. At the same time, though, it has to be considered how due attention can be paid to a legitimate interest in the recognition of diversity. Another challenge arises out of a particular conception of *culture*. For as long as one underestimates the reflective potential of cultural life, one has to treat culture and theology as two distinct discourses: one as the performance and the other as a critical contemplation of cultural practices. A more sophisticated understanding of culture, by contrast, would show in which way public theology itself partakes in a culture's search for self-understanding. When it comes to *economics*, economic issues cannot be neglected by theologians who attempt to take normative stances towards public life. A similar pattern seems to apply to *ecology*, for at first glance public theology cannot be equated with whatever environmental policy. Yet, as soon as one takes on a theological point of view and realizes the interconnectedness of all created beings, it becomes clear that ecology is more an ontological than a political concept. Hence, the challenge for public theology is to make this perspective plausible. Quite another topic is *sports*. Admittedly, until now, sports has scarcely been viewed as a challenge that public theology should address. However, particularly this realm of public life combines political, cultural, gender, economic and ecological aspects as probably no other field of common interest. Furthermore, the staging of great sports events exhibits all too often religious traits so that public theology cannot but be concerned with this prominent cultural phenomenon.

As has been indicated, there are multiple publics with specific languages, intellectual presumptions, topical emphases and discursive dynamics. The notion of the public thus only makes sense if used in the plural. Since public theology seeks to be part of all those debates, it also presents itself in a pluralist shape. At the same time, the discipline is driven by an overall concern, namely to communicate Christ to the margins of all publics. This has geographical implications so that one can rightly speak of the 'International Scope of Public Theology'. Outlining this scope properly would, strictly speaking, entail to depict public discourses in all regions and on all levels, from the global to the local, which is impossible. The handbook, therefore, restricts itself to an overview of how the discipline's situatedness in different continents, and, accordingly, contains chapters on the public theologies of *Africa*, *Asia*, *Australia*, *Europe*, *North America* and *Latin America*. Evidentially, such a coarse grid cannot fully do justice to the internal diversity of the respective discourses. Nonetheless, it will become conspicuous in what way and to which extent public theology, due to the multiformity of local and national challenges, exhibits a very peculiar shape within each of the continental settings.

Portraying public theology by presenting its self-positioning, its ecumenical character, its theological tenets, its challenges and its international scope is surely not the only way to make interested readers – students, scholars, church activists and others – acquainted with the peculiarities of the discipline. That it still is a way – and perhaps not the worst – is not at least indicated by the confidence that the contributors, all renowned experts in their fields, have put into this project. We would like to express our deepest gratitude for their willingness to write and sometimes rewrite the chapters, for their stimulating discussions and for their patience. Also many thanks to Marieke Meijer-Bernard, who so devotedly took care of the editing of the texts. Last but not least we would like to thank Anna Turton and Sinead O'Connor for the excellent support without which this handbook would have never seen the light of day.

PART I
Conditions and self-positioning

Introduction

CHAPTER 1

The public sphere

MAUREEN JUNKER-KENNY

As a much used and perhaps 'ubiquitous'[1] concept, the 'public sphere' is determined quite differently in individual human sciences such as political theory, sociology and media studies. In order to mark the outlines of a consistent meaning, its philosophical foundations need to be established. It is useful for public theology to become aware of the different conceptions that have been elaborated since they show distinct ethical accentuations and put forward expectations to the fellow citizens participating in this informal political forum. Some are also aware that religions can bring unique contributions to it.

The origins of a modern understanding of 'public' in Kant's theory of reason and his deontological, cosmopolitan ethics will be examined first (1.1). In analyses of the 'public sphere' (*Öffentlichkeit*), Jürgen Habermas has investigated its normative character in relation to a deliberative theory of democracy (1.2). It will be compared to John Rawls's conceptions of 'public reason', located in state institutions, and of pluralist society as consisting of parallel 'comprehensive doctrines' (1.3). A further framework will be explored with Paul Ricoeur's hermeneutical approach to traditions as 'co-founders' of the public sphere, offering an alternative foundation to contract theory (1.4). Finally, approaches to theology will be viewed from the civic and the internal public sphere within Christianity (1.5).

---

[1]Kristin Merle, *Religion in der Öffentlichkeit. Digitalisierung als Herausforderung für kirchliche Kommunikationskulturen* (Berlin: De Gruyter, 2019), 30. Translations from German into English, unless otherwise indicated, are my own.

1.1 KANT'S CONCEPTIONS OF THE 'PUBLIC USE OF REASON', MORALITY AND LAW, AND THE NEED FOR AN 'ETHICAL COMMONWEALTH'

An inherent link of theoretical reason to a public framework for clarifying perceptions of issues is expounded by Kant (1.1.1). In practical reason, the inner freedom of each person is decisive and her conscience is insurmountable; yet the task of deepening one's moral sensitivity requires active listening to others as well as contributing to improving conditions for all to fulfil both strict and wide obligations. The categorical imperative to respect the other even when this recognition is not reciprocal contains two levels, one prohibiting instrumentalization, the other requiring active, imaginative support for the other's happiness (1.1.2).[2] His differentiated outline of law also in its anticipatory, enabling function for the external, civic role of humans in their morality includes the aim of a peaceful word order (1.1.3). Since this presupposes an internal orientation in the moral subject for working towards such an ambitious goal, he outlines the need for an 'ethical commonwealth' of communities which supports them in their task of promoting the ends of others. Thus, a philosophical concept of 'church' is founded alongside the civic demands to everyone as a member of a polity capable and in need of improvement (1.1.4).

1.1.1 The public signature of reason and the 'world concept' of philosophy

Already the effort needed to clarify intersubjectively the epistemological starting points and perspectives at work in rationality or purposive reason as an enterprise directed at reaching justifiable results in the sphere of objective knowledge gives it a necessarily public character. Just how fundamentally the 'public' dimension belongs to reason can be seen in Kant's distinction between philosophy as an expert domain and as a universally accessible 'world concept'. This understanding arises from the leading premise of human freedom that is marked both by the unconditionality of everyone's reason (*Vernunft*) and its outreach towards an ultimate purpose of its activity. François Marty explains this final orientation that characterizes the 'world concept' of philosophy: 'As a "freely acting" being, the human person enters the realm of the unconditioned (*Unbedingten*)' in which 'a "canon", that is, a legitimate use of pure reason as *practical* reason exists. . . . As the final purpose (*Endzweck*) of the whole

---

[2]Cf. Herta Nagl-Docekal, 'Why Ethics Needs Politics: A Cosmopolitan Perspective (With a Little Help from Kant)', in *Chiasmatic Encounters. Art, Ethics, Politics*, ed. Kuisma Korhonen, Arto Haapala, Sara Heinämaa, Kristian Klockars and Pajari Räsänen (Lanham, MD: Lexington Books, 2018), 149–66 (153).

activity of human reason it characterises all of philosophy in its *world concept*, its "conceptus cosmicus"'.³

The idea that everyone is a co-owner of reason with its ultimately practical destination is also reflected in two types of use: the 'private' use in a person's role as an employee and the 'public' use as a fellow citizen:

> the private use of reason may quite often be very narrowly restricted, however, without undue hindrance to the progress of enlightenment. But by the public use of one's reason I mean that use which anyone may make of it as a man of learning (*als Gelehrter*) addressing the entire reading public (*ganzen Publikum der Leserwelt*). What I term the private use of reason is that which a person may make of it in a particular civil post or office with which he is entrusted. . . . Thus the use which someone employed as a teacher makes of his reason in the presence of his congregation is purely private. . . . Conversely as a scholar addressing the real public (*eigentlichen Publikum*) (i.e. the world at large) through his writings, the clergyman making public use of his reason enjoys unlimited freedom to use his own reason and to speak in his own person.⁴

Engaging in the latter use creates a public domain of interaction, which is the basis for growth in object-related and moral insight:

> There is more chance of an entire public enlightening itself. This is indeed almost inevitable, if only the public concerned is left in freedom.

> For enlightenment of this kind, all that is needed is *freedom*. And the freedom in question is the most innocuous (*unschädlichste*) form of all – freedom to make public use of one's reason in all matters. . . . The public use of man's reason must always be free, and it alone can bring about enlightenment (cf. *unter Menschen*).⁵

1.1.2 Law developed from a moral foundation

Second, it is noteworthy that Kant accesses law from the perspective of morality also by assigning an 'anticipatory' dimension to the establishment of

---

³François Marty, 'Die Analogie zwischen "ethischem" und "bürgerlichem" gemeinen Wesen. Ein Beitrag zur Frage der Erreichbarkeit des höchsten politischen Gutes', in *Recht – Geschichte – Religion. Die Bedeutung Kants für die Gegenwart*, ed. Herta Nagl-Docekal and Rudolf Langthaler (Berlin: Akademie Verlag, 2004), 63–70 (64), with reference to Kant, Akademie-Ausgabe, vol. 3, 518 and 542–3.
⁴'"An Answer to the Question: "What is Enlightenment?"', in *Kant's Political Writings*, ed. with an Introduction, and Notes by Hans Reiss, trans. H. B. Nisbet (Cambridge: CUP, 1970), 54–60 (55. 57).
⁵Ibid., 55. Cf. also Sarah Holtman, 'Öffentlichkeit', in *Kant-Lexikon. Studienausgabe*, ed. Marcus Willaschek, Jürgen Stolzenberg, Georg Mohr and Stefano Bacin (Berlin: De Gruyter, 2017), 408–10.

legal structures.⁶ In opposition to Hobbes, the 'state of nature' is conceived as allowing for the anticipation of public law since individuals are envisaged as having an equal claim to the surface of the earth which carries and nourishes them. This prior recognition only has to be institutionalized in law but is not inaugurated by the state with its monopoly of violence, a political principle which is justified also for Kant. A further act of anticipation is that of a constitutional republic from within a state marked by authoritarian governance (*Obrigkeitsstaat*). The medium of the process of reform is the public use of reason by the citizens.

1.1.3 The cosmopolitan horizon of a peaceful world order

The widest sphere of anticipation established by legal structures is to be found in the external relations between such free republics, oriented towards a league of individual states which is designed to avert war.⁷ This is not regarded as a 'utopian ideal' but as already possessing a legally obliging character. While a unitary world state is feared as amounting to 'soulless despotism', the 'Right of Nations (*Völkerrecht*) shall be based on a Federation of Free States'.⁸

Based on the equal, common ownership of the earth, colonialism is rejected and the right of each human to be received as a guest, not an enemy, established, giving a right to visit, though the right to stay needs the agreement of the host.⁹ Thus, a cosmopolitan framework of intercultural recognition and justice is outlined as a consequence of citizens advancing their states through the public use of reason. They direct it towards a constitution in which their freedom and equality are respected, and an international setting of cooperation that limits the unleashing of unrestricted violence in war.¹⁰ Yet while the 'highest political good consists in attaining perpetual peace', its 'realisation remains problematic

---

⁶In Heiner Bielefeldt, 'Verrechtlichung als Reformprozess. Kants Konstruktion der Rechtsentwicklung', in *Recht – Geschichte – Religion. Die Bedeutung Kants für die Gegenwart*, ed. Herta Nagl-Docekal and Rudolf Langthaler (Berlin: Akademie Verlag, 2004) (cf. note 3), 73–84 (75–83), Heiner Bielefeldt distinguishes the following three stages: overcoming the state of nature, working towards a republic and devising international law.
⁷Cf. Bielefeldt, 'Verrechtlichung', 75–83.
⁸Cf. Bielefeldt, 'Verrechtlichung', 81, with reference to 'Perpetual Peace: A Philosophical Sketch', in *Kant's Political Writings*, 93–130 (102) (Second Definitive Article).
⁹In Nagl-Docekal, 'Why Ethics Needs Politics', 156, Nagl-Docekal refers to Hannah Arendt's conclusion of the 'right to go visit', which includes the faculty of imagination: 'With reference to Kant's thoughts on "the right to visit," formulated in his study on "Perpetual Peace," Arendt summarizes: "To think with an enlarged mentality means that one trains one's imagination to go visiting"', with reference to Arendt, *Lectures on Kant's Political Philosophy* (Chicago: The University of Chicago Press, 1982), 43.
¹⁰Cf. Kant, 'Perpetual Peace', 120–1, notes: 'In the external relationships between *states*, this wickedness is quite undisguisedly and irrefutably apparent. Within each individual state, it is concealed by the coercion embodied in the civil laws.'

since the development of law inevitably reaches a cul de sac'.[11] This is where a change of attitude is required that calls for a different medium.

1.1.4 Religions as communities constituting an 'ethical commonwealth'

Within the universal scope of the moral and the legal frameworks, religions are assigned a non-substitutable function as communities capable of renewing virtue and marked by a hope in the ultimate fulfilment of human endeavours. As public communities they are seen as fostering an 'ethical commonwealth' alongside the realm of state and society:

> As Kant explains, such an 'ethico-civil state' is clearly distinguished from a 'juridico-civil (political) state,' since it unites people 'under laws of virtue alone' (RR, 106). This implies that the task of establishing an 'ethical community' cannot be performed by means of politics. . . . In Kant's view, our duty to engage in developing an 'ethico-civil state' is tantamount to the obligation of 'founding a kingdom of God on earth,' which needs to be expounded in terms of a philosophy of religion.[12]

The key term of this philosophy of religion that is an integral part of Kant's philosophy of autonomy is 'hope'. Here a dimension that was already identified in Section I comes to play its part. The outreach of reason towards the unconditioned poses an irrefutable question: 'With an internal necessity, the essence of morality raises the question of meaning . . . the problem what the ultimate purpose of all moral action is. . . . The practical interest of reason not only announces itself in the question of obligation (*Sollen*) but at least as urgently in the question of hope.'[13]

While each of the four aspects would need to be developed further, they provide enough of a basis for comparing the new departures taken by philosophers in the second half of the twentieth century. How do Habermas, Rawls and Ricoeur take on board the dimensions within which Kant locates the 'public use of reason': its link to law, its global scope, and the question of meaning in the face of the antinomy of practical reason between the purity of moral motivation and the experience of their frequent failure that leads to the postulate of God?

---

[11] Marty, 'Die Analogie', 63.
[12] Nagl-Docekal, 'Why Ethics Needs Politics', 168.
[13] Christoph Hübenthal, 'Autonomie als Prinzip. Zur Neubegründung der Moralität bei Kant', in *Kant und die Theologie*, ed. Georg Essen and Magnus Striet (Darmstadt: WBG, 2005), 95–128 (115).

1.2 JÜRGEN HABERMAS'S CONCEPTION OF THE PUBLIC SPHERE

The significance of this concept established as the centre of a theory of democracy by Jürgen Habermas has been compared to that of a 'discovery in the natural sciences'.[14] First, its place in his developed social theory (1.2.1), then its distinction from the functions of the state and from aspects of 'the private' will be outlined (1.2.2), before the issue of its universal standing, relevant for global and intercultural settings, is examined (1.2.3). After treating the final aspect, religion (1.2.4), I will take stock of key critiques of what is assumed as the counterpart to 'public', the 'private': as the home space, as individual morality, as cultural conventions and as religion (1.2.5).

1.2.1 Key features

Habermas's analysis of the public sphere and of the structural changes it has undergone since the seventeenth and eighteenth centuries predates his turn to researching the capabilities of communicative rationality that human beings are endowed with.[15] While his subsequent move to communicative reason implies a shift in method, there is a connection between the two in the underlying human ability, which also the 1961 monograph draws on. The capability to 'reason publicly' called on by Kant in its constitutive significance for mutual enlightenment is operative when engaging in a civic discussion: in it, existing social and political arrangements are questioned, validity claims are raised in terms of criteria of rationality, not of social standing, and the level of a universally justifiable proposal for practical reform is taken as the benchmark. The theme is the first of a 'trias' that sums up the constellation of Habermas's social and political philosophy: 'public sphere – discourse – reason'.[16] Its key feature is the 'generation of social space', leading to 'metaphors like fora, stages, arenas'.[17] On the one hand, it is distinguished from the private realm, on the other, from strategic communication that uses an already existing public space for its own interests.[18] By engaging in action oriented towards understanding, it is close to the 'lifeworld'. Distinguished from the 'systems' of politics and economics

---

[14]Nancy Fraser, 'Theorie der Öffentlichkeit', in *Habermas-Handbuch. Leben – Werk – Wirkung*, ed. Hauke Brunkhorst, Regina Kreide and Cristina Lafont (Darmstadt: WBG, 2009), 148–55 (148).
[15]Jürgen Habermas, *The Structural Transformation of the Public Sphere*, trans. Thomas Burger (Cambridge, MA: MIT Press, 1989) (German original 1961). Ibid., *Communication and the Evolution of Society*, trans. Thomas McCarthy (Boston: Beacon Press, 1979), 1–68.
[16]André Munzinger, *Gemeinsame Welt denken. Bedingungen interkultureller Koexistenz bei Jürgen Habermas und Eilert Herms* (Tübingen: Mohr Siebeck, 2015), 43.
[17]Jürgen Habermas, *Between Facts and Norms. Contributions to a Discourse Theory of Law and Democracy*, trans. William Rehg (Cambridge: Polity Press, 1996), 360.
[18]Ibid., 369–70. 375.

which do not use communicative interaction but the media of administrative power and money, the 'lifeworld' is given the standing of an immediate sphere of exchange. Public space, by contrast, also functions beyond those 'physically present', extending to the 'virtual presence of dispersed readers, listeners and spectators'. It cannot, however, without being subverted, be robbed of the principled openness and equality of consideration for everyone affected.

1.2.2 Between the state and private life: Exchanges among equals forging the democratic bond

The social space opened up is assigned a 'dual orientation': participants 'directly influence the political system, but at the same time they are also reflexively concerned with revitalizing and enlarging civil society and the public sphere as well as with confirming their own identities and capacities to act'.[19] This double direction explains that in it not only questions of the just, of rights and obligations directed at the political system, arising from the effects of its shortcomings on everyday life, are thematized. Also, issues that are not objects of collective action are treated: cultural, literary, artistic and religious dimensions between participants that shape their practical self-understandings. It 'can be easily missed', that, apart from politics, 'the lifeworld' itself is its subject.[20] Public spheres 'are not only arenas for the formation of discursive opinions; in addition, they are arenas for the formation and enactment of social identities'.[21] Analysing, comparing, reflecting on the self-conceptions of agents is a key theme that relies on communicative resources and cannot be provided merely from an observer's position.

The problem spotting and heuristic insights that can only arise in the lifeworld – its metaphorical 'antennae' – use 'existential language' to identify dysfunctionalities.[22] Such exchanges that flow into public opinion formation manifest an origin which needs to be defended against 'markets' that 'cannot be democratized'. It has consequences for the normative foundations of democracy when markets assume 'regulatory functions in domains of life that used to be held together by norms – in other words, by political means or through pre-political forms of communication'. Habermas warns against 'an uncontrolled [entgleisende] modernization of society' that could 'undermine the form of solidarity on which the democratic state depends even if it cannot enforce

---

[19]Ibid., 370.
[20]Bernhard Laux, 'Massenkommunikation im Spannungsfeld von Öffentlichkeit, Markt und Macht', in *Theologische Ethik im Diskurs*, ed. Walter Lesch and Alberto Bondolfi (Paderborn: UTB, 1995), 269–91 (273).
[21]Nancy Fraser, 'Rethinking the Public Sphere', in *Habermas and the Public Sphere*, ed. Craig Calhoun (Cambridge, MA: MIT Press, 1992), 109–42 (125).
[22]Habermas, *Between Facts and Norms*, 365.

it'.²³ The social bond as distinct from a mutually disinterested contract can only be established and reinvigorated in a public space that is able to identify instrumentalizing forces which subvert its inter-civic egalitarian constitution.

1.2.3 Universality through new theory foundations

The critique of mechanisms replacing processes conducted at an interactive level of uncoerced sharing of insights is motivated by Habermas's interest in the possibilities of agency. Craig Calhoun analyses how Habermas has shifted 'attention from the institutional construction of a public sphere as the basis for democratic will formation to the validity claims universally implicit in all speech'.²⁴ The first book was a study of a specific historical period from which normative conclusions were drawn. The next step was to work out at what level the resources animating the public sphere are anchored, in 'a transhistorical capacity of human communication.'²⁵ Thus, a universal basis has been identified in capacities of the human species, providing a foundation for statements beyond the period of European modernity. Does this move to specify agency-enabling conditions take up the 'world concept of philosophy' advocated by Kant, claimed as a possibility for every moral agent? It opens up a horizon of universality from which all cultural formations can be seen as distinctive variants. But does it also contain the dimension which belongs to it in Kant, the idea of a God who could safeguard the moral efforts of humans?²⁶

1.2.4 Religions as resources for insight and motivation

The extent to which cultural understandings, symbolic and semantic resources present in the modern public sphere are owed to biblical monotheism has been pointed out repeatedly by Habermas. Conversations with theologians such as Johann Baptist Metz and Helmut Peukert since the mid-1970s have expressed a clear recognition of the role of 'Jerusalem' for 'Athens'.²⁷ This appreciation is in

---

²³Jürgen Habermas, *Between Naturalism and Religion*, trans. Ciaran Cronin (Cambridge: Polity, 2008), 107.
²⁴Craig Calhoun, 'Introduction', in *Habermas and the Public Sphere*, ed. Craig Calhoun (Cambridge, MA: MIT Press, 1992), 1–48 (31).
²⁵Ibid., 31.
²⁶Among the philosophers who ask this question is also Jürgen Stolzenberg. Cf. his analysis of the implications of the 'world concept' of philosophy in '"Was jedermann notwendig interessiert". Kants Weltbegriff der Philosophie', in *Protestantismus zwischen Aufklärung und Moderne (FS Ulrich Barth)*, ed. Roderich Barth, Claus-Dieter Osthövener und Arnulf von Scheliha (Frankfurt: P. Lang, 2005), 83–94.
²⁷Jürgen Habermas, 'Jerusalem or Athens: Where Does Anamnestic Reason Belong? Johann Baptist Metz on Unity amidst Multicultural Plurality', in *Religion and Rationality. Essays on Reason, God and Modernity* (Cambridge: Polity, 2002), 129–38.

contrast to the reconstructions offered in *Structural Transformation*, where, as his American interlocutors in 1989 comment, the role of religion as a factor in forging the public sphere has not been accounted for.[28] Since around 2000, the third phase of his view of religion includes the demand for mutual translations between religious and secular fellow citizens. The world-disclosing potential of religious language and the heuristic and motivating capacities religions make available are needed to re-energize the social bond and the normative consciousness which is threatened by 'pathologies of rationalisation': 'Pure practical reason can no longer be so confident in its ability to counteract a modernization spinning out of control armed solely with the insights of a theory of justice. The latter lacks the creativity of linguistic world-disclosure that a normative consciousness afflicted with accelerating decline requires in order to regenerate itself.'[29] Yet, despite being accredited with sharing its origin with philosophy in a new conception of self, world and ultimate horizon since the axial age, and being accorded a 'dilatory plea' (*aufschiebendes Veto*)[30] in discussions on future technologies, its basis is established as the 'other' of rational communication. Which concept of reason (*Vernunft*) is in play when its questioning beyond everything conditioned – which defined it for Kant – is foreshortened?

1.2.5 Questions regarding the counterpart to 'public'

The public–private distinction presupposed has been problematized in several respects. As a *sociological–empirical* concept, it could already result from structures of domination that relegate to an internal 'private' sphere what are changeable political and economic impositions, especially on women.[31] The ideal of a singular public sphere has been rejected in favour of multiple 'subaltern counter-publics'[32] that are better able to fulfil the normative remit to let the voices of everyone affected be heard.

---

[28]Calhoun, 'Introduction', 43, n. 16: 'It is remarkable that Habermas's account of how the family helped to give rise to a notion of "pure" and undifferentiated humanity does not betray any sense of the role of religion in helping to produce this result. Yet the tradition of interiority was pioneered by Augustine, and during the Protestant Reformation it was given decisive new form as something shared equivalently among all people.' In 'Religion, Science, and Printing in the Public Spheres in Seventeenth Century England' (212–35), David Zaret examines all three factors as constitutive for the emergence of a public sphere, despite the Puritan distrust of reason as part of the 'innate corruption of human nature' (224).
[29]Habermas, *Between Religion and Naturalism*, 211.
[30]Jürgen Habermas, *The Future of Human Nature* (Cambridge: Polity Press, 2003), 109.
[31]Seyla Benhabib, 'Models of Public Space: Hannah Arendt, the Liberal Tradition, and Jürgen Habermas', in *Habermas*, ed. Calhoun, 73–99 (89–95).
[32]Fraser, 'Rethinking', 127.

Despite Habermas's attention to subjectivity in eighteenth-century literature, the important role of the *cultural* sphere for the political is seen to be underestimated.[33] This is not only true for the semantic heritage of religious concepts and foundational stories which are part of public background understandings, supplying resources that are more than the 'conventions' which are positioned as the counterpart to 'critical-reflective' reason. It also affects the ranking of 'conversation' which should be seen as foundational and prior to 'discourse' about validity claims regarding contested norms.[34]

The theory decision to take communicative action as the starting point for analysis affects the *moral* dimension in a significant way. It supersedes the individual subject who became engaged in the public sphere as a 'private' person by focusing solely on intersubjectivity and on grammatical structures seen as offering 'public' accessibility. This subordination risks undermining the key qualification of citizens as both 'authors and addressees' of laws; from a Kantian perspective, it incurs the concern that moving the testing of the categorical imperative to real discourse submits it to the charge of 'heteronomy'.[35] What is 'public' for Kant is each individual's capacity to use his or her reason. The factual consensus reached by the discourse partners appears as 'arbitrary'. A connected problem is that it is owed to a split between 'discourses of justification' and of 'application'. The critical conclusion is that the 'procedural character' claimed as a proper substitution of individual reflection on the universalisability of maxims cannot in fact deliver the moral standard sought. What should be 'non-negotiable' and in need of being secured before the discourse takes place is the 'deontological framework which already includes substantial stipulations'.[36]

Also, *religious* convictions are qualified as 'private', and monolingual citizens are not expected to translate their views in the informal public sphere. This protection, however, can be critiqued as being built on not crediting religious persons with being naturally bilingual from their innate moral capacity. Part of the principled contrast between 'publicly accessible' and 'opaque religious' statements derives from the insistence that grammar is visible, while subjectivity is not. The reason for their unbreachable distance is dual: an underestimation of reason (*Vernunft*) as located in each individual,

---

[33]Peter Uwe Hohendahl, 'The Public Sphere: Models and Boundaries', in *Habermas*, ed. Calhoun, 99–108. Fraser, 'Rethinking', 120. 126.

[34]David Tracy, 'Theology, Critical Social Theory and the Public Realm', in *Habermas, Modernity, and Public Theology*, ed. Don Browning and Francis Schüssler Fiorenza (New York: Crossroad, 1992), 19–42.

[35]Cf. Herta Nagl-Docekal, *Innere Freiheit. Grenzen der nachmetaphysischen Moralkonzeptionen* (Deutsche Zeitschrift für Philosophie Sonderband 36) (Berlin/Boston: De Gruyter, 2014), 85.

[36]Christoph Hübenthal, *Grundlegung der christlichen Sozialethik. Versuch eines freiheitsanalytisch-handlungsreflexiven Ansatzes* (Münster: Aschendorff, 2006), 364.

and of religious traditions as being able to contribute from their own resources to what is needed beyond a procedural account: a 'philosophically justified substantial morality'.[37]

1.3 CONTRACT, COMPREHENSIVE DOCTRINES AND PUBLIC REASON IN RAWLS

Is there an equivalent in Rawls's social philosophy to the concept of the public sphere as developed by Habermas? The solutions Rawls offers regarding the voice accorded to different traditions in a society will be investigated in four sections. First, the change of approach that takes place between *A Theory of Justice* (1971) and *Political Liberalism* (1993) will be outlined (1.3.1), followed by an enquiry into how the citizen is conceived of in relation to the state and the background culture (1.3.2). The question of how a liberal framework based on negative rights determines the scope of ethics between the national and the global will be discussed next (1.3.3). Finally, the perspective on religions as one group of traditions among the other comprehensive doctrines is evaluated (1.3.4).

1.3.1 Two foundations: Contract and context

Already in the first book that proposes a conception of justice as 'fairness', two foundations are laid: the first is contract, reenvisaged as an 'original position' with 'heads of household' deciding behind a 'veil of ignorance' on the principles that would guide their society. Second, 'considered convictions' are drawn on, that is, judgements based on culturally available values, arising from a sense of justice and from a person's conception of the good. Twenty years on, they are extended into a new category, 'comprehensive doctrines', in which these conceptions are all embedded, whether secular or religious.[38]

Relevant for assumptions on civic interactions is the justification given in *Theory of Justice* for the 'contract'. How is the 'veil of ignorance' behind which 'rational', that is, self-interested and cautious agents, choose principles, to be interpreted? Is it a device in the sense of a 'ruse', as Höffe holds, or does it reveal a basic anthropology of competitive individuals who strive to 'maximise the minimum'?[39] The outcome is two principles: the first of liberty, as maximal as possible while still remaining compatible with others; the second one of

---

[37]Ibid., 365.
[38]John Rawls, *A Theory of Justice* (Cambridge, MA: Belknap Press, 1971), 11–22. Ibid., *Political Liberalism* (New York: Columbia University Press, 1993).
[39]Cf. Rawls, *Theory*, 152–3. In *Religion and Public Reason. A Comparison of the Positions of John Rawls, Jürgen Habermas and Paul Ricoeur* (Berlin/Boston: De Gruyter, 2014), 8–22, I compare the

justice, including the 'difference principle' to allow for inequalities that benefit the worst off. A socially responsible democratic society appears as the most advisable bet in a construction based on contract between individuals without the premise of a moral motivation or a social bond. The second foundation is on the coherence of an individual's reflected values and principles. The early definition of 'rational' as self-interested recedes with the subsequent realization that societies are marked by a profound pluralism in which stability between 'reasonable' doctrines has to be actively fostered. Yet the question remains how to get insight into other citizens' outlooks.

1.3.2 Conceptualizing the citizen in relation to the state and the background culture

The contract foundation's portrayal of citizens as 'mutually disinterested' and as guided by a self-serving calculation offers no basis for communication with others as morally conscious fellow humans. It takes them seriously as legally equal fellow citizens on the basis of external reciprocity. Can a concept of public space be reached on the basis of these assumptions?

In Ricoeur's assessment, they give rise to two alternative understandings, as summarized by Christof Mandry: 'Behind the question about the justification status of the contract and of the maximin argument lies the question about the coherence of the community (*Gemeinwesen*) itself – is it a cooperative enterprise whose bonding power must be strengthened, or a connection of mutually disinterested individuals oriented towards their self-interest?'[40] Habermas, in contrast, saw 'social space' as only being able to emerge as the third feature of the structure of communicative action, following 'functions' and 'contents' of everyday speech oriented towards understanding.[41] Precisely because of the normative standard inherent in communication, could Habermas identify the intrusion of a market logic as a pathological replacement of pre-political exchanges and principled discourse. These receive their energy from the vision of democracy as a joint project. If Rawls's liberal (as distinct from a deontological) perspective is based on the priority of individual rights, does the subsequent embedding of the citizens' individual outlooks in 'comprehensive doctrines' allow for a more communal orientation? In *Political Liberalism*, Rawls sees these formations as making up the 'background culture', but not

---

critiques of the assumptions made in the 'original position' by Onora O'Neill, Otfried Höffe and Paul Ricoeur.
[40]Christof Mandry, *Ethische Identität und christlicher Glaube* (Mainz: Grünewald, 2002), 189, with reference to Ricoeur, *Oneself as Another*, trans. Kathleen Blamey (Chicago: University of Chicago Press, 1992), 250.
[41]Habermas, *Between Facts and Norms*, 360.

as continually productive and interactive traditions. It is in keeping with this view that the main reference of 'public' is to officeholders of the state, while Habermas's civic forum becomes the 'non-public' background culture,[42] together with universities and professional associations that are distinct from the 'private'. However, comprehensive traditions are attributed the ability to translate their worldviews into 'public conceptions of justice', relating to the political values of liberty and equality from their own grounds. This makes it possible to reach an 'overlapping consensus' on specific issues, with the overlap being identified from an observer's position, as an at least minimal basis of agreement.

1.3.3 Bounded or cosmopolitan scope of justice?

This overlap is less than the benchmark of the universalization test which Kant and Habermas maintain for judging which maxims or policy proposals can be justified.[43] From a Rawlsian position, their moral expectation already within their own society seems exaggerated. Catherine Audard interprets Habermas as demanding 'civic friendship',[44] when what he is outlining as the norm for interaction also between strangers is in fact a Kantian premise of morality. Since also philosophy is deemed to fall under 'comprehensive doctrines', there is no critical medium left for adjudicating truth-claims. The aims of cosmopolitan peace and justice no longer form the horizon of the 'public use of reason' which relates instead to a bounded society. A global perspective would require taking a different starting point than the individuals' regard for their rights, for what is theirs in private law. Here, the difference between Locke and Kant is relevant; the latter conceives of 'private law in a cosmopolitan way, not as defense of private property. The solid ground of law is the regulation of the relationship to the ground (*Boden*) that is shared by all human beings'.[45] This enlarges the scope of responsible agency far beyond individuals' rights towards the state and each other, where the liberal prohibition of harming the other only extends to fellow citizens.

---

[42]Cf. Rawls, *Political Liberalism*, 220.
[43]In volume I, *Die okzidentale Konstellation von Glauben und Wissen*, of his new work, *Auch eine Geschichte der Philosophie*, 2 vols. (Berlin: Suhrkamp, 2019), 91–100 (99), Habermas portrays the shared elements with Rawls but concludes that 'in my view, an autonomous use of reason in intercultural discourses has to be imagined differently'.
[44]Catherine Audard, 'Rawls and Habermas on the Place of Religion in the Political Domain', in *Habermas and Rawls. Disputing the Political*, ed. James Gordon Finlayson and Fabian Freyenhagen with help from James Gledhill (London: Routledge, 2011), 224–46 (243).
[45]Marty, 'Die Analogie', 64. Cf. Bielefeldt, 'Verrechtlichung', 77.

1.3.4 Religions as comprehensive doctrines translating individually into political conceptions

On the one hand, religions are seen as significant factors in the social and political life of a pluralist democracy. As comprehensive doctrines with histories longer than many states, they are taken as external social facts which may also be reasonable and able to connect with the democratic values of liberty and equality. The question 'What gives them the capability to "translate"?' is not asked.[46]

At the same time, the path to linking the faith they confess to a demand of reason is cut off. Similar to Habermas, Rawls rejects Kant's postulate of God as well as the antinomy of practical reason from which it arises, replacing the alternative between absurdity and hope for meaning with a trust in incremental progress.[47]

The question put by Herta Nagl-Docekal to Habermas in view of earlier positions within the Frankfurt School can be extended to Rawls: 'Also on this point Horkheimer agrees with Adorno, who claims: "The question about the meaning of life cannot be pacified (*ruhig gestellt werden*) in a collective, amelioristic concept of action."'[48]

Thus, without a shared, not just a partially overlapping, capacity of reason to relate to, religions lose the chance to offer their unique contribution to the project of social and global justice. While they coexist in the background culture, the concept of a shared public space and metaphors like forum, arena or stage are missing in Rawls's approach. This means that there is no civic place in which conversations and discourses involving encounters, mutual listening and a joint identification of problems can happen. Is the elaboration of ground rules for contributing, such as endorsing democratic values and avoiding conflicts about guiding visions of the 'good', too modest for the tasks at stake?[49]

---

[46]Herta Nagl-Docekal, 'Moral und Religion aus der Optik der heutigen rechtsphilosophischen Debatte', *Deutsche Zeitschrift für Philosophie* 56 (2008): 843–55 (854).

[47]John Rawls, *Lectures on the History of Moral Philosophy*, ed. Barbara Herman (Cambridge, MA: Harvard University Press, 2000), 319–22. I have treated Kant's argumentation in 'What Scope for Ethics in the Public Sphere? Principled Autonomy and the Antinomy of Practical Reason', in ed. Christoph Hübenthal, Special Issue, Theology and Reason in the Public Sphere, *Studies in Christian Ethics* 32 (2019): 485–98.

[48]Herta Nagl-Docekal, 'Nach einer erneuten Lektüre: Max Horkheimer, *Die Sehnsucht nach dem ganz Anderen*', *Deutsche Zeitschrift für Philosophie* 68 (2020) (in print), quoting Ludwig Nagl's summary of this point in Adorno in L. Nagl, *Das verhüllte Absolute. Essays zur zeitgenössischen Religionsphilosophie* (Frankfurt a.M.: Peter Lang, 2010), 29.

[49]In *The Common Good and Christian Ethics* (Cambridge: CUP, 2002), 137–70, David Hollenbach outlines 'intellectual solidarity' as an alternative to Rawls's 'method of avoidance'.

1.4 CONSTITUTED BY TRADITIONS – RICOEUR'S HERMENEUTICAL CONCEPTION OF THE PUBLIC SPHERE

The philosophical addition that Ricoeur brings to the demarcation of a 'public sphere' is the inclusion of both a theory of subjectivity and of hermeneutics (1.4.1). These resources allow for a decisively different conception of public space: it is constituted by traditions as 'co-founders' (1.4.2). The immediate awareness of living in a context of diverse cultures calls for a cosmopolitan scale of recognition (1.4.3). It allows for religions to be approached not merely as historical and sociological entities but from an interest in the internal motivation of the believers (1.4.4).

1.4.1 A framework encompassing philosophy of reflection and hermeneutics of cultures

The self-reflection increasingly called for also by Habermas but undermined by his reduction of the equally original reflexivity of the self to its counterpart, intersubjectivity, is analysed in its conditions. Ricoeur 'will always argue for a more interactive theory, one where neither the ego nor the other takes precedence but also where there is something singular about the self that is not reducible to intersubjective relations'.[50] Not used by Rawls and deemed part of a superseded philosophy of consciousness by Habermas are a phenomenological enquiry into the self's intentionality, oriented towards the will, and a hermeneutics of symbols operative in the conceptualization of a world. Together they allow to approach the public space not as an initially empty stage but as always prefigured by the symbolic heritages of different traditions. These are not simply conventions but horizons for agents with both ideologies and utopias to rationalize and devise alternatives to existing power arrangements.[51] Starting the analysis from an agent-centred viewpoint already questions an objectivizing stance; for example, Max Weber's concept of unilateral domination (*Herrschaft*) received with 'obedience' overlooks the irrepressible negotiations evident at the level of micro-history.[52] Ricoeur's ability to identify polarities in a dialectic has the potential to undermine dualistic constructions with determinate roles, such as 'system' and 'lifeworld'. The naturalization of morality in Habermas's universal pragmatics and the ambiguity of Rawls's contract foundation between

---

[50] David Pellauer, *Ricoeur – A Guide for the Perplexed* (New York: Continuum, 2007), 142, n. 8.
[51] Paul Ricoeur, *Hermeneutics and the Social Sciences*, ed. and trans. John B. Thompson (Cambridge, MA: MIT Press, 1981), 63–100. Ibid., *Lectures on Ideology and Utopia*, ed. George H. Taylor (New York: Columbia Press, 1986).
[52] Paul Ricoeur, *Reflections on the Just*, trans. David Pellauer (Chicago: University of Chicago Press, 2007), 133–48. 149–55.

'exchange relations' and 'deontological intention'[53] are both resisted in an ethics of practical reason ordered in three steps: from 'striving to live well with and for others in just institutions', to a necessary deontological check of intentions through the 'sieve of the norm', towards reflective judgement combining the two.[54] These categories provide a profound and nuanced method of assessing public issues, such as events of commemoration between a state's legitimation interests, the victims of its frequently violent foundation and of subsequent conflicts, and efforts of active reconciliation that are deeper than a 'commanded amnesty'.[55]

1.4.2 Traditions as co-founders of the public sphere

From the range and depth of Ricoeur's work, elements encountered in the previous theories can be reconceived and brought together in one consistent framework. The multiple dimensions of the public sphere include the material, that is, a 'townhall', square or virtual gathering point; the symbolic, consisting of the narratives and specific concepts of its participants; the discursive, as it appears in the actual argumentations, as well as the practical–political outcomes in the structures and directions for solutions produced.

With his interest in practical self-understandings, Ricoeur has highlighted the enabling role of symbolic resources owed to historical constellations of encounters with others; biblical monotheism, Greek philosophy and Roman law are a case in point, with alternate ways of envisaging and realizing the social bond. Between the three authors, it is Ricoeur who develops the most dynamic conception of public space: it is cofounded by distinct traditions and contains the latent normative heritage of their sources. They are marked by internal struggles between opposed interpretations from which defeated elements may reappear in subsequent eras. Their appeal is at the 'enunciative' level, as distinct from the 'institutional authority' of government.[56] The realm of 'enunciative authority' of these movements parallels Habermas's 'informal' or 'wild' public sphere with its heuristic capacity of discovering new trends and future issues for moral discourse which the 'formal public sphere' beyond the 'institutional threshold' of democratic office must recognize as relevant. Ricoeur includes as an additional factor not thematized in the other two political theories the origin of their members' commitment: the lost causes and unkept promises to which

---

[53]Paul Ricoeur, *The Just*, trans. David Pellauer (Chicago: University of Chicago Press, 2000), 58.
[54]Ricoeur, *Oneself as Another*, 170, 172.
[55]Paul Ricoeur, 'Reflections on a New Europe', in *Paul Ricoeur: The Hermeneutics of Action*, trans. E. Brennan, ed. Richard Kearney (London: Sage Publ., 1996), 3–13. *Memory, History, Forgetting*, trans. Kathleen Blamey and David Pellauer (Chicago: University of Chicago Press, 2004), 452–6.
[56]Ricoeur, *Reflections on the Just*, 91–105.

they feel indebted, motivating them to avail of further chances to realize what was missed before.

1.4.3 Diverse cultures in a cosmopolitan framework of recognition

The Kantian heritage shared by Habermas and Ricoeur that the horizon also of the local public sphere is the planet is further specified by two tenets: that diversity is meant to be, and that in principle, communicability exists between humans;[57] even with the so-called 'exotic' other,[58] imagination enables the hermeneutic capacity to discover analogies in foreign languages and life forms. The appreciation of the distinct cultural traditions into which humanity has 'congealed'[59] is based on the 'wager' that these heritages in their particularity have at least the potential for universality within them. Their particularity consists not only in different features; it is located in a core from which it is renewed in contingent ways, based on the challenges and chances arising through the eras for their adherents. Symbols are not the 'other' of reason, they give 'rise to thought', as Ricoeur notes with a Kantian expression.[60]

Thus, there can be no fixed target language for translations between them, but only a reflexive account of how specific terms – freedom, justice, the self, the reign of God, . . . – gained their currency.[61] While Rawls's interest in a minimum of compatibility between comprehensive doctrines is understandable, it does not capture their productivity to think of their contributions as segments of an overlapping consensus. They are each original co-founders of the very space of exchange in which they engage both with their counterparts and with their own foundational story in identifying impasses, directions and promising steps.

1.4.4 Renewed from their fonds mystique: The significance of religions for human agency

From a cultural perspective, as distinct from an empirical sociology of membership patterns, religious traditions are already present in the public

---

[57]Whether the 'other' is conceived as an enemy in a naturalizing account like Hobbes's, or in frameworks of recognition, as Kant and Hegel do, is a basic choice: cf. Paul Ricoeur, *The Course of Recognition*, trans. David Pellauer (Cambridge, MA: Harvard University Press, 2005), 152.
[58]Ricoeur, *Oneself as Another*, 289.
[59]Ricoeur, *History and Truth*, trans. and intro. Charles A. Kelbley (Evanston: Northwestern University Press. 1965), 280.
[60]Paul Ricoeur, *The Symbolism of Evil*, trans. Emerson Buchanan (Boston: Beacon Press, 1967), 347–57.
[61]For a discussion on whether 'general' categories are in fact 'Eurocentric', cf. Habermas, 'The New Philosophical Interest in Religion: A Conversation with Eduardo Mendieta', in *Postmetaphysical Thinking II*, trans. Ciaran Cronin (Cambridge: Polity, 2017), 59–76. See also Jürgen Habermas, *Auch eine Geschichte der Philosophie*, vol. I, 110–35 (3. Der okzidentale Entwicklungspfad und der Universalitätsanspruch nachmetaphysischen Denkens).

sphere since they are part of the symbolic worlds from which the categories and life forms of a polity emerge. Ricoeur encourages religions to get used to having lost institutional authority, as Christianity did in Europe, now only being one among other traditions in civic society, and to compete with other movements 'without hang-ups' in the public space.[62] Their enunciative authority, however, can draw from being anchored at a deeper level than other public purpose-means considerations. Ricoeur explores the genres of their texts for the literary variety they encompass, the sense of time and the conceptions of life they offer; across historical periods they are renewed from a core which remains a mystery. While this original foundation cannot be rationalized, it can be argued with reasons at which point they connect to human agency: not at the moral, but at the 'poetic' level, where imagination gives orientation to the will. By fulfilling an agent's hope for forgiveness, they reopen the sources of goodness after failure, thus holding the key to revived human agency. Religions harbour a depth that is crucial for human action: a sense of the possible.

1.5 THEOLOGICAL APPROACHES TO THE PUBLIC SPHERE

It will become clear in the following chapters how different theological approaches conceive of the 'public' as a theoretical concept, and with which constituencies in the 'public realm' they wish to engage. A crucial question arising about the term 'public' concerns the concept of truth it implies. How does theology relate to the general consciousness of truth expounded in philosophy, deriving from the human capacity for reason? It has become evident in relation to Habermas and Rawls that faith traditions need to insist on the full extent of reason with its outreach towards the unconditioned. Yet not only philosophical approaches can fall short of the Kantian scope of human questioning that leads to the questions of meaning and of God. There are also theological positions that dismiss the human capability for morality which is shared with non-believers. Which message do Christian traditions wish to portray?

One view, critical of the public sphere since it still expresses expectations to the state, is that political governance in its neutrality towards worldviews cannot be a dialogue partner. It is merely 'statecraft', oriented as such towards war. Daniel Bell contrasts two understandings of political theology: the 'dominant' tradition and the 'emergent' one:

---

[62]Ricoeur, *Reflections on the Just*, 105.

the dominant tradition conceives of Christian political engagement on the world's terms (Milbank 1990). Indeed, each strand is quite explicit in its embrace of modernity's cartography of social and political space . . . each strand is equally vehement in its denunciation as sectarian or narcissistically ecclesiocentric of any effort to articulate Christian political engagement on terms other than those circumscribed by the modern *mythos* of statecraft. . . . The modern differentiation of life into autonomous spheres, the separation of theology and politics, is a ruse. . . . Refusing the modern nation-state's claim to the right to organise human community in its own image, the emergent tradition sees in the practices of the church the true politics.[63]

No remedy is expected from the citizens' 'public use of reason' in interaction with their different insights. This is similar to the way in which Stanley Hauerwas attempts to replace the function of a theological anthropology through the church. Also here, ecclesiology is charged with properties that belong to Christology and to an analysis of the human openness for the question of God from a reflection on their own existence.[64] Collapsing these different enquiries in dogmatic theology and its hermeneutics into a theory of church bears the hallmarks of an integralist approach.

A further example where a degeneration of the public sphere is assisted by an entrenched religious position is the modern occurrence of fundamentalist versions of world religions. As a theorist of religious education, Rolf Schieder observes:

> The key problem of fundamentalism is its nativism: It claims that its selective and arbitrary recourse to tradition is the sign of a special loyalty, for example to the biblical texts. . . . A Manichean-dualistic image of the world and apocalyptic scenarios for the future could, if the level of theological education were higher, be seen through as typical reactions to an unsettling societal development in which one positions oneself on the side of the losers.[65]

---

[63] Daniel Bell, 'State and Civil Society', in *The Blackwell Companion to Political Theology*, ed. Peter M. Scott and William Cavanaugh (Oxford: Blackwell, 2004), 434–5.
[64] Cf. Christofer Frey, 'Konvergenz und Divergenz von Ethik und Praktischer Theologie', in *Reconsidering the Boundaries between Theological Disciplines*, ed. Michael Welker and Friedrich Schweitzer (Münster: LIT Verlag, 2005), 113–22 (122). Hauerwas's approach and Radical Orthodoxy are among the positions I compare in *Approaches to Theological Ethics. Sources, Traditions, Visions* (London/New York: T&T Clark, 2019).
[65] Rolf Schieder, 'Die Zivilisierung der Religion durch Bildung in Deutschland', in *Wie viel Religion verträgt der Staat?*, ed. Winfried Kretschmann and Verena Wodtke-Werner (Ostfildern: Grünewald, 2014), 163–70 (166).

In contrast to these understandings of Christian identity, the theological ethicist Robert Gascoigne points to the potential of symbolic traditions with their world structuring, socializing and empowering orientations to keep a participative democracy inspired towards goals beyond stability:

> What are the visions of humanity, the sources of life, which can inspire social discourse to become a genuine forum of civil respect, a community of justice and generosity – even of willingness to sacrifice interests for the sake of the need of others? . . . Understandings of the human person are formed by historical traditions, so that any commonality must be the result of a dialogue between traditions.[66]

These models show through their mutual opposition that an internal public sphere within the religions is required to argue out their divergent understandings. Friedrich Schleiermacher – defender of the public function of religion in modernity and author of the first Christian dogmatics after the anthropological turn – welcomed the need to justify one's interpretation of the contested essence of Christianity between the different quarters in inner-Christian debate: 'Blessed be this dispute among us . . . it is a precious good.' It manifests, as Claus-Dieter Osthövener concludes for these ultimately Christological debates, that 'the plurality of faithful understandings is not an obstacle but an element of life in the church'.[67]

---

[66] Robert Gascoigne, *The Public Forum and Christian Ethics* (Cambridge: CUP, 2001), 3.42.
[67] Claus-Dieter Osthövener, 'Der christliche Glaube – Dogmatik II: Materiale Entfaltung der "Glaubenslehre"', in *Schleiermacher Handbuch*, ed. Martin Ohst (Tübingen: Mohr Siebeck, 2017), 362–83 (369–70), quoting from a text of 1832. In *Self, Christ and God in Schleiermacher's Dogmatics. A Theology Reconceived for Modernity* (Berlin and Boston: De Gruyter, 2020), I treat his concept of religion, his Christology and doctrine of God and some of the divergent history of reception of *The Christian Faith*, which celebrates the 200th anniversary of the publication of its first edition in 2021/2.

CHAPTER 2

Liberal democracy

HANS-MARTIEN TEN NAPEL

2.1 INTRODUCTION

The author of this chapter is on record for arguing that some of the most valuable books on liberal democracy in recent years have been written by, for example, philosophers and theologians, rather than by legal scholars and political scientists.[1] Hence, this chapter approaches the topic of liberal democracy in view of a philosophical topic, namely the pursuit of happiness. The concept of the pursuit of happiness allows us to examine liberal democracy within a broader timeframe than would be possible when 'only' dealing with liberal democracy per se. While the pursuit of happiness is characteristic of liberal democracy, Aristotle (384–322 BCE) already identified the facilitating of happiness as the goal of political life in general. The question then is how liberal democracy can best enable citizens to pursue and achieve happiness.

Viewed within this broader timeframe, liberal democracy, for the first time in history, distinguishes between an objective and a subjective definition of happiness, while aiming to achieve both. For the better part of history, the idea of happiness was defined objectively. Citizens had to learn what the arguably evident elements of happiness were and practice these. Only with the advent of modernity, the idea arose that happiness could be defined subjectively and that the state should help citizens to pursue their subjective definitions of happiness.

---

[1] Hans-Martien ten Napel, *Constitutionalism, Democracy and Religious Freedom: To Be Fully Human* (London and New York: Routledge, 2017), 13.

At the same time, liberal democracy maintained the idea that the government should conform to the traditional, objective definition of happiness as it had developed over the centuries. This dual nature of the pursuit of happiness in liberal democracy will be explained in more detail in Section 2.2.

Section 2.3 of this chapter then proceeds to examine how liberal democracy has developed during the roughly 250 years since its origins in the American and French Revolutions. Since the scope of this chapter does not allow for a detailed overview of this development with all its aspects, the focus will be solely on the pursuit of happiness and the treatment will remain schematic. I will argue that, in the course of this period, the objective definition of happiness somehow disappeared, even as a point of reference for the state. As this chapter will point out, the Progressive Era (1890–1920) marks a paradigm shift as it sought to abandon the natural law tradition to which both the classics and Christianity belong. Through the centuries, it has been at the heart of the objective definition of happiness. At the same time, however, the idea of a shared conception of happiness pursued by the state remained in place during the Progressive Era. With the advantage of hindsight, we can now see how this paradigm shift paved the way for a fundamental change of liberal democracy after the Second World War, particularly during the Cultural Revolution of the 1960s. Paradoxically, although democratization was one of the goals of this epoch, its result was a more undemocratic form of liberalism than had previously existed.

Section 2.4 will analyse the varied reactions that have been provoked by this undemocratic form of liberalism. The renewed wave of populism that is currently hitting the West can be regarded as one such reaction. While extremist and racist elements of populism can no longer be meaningfully related to the pursuit of happiness, some other of the populist criticisms can be regarded as a reaction to the undemocratic form of liberalism after the Second World War. In this latter vein, populist movements could be constructively married to some kinds of post-liberal thought. Catholic integralism as one rising strand of post-liberal thought seeks to reintroduce the notion of common good into politics. This can be seen as one variant of reintroducing an objective definition of happiness in state politics and perhaps even on the individual level.

The chapter ends with a conclusion.

2.2 LIBERAL DEMOCRACY AND THE NATURAL LAW TRADITION

Liberal democracy has always been and still is about facilitating the pursuit of happiness by its citizens. As such, we consider liberal democracy as the fruit of the American and French Revolutions of the late eighteenth century. According to the Declaration of Independence (1776), the raison d'être of the new republic was to guarantee 'Life, Liberty, and the pursuit of Happiness'.[2] *The Federalist Papers* (1887–8) can be considered to be the first modern constitutional treatise.[3]

Why would it need to be *argued* that liberal democracy is, essentially, about the pursuit of happiness? Most of the legal and social science literature on liberal democracy is concerned with institutional and procedural arrangements, such as the legality principle, the separation of powers and the judiciary's independence. The respect for fundamental rights is of a more substantial nature. Yet, this focus on procedures comes with an ethical vacuum concerning the public square, which is often viewed as a major advantage of liberal democracy, as it supposedly leaves room for as much individual freedom for its citizens as possible.

In this light, there are at least two reasons for emphasizing that liberal democracy is concerned with the pursuit of happiness. First, it clarifies that, although institutional and procedural safeguards are without doubt of relevance, these are not what liberal democracy is ultimately about. The institutional and procedural safeguards serve to facilitate the pursuit of a more substantive goal at the heart of liberal democracy. Second, this more substantive goal is not, merely, freedom, but happiness. If today, the goal of liberal democracy is most often associated with freedom, this means that the nature of liberal democracy has somehow changed.

The American Founding was not the first time in history that the purpose of government was defined as enabling the pursuit of happiness.[4] 'Now it is clear that the best constitution is the system under which anybody whatsoever would be best off and would live in felicity,' Aristotle writes already in his *Politics*.[5] The Founders were well aware of this, of course, as Aristotle was a highly authoritative figure for them.[6] In general, the Founders frequently referred to previous political orders, such as the Greek democracies, the Roman Empire and the Italian city states of the fourteenth and fifteenth centuries. This keen historical awareness contrasts today's liberal democrats, who often appear to believe that political thought started with the invention of liberal democracy. This unhistorical approach is symptomatic of a misplaced idea

---

[2] https://www.archives.gov/founding-docs/declaration (last accessed 6 January 2021).
[3] Andreas Kinneging, 'Bijbel van het moderne constitutionalisme', in *De Federalist Papers. Bakermat van het moderne constitutionalisme*, ed. Paul de Hert, Andreas Kinneging and Gerard Versluis (s.l.: Damon, 2018), 305–25 (305).
[4] Cf. Ryan Rynbrandt, 'The Pursuit of Happiness', paper prepared for the Western Political Science Association 2016 Annual Conference in San Diego, CA, 25 March 2016.
[5] Book 7, Section 1324a.
[6] Michael Pakaluk, 'Aristotle, Natural Law, and the Founders,' https://www.nlnrac.org/classical/aristotle (last accessed 6 January 2021).

of the superiority of liberal democracy, especially in comparison with earlier forms of constitutionalism.

There is some continuity between the modern constitutionalism that arose in the late eighteenth century and so-called ancient constitutionalism. Both aim to facilitate the pursuit of happiness, albeit in very different ways. The Founders maintained the idea that the purpose of government was to guarantee the pursuit of happiness. Moreover, the Founders – like the classics – believed that happiness, or the good life, is an objective concept. As Thomas G. West has convincingly demonstrated, the theoretical framework within which the Founders acted and thought was very much that of the natural rights tradition.[7] Although the notion of rights marked a conceptual departure from the natural law tradition of the classics and Christianity, which focused on virtues and duties, it did not intend to break with it altogether. The main characteristic of both the natural law and the natural rights tradition is the idea that there are particular truths concerning the human condition that can and will not change over time or differ from place to place.[8]

The idea that there are 'natural laws' regarding the human condition implies that it is possible to determine what constitutes the good life objectively. If, as the natural law tradition supposes, humankind is created for a particular purpose, it follows that we can only become happy when achieving this purpose. Furthermore, both the classics and Christianity conceive of individual happiness as intrinsically related to the happiness of the community to which a person belongs. According to both the classics and great parts of the Christian tradition, the happiness of a person is at least partly dependent on whether s/he contributes to the common good. At this point, we meet a potential tension between liberalism and the natural law and natural rights tradition. The liberal emphasis on subjective happiness might jeopardize the priority of the common good over the pursuit of sheer individual happiness.

While the modern constitutionalism that arose in the United States in the late eighteenth century remained in continuity with the ancient idea of the objective character of happiness, it introduced the new idea that everyone could follow their own path to happiness; that is to say, it subjectified happiness at the individual level. This innovation begs the question of whether liberalism can be compatible with the natural law and natural rights tradition: What remains of the collective, objective concept of happiness, if each individual is allowed to pursue their subjective understanding of happiness? The Founders might not have considered a possible clash, as they were convinced that the population

---

[7]Thomas G. West, *The Political Theory of the American Founding. Natural Rights, Public Policy, and the Moral Conditions of Freedom* (Cambridge: Cambridge University Press, 2017).
[8]https://www.nlnrac.org/about (last accessed 6 January 2021).

would, through education, remain firmly rooted in the classical and Christian worldviews prevalent at their time.

So profound were the societal changes in the 1960s that it is challenging for readers in the twenty-first century to imagine what the state's adherence to an objective definition of happiness meant 250 years ago. As the United States is a federation, the relevant provisions to regulate morality are not as much in the US Constitution as they belonged to the competence of the states. For example, these tended to make adultery or overt homosexual behaviour punishable. More restrictions were in place concerning the opening hours of shops or the selling of liquor. This active role of the government in matters of morality is all the more interesting, as the United States is widely perceived as the prototype of a limited government system.[9]

2.3 THE RISE OF UNDEMOCRATIC LIBERALISM

2.3.1 The Progressive Era

With the advantage of hindsight, it is easy to see that the Founders were mistaken in believing that the population at large would remain firmly rooted in the classical and Christian worldviews prevalent at their time.

The genius of modern constitutionalism was that it remained in continuity with the ancient idea of the objective character of happiness while subjectifying happiness at the individual level. The first major pushback on its dual nature occurred during the Progressive Era. Although this period would deserve a much more elaborate treatment than can be offered here, for the purpose of this argument it suffices to note that the Progressive Era by and large abandoned the anthropology of the Founders. The objective definition of happiness presupposed a rather pessimistic anthropology. As the classics already argued, human beings are not naturally inclined to behave virtuously. Instead, they must be educated, and not everyone will be suited to be so trained. In Christianity, the doctrine of original sin defines human beings as innately sinful and in need of a rebirth. What concerns politics, this pessimistic vision of humankind implies that there must be checks to keep both rulers and the ruled under control. Initially, ancient constitutionalism conceived of these checks as internal checks. Man's willpower can control his desires as long as it cooperates with the mind, which sets the limit. Liberal democracy externalized these checks, with the help of the doctrine of the separation of powers. The state's role would have to remain limited to minimize the risks involved in granting people the authority to rule. Moreover, even this limited state had to be divided into three branches,

---

[9]West, *The Political Theory of the American Founding*, Parts II and III.

that is, the legislature, the executive and the judiciary, which could control and balance each other.

During the Progressive Era, the state was given a more critical role to play in the economy, among other things.[10] While the Founders had already envisaged a role for the state in the economy, it was only the ideas of, for example, President Theodore Roosevelt (1901–8) and President Woodrow Wilson (1913–21) which laid the intellectual basis for the modern 'administrative state'. This shift presupposed a change of the traditional, fixed view of human nature.

With their more optimistic anthropology, the Progressives could further depart from the traditional, objective definition of happiness as well. An intrinsically good human being could be trusted to pursue his or her own idea of happiness without thereby automatically creating great damage for themselves and others. Nonetheless, this was still very much a collective attempt at formulating a new definition of happiness. Moreover, the attempt took place in an overwhelmingly Christian society, preventing any complete departure from the natural law and natural rights tradition. Some even argue that the ideas of the Progressives were more in conformity with Catholic Social Teaching as it had arisen in the late nineteenth century than those of the Founders.[11]

2.3.2 The 1960s

A different shift occurred with the Cultural Revolution of the 1960s. In Europe, this revolution accelerated the process of secularization of society. This secularization process did not occur in the same manner in the United States, which has seen a rise of 'nones', that is, people who in surveys answer that they do not belong to a specific denomination only recently.[12] A second secularization process sees to the equally significant development that the 1960s also marked a farewell to the classical education enjoyed by Western elites for centuries.[13] In combination, the abandonment of both the classics and Christianity means that the whole cultural environment of modern constitutionalism has radically changed.

As part of this changed cultural environment, the entire concept of happiness has become subjective. As noted before, modern constitutionalism already introduced at least some tension between an objective concept of happiness to be pursued collectively and the freedom to define happiness subjectively at the

---

[10]Ronald J. Pestritto and William J. Atto, eds., *American Progressivism: A Reader* (Lanham, MD: Lexington Books, 2008).

[11]John F. Woolverton and James D. Bratt, *A Christian and a Democrat. A Religious Biography of Franklin D. Roosevelt* (Grand Rapids, MI: William B. Eerdmans Publishing Company, 2019).

[12]Jack Jenkins, '"Nones" Now as Big as Evangelicals, Catholics in the US', *Religion News Service*, 21 March 2019.

[13]Stanley Kurtz, *The Lost History of Western Civilization* (National Association of Scholars, 2020).

individual level. As long as the classics and Christianity continued to inform most people's ideas about what happiness involves, this tension remained manageable. During this period, Christianity was informally very much the 'political theology' of liberal democracy if political theology is defined as 'bringing the disciplines of theology and critical thought to bear on the relation between politics and religion'.[14] As several theologians, notably Oliver O'Donovan,[15] have highlighted, many of the critical concepts of liberal democracy cannot be fully understood without historical reference to Christianity. Examples include the concepts of representation and accountability. According to these theologians, liberal democracy faces a problem when the Christian tradition begins to fade.[16]

With the fading of the natural law and natural rights tradition the concept of happiness became subjective, and the rupture between modern and ancient constitutionalism complete. This rupture begs the question of whether it is still appropriate to speak of modern constitutionalism. Thus far, the term 'liberal democracy' has been used as synonymous with modern constitutionalism. While modern constitutionalism demonstrates both continuity and change in respect to ancient constitutionalism, postmodern constitutionalism sides one-sidedly for change.

Yet, postliberalism is a term used by critics of liberalism in search of an alternative. What present-day Western democracies are currently experiencing, however, is a more radical version of liberal democracy than has existed before, that is, secularized, liberal democracy. If the term 'modern' denotes a mixture of Christianity and Enlightenment thought, then, at present, only the second part of modernity appears to remain. This Enlightenment part has, moreover, broken with the classics.

With this terminological problematic in the background, we could refer to constitutional democracy when talking about the order initiated by modern constitutionalism. A constitutional democracy is liberal only insofar as government is limited by the Constitution. After all, this is the original political meaning of 'liberal'. It wants to limit the state's role through a constitution, among other things. From this perspective, Western political orders have transformed from constitutional into more comprehensively liberal democracies. The latter remain constitutional, but the role of government in society has been considerably enhanced. Government in liberal democracies is

---

[14]Max Stackhouse, 'Civil Religion, Political Theology and Public Theology: What's the Difference?', *Political Theology* 5 (2004): 275–93.
[15]Oliver O' Donovan, *The Desire of the Nations. Rediscovering the Roots of Political Theology* (Cambridge: Cambridge University Press, 1996).
[16]Cf. Hans-Martien ten Napel, 'Review Essay: Theological Medicine for Liberal Democracy', *Journal of Markets & Morality* 22 (2019): 169–81.

only still limited when compared to authoritarian regimes. There may be valid reasons, also in a democracy, to advocate a significantly enhanced increased role for the government. One way of keeping government within certain limits, as in authoritarian regimes, is by ensuring that it remains within a 'thin' definition of the rule of law.[17]

2.3.3 Legitimacy crisis

The transformation of Western political orders from constitutional into more comprehensively liberal democracies is a development that did not happen overnight. The growth of the state's role started in the United States, already during the Progressive Era. This era resulted in the modern administrative state, membership in a range of international institutions and organizations, and, last but not least, the codification of an ever-expanding number of human rights. In combination, these developments impacted the separation of powers that was the hallmark of limited government. The legislature, which had initially been the most crucial branch of government, became increasingly replaced by the executive and the judiciary. The term 'executive' no longer adequately describes the role of this branch of government, as it has acquired significant legislative powers. Admittedly, modern governments cannot exist without a certain degree of bureaucracy. This administrative state resulted, however, in a more technocratic character of the decision-making process. The same can be said for the process of internationalization that originated after the Second World War. Some form of international cooperation is necessary in order to achieve the policy goals of states. At the same time, the internationalization process further strengthens the executive, whose position had already become stronger with the rise of the administrative state. International relations have traditionally been the domain of governments. Ministers, civil servants and diplomats dominate, for example, Europe's negotiating tables. At the same time, the birth of the modern human rights movement after the Second World War led to a more critical role of the judiciary in the modern state. Because of the proliferation of human rights, many political decisions became legalized. As a result, several academics have noted the birth of 'juristocracies'.[18] The judiciary then became a potential counterweight to the executive's growing dominance, enhancing the courts' role within the political order further. In sum, a relatively technocratic form of government has arisen that is markedly different from the modern constitutionalism that had been designed 250 years ago.

---

[17]Cass R. Sunstein and Adrian Vermeule, *Law and Leviathan. Redeeming the Administrative State* (Cambridge, MA: Harvard University Press, 2020).
[18]Ran Hirschl, *Towards Juristocracy. The Origins and Consequences of the New Constitutionalism* (Cambridge, MA: Harvard University Press, 2007).

In response to the ideological vacuum at the heart of liberal democracies, the past decade has witnessed the growth of both left-wing and right-wing populist movements across the West. Although 'populism' is a complicated phenomenon with many different dimensions, what is relevant for present purposes is its resolve to 're-enchant democracy' by restoring the primacy of politics in decision-making processes.[19] Instead of Christianity as its political theology, or indeed liberalism,[20] populists note the absence of any political theology. To the extent that populist movements try to fill the void, they sometimes make use of Christian references and symbols. Yet, many populist leaders, although paying lip service to Christian ideals, do not self-identify as Christians. The resulting political theology thus quickly becomes a peculiar mixture of Christian notions and, for example, a right-wing ideology that sometimes actually contradicts Christian doctrine.

It seems puzzling how liberal democracy can both be liberal to the extreme, on the one hand, and demonstrate an ideological vacuum, on the other. Paradoxically, the desire to liberate all people from whatever bonds requires an eventually almost (soft-) totalitarian state.[21] At a minimum, to achieve its ideals, a secularized liberalism must become a technocratic political order. In light of this state of affairs, one of the most pressing questions of our time is whether the modern constitutionalism that originated under very different cultural circumstances from ours will continue to function in our time.

At the moment, there are ever more pessimistic views concerning the future of liberal democracy. Since about 2006, several authoritative reports have signalled a global democratic recession. The headlines in the latest editions of these reports confirm this trend. In its report *Freedom in the World 2020*, Freedom House warns in no uncertain terms: 'Democracy and pluralism under assault'; '14 years of democratic decline'; 'an unsteady beacon of freedom in the United States'; 'division and dysfunction in democracies' and 'Illiberal populists defend or gain their power, threatening democratic norms'.[22] Almost exclusively these headlines relate to the cradle of liberal democracy: the West. The *Democracy Index 2019*, compiled by the Intelligence Unit of the

---

[19] Paul Blokker, 'Populism as a Constitutional Project', *International Journal of Constitutional Law* 17 (2019): 535–53, at 536.
[20] See Section 2.4.
[21] Ryszard Legutko, *The Demon in Democracy: Totalitarian Temptations in Free Societies* (New York & London: Encounter Books, 2016).
[22] Freedom House, *Freedom in the World 2020. A Leaderless Struggle for Democracy*, https://freedomhouse.org/report/freedom-world/2020/leaderless-struggle-democracy (last accessed 11 January 2021).

international journal *The Economist*, speaks of 'A year of democratic setbacks and popular protest'.[23]

The democratic decline as stated by the *Democracy Index 2019* concerns factors like:

- an increasing emphasis on elite/expert governance rather than popular participatory democracy;
- a growing influence of unelected, unaccountable institutions and expert bodies;
- the removal of substantive issues of national importance from the political arena to be decided by politicians, experts or supranational bodies behind closed doors;
- a widening gap between political elites and parties, on the one hand, and national electorates, on the other.[24]

It takes little effort to visualize how developments such as the coronavirus pandemic can exacerbate some of these trends. The famous Carnegie think tank is not at all assured about what the long-term consequences could be. Governments use the pandemic to increase their executive powers and limit individual rights. Furthermore, that is just the tip of the iceberg, according to the think tank.[25]

While the literature sometimes all too easily assumes that populism constitutes a significant threat to liberal democracy, we should ask whether liberal democracy itself has started to show certain flaws and whether some forms of populism could correct that. Seen from one angle, liberal democracy is now experiencing the deleterious consequences of the rise of populism, or is the rise of populist constitutionalism – which wants to revive democracy and to reduce the divide between citizens and professional politicians – the result of shortcomings of liberal democracy? Populism could impact negatively on liberal democracy in the sense of a shift towards a more authoritarian rule. Moreover, right-wing extremisms are incompatible with the foundational principles of liberal democracy. And yet, as argued earlier, the increasingly undemocratic character of liberalism since the Progressive Era and the ideological vacuum that arose in the 1960s lies at the root of the current rise of populism.

---

[23]This overview counts only twenty-two full democracies worldwide, representing just 5.7 per cent of the world's population. Economist Intelligence Unit, *Democracy Index 2019*, https://www.eiu.com/topic/democracy-index (last accessed 11 January 2021).
[24]Ibid., 6.
[25]Carnegie Endowment for International Peace, 'How Will the Coronavirus Reshape Democracy and Governance Globally?' 7 April 2020.

2.4 POSTLIBERALISM

While some lament only the new cultural conditions under which modern constitutionalism must function nowadays and support nevertheless the more original idea and form of modern constitutionalism, others adopt a more critical attitude towards liberal democracy altogether.[26] Post-liberals are critical of modernity as such, because of its supposed departure from the classics and Christianity. Since they associate the classics and Christianity with the truth about the human condition, a constitutional order based on a partial denial of that truth is doomed to fail. From this perspective, thus, modern constitutionalism was destined to fail from the very beginning. Recent developments such as the Cultural Revolution of the 1960s are hardly a surprise from this perspective. It is more surprising that liberal democracy has been able to hold sway for some 250 years.

According to its critics, the experiment of modern constitutionalism was bound to fail from the beginning, because the underlying political theology of liberalism abandons precisely the moral and religious resources that it needs to survive. Because liberalism limits religious beliefs to the private sphere,[27] it becomes more difficult for religion to promote the ethos needed to sustain a genuinely liberal society. In this way, liberalism almost necessarily becomes Christianity's rival. According to post-liberals, Christianity must be at the centre, and liberalism prevents Christianity from inhabiting this position. Thus, liberalism functions like a political theology.

Constitutional lawyer Adrian Vermeule of Harvard Law School is among the authors who have elaborated upon this quasi-religious character of liberalism.[28] He and others have analysed how liberalism, like other religions, possesses its liturgy, sacraments and rituals. This comparison is an eye-opener, especially for the many who still believe that liberalism stands for neutrality in the public sphere, among other things. This religious character of liberalism contrasts the view discussed in the previous section that the Cultural Revolution of the 1960s led to an ideological vacuum that populist movements subsequently attempt to fill. However, it is in line with the idea that, since the demise of Christianity, liberalism has become the dominant cultural force in modern societies.

It is not entirely clear what post-liberal thought envisages as alternative system of government. Postliberalism comes in many different shades and, apart from similarities, differences abound. Theoretically, it is possible to return to pre-modern times. One could advocate the kind of ancient constitutionalism

---

[26]Patrick J. Deneen, *Why Liberalism Failed* (New Haven and London: Yale University Press, 2018).
[27]John Rawls, *Political Liberalism* (New York: Columbia University Press, 2003; expanded edition).
[28]Adrian Vermeule, 'All Human Conflict Is Ultimately Theological', *Church Life Journal*, 26 July 2019.

that the Founders did not want to abandon altogether.[29] One could even conceive of a form of a 'regimen mixtum', as was advocated by Cicero (106–143 BCE),[30] a mix of monarchal, aristocratic and democratic elements. Yet, in practice, it is impossible to turn the clock back to before the rise of modernity. Even though reforms can be abolished and regression is as much part of history as progression, undoing the many changes modernity has brought remains an imaginative option.

Consequently, any post-liberal political order will somehow have to build on the foundation of modernity. This diminishes the difference between postliberalism and the original idea of liberal democracy. Adrian Vermeule's recent proposal of a 'common good constitutionalism'[31] can illustrate this. This term suggests that substantive goals, such as 'abundance' and health and safety, should henceforth guide the various policies again. Liberalism is typically very hesitant to formulate such goals, although this hesitancy can be seen as a substantive goal in its own right. Also, liberalism might even pursue further substantive goals against its own intentions. This raises the question concerning the difference between the substantive goals of liberalism and the idea of the common good as advocated by Vermeule. The answer is that liberal policies are an aggregation of different individual wills that exist within a society, while common good constitutionalism seeks to strike a balance between those interests that surpass the sum of individual wills. This balance is meant to serve the shared interests of the population.

To a certain extent, the idea of common good constitutionalism resembles the Founders' idea to combine an objective definition of happiness at the state level with more subjective formulations at the individual level. Among the camp of post-liberal thinkers, Vermeule belongs to recent proponents of Catholic integralism.[32] Catholic integralism wants the Catholic tradition to inform government policies, as Catholicism supposedly represents the truth concerning the human condition. Although this is anathema to many twenty-first-century readers, it nevertheless goes back to classical and Christian thought that has always held that true freedom existed in the desire to act in conformity with truth and goodness. The idea that government policies should be based on the truth guided also the Founders' affiliation to the natural law and natural rights tradition at the collective level. Unlike Catholic integralism, however,

---

[29]Bruce P. Frohnen, 'Is Constitutionalism Liberal?', *Campbell Law Review* 33 (2011): 529–58.
[30]*De Re Publica* (54–51 BCE).
[31]Adrian Vermeule, 'Beyond Originalism. The Dominant Conservative Philosophy for Interpreting the Constitution has Served Its Purpose, and Scholars Ought to Develop a More Moral Framework', *The Atlantic*, 31 March 2020.
[32]Theologian and philosopher John Milbank represents a Protestant – Anglican – strand of post-liberal thought.

the Founders wanted to grant considerable freedom at the individual level to depart from this collectively acknowledged truth.

2.5 IN CONCLUSION

As we have seen, liberal democracy began as a system that, in continuity with ancient constitutionalism, defined happiness objectively at the collective level. The new, modern element consisted of the fact that individual members of society were allowed to pursue happiness in their own, subjective ways. For a considerable period, Christianity served as the political theology of this order, thus guaranteeing its legitimacy.

Over time, constitutional democracy transformed into a secular, liberal democracy inasmuch as the quest for happiness acquired a subjective character even at the collective level. Although, in theory, this should have led to more freedom, the state soon paradoxically acquired an ever more powerful role, in order to realize its liberal goals. Liberal democracies turned into increasingly technocratic forms of government, with a consequent decline in legitimacy. Populist movements reacted with alternatives in the form of quasi-Christian political theologies. There is not much reason to assume that such populist political orders would be able to maintain democratic legitimacy in the long run, either. There appear to be roughly two possible directions in which populist-led orders might develop. Either they become constitutional democracies again or they develop into authoritarian regimes. As constitutional democracy requires a high level of political sophistication and indeed education at the level of the population, the second option seems more likely.

Such a scenario demonstrates the importance of political theology for constitutional orders. A constitutional democracy can probably not exist for long without the role that the natural law and natural rights tradition has played in the past. Liberalism proves to be unable to serve as a secular substitute for Christianity in liberal democracies. Populist movements try to fill the religious void. In other words, to the extent that liberalism tends to undermine the role that Christianity has historically played in the public sphere, it actively undermines itself.

The West, then, finds itself yet again at a historical turning point. If the most recent turning point occurred 250 years ago with the rise of modernity, today, the question is whether modernity can produce a viable liberal democratic political order if both its classical and Christian roots are being cut off. Those who appreciate the blessings of liberal democracy must hope for a revival of the natural law and natural rights tradition. The elites might, for example, somehow have to allow Christianity to play a role in public life again, despite its decreased numerical significance. Thus, the English system of state-church relations is not the least plausible option for today.³³ Of course, this system is often criticized for being out of touch with the developments in society. Indeed, the Church of England no longer represents more than a minority of the population. Nevertheless, by safeguarding the church's constitutional role, Britain creates a space in public life not just for Christianity but also for other religions and, indirectly, the classics. Great Britain may not just be the birthplace of democracy but also the place where it will last the longest in its contemporary form of liberal democracy.

This somewhat unexpected conclusion is the result of the external perspective that this chapter has adopted. Legal scholars and political scientists may accumulate much knowledge about the functioning of liberal democracies and the contributions of the Constitution to their legitimacy. These disciplines have difficulties assessing the current legitimacy crisis of liberal democracy, because of their often internal perspectives. Normatively, most constitutional lawyers and political scientists adhere to the ideals of liberal democracy, which equally makes it challenging to be as critical as is required for academic treatments of the topic.

Paradoxically, philosophers and theologians sometimes write more valuable commentaries on the state of liberal democracy, because they do not always fully adhere to the ideals of liberal democracy themselves. Even though, since Vatican II, the Roman Catholic Church has moved closer to liberal democracy by acknowledging, for example, the freedom of religion, it has maintained some reservations. These reservations may grow more robust, now that liberal democracy is turning into a secular liberal form of government. Although it is too soon to tell whether integralism will gain even more momentum, it is somehow telling that this is a movement within the Roman Catholic Church.³⁴

Adopting an external perspective also allows us to acknowledge the role of political theologies within liberal democracies. This chapter has identified at least three different political theologies that explain the way liberal democracy has developed historically: Christianity, liberalism and populism. If the analysis presented earlier is correct, it is crucial to recognize the political–theological character of both liberalism and populism. It is also vital to acknowledge the historical and present role of Christianity in legitimating and maintaining liberal democracy.

If Max Stackhouse is correct that political theology 'too often equates or reduces the public to partisan or governmental policy, and understands the state

---

³³Cf. Roger Trigg, *Religion in Public Life. Must Faith Be Privatized?* (Oxford: Oxford University Press, 2007).
³⁴For an excellent collection of essays by a Protestant philosopher and theologian, see Nicholas Wolterstorff, *Understanding Liberal Democracy. Essays in Political Philosophy* (Oxford: Oxford University Press, 2012).

as the institution that comprehends and guides all other spheres of society', there is a contribution to be made by public theology as well. According to Stackhouse,

> [p]ublic theology seeks to remedy this by insisting that institutions of civil society precede regimes both in order of occurrence and by right, and insists that theology, in dialogue with other fields of thought, carries indispensable resources for forming, ethically ordering and morally guiding the institutions of religion and civil society as well as the vocations of the persons in these various spheres of life.[35]

At this moment in time, when liberal states suffer from a legitimacy crisis, the key to facilitating the pursuit of happiness in the foreseeable future is likely to lie in civil society and, thus, in public theology.[36]

---

[35] Stackhouse, 'Civil Religion, Political Theology and Public Theology'.
[36] Cf. Miroslav Volf and Matthew Croasmun, *For the Life of the World. Theology That Makes a Difference* (Grand Rapids, MI: Brazos Press, 2019).

CHAPTER 3

The secular

CHRISTOPH HÜBENTHAL

Until today, the concept of the secular has not played a major role in the debates on public theology; and it has certainly not been viewed as the key concept upon which public theology can be built. In contrast to this widespread neglect, in the present chapter I will argue that the secular can be taken as the central notion to determine what public theology is. For if public theology claims to be genuine theology, it must be based on a *comprehensive account of Christian faith* as it is usually articulated by systematic theology. This includes an account of the *relationship between the creator and his creation*, the *place of the human being* within the whole of creation, the *concrete historical shape that this place has taken on today* and the *responsibilities and aspirations* that the human being has in face of this concrete place. My suggestion is that the place of the human being and the corresponding responsibilities and aspirations can best be summed up in the concept of the secular.

In order to substantiate this claim, in Section 3.1, I will take a brief look at the *historical processes* that have shaped the secular. Next to providing a better understanding of how the secular has come about, this section will also collect some important motifs which are needed to develop a *theological concept of the secular*. In Section 3.2, I will try to systematically carve out this concept. The aim is thus to determine the place of the human being within the whole of God's creation and to infer from that its responsibilities and aspirations. Paradoxically, though, the essence of the secular is hardly known to the secular itself. Therefore, as I will argue in Section 3.3, *the secular has to be enlightened about itself*. Exactly this is the task of public theology. More specifically, I will show that public theology has to enlighten the secular about its distortions, its core and its aspirations.

3.1 THE WAY TO THE SECULAR

3.1.1 'Secularization' – a contested concept

Discriminating the age we live in from the processes that have brought this age about entails making a distinction between the *secular* and *secularization*. 'Secularization', however, is not an uncontested term. Hans Joas, for example, has recently put forward an astute critique on 'processual nouns' (*Prozesssubstantive*) like 'disenchantment', 'modernisation', 'rationalization' or 'secularization' since they all insinuate a mono-linear development of the history of religion.[1] According to Joas, religious history must be taken as a permanent alteration between processes of sacralization and de-sacralization. Although this view tends to overemphasize historical contingencies and to overlook continuities, Joas is still right to condemn the assumption of a mono-linear development. This holds particularly true for accounts which employ a straight-lined secularization narrative in order to motivate a one-sidedly positive or negative judgement about its present outcome. Whereas Hans Blumenberg, for instance, affirmatively emphasized the self-assertion of modernity over against the theological absolutism of the late Middle Ages,[2] authors like Carl Schmitt, Leo Strauss, Karl Löwith and Eric Voegelin held the history of secularization responsible for what they respectively identified as the crisis of modernity.[3] In the same vein, theologians like Friedrich Gogarten, Wolfhart Pannenberg and Jürgen Moltmann valued the secularization project as 'the birth of the modern world out of the spirit of the messianic hope'.[4] Others, in contrast, fiercely disapproved the process of secularization as the linear unfolding of a disastrous theological course-setting which eventually resulted in a godless, nihilistic and violent myth.[5] In all these cases, however, the problem is not, as Joas suggests,

---

[1] Hans Joas, *Die Macht des Heiligen: Eine Alternative zur Geschichte von der Entzauberung* (Berlin: Suhrkamp, 2017), 355–417.
[2] Hans Blumenberg, *Die Legitimität der Neuzeit*, 3rd edn. (Frankfurt a. M.: Suhrkamp, 1997).
[3] See Giaccomo Marramao, 'Säkularisierung', in *Historisches Wörterbuch der Philosophie*, ed. Joachim Ritter und Karlfried Gründer, vol. 8 (Basel: Schwabe, 1992), cols. 1133–61.
[4] Jürgen Moltmann, *God for a Secular Society: The Public Relevance of Theology*, trans. Margaret Kohl (London: SCM Press, 1999), 6.
[5] See, for instance, John Milbank, *Theology and Social Theory: Beyond Secular Reason*, 2nd edn. (Malden, MA: Blackwell, 2006); Conor Cunningham, *Genealogy of Nihilism: Philosophies of Nothing and the Difference of Theology* (London: Routledge, 2002); Brad S. Gregory, *The Unintended Reformation: How a Religious Revolution Secularized Society* (Cambridge, MS: Harvard University Press, 2012).

the use of the processual noun 'secularization' as such but rather its mono-linear interpretation which is motivated by a partisan evaluation of its result.

The secularization thesis, therefore, needs not to be denounced but must be revised. Instead of narrating a straight-lined story which ends up in an unambiguously desirable or detrimental state of affairs, secularization has to be conceived of as a multidimensional process whose current outcome is a situation of high ambivalence. Such narratives are available. Taylor's magisterial work *A Secular Age* is certainly an impressive example hereof.[6] Likewise, Jürgen Habermas has recently presented a large-scale genealogy of post-metaphysical thinking.[7] Particularly, this work might be of interest to us since it depicts the genealogy in question as an *'internally comprehensible, but not exclusively internally directed* learning process'.[8] This means that the intellectual history of Europe can be construed as a consistent learning process which was intrinsically perspicuous to the protagonists involved. However, it must not be taken as a mono-linear development, since the process was also informed by external factors, particularly by the contingencies of the *social evolution* and the *accumulation of world knowledge*. Habermas's genealogy of post-metaphysical thinking thus portrays a learning process towards the secular whose exponents innovatively reacted to the theories of their predecessors and contemporaries, as well as to the varying challenges of the social and scientific evolution.

In what follows, I will build on the idea that secularization can be described as a complex interplay of the accumulation of world knowledge, the social evolution and accompanying intellectual learning processes. Of course, I do not pretend to give a full account of the different secularization strands and their interconnections. I only want to highlight important intellectual shifts and collect some crucial motifs, which then can be used to develop a theological concept of the secular.

3.1.2 *The accumulation of world knowledge*

That modernity saw the light of day long before it became aware of itself in the sixteenth and seventeenth centuries is a widely held view. Michael Allen Gillespie has pointed out that already the *nominalist revolution* in the fourteenth century marked the advent of modernity.[9] According to him, it was Willem of Ockham who 'destroyed the order of the world that scholasticism

---

[6]Charles Taylor, *A Secular Age* (Cambridge, MA: The Belknap Press of Harvard University Press, 2007).
[7]Jürgen Habermas, *Auch eine Geschichte der Philosophie*, 2 vols. (Berlin: Suhrkamp, 2019).
[8]Ibid., vol. 1, 39 – all translations are mine.
[9]See Michael Allen Gillespie, *The Theological Origins of Modernity* (Chicago: Chicago University Press, 2008), 19–43.

had imagined to mediate between God and man and replaced it with a chaos of radically individual beings'.[10] Though this judgement sounds rather harsh, Gillespie is not mistaken in contending that Ockham's nominalism heralded the decline of the Neoplatonic–Aristotelian metaphysics and inaugurated a completely novel world view which was soon designated as the *via moderna*. This 'modern way' denied the reality of ontological universals and advocated a strict distinction between theology and philosophy.[11] In the long run, the focus on individual entities and the growing autonomy of philosophy gave rise to a decidedly empirical and non-theological way of gaining knowledge about the world, that is, the modern sciences.

Perhaps the most revolutionary step on this path was Copernicus' replacement of the geocentric by the *heliocentric system*.[12] As such, heliocentrism was not unprecedented,[13] but its opposition to the theological world view became not visible before Copernicus' empirically and mathematically well-substantiated findings reached a wider audience. Remarkably, however, it took more than seventy years until Copernicus' work and other publications endorsing heliocentrism were placed on the index. The occasion was the first trial of Galileo Galilei. On the surface, this conflict pertained to the correct interpretation of the Bible, but in fact there was more at stake. For Galilei was not only interested in astronomic but also in terrestrial phenomena. He thus systematically employed hypotheses, experiments, accurate observations, exact measurements and mathematical methods in order to interpret virtually every appearance of the celestial and sublunary world. So, it was not without good reasons that he was suspected of having laid the foundation of an irresistible disenchantment of God's creation. Notwithstanding his personal beliefs, therefore, he rightly counts as the founder of the modern sciences and as the instigator of a project that would soon lead to a tremendous accumulation of secular world knowledge.

Yet, for the time being, even the factual exodus of the sciences from the sacral complex did not account for their comprehensive theoretical emancipation. Copernicus, Kepler and Galilei were all convinced that they were just spelling out the divine blueprint of creation. This was a more or less personal view, but from Descartes' work it became obvious that there was indeed a fundamental

---

[10]Ibid., 27.
[11]Sigrid Müller, *Theologie und Philosophie im Spätmittelalter: Die Anfänge der via moderna und ihre Bedeutung für die Entwicklung der Moraltheologie (1380–1450)* (Münster: Aschendorff, 2018).
[12]For the complicated dependecy of Copernicus on the *via moderna*, see Heinrich Rombach, *Substanz, System, Struktur: Die Ontologie des Funktionalismus und der philosophische Hintergrund der modernen Wissenschaften*, vol. 1, 2nd edn. (Freiburg, München: Karl Alber, 1981), 75–288.
[13]Astriarchus of Samos advocated heliocentrism already in the third century BCE. And Nicolaus of Oresme, a *via moderna* thinker of the fourteenth century, also discussed the possibility of a heliocentric system.

theoretical problem which impeded the final secularization of the sciences.[14] In line with his predecessors and contemporaries, Descartes pursued a scientific description of the astronomic and terrestrial world, the so-called *mathesis universalis*. Yet from the *via moderna* Descartes had also inherited the idea of the world's absolute contingency. For that reason, he deployed his method of radical doubt in order to find a non-contingent fundament on the basis of which the mathematical structure of reality could be ensured. He found this fundament in the self-consciousness of the thinking subject, the famous *cogito*. But still there was no warranty that the clear and distinct concepts of the thinking subject would correspond to the structure of the extra-mental world. To safeguard this correspondence, therefore, Descartes had to invoke a proof of God's existence which, moreover, made sure that the deity is not an evil genius but a benevolent God who ensures the congruity of our mathematically informed sensations and the actual make-up of reality. Only on this theological assumption Descartes believed the *mathesis universalis* to be able to produce truthful knowledge. As far as their philosophical foundation was concerned, the sciences were thus not yet completely secularized. By the same token, many prominent successors of Descartes such as Pascal, Spinoza, Leibniz and Newton adhered to the opinion that the sciences need some kind of metaphysical foundation. Though they all made significant contributions to the augmentation and factual secularization of the sciences, on a fundamental theoretical level, they still connected the accumulation of world knowledge with the sacral complex.

3.1.3 The social evolution

Interestingly, it was again the nominalist revolution which – albeit in a more indirect way – had an impact on a second strand of the secularizing process, namely the social evolution. And again, it was Ockham who played an important role because he, for contingent biographical reasons, dedicated the second half of his creative life to political issues.[15] By building on his nominalist critique of the Neoplatonic–Aristotelian metaphysics and on a demanding concept of human freedom, he developed a theory of ecclesial and state power which accentuated the right of the subjects to freely elect their rulers in both realms. Likewise, he provided an elaborate account of the separation of church and state. Even a step further went his contemporary Marsilius of Padua who not only advocated the separation of church and state but also campaigned for the church's subordination under the secular authority. The reason for this was his conviction that the persistence of a society can be safeguarded only if coercive

---

[14]For the following, see Rombach, *Substanz, System, Struktur*, 355–513; Gillespie, *The Theological Origins of Modernity*, 170–206.
[15]See Jürgen Miethke, *Ockhams Weg zur Sozialphilosophie* (Berlin: De Gruyter, 1969).

power is exercised by a single state authority which in turn has to be legitimized by the rational will of the people. Furthermore, he asserted that even in religious matters the rational will of the people is a better means to maintain the organizational structure of the church than the papal primacy alone.[16] Against this background, Johannes Fried rightly observes that already at the beginning of the fourteenth century 'a tendency towards de-hierarchization intensified and shaped a polycentric order of the world which sought to legitimize and organize – even below the level of kings and princes – the participation of the many in the exercise of power'.[17]

In spite of the visionary accounts of Ockham and Marsilius, however, a broader societal debate on the legitimation of power occurred not before the sixteenth century. At that time, a public opinion began to form, which demanded a reasonable justification of governmental interferences in the light of any information available.[18] In the seventeenth and eighteenth centuries – supported by the increase of independent newspapers, the general growth of literacy and the establishment of learned circles – the idea of a *public sphere* took shape, that is, the idea of a virtual forum at which all issues of common interest can be discussed through the exchange of rational arguments and at which authoritative decisions are prepared by providing them with a rational basis. Moreover, this forum was believed to be accessible to everyone. On the social level the secularization process thus saw the formation of a *public sphere* which was meant to serve as a *common body of reflection*. Ideally speaking, this body alone could justify public decisions and the exercise of power, for only this body was able to warrant the commonality of the justifying reasons.

3.1.4 Intellectual learning processes

With regard to the intellectual learning processes that propelled secular thinking, I will confine myself to two seminal positions which marked, as it were, the beginning and the high point of secularization. From the previous remarks it became already clear that the nominalist revolution played a pivotal role in the onset of multiple secularizing strands. However, this revolution did not come out of the blue. In fact, it had been prepared by a rediscovery and novel articulation of central elements of Christian faith and practice. Accordingly, the very origins of all the branches of secularization can be traced back to a vital *theological learning process*.

---

[16]Alan Gewirth, 'Introduction', in Marsilius of Padua, *Defensor Pacis*, trans. Alan Gewirth (New York, NY: Columbia University Press, 1956), xix–xci.
[17]Johannes Fried, *Das Mittelalter: Geschichte und Kultur* (München: C.H. Beck, 2008), 344.
[18]Jürgen Habermas, *Strukturwandel der Öffentlichkeit: Untersuchungen zu einer Kategorie der bürgerlichen Gesellschaft*, reprint (Frankfurt a. M.: Suhrkamp, 1990).

The main instigator of the nominalist revolution was John Duns Scotus, though he himself was not a nominalist. One of his decisive achievements consisted in the replacement of an 'epistemological way to salvation', as it was propagated within the Neoplatonic–Aristotelian framework, by a 'communicative way'.[19] In fact, he provided the theoretical tools to comprehend the relationship between God and humans as *personal encounter* and not merely as *radical dependency* on the part of creature. To achieve this, Scotus did away with the metaphysics of the *analogia entis* which had put the creature in an ontological dependency relation with its divine ground of being. This ground, in turn, was taken as exhibiting similarities as well as – ever greater – dissimilarities with creaturely being. The corresponding epistemological way to salvation was thus to gain knowledge of the creature's analogical ground of being. In Scotus's view, however, such a metaphysical conception could neither do justice to God as he was reported in the Scriptures nor to the peculiarities of Christian piety. On this account, he disrupted the ontological bond and emphasized the independence of the creaturely realm. For the same reason, he introduced a quite innovative understanding of *human freedom*. While the Neoplatonic–Aristotelian tradition had considered the human will as a kind of natural inclination directed towards the good, Scotus regarded it as the faculty to freely determine itself. In doing so, he was able to conceptualize salvation as the human's free consent to God's gratuitous self-giving. The soteriological importance of this account becomes clear from his Christology.[20] Here, he not only showed that the unity of Christ's divine and human nature is nothing but a *unity of love*, but he also contended that every human being is called to enter into such a Christ-like unity.

The paradigm shift that Scotus prepared indicates a substantial theological learning process since it replaced the model of an *already existing metaphysical unity* by the vision of a *personal unity that is yet to be achieved* in that the creature freely engages with God's antecedent love. Apparently, this vision corresponded much better with biblically informed believes and practices. More importantly, however, it also entailed the *theological justification* of an independent creaturely realm because, in Scotus's view, it was the intention of the creator to lovingly unite with his creation through the creature's free-loving response. If we thus take the theological idea of a creaturely realm which is metaphysically detached from the divine as to epitomize the *conceptual nucleus of the secular*, and if we, moreover, agree with Habermas that this shift was indeed an essential breakthrough on the long way to secular thinking, then we may contend that the process of secularization originated from a theological

---

[19]Habermas, *Auch eine Geschichte der Philosophie*, vol. 1, 781–2.
[20]See Richard Cross, *The Metaphysics of Incarnation: Thomas Aquinas to Duns Scotus* (Oxford: Oxford University Press, 2002).

discovery and justification of the secular itself.[21] In any event, Scotus's departure from the metaphysics of the *analogia entis* and his seminal redefinition of freedom marked, as Habermas holds, the 'release of the fallen creature into the demanding freedom of a morally bound self-determination by virtue of which humans have to self-manage their social and political life in face of practical necessities'.[22]

It is surely not mistaken to assert that Immanuel Kant was the one who eventually consummated this release into secular freedom. In fact, he put together the different branches of the secularization process and provided them with a robust philosophical foundation. His transcendental reflections on the possibility conditions of human knowledge, for instance, definitely ratified the break with the analogical metaphysics that Scotus and the nominalists had launched. In contrast to Descartes, Spinoza or Leibniz, Kant was also able to show that the sciences are not in need of any metaphysical grounding. For true knowledge, as he claimed, is only possible if intuition and concept work together. While the sciences adhered to that tenet and so made progress, metaphysics did not and was thus 'mere groping, and what is the worst, a groping among mere concepts'.[23]

Kant's unequivocal statement against metaphysics and for the sciences resembles an equally clear affirmation of the social evolution hitherto. In his little piece on Enlightenment, for example, Kant remarked that 'for many affairs conducted in the interest of a commonwealth a certain mechanism is necessary', a mechanism which compels the functionaries to simply obey the internal logic of the relevant sphere.[24] At the same time, however, he stressed that as educated private people the same functionaries are entitled to publicly criticize such logics, and this applies to all societal spheres such as politics, law, economy, military and religion. Furthermore, it is the *public sphere* within which such private views are discursively mediated into a reasonable public opinion, and this opinion is the ultimate instance in face of which the exercise of power is to be legitimized.[25]

The obligation to reasonably justify all kinds of common activities, however, does not stand on its own feet but is rather a derivative of each individual's duty to freely submit his or her will to the universal laws of reason. Every human

---

[21]See Christoph Hübenthal, 'The Theological Significance of the Secular', *Studies in Christian Ethics* 32 (2019): 455–69.
[22]Habermas, *Auch eine Geschichte der Philosophie*, vol. 1, 803.
[23]Immanuel Kant, *Critique of Pure Reason*, trans. Paul Guyer and Allen W. Wood (Cambridge: Cambridge University Press, 1998), B XVI, 110.
[24]Immanuel Kant, 'An Answer to the Question: What Is Enlightenment?', in *Practical Philosophy*, trans. Mary J. Gregor (Cambridge: Cambridge University Press, 1996), 15–22 (18).
[25]Habermas, *Strukturwandel der Öffentlichkeit*, 178–95.

being is thus supposed to live autonomously. The possibility of autonomy, in turn, rested for Kant on the – theoretically unprovable, but practically necessary – assumption that the human being is unconditionally free, because the spontaneity of freedom cannot be caused by whatever condition. As exempt from all conditionalities, furthermore, freedom cannot be considered as an empirical skill but must be conceived of as a transcendental faculty. It is here that we touch upon the very heart of Kant's philosophy, since *transcendental freedom* turns out to be the final ground of all our theoretical and practical operations.[26] More important, though, this principle also reveals in which way Kant can be said to have consummated the secularization process. For if it is transcendental freedom that constitutes the whole realm which is theoretically and practically accessible to us, then the human world can be reduced to this immanent principle. Kant, therefore, definitely confirmed the tendency towards a decidedly *immanentist* determination of the human's position in the world.

However, Kant not only sought to answer the questions of what we can know and what we should do but also of what we may hope.[27] All these questions, he claimed, express a necessary interest of reason so that they must find an answer. His own attempt to resolve the third question started again from the notion of transcendental freedom. Here, he showed that freedom is obligated to pursue the highest good which, however, can never be achieved through freedom's own efforts. To warrant the possibility of the highest good, therefore, the existence of a personal God had to be postulated.[28] Despite some problems that this answer might bear,[29] Kant nonetheless provided an insight whose significance can hardly be overestimated. In fact, he demonstrated that transcendental freedom is the principle which *confirms the secular's immanentism* but at the same time *disrupts this immanentism* in that it necessarily strives for an ultimate fulfilment which corresponds to its own unconditionedness. Since this unconditionedness only refers to its primordial spontaneity but not to its factual possibilities which are confined to the empirical world, transcendental freedom can never accomplish its own fulfilment. Rather its *fulfilment condition*, as one might call it, lies in an *absolute freedom* which is not subjected to the limitations of space and time and thus proves to be *almighty* and *morally good*.

To sum up, secularization as an intellectual learning process from Scotus to Kant can be depicted as the unleashing and gradual development of an autonomous realm. First, this unleashing was meant to warrant the possibility

---

[26]Herbert Meyer, *Kants transzendentale Freiheitslehre* (Freiburg, München: Alber, 1994).
[27]Kant, *Critique of Pure Reason*, A 805 / B 833, 677.
[28]Immanuel Kant, *Critique of Practical Reason*, in Kant, *Practical Philosophy*, 133–271 (228–58).
[29]Christoph Hübenthal, 'Autonomie als Prinzip: Zur Neubegründung der Moralität bei Kant', in *Kant und die Theologie*, ed. Georg Essen and Magnus Striet (Darmstadt: Wissenschaftliche Buchgesellschaft, 2005), 95–128.

of a loving unification of God and humans. For this purpose, Scotus not only broke open an already existing metaphysical unity but also reinterpreted human freedom as the faculty of self-determination. Step by step, the autonomy of the secular unfolded its own dynamics, not least because the other branches of secularization – the accumulation of world knowledge and the social evolution – tended into the same direction. At the provisional end point of this process, Kant provided all secularizing strands with a philosophical foundation which, moreover, terminated in the notion of transcendental freedom. Remarkably, it was this principle which at the same time consummated and disrupted the immanentism of the secular realm, because it constitutes the empirical world and nonetheless points to a divine fulfilment condition which lies beyond this world.

3.2 TOWARDS A THEOLOGICAL CONCEPTION OF THE SECULAR

3.2.1 The inevitability of a transcendental understanding of freedom

Of course, the previous account of secularization remains terribly incomplete. Much more should be said about the different branches and their interweaving. Likewise, secularization did not stop with Kant. However, whereas the scientific and the social evolution after Kant mostly accelerated previous trends, the intellectual learning process was characterized by an increasing renunciation of Kant's transcendentalism. This *de-transcendentalization*, as Habermas calls it,[30] generated lots of indispensable insights such as the turn to linguistics and hermeneutics, the discovery of the objective spirit and the intuition of a communicative mediation of truth. Yet, the abandonment of transcendental thinking also resulted in a mindset which eclipsed the quest for freedom's ultimate fulfilment. For as soon as freedom is deprived of its transcendental unconditionedness, it will necessarily be reduced to an inner-worldly faculty whereby its fulfilment condition will no longer be located beyond the scope of its own power.

Habermas nevertheless endorses the de-transcendentalization process because he thinks that every performance of freedom is embedded in an intersubjective setting. Kant's approach, in contrast, represents for him a merely solitary and detached view. However, the legitimate claim that any contemplation about the reasonableness of decisions should be an intersubjective endeavour does not entail that the transcendental status of freedom can be abandoned. Thomas Nagel has rightly pointed out that Kant's *fact of reason* inevitably 'reveals

---

[30]Habermas, *Auch eine Geschichte der Philosophie*, vol. 2, 375–766.

itself in decision not in contemplation'.[31] Freedom thus necessarily exhibits a transcendental standpoint over against all factors conditioning or motivating our decisions, including reason. But this is not to say that the exercise of freedom is irrational. By building on Fichte, Stephen Darwall has highlighted that transcendental freedom always stands in an authority and accountability relation to other freedom by which it is summoned to commit itself to reasons that can intersubjectively be shared.[32] Likewise building on Fichte, Hermann Krings has even shown that transcendental freedom properly determines itself only through the unrestricted recognition of other freedom, whereby this recognition finds its expression in an engagement with intersubjectively shared reasons.[33]

In so arguing, Darwall and Krings have successfully reconciled Kant's transcendentalism with Habermas's claim for intersubjectivity. But there is more to it. Particularly Krings has also offered a novel understanding of the fulfilment condition of freedom.[34] Whereas in Kant's account God only plays an instrumental role in the realization of the highest good, Krings has demonstrated that God's absolute freedom itself is the ultimate fulfilment of human freedom. For the unrestricted recognition of any other freedom (to which finite human freedom is obligated by virtue of its own unconditionedness) is ultimately possible only on the assumption that there is an absolute divine freedom which already recognizes finite freedom unconditionally.[35] Hence, it is this absolute freedom which constitutes the ultimate fulfilment of human freedom. Although Krings makes no affirmative statement about God's existence or the necessity to postulate it, his considerations still amount to the *hypothetical* assertion that *if* transcendental freedom ever will enjoy ultimate fulfilment, *then* this fulfilment consists in an incessant communion with God.

In spite of the factual secularization process after Kant, the notion of transcendental freedom thus cannot be given up. It is, so to speak, the *hidden core of the secular* which prevents it from a total encapsulation in the 'iron

---

[31]Thomas Nagel, *The Last Word* (Oxford: Oxford University Press, 1997), 117.
[32]Stephen Darwall, *The Second-Person Standpoint: Morality, Respect, and Accountability* (Cambridge, MA: Harvard University Press, 2006).
[33]Hermann Krings, *System und Freiheit: Gesammelte Aufsätze* (Freiburg, München: Karl Alber, 1980).
[34]Hermann Krings and Eberhard Simons, 'Gott', in *Handbuch philosophischer Grundbegriffe*, ed. Hermann Krings, Hans Michael Baumgartner and Christoph Wild, vol. 3 (München: Kösel, 1973), 614–41.
[35]It should be mentioned that Krings makes a distinction between *finite freedom* and *absolute freedom*. Finite (human) freedom is 'formally unconditioned' because there are no conditions that can causally determine its execution; at the same time, however, it is 'materially conditioned' as its factual exercise is subjected to the limits of space, time or the laws of nature. Absolute (divine) freedom, in contrast, proves to be formally and materially unconditioned.

cage' (Max Weber) of immanentism. Admittedly, in contrast to Kant's view, the notion of transcendental freedom does not allow for an affirmative statement about the reality of a transcendent God, but still it shows that the secular itself cannot provide for the ultimate fulfilment of the human existence.

3.2.2 Freedom and the public sphere

Theological critics have observed that the secular builds on a distorted conception of freedom. William Cavanaugh, for instance, stressed that modern people 'falsely imagine that freedom means . . . being the source of their own being'.[36] In a similar vein, John Milbank contended that 'the modern is based upon the promotion of a non-teleological freedom'.[37] And Rowan Williams asserted 'that "secular" freedom is not enough; that this account of the liberal society dangerously simplifies the notion of freedom and ends up diminishing our understanding of the human person'.[38] These and other commentators make a good point in that the secular's average comprehension of freedom indeed hardly exceeds the idea of being able to do whatever one wants to do. And the critics are also right in complaining that a selfish understanding of freedom accounts for the ugly face of the secular in that it breeds the alienated, violent and exploitative relations that we maintain towards ourselves, our fellow human beings and the non-human nature.

Yet, we must not take the surface for the essence. The hidden core of the secular is not, as we have noticed, the superficial appearance of freedom that we come across everywhere. Instead, it is made up by the unconditioned human faculty to properly determine itself through the unrestricted recognition of others and to reach out for the gift of being unconditionally recognized by absolute freedom. On that account, the secular bears the intrinsic obligation of establishing a *social order* which gives full expression to the unrestricted recognition of freedom. As from the Kantian and Fichteian legacy can be learnt, such recognition is mediated by a voluntary commitment to *rules* that can reasonably be endorsed by everyone. Conversely, this means that every rule regulating the exercise of freedom must at the same time serve its unrestricted recognition. Krings called this the 'transcendental rule of every rule-setting' and pointed out that each norm, precept, regulation or law which guides the conduct of individuals, the operations of institutions or the functionings of

---

[36] William Cavanaugh, *Field Hospital: The Church's Engagement with a Wounded World* (Grand Rapids, MI: Eerdmans, 2016), 89.
[37] John Milbank, *Beyond Secular Reason: The Representation of Being and the Representation of the People* (Malden, MA: Wiley-Blackwell, 2013), 131.
[38] Rowan Williams, *Faith in the Public Square* (London: Bloomsbury, 2014), 24.

the (global) society must comply with this transcendental rule.[39] The question is thus of how concrete rules can be generated so that they accord with this transcendental requirement. At that point, Habermas's critique on Kant is in the right because merely solitary considerations cannot allow for a common rule-setting.[40] Rather, the acceptability of rules is to be determined by a *discursive exchange of reasons* in which virtually everyone who will be subjected to the rules can participate. Therefore, only rules that emanate from reasonable discourses can count as generally justified. And as the discursive exchange of reasons necessarily creates a *public*, it is the *public sphere* where the production and legitimation of rules have to happen. The public sphere thus constitutes the appropriate space within which the universal and unrestricted recognition of freedom on all levels is to be mediated by a rule-setting that regulates personal conduct, institutional operations and societal functions.[41]

It is important to note, though, that the reflective potential of the public sphere must not be restrained to the creation and justification of rules. For unrestrictedly recognizing every instantiation of freedom also entails enabling every human being to lead a *good, fulfilled or meaningful life*. If, therefore, the public sphere is the appropriate space to mediate the unrestricted recognition of freedom, public discourses have to serve this purpose too. Per Bauhn, for example, has pointed out that there is an existential 'need for meaning'[42] which involves the moral obligation to make one's life meaningful. In line with Paul Ricoeur or Charles Taylor, he furthermore argued that the personal identity of a self exhibits a *narrative structure* whose genuine author is the individual self. Accordingly, to lead a meaningful life implies telling the story of one's life in a way that gives expression to its internal meaning. 'Because I am an agent capable of creativity', Bauhn says, 'I ought to make my life narrative beautiful in form as well as in content.'[43] Though the self is the genuine author of its story, however, narrating one's life is not a solitary enterprise as every individual biography relates to greater communal or cultural narratives which 'provide the more specific narratives of individual agents and their lives with a culturally flavoured content'.[44] Or, as Ricoeur puts it, 'the life history of each of us is caught up in the histories of others.'[45] To lead and tell a good, meaningful and fulfilled life

---

[39]Krings, *System und Freiheit*, 94–8.
[40]For this critique on Kant, see also Karl-Otto Apel, *Diskurs und Verantwortung: Das Problem des Übergangs zu einer postkonventionellen Moral* (Frankfurt a. M.: Suhrkamp, 1988).
[41]Jürgen Habermas, *Faktizität und Geltung: Beiträge zur Diskurstheorie des Rechts und des demokratischen Rechtsstaats* (Frankfurt a. M.: Suhrkamp, 1992), 399–467.
[42]Per Bauhn, *Normative Identity* (London: Rowman & Littlefield, 2017), 15–27.
[43]Ibid., 137.
[44]Ibid., 31.
[45]Paul Ricoeur, *Oneself as Another*, trans. Kathleen Blamey (Chicago: Chicago University Press, 1992), 161.

thus necessarily exhibits a social dimension. But this does not yet explain why a public conversation is needed to support the individual self in its quest for a meaningful life and so to express the unrestricted recognition of its freedom. A decisive hint has been given here by Alan Gewirth. In addition to the aesthetic character of a life story that Bauhn calls for, Gewirth points out that the values and purposes which account for the evaluative quality of a narrative identity 'must not be a miscellaneous assortment of purposes; they should be organized according to some general plan that is intelligible and indeed compelling to the agent'.[46] Likewise, these 'purposes must be, and be regarded as, attainable by the agent'.[47] Gewirth also insists that every self is morally entitled to the social preconditions necessary to compose a beautiful, well-organized, intelligible and attainable life narrative. As he defines such entitlements in terms of human rights, he primarily thinks of preconditions like covering basic needs, political and social rights, security, education and so on.[48] But at the backdrop of what has just been said, it is easy to see that such preconditions also include greater cultural narratives without which a self cannot tell its own story in a substantial way.

It is here that the public sphere comes into play. For mediating the recognition of anyone's freedom does not only entail generating rules but also encouraging the *public narration of greater narratives of meaning*. The public availability of greater stories that spell out what human life is about and what accounts for its beauty, meaning and purpose form an indispensable element of the recognition of every individual self. If such stories are inaccessible, the individual self will simply not be capable of creating its own narrative. Apparently, there is no other place than the public sphere where narratives of meaning can be made available. But providing a forum for the narration of greater stories is not the only task of the public sphere. Since individual narratives must meet the requirements of beauty, meaningfulness, attainability, coherence, intelligibility and so on, the greater narratives too must comply with these conditions. For this purpose, public discourses also seek to verify whether greater narratives fulfil these prerequisites and – if they do not or not to the full extent – also help to enhance their intrinsic quality.[49] In this way, the individual self will be empowered to freely compose its own narrative and so to lead a good, fulfilled and meaningful life.

---

[46] Alan Gewirth, *Self-Fulfillment* (Princeton: Princeton University Press, 1998), 186.
[47] Ibid., 187.
[48] See Ibid., 189–99.
[49] Comparative theology is an interesting approach to enact such discourses. See Klaus von Stosch, *Komparative Theologie als Wegweiser in der Welt der Religionen* (Paderborn: Schöningh, 2012).

3.2.3 The theological concept of the secular

The line of thought expounded thus far identified a transcendental understanding of freedom as the hidden but nonetheless indispensable core of the secular. Likewise, it became clear that, by virtue of its own unconditionedness, freedom is obligated to recognize every other instantiation of freedom unrestrictedly. Such recognition is mediated by public discourses which justify normative frameworks and provide intelligible narratives of meaning so that the individual self can – as Ricoeur phrased it – aim 'at the "good life" with and for others in just institutions'.[50] However, a good, fulfilled and meaningful life is not the final goal of the human existence. Ultimately, transcendental freedom longs for unconditioned recognition by absolute divine freedom. And though it is true that the reality of divine freedom remains just a hypothesis for secular thinking, this hypothesis still prevents it from being locked up in the self-enclosed immanentism towards which the secularization process so long tended.

The different strands of this process emerged, as we saw, from a theological learning process in the late Middle Ages. Here, the analogical model which had situated the creature in a radical ontological dependency relation with the divine was replaced by a model that emphasized God's will to have true human 'co-lovers'.[51] Mutual love, however, presupposes unconditioned freedom on both sides, for otherwise human love would be just an affection caused by God. With this model, it became possible to comprehend orthodox Christian faith and practice in a coherent and consistent manner. *Creation*, for instance, could now be taken as the *ex nihilo* origination of a non-divine realm, whereby God wanted to make room for another freedom next to himself. Likewise, *sin* no longer needed to be thought of as a kind of intellectual error but could be cognized as a free refusal of divine love. Likewise, *Christ* appeared to be the ultimate unity of divine and human love. And the *eschaton* could be conceived of as the Christ-like unification of God with the whole of his creation.[52] Hence, the essential achievement of this learning process was that it redefined the relationship between God and humans by replacing metaphysical dependency with personal relationality. As relationality implies an autonomous standing of both partners, the new model discovered the existence of a non-divine sphere which is decidedly willed by God and which he entrusted to human freedom. It was this discovery out of which the secular gradually developed. Hence, *the historical process of secularization emerged from a theological conceptualization and justification of the secular itself.*

---

[50]Ricoeur, *Onself as Another*, 172.
[51]John Duns Scotus, *Ordinatio III*, d. 32, q. un. (ed. Viv. XI, 433).
[52]For a comprehensive theological account based on the principle of human freedom, see Thomas Pröpper, *Theologische Anthropologie*, 2 vols. (Freiburg: Herder, 2011).

Against this backdrop, now the *theological concept of the secular* can be spelt out. In short, the secular can be depicted as the *scope of human freedom*, whereby freedom must not primarily be taken in the superficial form of mere freedom of choice or freedom of action but mainly as the transcendental faculty to unconditionally determine itself. In spite of this transcendental unconditionedness, though, the empirical effects of free choices and free actions are still subjected to the constraints of space and time which is why human freedom proves to be *finite freedom*. Due to this finitude, freedom's ultimate fulfilment lies beyond the scope of its own power, namely in the unconditioned recognition by absolute divine freedom. From a theological point of view, the existence of absolute freedom is not just a hypothesis as it is for philosophical thinking. Rather, theology starts from the belief that God definitely revealed himself in Jesus Christ as unconditioned love for every human being.[53] Accordingly, God's self-manifestation, as well as the communication of his unconditioned recognition of human freedom, is the content of revelation which as such is meant to invite human freedom to lovingly respond to the unconditioned recognition and love it has received. Seen in that light, the secular turns out to be *the scope that God has entrusted to human freedom*. And as the proper performance of human freedom entails the mutual and unrestricted recognition of every manifestation of freedom, the secular needs to give expression to such recognition. The realm to mediate recognition is, as we have seen, the *public sphere* as the secular's common body of reflection. In that sphere, *reasonable rules* have to be generated which regulate the use of freedom on the individual, communal, institutional and global level. On the other hand, the public sphere also has to create various fora at which *greater narratives of meaning* can be told and discursively be evaluated in terms of their internal coherence, intelligibility and beauty so that the individual self is empowered to narrate a meaningful story of its own life.

The secular, so we may conclude, is the scope that God has entrusted to human freedom. But this does not mean that God is absent from the secular. On the contrary. As courting love he is omnipresent, for he wills that every single manifestation of human freedom, as well as the secular in total, eventually will enter into a Christ-like unity with himself.

3.3 PUBLIC THEOLOGY IN THE FACE OF THE SECULAR

If, theologically speaking, the secular is the scope that God has entrusted to human freedom; if, moreover, the proper use of freedom consists in the

---

[53]Thomas Pröpper, *Evangelium und freie Vernunft* (Freiburg: Herder, 2001), 42–5.

unrestricted recognition of any instantiation of freedom and ultimately longs for an unconditioned recognition by God himself; and if, finally, the adequate use of freedom is mediated by the public sphere – what, then, are the tasks of public theology? The short answer is: it has to *enlighten the secular about itself*. As astonishing as this answer may seem at first glance in that it hardly resembles traditional attempts to determine the business of public theology,[54] it does not at all announce a revolution. On closer inspection, it turns even out that the enlightenment of the secular describes a multidimensional enterprise to which almost all traditional tasks of public theology can easily be assigned. More precisely, it entails enlightening the secular about its *distortions*, its *core* and its *aspirations*, whereby the first dimension largely coincides with the critical and prophetic task, the second with the ethical and political task and the third with the pastoral and apologetic task of public theology.

3.3.1 Enlightening the secular about its distortions

To enlighten the secular about its distortions means, first of all, to *criticize* secular thinking and behaviour whenever they turn out to disfigure the relations that we maintain towards ourselves, towards others and towards the non-human nature. More important, though, it also has to lay bare the *ideological roots* from which such disfigured theory and praxis spring. In that respect, it would seem as if public theology could learn a lot from post-liberal theologians who have invested intellectual rigour to reveal the secular's basic failures. Yet, however helpful such analyses may be in order to diagnose all kinds of pathologies, post-liberal theology is nonetheless incapable of properly enlightening the secular. In the wake of poststructuralism and postmodernism, post-liberal theology denies the very possibility of an overall, reasonable and truth-oriented discourse. Milbank, for instance, celebrates the 'end of a single system of truth based on universal reason, which tells us what reality is like'. Consequently, he endorses the postmodern mindset, because '[i]n postmodernity there are infinitely many possible versions of truth, inseparable from particular narratives'.[55] It is easy to see that on this assumption it is impossible to criticize secular thought in such a way that the secular is enlightened by this critique. When Milbank thus asserts that '[t]he secular *episteme* is a post-Christian paganism . . . a refusal

---

[54]See, for instance, Chul Ho Youn, 'The Points and Tasks of Public Theology', *International Journal of Public Theology* 11 (2017): 64–87; Ted Peters, 'Public Theology: Its Pastoral, Apologetic, Scientific, Political, and Prophetic Tasks', *International Journal of Public Theology* 12 (2018): 153–77.
[55]John Milbank, 'Postmodern Critical Augustianism: A Short Summa in Forty-Two Responses to Unasked Questions', in *The Radical Orthodox Reader*, ed. John Milbank and Simon Oliver (London: Routledge, 2009), 49–61 (49).

of Christianity and an invention of an "Anti-Christianity'",[56] then this can only be taken as a theologian's miffed lamentation about his non-Christian environment, but not as a meaningful analysis which makes any sense outside the particular theological narrative.

About its distortions the secular can thus only be enlightened by means of a discourse that takes place within the secular's common body of reflection, that is, the public sphere. Accordingly, the enlightenment in question proves to be a *self-enlightenment*, performed by secular itself. The specific role of public theology then is to initiate and foster this discourse just because it, by virtue of its own *theological* conception of the secular, knows about the necessity of such self-enlightenment. In close cooperation with other disciplines (e.g. philosophy, historiography and sociology), public theology openly communicates what went wrong with secular theory and practice. If the aforementioned analysis is sound, it is primarily a truncated understanding of freedom from which these distortions emerge. Hence, public theology decidedly defends the thesis that the concept of freedom is entirely misconstrued when it is taken as the mere faculty of *power, possession* or *self-sufficiency*. On this basis, for instance, it can be revealed what the driving force behind a perverted *power politics* is that leads to the sacralization of the nation, the state, the race or whichever idolatrous object. Likewise, it can be explained why the mercilessness of a lunatic *capitalism* preserves neither humans nor the non-human nature. And it can also be shown in which way the parochialism of a blind *scientism* tends to dangerously downsize the human self-understanding.

Public theology, therefore, enlightens the secular about its distortions not by telling a self-referential story which, on the one hand, paints the gloomiest possible picture of the secular but, on the other, does not even claim that the secular can recognize itself in this picture. Rather, inspired by its own theological concept of the secular, public theology promotes the secular's self-enlightenment. It does so by initiating and fostering public discourses about the deformations of secular thought and practice which find their cause in a reductionist understanding of freedom.

3.3.2 Enlightening the secular about its core

As has now repeatedly been shown, the core of the secular consists in a transcendental – though mostly concealed – understanding of freedom, which contains far-reaching ethical and political implications. To enlighten the secular in this regard thus requires publicly challenging truncated conceptions of freedom and revealing its deeper meaning. Next to the ideology-critical

---

[56]Milbank, *Theology and Social Theory*, 280.

undertakings that we have just discussed, this goal can best be achieved by engaging in *ethical and political debates*, because here the proper use and the unrestricted recognition of freedom are at stake. Since, moreover, ethical and political engagement has traditionally been viewed as the central task of public theology,[57] enlightening the secular about its core perfectly matches with this conventional understanding.

Public theology's basic guideline in such debates is the 'transcendental rule of every rule-setting', that is, ethical norms and political arrangements have to give expression to the unrestricted recognition of *every* instantiation of freedom. The scope of ethics and politics is thus *universal*. At the same time, however, every instantiation of freedom is necessarily situated within a unique bodily, biographical, cultural or historical setting so that it is always a *particular* person or group of persons whose recognition is at stake. Ideally, the tension between particularism and universalism can be bridged by enabling everyone to participate in ethical and political debates. For as soon as the universal validity of rules and arrangements can reasonably be affirmed from each particular perspective, the tension between universalism and particularism has withered away.

But, of course, things are not ideal. The lack of personal skills, imbalances of power or social and cultural biases effectively exclude multiple persons and groups from a free and equal participation in public debates. On this account, public theology's engagement in such debates aims, above all, at making the excluded voices heard. 'The presence of minorities', Clive Pearson rightly states, 'is likely to release a hermeneutic that will advocate for the stranger, the poor, those who are disadvantaged and the coming together of those whose cultural and linguistic backgrounds differ'.[58] Public theology thus strongly pursues the inclusion of the excluded. Sometimes, however, the voices of the excluded cannot be made audible even by providing them access to public debates. Due to a lack of education, traumatic experiences or a deep-rooted self-underestimation individuals and groups may not be able to adequately articulate their concerns. In such cases, public theology not only has to encourage and support the excluded but must act as their mouthpiece and advocate.

---

[57]See, for instance, E. Harold Breitenberg, 'What Is Public Theology?', in *Public Theology for a Global Society: Essays in Honor of Max L. Stackhouse*, ed. Deirdre King Hainsworth and Scott R. Paeth (Grand Rapids, MI: Eerdmans, 2010), 3–17; Hak Joon Lee, 'Public Theology', in *The Cambridge Companion to Christian Political Theology*, ed. Craig Hovey and Elizabeth Phillips (Cambridge: Cambridge University Press, 2015), 44–65; Florian Höhne, *Öffentliche Theologie: Begriffsgeschichte und Grundfragen* (Leipzig: Evangelische Verlagsanstalt, 2015), 43–75.

[58]Clive Pearsons, 'The Quest for a Coalitional Praxis: Examining the Attraction of a Public Theology from the Perspective of Minorities', in *A Companion to Public Theology*, ed. Sebastian Kim and Katie Day (Leiden: Brill, 2017), 418–40 (418).

The enlightenment of the secular about its core thus primarily takes place within ethical and political debates which bring to the surface what true freedom is, how it ought to be used and how it should universally and unrestrictedly be recognized. To comprehensively warrant this universalism, special attention is to be given to those instantiations of freedom that can hardly or not at all speak for themselves.

3.3.3 Enlightening the secular about its aspirations

Up to this point it might seem as if enlightening the secular was not a specific theological task but could just as well be performed by other disciplines and actors. It must be kept in mind, however, that all these accomplishments build on a decidedly theological concept of the secular so that public theology's ideology-critical, ethical or political engagement can by no means be taken as a secularist accommodation to penultimate needs and challenges.[59] Nonetheless, the genuine theological task of public theology is, of course, to enlighten the secular about its aspirations and, above all, about its final aspiration. Recall that human freedom in its transcendental understanding forms the core of the secular and that human freedom ultimately aspires to being unconditionally recognized by absolute divine freedom. Being unconditionally recognized by God thus makes up the final aspiration of the secular. But, as we have seen, it is by no means clear that this aspiration can be satisfied, for there is no rational evidence that God exists. And yet, although God's existence cannot compellingly be proven, it can still be witnessed to by publicly narrating an intelligible, coherent and beautiful story of meaning and by credibly living individual and communal lives in accordance with this narrative.

Enlightening the secular about its aspiration, therefore, entails a threefold challenge to public theology. *First*, the entire story of Christian faith has to publicly be narrated in an intelligible, coherent and beautiful manner. For this purpose, public theology must employ a systematic account which comprises all treatises of Christian doctrine, from Trinity and creation through revelation, Christology and ecclesiology to soteriology and eschatology. At the same time, it must become clear why this story provides an adequate response to the quest for meaning and to human freedom's longing for fulfilment. *Second*, however convincing and attractive such a narrative may be, without a corresponding practice it will barely be credible. Accordingly, public theology has to make sure that individual and communal ways of Christian life, as well as the institutional presence of the church, trustworthily express the truth of the story told. Rightly

---

[59] For a critique on accommodationist approaches, see Miroslav Volf, *A Public Faith: How Followers of Christ Should Serve the Common Good* (Grand Rapids, MI: Brazos Press, 2011), 84–5.

understood, public theology therefore not only has an external but also an internal task to fulfil. *Third*, in a pluralistic setting, the Christian narrative of meaning necessarily competes with other religious and non-religious world views. Hence, enlightening the secular about its aspiration also exhibits an apologetic dimension. After all, it can hardly be denied that the public narration of an intelligible, coherent and beautiful story about ultimate meaning implies a profound truth claim concerning the story's theoretical content and its practical adequacy. Therefore, apologetically defending this truth is the task of public theology.[60] But every articulation of truth remains fallible. In fact, there is no theological account which can claim to narrate the Christian story in a definite and insurmountable manner. For this reason, public theology's apologetic communication must keep itself open for external critique. When apologetically competing with other religious and non-religious world views for the best answer to the quest for meaning, therefore, public theology is not merely in a teaching but always also in a learning position.

At the end of the day, enlightening the secular about its distortions, its core and its aspirations aims at enabling secular people to make a free, informed and well-considered decision on whether or not they will tell the story of their life by inscribing it into the greater Christian narrative of meaning.

---

[60]Christoph Hübenthal, 'Apologetic Communication', *International Journal of Public Theology* 10 (2016): 7–27.

CHAPTER 4

Post-secularity and the pluralization of public theology

WILLIAM BARBIERI

Christians have long taken an interest in worldly affairs, including the affairs of the *polis*. But this interest has manifested itself in the form known as 'public theology' only in a particular time and place – namely, Western secular modernity, and more specifically contemporary pluralistic liberal democracies. Public theology is a flower that blossomed in an ecosystem with particular types of secularity, particular forms of publicness, particular levels of religious diversity and particular theological sensibilities. What happens, then, when these conditions change? This chapter considers the implications for public theology of a constellation of changes affecting secularity that have led numerous commentators to proclaim the advent of a post-secular dispensation.

The chapter proceeds in three stages. First, I will provide a characterization of those shifts across a range of social arenas and intellectual fields that together constitute what I will call the post-secular constellation. I will then explore how this emergent situation bears on the character and tasks of public theology, first tracing areas of change and renewal and then commenting on core commitments that can be expected to persist. Lastly, I will discuss as an illustrative case how post-secular conditions can be expected to inform the public engagement of churches and other religious actors with ecological issues. The main theme of my treatment is that the post-secular context provides new opportunities for public theology even as it pushes this project to adopt an ethos of internal pluralism.

4.1 THE POST-SECULAR CONSTELLATION

Among the various conditions and concerns that have been associated with the enterprise of public theology over the past half-century – pluralism, liberalism, a politics of the common good and so on – it seems hard to deny that secularity is the most crucial. One might make an alternative case for the centrality of the public–private distinction characterizing modern Western societies; but this, in the end, is itself largely a product of secularization processes.

Both the occasion and the need for public theology arose in response to the historical emergence of secular modernity in the West, a process that can be thought of as the Great Disentangling. One of the principal effects of the dialectic of the Enlightenment was a progressive sorting- and separating-out of previously more or less integrated realms. Thus were 'public' and 'private' distinguished, facts separated from values, philosophy and reason detached from theology and faith, science set off from metaphysics, politics insulated from the churches and a divide posited between religion and the (formerly religious) category of the secular. The product of this history of cultural unravelling is what Charles Taylor has characterized as 'a secular age', an epoch marked by interrelated processes of secularization in which Christian power and influence have been extracted or banished from political authority and autonomous social spheres; levels of religious affiliation, practice and belief have tailed off; attunement to salvation history and a sacred cosmos has given way to the exclusive perception of mundane time and a disenchanted universe; and the 'conditions of belief' underlying experience and thought have shifted in a manner demoting faith in a transcendent God to a mere option among many immanent alternatives.[1] These modes of secularity have originated in the United States and other post-Christian nations, but through a globalizing dynamic have found their way to varying degrees into the modernization paths of countries around the world. The quest to articulate an effective religious witness to how to pursue the collective worldly good under these broad conditions has defined the task of public theology.

Given this account of secularity, what, then, does it mean to speak, as many recently have, of *post-secularity*? Talk of the post-secular has become inevitable in recent decades, as the 'secularization thesis' popularized by sociologists

---

[1] Charles Taylor, *A Secular Age* (Cambridge, MA: Harvard University Press, 2007); see also Hent de Vries, 'The Deep Conditions of Secularity', *Modern Theology* 26, no. 3 (2010): 382–403.

anticipating the demise of religion in modern societies has collapsed, as the prevalence and societal impact of religious movements has surged around the world and as secularist political philosophers such as Jürgen Habermas have been obliged to move to a grudging acceptance of a role for religious perspectives in the public sphere.[2] It is hard to maintain a view of the political culture as wholly secular or of religion as strictly privatized and marginalized today, especially in an American context in which religious liberty claims are in the ascendant, the National Prayer Breakfast serves as a venue for presidential politicking, government agencies incorporate offices for interacting with faith-based service providers and other actors, and appeals to religion by political candidates are legion. It is no wonder that academicians across a broad range of fields, in attempting to characterize this moment, have broached the idiom of post-secularity.

Such is the diversity of accounts of post-secularity that it is hardly practicable to identify a single coherent and all-encompassing definition of the term. Still, it is possible to make a few generalizations about its overarching significance. At the outset it is necessary to dispel the idea that 'post-secular' somehow denotes the end of the secular era or the rise of a non-secular civilization. Rather, in a general way post-secularity represents a qualification of the secular, a decentring of many of secularity's focal points, a corrective to some of the excesses of the Great Disentangling. The thrust of many of the themes and proposals associated with post-secularity is to challenge binary conceptions associated with secularity such as the public–private distinction and the religion–secular divide itself. Post-secular theorists contest the assumptions of secularist epistemology concerning reason and the 'end of metaphysics'. They propose new narratives regarding the march of secularization and highlight countervailing forces acting against secularizing tendencies in power relations, globalization, nationalism and perceptions of spatiality and temporality. And they raise new possibilities for defining and mapping religion against the backdrop of an intensifying pluralization of spiritual practices. Importantly, post-secularity describes a moment that opens up new possibilities for the 'reformatting'[3] of religions and the renegotiation of the relations between faith and politics.

Accounts of post-secularity make up a constellation that stretches across a variety of academic disciplines and fields. Discourses regarding the post-secular have drawn in scholars of politics, political theory, sociology, philosophy,

---

[2]Jürgen Habermas, *Auch eine Geschichte der Philosophie*, vol. 1 (Frankfurt: Suhrkamp, 2019), 75–109.
[3]I borrow the term, following Linell Cady, from Olivier Roy, *Holy Ignorance: When Religion and Culture Part Ways*, trans. Ros Schwartz (Oxford: Oxford University Press, 2013).

epistemology, literary theory, theology and religious studies.[4] For purposes of exploring the ramifications of post-secularity for public theology, five of these discourses are especially worthy of commentary.

Public Post-Secularity. In coining the phrase 'post-secular society', Habermas has signalled a reassessment of the principle of secularism as an article of faith for modern liberal societies.[5] His phrase is both descriptive and prescriptive: it describes the resurgent influence of religious communities in the public sphere in North Atlantic countries, but it also acknowledges the normative case for granting greater legitimacy to religious perspectives in the political life of constitutional democracies. As religious institutions and actors become more visible and influential in public affairs, they contribute to a push to renegotiate the various arrangements across Western states for balancing religion and politics and to recalibrate the degrees of separation maintained between church and state. As a consequence, the very rationale for separationism is opened up for debate, along with associated doctrines of secularism such as the Rawlsian insistence on a neutral language of "public reason" for resolving common affairs.

Theological Post-Secularity. Another energetic strand of post-secularity has brought together theologians and postmodern critics of the Enlightenment in an attack on the epistemological foundations of the secular. These thinkers contest the plausibility of the model of universal, religiously neutral reason advanced as a key building block of the secular political order, challenging both its claim to self-sufficiency and its capacity to generate just results over time. In taking aim at what they view as the pretensions of autonomous human reason, value-free science and the modern myth of human progress, theological proponents of Radical Orthodoxy and like-minded programmes of Christian renewal have pursued a diverse set of strategies for restoring the credibility of traditional religion. One approach is to attempt to unmask the hidden – and 'heretical'[6] – theological underpinnings of secular modernity. Another is to try to generate new modes and structures of belief that can help reconstitute the social imaginary and conditions of belief Taylor pointed to as crucial underpinnings of secularity.

Sociological Post-Secularity. The principal problematic of post-secularity from the standpoint of sociology stems from a recognition of the limits of secularization processes. Sociologists of religion have been obliged to acknowledge not only that the religious impulse seems to be alive and well in many regions around the

---

[4] One useful overview of this disciplinary map is James Beckford, 'Public Religions and the Post-Secular: Critical Reflections', *Journal for the Scientific Study of Religion* 51, no. 1 (2012): 1–19.
[5] Jürgen Habermas, 'Notes on a Post-Secular Society', *New Perspectives Quarterly* 25, no. 4 (2008): 17–29.
[6] John Milbank, *Theology and Social Theory: Beyond Secular Reason*, 2nd edn. (Malden, MA: Blackwell, 2006), 3.

world – if it had ever wavered – but also that the announcement of religion's demise in Western societies as a result of modernization was premature. Indeed, some have spoken explicitly of desecularization.⁷ This should not be taken to mean, however, that secularity has somehow been set aside; rather, what seems evident is that *pluralization* along various lines is taking place with respect to religion and modernization. The discourse of sociological post-secularity thus extends to debates about multiple modernities as well as studies of new religious movements, of people who claim to be 'spiritual but not religious' and of increasing levels of religious diversity produced by mass migrations. What is emerging is a recognition that secular and religious elements are interacting in modern societies in new and complex ways, and that, as José Casanova puts it, 'as the rest of the world modernizes, people . . . are becoming simultaneously both more secular and more religious'.⁸

Political Post-Secularity. One mark of a post-secular turn in political theory is the surge of interest in recent decades in the topic of political theology. Here, political theorists have requited the interest in political thought and action expressed by religious thinkers in such forms as European political theology, Latin American liberation theology and various US movements of contextual theology along with, of course, public theology, 'theopolitics' and civil religion. Their response has been to mine a theological vein in the theory of politics most influentially identified by Carl Schmitt.⁹ Working in this mode, thinkers such as Claude Lefort and William Connolly have sought to unearth genealogical and structural connections between modern politics and religion while at the same time attacking the propensity of secularism to cover over and attempt to efface the plurality of deeply different religious and non-religious outlooks in contemporary liberal societies.¹⁰ Even as these sorts of critiques question the received assumption that religion and politics occupy separate realms, they also aim to facilitate intellectual cross-pollination between them.

Religious Post-Secularity. Post-secular thought in the field of religious studies has been downright subversive inasmuch as it has focused on criticizing the very

---

⁷Peter Berger, ed., *The Desecularization of the World: Resurgent Religion and World Politics* (Grand Rapids, MI: Eerdmans, 1999).
⁸José Casanova, 'Are We Still Secular? Explorations on the Secular and the Post-Secular', in *Post-Secular Society*, ed. Peter Nynäs, Mika Lassander, and Terhi Utriainen (New Brunswick, NJ: Transaction, 2012), 41. See also Michael Walzer, *The Paradox of Liberation: Secular Revolutions and Religious Counterrevolutions* (New Haven, CT: Yale University Press, 2015).
⁹Carl Schmitt, *Political Theology: Four Chapters on the Concept of Sovereignty*, trans. George Schwab (Chicago: University of Chicago Press, 2005 [1922]).
¹⁰Claude Lefort, 'The Permanence of the Theologico-Political?' trans. David Macey, in *Political Theologies: Public Religions in a Post-Secular World*, ed. Hent de Vries and Lawrence E. Sullivan (New York: Fordham University Press, 2006), 148–87; William Connolly, *Why I Am Not a Secularist* (Minneapolis, MN: University of Minnesota Press, 1999).

notions of 'religion' and 'the secular' themselves. Critics of the religion–secular distinction have deconstructed the dyadic relation of the terms and sought to expose their implication in a history of power bound up with the emergence of the modern nation state.[11] The genealogical investigations of Talal Asad, for example, highlight how the binary relation of the two terms bound their evolution together as they emerged from the Western Christian context and, concealing their own origins, took on a putative universality.[12] Their sociopolitical construction links religion with an emergent private sphere, while attributing secularity to the public realm. As an ideological configuration serving the interests of colonial control and capital, the religion–secular distinction has naturalized itself, established a purportedly neutral objectivity and authority for secularity and associated religion with otherness and violence. The post-secular demystification of this distinction seeks, in response, to open new spaces for the reconceptualization of relations between traditions of sacredness and worldly affairs.

Signs of the post-secular constellation are thus visible in daily life and politics, as well as in scholarly reflections, in a plethora of ways that do not always cohere with one another. They manifest a labile situation in which religious energies are declining in some ways, while reasserting themselves in other ways. Traditional religious institutions and practices are undergoing a process of transformation; even the idea of religion itself is being contested anew and renegotiated, not only in the academy but through tortuous – and at times torturous – legal proceedings.[13] The predominant trajectory in post-secular society towards the pluralization of religion and culture does not make the task of public theology any easier. But it does carry with it new possibilities and openings for action.

4.2 POST-SECULAR PUBLIC THEOLOGY

How does the post-secular constellation affect the undertaking of public theology? Or – to put the question another way – within this setting, what is an appropriate role for engaged theology? It might be tempting, for some,

---

[11]On this history, see, for example, Timothy Fitzgerald, *Discourse on Civility and Barbarity: A Critical History of Religion and Related Categories* (Oxford: Oxford University Press, 2007); and Brent Nongbri, *Before Religion: A History of a Modern Concept* (New Haven, CT: Yale University Press, 2013).

[12]Talal Asad, *Formations of the Secular: Christianity, Islam, Modernity* (Stanford, CA: Stanford University Press, 2003).

[13]Robert A. Orsi, *Between Heaven and Earth: The Religious Worlds People Make and the Scholars Who Study Them* (Princeton, NJ: Princeton University Press, 2005); Winnifred Fallers Sullivan, *The Impossibility of Religious Liberty* (Princeton, NJ: Princeton University Press, 2005).

to hold up public theology as a means for working against the diversification and fragmentation of modern society by providing a unified front modelling a social ethic rooted in Christian commitments and virtues. I am not, however, convinced that this is a viable strategy. Instead, I will argue that a more fitting response to the contemporary post-secular forces of pluralization is for public theology to adopt a reflexive pluralism itself. Distributing the tasks of public theology among different bodies, genres, publics and models of religion and reason can afford public theologians the flexibility and nimbleness required to creatively respond to the conditions and possibilities of post-secularity in pursuit of the common good. That said, this response will still depend on maintaining certain core values as defining the enterprise of post-secular public theology.

The impact on public theology of the pluralization attending post-secular climes begins with conceptions of church and religion. If public theology concerns the mediation of a revelatory wisdom and ethos – rooted in divine transcendence – into civil society and the political life of modern democracies, then this task cannot help but be affected by changing understandings of religion and Christian faith. Under post-secular conditions, the traditional institutional Christian churches as the locus of this activity become decentred. This occurs in two ways. On the one hand, religiously diverse societies provide opportunities for other established traditions such as Judaism,[14] Islam and Confucianism[15] to engage Christianity or draw on their own resources to produce prophetic interventions in public life.[16] Christianity does not enjoy a monopoly on theologizing. On the other hand, new, unconventional Christian voices are emerging as traditional denominations progressively lose influence and relevance. Non-institutional collectivities such as the Emerging Church movement, house churches and intentional eucharistic communities become important sources of social action. In the United States and Western Europe, the picture is further complicated by large numbers of 'nones', populations of the religiously unaffiliated who nonetheless frequently maintain a generically Christian or 'spiritual but not religious' orientation that remains capable of generating civic involvement. Finally, one of the hallmarks of sociological post-secularity is that the divide between believers and non-believers becomes

---

[14]Abraham Unger, *A Jewish Political Theology: God and the Global City* (Lanham, MD: Lexington Books, 2019).

[15]Alexander Chow, *Chinese Public Theology: Generational Shifts and Confucian Imagination in Chinese Christianity* (Oxford: Oxford University Press, 2018); Zhibin Xie, 'Why Public and Theological? The Problem of Public Theology in the Chinese Context', *International Journal of Public Theology* 11 (2017): 381–404.

[16]In this respect, Gandhi – who often invoked the Sermon on the Mount – could be considered an exemplary public theologian.

ambiguous.[17] In the resulting picture, religious impulses can enter public discourse from many different points.

A further feature of public theology under the post-secular dispensation is that these impulses can be embodied by different sorts of personages. Alongside academic theologians and ecclesial officials or bodies, a broad range of actors come into play. First and foremost, embodied public witness in the form of activists engaging in political advocacy, providing sanctuary or deploying their bodies in acts of solidarity models a pluralistic mode of public theology.[18] As Will Storrar has pointed out, contemporary public theology is – far from being an elite activity – the business of social networks and movements, 'led by the local organizers of collective action and global enablers of collaborative thinking'.[19] If the received canon of public theology is dominated by male voices, it is important to point out a growing acknowledgement of the prevalence of women in the trenches and to self-consciously take advantage of the opportunities made available by post-secular thought to reconfigure gendered modes of understanding religious action.[20]

In addition to this expanded cast of characters, post-secular public theology admits a variety of genres of theologizing. Alongside traditional forms – preaching, apologetics, jeremiads[21] – post-secularity places a premium on action and pragmatics.[22] Elaine Graham, for instance, identifies as a site of public theology the 'apologetics of presence': that is, a 'praxis of discipleship' involving a 'giving an account of oneself' enacted primarily by laypeople exercising their civic vocation as a habitus or way of life.[23] Similarly, Mike

---

[17]As the Czech sociologist, public theologian and Templeton Prize laureate Tomáš Halík put it, 'Believers and unbelievers are not two clearly separate groups like two soccer teams. The playing field for the contest between belief and unbelief is within each individual human heart and human mind.' Quoted in Chris Herlinger, 'Czech Priest, Philosopher Tomáš Halík wins 2014 Templeton Prize', *The Washington Post*, 13 March 2014.

[18]For a perceptive commentary advocating for the 'full range of cultural expressions and genres' of public theology, see Linell Cady, 'Public Theology and the Postsecular Turn', *International Journal of Public Theology* 8 (2014): 292–312.

[19]William Storrar, 'Foreword', in *A Companion to Public Theology*, ed. Sebastian Kim and Katie Day (Leiden: Brill, 2017), x.

[20]Elaine Graham provides some cautionary remarks and constructive proposals regarding how post-secular thought might retain a critique of gender in her 'What's Missing? Gender, Reason, and the Post-Secular', *Political Theology* 13, no. 2 (2012): 233–45. See also Rosi Braidotti, 'The Post-Secular Turn in Feminism', in *Contesting Secularism: Comparative Perspectives*, ed. Anders Berg-Sorensen (Burlington, VT: Ashgate Publishing, 2013), 87–109.

[21]On the politics of jeremiads, see Cathleen Kaveny, *Prophecy Without Contempt: Religious Discourse in the Public Sphere* (Cambridge, MA: Harvard University Press, 2016).

[22]See Michael S. Hogue, 'After the Secular: Toward a Pragmatic Public Theology', *Journal of the American Academy of Religion* 78, no. 2 (2010): 346–74. For Hogue, the Chicago-based Interfaith Youth Core exemplifies a constructive programme of post-secular public theology.

[23]Elaine Graham, *Between a Rock and a Hard Place: Public Theology in a Post-Secular Age* (London: SCM Press, 2013), 212.

Grimshaw has defended a mode of Christian witness rooted in a mode of 'response' and interpretation rather than 'belief' and exclusivity.[24]

A suitable image of post-secular public theology in this vein could be the sort of scene that often transpires today in the United States and other democratic societies of a local civic meeting bringing together churches and other faith communities, government officials, and representatives of schools, housing associations and other civil society organizations to testify (including in a religious sense) and deliberate about matters of common concern.[25] But it is important to mention a corollary feature of this understanding: pluralistic public theology does not affirm a single party-line interpretation of the liberal-progressive implications of faith for today's enlightened democracies but, rather, nurtures divergent and even contradictory readings and prescriptions. Thus, other manifestations of public theology might look like the 2017 human chain of Catholics organized by a lay organization to surround Poland and pray the rosary 'to save Poland and the World' – primarily against secularization and a feared Islamization of Europe.[26]

Another dimension in which public theology is faced with a dynamic of internal pluralization revolves around the idea of the public itself. As noted, an important element of post-secular thought is its challenge to received binary presuppositions including the public–private distinction. Of course, public theologians have in the past hardly confined their concerns to a rigid, narrowly defined public realm. After all, many have supported the notion that Christian theology properly takes into its ambit not only the sort of governmental matters defining the category of public order but also the much broader field of civic culture and civil society. Indeed, the eminent public theologian David Tracy seminally identified the primary publics to which theology responds as comprising church, academy and the 'wider society' – which includes the

---

[24]Mike Grimshaw, 'Responding Not Believing: Political Theology and Post-Secular Society', *Political Theology* 10, no. 3 (2009): 537–57.

[25]On these dynamics in the United States, United Kingdom and elsewhere, see Jeffrey Stout, *Blessed Are the Organized: Grassroots Democracy in America* (Princeton, NJ: Princeton University Press, 2010), especially 196–209; Luke Bretherton, *Christianity and Contemporary Politics: The Conditions and Possibilities of Faithful Witness* (Oxford: Wiley-Blackwell, 2010) and *Resurrecting Democracy: Faith, Citizenship, and the Politics of a Common Life* (Cambridge: Cambridge University Press, 2014); Paul Cloke and Justin Beaumont, eds, *Faith-Based Organizations and Exclusion in European Cities* (London: Policy Press, 2012); and Elaine Graham, 'Reflexivity and Rapprochement: Explorations of a 'Postsecular' Public Theology', *International Journal of Public Theology* 11 (2017): 277–89.

[26]Joanna Berendt and Megan Specia, 'Polish Catholics Gather at the Border for Vast Rosary Prayer Event', *New York Times*, 7 October 2017. For a nuanced analysis of far-right claims to embody Christianity across Europe, see Ulrich Schmiedel and Hannah Strommen, *The Claim to Christianity: Responding to the Far Right* (London: SCM Press, 2020).

techno-economic, political and cultural realms.²⁷ Still, there continue to be emerging features of publicness that theology needs to take into account. One of these is the importance of newer dimensions of publicness: of transnational or virtual publics, or of what Michael Warner has called 'counterpublics', that is, subpublics that emerge out of conflictual relations with the broader public, and which often have a liberative agenda of the sort in which Christian social witness might have a stake.²⁸ Another is the comprehensive critique of the public–private binary that has been mounted by feminists who have placed in relief its relation to gender injustice. But what few theologians have taken account of – and what is most central for our purposes here – is the internal relation between publicness and religion in secular modernity. If, historically, the public sphere in which modern democracies informed themselves about, debated and pursued solutions to common problems was designed to exclude religion,²⁹ recent times have been marked by the reassertion of 'public religions'.³⁰ The 'deprivatization' of religion is symptomatic of a post-secular environment in which a host of new possible relations between theology and the public has opened up.

Another important way in which publicness has been renegotiated concerns contemporary modes of membership. Public theology was constructed in reference to an ethos of civic engagement and commitment to the common good. However, the political imaginary that shaped public theology at its inception reflected the nation-state model of citizenship, and in the meantime mass migrations, the rise of 'social citizenship' and other modes of partial belonging, and various processes of regional organization (such as with the European Union) and globalization have added layers to the ideal of civic involvement or virtue. At the same time, influential religious entities such as the Catholic Church and the World Council of Churches have progressively modified their understanding of the common good, from a state basis to including international society, the global community and, finally – as I will discuss later in the chapter – the earth community. The result is that post-secular public theology must be informed by a layered account of the common good.

---

²⁷David Tracy, *The Analogical Imagination: Christian Theology and the Culture of Pluralism* (New York: Crossroad, 1981).

²⁸Michael Warner, *Publics and Counterpublics* (London: Zone, 2005). The idea of 'subpublics' is developed in Martin Marty, 'The *the* Public and the Public's Publics', in *The Power of Religious Publics: Staking Claims in American Society*, ed. William H. Swatos Jr. and James K. Wellman Jr. (Westport, CT: Praeger, 1999), 1–18.

²⁹On this point, see John Dewey, *A Common Faith*, 2nd edn. (New Haven, CT: Yale University Press, 2013 [1934]); see also Jürgen Habermas, *The Transformation of the Public Sphere: An Inquiry into a Category of Bourgeois Society*, trans. Thomas Burger (Cambridge, MA: MIT Press, 1989).

³⁰José Casanova, *Public Religions in the Modern World* (Chicago: University of Chicago Press, 1994).

The resurgence of nationalism in recent years sets up a tension between levels that can be acute, since some form of patriotism has often been a conditional value for public theologians.[31]

A final arena in which public theology confronts the force of pluralization is that of epistemology and hermeneutics, where theological post-secularity and religious post-secularity collaborate in contesting the presumed neutrality and impartiality of secular reason. An implication of post-secularity is that, as Alasdair MacIntyre has argued, there are plural forms of rationality – and accompanying models of ethics and justice – that interact in public debate.[32] The postmodern critique of public reason also implies that there can be different languages, logics or idioms used to convey religious outlooks in common deliberation, even as sociological post-secularity upholds the idea that there are multiple modernities that can engage religion in varying ways. In the face of these plural trajectories, however, public theologians need not subscribe to MacIntyre's view that these different modes are likely to be incommensurable. The task of fostering translation, dialogue and argument is a difficult one, but it has always been a central function of both the public sphere in general and public theology in particular. Likewise, the problem of limiting the effects of either totalizing secular reason or theocratic fundamentalism is not new for democracies, however thorny it may be.

In this picture of divergent mechanisms, means, modes and mediators, what remains constant and lends definition and contour to the pursuit of public theology? In fact, even under the changed conditions of post-secularity many of the distinguishing characteristics of public theology remain essentially unchanged. A number of these characteristics have to do with the objects or aims of the undertaking. For example, despite the shifting contours of publicness the central concern of public theology remains with *civic engagement* – and more specifically, with pursuing justice in connection with the apparatuses through which governments and the powers-that-be establish the rules and conditions for common life. This means, further, that public theology remains committed to 'speaking truth to power', and, more broadly, to critiquing power relations and combating abuses of power. To exercise this role, public theology – in contrast to, say, civil religion or religious nationalism – must retain a base that is autonomous from institutions of the state. And, just as important, it must conceive of its objectives in communitarian terms, as oriented to the common good – even as it acknowledges the diversification and layering of

---

[31] See for example, the discussion of nationalism and patriotism in Michael J. Himes and Kenneth R. Himes, *The Fullness of Faith: The Public Significance of Theology* (Mahwah, NJ: Paulist Press, 1993), 125–56.
[32] Alasdair MacIntyre, *Whose Justice? Which Rationality?* (Notre Dame, IN: University of Notre Dame Press, 1988).

the moral communities whose good is sought. Put a bit differently, post-secular public theology continues to eschew pursuing ecclesial, religious or otherwise parochial interests in favour of working for the good of all.

A second set of defining features has to do with what grounds public theology. While the enterprise may not remain the exclusive preserve of the Christian churches under conditions of post-secularity, it will still generally authorize itself with reference to some sort of divine or transcendent source, as mediated by enough organization and tradition to make possible theological discourse. This holds, I think, even in a setting in which the category of religion is deeply contested and, indeed, the transcendent–immanent dyad itself has been called into question. A related feature is a commitment to an ethical universalism, of the sort typifying the spiritual and philosophical traditions that emerged in the so-called Axial Age. And although it is perhaps not conceptually required, a further attribute defining post-secular public theology remains a special, 'preferential' bias in favour of the poor and marginalized. Of course, this is an abiding common feature of many major religious communities. One more distinguishing mark worth mentioning here is the *transformative* aim of public theology. A post-secular public theology aims not simply to inform or persuade but to provide a prophetic witness and to inspire, motivate and convert those in power to an alignment with the virtues of worldly justice.

A last set of characteristics has to do with the means and methods of public theology. A crucial function of public theology has been, and remains, the hermeneutical task of aiding communication between the sources of public theological positions and the realm of public discourse. This is a two-way street: the culture and humanistic predilections of liberal pluralist societies must be conveyed persuasively to a religious frame of reference, but by the same token the corresponding theological framework must be made intelligible to a non-religious audience. It is, perhaps, a boon of the post-secular environment that it has been accompanied by stiff challenges to claims that religious discourse must be couched in neutral secular terms in order to be accepted in the public sphere. Beyond this task of mutual translation, finally, it remains a requisite task of public theology to promote genuine dialogue between theological and non-theological perspectives, in a context of pluralism and toleration.[33]

I grant that the overall portrayal I am offering – of a complexifying theological enterprise beset by multiple processes of pluralization – may seem hopelessly variegated and diffuse. I would like to point out, though, that post-secular public theology naturally still prominently includes paradigmatic modes in which official

---

[33]For some discerning accounts of toleration in modern societies, see Michael Walzer, *On Toleration* (New Haven, CT: Yale University Press, 1997); and Rainer Forst, *Toleration in Conflict: Past and Present*, trans. Ciaran Cronin (Cambridge: Cambridge University Press, 2013).

church bodies or confessional theologians produce statements and arguments about pressing matters of public interest. Yet it is in the new forms of expression, organization and engagement that emerge under conditions of post-secularity, I would argue, that the most fertile possibilities for public theology arise, and where the opportunities for effective interventions in public life are greatest.

4.3 THE GREENING OF PUBLIC THEOLOGY

Inasmuch as the discussion thus far has been rather general and abstract, it may be helpful to consider what post-secular public theology looks like in practice by considering a specific case: theological eco-activism. Among the various issues that public theologians have typically addressed – economic injustice, racism, war, bioethics and so on – there can be no question that environmental issues have taken on increasing prominence in recent years. It may be true, on the one hand, that Christian leaders were slow to board the bandwagon of environmentalism, which in the United States and Western Europe initially took shape as a largely secular movement. On the other hand, recent decades have been characterized by a remarkable 'greening of religions'[34] in which the Christian churches – and other major religious traditions and interfaith bodies – have turned their attention to environmental concerns, initiating internal processes reassessing and revising their teachings on nature, creation and ecological ethics, and eventually seeking to exercise public influence on pressing issues of the day such as climate change. Two decades into the twenty-first century, the environmental movement has become a striking post-secular phenomenon, with a broad coalition of religious organizations, state agencies, secular NGOs and activists inspired by various modes of green spirituality[35] working together under the injunction of a recent US president to 'preserve our planet, commanded to our care by God'.[36]

The application of public theology to environmental concerns has been advanced by religious leaders such as the 'Green Patriarch', Ecumenical Patriarch Bartholomew of the Orthodox Church, who has used his office to promote environmentalism since the early 1990s; the Dalai Lama, who has taught ecological responsibility and advocated for the transformation of Tibet into a

---

[34] Roderick Nash, *The Rights of Nature: A History of Environmental Ethics* (Madison, WI: University of Wisconsin Press, 1989); Roger S. Gottlieb, *A Greener Faith: Religious Environmentalism and Our Planet's Future* (Oxford: Oxford University Press, 2006).
[35] Bron Taylor, *Dark Green Religion: Nature Spirituality and the Planetary Future* (Berkeley, CA: University of California Press, 2009).
[36] Second Inaugural Address by President Barack Obama, https://obamawhitehouse.archives.gov/the-press-office/2013/01/21/inaugural-address-president-barack-obama (last accessed 17 December 2020).

'zone of peace' and environmental sanctuary; and the 'Green Pope', Benedict XVI, who advocated for the 'care of creation' in his writings and undertook to make Vatican City carbon-neutral. But no figure has done more to harness religious teaching to the battle against ecological degradation than Pope Francis, as is exemplified by his 2015 encyclical letter *Laudato si'*, 'On Care for Our Common Home'. *Laudato si'* is in the tradition of other seminal instruments of Catholic social teaching, such as the US Catholic bishops' pastoral letter 'The Challenge of Peace' (1983) and Pope John Paul II's encyclical *Centesimus Annus* (1991), that have helped define the genre of public theology. At the same time, it is a document that exhibits decidedly post-secular features.

Laudato si''s bona fides as an exercise in public theology can be readily enumerated. The document aims squarely at promoting collective solutions to environmental problems; indeed, it was rolled out in a strategically planned process involving addresses to the US Congress and the United Nations timed to influence deliberations on the Paris Accord on climate change as well as an inter-religious statement with 1.7 million signatures. *Laudato si'* thus represents an intervention by a non-state actor, the global Catholic Church, bringing its religio-moral voice to bear in a critique of the regnant 'technocratic paradigm' and the powers that support it. Its commitment to promoting the common good is made transparent by the fact that it is addressed, not to Catholics or Christians, but to 'every person living on this planet' (3); in addition, it identifies climate as a common good (23–6) and extends the notion to future generations (159) and, some would argue, the earth itself.[37] A striking feature of Pope Francis's missive is the manner in which it integrates the transcendent horizon of Christian doctrine and biblical hermeneutics with an informed discussion of climatology, earth science and economics. This feature allows the document to mediate its theological outlook to a broader public while communicating a scientific perspective to the faithful. Moreover, a cornerstone of the encyclical remains a universal ethic rooted in a layered conception of 'integral ecology' unifying normative accounts of environmental, economic, social, cultural and human ecology. True to form, and in keeping with the principal themes of Francis's papacy, a central preoccupation of his message is with the downtrodden and marginalized and the deep connection between the 'cry of the poor' and the 'cry of the earth' (49). In the tradition of the best public theology, Francis continually emphasizes the importance of dialogue – in international relations (164), within nations and localities (176),

---

[37] A persuasive case that Catholic social thought points in the direction of not just the international or global but the 'cosmic common good' – and that this value can also be rooted in other religious traditions – is made by Daniel Scheid in *The Cosmic Common Good: Religious Grounds for Ecological Ethics* (Oxford: Oxford University Press, 2016).

among economic actors (182), between religion and science (199), and among ecological movements (201). And finally, the transformative aim of *Laudato si'* is made clear in Francis's unambiguous appeal for 'ecological conversion' (216–21). While it is difficult to measure the impact of such a document, there can be no doubt that it has raised the visibility of faith-based approaches to combating environmental injustice and ecological destruction.[38]

What is post-secular about *Laudato si'* and the broad movement it has spearheaded? The encyclical itself operates on the assumption that religious convictions need not be translated into some neutral idiom of secular reason in order to be taken seriously in public discourse.[39] 'Why should this document, addressed to all people of goodwill, include a chapter dealing with the convictions of believers?' Francis asks, before replying, 'If we are truly concerned to develop an ecology capable of remedying the damage we have done, no branch of the sciences and no form of wisdom can be left out, and that includes religion and the language particular to it' (62–3). *Laudato si'* also reflects the increasingly inter-religious framing of the environmental movement: Francis comments on how faith commitments regarding the gift of creation can motivate 'Christians and some other believers as well' (64) and suggests that believers of all stripes share a commitment to protecting nature and defending the poor (201).

His remarks reflect the reality on the ground of a growing nexus of religious environmentalist thinkers and activists. A bevy of different types of religious actors now works to promote environmentalism or 'care of creation' in public policy and civil society. These include interfaith projects such as Interfaith Power and Light, the National Religious Partnership for the Environment, the International Network for Religion and Conservation and the Yale Forum on Religion and Ecology. The UN Environment Programme's Faith for Earth Initiative has built a cooperative arrangement with over 135 environmental faith-based organizations guided by the values of 'CREATION': Communicate, Respect, Empower, Act, Transform, Inspire, Organize and Network. In the ecological sphere, the post-secular pluralization of actors in the domain of public theology has seen the emergence of 'green sisters',[40] indigenous activists and lay

---

[38] On the difficulty of gauging the concrete effects of Catholic public theology, see Richard L. Wood, 'Public Catholicism: Contemporary Presence and Future Promise', in *The Future of Catholicism in America*, ed. Patricia O'Connell Killen and Mark Silk (New York: Columbia University Press, 2019), 276–330.

[39] On *Laudato si'* see for a commentary on this aspect of the document, and on how Francis positions theology as a partner of other sciences in an interdisciplinary approach to understanding and responding to climate change, see George B. Handley, '"Laudato si" and the Postsecularism of the Environmental Humanities', *Environmental Humanities* 8, no. 2 (2016): 277–84.

[40] The ecological innovations of several communities of religious women are profiled in Sarah McFarland Taylor, *Green Sisters: A Spiritual Ecology* (Cambridge, MA: Harvard University Press, 2009).

initiatives of all sorts. These developments have been supported by scholarly work reassessing the human–nature relation,[41] extolling the religious insights generated by grassroots organizing,[42] extending the critique of ecofeminism,[43] probing new forms of spirituality and activism emerging from concern for the environment,[44] articulating a theologically informed earth ethic[45] and extracting the religious significance of the Anthropocene.[46] Modes of public eco-theology range from church statements to interfaith prayer to eating practices[47] to civil disobedience. In keeping with the manner in which the force majeure of climate change has strengthened the existential foundations for a global community, environmental public theology now addresses new publics and counter-publics. These include non-human creation, the intrinsic value of which has been affirmed by *Laudato si'* and many other religious statements.

In our present era, as Larry Rasmussen has argued, the field of social ethics traditionally so valued by public theology is in the process of being transformed into creation ethics.[48] At the same time, under post-secular conditions, public theology itself has become a sort of moral ecology, a normative ecosystem that thrives on diversity, but unites its plural energies under an integral vision that holds an appreciation of the sacred origins and horizon of the natural world to be inseparable from the quest to fight injustice and uphold human dignity. Within this context, theological eco-activism has the potential to play an invaluable role in the environmental movement by bridging the gap between an environmental justice movement focused on the disproportionate harms inflicted on the poor, and a land ethic or deep ecology inspired by a sense of the

---

[41] Whitney Bauman, *Religion and Ecology: Developing a Planetary Ethic* (New York: Columbia University Press, 2014); Patrick Curry, *Ecological Ethics: An Introduction* (Cambridge: Polity Press, 2011), especially 162–80.
[42] Willis Jenkins, *The Future of Ethics: Sustainability, Social Justice, and Religious Creativity* (Washington, DC: Georgetown University Press, 2013).
[43] Elizabeth Johnson, *Ask the Beasts: Darwin and the God of Love* (London: Bloomsbury, 2014); Catherine Keller, *Political Theology of the Earth: Our Planetary Emergency and the Struggle for a New Public* (New York: Columbia University Press, 2018).
[44] Krista E. Hughes, Dhawn B. Martin, and Elaine Padilla, eds, *Ecological Solidarities: Mobilizing Faith and Justice for an Entangled World* (University Park, PA: The Pennsylvania State University Press, 2019).
[45] Larry L. Rasmussen, *Earth-Honoring Faith: Religious Ethics in a New Key* (Oxford: Oxford University Press, 2015); see also Markus Vogt, Christliche Umweltethik (Freiburg i. B.: Herder, 2021).
[46] See, for example, Celia Deane-Drummond, Sigurd Bergmann and Markus Vogt, eds, *Religion in the Anthropocene* (Cambridge: The Lutterworth Press, 2018), especially the contributions by Michael Northcott and Markus Vogt; and Kjetil Fretheim, 'Democracy and Climate Justice: Public Theology in the Anthropocene', *International Journal of Public Theology* 12 (2018): 56–72.
[47] Norman Wirzba, *Food and Faith: A Theology of Eating*, 2nd edn. (Cambridge: Cambridge University Press, 2019).
[48] Larry L. Rasmussen, 'From Social Justice to Creation Justice in the Anthropocene', in *The Wiley Blackwell Companion to Religion and Ecology*, ed. John Hart (Oxford: Wiley, 2017), 239–55.

inherent goodness of the earth and all its non-human denizens. By providing this sort of 'ecosystem service', public theology has the potential to re-establish its relevance and value in a post-secular environment.

The portrait I have provided of religious eco-activism as post-secular public theology could be redrawn to display similar developments in the fields of migration, peacebuilding, race relations, economics and other traditional areas of political concern. In today's pluralistic democratic societies, religious voices and energies in the public sphere remain abundant. It may be, in conclusion, that the most incisive question raised for public theology by the post-secular constellation is not whether, or even how, Christian faith will continue to exercise a critical influence on public affairs. Rather, in light of the pluralization of faith-based forms of public witness and in the wake of the post-secular critique of the construction of religion and politics, the question may be how public engagement will transform Christianity.

CHAPTER 5

The distinction of public theology from political and liberation theologies

GASPAR MARTINEZ

Defining 'public theology' is becoming increasingly difficult. What, technically speaking, was born on American soil has spread across every world region, colouring the term variously, thus blurring its original American contours.[1] Something similar, albeit in a more restricted way, applies to 'liberation theology', an endeavour born in Peru, thereafter present also in every continent and adapted to the respective context. Even far more restricted has been the spread of 'political theology' in its specificity, although the adjective 'political' carries a plethora of meanings.

In general terms, these three theologies are public, because, in their inception and vocation, they relate to the public realm or *polis*. They all want to take part in the public discussions that define a just and fair society, and they address

---

[1] See, for instance, the breadth of topics, approaches and geographical locations gathered around the *International Journal of Public Theology*. The journal is affiliated with the *Global Network for Public Theology*, with member institutions from every continent. See also Sebastian C. H. Kim, *Theology in the Public Sphere* (London: SMC Press, 2011); Sebastian Kim, 'Public Theology in the History of Christianity', in *A Companion to Public Theology*, ed. Sebastian Kim and Katie Day (Leiden and Boston: Brill, 2017), 40–66, where the author shows how the understanding and development of public theology have expanded.

not only their own religious fellowships but those specific publics that define or/and share in the prevailing social narrative. Their differences lie in the context from which they stem, in the problems they focus on and want to address, and in their theological *locus*, approach and scope.

5.1 PUBLICNESS AND THE MAIN TASKS OF THEOLOGY

One way of looking at the purpose of theology is to focus on how it justifies its claims. In this respect, three different tasks come to the fore. The first is to show the inner cogency of the *depositum fidei*, defining its content, interpreting it and making its various elements mutually coherent. As Jaroslav Pelikan has masterfully shown,[2] most ecumenical councils up to Constantinople III were devoted to defining and interpreting the content of the *depositum*. Working with those doctrinal milestones, systematic theology has tried to figure, order and relate them in such a way that they mutually hold. Origen's Περὶ Ἀρχῶν, Aquinas' *Summa theologiae*, Calvin's *Institutio christianae religionis*, Schleiermacher's *Glaubenslehre*, Tillich's *Systematic Theology* and Rahner's *Grundkurs des Glaubens* are classic examples of this first task of theology.

Systematic theology's main goal is rather *ad intra* than *ad extra*. Using the tools and rules of the theological art, it endeavours to show that the key doctrinal tenets of Christianity cohere mutually and offer a consistent picture of reality as a whole. Although with an undeniable external projection, systematic theology primarily addresses itself both to the Christian-denominational community at large and, particularly, to the community of theologians.

The second task of theology has an apologetic character, rather *ad extra* than *ad intra*. One branch of apologetics aims to show the appropriateness of the Christian tenets and world view with respect to other culturally relevant explanations of reality. A second branch tries to do the same in relation either to other denominations of the same faith (intrafaith apologetics) or to other faiths (interfaith apologetics).

Apologetics was essential in the first centuries of Christianity, in the midst of an intellectually more powerful culture. Apologists like Justin, Tertullian and Origen endeavoured to legitimize Christianity publicly, countering anti-Christian views and imperial persecution. In the aftermath of the sack of Rome (410 CE), Augustine came up with *De Civitate Dei contra paganos*, a masterpiece of Christian apologetics, highly influential throughout history.

---

[2]Jaroslav Pelikan, *The Christian Tradition: A History of the Development of Doctrine, Volume 1: The Emergence of the Catholic Tradition (100–600)* (Chicago: University of Chicago Press, 1971).

The second branch of apologetics, defending the legitimacy of Christian or Christian-denominational claims with regard to other faiths or other Christian denominations, started with the writings of the New Testament in the Apostolic Era. Paul's *Letter to the Romans* is its clearest example. Afterwards, trying to define the symbols of faith up to the seventh century, practically every major theologian became involved in doctrinal controversies. Intra-Christian controversies, which flared again in the East–West division of Christianity in the eleventh century, and once more with the Reformation in the sixteenth century, have continued until the present time.[3] Interfaith apologetics, related both to Judaism and to the gentiles, was also present in the Apostolic and Patristic eras, getting renewed attention with the rapid spread of Islam and its European inroads. Aquinas' *Summa contra gentiles* is a paradigmatic example of this kind of apologetics.

The third task of theology is to present its claims in the public arena. This task, clearly *ad extra*, can adopt a manifold expression. In terms of classical ways of dividing the specialties of theology, whereas systematic theology would be the most proper for the first task and fundamental-systematic for the second one, this third task asks for the deployment of both fundamental and practical theology. Fundamental theology is the best way of justifying theological claims with respect to other overall world views, mostly of a philosophical nature. When the task, though, applies to the way society must be ordered, according to human rights, justice, equity and the Christian preferential option for the poor, practical theology takes centre stage.[4]

There has been a myriad of public theology works throughout history. One reason is that almost every theological work has an embedded public dimension, irrespective of its main focus. An excellent instance is one of the most classical works of systematic theology, Aquinas' *Summa theologiae*. Its method is an argumentative sorting out of the conflicting answers – biblical, theological and philosophical – to the different questions that come up when trying to build an ordered and coherent theological tree that comprises the different parts of Christian doctrine: God (one and triune), Creation (angels, world, humanity), creation's alienation (the Fall), salvation (Jesus Christ, grace, sacraments, moral life) and consummation. On this *exitus-reditus* Platonic canvas, Aquinas draws the *Summa* tree by dealing with the different books of the Bible, which he quotes extensively, and in dialogue with every major author, from Aristotle to Peter Lombard, that is relevant to the question under examination. In other

---

[3]See, for instance, Newman's classic, *Apologia pro Vita Sua*.
[4]Metz fuses both when he refers to political theology as a practical fundamental theology. See Johann Baptist Metz, *Faith in History and Society: Toward a Practical Fundamental Theology*, trans. Matthew Ashley (New York: Herder & Herder, 2007), especially Chapter 4.

words, despite being a dogmatic-systematic work, it is also a great example of both apologetics and public theology. The corollary is that the distinction of the three tasks does not entail their mutual separation but, rather, an intertwining that is different for each task yet integral to all of them.

5.2 THEOLOGICAL APPROACH: TRANSCENDENTAL *VERSUS* CONTEXTUAL THEOLOGY

Starting with Paul, every mystical–existential theology entails a transcendental dimension. Augustine discovered that the answer to his anxieties, both existential and intellectual, lies not outside but inside the self. He also discovered that the bottom of that inner self was the unencompassable God, who, in turn, encompasses the self.

In an era when modern, self-referential reason became the access to sure knowledge, Pascal countered that 'The heart has its reasons, which reason does not know'. At the height of the Enlightenment, Schleiermacher changed the rules of how to approach and understand religion. Opposing those who, considering themselves enlightened, despised religion, he shifted from dogmatic to anthropological grounds to show that religion, the unmediated feeling of dependency, is intrinsic to the human being.

In Catholic philosophical and theological quarters, an analogous move by Blondel, Maréchal, De Lubac and Rahner made God and grace intrinsic to being, thus radically inserting God in the creature and doing away with the nature-grace separation, while keeping the distinction between both terms.

The horrors of the twentieth century confronted the ahistorical approach of transcendental theology, which seemed totally unconcerned by the massive suffering and tragedies in history. Radical evil showed its true face and power in the horrors of the two world wars and, most especially, in the abysmal *Shoah* of a methodically planned *Endlösung*. Could the God-talk continue undeterred by such a horror?

Very rapidly after the 1960s, the unpaid bills of the ignored historical grievances and wounds landed on the table of both modernity and its theological counterpart, not only asking for a place at the table but also demanding the table to be overturned. From Latin America to South Africa, through Korea, India, the United States and Europe, the repressed voices of the oppressed, excluded and forgotten populated the world of contextual theology in many different ways and shapes: liberation theology, black theology, Native American theology, *Minjung* theology, Dalit theology, feminist, womanist, mujerista theologies, postcolonial theology, environmental-Anthropocene theology and so on. In each case, the context asked for a particular cultural and theological narrative, replacing the hitherto reigning one.

5.3 PUBLIC, POLITICAL AND LIBERATION THEOLOGIES IN DIALOGUE

Given the global spread and intertwining of these theologies over the last two decades, the analysis of how they relate to each other will be restricted, for the purpose of this chapter, to their original contextual setting and development: the United States, Germany and Latin America.

In general terms, these three theologies defend the legitimacy of their presence in the public realm. In this sense, they are apologetic: religion is not a matter pertaining only to the private realm of either the believer or the community of believers. Every religion, and certainly the prophetic Judeo-Christian tradition, makes claims about the world, its origin, order and end, and about how it should function, especially with respect to human affairs, both personal and societal.

At the same time, none of the three defends a hierocratic view of a society that makes the *polis*, its organization and ruling, dependent on religion. There is an autonomous public realm, but religion cannot be excluded from it. In positive terms, these three theologies claim that the resources of religion, especially transcendence, are valuable for grounding human dignity and for advancing a just and solidary society, countering the permanent threat that stems from the sheer will to power operating in history.

5.3.1 Three different contexts

Context does not determine theology. The latter is anchored primarily in the Word and in the way that Word has been understood, celebrated and interpreted across centuries by the various Christian traditions. However, context is the necessary concrete place (situational square) where theological reflection (witness Augustine's *City of God*) is played out. From that concrete situational square stem the challenges to which theology must respond.

5.3.1.1 United States: The experiment Martin Marty has been credited with the coinage of the term 'public theology'.[5] A key factor in assessing the public dimension of religion in the United States is the crucial role played by

---

[5] See Robert W. McElroy, *Search for an American Public Theology: The Contribution of John Courtney Murray* (Mahwah, NJ: Paulist Press, 1989), 4. For McElroy, the term 'public theology' 'has come to apply to an effort by non-Evangelical Christian theologians to steer a course between the fundamentalist approach to social reconstruction and the secular notion that spiritual values should not influence public policy or the constitution of society' (Ibid., 185, n12).

Christian Protestantism both in forging the ethos of the nation and in defining its constitutional form of government.[6]

Lincoln's famous Second Inaugural Address is a paramount example of it: a religiously non-affiliated president becomes the highest moral authority in the country. Lincoln mentions God fourteen times, quotes the Bible four times and invokes prayer three times in an otherwise one-page-brief address. He reads the war biblically, focusing on a provident God whose justice is absolute and whose ways cannot be humanly discerned, refusing to judge the other side and ending with a call to inclusiveness in his legendary 'With malice to none with charity to all' final paragraph.[7]

Lincoln's case shows that religion is not, pace Jefferson, just a private matter but one that has been constantly and relevantly present in American life and politics. However, this foundational religious dimension, quasi-natural to the American experiment, is neither of a monolithic nature nor the only one dimension in defining that experiment. A second trait of the nation is its original diversity, encompassing different Christian denominations, various political visions and deistic ideas. A third characteristic is the secular nature of power, following the ideas of Hume, Locke, Rousseau, etc. Given this diversity, the US Constitution and the Amendments to it have been a consensual instrument to formulate an original political experiment, commonly shared in its vision and purpose, while, at the same time, preserving the religious and ideological diversity and freedom of the citizenry.[8] In this framework, public theology seeks to establish an effective link between the particularity of the religious tradition/denomination and the commonality of the experiment.

5.3.1.2 Germany: The ambiguities and horrors of modernity Political theology can be analysed from many different perspectives and its roots may be defined variously, depending on the viewpoint and the approach.[9] In the last third of the twentieth century, the Catholic theologian Johann Baptist Metz gave form to his *Neue Politische Theologie*. His Lutheran contemporaries, Dorothee Sölle and Jürgen Moltmann, also elaborated a politically responsive theology.

The experience of deep evil and total moral corruption at the national level under the Nazi regime brought about fundamental questions, compounded with

---

[6]See H. Richard Niebuhr, *The Kingdom of God in America* (Chicago; New York: Willett, Clark & Company, 1937).
[7]Library of Congress, *Abraham Lincoln papers, Second Inaugural Address* https://tile.loc.gov/storage-services/service/mss/mal/436/4361300/4361300.pdf (consulted on 23 August 2021).
[8]First Amendment to the Constitution of The United States of America: 'Congress shall make no law respecting an establishment of religion, or prohibiting the free exercise thereof.'
[9]See Francis S. Fiorenza, 'Political Theology as Foundational Theology: An Inquiry into Their Fundamental Meaning', *Proceedings of the Catholic Theological Society of America* 32 (1977): 142–77.

a profound sense of hopelessness that, in the last analysis, asked if believing in God was possible after the *Shoah*. Germany was the soil where Kant, reviving Horace, proclaimed his famous *sapere aude!*, formulated the unrenounceable obligation to become a responsible, autonomous moral self and announced the promise of universal peace. Hegel went even further, creating the grand narrative of the spirit that, coming to its total self-realization, fulfils itself in history.

However, the promises of an enlightened self and an enlightened society did not preclude two devastating wars in Europe and, even worse, the triumph of a totalitarian political party that, once in power, sought to conquer the whole of Europe and put into practice the *Endlösung* for the extermination of Jews and other 'perverted' minorities. Moral bankruptcy extended also to the Christian churches, although there were some heroic few, like Bonhoeffer and other members of the *Bekennende Kirche*, who paid the price of their lives for their active resistance to the Nazi regime.

The Frankfurt School developed a critical social theory, made explicit by Horkheimer and Adorno in their work *Dialektik der Aufklärung*, written in exile in 1944, at the height of madness in Nazi Germany. In the opening sentence, they state the total failure of the emancipatory goal of the Enlightenment: 'Enlightenment, understood in the widest sense as the advance of thought, has always aimed at liberating human beings from fear and installing them as masters. Yet the wholly enlightened earth is radiant with triumphant calamity.'[10] Primary tenets of this work are the dissolution of the self and the hegemony of instrumental reason. Far from being emancipatory, the Enlightenment had become an inescapable force of destruction and sheer human alienation.

5.3.1.3 Latin America: The cry of the poor Awareness of what Frantz Fanon termed the *wretched of the earth*[11] grew at a fast pace in the late 1950s and the 1960s of the last century. Cries for the liberation from all forms of subjugation, colonization and destitution spread all over the world, from every corner in Africa to Latin America and Asia. This movement was a powerful critique of a modernity used by the enlightened Europeans and Americans as an instrument of domination.

In Latin America, that cry was amplified by the Cuban revolution and the revolt it set off against all forms of oppression: *un grito destinado a crecer y a estallar*.[12] The goal of the revolt was not to address the symptom of poverty

---

[10] Max Horkheimer and Theodor W. Adorno, *Dialectic of Enlightenment: Philosophical Fragments* (Stanford, CA: Stanford University Press, 2002), 1.
[11] Frantz Fanon, *The Wretched of the Earth* (New York: Grove Press, 1963).
[12] 'A cry destined to grow and to explode', in the words of the singer Mercedes Sosa, in his famous hymn *Canción con todos*, included in her 1970 album *El grito de la tierra*.

but its structural causes. Some thinkers at UN's ECLA (Economic Commission for Latin America) developed the influential theory of dependency. The core of the theory held that economic dependency, far from being an extrinsic factor, was systemic, ingrained in the institutional ways in which the global economic markets, rules, practices and institutions were organized.[13]

All over Latin America, racial discrimination was another structural factor to redress. Vast indigenous populations from Mexico to Argentina were systemically marginalized – culturally, linguistically, economically and politically. This marginalization was deeply embedded in the cultural and political ways those countries had inherited from their former colonial masters.

5.3.2 Modernity paradigm

The three theologies assess modernity in different ways. All of them accept its emancipatory drive and see it, in principle, as a positive and necessary development, even though they are highly critical of its ambiguities. In this respect, they are different from other theological positions for which modernity is intrinsically wrong, and, therefore, its fatal flaws must be exposed and its paradigm rejected.

5.3.2.1 United States: Dialogue and critique In the first quarter of the twentieth century, modernity had transformed the social, cultural and economic US situation. New problems, most of them stemming from social dislocation, had to be met with new solutions. At the same time, old forms of oppression linked with the origin and development of the nation continued to afflict the Native American and African American people. Confronting these problems, the Social Gospel movement had an important public impact in promoting social justice, racial equality and solidarity.[14] In secular quarters, change was proposed on the basis of social engineering.[15] Both, Christians and seculars, though, shared a progressive and liberal view of human nature and of its ability to overcome its ailments.

The neo-orthodox Niebuhr brothers countered this liberal view in different ways. Reinhold exposed theologically the anthropological and moral frailties intrinsic to humankind.[16] He became a most prominent public theologian, whose

---

[13]For a good summary of the theory, see Steven Schmidt, 'Latin American Dependency Theory' at https://globalsouthstudies.as.virginia.edu/key-thinkers/latin-american-dependency-theory (consulted on 22 March 2021). The author includes a good bibliography.
[14]See especially Walter Rauschenbusch, *A Theology for the Social Gospel* (New York: The Macmillan Company, 1917).
[15]See John Dewey, *A Common Faith* (New Haven, CT: Yale University Press, 1934).
[16]Reinhold Niebuhr, *The Nature and Destiny of Man: A Christian Interpretation* (New York: C. Scribner's Sons, 1949).

'Christian realism' was deeply influential.[17] For his part, his brother H. Richard criticized liberal Christianity as a mere adaptation to secular modernity.[18]

For its part, Roman Catholic public discourse in the United States developed along the lines of Catholic Social Teaching. Unlike its Protestant counterpart, it was more philosophical than theological, based on natural law and human rights. However, Vatican II made it more explicitly theological. Both forms of public discourse have been influential in the United States.[19] Whereas John Courtney Murray leaned more on the former, the American bishops produced two excellent pieces of the latter.[20]

A third form of Catholic public theology in the United States, rather than seeking to dialogue with the modern 'American Proposition',[21] sought to challenge it in a prophetic way. Dorothy Day and the Catholic Worker movement are two examples of this radical–prophetic form of public theology, which, under many forms, has taken root in different Christian denominations.[22]

A final example of public theology, in dialogue with culture, is correlational theology, which tries to establish a correlation between the human situation and the Christian message, seeking to make that message meaningful. Paul Tillich formulated it, addressing the challenges of modernity. David Tracy has reformulated it, combining the resources of philosophy, theology, science,

---

[17]See Reinhold Niebuhr, *Christian Realism and Political Problems* (New York: Charles Scribner's Sons, 1953).

[18]See H. Richard Niebuhr, *The Kingdom of God in America* (New York: Harper & Row, 1937), where, he writes, 'A God without wrath brought men without sin into a kingdom without judgment through the ministrations of a Christ without a cross' (193).

[19]See J. Bryan Hehir's contribution in 'Forum: Public Theology in Contemporary America', *Religion and American Culture: A Journal of Interpretation* 10, no. 1 (2000): 20–7.

[20]See John Courtney Murray, *We Hold These Truths: Catholic Reflections on the American Proposition* (Kansas City, MO: Sheed and Ward, 1960); National Conference of Catholic Bishops, *The Challenge of Peace: God's Promise and Our Response* (Washington, DC: United States Catholic Conference, 1983); National Conference of Catholic Bishops, *Economic Justice for All: Pastoral Letter on Catholic Social Teaching and the U.S. Economy* (Washington: United States Catholic Conference, 1986).

[21]Murray, in *We Hold these Truths*, coined this phrase, by which he claimed that the American experiment, as a political project, had to be understood in the light of the truths that the Founders thought to be self-evident. Such truths were, so to speak, the ideal or soul of the political experiment.

[22]See Kristin E. Heyer, 'Bridging the Divide in Contemporary U.S. Catholic Social Ethics', *Theological Studies* 66 (2005): 401–40. Two other examples of prophetic public theology in the United States are Black liberation theology and the different forms of theologies related to the discrimination of women: feminist, womanist and mujerista theologies. Without denying their evident publicness, they are technically considered different from public theology within the umbrella of contextual theology. Some foundational works of these theologies are: James H. Cone, *A Black Theology of Liberation* (Philadelphia: Lippincott, 1970); Rosemary Radford Ruether, *Sexism and God-talk: Towards a Feminist Theology* (Boston: Beacon Press, 1983); Delores S. Williams, *Sisters in the Wilderness: The Challenge of Womanist God-Talk* (Maryknoll, NY: Orbis Books, 1993); Ada María Isasi-Díaz, *Mujerista Theology: A Theology for Twenty-first Century* (Maryknoll, NY: Orbis Books, 1996).

literature and art in interpreting the cultural meaningfulness of the 'Christian classics' (the keystone of which is for him the 'Christ event') in a postmodern culture. Suspicious of all forms of systemic distortion (included those embedded in the 'Christian classics'), he advocates the liberating power of fragments ('frag-events') in front of every form of hegemonic ideology, especially that of modernity.[23]

5.3.2.2 A truncated modernity The leading political theologians, the Lutheran Dorothee Sölle and Jürgen Moltmann and the Catholic Johann Baptist Metz, forged their theology in a Germany that was in tatters in every respect (especially morally) after the Second World War. For these three authors, political theology is not just a theological speciality or branch. For them, every theology has an intrinsic political dimension; therefore, theology is always political.[24] However, their political theology developed out of a painful historical situation, in confrontation with the tragic effects of the ambiguities of modernity.

The promise of the *Aufklärung* had gone through the Napoleonic invasion, the social revolt of 1848–9, the First World War and its subsequent humiliating Versailles treaty, the weak Weimar Republic and, most ominous of all, the Nazi regime (strongly backed by the population), the *Shoa* and the great war defeat. That promise ended not in a mere deception but in utter monstrosity. How could this promise of liberation become so perverted? But, beyond that, how could systemic-to-perfection evil come to dominate the soul of a Christian nation? Death, with the dutiful collaboration of Christian servants, had once again shown its powerful sting in history, thus defying Christ's victory on the cross (1 Cor. 15.55). Where was God in Auschwitz? How to respond to that theologically?

Past the Adenauer years, closely following social critical theory, political theology exposed the contradictions between the proclaimed ideals of the

---

[23]See David Tracy's two collections of essays, *Fragments: The Existential Situation of Our Time* (Chicago: Chicago University Press, 2019) and *Filaments: Theological Profiles* (Chicago: Chicago University Press, 2019).

[24]See Dorothee Sölle, *Politische Theologie* (Stuttgart: Kreuz Verlag, 1982), 12, where she writes that political theology 'sich nicht als Teilbereich, sondern als wesentliche theologische Fragstellung versteht'; Jürgen Moltmann, *Politische Theologie – Politische Ethik* (Munich; Mainz: Kaiser Verlag; Matthias-Grünewald Verlag, 1984), 9: 'Politische Theologie ist keine neue theologische Richtung und auch keine besondere theologische Disziplin, sondern das Bewußtsein der politischen Relevanz jeglicher Theologie. Jede Theologie ist auf ihre eigene Weise politische Theologie'; Johann Baptist Metz, *A Passion for God: The Mystical-Political Dimension of Christianity* (Mahwah, NJ: Paulist Press, 1998), 23: '[political theology] aspires to be nothing other than theology, discourse about God in our times . . . a corrective to situationless theologies. . . . In that sense this theology considers itself to be "postidealist"'. For a short but comprehensive understanding of political theology, see Johann Baptist Metz and Werner Kroh, 'Politische Theologie', *Evangelisches Kirchenlexikon III* (Göttingen: Vandenhoeck und Ruprecht, 1992), 1261–5.

Enlightenment and the de facto development of a free-riding reason, become mostly instrumental at the service of a system tailored to the needs of the market economy. Modern reason challenged all kinds of dogmatisms and rebelled against tradition. But, in his pursuit of a new autonomous subject on the basis of a self-referential reason, it dangerously weakened the crucial role memory plays in the formation of reason. Without memory, the modern subject was rootless, becoming a mere experiment, always projected forward into a limitless future. Without any firm anchoring, the self lost its own consciousness and control, becoming easy prey to the forces of a disfigured market-led-instrumental modernity. Reason had promised to liberate humankind; instead, it produced monsters.[25]

5.3.2.3 The underside of history If modernity became the ruling paradigm and narrative for both Europe and the United States, what about those outside these two? Gutiérrez came up with a new narrative from '*el reverso de la historia*' (the underside of history). In his own words, 'what was a movement for liberty in some parts of the world, when seen from the other side of the world, from beneath, from the popular classes, only meant new and more refined forms of exploitation of the very poorest – of the wretched of the earth'.[26] He goes on to say, 'The exploitation carried on among us by the modern nations – those shining knights of "liberty" – occasioned a traumatic experience not easy to forget about when we hear of "freedom and democracy".'[27] For him, 'This is the context in which the theology of liberation was born and grew. . . . These struggles are the locus . . . of a new manner of living the faith. . . . It is the spiritual experience . . . , in solidarity with "history's absent ones", the very spring and source of our new theological effort.'[28]

5.3.3 Main focus and goals

Born in different contexts, public, political and liberation theologies have also different focuses and goals, sharing, nevertheless, in their effort to overcome the privatization of religion fostered by modernity.

---

[25]Metz kept in his office at the Katholisch-Theologische Fakultät – Universität Münster, a poster of Goya's etching, *El sueño de la razón produce monstruos* from Goya's *Caprichos* series. Although the exact meaning of the work remains debatable (the Spanish term *sueño* can mean either slumber or dream), Metz meant by it that reason, if abandoned to its own Promethean dreams, ends up in sheer monstrosity.
[26]Gustavo Gutiérrez, *The Power of the Poor in History* (Maryknoll, NY: Orbis Books, 1990), 186.
[27]Ibid., 188.
[28]Ibid., 191.

5.3.3.1 Contribution to the experiment: Making the particular publicly shareable Public theology, born in the soil of the American experiment, seeks to contribute, on theological terms, to the public realm – understood as *polis* or common *res publica* – at the service of the fulfilment ('Life, Liberty and the pursuit of Happiness')[29] of all its members. Although, over the last decades, the experiment has been losing progressively its innocence, and has had to confront its own sins and pride, it has not reached the point of either radical scepticism or cynicism to the extent of becoming irretrievable.[30] Public theology, therefore, although beyond every naiveté, keeping always also a prophetic stand, retains a somewhat positive view of the experiment and wants to contribute to its purification and deployment, based on the particular Christian experience and tradition.

Within this overall approach, public theology has sharpened its critical spirit, reclaiming the voices of every 'other' to be heard. Becoming more and more prophetic and challenging, it demands a conversion and social transformation that entails the recognition of the concrete modes of oppression exerted throughout history by the mainstream American experiment on the 'others': natives, slaves, immigrants, workers, women, LGBTQ people, other countries and cultures, etc.

5.3.3.2 The reconstruction of reason, the self and society For political theology, the question is not how to improve the modern experiment but how to understand and to respond to the horrific bankruptcy of reason, the self and society. Can there be still hope? Is the *Gottesrede* possible after Auschwitz? On which grounds? Have the Christian churches been co-opted by a modernity that has fallen prey to instrumental reason?

The goal of political theology is to offer the Christian resources for rescuing reason, the self and society from their total annihilation. The postmodern, radical critique of modernity does not, in the last analysis, lead to true emancipation but to polymythology, nihilism and a second *Unmündigkeit*, that is, a return to a condition of minority from the much sought and proclaimed coming of age of the modern project.[31]

---

[29]Second Continental Congress, *The United States Declaration of Independence*, Philadelphia, Pennsylvania, 4 July 1776.
[30]See President Biden's Inaugural Address, https://www.whitehouse.gov/briefing-room/speeches-remarks/2021/01/20/inaugural-address-by-president-joseph-r-biden-jr/ (consulted on 24 August 2021).
[31]See Johann Baptist Metz and Jürgen Moltmann, *Faith and the Future: Essays on Theology, Solidarity, and Modernity* (Maryknoll, NY: Orbis Books, 1995), especially 49–56 and 72–8; *A Passion for God*, 72–91; Johan Baptist Metz, 'Wider die zweite Unmündigkeit: Zum Verhältnis von Aufklärung und Christentum', in *Die Zukunft der Aufklärung*, ed. Rüsen, Lämmert, and Glotz (Frankfurt: Suhrkamp, 1988).

5.3.3.3 The liberation of the poor and the oppressed Public theology focuses on the modern American experiment, strives for its fulfilment and reclaims the role of both the Christian resources and theology in the public sphere. Political theology focuses on the bankruptcy of the modern project, and the loss of both reason and the self, showing the necessity of recovering Christian memory, solidarity and hope, in order to rescue reason, the self and society from instrumentalization, nihilism and sheer 'will to power'. Liberation theology focuses on the situation of oppression of the poor and destitute in Latin America and reads history from their viewpoint (from below), concluding that modernity, with its claims to freedom and reason, has been an instrument of oppression at the service of the different colonizing powers throughout history. Its primary goal is the full liberation of the poor on the basis of a Christian message that is lived out (praxis) and reflected upon by a solidary Christian community guided by a preferential option for the poor.

5.3.4 Theological themes and categories

Depending on its locus, its focus and its goal, each theology underlines a preferred symbol or a special dimension of it among the principal ones: the Trinitarian God, Creation, the Fall, the covenant, the event Jesus Christ, the church, eschatological fulfilment.

5.3.4.1 The different theological approaches to publicness in the United States Public theology in the United States, as pointed out earlier, adopts different forms. No single interpretation of it can do justice to this plurality, which mirrors the plural nature of the nation, of its democracy and of its religious traditions. A good example of this diversity (among the many possible ones) is the work of Reinhold Niebuhr, John Courtney Murray and David Tracy.

Niebuhr and Murray developed their work mostly between 1930 and the mid-1960s, becoming the two leading figures on how religion related to public life. Both were ordained ministers. Whereas Murray was a Catholic Jesuit priest, Niebuhr came from a Lutheran-Reformed denomination. Both had a remarkable academic and intellectual life with ample public recognition.[32] Their work was of practical influence in the public arena, far beyond their denominational boundaries. Both were supportive of the American experiment,[33] while adopting at times a highly critical position towards what they considered a hypocritical–imperialist corruption of that experiment. Neither of them agreed with the

---

[32] Both appeared on the cover of *Time* magazine: Niebuhr on 8 March 1948 and Murray on 12 December 1960.
[33] Murray's term was 'The American proposition'.

optimistic liberal view of human nature and society. Although they disagreed on their approach, their ethical views on public issues were often rather close.

Niebuhr based his ethical views on Augustine's notions of the self and of society.[34] His major theological work, *The Nature and Destiny of Man*, is an interpretation of the Christian *exitus-reditus* view of God's creation. Within this view, he focused on the myths of Creation and the Fall. Fully accepting the original goodness of Creation, Niebuhr affirmed, nevertheless, that sin, although not necessary, was inevitable. Human finiteness and freedom, combined with the deep-seated longing for fulfilment, is the origin of anxiety, indeterminacy, confusion and radical ambiguity from which temptation stems, paving the way to sin.[35] Moreover, society compounds this sinful dimension of humankind with the difficulties and traps of social dynamics.[36] Although Niebuhr criticizes some aspects of his thought,[37] he considers that Augustine is realistic in assessing human anxiety, pride and sensuality, as well as the deep ambiguity ingrained in society, understood as 'earthly city'. This biblically rooted realism is, in Niebuhr's view, the best way to overcome the deceitful optimism of both modern liberals and Catholic natural law.

Murray agrees with Niebuhr in affirming the transcendent nature of both the self and society with respect to their origin and destiny. For both of them, transcendence must be predicated of God together with God's total relatedness to creation. They equally agree on the intrinsic social dimension of the self. They disagree, however, in their approach to social ethics, reflecting the different traditions from which they come.

Murray directly criticizes Niebuhr's views on anxiety and ambiguity when it comes to questions pertaining to the *polis*. In his view, the moral precepts of the Gospel do not apply directly to society and the state. These 'are understood to be natural institutions with their relative autonomous ends and purposes.... These purposes are public, not private ... they are not coextensive with the ends of the human person as such'.[38] Consequently, 'the imperatives of political and social morality derive from the inherent order of political and social reality itself ... in the light of the fivefold structure of obligatory political ends – justice, freedom, security, the general welfare, and civil unity or peace'.[39]

---

[34] See *Christian Realism and Political Problems*, 119–46.
[35] See Reinhold Niebuhr, *The Nature and Destiny of Man. Vol I, Human Nature* (New York: Charles Scribner's Sons, 1941), 179–86 and 255–64. For an insightful analysis of Niebuhr's theology, see Langdon Gilkey, *On Niebuhr: A Theological Study* (Chicago; London: The University Chicago Press, 2001).
[36] *Nature and Destiny I*, 208–19.
[37] *Christian Realism and Political Problems*, 137–42.
[38] *We Hold These Truths*, 286.
[39] Ibid.

This 'natural law' approach has a theological foundation: the whole of creation is divinely ordered and this divine order is both inherent and suitably adapted to the natural order, and, although imperfectly, universally accessible to human reason. Sin has obscured the light of reason but not to the extent of preventing it from accessing the laws of the natural order. Furthermore, redemptive grace helps to counter the darkening effects of sin.

Two conclusions follow. First, only when its transcendent root is explicitly acknowledged can natural law hold publicly and universally. Otherwise, it becomes thin, subjective and private. The second conclusion is that the Christian view on social ethics is constitutively public, since it is based on a natural law universally accessible. A third conclusion, according to Murray, derives from these two: the Catholic community's contribution to public reason and public good must be particularly acknowledged, because the tradition of natural law 'has found and still finds its intellectual home within the Catholic Church'.[40]

David Tracy is also an acclaimed theologian that has explicitly worked in the field of public theology. Unlike Niebuhr and Murray, whose primary focus was on theological ethics, his main goal has been the relentless pursuit of the meaningfulness of Christian faith in our postmodern situation. From his early revisionist project[41] to his current exploration of 'fragments', he has sought to establish a two-way dialogue between the main cultural world views (modern-postmodern) and the Christian one. In this regard, he has seen his project throughout as both theological and public.

Publicness is referred to three main addressees: the public of the academy, the public of the church and the public of society. A related question is how to share the relevance of Christian faith with these three publics? How is publicness to be attained?

In the context of a pluralistic, democratic society, Tracy understands publicness as public reason. He explores three sources and ways of it[42] that mostly correspond with the different phases of Tracy's correlational project: rational inquiry, dialogical conversation and what might be termed 'the reason of otherness'.[43] The first one is the Kantian-enlightened one. Although necessary and helpful, it risks becoming the prisoner of its own cage. The second one is

---

[40]Ibid., 41.
[41]David Tracy, *Blessed Rage for Order: The New Pluralism in Theology* (Minneapolis, MN: The Seabury Press, 1975).
[42]*Fragments*, 269–87.
[43]For an excellent synoptic view of the evolution of Tracy's correlational project, see Younhee Kim, *The Quest for Plausible Christian Discourse in a World of Pluralities: The Evolution of David Tracy's Understanding of 'Public Theology'* (Oxford; Bern; Berlin; Bruxelles; Frankfurt am Main; New York; Wien: Peter Lang, 2008), 386.

hermeneutical. It acknowledges that truth can manifest itself and, in fact, is made manifest by the classics. Conversation with them (which may include argument and critique) is a way to reach out to their publicness. The third one is, rather than a commonly accepted public reason, an opportunity to have access to the 'special reason' – or privileged window to knowledge and wisdom – of those others that were expelled from the modern public sphere: mystics, prophets, meditative thinkers, etc. The riches of faith are made publicly available using these three 'ways of reason'.

Concerning his main theological themes, Tracy's theological cornerstone is the *analogia entis*. The human creature is *imago Dei*. This original God-likeness is the primary access to God. The Fall has dimmed, but has not destroyed, it. The relation of the Creator to the creature is indestructible. It finds its ultimate expression in the Jesus Christ event, God incarnate, which is the core of, and the key to interpret, the 'Christian texts'. Reason, albeit gropingly in the midst of indeterminacy, never loses its original relation to the divine *Logos*.

Confronted with the horrors of history, Tracy is fully aware not only of the failure of the promise of modernity but also of the deep crisis of hope that nests in the postmodern *ethos*. Responding to this 'existential situation of our time' has become the core of Tracy's publicness. It certainly has to do with the American experiment, which has lost its innocence and must respond to its grave original and historical sins, but it goes beyond it, joining the effort of all those, who, from different angles and traditions, strive to give hope a reliable basis in a dispirited, cynicism-tempted, cultural-spiritual situation.

The publicness of hope, in this situation, is not achieved within a clear system of meaning, but through those 'fragments', mostly stemming from 'otherness', that hold the promise of new possibilities of being. They belong to the third form of public reason. Theologically, those fragments (meditative, mystical, prophetical, apocalyptical) open new ways to speak about the Christian God manifested in the Jesus Christ event. In this 'fragment'-driven naming of God, Tracy restates his fundamental conviction: 'Theology should in principle be expressed as both highly particular in origin and public in effect.'[44] In this respect, 'The notion of fragment as frag-event is one way to aid the hermeneutical task of all theology. The alternative is whistling in the dark.'[45]

---

[44]*Fragments*, 14.
[45]Ibid, 15. See in this respect the insightful analysis of Tracy's understanding of the 'classic' and the 'fragment' in Stephen Okey, *A Theology of Conversation: An Introduction to David Tracy* (Collegevielle, MN: Liturgical Press Academic, 2018), 76–97.

5.3.4.2 Facing radical evil: Memory, hope and solidary praxis Political theology deals with the presence of radical evil in history, especially manifested in the *Shoah*. There are some questions related to that radical evil, which are the direct object of theological reflection: the origin of evil, the question of suffering, the nature of salvation, the role of the church, the meaning and end of history and the understanding of the Christian God.

Moltmann and Metz, conscripted as soldiers in their teens, experienced sheer horror and catastrophe during the war. Those personal memories have both haunted them and played a primary role in their theological projects, bringing theodicy to the fore.[46] For Metz, theology must be 'discourse about God as the cry for the salvation of others, of those who suffer unjustly, of the victims and the vanquished in our history'.[47] That discourse is not of a theoretical kind: 'The truth that guides it is known only in committed resistance against every form of injustice that creates suffering.'[48] That cry involves an unavoidable 'why?' directly addressed to God. Metz does not agree with Augustine's understanding of original sin, that put all blame of every evil and suffering on the creature and exonerates God. Theology cannot close theodicy with a proper answer. That question remains always open, directed to God. Metz concludes, 'There is a hint of something unreconciled in Christianity. To banish this would be an expression not of faith, but of a smallness of faith.'[49]

For both, Metz and Moltmann, hope is a major theological category. Bloch's work *Das Prinzip Hoffnung*[50] influenced both of them. In interpreting Christian hope, both stress its eschatological nature. However, whereas Metz underlines the interruptive–apocalyptical trait of the eschatological,[51] Moltmann distances himself from that trait and seeks to establish a link between the new creation (beginning) and the end of the original one (end), rejecting the naked apocalyptical imagery and its literal understanding.[52]

This different understanding of the eschatological nature of Christian hope is not alien to the way they interpret the question of suffering. Metz disagrees

---

[46]See Jürgen Moltmann, *In the End-The Beginning: The Life of Hope* (Minneapolis, MN: Fortress Press, 2004), 33–6; Metz, *A Passion for God*, 1–2.

[47]*A Passion for God*, 55. For Metz, the universal history of the victims is (using the title of a poem by Nelly Sachs) a *'Landschaft aus Schreien'*, a 'landscape of screams' addressed to God. See in this respect Joahnn Baptist Metz, ed., *'Landschaft aus Schreien'. Zur Dramatik der Theodizeefrage* (Matthias-Grünewald-Verlag: Mainz, 1995), 85–7.

[48]*A Passion for God*, 55.

[49]Ibid., 56.

[50]Enst Bloch, *Das Prinzip Hoffnung* (Berlin: Aufbau-Verlag, 1953).

[51]*Faith in History and Society*, chapter 10.

[52]*In the End-The Beginning*, IX–X.

with Moltmann's *Leiden in Gott* and shifts that suffering to a *Leiden an Gott*,[53] which is a sort of cosmic cry to God stemming from the 'landscape of screams' of the entire human history. For him, the question of suffering cannot be pacified by placing it within the Trinity. God cannot be blamed for human suffering but neither is God unrelated to it. Therefore, asking God *Why?*, like Job and like Jesus on the cross, is not only legitimate but also a necessary way of praying, thus essentially relating human life, every innocent suffering and all forms of meaninglessness to God.

For Metz, apocalyptical interruption and memory of suffering are the firm bases for a theology that is fully responsive both to every victim in history and to a historical hope anchored in the permanent awaiting of the imminent advent of God[54] – a hope that radically interrupts a 'Time without Finale'.[55]

For Sölle, Moltmann and Metz, the church must avoid adapting to the mores and values of modern society, becoming instead the bearer of hope against all kinds of historical injustice, oppression and suffering. Believing implies a praxis of solidarity with past and present victims. Such a praxis constitutes the self, resists the naked will to power in history and keeps hope alive in the midst of every form of despair and resignation.[56]

5.3.4.3 Facing systemic poverty and oppression: The crucified–liberating Christ and the preferential option for the poor   Liberation theology, which shares with political theology the critique of modernity, the theological primacy of the victims and the praxis of solidarity and struggle for justice, has its own special traits: the theological importance of systemic poverty, its Christological centre and the constitutive importance, both theoretical and practical, of the church.

The poor and the oppressed (both systemic) are the historical *locus theologicus* of liberation theology. Poverty and oppression are constitutive of the process of colonization of Latin America. The conquest (called 'discovery' by the European colonizers), far from being an encounter, was a ruthless enterprise aimed primarily at the exploitation of natural resources. Theologically important is the fact that this enterprise was developed under the pretence of

---

[53] *A Passion for God*, 69–71. *Leiden an Gott* means that, for the sufferer, God is somehow the cause of suffering.
[54] See the similarity with Benjamin's 'For every second of time was the strait gate through which the Messiah might enter' (Benjamin's *Theses on the Philosophy of History*, XVIII B).
[55] Johann Baptist Metz; Jürgen Moltmann, *Faith and the Future: Essays on Theology, Solidarity, and Modernity* (Maryknoll, NY: Orbis Books, 1995), 79–86.
[56] Sölle comes ahead of the three as a practitioner of public grassroot actions addressed both to the Christian communities and to society. She co-organized three times the *Politisches Nachtgebet in Köln*, to express and make public this solidarity with the victims and to advocate for justice and peace. See *Politische Theologie*, 113–82.

'evangelizing the *Indios*', even to the point of trying to justify on philosophical and theological bases the inferior humanness of the *Indios*.[57]

The integral liberation of the poor is the goal of liberation theology. The Christ event is its focal symbol. Boff, Gutiérrez, Sobrino and Segundo are the leading authors of this Christology of liberation.[58] The poor identify themselves with the crucified God, condemned by civil and religious authorities, powerlessly hanging on the cross. Gutiérrez shows such an identification already in the sixteenth-century Spanish Dominican Bartolomé de Las Casas, for whom Christ was being slapped, scourged and crucified again in every 'Indian'.[59]

The passion as well as crucifixion of Jesus is the consequence of his prophetic message and actions in favour of the poor and of the least ones. The Kingdom Jesus announces and realizes through his actions upends the established social and religious values and takes on a liberating dimension. His entire life and mission have a martyrial (witnessing) character, thus inaugurating a church as a community of martyrs (witnesses) of the Kingdom of God. Jesus' resurrection inaugurates the era of full liberation, understood as invincible hope that, carried on by the martyrial church, will be eschatologically fulfilled.[60]

The church must be fully renewed and purified to become the church of the crucified Christ, fleshed out in all those in whom Christ is crucified again and again in human history. This church of the poor, constituted by living grassroot communities, is a church 'from below'. The mission of this martyrial church is to carry on in history the liberating mission of Christ from all kinds of poverty and oppression. It is a church aligned with the poor. It drinks from its own spiritual wells,[61] constantly renewed and strengthened by a discipleship fleshed out in liberating praxis.[62]

A final trait of this ecclesial dimension of liberation theology is the chief role it has played in defining the identity and the mission of the Roman

---

[57]See Leonardo Boff; Virgil Elizondo, eds, *1492–1992: The Voice of the Victims* (London: SMC Press, 1990); Gustavo Gutiérrez, *Las Casas: In Search of the Poor of Jesus Christ* (Maryknoll, NY: Orbis Books, 1993), especially 291–300.

[58]For the importance of Christology in liberation theology, see Julio Lois, 'Christology in the Theology of Liberation', in *Mysterium Liberationis: Fundamental Concepts of Liberation Theology*, ed. Ignacio Ellacuria and Jon Sobrino (Maryknoll, NY: Orbis Books, 1993), 168–93.

[59]See *Las Casas: In Search of the Poor of Jesus Christ*, 61–4.

[60]See Carlos Bravo, 'Jesus of Nazareth, Christ the Liberator', in *Mysterium Liberationis*, 420–39; Jon Sobrino, 'Systematic Christology: Jesus Christ, the Absolute mediator of the Reign of God', in *Mysterium Liberationis*, 440–61; Gustavo Gutiérrez, *A Theology of Liberation: History, Politics, and Salvation* (Maryknoll, NY: Orbis Books, 1988), 97–105.

[61]Gustavo Gutiérrez, *We Drink from Our Own Wells: The Spiritual Journey of a People* (Maryknoll, NY: Orbis Books, 1984).

[62]See Gustavo Gutiérrez; James B. Nickoloff, ed., *Essential Writings* (Minneapolis, MN: Fortress Press, 1996), 236–85.

Catholic Church.[63] Every General Conference of Latin American Bishops, from Medellin (1968) to Aparecida (2007), has been a new step in the process of receiving, understanding and applying the main tenets of liberation theology to the pastoral praxis of the church in Latin America.[64] However, liberation theology has gone beyond the boundaries of Latin America and become relevant for the entire Roman Catholic Church. John Paul II made a central piece of liberation theology, the preferential option of the church for the poor, a guiding theological category for the universal mission of the church.[65]

5.4 CONCLUDING REMARKS

In some sense, public, political and liberation theologies are public. As such, they relate to the *polis* and, in this respect, they are also political. Their publicness has a twofold character: apologetical and propositional. Apologetically, they oppose the modern privatization of religion. Propositionally, they seek to contribute to the public realm, although in different ways: foundational, critical, prophetical and radically transformational.

These three theologies have another common trait, which is the way they critically relate to modernity. Starting with Schleiermacher, theology responded to the modern critique of religion (spearheaded by Hume, Kant and Hegel) by making the religious experience the ground and horizon of the self: God's presence in the self is not secondary or derivative but original and constitutive. However, this transcendental theology seemed unable to respond to the historical challenges that confront its foundational–transcendental tenets, most especially the horrors and the widespread, scandalous innocent suffering that, although always present in history, reached an abysmal peak throughout the utmost modern twentieth century. Theology was, therefore, forced to become situational, historical and politically responsive. This is the matrix of every contextual theology. From this contextual standpoint, public theology, political theology and liberation theology must be distinguished according to the *locus*, the main concern, the goal and the theological emphasis of each one of them.

Public theology differs from the other two in its origin: The American experiment, marked by a constitutive plurality, an ambiguous, optimistic narrative and the necessity to justify the public value of the particular Christian tradition/denomination. The other two have a different origin: political theology stems from the particular situation of a morally broken Germany that has gone through

---

[63] On the reception of liberation theology in the Roman Catholic Church, see Alfred T. Hennelly, ed., *Liberation Theology: A Documentary History* (Maryknoll, NY: Orbis Books, 1990).
[64] Gustavo Gutiérrez, *De Medellín a Aparecida. Artículos reunidos* (Lima: CEP- IBC – Fondo Editorial de la PUCP, 2018).
[65] John Paul II, *Encyclical Letter Sollicitudo Rei Socialis*, 1987, nn 42–7.

the horrors of Nazism and the *Shoah*, while liberation theology is born of the dire situation of the poor and oppressed cultures and peoples in Latin America.

Although the three theologies are critical of modernity, political and liberation theologies see modernity's flaws as being systemic, therefore asking for a radical upending of its domineering narrative. This also has an impact on their goals. Whereas public theology seeks mainly (although not only) to correct, purify and fulfil the promise of the American experiment, political theology, having always presented the dangerous memories of the victims, pursues the reconstitution of the self, reason and society. For its part, liberation theology, interpreting reality from 'the underside of history', aims at overcoming all forms of systemic oppression in Latin America.

Since plurality is one of the main traits of US society, the diversity of theological projects is greater in the case of public theology than in the case of the other two contextual theologies. This plurality affects not only to the approach but also to the theological content of public theology in the United States. With respect to the approach, there are two main focuses: the ethical-political (best represented by Niebuhr and Murray) and the cultural-correlational (Tillich and Tracy are good examples). As for the theological content, Catholic public theologians tend to be analogical (foundational *analogia entis*), while Protestant public theology (exemplified by the Niebuhr brothers) stresses the radical ambiguity inherent in both human beings and history.

The three theologies affirm the centrality of the Jesus Christ event. However, they approach that event differently. Public theology focuses rather on the original condition of reality and history: creation's original grace and its corruption by sin. Political theology stresses hope, either eschatological or radically apocalyptical, and solidarity with the victims. Liberation theology's main symbol is Christ the liberator, who calls the church to make an option for the poor, fleshed out in solidary praxis.

A final remark, coming back to the beginning of this chapter: more and more, publicness has come to encompass most forms of contextual theology, either cultural (modern or postmodern), otherness related (gender, postcolonial, racial etc.), or liberationist (systemic injustice). There is no denying of the publicness of all these theologies. However, paying close attention to the concrete matrix from which each contextual theology stems might help to understand the particular nature and theological contribution of each of them.

CHAPTER 6

Public theology as apologetics

ELAINE GRAHAM

6.1 INTRODUCTION

In this chapter, I will consider what it means for public theology to demonstrate an apologetic function or quality. Apologetic public theology upholds the correlational and dialogical basis of theological understanding in relation to wider cultural discourse by seeking to communicate itself in ways that are comprehensible to a non-religious audience while remaining faithful to its Christian heritage.

This notion of public theology as having an apologetic dimension has been attributed to, among others, the Reformed scholar Max Stackhouse (1935–2016). We may ask, however, why Stackhouse intentionally adopts the notion of 'apologetics' rather than other terms current within public theology, such as 'correlation', 'mediation' and 'bilingualism'. What is it about the notion of apologetics that might be significant for the identity of public theology? For Stackhouse and others, it certainly embraces understandings of theology as having 'public' import rather than being merely a matter of personal or privatized belief. It also eschews assumptions that theology is simply an ecclesial discourse, 'a closed group's spiritual language',[1] stressing its accessibility and accountability to

---

[1] Malcolm Torry, 'On Completing the Apologetic Spectrum', *Theology* 103, no. 812 (2000): 108–15 (108).

non-theological insights. Yet beyond that, this emphasis on apologetic discourse implies, further, that public theological discourse should embrace a degree of self-justification on the part of Christian theology as a credible form of public reasoning. All the more so in the contemporary West, where, due to globalization and cultural pluralism, religion is newly prominent in public affairs but where large parts of civil society, academic discourse and policymaking remain reluctant to grant it legitimacy. This necessarily entails renewed attention to the way in which religious values and practices are mediated into the public domain.

In seeking to communicate with a secular, pluralist audience unfamiliar with its basic premises, contemporary public theology bears some similarity to the experiences of early Christianity. The emergence of Christian apologetics from the second century CE may well prove instructive for the present day, therefore, insofar as its proponents were also called upon to defend and commend the Gospel to a wide range of civic and political interlocutors. Since the earliest years of Christianity, apologetics has been both intellectual discourse and appeal to the prevailing civil and political powers. Prior to Christianity becoming the state religion of Rome under Theodosius I in 380 CE, Christians were required to justify their existence within a climate of 'plurality and conflict'[2] in which their faith held no automatic privilege or credence. In the face of accusations that Christians were disloyal to the Empire, apologists followed the injunction of the first letter of Peter to 'give an account of the hope that is within you'.[3] Christian apologetics has always been a form of public rhetoric, charged with the task of defending and commending its existence against a variety of non-believers, detractors and persecutors: 'Jews, pagans, sceptics and Emperors'.[4] In engaging with the interlocutors of their day, therefore, Christian apologists were essentially doing their theology in public, justifying their faith not only on philosophical grounds but to prove the political and civil probity of the church and its members.

While this provides historical precedent for public theology to reaffirm its task of 'translating' or mediating religious beliefs into terms that are comprehensible to others and compatible with the precepts of liberal democracy, there are further challenges for the conduct of apologetic public theology today. We need to ask exactly how religious voices might be mediated into the public square in the context of 'post-secular' civil society in which people are both 'fascinated' and 'troubled' by religion.[5] The questions are, how

---

[2]Cullan Joyce, 'The Seeds of Dialogue in Justin Martyr', *Australian eJournal of Theology* 7 (2006): 1–11 (2).
[3]1 Pet. 3.15 (NIV edition).
[4]Elaine Graham, *Between a Rock and a Hard Place* (London: SCM Press, 2013).
[5]Elaine Graham, *Apologetics without Apology: Speaking of God in a World Troubled by Religion* (Eugene, ON: Cascade, 2017). See also Linell E. Cady, 'Public Theology and the Postsecular Turn',

this might work in practice, and whether it requires a level of compromise with the world views of secular discourse that proves impossible if religious groups are still to retain a degree of fidelity to the precepts of their faith. Are secular institutions capable of summoning up sufficient levels of 'religious literacy' to engage with and understand their religious neighbours? Or, in short, will such communicative and apologetic public theology simply get 'lost in translation'?

6.2 FUNCTIONS OF PUBLIC THEOLOGY

It is true that theology has 'always had a public character',[6] but the academic discipline of public theology has emerged over the past fifty years to address questions of what relevance theology might have to issues of public policy and practice, to the nature of global civil society and, increasingly, the terms and conditions on which that contribution – in word and deed – might take place.[7]

In commenting on contemporary issues, public theology regards itself as a synthesis of theological sources and contextual analysis. Public theology 'must both be rooted in a valid theological stance and . . . able to engage the empirical conditions it purports to address.'[8] The task of 'reading the signs of the times' in terms of understanding the contemporary context requires a range of tools of interpretation, deploying multidisciplinary enquiry. The sources and norms of Christian tradition can then be brought to bear in an act of 'active discernment of God's action in the world',[9] which in turn lead to forms of social action.

This is about the nature of theological understanding, as necessarily a dialogue between the imperatives of the situation and the wisdom of received tradition. Public theology has adopted the correlational method popularized by Paul Tillich and David Tracy in the last half of the twentieth century.[10] The theologian is alert to multiple voices or sources of understanding, including cultural information, Scripture, traditions of Christian teaching and practice.

International Journal of Public Theology 8, no. 3 (2014): 292–312.
[6]Scott R. Paeth, 'Whose Public? Which Theology? Signposts on the Way to a 21st Century Public Theology', *International Journal of Public Theology* 10, no. 4 (2016): 461–85 (461).
[7]Heinrich Bedford-Strohm, 'Nurturing Reason: The Public Role of Religion in the Liberal State', *Ned Geref Teologiese Tydskrif* 48, no. 1–2 (2007): 25–41; John W. de Gruchy, 'Public Theology as Christian Witness: Exploring the Genre', *International Journal of Public Theology* 1, no. 1 (2007): 26–41; Duncan B. Forrester, 'The Scope of Public Theology', *Studies in Christian Ethics* 17, no. 2 (2004): 5–19; Sebastian Kim, *Theology in the Public Sphere* (London: SCM, 2011); Paeth, 'Whose Public?'; Ted Peters, 'Public Theology: Its Pastoral, Apologetic, Scientific, Political, and Prophetic Tasks', *International Journal of Public Theology* 12, no. 2 (2018): 153–77.
[8]Max Stackhouse, *God and Globalization, Volume 4: Globalization and Grace* (New York: Continuum, 2007), 35.
[9]Paeth, 'Whose Public?' 466.
[10]David Tracy, *The Analogical Imagination: Christian Theology and the Culture of Pluralism* (London: SCM Press, 1981).

Such a process is consistent with high theologies of creation and incarnation, in which God's self-revelation is evident within the unfolding events and insights of human history and intellectual achievement, albeit subjected to the critical insights of Scripture and theological traditions. For Tracy, and others, cultural and intellectual movements have the potential to correct and augment the received tradition of faith.[11]

Like other practical and contextual theologies, then, public theology rests on a bedrock of normative understanding, but one that is mindful of the pluralism of its own tradition as well as the need to incorporate and listen to non-theological voices. This is theology about public issues, but also a theology that must do its work 'in public'; not least, as I shall indicate, in a time when the relevance of religion to wider society has come under unprecedented scrutiny.

Public theology also involves a range of actors and protagonists and may take a number of forms. It is articulated through the official reports and statements of church leaders and organizations.[12] While these often serve as teaching documents to the faithful and serve to provide general guidance or principles – such as J. H. Oldham's 'middle axioms'[13] – while stopping short of specific policy recommendations, there have been times when religious leaders have 'spoken truth to power' and engaged in explicit critique, even condemnation, of government policy. Nevertheless, they are often intended as contributions to the shaping of a particular debate, seeking to address the implicit theologies at work in public discourse, as well as drawing out the implications of Christian teaching for a particular issue. It is not a matter of making converts but of seeking 'to demonstrate to the widest possible public that Christian symbols and doctrines shed light on our common human self-understanding'.[14]

Public theologians have also interested themselves in how the statements of world politicians might mediate questions of religious faith, and in particular how a leader's own personal convictions might be mediated into the public square.[15] Given liberal democratic conventions in many countries that require a degree of neutrality towards conviction politics – especially religious belief –

---

[11]Tracy, *The Analogical Imagination*; see also de Gruchy, 'Public Theology as Christian Witness'; Kim, *Theology in the Public Sphere*; and Peters, 'Public Theology'.

[12]See, for example: Robert McAfee Brown, ed., *Kairos: Three prophetic challenges to the Church* (Grand Rapids, MI: Eerdmans, 1990); US Catholic Bishops, 'Economic Justice For All: Pastoral Letter on Catholic Social Teaching and the US Economy', *St. Paul and Minneapolis Office for Social Justice* (1986); Pope Francis, *Praise Be to You: Laudato si': On Care for Our Common Home* (Ignatius Press, 2015).

[13]Ronald H. P. Preston, 'Middle Axioms in Christian Social Ethics', in *Social Christianity: A Reader*, ed. John Atherton (London: SPCK), 144–53.

[14]Peters, 'Public Theology', 163.

[15]Nick Spencer, ed., *The Mighty and the Almighty: How Political Leaders Do God* (London: Biteback, 2017).

this may prove controversial. It serves to demonstrate how personal religious commitment might still be mediated into a pluralist public square. It considers the extent to which mainstream political leaders make use of implicit religious or theological ideas and may provide some measure of how far such values still resonate with the wider public and how far a secular electorate might still retain residual religious sympathies.

Public theology also has a 'performative' dimension, insofar as the actions and practices of local faith communities constitute an enactment of their core values. Campaigns to alert public opinion to the realities of climate emergency may use elements of ritual or symbolism. Local churches have an incarnational presence in their neighbourhoods, expressed tangibly in forms of human capital such as the ability to summon up volunteer labour, or in the ways in which physical capital such as historic buildings can be put at the disposal of communities in need.[16] Or it may be that actions simply speak louder than words: many people of faith may not be able to articulate the source of their concern in formal theological terms but nevertheless regard their commitment to social action as a natural outworking of their faith in Christ, something to which I shall return later.

6.3 MAX STACKHOUSE ON APOLOGETIC PUBLIC THEOLOGY

Max Stackhouse states, 'it is difficult to understand how an intense conviction could form or guide a society or civilization without having an argument as to why it should be believed'.[17] For Max Stackhouse, public theology draws on dogmatic and doctrinal theology, insofar as it mediates the core convictions of the Christian tradition into contemporary contexts. Equally, it is also a form of contextual theology, since it is always rooted in, and addressed to, specific economic, political, geographical and cultural circumstances. Similarly, it is practical in that it seeks to build up 'theologically based practices of faith' in the church and the world. These correspond with my earlier discussion of normative and formative dimensions of public theology, in its need to be rooted both in tradition and context, and to inform practices of discipleship. However, Stackhouse insists that the 'primary focus'[18] of public theology must be on apologetics.

This is not simply about demonstrating the internal logic of Christianity to those who are already familiar with theological language, or using 'theology

---

[16] Alan Everett, *After the Fire: Finding words for Grenfell* (London: Canterbury Press, 2018).
[17] Stackhouse, *God and Globalization*, 78.
[18] Ibid., 107.

as a megaphone'.[19] Rather, it aims to persuade Christians to move beyond the confines of internal debate and preoccupation with church life, towards convincing their non-religious neighbours of the legitimacy of religious insights.

> Apologetics seeks to speak in ways that can be grasped by those who doubt or do not share the faith. It thus tests the reasonability and morality of the faith and those who hold it by engaging those who are not already convinced. It acknowledges that if it is in principle impossible to make a case for the truth or justice of theology, others are under no obligation to take it seriously.[20]

In other words, its justification rests in its ability to transcend its own circumstances in order to contribute constructively to a wider 'common good'. Thus, apologetic public theology defends the terms on which religion might contribute to the public square, but it also regards such justification as going beyond mere persuasion into the promotion of a constructive civil conversation that seeks the enrichment of the *res publica* for the sake of the common good.[21] Public theology understands that civilizations, both in material and cultural terms, have, for good or ill, already been decisively shaped by Christianity. 'Every theology . . . has to meet the test of public reception',[22] therefore, not least precisely because it tries to reflect more than the sectional opinions of inconsequential communities and instead attempts to convey practical and normative proposals for policy and action on the wider political stage.

6.4 PLURALISM, SCEPTICISM AND POSTSECULARISM

It is notable that religion and belief are once again prominent throughout the world, despite predictions that the processes of secularization – at least in Western societies – would lead to its virtual disappearance from public life. This is not, however, simply a question of 'desecularization' as Peter Berger has famously argued,[23] although it is certainly possible to see the global influence of religiously motivated political movements, such as the rise of radical Islamicist movements, the political heft of Christian Evangelical Right in US politics and the rise of Hindu 'identity politics' in India as signs of resurgence. Another determining factor has been that of globalization. Global migration has fostered

---

[19]Ibid., 39.
[20]Stackhouse, 'Public Theology and Ethical Judgement', 168, n.6.
[21]Ibid., 107; Kim, *Theology in the Public Sphere*, 3.
[22]Stackhouse, *God and Globalization*, 84.
[23]Peter L. Berger, 'The Desecularization of the World: A Global Overview', in *The Desecularization of the World: Resurgent Religion and World Politics*, ed. Peter L. Berger (Grand Rapids, MI: William B. Eerdmans, 1999), 1–18.

religious diversity and heightened awareness of the links between religious profession and cultural or ethnic identity.[24]

Religion continues to be a potent force in many aspects of global civil society and is increasingly identified by governments as a significant source of social capital and political mobilization. Similarly, while patterns of religious observance and affiliation may be declining at an accelerating rate,[25] other indicators suggest greater complexity. Interest in personal spirituality beyond creedal and institutional expressions of religion continues to be strong,[26] especially in the way concepts of mindfulness, spiritual well-being and spiritual care have come to suffuse professional practice and institutional provision.[27]

This 'post-secular' turn in civil society signifies a number of phenomena, therefore. It is in part an acknowledgement of the persistence of conventional religious beliefs and practices alongside the emergence of novel forms of religious engagement with the public square. But it also represents a collapse of the binaries of religion and secularity that have characterized Western modernity. As Charles Taylor has argued, 'the interesting story is not simply one of decline, but also of a new placement of the sacred or spiritual in relation to individual and social life. This new placement is now the occasion for recompositions of spiritual life in new forms, and for new ways of existing both in and out of relation to God.'[28] Many Western democracies continue to be, at the level of government and policymaking, shaped by default by the paradigm of secular*ism*, even if the predictions of secular*ization* have been revised.[29] If religion is a resurgent political force, this is occurring against a backdrop of religious scepticism and reluctance to accommodate religious actors and practices into what is still, an operationally secular body politic. While scholars such as Jürgen Habermas have called for the reintroduction of religious actors into the formerly secular, liberal public square,[30] the debate continues as to how,

---

[24]Titus Hjelm, ed., *Is God Back? Reconsidering the New Visibility of Religion* (London: Bloomsbury, 2015).
[25]National Centre for Social Research, *British Social Attitudes 36th Edition* (London: NatCen Social Research, 2019); Linda Woodhead, 'What People Really Belive about God, Religion and Authority', *Modern Believing* 55, no. 1 (2014): 49–58.
[26]ComRes, *The Spirit of Things Unseen Spirituality Survey* (London: Theos, 2013).
[27]Gordon Lynch, *The New Spirituality: An Introduction to Progressive Belief in the Twenty-first Century* (London: I.B. Tauris, 2007); Gillian White, *Talking about Spirituality in Health Care Practice* (London: Jessica Kingsley, 2006); Laszlo Zsolnai and Bernadette Flanagan, eds, *The Routledge International Handbook of Spirituality in Society and the Professions* (London: Routledge, 2019).
[28]Charles Taylor, *A Secular Age* (Cambridge, MA: Harvard University Press, 2007), 437.
[29]Talal Asad, *Formations of the Secular* (Stanford, CA: Stanford University Press, 2003); Hjelm, *Is God Back?*.
[30]Jürgen Habermas, 'Religion in the Public Sphere: Cognitive Presuppositions for the "Public Use of Reason" by Religious and Secular Citizens', in *Between Naturalism and Religion: Philosophical*

and on what terms, such faith-based reasoning might be communicated, and in particular whether religious communities should be expected to accommodate themselves to alternative views.

This is familiar territory for public theologians who insist that Christians must articulate their core principles in terms that are accessible to pluralist, secular society. Perhaps, then, this will entail a renewal of the practice of Christian apologetics, 'essentially a question of how to engage with a non-Christian interlocutor in order to persuade that person of the validity of Christian faith and practice'.[31] The early Christian epistle, the first letter of Peter, summarizes this imperative as follows: *Always be prepared to give an answer to everyone who asks you to give the reason for the hope that you have* (1 Pet. 3.15, NIV). Is there sufficient historical precedent to imagine that this early Christian history has something to say to the challenges of post-secularity?

6.5 ORIGINS OF CHRISTIAN APOLOGETICS

Avery Dulles's *History of Apologetics*, first published in 1971, provides a useful entry point to considering the nature and scope of early Christian apologetics. From a focus on forming the beliefs and practices of the Christian community during the first two centuries of its existence – concerning questions of Christian induction and nurture and the life of the church – writers then began to turn to debates with the world beyond the church, until by the middle of the second century 'apologetics became the most characteristic form of Christian writing'.[32] Such literature, Dulles argues, addressed a range of interlocutors, from educated converts and philosophical teachers to Jews and the Imperial powers. While some apologies were directed towards conversion and intellectual defences, there were also political apologies, 'designed to win civil tolerance'.[33] This alerts us to the fact that once the first Christian communities had become established, an important aspect of early Christian apologetics was to gain recognition from the civil authorities and win protection against persecution and slander.

The New Testament provides some early indications of what we might term an apologetic approach, conducted in the pluralist, public square. On the day

---

Essays, ed. Jürgen Habermas (London: Routledge, 2008), 114–47; Jürgen Habermas, 'An Awareness of what is Missing', in *An Awareness of what is Missing: Faith and Reason in a Post-Secular Age*, ed. Jürgen Habermas et al. (Cambridge: Polity, 2010), 15–23; Michael Reder and Josef Schmidt, 'Habermas and Religion', in *An Awareness of What Is Missing*, ed. Jürgen Habermas et al. (Cambridge: Polity, 2010), 1–14.

[31]Graham, *Apologetics without Apology*, 6–7.

[32]Avery Dulles, *History of Apologetics*. First published 1971 (Eugene, ON: Wipf and Stock, 1999), 27.

[33]Ibid., 28.

of Pentecost[34] the disciples address a multicultural assembly in a diversity of languages: a sign of the power of the Holy Spirit to unite human divisions and of the universal nature of salvation in Christ. This power to transcend cultural difference, however, extends also to Peter's use of his audience's pre-existing religious world view, as he cites the Hebrew prophets to proclaim Jesus as the promised Messiah, the fulfilment of Scriptures.[35]

Similarly, when preaching in Athens,[36] the apostle Paul speaks first at the synagogue, presenting the Gospel as the fulfilment of the Hebrew scriptures. In his speech to the pagan, pluralist crowd at the Areopagus, or market place, however, he emphasizes how their monument 'To an Unknown God' is ancient philosophy essentially prefigures the revelation of Jesus Christ.[37] The good news is not an esoteric secret but intelligible to all reasonable people, and what Justin Martyr later termed 'the seeds of the Word' (*semina Verbi*)[38] are present in other sacred traditions.

Another clue to the significance of apologetics – as justification and public discourse – for emerging Christian identity comes from the first letter of Peter, thought to date from the end of the first century CE. It was probably addressed to a group of churches in Asia Minor, undergoing a period of privation and hostility due to their refusal to participate in certain civic rites honouring the emperor. The writer of the letter attempts to offer advice and encouragement to communities facing such treatment.

Against accusations that the early Christians engaged in scandalous cultic practices, it was expedient to be answerable to public scrutiny. 'For it is God's will that by doing right you should put to silence the ignorance of foolish men. Live as free men, yet without using your freedom as a pretext for evil; but live as servants of God.'[39] Christians are exhorted 'to think through the meaning of their faith and its relation to public life, and be prepared to respond intelligently when asked'.[40] And yet the warrant, or exoneration, for Christ crucified is the exemplary behaviour of the church. 'By living distinctive and exemplary lives, refusing either to submit to persecution or assimilate to ungodly values, these communities are urged to identify with Christ's redemptive suffering, thereby pledging their hope in the ultimate victory of the Cross.'[41] In the face of persecution, however hard their privations, Christians can be assured that they

---

[34] Acts 2.1–12.
[35] Acts 2.14–40.
[36] Acts 17.16–34.
[37] Graham, *Apologetics without Apology*, 75–8.
[38] Joyce, 'The Seeds of Dialogue'.
[39] 1 Pet. 2.16-17 (New International Version).
[40] Peter H. Davids, *The First Epistle of Peter* (Grand Rapids: William B. Eerdmans, 1990), 132.
[41] Graham, *Apologetics Without Apology*, 81.

share in the sufferings of Christ crucified; and that they, too, participate in the 'hope' of the resurrection, which forms the basis of their apologetic.

> Who is going to harm you if you are eager to do good? But even if you should suffer for what is right, you are blessed. Do not fear their threats; do not be frightened. But in your hearts revere Christ as Lord. *Always be prepared to give an answer to everyone who asks you to give the reason for the hope that you have.* But do this with gentleness and respect, keeping a clear conscience, so that those who speak maliciously against your good behaviour in Christ may be ashamed of their slander.[42]

This echoes a rabbinic saying, 'Be alert to study the Law and know how to make an answer for the believer.'[43] Such a 'defence' of Christian faith could be either formal and legal or personal.[44] Indeed, the origins of the very term 'apologetics' (απολογια) or *apologia* has associations with the kind of defence mounted in a (secular) court of law.[45] The term itself only emerges quite late, in the writings of Eusebius of Caesarea in the early fourth century, who argued that the *apologia*, by definition, implied some kind of public petition to the emperor.[46]

Whether or not such texts literally had to be handed over to the emperor in person is a matter of debate, but it is certainly clear that, probably beginning with the writings of Justin Martyr (*c*. 100–167 CE) through to Augustine of Hippo (354–430 CE), this genre appeals to the powers-that-be against charges of immorality, sedition and – perhaps surprisingly – atheism formed a significant part of the apologetic literature. Such defences refuting Christians' political disloyalty by demonstrating their public probity thus formed a significant part of apologetic defences.

Why were Christians persecuted and treated with suspicion? Much of this came from Christians' refusal to participate in Imperial cults in which the emperor was venerated as a god. Christians' allegiance to the Lordship of Christ forbade them to acknowledge any rival heavenly or earthly authority; something which, to the Romans, was tantamount to sedition. Since rituals of fidelity to the emperor were regarded as guarantees of social cohesion, many

---

[42]1 Pet. 3.13-17 (New International Version).
[43]Davids, *The First Epistle of Peter*, 132.
[44]Ibid., 131.
[45]Jörg Ulrich, 'Apologists and Apologetics in the Second Century', in *In Defence of Christianity: Early Christian Apologists*, ed. Jakob Engberg, Anders-Christian Jacobsen and Jörg Ulrich (Frankfurt: Peter Lang, 2014), 1–32 (8).
[46]Oscar Skarsaune, 'Justin and the Apologists', in *Routledge Companion to Early Christian Thought*, ed. D. Jeffrey Bingham (London: Routledge, 2010), 121–36 (121–3).

feared that such a show of non-compliance might incur divine retribution in the form of disease, natural disaster and economic ruin.[47] Some commentators argue that such antipathy operated more at the level of local harassment than outright state persecution;[48] but even so, Christian writers felt it expedient to protest to the highest authorities against their treatment. The apology of Athenagoras the Athenian, *A Plea for the Christians*, dating from the second century CE, appeals to the powers-that-be as defenders of liberty and lovers of truth. He asks why Christians have seemingly been singled out for prosecution and defamation when other citizens enjoy freedom of expression, or at the least, a fair trial:

> If, indeed, anyone can convict us of a crime, be it small or great, we do not ask to be excused from punishment, but are prepared to undergo the sharpest and most merciless inflictions. But if the accusation relates merely to our name . . . it will devolve on you, illustrious and benevolent and most-learned sovereigns, to remove by law this most despiteful treatment, so that, as throughout the world both individuals and citizens partake of your beneficence, we also may feel grateful to you, exulting that we are no longer the victims of false accusation.[49]

Tertullian in his second apology argues similarly:

> If . . . it is certain that we are the most wicked of men, why do you treat us so differently from our fellows, that is, from other criminals, it being only fair that the same crime should get the same treatment? When the charges made against us are made against others, they are permitted to make use both of their own lips and of hired pleaders to show their innocence. They have full opportunity of answer and debate; in fact, it is against the law to condemn anybody undefended and unheard. Christians alone are forbidden to say anything in exculpation of themselves, in defense of the truth, to help the judge to a righteous decision; all that is cared about is having what the public hatred demands – the confession of the name, not examination of the charge.[50]

---

[47]Paul Middleton, *Radical Martyrdom and Cosmic Conflict in Early Christianity* (London: T&T Clark, 2006), 46.
[48]Ibid.
[49]Athenagoras, 'A Plea for the Christians', in *Classical Readings in Christian Apologetics AD 100–1800*, ed. Luther Russ Bush (Grand Rapids, MN: Academie Books, 1983), 35–61.
[50]Tertullian, 'Apology II', in *From Ante-Nicene Fathers*, Vol. 3, ed. Alexander Roberts, James Donaldson and Arthur Cleveland Coxe, trans. Sydney Thelwall, revised and edited for New Advent by Kevin Knight (Buffalo, NY: Christian Literature Publishing Co., 1885), Chapter 2.

Having pleaded for the right of a fair trial, Tertullian goes on to expound the positive virtues of the Christian community and its positive contributions to society.[51] Aristides' apology, dating from around 125 CE, is believed to have been addressed to the Emperor Hadrian.[52] Along with philosophical proofs for the existence of God, Aristides commends the cultural and moral superiority of Christianity. Contrary to popular slander, Christians are good citizens, honest and compassionate. The quality of their fellowship should be an example to the whole Empire.

In the face of accusations that Christianity was an esoteric or secret society, apologists such as Tertullian argued that Christian communities were civic associations like any other. Not a political faction or conspiracy (*factio*), they were bodies 'based on a prudential regard to public order'.[53] Similarly, Justin Martyr argued that the virtues of 'piety, justice, philanthropy, faith and hope'[54] rendered Christians every bit as respectable as other citizens. He argues that in their care for one another, concern for the poor and their sexual continence, they put the pagans to shame. He offers several stories of exemplary Christian behaviour, including that of a Christian woman, divorced by her husband for converting, who renounced her previously hedonistic lifestyle and petitioned the emperor to reclaim her dowry and clear her name.[55]

The conjunction of public theology and apologetics in these writings can be seen in the apologists' defence of Christians' moral and civic integrity to both Imperial and intellectual publics alike. While early Christian apologies defended the intellectual coherence and Scriptural provenance of their faith, their arguments were also directed towards offering a theologically reasoned rationale for the right to identify both as persons of faith and practice as legitimate citizens. In addition, they appealed to ideals of natural justice in their petitions regarding the way in which all reasonable citizens might expect Imperial power to be exercised.[56] Furthermore, these early Christian apologies prefigured the dialogical and 'bilingual' qualities of modern public theologies in that they affirmed the need to adopt the world views and presuppositions of their interlocutors.

---

[51] Tertullian, 'Apology II', Chapter 39.
[52] Nils Arne Pedersen, 'Aristides', in *In Defence of Christianity: Early Christian Apologists*, ed. Jakob Engberg, Anders-Christian Jacobsen and Jörg Ulrich (Frankfurt am Main: Peter Lang, 2014), 35–50 (36–7).
[53] Tertullian, *Apology II*, Chapter 38.
[54] Justin Martyr, *Dialogue*, 110.3.
[55] Grant, *Greek Apologists of the Second Century*, 69–72.
[56] Skarsaune, 'Justin and the Apologists', 125–9.

6.6 CONTEMPORARY EXPRESSIONS AND FUTURE CHALLENGES

Some contemporary theologians have been sceptical of the possibility of apologetics, since it presupposes a shared territory of common reason between church and world.[57] Similarly, public theology's bilingual and dialogical stance has been accused of an unacceptable deference towards secular reason. Yet the very essence of the apologetic approach to public theology guarantees the integrity of both sides of the tradition. No theological discourse is self-sufficient or free of its context. It is possible to conduct apologetic dialogue without surrendering the basis of one's own convictions. For Stackhouse, public theology steers a path between religious dogmatism and fideism that sees 'no possibility of providing publicly defensible warrants'[58] on the one hand, and on the other, collusion with secularist perspectives that would reject out of hand any question of religion being admitted into public discourse. To those within the churches who assume, then, even in a post-secular society, that their truth-claims will be self-evident, public theologians argue that they have to make them accessible and credible to non-theological audiences in order to speak across the post-secular divide. And to those who suspect that it is enough for Christians to demonstrate their sincerity through the integrity of their actions without having to express more substantively in words, public theologians insist on showing how procedural questions of social justice and the common good rest on matters of ultimate value rooted in Christian teaching.[59]

A particular strand of Christian apologetics, popular within some Evangelical circles, engage 'believers, inquirers and adversaries'[60] with a defence of the faith premised on the truths set out in Scripture and doctrine. Such apologists rely on the epistemological authority of Scripture to counter scientific world views, use logical argument to prove the existence of God and deploy evidentialist arguments in support of the historicity of the resurrection and miracles.[61]

However, many critics regard this particular kind of apologetic reasoning based on logic and positivist evidence as representing a narrowing of the apologetic tradition. This strand of apologetics has allowed itself to be captured

---

[57]William Werpehowski, 'Ad Hoc Apologetics', *Journal of Religion* 66, no. 3 (1986): 282–301 (287).
[58]Stackhouse, *God and Globalization*, 110.
[59]Christoph Hübenthal, 'Apologetic Communication', *International Journal of Public Theology* 10, no. 1 (2016): 7–27.
[60]James K. Beilby, *Thinking about Christian Apologetics* (Downers Grove, IL: Inter-Varsity Press, 2011), 37.
[61]Peter Kreeft and Ronald K. Tacelli, *Pocket Handbook of Christian Apologetics* (Downers Grove, IL: Inter-Varsity Press, 2003); Stephen B. Cowan, ed., *Five Views on Apologetics* (Grand Rapids, MI: Zondervan, 2000).

by the logic of modern secular reason that represents 'a kind of *apologetic positivism* . . . according to which Christian beliefs must be demonstrably rational to be accepted'.⁶² Myron Penner calls for a departure from this kind of adversarial, rationalist tradition of apologetics, in which 'being a Christian amounts to giving intellectual assent to specific propositions'.⁶³ Engagement with cultural forms such as the arts as common spaces of shared meaning, with motifs such as narrative, imagination and performativity as the means of mediation, are therefore emerging alongside rationalist, propositional and positivist evidential methods.⁶⁴ A new generation of Christian apologists are addressing non-religious 'publics' in ways that continue the task of defending and commending religious faith, but in more conversational and irenic ways. For example, Krista Tippett, a broadcaster with US Public Radio, calls upon her listeners to occupy the 'vast middle' of religious commitment which avoids the extremes of proofs and certainties in favour of a model of faith that privileges religious faith as a form of practical wisdom over cognitive knowing:

> In the vast middle, faith is as much about questions as it is about answers. It is possible to be a believer and a listener at the same time, to be both fervent and searching, to honor the truth of one's own convictions and the mystery of the convictions of others. The context of most religious virtue is relationship – practical love in families and communities, and care for the suffering and the stranger beyond the bounds of one's own identity. . . . These qualities of religion should enlarge, not narrow, our public conversation about all of the important issues before us.⁶⁵

Her approach affirms 'the conversational nature of reality' at the intersection of religion, literature, science and politics, between faith traditions and across the sacred–secular divide. Dialogue is the way we construct meaning for ourselves, how we explore what it means to be human and, Tippett would attest, where people encounter the divine. This is a more irenic and 'civil' way of learning: 'Developing eyes and ears for moderation does not mean denying the importance of religion in human life. It means inviting and enabling the devout to bring the best of their tradition to bear in the world.'⁶⁶

---

⁶²Myron B. Penner, *The End of Apologetics: Christian Witness in a Postmodern World* (Baker Academic, 2013), 44.
⁶³Ibid., 31.
⁶⁴Andrew Davison, ed., *Imaginative Apologetics: Theology, Philosophy and the Catholic Tradition* (London: SCM Press, 2011).
⁶⁵Krista Tippett, *Speaking of Faith: Why Religion Matters – and How to Talk about It* (New York: Penguin, 2007), 3.
⁶⁶Tippett, *Speaking of Faith*, 156.

Tippett's radio programme, *On Being*, and associated website[67] use the media to construct a quintessential form of public theology that is both conducted in a public forum and which, frequently, invites public figures (including politicians) to 'give an account' of their convictions – but always in dialogical and non-dogmatic fashion.

The title of Francis Spufford's book, *Unapologetic*, might be seen as an ironic rejection of forms of apologetics that proceed on propositional and rationalist grounds. Apologetics based on evidentialist and rationalist proofs is futile, because, for him, what matters is 'what Christianity feels like from the inside'.

> The point is that from outside, belief looks like a set of ideas about the nature of the universe for which a truth-claim is being made, a set of propositions that you sign up to. . . . But it is still a mistake to suppose that it is assent to the propositions that makes you a believer. It is the feelings that are primary. I assent to the ideas because I have the feelings; I don't have the feelings because I've assented to the ideas.[68]

David Bentley Hart's refutation of new atheism focuses on religion as a public good. 'As a historical force, religion has been neither simply good nor simply evil but has merely reflected human nature in all its dimensions.'[69] Without some kind of transcendental referent, he argues, humanity's most profound moral convictions lack anchorage and descend into relativism or personal preference. The social goods of virtue, compassion and charity 'are not objects found in nature . . . but are historically contingent conventions of belief and practice, formed by cultural conventions that need never have arisen at all.'[70] Left to its own devices, there is no guarantee (beyond a particular, historically contingent, materialist, scientific-rationalist belief in the perfectibility of human nature) that humanity is capable of selfless, disinterested or charitable behaviour. The power of faith traditions to cultivate civic virtue is tribute to religion's capacity to broaden and deepen the moral imagination.

In an echo of the earliest Christian apologists, Hart argues that the public probity of the church will be judged according to the logic not of its propositional truth-claims but by the quality of its civic engagement. This also heralds a more

---

[67] https://onbeing.org/ (last accessed 3 December 2020).
[68] Francis Spufford, *Unapologetic: Why, Despite Everything, Christianity Can Still Make Surprising Emotional Sense* (London: Faber & Faber, 2012), 17–18; see also Rupert Shortt, *Outgrowing Dawkins: God for Grown-Ups* (London: SPCK, 2019), 17.
[69] David Bentley Hart, *Atheist Delusions: The Christian Revolution and Its Fashionable Enemies* (New Haven: Yale University Press, 2010).
[70] Bentley Hart, *Atheist Delusions*, 16.

'performative' emphasis within postmodern and post-secular apologetics.[71] Public theology as apologetics operates as a kind of 'practical wisdom' oriented as much to mobilizing performative values of compassion, justice, solidarity and altruism as debating scientific evidence: 'Apologetics is a matter of being able to demonstrate . . . how faith might make a difference to individuals and communities.'[72] Just as God encounters human beings in personal, concrete and specific ways through the incarnation, so any really effective apology will exhibit a similarly embedded and sacramental quality.

Van Putten, Overeem and van Steden's study of the Street Pastors movement serves as an illustration of how religious practices might be mediated into a pluralistic and post-secular public square.[73] As a ministry of presence and pastoral care within the urban night-time economy, Street Pastors take a non-partisan and broad-based approach; but one nonetheless authentically grounded in religious conviction.

> The immediate implication of this faith-based engagement is that Street Pastors do their work explicitly as Christians: their faith is the key driver behind their desire to help vulnerable youngsters [in] the night-life economy. They do so not by handing out Bibles, but simply by acting as Good Samaritans who care about people in their local communities.[74]

Further examples of such apologetic public theology can be seen at work in the pragmatic collaborations between diverse stakeholders in local civil society, spanning the 'interconnections between religious, humanist and secularist positionalities in the dynamic geographies of the city'.[75] The practical side of this is to be found in projects like food banks, youth training, mental health projects and work with migrants; but this goes alongside an ongoing commitment to deep conversation about the underlying values – religious and non-religious – that motivate such collaborations.[76]

All these examples affirm the claims of public theologians that truth is achieved through dialogue and mutual comprehension. Christian witnesses must pass the test of public accountability. For these writers, that kind of

---

[71] Graham, *Apologetics without Apology*, 124–50.
[72] Ibid., 12.
[73] Robert van Putten, Patrick Overeem and Ronald van Steden, 'Where Public Theology and Public Administration Meet', *International Journal of Public Theology* 13, no. 1 (2019): 5–24 (18).
[74] Ibid., 21.
[75] Justin Beaumont and Paul Cloke, 'Introduction to the Study of Faith-Based Organizations and Exclusion in European Cities', in *Faith-Based Organizations and Exclusion in European Cities*, ed. Paul Cloke and Justin Beaumont (London: Policy Press, 2012), 1–36 (32).
[76] Chris Baker and Jonathan Miles-Watson, 'Faith and Traditional Capitals', *Implicit Religion* (2010): 17–69.

apologetic dialogue emerges from the lived experience of a community whose faith is attested to by the quality of its life together. Its witness to that faith, nurtured by that common life, will rest in the social goods it promotes.[77]

This begs the question of how far the laity, who are after all at the interface of church and world, are sufficiently supported to connect the sources and resources of faith with the practical challenges of everyday life. It leads to consideration of the extent to which public theology should exercise a formative and pedagogical function. This might be how to respond to big issues such as poverty, racism, environmental crisis; or how to discharge their responsibilities at work; how to spend and save money wisely; how to engage with social media; how to be good parents. Work in the area of Christian formation and adult nurture has a direct relevance, therefore, in helping ordinary Christians to make the transition from personal 'discipleship' to informed and confident 'citizenship',[78] bridging sacred and secular, something which is after all at the very heart of public theology.

However, there is a danger that a personal motivation for engaging in social action remains largely 'intrinsic' and implicit. How far does such a performative apology still have to be couched in words and put to the test in a public arena? Elaine Graham's solution is to root apologetic public theology in the theological concept of the *missio Dei*, in which a threefold activity of 'discernment, participation and witness' informs the social praxis of the church.[79] This ensures that apologetics is communicated in deed *and* word; but it will require a degree of theological literacy on the part of ordinary lay Christians if the message is not to be 'lost in translation'.[80]

6.7 CONCLUSION

As well as framing public theology as ecclesial commentary on public affairs from a religious standpoint, I have been arguing for a further task of public theology as one of apologetic dialogue. In a religiously pluralist, global context it is expedient to articulate (and to defend) the values that inform Christian statements about, and interventions in, the public realm. This apologetic function reflects a commitment on the part of public theologians to conduct debates about the public trajectories of faith and practice in ways that are transparent and publicly accessible and defensible. It follows, too, that public theology is

---

[77]Graham, *Apologetics without Apology*, 13.
[78]Malcolm Brown, Stephen Pattison and Graeme Smith, 'The Possibility of Citizen Theology: Public Theology after Christendom and the Enlightenment', *International Journal of Public Theology* 6, no. 2 (2012): 183–204.
[79]Graham, *Apologetics without Apology*, 9.
[80]Graham, *Between a Rock and a Hard Place*, 69–105.

less concerned with defending the interests of specific faith communities than generating informed analyses of the moral and religious dimensions of public issues and communicating these in language that is accessible to different intellectual disciplines and faith traditions.

I have argued that some of the most significant and foundational events and texts of early Christianity were apologetic in nature. This historic understanding of early Christian apologists as petitioners to the powers-that-be, calling for justice and civil freedoms must remain a major part of the work of public theologians today, not simply as a matter of self-interest but as something that is advocated as a 'gift' to the larger body politic. It represents a historical precedent for public theology to reassume its apologetic role, to render Christian faith intelligible and credible in a world in which religion is newly and urgently relevant.

Christian apologetics in the modern era has largely been dominated by forms of propositional deductive argument, often based on understandings of the inerrancy of Scripture designed to win converts. Yet alternative strands are beginning to emerge which adopt a more conversational, dialogical approach. In many respects these are more faithful to the pattern established within early Christianity, on apologetics as a form of public speech, addressed to civil authorities.

Apologetic public theology may still not resolve some of the impediments to real dialogue caused by mutual incomprehension or sheer intransigence on the part of religious and secular bodies alike. But in pragmatic, performative terms, this overriding commitment to the creation of shared public space – both physical and discursive – in which the practices and principles of citizenship can be exercised represents a serious attempt to give substance to a theological praxis that is dialogical, interdisciplinary, pluralistic and directed towards the achievement of shared goods.

PART II

The ecumenical scope of public theology

CHAPTER 7

The legacy of theological liberalism

A ghost in public theology

ULRICH SCHMIEDEL

'I am the chosen one', claimed the former president of the United States, Donald J. Trump.[1] It is a cliché to call on Trump when considering the current controversies stirred up by religion in the public square. But if theology is thinking and talking about God, then Trump is a theologian of sorts (even if there might be more talking than thinking in his case). *The Washington Post* analysed Trump's claim, arguing it is nothing special for a US president to call on God for political purposes.[2] What is special about Trump's claim is that it is staked in a context characterized by the construct of a clash of civilizations. Although one would be hard-pressed to find political theorists or public theologians who agree with Samuel P. Huntington's construction,[3]

---

[1] See Sarah Pulliam Bailey, '"I am the Chosen One": Trump Again Plays on Messianic Claims as He Embraces "King of Israel" Title', *The Washington Post*, 21 August 2019, https://www.washingtonpost.com/religion/2019/08/21/i-am-chosen-one-trump-again-plays-messianic-claims-he-embraces-king-israel-title/ (accessed 20 January 2020).
[2] Ibid.
[3] Samuel P. Huntington, 'The Clash of Civilizations', in *The Clash of Civilizations? The Debate*, ed. Samuel P. Huntington (New York: Foreign Affairs, 1993), 22–49. See also Samuel P. Huntington, *The Clash of Civilizations and the Remaking of World Order* (New York: Simon & Schuster, 1996).

the construct of a clash is contagious. What is at stake with the construct are competing and conflicting theologies in the public square,[4] a 'return of political theology' in which Christianity clashes with Islam as much as Islam clashes with Christianity.[5] As Wendy Brown argues, politicians continue to 'cloak themselves in God talk' in order to present and prop up their power politics.[6] 'Conflicting sovereign and would-be sovereign powers', she asserts, 'appear to serve warring godheads . . ., even if these godheads do not align precisely with nation states'.[7] The contagious construct of a clash of civilizations prejudices internal and external politics. Trump's claim to be chosen by God concurrently perceives and produces the construct, while cashing in on the clash. What do we – by 'we', I mean public theologians in the academy who aim to analyse and assess the significance of theology for the public square – do with such a public theology? How should public theologians respond? How should public theologians not respond? Is there a criterion for our response?

In order to ask and answer these questions, I return to a conversation about religion in the public square from the 1960s and 1970s. It is the conversation between Robert Bellah and Martin Marty in which Marty invoked the figure of the 'public theologian' for the first time, coining the combination of 'public' with 'theology' and 'theology' with 'public'. Since the concept was coined, I contend, public theologians have been haunted by a ghost – the ghost of theological liberalism, concretized in Paul Tillich. My core concern in this chapter is historical or hauntological.[8] Regardless of whether we like or dislike being haunted by the legacy of liberalism – although it arguably rests on this legacy, the American Academy of Religion recently closed its 'Liberal Theologies Unit' – it continues to haunt us. I chart the impact of this legacy on the conceptualization of public theology, but *not* in order to cast out the ghost.[9] On the contrary, I claim that the legacy is crucial to carve out the contours

---

[4]See Arshin Adib-Moghaddam, *A Metahistory of the Clash of Civilizations: Us and Them Beyond Orientalism* (Oxford: Oxford University Press, 2014).
[5]See Seyla Benhabib, 'The Return of Political Theology: The Scarf Affair in Comparative Constitutional Perspective', *Philosophy and Social Criticism* 36, no. 3–4 (2010): 451–71; Wendy Brown, 'Subjects of Tolerance: "Why We Are Civilized and They Are the Barbarians"', in *Political Theologies: Public Religions in a Post-Secular World*, ed. Hent de Vries and Lawrence E. Sullivan (New York: Fordham University Press, 2006), 298–317.
[6]Wendy Brown, *Walled States, Waning Sovereignty* (New York: Zone Books, 2010), 64.
[7]Ibid., 63.
[8]I borrow the concept of hauntology from Jacques Derrida, *Specters of Marx: The State of the Debt, the Work of Mourning, and the New International*, trans. Peggy Kamuf (London: Routledge, 1994).
[9]In Ulrich Schmiedel, 'Kirche im Kreuzfeuer: Potenziale liberaler Theologie in postmigrantischen Gesellschaften', in *Liberale Theologie heute / Liberal Theology Today*, ed. Jörg Lauster, Ulrich Schmiedel and Peter Schüz (Tübingen: Mohr Siebeck, 2019), 351–66, I have pointed to the significance of the legacy of theological liberalism for public theology today, but without presenting it in historical detail or hauntological depth.

of a criterion that allows for critical analyses and constructive assessments of theologies in the public square today: openness to otherness. If public theologies are opened to the other, they can resist the interpretation and instrumentalization of theologies for the contagious construct of the clash of civilizations by calling for coalitions between Christians and non-Christians. In the current context, coalitions with Muslims will be the most provocative and the most productive.[10] The legacy of liberalism calls public theologians inside and outside the academy to introduce these productive provocations into the public square.

7.1 LIBERAL THEOLOGY: LABEL AND LEGACY

In *Critics not Caretakers: Redescribing the Public Study of Religion*, Russel T. McCutcheon complains that 'the ghost of Paul Tillich yet haunts the field'.[11] McCutcheon compiles a long list of liberals concluding with Martin E. Marty, 'perhaps the best-known scholar of religion in the United States'.[12] If the scholar who coined and conceptualized 'public theology' was a Tillichian, is Tillich's ghost haunting public theology?

Marty works in the wake of the turn to experience which both its defenders and its despisers consider the core characteristic of the legacy of theological liberalism.[13] It can be traced back to Friedrich Schleiermacher's speeches *On Religion*, which shifted from revelation to religion as the central category of theology.[14] According to McCutcheon, Marty distinguishes between religion as experience and religion as expression. Religion is about a transcendence – 'the

---

[10]See also Ulrich Schmiedel, '"Take Up Your Cross" Public Theology between Populism and Pluralism in the Post-Migrant Context', *International Journal of Public Theology* 13, no. 2 (2019): 140–62. My account of public theology in this chapter builds on the analyses of Robert Bellah and Martin Marty I offer in that article.

[11]Russell T. McCutcheon, *Critics Not Caretakers: Redescribing the Public Study of Religion* (Albany: State University of New York Press, 2001), 180, where McCutchen cites Jonathan Z. Smith from memory.

[12]Ibid., 5.

[13]Ibid. For the significance of the turn to experience, see Jörg Lauster, 'Liberale Theologie: Eine Ermunterung', *Neue Zeitschrift für Systematische Theologie und Religionsphilosophie* 49, no. 3 (2008): 291–307. Lauster analyses liberalism in the history of theology as an 'attitude' or an 'approach', 'Haltung' in German. It is marked by the differentiation between experience and expression which in turn demands a critical and self-critical exploration of theological claims to truth.

[14]McCutcheon, *Critics not Caretakers*, 4. See Friedrich Schleiermacher, *On Religion: Speeches to the Cultured Among Its Despisers*, trans. Richard Crouter (Cambridge: Cambridge University Press, 2003). See also the contributions to Dietrich Korsch and Amber Griffioen, eds, *Interpreting Religion: The Significance of Friedrich Schleiermacher's 'Reden über die Religion'* (Tübingen: Mohr Siebeck, 2011).

ultimate', in Tillich's terminology[15] – that can be experienced, but that cannot be expressed. For McCutcheon, however, transcendence is a trick: when the experience is considered central (although it cannot be expressed), while the expression is considered not central (although it can be expressed), then the centre of religion is rendered inaccessible to scholarship. While all the 'modern day Tillichians'[16] agree, McCutcheon asks: Why should scholars assume that there is a transcendence in the first place, if all that is accessible to scholarship are, after all, only echoes of it?[17] For McCutcheon, Tillich's claim to the ultimate is 'empty'.[18] It is indeed a ghost – the ghost of theological liberalism that needs to be exorcized from the study of religion.[19]

While McCutcheon's criticism promotes a concept of the study of religion that contrasts and conflicts with theology, there are trajectories and trends in the history of theology which support his exorcism of the legacy of theological liberalism. Within theology, both the neo-orthodox and the neo-neo-orthodox critics of liberalism concentrate their critique on Schleiermacher's turn to experience.[20] George Lindbeck's post-liberal theology has been dynamite for theologians' understanding of theology in contrast to religious studies (and religious studies in contrast to theology).[21] At least since Lindbeck, then, theologians and non-theologians can agree that ghost busters should stop the legacy of liberalism from spooking around in their research on religion, regardless of whether it is theological or non-theological. Both agree that Tillichian transcendence is empty.[22]

---

[15] Martin Leiner, 'Tillich on God', in *The Cambridge Companion to Paul Tillich*, ed. Russell Re Manning (Cambridge: Cambridge University Press, 2009), 37–55 (50), points to a subtle but significant shift in Tillich's terminology: from 'the unconditional (*das Unbedingte*)' to 'the ultimate concern (*das, was uns unbedingt angeht*)' which emphasizes the relationality between the concern and the concerned.
[16] McCutcheon, *Critics Not Caretakers*, 165.
[17] Ibid., 3–20. See also the polemic in Russell T. McCutcheon, 'I Have a Hunch', in *Religious Experience: A Reader*, ed. Craig Martin, Russell T. McCutcheon and Leslie Dorrough Smith (London: Equinox, 2012), 199–202. For a critique of McCutcheon's conceptualization of experience, see Thomas Hardtke, Ulrich Schmiedel and Tobias Tan, 'Introduction: Experience or Expression? A Puzzling Oversight" and "Conclusion: Experience or Expression? Preserving the Puzzle"', in *Religious Experience Revisited: Expressing the Inexpressible?*, ed. Thomas Hardtke, Ulrich Schmiedel and Tobias Tan (Leiden: Brill, 2016), 1–13 and 262–73.
[18] McCutcheon, *Critics Not Caretakers*, 207.
[19] Ibid., 106.
[20] See the neo-orthodox critique by Karl Barth, *Church Dogmatics*, vol. I/2, trans. Geoffrey W. Bromiley (Edinburgh: T&T Clark, 2004 [1956]), 280–360 and the neo-neo-orthodox critique by George R. Lindbeck, *The Nature of Doctrine: Religion and Theology in a Postliberal Age* (Louisville, KY: Westminster John Knox Press, 1984), 30–72.
[21] Lindbeck, *The Nature of Doctrine*, 30–45 and 112–38.
[22] See Gorazd Andrejč, 'Liberal Theology as a Slippery Slope: What's in the Metaphor?', in *Liberale Theologie heute / Liberal Theology Today*, 215–26.

Crucially, the critique of liberalism has led theologians to criticize the project and the programme of public theology. Liberalism is so ingrained in the concerns and the concepts of the field that even exorcism cannot save it. Lindbeck insisted that public theology is problematic, because the issue is not how theology enters the public but how the public enters theology.[23] Insisting on the identity and the integrity of the church, Lindbeck's theology is not interested in a conversation but in a conversion – the conversion of the public.[24] However, theologians who are commonly considered liberal criticized the label of liberalism themselves. Tillich spurned the label too.[25] It was Rudolf Bultmann who branded theologians working in the wake of Schleiermacher as liberals.[26] Bultmann conjured up a tradition of liberal theology that never existed as a unified and unifying whole in order to present his 'new theological movement' in contrast and contradiction to it.[27] Both in the past and in the present, then, the characterizations of the legacy of theological liberalism come from its critics rather than its caretakers, so one could argue that critiques of liberalism (as a label) are characteristic of liberalism (as a legacy).[28] If nobody – not even liberals – wants to be labelled 'liberal', what is the ghost that haunts the field?

In *Dynamics of Faith*, Tillich conceptualized religion through his theory of symbols.[29] In as much as it draws or redraws the distinction between experience and expression, Tillich's theory of symbols can be considered his own creative and constructive contribution to the legacy of theological liberalism. According to Tillich, the core characteristic of symbols is participation.[30] While symbols and signs point beyond themselves, the

---

[23] Lindbeck, *The Nature of Doctrine*, 30–45 and 112–38.
[24] See Kristin Heyer, 'How Does Theology Go Public? Rethinking the Debate between David Tracy and George Lindbeck', *Political Theology* 5, no. 3 (2004): 307–27. Heyer argues that, despite the contrast between post-liberal and public theology that is set up by Lindbeck, 'postliberal theology's very emphasis on the distinctiveness of the Christian community . . . serves as its "public theology"'. (Ibid., 322).
[25] Tillich saw himself as a mediator between liberal theology, on the one hand, and the critics of liberal theology, on the other. See the programmatic statement in Paul Tillich, *A History of Christian Thought: From its Judaic and Hellenistic Origins to Existentialism*, ed. Carl E. Braaten (New York: Simon & Schuster, 1967), 27.
[26] Rudolf Bultmann, 'Die liberale Theologie und die jüngste theologische Bewegung', in Rudolf Bultmann, *Glauben und Verstehen*, vol. 1 (Tübingen: Mohr Siebeck, 1980 [1933]), 1–25.
[27] Ibid.
[28] See also Lauster, 'Liberale Theologie', 291–2.
[29] Paul Tillich, *Dynamics of Faith* (New York: Harper, 1956). Tillich published his theory of symbols for the first time in 1928 in German. In English it was published a number of times, including Paul Tillich, 'The Religious Symbol', *Daedalus* 87, no. 3 (1958): 3–21. About a decade later, *Daedalus* will also publish Robert Bellah's account of religion in the public square.
[30] Tillich, *Dynamics of Faith*, 41–53. For the significance of Platonism for Tillich's theory of the symbol, see Douglas Hedley, 'Tillich and Participation', in *Returning to Tillich: Theology and Legacy in Transition*, eds. Russell Re Manning and Samuel A. Shearn (Berlin: De Gruyter, 2018), 31–40.

pointing of symbols in contrast to the pointing of signs is *not* arbitrary, because the symbol participates in the symbolized. In the case of religion, God is the central symbol.[31] What Tillich characterizes as 'the ultimate' is experienced as a concrete concern. Analytically, the 'that' and the 'what', the concern and the concrete, can be distinguished.[32] The concept of the symbol draws the distinction. When Tillich explains that the symbol of God points beyond the symbol of God to God, his explanation implies that the concrete points beyond the concrete to the concern – which is to say, to the ultimate.[33] If theologians are interested in transcendence, they have to put the 'that' above the 'what', the concern above the concrete, or 'God above God'.[34] Described differently, as a 'symbol for what concerns us ultimately', God (as a concrete concept) points beyond God (as a concrete concept) towards God (the ultimate concern that Tillich understands as the 'God above God').

Tillich's 'God above God' is a complex and complicated category which was conceptualized alongside his theory of symbols.[35] He connects components from negative and positive theology dialectically and dynamically in his theory of the symbol of God.[36] The God above God stands for the resistance of transcendence to being captured or confined by concepts. God remains other, so Tillich calls theologians who think and talk about God to remain open to God's otherness. Crucially, openness is not emptiness. In Tillich's theory of symbols, the concrete captures the concern, while the concern critiques the concrete. Taking the concrete as a propositional category and the concern as a performative category, it could be concluded that, for Tillich, the ultimate must be propositionally empty in order to be performatively.

---

[31] Tillich, *The Dynamics of Faith*, 44–8. According to Paul Tillich, *Systematic Theology*, vol. 1 (Chicago: The University of Chicago Press, 1951), 238–9, only 'the statement that God is being-itself is a non-symbolic statement. . . . However, . . . nothing else can be said about God which is not symbolic'.

[32] Tillich, *Dynamics of Faith*, 102–3. I am drawing on Marijn de Jong and Ulrich Schmiedel, 'Compromised Correlation? Experience in Paul Tillich's Concept of Correlation', in *Returning to Tillich: Theology and Legacy in Transition*, ed. Russell Re Manning and Samuel A. Shearn (Berlin: De Gruyter, 2018), 41–51, here.

[33] Tillich, *Dynamics of Faith*, 46: 'It is obvious that such an understanding of the meaning of God makes the discussions about the existence or non-existence of God meaningless. It is meaningless to question the ultimacy of an ultimate concern.'

[34] The 'God above God' is a central concept for Tillich. See Paul Tillich, *The Courage to Be* (New Haven: Yale University Press, 1952), 186–90.

[35] For a comprehensive account, see Lars Christian Heinemann, *Sinn – Geist – Symbol: Eine systematisch-genetische Rekonstruktion der frühen Symboltheorie Paul Tillichs* (Berlin: De Gruyter, 2018). For the significance of this category as a pastoral response to doubt, see Samuel A. Shearn, *Pastor Tillich: The Justification of the Doubter* (Oxford: Oxford University Press, 2022).

[36] Hedley, 'Tillich and Participation', 37–8.

Critics such as McCutcheon argue that the assumption that there is a transcendence cannot be proven. It is a ghost. Yet McCutcheon overlooks that the God above God functions as a *normative* category for Tillich. If scholars accept that there is a God above God who can neither be confined nor captured by concepts, scholars have a criterion to analyse and assess the practice of religions. Through his concept of the symbol, Tillich shifts from a descriptive to a prescriptive register when he suggests that the concern (the symbolized) must criticize the concrete (the symbols).[37] Against what Tillich interprets as the 'idolatry' of identifying the concrete with the concern, he argues that the 'criterion of the truth of faith' is the critique of the concrete through the concern.[38] Normatively, then, whether faith is true or untrue to itself depends on whether it criticizes itself in relation to the ultimate.[39] What Tillich formulates as the 'dynamics of faith' – the constant movement from the propositional concrete to the performative concern and from the performative concern to the propositional concrete that opens religion to the other – is fuelled by his theory of symbols. While Tillich is interested in the dynamics of faith inside rather than outside churches, his criterion has consequences for religion in the public sphere. Both where theologians are interested in studying what public theology is and where theologians are interested in shaping what public theology is, they will encounter the ghost of Tillich.

7.2 THE GHOST OF PAUL TILLICH IN PUBLIC THEOLOGY: A HAUNTOLOGY

Paul Tillich's criterion for the truth of faith runs through Robert N. Bellah's and Martin E. Marty's characterizations of religion in the public square, terminologically and theoretically. Critics such as McCutcheon complain that Tillich's criterion for faith transgresses the standards of scholarship because there is no proof for the God above God. Of course, the proof of the ultimate would miss the point of the ultimate – which is, the pointing. A hauntology might be capable of exploring and examining the criterion for public theology that comes to the fore in the liberal theological legacy: openness to otherness.[40]

---

[37]Tillich, *Dynamics of Faith*, 52.
[38]Ibid., 97.
[39]Ibid. See also ibid., 29, where Tillich insists that the 'creedal expressions of the ultimate concern of the community must include their own criticism. It must become obvious in all of them . . . that they are not ultimate. Rather, their function is to point to the ultimate which is beyond all of them'.
[40]Derrida, *Specters of Marx*, 9, coined the concept of hauntology to characterize Marxism as a ghost that haunts political philosophy in the past and the present. Although I am less interested in ontology than Derrida, I borrow his concept because his answer to the question of 'What does it mean to follow a ghost?' allows for a tentative distinction between history and hauntology (ibid).

If the current context is characterized by the contagious construct of the clash of civilizations, public theology is instructive precisely because it transgresses the standards of scholarship.

7.2.1 Robert N. Bellah

In his seminal study, 'Civil Religion in America', published in the 1960s, Robert N. Bellah presents and promotes a concept that he had borrowed from Jean-Jacques Rousseau's *The Social Contract*:[41] 'civil' in contrast to 'confessional' religion.[42] Bellah proposes that confessional religion is tied to specific ecclesial institutions, while civil religion is not tied to specific ecclesial institutions. It is religion in the public square. Both require 'the same care in understanding'.[43] Tillich is not mentioned, but the ghost of Tillich haunts Bellah's study.[44]

President John F. Kennedy's inauguration serves as an empirical example for the civil in contrast to the confessional role of religion in the United States. Bellah is struck by Kennedy's repeated reference to God. Since 'God' is a concept that 'almost all Americans can accept', Bellah suggests, it connects Christians and non-Christians.[45] Although Kennedy was a Christian, the God of his address could be accepted by both Christians and non-Christians, because Kennedy invoked public civil religion rather than private confessional religion. Bellah admits that the civil-religious (in contrast to the confessional-religious) concept of God 'means so many different things to so many different people that it is almost an empty sign' but argues that the emptiness of the sign is significant.[46] It can be accepted by almost all Americans because of its openness. '"God" has clearly been a central symbol' for religion in the public square.[47]

Although acceptable to almost all Americans, Bellah argues that the concept of God claimed by politicians like Kennedy has theological and anthropological

---

A hauntology has to do with traces of theories or thinkers rather than theories or thinkers, traces which always already influence the one who traces them (see ibid., 63–5 and 201–3).

[41] Jean-Jacques Rousseau, *The Social Contract*, trans. Christopher Betts (Oxford: Oxford University Press, 1994), 158–67.

[42] Robert N. Bellah, 'Civil Religion in America', *Daedalus* 96, no. 1 (1967): 1–21. Bellah developed and discussed his concept, especially in Robert N. Bellah, *The Broken Covenant: American Civil Religion in Time of Trial* (Chicago: The University of Chicago Press, 1975); Robert N. Bellah and Philip E. Hammond, *Varieties of Civil Religion* (New York: Harper & Row, 1980), and also Robert N. Bellah, *Beyond Belief: Essays on Religion in a Post-Traditionalist World* (Berkley: University of California Press, 1991).

[43] Bellah, 'Civil Religion in America', 1.

[44] Matteo Bortonlini, *A Joyfully Serious Man: The Life of Robert Bellah* (Princeton: Princeton University Press, 2021) was published after I finished this chapter. In this masterful biography, Tillich's personal and professional influence on Bellah features prominently.

[45] Ibid., 3.

[46] Ibid. Bellah uses 'sign' and 'symbol' synonymously here.

[47] Bellah, 'Civil Religion in America', 15.

content. Drawing on documents from the history of the United States, he specifies the civil-religious in contrast to the confessional-religious concept of God: 'Even though he is somewhat deist in cast', Bellah (for whom God is apparently a 'he' rather than a 'she') writes, 'he is by no means simply a watchmaker'.[48] On the contrary, God is interested and intervenes in the fate of 'American Israel'.[49] There is a relation between religion and nation that is reflected in Kennedy's address: 'The whole address can be understood as only the most recent statement of a theme that lies very deep in the American tradition, namely the obligation . . . to carry out God's will on earth. This was the motivating spirit of those who founded America.'[50]

Bellah stresses that both civil religion and confessional religion are avenues to God.[51] While the sociologist is careful with theological terminology – to be precise, Bellah proposes that 'one could almost say' that transcendence is 'revealed through the experience of the American people'[52] – he specifies transcendence in Tillichian terminology as 'ultimate'.[53] The ultimate is a 'reality' that is transcendent rather than immanent.[54] Bellah contends that 'civil religion at its best is a genuine apprehension' of it.[55] The constraining 'at its best' is crucial. It clarifies that Bellah has a criterion to distinguish between a civil religion that is and a civil religion that is not 'at its best', even if the criterion is implicit rather than explicit.[56] Bellah's criterion can be gauged where he cautions against ideological instrumentalizations of the ultimate. In the case of the United States, these 'idolizations' can be found both in national and in international politics.[57] Writing during the Cold War, Bellah points to 'adventures in imperialism', such as the war in Vietnam,[58] warning that religion in the public square runs rogue when Americans instrumentalize it to distinguish the free world from the unfree world in order to prop up their own power politics.[59] In these instrumentalizations, religion is reduced to a celebration of the nation rather than a critique of the

---

[48]Ibid., 7.
[49]Ibid.
[50]Ibid., 5.
[51]Ibid., 12. See also Russell E. Richey and Donald G. Jones, 'The Civil Religion Debate', in *American Civil Religion*, ed. Russell E. Richey and Donald G. Jones (New York: Harper, 1974), 3–20 (6).
[52]Bellah, 'Civil Religion in America', 12.
[53]Ibid., 18.
[54]Ibid., 12.
[55]Ibid.
[56]For the normativity inherent in the concept, see Philip Gorski, *American Covenant: A History of Civil Religion from the Puritans to the Present* (Princeton: Princeton University Press, 2017), 13–36.
[57]Bellah, 'Civil Religion in America', 14–16.
[58]Ibid., 14.
[59]Ibid., 15. See also Bellah's critique of Richard M. Nixon's references to religion in Robert N. Bellah, 'American Civil Religion in the 1970s', in *American Civil Religion*, ed. Russell E. Richey and Donald G. Jones (New York: Harper, 1974), 255–72.

nation: it revels in its God-given rights but rejects its God-given responsibilities.[60] Normatively, then, it is crucial for Bellah that the avenue to the ultimate that is provided by religion in the public square allows for both the critique of the nation and the celebration of the nation.

Bellah's account of sovereignty illustrates the simultaneity of celebration and critique. 'What difference does it make that sovereignty belongs to God?'[61] While Bellah accepts that in 'American political theory, sovereignty rests, of course, with the people', he answers that the transfer of sovereignty to a transcendence clarifies that 'the will of the people is not itself the criterion. . . . There is a higher criterion in terms of which this will can be judged'.[62] The consequence is both positive and negative: there are God-given rights and God-given responsibilities for any people under God. What is at stake here is Tillich's God above God who cannot be confined by concepts. Remaining other, the ultimate works in two ways: one can refer to it in order to celebrate the nation (pointing to where God is revealed in the nation) and one can refer to it in order to criticize the nation (pointing to where God is not revealed in the nation, where the nation is lagging behind). Given that the God above God is in principle and practice beyond reach, the nation is ceaselessly called to improve. According to Bellah, the ultimacy of the ultimate – the fact that it can be neither captured nor confined – is the criterion for civil in contrast to confessional religion 'at its best', religion as it ought to present itself in the public square.

Overall, Bellah's criterion resonates with Tillich's terminology and with Tillich's theory. Bellah transposes Tillich's concept of the symbol from confessional to civil religion. In the public square of the United States, the symbol of God is claimed for the nation. Since the symbol points beyond the symbol to what it symbolizes, the symbol should allow Americans to resist any identification and any instrumentalization of God for America. God is always already more than can be said about God. What Tillich calls the concrete is there to allow for celebration and what Tillich calls the concern is there to allow for critique. At its best, civil religion holds a balance between the two.[63] It is not surprising that the ghost of Tillich runs through Bellah's concept of religion in the public square. Bellah repeatedly referred to Tillich as 'one of my three great teachers'.[64] The two were colleagues at Harvard Divinity School, where Tillich

---

[60]Bellah, 'Civil Religion in America', 12, where Bellah refers to 'deformation', 'distortion', and – in Tillichian terminology – 'demonic'.
[61]Ibid., 4.
[62]Ibid.
[63]Ibid., 12.
[64]Robert N. Bellah, *Religion in Human Evolution: From the Paleolithic to the Axial Age* (Cambridge, MA: Harvard University Press, 2011), xxvi, listing Tillich next to Talcott Parsons and Wilfred Cantwell Smith.

taught from 1955 to 1962. There is so much of the liberal theological legacy in Bellah that he himself has been labelled a 'liberal' by his critics.[65] Bellah took the label as a compliment rather than a criticism but clarified that he 'would like to decline the honor'.[66] Nonetheless, systematically, it is the dynamics of faith in Tillich's theory of symbols – the constant movement from the propositional concrete to the performative concern and from the performative concern to the propositional concrete that keeps religion open to the other – that Bellah spells out for religion in the public square. Bellah's account, then, is haunted by the legacy of theological liberalism.

7.2.2 Martin E. Marty

Martin E. Marty's 'Two Kinds of Two Kinds of Civil Religion', published in the 1970s, engaged Bellah's conceptualization of religion in the public square both critically and constructively.[67] In response to Bellah, Marty coined the concept of public theology – a concept that Bellah then called 'a major contribution' to the study of religion in the public square.[68] Marty is also haunted by the ghost of Tillich, although he names the ghost only once.

Marty studies Bellah's concept of civil in contrast to confessional religion as a 'social construction'.[69] He suggests that 'it remains . . . the product of the scholars' world' since 'the man' (for Marty there seems to be no woman) 'on the street would be surprised to learn of its existence'.[70] Marty is keen to avoid definitions of religion that are incapable of distinguishing between what is religious and what is non-religious: 'ultimacy', he proposes, makes the difference.[71] Marty's core concern is that Bellah's conceptualization of religion in the public square can be considered positively or negatively: 'liberal

---

[65]See Bellah's response to Paul Griffith in the symposium on *Religion in Human Evolution* in *First Things*, Robert N. Bellah, 'A Reply to My Critics: Responses to Thomas Joseph White, Francesca Aran Murphy, and Paul Griffith', *First Things* (June 2013), https://www.firstthings.com/article/2013/06/a-reply-to-my-critics (accessed 20 January 2020).
[66]Ibid.
[67]Martin E. Marty, 'Two Kinds of Two Kinds of Civil Religion', in *American Civil Religion*, ed. Russell E. Richey and Donald G. Jones (New York: Harper, 1974), 139–57. Florian Höhne, *Öffentliche Theologie: Begriffsgeschichte und Grundfragen* (Leipzig: Evangelische Verlagsanstalt, 2015), 15 (fn. 11), clarified that the article is the publication of a lecture that Marty delivered at Drew University. The lecture is the first time that 'public theologian' (not yet 'public theology') is used by Marty.
[68]Bellah, 'American Civil Religion in the 1970s', 258.
[69]Marty, 'Two Kinds of Two Kinds of Civil Religion', 141, referencing Peter L. Berger and Thomas Luckmann, The *Social Construction of Reality*: *A Treatise in the Sociology of Knowledge* (New York: Doubleday, 1966). Bellah, 'American Civil Religion in the 1970s', 256, accepts Marty's suggestion.
[70]Marty, 'Two Kinds of Two Kinds of Civil Religion', 141.
[71]Ibid., 139.

intellectuals in the academy', Marty quips, have different opinions: if the president is a liberal (and like them), they will consider civil religion favourably and if the president is not a liberal (and unlike them), they will consider civil religion unfavourably – they will 'flee for cover'.[72] Against the normativity in Bellah's conceptualization,[73] Marty insists that both civil and confessional religion should be studied according to what they do rather than according to what scholars say they should do. Marty offers a typology in which 'there are two kinds of two kinds of civil religion'.[74] The typology organizes the types of civil religion according to their substance and their style. Considering that Marty is credited with coining a new concept, it is surprising that he adds: 'I shall eschew neologisms – let me disappoint those who are seeking novel designations. The stress is here on common sense.'[75]

Substantially, Marty distinguishes between a type of civil religion in which God and the nation diverge and a type of civil religion in which God and the nation converge.[76] He refers to the 'transcendence' of the nation, on the one hand, and the 'self-transcendence' of the nation, on the other hand.[77] Described differently, civil religion can revolve around a God-above-the-nation or a God-as-the-nation.[78] Tillich's concept of the symbol runs through Marty's connection between religion and nation. What is the ultimate? If civil religion works with a God-above-the nation, the nation itself is not ultimate, but the transcendence is – God and the nation diverge. If civil religion works with a God-as-the-nation, the nation itself is ultimate, the transcendence is not: the nation is transcendence – God and the nation converge. Tillich's God above God is what is at stake here. But what Tillich – and following Tillich, Bellah – normatively assess as either positive (God-above-the-nation) or negative (God-as-the-nation) configurations of religion in the public square, Marty approaches more descriptively than prescriptively. He is interested in a neutral account of civil religion.

Stylistically, Marty distinguishes between a type of civil religion in which the celebration of the nation is central and a type of civil religion in which the critique of the nation is central.[79] 'Within each of these two kinds', Marty

---

[72]Ibid., 142.
[73]In response to Marty, Bellah, 'American Civil Religion in the 1970s', 257, admits that he mixed epistemological and evaluative categories in the article in *Daedalus*, but argues that 'the notion of civil religion . . . is an analytical tool for the understanding of something that exists, which, like all things human, is sometimes good and sometimes bad'.
[74]Marty, 'Two Kinds of Two Kinds of Civil Religion', 144.
[75]Ibid.
[76]Ibid.
[77]Ibid.
[78]Ibid.
[79]Ibid., 144–5.

argues regarding the types of a civil-religious God-above-the-nation and a civil-religious God-as-the-nation, 'there are two kinds of approaches or analyses. . . . Let us speak of these as "priestly" and "prophetic"'.[80] Described differently, Marty discusses the categories of America's God-given rights and America's God-given responsibilities that Bellah delineates in his account of the history of the United States as two styles of religion in the public square: 'the one comforts the afflicted; the other afflicts the comfortable'.[81] The criterion that Tillich constructed through his theory of symbols – the criterion that Bellah then turned from confessional to civil religion – is interpreted in a way that allows Marty to distinguish between two styles of religion in the public square. Here he references Tillich, pointing to Tillich's 'Protestant Principle' as a marker of the prophetic rather than the priestly.[82] Again avoiding the normative assumption that the prophetic is positive while the priestly is negative, Marty argues: 'If the two elements can be built into civil religion, it will not be so ominous to its critics.'[83]

Marty offers a detailed discussion of the four configurations of civil religion in the history of the United States, outlining his distinction between two substances and two styles of religion in the public square. Interestingly, the concept of public theology that he coins in his discussion is not his core concern. He seems unaware of the impact his concept would have on the study of religion. What, then, is public theology?

Although Marty seems to suggest that public theology differs from civil religion as much as civil religion differs from public theology – there is a 'perhaps' in the sentence that draws this distinction, so it is not clear how convinced he is himself[84] – the concept of public theology can be characterized with his typology of civil religion, but the characterization hovers between the types.[85] Public theologians operate with a God above God as they opt for a God-above-the-nation rather than a God-as-the-nation. The nation is considered to be 'under God'.[86] This consideration allows public theologians to engage in priestly celebration *and* prophetic critique *at the same time*.[87] The combination

---

[80]Ibid.
[81]Ibid., 145.
[82]Ibid., 154.
[83]Ibid., 155.
[84]Ibid., 148.
[85]Accordingly, Marty's types are ideal-types. For Max Weber, ideal-types are *not* supposed to characterize empirical cases. Only when the case differs from its characterization can the ideal-type become a hermeneutic and heuristic tool. See Max Weber, 'The "Objectivity" of Knowledge in Social Sciences and Social Policy', in Max Weber, *Collected Methodological Writings*, trans. Hans Henrik Bruun, eds. Hans Henrik Bruun and Sam Whimster (London: Routledge, 2012), 100–38.
[86]Marty, 'Two Kinds of Two Kinds of Civil Religion', 147.
[87]Ibid., 148.

of celebration and critique is the core characteristic of public theology for Marty. The prophetic approach to the nation alone would be critical but would not be received by the people. The priestly approach to the nation alone would be received by the people but would not be critical. Hence, public theology has to be prophetic and priestly; at the same time, it 'has to be dialectical'.[88]

What Marty suggested about the priestly and the prophetic in his account of civil religion – 'If the two elements can be built into civil religion, it will not be so ominous to its critics'[89] – now re-enters his reflections as the core characteristic of public theology. Yet there is a twist to the re-entry: Marty's study of religion in the public sphere – of civil as opposed to confessional religion – insisted on neutrality, but when it comes to public theology, Marty presents the dialectics of priestly and prophetic as a *normative* marker of public theology. Normativity, then, is reserved for theology.

The normativity that Marty integrates into the concept of public theology is illustrated by his interpretation of Reinhold Niebuhr as 'a paradigm for public theology'.[90] According to Marty, Niebuhr reflected on the life of the American people 'in light of some transcendent reference',[91] joining 'in his person the two main approaches to public theology in America' – namely one that draws on confessional and one that draws on non-confessional resources.[92] Niebuhr stands for a 'relocation of theology'.[93] While some theologians criticized Niebuhr for moving theology from the inside to the outside of the church, Marty defends Niebuhr. Against the critics who complain about a lack of ecclesiology, he insists that Niebuhr's concept of the church comes close to Tillich's.[94] Niebuhr 'had an undeveloped sense . . . about the borders of the church',[95] but the blurred boundaries enabled and equipped his theology to go public in the first place.

Marty points out that for Niebuhr 'the Church is that place in human society where men are disturbed by the word of the eternal God'.[96] Presumably the word of God disturbs both men and women, but Niebuhr's point is nonetheless perceptive: the disturbance can occur inside and outside the institutional church,

---

[88]Ibid., 149.
[89]Ibid., 155.
[90]Martin E. Marty, 'Reinhold Niebuhr: Public Theology and the American Experience', *Journal of Religion* 54, no. 4 (1974): 332–59 (359).
[91]Ibid., 332.
[92]Ibid., 359.
[93]Ibid., 338.
[94]Ibid., 341, referencing Harold R. Landon, 'Introduction', in *Reinhold Niebuhr: A Prophetic Voice in our Time*, ed. Harold R. Landon (New York: Seaburg Press, 1962), 11–26.
[95]Marty, 'Reinhold Niebuhr: Public Theology and the American Experience', 341.
[96]Ibid., citing Reinhold Niebuhr, *Beyond Tragedy: Essays on the Christian Interpretation of History* (New York: Charles Scribner's Sons, 1965 [1937]), 62.

so it makes little sense to separate confessional religion from non-confessional religion. Religion is always already in the public square. According to Marty, Niebuhr appreciated the need for acknowledging and analysing the nation as a repository of religion, which is to say he turned more and more towards religion in the public square.[97] Marty concludes that 'Niebuhr kept the tension between the two spheres', which is what makes his theology the paradigm of public theology in the United States.[98]

Crucially, Marty argues that Niebuhr's paradigmatic public theology agrees with Tillich in as much as it finds the ultimate both outside and inside the churches.[99] Tillich is invoked where Marty insists on Niebuhr's critique of 'idolatry' in American public life, as spelt out in his critique of the racism that runs through the history of the United States from the past to the present.[100] The invocation of Tillich suggests that it is the criterion in Tillich's theory of symbols that underscores Niebuhr's public theology in its dialectic of the priestly and the prophetic. According to Marty, Niebuhr calls for the constant movement from the concrete to the concern and from the concern to the concrete that keeps religion open to the other. Niebuhr calls for the dynamics of faith as a catalyst for the dialectics of public theology. There is a lot of haunting here. Tillich's ghost haunts both of the sources that Marty considers for his conceptualization of public theology: Niebuhr and – after Niebuhr[101] – Bellah.

Overall, Marty's criterion for public theology resonates with Bellah's criterion for civil in contrast to confessional religion. Florian Höhne has clarified how the hidden normativity that runs through Bellah's account of religion in the public square is taken out of the concept of civil religion by Marty in order to put it into public theology.[102] As a consequence, the field of public theology suffers from the same lack of clarity that characterized the concept of civil (in contrast to confessional) religion: it is unclear whether

---

[97]Marty, 'Reinhold Niebuhr: Public Theology and the American Experience', 356–8. Interestingly, Reinhold Niebuhr, *Christianity and Power Politics* (New York: Charles Scribner's Sons, 1940), 109, criticized the liberalism of the churches in this context: 'If the modern churches were to scrutinize their true faith they would take the crucifix from their altars' in order to replace it with 'the three little monkeys who counsel men to "speak no evil, hear no evil, see no evil."' The critique is cited by Marty, 'Reinhold Niebuhr: Public Theology and the American Experience', 353. Disappointed with the liberal lack of politics in the churches, Niebuhr turns from the confessional to the civil, but without denying the 'custodial responsibilities of the Christian believing community' (Marty, 'Reinhold Niebuhr: Public Theology and the American Experience', 353).
[98]Marty, 'Reinhold Niebuhr: Public Theology and the American Experience', 354.
[99]Ibid., 355.
[100]Ibid., referencing Niebuhr, *Beyond Tragedy*, 53 and 85.
[101]For Niebuhr's take on liberalism in theology, see Gary Dorrien, *The Making of American Liberal Theology: Idealism, Realism and Modernity. 1900–1950* (Louisville: Westminster John Knox, 2003), 435–58.
[102]Höhne, *Öffentliche Theologie*, 20.

the field is about studying or about shaping religion in the public square.[103] Crucially, it is the ghost of Tillich which is responsible for the lack of clarity in public theology, because Tillich's God above God fulfils both a descriptive and a prescriptive function in his theory of symbols. Against a clear-cut separation, Tillich would suggest that we should remain open to the other, because God remains other. His prescriptive theology is rooted in his descriptive theology. In any case, in *The Public Church*, Marty will refrain from using Bellah's concept at all, pointing instead to public theology as an 'effort to interpret the life of a people in the light of a transcendent reference' that draws on both confessional and non-confessional resources.[104] It is not surprising that Marty's reflections on public theology resonate with the Tillichian terminology and the Tillichian theory in Bellah's account of religion. Marty, too, was a colleague of Tillich who taught at Chicago Divinity School from 1962 to 1965.[105] Systematically, Tillich's theory of symbols underlies Marty's core characteristic of public theology. God is always already more than can be said about God: God above God. What Tillich considers the propositional concrete enables the priestly celebration of the nation and what Tillich considers the performative concern enables the prophetic critique of the nation. What Tillich calls 'dynamics of faith' enters or re-enters public theology as the 'dialectics' between the priestly and the prophetic. Public theology, then, is haunted by the legacy of theological liberalism.

7.3 LEARNING FROM THE GHOST: LIVING WITH THE LEGACY

To summarize, I have argued so far that the legacy of theological liberalism, personified by Tillich, haunts public theology. When Marty coined the concept of public theology, he took Tillich's creative and constructive contribution to the legacy of liberalism – Tillich's theory of symbols – out of Bellah's account of religion in the public square in order to incorporate it into public theology. Under the new name of 'dialectics', Tillich's dynamics of faith is conceptualized as the normative core characteristic of public theology. Public theology, then, is where theological resources, either from the confessional realm (which is to say, from inside institutional churches) or from the non-confessional realm (which is to say, from outside institutional

---

[103]Ibid., 24. Höhne follows Rolf Schieder, *Civil Religion: Die religiöse Dimension der politischen Kultur* (Gütersloh: Gütersloher Verlagshaus, 1987).

[104]Martin E. Marty, *The Public Church: Mainline, Evangelical, Catholic* (New York: Crossroad, 1981). See also Höhne, *Öffentliche Theologie*, 22, for a succinct summary.

[105]See the report about their encounter in Martin E. Marty, 'The Tillich Legacy', *The Christian Century* (August–September, 1986), 732–3.

churches), are taken up in a dialectics that combines a celebration and a critique of a nation's public and political positions in relation to transcendence. Why, then, would scholars of religion want to exorcise the ghost of Tillich?

McCutcheon mocks scholars who work in the wake of Tillich for maintaining that religion is about a transcendence that transgresses its confessional-religious and its civil-religious conceptualizations as a 'repackaging of the old social gospel movement'.[106] He cautions against the consequences of Tillichian transcendence for the study of religion in the public square.[107] Marty, McCutcheon contends, puts himself in the position of the authority that decides who can and who cannot be invited into the public square. Only those who are playing according to Marty's rules – the rules that are determined by the ghost of Tillich – 'are invited to mount the public square's soap box'.[108] The hidden but haunting normativity in Marty's public theology is what is at stake here. I am not convinced that McCutcheon's critique of Marty is correct, but it is nonetheless important and instructive for the point and the profile of public theology.

The study of theology in the public square has to investigate the theologies with which we agree and the theologies with which we disagree. Consider Trump's claim to be the chosen one. It is no surprise that it is a claim in which faith is – if we return to Tillich – untrue to itself rather than true to itself, because it is no surprise that Trump is not a liberal theologian. However, taking account of the legacy of theological liberalism, public theologians can explain *why* Trump's theology has to be resisted. There is no openness to otherness in Trump's claim to God. Instead, God is anything but other. Trump identifies and instrumentalizes God for his political purposes, so as to rule out any civil (or not so civil) disobedience against his presidency. His 'theology' is idolatrous. Tillichian transcendence, then, is crucial for a critique of Trump as a theologian of sorts. Countering McCutcheon, I would suggest that the transgression of the standards of scholarship – the thinking and the talking about God termed 'theology' that goes beyond statements for which there is watertight proof – is necessary to explain by which criterion Trump's claim to God is resisted. Trump's 'theology' is about the propositional concrete rather than the performative concern, without the dynamics or the dialectics of public theology. It is helpful to be haunted by the ghost of Tillich, then, as long as the origin and the operation of the criterion are made clear.

However, as mentioned earlier, what is interesting and instructive about Trump's claim is not the claim itself, but that it is staked in a context characterized

---

[106]McCutcheon, *Critics not Caretakers*, 158.
[107]Ibid., 161.
[108]Ibid., 162, concentrating on Martin E. Marty, *The One and the Many: America's Struggle for the Common Good* (Cambridge, MA: Harvard University Press, 1982).

by the construct of a clash of civilizations. Here, McCutcheon's criticism is more perceptive and more problematic for the legacy of theological liberalism. Tillich is a case in point. He proposes that the symbol of the cross is crucial for Christianity because it symbolizes the criticism of the concrete through the concern. Christianity 'stands "under the Cross"': the cross communicates the critique of the expression of Jesus Christ as God for the sake of the experience of Jesus Christ as God.[109] Hence, 'in the picture of the Christ itself the criterion against its idolatrous abuse is given – the Cross'.[110] According to Tillich, then, the cross is what is missing in Trump's 'theology'. I cannot discuss Tillich's Christology here, but I can point to its consequences in a context characterized by the clash of civilizations.

Tillich contents that Christianity has a symbol that creates a 'contrast to all other religions, namely, . . . the Cross of the Christ'.[111] He concentrates on the cross in order to criticize Christian rather than non-Christian religions, but he nonetheless constructs a contrast that puts Christianity *against* and *above* all others. Christianity is the one and only religion that has the symbol of the cross. When Tillich connects the 'source of idolatry' to the 'source of intolerance' by claiming that both take the propositional concrete rather than the performative concern to be the ultimate – which is to say that both are in need of critique through the cross[112] – it could be concluded that *only* Christians have a faith that is true rather than untrue to itself. Although not intended by Tillich, his interpretation of Christianity can be co-opted by the constructors of the clash of civilization that put the tolerant Christian against the intolerant non-Christian. Once such a clash of civilizations is operative in the public square, politicians and pundits will be quick to caution against public or political Islam. Bernard Lewis, who coined the concept of the clash of civilizations that Huntington popularized, makes such a case when he writes about 'The Roots of Muslim Rage'.[113] Only those who adhere to the criterion of the cross are allowed to 'mount the public squares soap box'. Here, the criterion of the legacy of liberalism can critique Trump's claim to be the chosen one, but the critique runs the risk of confirming rather than criticizing the clash of civilizations in which the claim is couched. McCutcheon's call for exorcism, then, has a point. The legacy of theological liberalism is ambiguous. However, by way of conclusion, I would like to propose that the point has already been made – namely by the

---

[109]Tillich, *Dynamics of Faith*, 29.
[110]Ibid., 104.
[111]Ibid., 97.
[112]Ibid., 122.
[113]Bernard Lewis, 'The Roots of Muslim Rage', *The Atlantic* (September 1990), 47–54, taken up by Huntington, 'The Clash of Civilizations', 31.

two public theologians who work in the legacy of liberalism. The ghost of Tillich holds both a problem and a promise for public theology.

In the 1970s, Bellah suggests that 'it is essential that the transcendence which is a constitutive part of the democratic process remain symbolically empty, for particularity of content would operate to prevent precisely the openness it is meant to guarantee'.[114] Bellah calls for a 'new set of symbolic forms' that could lead to a 'world civil religion'.[115] He clarifies that his core concern is 'that we open our search . . . beyond the ambit of our own tradition' so as to connect different and diverse traditions in a 'movement toward human liberation'.[116] Marty is more cautious and more careful. In response to Bellah, he suggests that the future can draw neither only on a universalized (civil) religion nor only on a particularized (confessional) religion.[117] The 'future belongs, no doubt, to neither but only both'.[118] But in spite of their different programmes and their distinct prognoses, both see the promise of public theology for the future. As Bellah argues, a 'variety of interpretations . . . is not inconsistent with the openness of . . . transcendence as long as no public theological position is institutionalized as . . . orthodoxy. Indeed, a variety of public theologies is a guarantee of the openness of civil religion'.[119] Accordingly, public theologies – in the plural rather than the singular – are crucial to keep religion in the public square open to the other.[120] Public theologians enrich religion in the public square through their different and diverse interpretations of transcendence, 'while never making their interpretations normative for others'.[121] Openness to otherness, then, is the criterion that demands and defines a *pluralist* position of public theology.

In her reflections on the return of political theology in the construct of the clash of civilizations, Brown argues that 'the alternative' to a political liberalism that lives from the construct of the clash 'is not abandoning . . . liberalism, but, rather, using the occasion to open liberal regimes to self-reflection'.[122] While Brown is interested in liberalism in political philosophy, her argument resonates

---

[114]Bellah, 'American Civil Religion in the 1970s', 258.
[115]Bellah, 'Civil Religion in America', 18.
[116]Bellah, 'American Civil Religion in the 1970s', 266.
[117]Marty, 'Two Kinds of Two Kinds of Civil Religion', 155–6.
[118]Ibid., 156.
[119]Bellah, 'American Civil Religion in the 1970s', 259. Bellah responds to the theological critique of his category by Herbert Richardson, 'Civil Religion in Theological Perspective', in *American Civil Religion*, ed. Russell E. Richey and Donald G. Jones (New York: Harper, 1974), 161–84.
[120]Mapping out a 'mediated realism' that comes close to Tillich's, Jörg Lauster, 'How to do Transcendence with Words? The Problem of Articulation in Religious Experience', in *Religious Experience Revisited: Expressing the Inexpressible?*, ed. Thomas Hardtke, Ulrich Schmiedel and Tobias Tan (Leiden: Brill, 2016), 15–29, points out that articulations of transcendence are, by necessity and by nature of the transcendent, plural.
[121]Bellah, 'American Civil Religion in the 1970s', 259.
[122]Brown, 'Subjects of Tolerance', 316.

with the legacy of liberalism in theology. Liberalism has to be 'transformed', she argues, by the 'encounter with what liberalism has conventionally taken to be its constitutive', its 'outside' or its 'other'.¹²³ Turned theologically, in order to make sure that God remains other – that God is neither interpreted nor instrumentalized for political purposes – Christian public theology needs non-Christian public theology. Both systematically and structurally, openness to otherness, the criterion for public theology that comes out of the legacy of theological liberalism, then, calls for coalitions between Christians and non-Christians. According to Brown, 'this would be a liberalism potentially more modest, more restrained in its imperial and colonial impulses, but also one more capable of the multicultural justice to which it aspires' because it would criticize rather than confirm constructs of the clash of civilizations.¹²⁴ What would it look like in practice?

Public theologies such as Trump's can be tackled indirectly rather than directly. It seems to me that there is not much point in calling Trump out for not being open to the other. However, there is a point in criticizing and checking theologies – both the ones that come from the inside and the ones that come from the outside of the academy, from churches – for how inviting they are to the other. What if Christian public theologians would work with this criterion by making room for Muslims in the public square? What if they got down from their soapbox to invite the other? The pluralization of public theology could be spelt out for a variety of religious or non-religious positions. A public church, characterized by the legacy of theological liberalism, could be a crucial catalyst for such coalitions in civil society.¹²⁵ Thomas Schlag contends that the openness to otherness that is so crucial to the legacy of theological liberalism is central for the practices of public church, thus countering ecclesiologies that call for clear-cut concepts of the identity of the church that confirm a contrast between what they consider Christian and what they consider non-Christian.¹²⁶ The public church begins with open and open-ended practice. Given the prevalence of the clash of civilizations in the current context, a coalition with Islam might be the most pertinent and the most provocative for Christian public theologians inside and outside churches. If Christian public theologians are committed to open their theologies up to a God who remains 'other', what speaks against such coalitions? What speaks for them is the legacy of theological liberalism that haunts the field of public theology. Public theology can welcome the ghost that has invited the other.

---

¹²³Ibid.
¹²⁴Ibid., 317.
¹²⁵See Thomas Schlag, *Öffentliche Kirche: Grunddimensionen einer praktisch-theologischen Kirchentheorie* (Zurich: TVZ, 2012), 30–6, where Schlag draws on Marty to describe and define the contribution of a public church to a pluralized and pluralizing civil society.
¹²⁶Ibid., 58–60.

CHAPTER 8

Public theology in the Catholic tradition

KATIE DUNNE

8.1 INTRODUCTORY REMARKS

This chapter introduces the reader to the landscape of public theology in the Catholic tradition. It pays particular attention to two areas central to public theology: Catholic Social Teaching (hereafter CST) and the common good. It will be useful, right at the beginning, to outline the contested nature of public theology. In many ways, public theology is best understood, not as a unified theological discourse but as an 'umbrella' term. Indeed, the lack of any agreed-upon definition is a prevailing characteristic of the discipline. Dirk J. Smit helpfully explains that confusion often abounds: there are those who seem to engage in public theology but never explicitly invoke the term; those who deliberately choose not to invoke it, and those who do, yet who fail to agree to a consensus on what is actually at stake in a public theological discourse.[1] Paradoxically, identifying what is normative in the discourse is not the most pressing challenge facing public theology. The more urgent concern is ensuring that the content of public theology is transformative and practical in the real world. Consequently, this chapter argues that Catholic public theology can draw helpful resources from CST and the principle of the common good.

---

[1] Dirk J. Smit, 'Does It Matter? On Whether There Is Method in the Madness', in *A Companion to Public Theology*, ed. Sebastian Kim and Katie Day (Leiden: Brill, 2017), 67–92 (67).

CST and particularly the principles of the church's social doctrine – human dignity, subsidiarity, solidarity, the common good and justice – are robust resources for public theology in the twenty-first century. In this globalized world, where 1.3 billion people are living in multidimensional poverty, stark inequalities characterize life.[2] In such an unequal world, it is difficult to overstate the urgent task of public theology to adequately confront deprivation. Irrespective of this inherent difficulty, the CST tradition is committed to the struggle for justice and promotes the notion of 'integral development' and takes the human person – their dignity, flourishing and well-being – as the basic premise of its teachings. Perhaps the most emphasized principle in this tradition is the common good, which documents the importance of conditions that enable people, as groups or individuals, to flourish. However, the language of the common good, while promoting just structures and fundamental freedoms, fails to comprehensively identify the requirements of a truly human life. Indeed, two lacunae have been identified in the discourse on the common good, particularly in terms of specificity and practicality.[3] This is remarkable given the centrality of the common good to the discipline of public theology. Therefore, this chapter aims to offer a constructive account of public theology in Catholic perspective by exploring the potential of incorporating the theoretical and practical framework of the capabilities approach (hereafter CA) with CST. This engagement offers a vision relevant for public theology, particularly in terms of the common good, which leads us to investigate the value of this dialogical approach to public theology.

It has been well established that, as a theoretical and practical framework, CA can enhance a theological analysis of human development.[4] With its predominant focus on agency and well-being, CA is also a significant resource for CST, and consequently public theology. In contrast to CST, writings based on CA have dealt with questions of achieving full justice by creating the appropriate space to analyse inequality and deprivation by focusing on human capabilities. As such, CA not only offers more substance to CST, it also provides a site for serious moral and political debate in terms of social justice and human development. Consequently, this chapter aims to explore the value of CA for

---

[2]Oxford Poverty and Human Development Initiative, 'Global MPI 2019', https://ophi.org.uk/wp-content/uploads/G-MPI_Report_2019_PDF.pdf
[3]Albino Barrera, *Modern Catholic Social Documents and Political Economy* (Washington: Georgetown University Press, 2001), 288.
[4]See, for example, Noah K. Tenai, 'Is Poverty a Matter of Perspective? Significance of Amartya Sen for the Church's Response to Poverty: A Public Practical Theological Reflection', *Theological Studies* 72, no. 2 (2016): 1–10; Joshua Schulz, 'The Capabilities Approach and Catholic Social Teaching: An Engagement', *Journal of Global Ethics* 12, no. 1 (2016): 29–47; Séverine Deneulin and Augusto Zampini Davies, 'Theology and Development as Capability Expansion', *Theological Studies* 72, no. 4 (2016): 1–9.

CST, particularly in terms of the demands of social justice, and to illuminate 'the practical theological questions of what is and what ought to be'.[5] In order to fulfil this aim, we proceed by exploring the scope and context of public theology in the Catholic tradition. The chapter then places a particular emphasis on CST and the common good, both integral components of any public social ethics in theological perspective. After this consideration, we explore the value of Martha Nussbaum's politically liberal (partial) theory of justice based on CA. The chapter concludes by proposing a constructive public theology, in dialogue with CA, that illuminates the social realities facing Catholic public theology in the twenty-first century.

8.2 THE SCOPE OF PUBLIC THEOLOGY

This chapter argues that CST enables the Catholic Church to do some good public theology. This, of course, is not to say that Catholic public theology is limited to CST. For example, John Courtney Murray and David Tracy are key protagonists in Catholic public theology. Courtney Murray's role in the production of the 'Declaration on Religious Freedom' (*Dignitatis Humanae*), at the Second Vatican Council, and his preoccupation with church–state relations remain hugely significant for the public life of Catholicism in a pluralist world.[6] Of similar significance for the Catholic strand of public theology is Tracy's *The Analogical Imagination: Christian Theology and the Culture of Pluralism*.[7] Here he argues that 'analogical imagination' is required to do systematic theology in the context of religious and cultural pluralism. His mapping of the three publics of Christian theology, (1) church, (2) society and (3) academy, serves to highlight the task of theology as public discourse.[8] Indeed, the theologian's accountability is to the church, academy and society in Tracy's theological method. Hence he argues that 'each theologian must attempt to articulate and defend an explicit method of inquiry, and use that method to interpret the

---

[5]Karl Rahner, 'Practical Theology Within the Totality of Theological Disciplines', in *Theological Investigations IX*, trans. Graham Harrison (London: Darton, Longman and Todd, 1972), 101–14 (102); Michael G. Lawler and Todd Salzman, 'Human Experience and Catholic Moral Theology', *Irish Theological Quarterly* 76 (2001): 35–56 (35).
[6]Thomas Hughson, 'Murray: Faithful to tradition in Context', in *Finding God in All Things: Celebrating Bernard Lonergan, John Courtney Murray, and Karl Rahner*, ed. Mark Bosco (New York: Fordham University Press, 2017), 109–21, (109). See John Courtney Murray, *We Hold These Truths: Catholic Reflections on the American Proposition* (Maryland: Rowman & Littlefield, 1960).
[7]David Tracy, *The Analogical Imagination: Christian Theology and the Culture of Pluralism* (New York: Crossroad, 1981).
[8]David Tracy, 'Three Kinds of Publicness in Public Theology', *International Journal of Public Theology* 8 (2014): 33–4.

symbols and texts of our common life and of Christianity'.[9] The significance of Tracy's concern for the public character of theology cannot be overstated. Thus, this chapter's focus on CST is not to depreciate the many other facets of the Catholic strands within the discourse. It is, rather, to highlight that CST is a promising contribution to public theology.

The struggle for justice is a fundamental commitment of Catholic theology. A key task of contemporary public theology is to articulate this commitment in the secular sphere. In short: confronting injustice is a constitutive dimension of public theology. Moreover, the essential Gospel demand, to love God and neighbour, compels the church to engage with secular society. It is the task of public theology, then, to articulate the hope of the transcendental and eschatological message of Christ. This concept of public theology, or theology in the secular, public sphere, is not a new one: The negotiation between the church and the world can be traced back to the very beginnings of the Christian tradition. These foundations have ensured that contemporary Catholic theology has rich resources for public theology such as the Catholic natural law tradition, its theory of reason and the principles of the church's social doctrine. More recently, in the wake of the global financial crisis of 2008, elements of the church's social doctrine have enjoyed renewed interest. CST constitutes the authoritative voice of the Catholic Church on interests of social concern. Values such as human dignity, the well-being of the common good, solidarity and care for creation permeate the Catholic perspective. In the context of the global financial crisis, CST extended beyond the prevailing paradigms that govern economic and political analysis. Indeed, the promotion of the well-being of all – the common good – enabled the Catholic Church to engage in the public forum and do some good public theology. Nicholas Sagovsky takes the point further: 'Catholic Social Teaching is the most powerful instrument of public theology today. Its key themes are human dignity, the common good, subsidiarity, and dialogue, together with a specific concern for the poor – themes about which all Christians, together with many others committed to social justice, can unite.'[10]

Of course, globalization is the inescapable context of public theology in the twenty-first century. The process has had a significant impact on the world economic system. As David Held and Anthony McGrew describe it,

> Globalization, simply put, denotes the expanding scale, growing magnitude, speeding up and deepening impact of transcontinental flows and patterns

---

[9]David Tracy, *Blessed Rage for Order: The New Pluralism in Theology* (New York: Crossroad, 1975), 3.
[10]Nicholas Sagovsky, 'Public Theology, the Public Sphere and the Struggle for Social Justice', in *A Companion to Public Theology*, 231–70 (267–8).

of social interaction. It refers to a shift or transformation in the scale of human organization that links distant communities and expands the reach of power relations across the world's regions and continents. But it should not be read as prefiguring the emergence of a harmonious world society or as a universal process of global integration in which there is a growing convergence of cultures and civilizations. For not only does the awareness of growing interconnectedness create new animosities and conflicts, it can fuel reactionary politics and deep-seated xenophobia. Since a substantial proportion of the world's population is largely excluded from the benefits of globalization, it is a deeply divisive and, consequently, vigorously contested process experienced uniformly across the planet.[11]

Contemporary global society is intrinsically connected fiscally and, yet, is disparate and pluralistic in terms of culture. Many debates surround economic development in this context, with the transformation of the economy seen as a significant result of globalization. From a theological perspective, the human person is at the heart of this globalizing process. Moreover, the depiction of the economy in theological perspective holds that the human person is the source, centre and purpose of all economic life. Indeed, the defence of the dignity of the human person, the rejection of exploitative economic systems and an appeal to the common good are three principles that ground the church's social tradition on the economy. One of the most emphasized principles in this area is the common good, which documents the importance of conditions that enable people, as groups or individuals, to flourish. As Linell E. Cady puts it,

> Public theology caught on among liberal religious thinkers as a compelling way to capture multiple features needed in contemporary theology; the capacity to pull together several strands under one rubric has accounted for much of its classificatory power. Public theology has been most strongly associated with issues and values of our shared life – the common good – not confined to the personal or private domain of the individual and their most proximate community.[12]

The church's commitment to the common good and shared values is at the heart of their response to the globalizing process. As a result, Catholic public theology has made substantial contributions to social ethics: authentic human

---

[11] David Held and Anthony McGrew, *Globalization/Anti-Globalization* (Cambridge: Polity Press, 2007), 1.
[12] Linell E. Cady, 'Public Theology and the Post-secular Turn', *International Journal of Public Theology* 8 (2014): 292–312 (294).

development, economic justice, equality of opportunity, human rights, religious freedom, sexual ethics, bioethics, war and peace, and ecological concern are highly significant areas of engagement for public theology.[13] Catholic moral theologians, in particular, have applied CST in social and political spheres to 'read the signs of the times', to borrow the language of *Gaudium et Spes*.[14]

8.3 CATHOLIC SOCIAL TEACHING: THE COMMON GOOD AND INTEGRAL DEVELOPMENT

CST and the principles of the church's social doctrine are significant resources for public theology in the twenty-first century. As a responsive tradition, social encyclicals, which form part of CST, are usually prefaced with the economic conditions at that particular time of promulgation. They document the trajectory of human progress, including worsening inequalities, the disparity between the rich and the poor, technological advances, and power dynamics.

While not being the first social encyclical, Leo XIII's *Rerum Novarum* (1891) is generally considered to signal a new era in the church's approach to modern social issues.[15] At this time, the nature of work was changing due to the transition from feudalism to capitalism in the context of the Industrial Revolution:[16]

> That the spirit of the revolutionary change, which has long been disturbing the nations of the world, should have passed beyond the sphere of politics and made its influence felt in the cognate sphere of practical economics is not surprising. The elements of the conflict now raging are unmistakable,

---

[13]Representative examples include Lisa Sowle Cahill, *Blessed Are the Peacemakers: Pacifism, Just War, and Peacebuilding* (Minneapolis: Fortress Press, 2019); David Hollenbach, *The Common Good and Christian Ethics* (Cambridge: Cambridge University Press, 2002); David Hollenbach, *The Global Face of Public Faith: Politics, Human Rights and Christian Ethics* (Washington: Georgetown University Press, 2003); Charles E. Curran, *The Development of Moral Theology: Five Strands* (Washington: Georgetown University Press, 2013); John Courtney Murray, *Religious Liberty: Catholic Struggles with Pluralism* (Louisville: John Knox Press, 1993); Michael Himes and Kenneth Himes, *The Fullness of Faith: The Public Significance of Theology* (New York: MacMillan, 1993).
[14]The Second Vatican Council, *Gaudium et Spes*, 4.
[15]John Sniegocki, *Catholic Social Teaching and Economic Globalization: The Quest for Alternatives* (Milwaukee: Marquette University Press, 2009), 105–6. The pre-Leonine period (1740–1877) saw 'nine popes produce seventy-seven letters antedating Leo XIII. There are thirty-four *litterae encyclicae* (letters to all bishops) and thirty-six *epistolae encyclicae* (letters to bishops of specific countries). Exceptions include five letters written to "all the faithful," one letter to missionaries, and one to heads of religious congregations'. For a detailed discussion of this period of CST, see Michael J. Schuck, *That They Be One: The Social Teaching of the Papal Encyclicals 1740–1989* (Washington: Georgetown University Press, 1991), 1–10.
[16]Kenneth R. Himes et al., *Modern Catholic Social Teaching: Commentaries and Interpretations* (Washington: Georgetown University Press, 2004), 128.

in the vast expansion of industrial pursuits and the marvellous discoveries of science; in the changed relations between masters and workmen; in the enormous fortunes of some individuals and the utter poverty of the masses; the increased self-reliance and closer mutual combination of the working classes. . . . Finally, in the prevailing moral degeneracy. . . . We thought it expedient now to speak on the condition of the working classes. . . . It is no easy matter to define the relative rights and mutual duties of the rich and of the poor, of capital and of labour. And the danger lies in this, that crafty agitators are intent on making use of these differences of opinion to pervert men's judgments and to stir up the people to revolt.[17]

Rerum Novarum was thus promulgated at a time of both political and economic turmoil, particularly in terms of the status of the industrial worker. To this end, the encyclical endorses and affirms the right and necessity of private property, the right of organized labour and argues for a 'living wage for workers'.[18] In seeking to challenge the economic structure, *Rerum Novarum* focuses on 'the relation between capital and labour, employee and employer [and], the wealthy and the poor'.[19] This intervention on behalf of the poor at this time signifies a profound shift in CST whereby the major social issues of the day are no longer deemed to be peripheral to church teaching. Commenting on the legacy of *Rerum Novarum*, Alec Vidler remarks that the encyclical 'had a truly epoch-making effect in driving home the idea that Catholics must have a social conscience'.[20]

Theological social commentary also appears subsequently in *Quadragesimo Anno* (1931). Similarly to *Rerum Novarum*, *Quadragesimo Anno* is addressed to the faithful. Over thirty years later, however, John XXIII initiates one of the most significant shifts in CST: *Pacem in Terris* (1963) is addressed not only to the faithful but to 'all men of good will'. This encyclical was not only well received but it was discussed in broader, secular society.[21] From this moment on, authoritative documents of CST are addressed to the public – to those both inside and outside the church. *Gaudium et Spes* makes the point explicitly:

> This Second Vatican Council, having probed more profoundly into the mystery of the Church now addresses itself without hesitation, not only to the sons of the Church and to all who invoke the name of Christ, but to

---

[17] Leo XIII, *Rerum Novarum*, 1 and 2.
[18] Himes et al., *Modern Catholic Social Teaching*, 127.
[19] Ibid.
[20] Alec R. Vidler, *A Century of Social Catholicism* (London: SPCK, 1964), 127.
[21] Charles E. Curran, *Catholic Social Teaching and Pope Benedict XVI* (Washington: Georgetown University Press, 2014), 15.

the whole of humanity. For the Council yearns to explain to everyone how it conceives of the presence and activity of the Church in the world today. Therefore, the council focuses its attention on the world of men, the whole human family along with the sum of those realities in the midst of which it lives.[22]

It continues by outlining the duty of the church in modern times:

The Church has always had the duty of scrutinizing the signs of the times and of interpreting them in light of the Gospel. Thus, in language intelligible to each generation, she can respond to the perennial questions which men ask about the present life and the life to come, and about the relationship of the one to the other, We must therefore recognize and understand the world in which we live, its explanations, its longings, and its often dramatic characteristics.[23]

As such, CST no longer speaks from the standpoint of moral privilege but engages with civil society in the pursuit of the common good. The principles of the church's social doctrine add unique value to this process by advocating that people ought to exercise their agency collectively and responsibly for the common good. It can reasonably be suggested, therefore, that the value of CST to public theology is found in the key concepts – human dignity, solidarity, the common good, subsidiarity – that it proposes. Moreover, CST is versatile and lends itself easily to interdisciplinarity. It is this dynamic nature of CST that allows it to address many diverse issues that are highly significant areas of engagement for public theology, including the economy, religious freedom, nuclear warfare, ecology, human rights and human development. One of the most valuable contributions of CST in this regard is the common good. Indeed, the common good is a central concern in most discussions of public theology.

8.4 THE COMMON GOOD

Several issues are unavoidable in mapping the complexity of the concept of the common good. The realities of pluralism, claims to universalism and accusations of paternalism permeate the search for the common good. How, for example, can we talk of common goods in the context of xenophobia and domestic conflict? A related question might also be raised regarding claims to universalism. Can we take refuge in Michael Sandel's claim that 'we can know

---

[22]The Second Vatican Council, *Gaudium et Spes*, 2.
[23]Ibid., 4.

a good in common that we cannot know alone' in a contemporary globalized society that is as diverse as it is vast?[24] Moreover, the common good can be interpreted as an ongoing, active dialogue on matters of justice.[25] Operating out of this context, and proposing a determinate account of the realities of human life, is ultimately an endeavour fraught with complexities. This may be why the discourse of the common good has remained rather vague in the CST tradition. As Patrick Riordan asks, 'What is this term which on the one hand can seem to convey so easily what its users wish to communicate, and on the other hand is so complex and confusing that it defies definition?'[26]

Irrespective of its characterization of the common good, CST has consistently held that the flourishing of each person is of fundamental importance. Underpinning the conditions for human flourishing is a concern, in both economic and social realms, for the dignity of the person, the vocation of the human person and the welfare of society as a whole.[27] The church's social doctrine builds on these presuppositions and explains that morality and the economy are intrinsically connected.[28] As such, the *Compendium of the Social Doctrine of the Church* explains that if economic activity is to have a moral character, it must be inclusive: 'Everyone has the right to participate in economic life and the duty to contribute, each according to his own capacity, to the progress of his own country and to that of the entire human family.'[29] Identifying the injustice of economic marginalization, John Paul II contends,

> The fact is that many people, perhaps the majority today, do not have the means which would enable them to take their place in an effective and humanly dignified way within a productive system in which work is truly central. . . . Thus, if not actually exploited, they are to a great extent marginalized; economic development takes place over their heads.[30]

The notion of integral development works to combat such marginalization by advocating that development requires that all aspects of human life, including the social, cultural, political, economic, moral and religious, deserve serious consideration. A core tenet, then, of CST is the common good, with its provision

---

[24]Michael Sandel, *Justice: What's the Right Thing to Do?* (New York: Farrar, Strauss and Giroux, 2009), 5.
[25]Hollenbach, *The Common Good and Christian Ethics*, 158.
[26]Patrick Riordan, *A Grammar of the Common Good: Speaking of Globalization* (New York: Continuum, 2008), 15–29.
[27]The Second Vatican Council, *Gaudium et Spes*, 63.
[28]See, Pontifical Council for Justice and Peace, *Compendium of the Social Doctrine of the Church* (Rome: Libreria Editrice Vaticana, 2004), 330–5.
[29]Ibid., 333.
[30]John Paul II, *Centesimus Annus*, 33.

that all people have the right to reach their fulfilment. It is most often defined as 'the sum total of social conditions which allow people, either as groups or as individuals, to reach their fulfilment more fully and more easily'.³¹ As early as 1961, John XXIII's *Mater et Magistra* includes the notion of just economic distribution, in an international context, within the notion of the common good.³² Paul VI's *Populorum Progressio* appeals for cooperation in international development, highlighting that the common good ought to be understood in universal terms.³³ These themes are reiterated in the Synod of Bishops' *Justitia in Mundo*: 'Economic injustice and lack of social participation keep a man [sic] from attaining his basic human and civil rights.'³⁴ More recently, Benedict XVI defines the common good as 'a good that is linked to living in society. . . . It is a good that is sought not for its own sake, but for the people who belong to the social community and who can only really and effectively pursue their good within it'.³⁵ More comprehensively, the Bishops' Conference of England and Wales offers a helpful explanation of the common good. Although long, it is relevant to frame the task at hand:

> The common good refers to what belongs to everyone by virtue of their common humanity. . . . Promoting the common good cannot be pursued by treating each individual separately and looking for the highest 'total benefit,' in some kind of utilitarian addition. Because we are interdependent, the common good is more like a multiplication sum, where if any one number is zero then the total is always zero. If anyone is left out or deprived of what is essential, then the common good has been betrayed. The common good is about how to live well together. It is the whole network of social conditions which enable human individuals and groups to flourish and live a full, genuinely human life. At the heart of the common good, solidarity acknowledges that all are responsible for all, not only as individuals but collectively at every level. The principle of the common good expands our understanding of who we are and opens up new sources of motivation. The fulfilment which the common good seeks to serve is the flourishing of humanity expressed in the phrase 'integral human development.' Such development requires that people are rescued from every form of poverty, from hunger to illiteracy; it requires the opportunities for education, creating a vision of true partnership and solidarity between peoples; it calls for active participation in economic and political processes and it recognises

---

³¹The Second Vatican Council, *Gaudium et Spes*, 26.
³²John XXIII, *Mater et Magistra*, 77–81.
³³Paul VI, *Populorum Progressio*, 21–6.
³⁴The Synod of Bishops, *Justitia in Mundo*, 9.
³⁵Benedict XVI, *Caritas in Veritate*, 7.

that every human person is a spiritual being with instincts for love and truth and aspirations for happiness.[36]

The basic approach of *Gaudium et Spes* echoes through these descriptions of the conditions for human flourishing. And, this promotion of the common good, which finds particular expression in CST, enables the church to bring a model for moral discourse to the public square. Moreover, using the common good as a framework for the interpretation of social justice presupposes two things. First, the dignity and the sociality of all people; second, that each person has rights and corresponding duties. Nevertheless, the language of the common good often remains rather vague.[37] Albino Barrera notes that there are two significant 'gaps' in the discourse on the common good:

> First, the concept itself has to be made more accessible for practical use by describing its content with greater specificity. What, for example, are the minimum conditions that must be satisfied in protecting and promoting the common good? What are its defining characteristics? Discourse on this subject matter has generally been so abstract as to make its application to particular issues frequently ad hoc. . . . There is a need for a more precise enumeration, to the extent possible, of the requirements imposed by legal, distributive, and commutative justice operating within the confines of the common good. A second gap is the pressing need to systematize the various warrants used extensively in the social documents . . . very little has been done to show how its principles and norms flow from the common good . . . unless the content of the common good is specified in a systematic and coherent way, it would be difficult to use the concept in a practical way or even sustain arguments made on its behalf.[38]

In some ways, the standpoint of the common good is sufficiently detailed insofar as it provides a sense of the need for conditions to flourish. Its inherent fluidity, however, is present in the CST tradition. As Barrera points out, CST does not articulate the components which enable individuals and groups to flourish. It is clear that CST is a rich tradition that works to ensure the commitment of Catholic public theology to social justice. However, the language of the common good, while promoting just structures and fundamental freedoms, fails to comprehensively identify the requirements of a truly human life. The

---

[36] Bishops' Conference of England and Wales, *Choosing the Common Good* (Stoke on Trent: Alive Publishing, 2010), 8–9. Emphasis added.
[37] See, in particular, Riordan, *A Grammar of the Common Good*, 15–29.
[38] Barrera, *Modern Catholic Social Documents*, 288.

capabilities perspective, however, gives a fuller account of the conditions for human flourishing. In this regard, CA offers CST the opportunity to create and sustain meaningful dialogue in the public square. As an evaluative framework that has practical value, CA can animate CST's mandate to act justly. In her attempt to build a partial theory of justice on the basis of CA, Nussbaum directly asks which capabilities are the most valuable for a life that is worthy of human dignity. As a set of interrelated opportunities, she proposes her ten central capabilities as ones that any just society ought to protect, promote and nurture so that human development can be authentic for all, especially women.[39] And, Nussbaum reacts to impoverishment and deprivation in comprehensive ways: her list of capabilities for a dignified life works to discern the necessary conditions for a just society and provides compelling reasons to engage the moral claims of human flourishing. On this point, in particular, it seems that CA is a natural interdisciplinary partner for public theology in Catholic perspective.

8.5 CAPABILITIES DISCOURSE: THE CENTRAL CAPABILITIES

A significant advantage of CA is its focus on what people are able to do and to be. By focusing on this, the approach foregrounds and addresses inequalities that persons suffer. In short, CA provides distinctive insight for ethical analyses because it recognizes that all persons should have an equality of basic opportunity. This fundamental aspect of the approach works to confront and respond to persistent inequality. Moreover, there is a strong ethical component in CA that mandates a confrontation of discrimination in all aspects of life. As Nussbaum explains of her approach,

> The capabilities approach is a powerful tool in crafting an adequate account of social justice. But the bare idea of capabilities as a space within which comparisons are made and inequalities assessed is insufficient. To get a vision of social justice that will have the requisite critical force and definiteness to direct social policy, we need to have an account, for political purposes of what the central human capabilities are, even if we know that this account will always be contested and remade.[40]

---

[39]Martha Nussbaum, *Creating Capabilities: The Human Development Approach* (Cambridge: Belknap, 2011), 18–19.
[40]Martha Nussbaum, 'Capabilities as Fundamental Entitlements: Sen and Social Justice', *Feminist Economics* 9 (2001): 33–59, (39).

In a world of inequalities, the capabilities perspective outlines a set of basic human capabilities, or entitlements, as a minimum of what justice requires for all.[41] Operating out of this context, it can be argued that the capabilities discourse is based on a vision of the common good. Perhaps it can also be suggested that capabilities can facilitate an approach to the common good: in a capability approach to the economy, what matters for economic and public policies is what a person can do and be. His or her achievement as a person, and the effective freedom that they command to achieve their goals, is of the utmost importance. Of note, Nussbaum's methodology is explicitly committed to involving women, especially those who are marginalized, in the process of defining capabilities essential to their own lives. She constructs her list of capabilities as a 'normative conception of social justice, with critical potential for gender issues'.[42] This is only the case, she points out, if a set of definite capabilities is specified.[43]

8.5.1 Ten central capabilities

According to Nussbaum, a life with or without dignity is easily identifiable. She therefore generates her list of central capabilities by asking 'which things are so important that we will not count a life as a human life without them?'[44] Her central capabilities signify both the freedoms and the opportunities to lead the life that one has reason to value. In her view, then, each capability is required in order for one to be capable of a truly human life. In other words, a life without any one of these capabilities on her list would not be recognizably dignified: Her ten capabilities are (1) life, (2) bodily health, (3) bodily integrity, (4) senses, imagination and thought, (5) emotions (6) practical reason, (7) affiliation, (8) other species, (9) play and (10) control over one's environment.[45] A fully human life requires certain things: adequate nutrition, education, liberty of speech and religious self-expression, freedom from discrimination, protection of bodily integrity and so forth. Nussbaum's list of capabilities provides a very clear picture of the basic conditions needed for human flourishing. This list functions as a focus for comparative quality of life assessment, and for the formulation of political principles.[46] All ten capabilities constitute dimensions of life that are recognized in all cultures across the world. Of course, how

---

[41]Martha Nussbaum, 'Beyond the Social Contract: Capabilities and Global Justice', *Oxford Development Studies* 32 (2004): 3–18.
[42]Ibid., 35.
[43]Ibid.
[44]Nussbaum, *Women and Human Development: The Capabilities Approach* (Cambridge: Cambridge University Press, 2000), 74.
[45]For a more detailed exposition of each capability, see Nussbaum, *Creating Capabilities*, 33–4.
[46]Nussbaum, 'Capabilities as Fundamental Entitlements', 40.

people experience these realities of embodiment, in the concrete circumstances of life, will inevitably differ from culture to culture or even within one particular society.[47] It is, however, reasonable to suggest that people share commonality in certain human experiences.

Specifically, in the pursuit of the common good, public theology confronts complex issues that often disproportionately affect the poor and the marginalized. From this perspective, the capabilities view can provide a useful avenue to imagine how a pluralistic society can uphold common values. A sense of inherent worth and dignity grounds Nussbaum's CA. Key to the central capabilities, then, is the notion of combined capabilities. In other words, people ought to actually be able to function in society – its structures and institutional environment must be conducive to genuine choice. Her CA, as an evaluative framework and a partial theory of justice, provides an important basis for thinking about the goals of authentic development. Consequently, Nussbaum's commitment to substance is hugely beneficial for Catholic public theology, and CST, in particular. It provides fresh insight into, and respect for, the dignity of the person and adds precision to the basic elements needed to ascertain the common good: Nussbaum's partial account of social justice causes her to name the capabilities that every person needs in order to live a full and dignified life. Conceptually, therefore, CA is well placed to diagnose, analyse and engage with the reality of oppression and deprivation – especially important themes of public theology.

8.5.2 Public theology and capabilities

What value does CA bring to public theology? Public theology, as already established, brings theological perspectives to its engagement to the common good, and CST is a cornerstone of public theology today. Without doubt, the promulgations in the CST body of thought present a rich understanding of the human person. As one would expect from theological pronouncements, the encyclicals pay particular attention to the transcendental and the eschatological dimensions of life. Viewing the common good, and human development, through this lens tends to shift development from the practical to the aspirational.[48] Indeed, to emphatically engage in the rhetoric of the eschatological in public theology would diminish the concrete circumstances of life that have a very real impact on well-being and the pursuit of the common good. And, the position of public theology must be a reasoned one:

---

[47]Nussbaum, *Women and Human Development*, 7.
[48]Kathryn Tanner, *The Politics of God: Christian Theologies and Social Justice* (Minneapolis: Fortress Press, 1992), 2.

CST, as a tradition of reflection and praxis, cannot be articulated in a way which would deny the diversity of modes of social life in different contexts, unless one is prepared to say that one single Catholic community culture for the whole world is still possible. In other words, if we want to understand how CST can become concrete and meaningful in the world of today, we cannot ignore the sociological background questions.[49]

Herein lies the value of CA for public theology. CA offers an avenue to address the relationship between CST and broader sociological issues. CST provides guiding principles that encourage people to participate fully in society and to confront injustice. These broad categories are hugely beneficial in the processes of development on both an individual and collective scale. Crucially, however, the principles of CST presume that the opportunity to exercise agency exists. Indeed, these principles rely on the existence of freedom and opportunity to participate, and yet there is no framework of opportunity, such as capabilities, provided to animate or secure the principles of CST. Consequently, incorporating capabilities into CST captures more concretely the multiple dimensions of well-being, human development and the common good. And, in this space, CA provides an important insight for theological engagement: by explicitly identifying the components that help promote the dignity of the person, CA provides a more determinate account of 'the good life' and the conditions of a life worthy of human dignity.

Participation of *all* members of society enables members of the community to share and enhance global common goods. CA, therefore, may act as a catalyst, empowering people to act together in shaping the common good by 'using information regarding who can in fact *do* what, and not just the way people *desire* or *react to* their ability or disability to do these things'.[50] This approach to human development coheres well with CST, and its relevance for public theology cannot be overstated. Indeed, the visible discontent, in recent years, with economic, social and political structures, at local, national and international level, has intensified in many parts of the world.[51] Despite the geographical spread of this problem, Séverine Deneulin argues that the common thread underlying these grievances is 'dissatisfaction with economic, political and social arrangements which are perceived to benefit a privileged

---

[49]Johan Verstraeten, 'Rethinking Catholic Social Thought as a Tradition', in *Catholic Social Thought: Twilight or Renaissance?*, ed. J. S. Boswell, F. P. McHugh and J. Verstraeten (Leuven: Leuven University Press, 2000), 59–77 (66).
[50]Amartya Sen, *Resources, Values and Development* (Cambridge: Harvard University Press, 1984), 309.
[51]Séverine Deneulin, *Wellbeing, Justice and Development Ethics* (New York: Routledge, 2014), 1.

minority disregarding the majority of the population'.[52] Shaping a common life amid such structural and personal injustices demands, in Nussbaum's words, 'thinking of what all human beings require to live a richly human life – a set of basic entitlements for all people – and . . . a conception of the purpose of social co-operation that focuses on fellowship as well as self-interest'.[53] CST also advocates this stance, albeit in a more general way, as has been illustrated by the representative definitions of the common good discussed earlier. CA can, however, offer more direction and precision to the concept of the common good by naming the requirements for a dignified life.

Unequal social and political circumstances ensure that there are millions of people living below threshold levels of capabilities. Nussbaum's list of central capabilities works to advance human development in this unequal context by focusing on the value dynamics needed to live a meaningful life. The values that are embodied in her capabilities are grounded in the notion of human dignity – a key concern of the common good. Nussbaum's theory provides an archetype for human flourishing and authentic human living. Sufficient attention is not paid to the conditions of human flourishing in the common good discourse as espoused by the CST tradition. And, given that the common good is central to the project of public theology, Nussbaum's methodology has much to offer. Her capabilities theory of development points towards a notion of the person that reaches well beyond the material. Indeed, her list of capabilities provides a noteworthy, partial, answer to the question of the good life. It gives specification to the notoriously vague concepts attached to the common good, such as well-being, flourishing and the quality of life.[54] This ultimately provides a holistic picture of personhood and the basic capacities that all should have the opportunity to avail of to flourish. It can reasonably be argued that Nussbaum's list of central human capabilities can offer precision to the common good and successfully promote social justice and human flourishing, given its broad specification and commitment to defining what a full human existence requires.

8.6 CONCLUDING REMARKS

Often the emphasis in public theology is, perhaps unsurprisingly, on praxis. As such, the conceptual contours of public theology are often delineated in terms of 'doing public theology'. Catholic public theology's commitment to the common good has enabled the Catholic Church to do some good public theology in recent years. Arguably, the Catholic tradition, capitalizing on its

---

[52]Ibid.
[53]Nussbaum, 'Beyond the Social Contract', 4.
[54]Ibid.

rich tradition of natural law and social teachings, is an early pioneer of public theology, long before the emergence of 'public theology' as a discipline. Indeed, CST is best characterized as a tradition of both thought and praxis, which has long been engaged in social action and public debate. Johan Verstraeten captures it well:

> The Catholic social tradition can be interpreted as a tradition which comprises a particular set of shared understandings about the human person, social goods and their distributive arrangements. This particular understanding is grounded in a living relation to the constitutive narratives provided by the Bible, integrated in a theoretical framework which makes it possible for the Catholic understanding to remain open to rational explanation and public debate. . . . Being a living narrative and reflective tradition, Catholic social thought can thus be described as an historically extended, socially embodied argument.[55]

This chapter has argued for incorporating the evaluative CA with CST to offer a robust resource for examining public issues in new ways and attending theologically to the 'signs of the times'. Indeed, in a dialogic framework, integrating CST and CA may have both a moral and practical appeal. In ways sympathetic to the CA, CST takes the human person – their flourishing and well-being – as the basic premise of its teachings. On this basis, it may be reasonable to suggest that, together, these discourses can impel the moral claims of human flourishing: CST offers a developmental framework that outlines the mutual responsibilities and rights of all living in an interdependent world. The duty of all to participate in the common good is one example of this. The requirements of the common good, however, remain rather vague. Nevertheless, CST's inherently social emphasis seems well placed to dialogue with the perspective of CA. Drawing on CA as a resource for public theology may give more specification to the complexities that surround human life, well-being and the search for the common good. Linking CST, then, with CA, may well enrich public theological discourse on social just.

---

[55] Verstraeten, 'Re-thinking Catholic Social Thought as Tradition', 64.

CHAPTER 9

A public Orthodox theology

ARISTOTLE PAPANIKOLAOU

The question of the role of the church in the public square presumes that there is such a thing as a 'public'. The question also presumes that the church's relation to such a public is homogeneous across space and time and does not consider how a particular 'public' shapes a particular church's understanding of itself. This chapter will interrogate the very category of public to examine if there is such a thing as *the* public. It will ask whether what is meant by 'public ecclesiology' depends on where the church is located. It will end by proposing an Orthodox 'public ecclesiology' across time and space through a case study of public issues surrounding homosexuality, such as laws against the so-called gay propaganda and gay marriage. I want to argue that Orthodox support of a public political space grounded in the sacredness of the person, as expressed in human rights language, especially rights to freedom and equality, is not necessarily being 'liberal' or 'western' but is Orthodox insofar as it is based on Orthodox ecclesiology and theological anthropology.

---

[1]This chapter was originally published under the title 'Whose Public? Which Ecclesiology?', in *Political Theologies in Orthodox Christianity*, ed. Kristina Stoeckl, Ingeborg Gabriel, and Aristotle Papanikolaou (New York: Bloomsbury, 2017), 229–42.

9.1 WHOSE PUBLIC?

In order to make sense of what we mean by 'public ecclesiology', we must first understand what we mean by 'public'. Public ecclesiology implies the presence or role of the church in public life. The very notion of public ecclesiology disputes the making of religion 'private' or the modern privatization of religion. It is well known, of course, that the general private/public distinction is an invention of modern Western thought, one that would have been unthinkable or would have assumed different forms in pre-modern societies, and even in many contemporary cultures. It is a distinction that contributed much to the creation of the modern notion of what Charles Taylor calls the 'buffered self' – an individualized self with clearly marked, though invisible, borders that serve to differentiate individuals from each other.[1] What is private are, thus, those aspects of the buffered self's life that are not exposed to other individuals and not part of the shared life one has with the aggregate of individuals. In terms of religion, what is private are one's beliefs about the whole, together with the norms by which one structures one's life and which are grounded in beliefs about the whole. What belongs to the public are those norms that structure the relations among individuals, and since not all individuals share the same religious beliefs, there are some who would argue that one's religious beliefs should not enter the public space as a way of structuring communal norms.

This public/private distinction in relation to religion has been recently one of the central themes under debate in Western political philosophy and has even come under attack in some forms of postmodern philosophy. On the individual level, it has been recognized that it is simply impossible to bracket or exclude one's religious beliefs as one deliberates how to participate or relate to others in the shared public space with other individuals. Contrary to the earlier thought of John Rawls, there is no 'original position' where one could deliberate about norms of a society that does not take into account the particulars of one's existence, including ethnicity, race and religious beliefs.[2] On the level of the individual, religious beliefs always affect public life, even when one decides, as an example, not to base her vote on her religious beliefs. It may, in fact, be her religious beliefs that influence her decision not to base her vote on religious beliefs. Thus, on the level of individual religious existence, the private/public distinction has rightly been interpreted as a myth used to exclude religion from the public sphere for very noble intentions of preserving civic peace and equality among individuals.[3]

---

[1] Charles Taylor, *A Secular Age* (Harvard University Press, 2007).
[2] John Rawls, *A Theory of Justice*, rev. edn. (Belknap Press, 1999).
[3] One could assert that the private/public distinction is operative in totalitarian regimes, where there may exist an intensification of a secret private life behind the public persona expected by

The fact, however, that the private/public distinction is a myth on the level of the individual does not mean that the notion of public itself is a myth, especially in terms of signifying broadly a shared communal life among individuals. Although there can be different interpretations of what is meant by the public political space, for the purposes of my argument, I mean society as a whole constituted as a shared communal life, which would include relations to state, culture and civic associations. In terms of the general definition of public as a shared communal life, it can also apply to the church, especially as it assembles in common worship, which is not to be differentiated from a *private* life, but from the space of interiority that is not accessible to other individuals in common worship even if it shapes how one relates to these same individuals in common worship. The church, then, is a kind of public in the sense of the realization of a shared communal life, most realized in the celebration of the Eucharist. When we speak of public ecclesiology, however, we do not mean the church as public, but the church *in* public, that is the church in the public political space of society as a whole. This implies that the church *as* public is in relation to the public political space that is society as a whole, which itself is constituted by multiple publics. This society as a whole that exists *as* multiple publics is different from the church in the sense that being constituted as and by multiple publics, it does not presuppose the shared common beliefs that would be evident in the church. When we speak of public ecclesiology, we mean the existence of the church as public in, through and within society as a whole, which is a common space in which the shared beliefs of the church are not presupposed, taken for granted or form a unified cultural, political or theological perspective.

There are those who have and would continue to argue that in order to maintain and preserve modern democratic principles of equality and freedom, there needs to exist a high wall of separation between the church as public and the public that is the political space in which the church exists in relation to other publics. While the situation in France indicates that it is possible to erect this high wall of separation through force in a way that is difficult on the level of the individual's interior life, José Casanova has shown that religion as an institutional and cultural presence in Brazil, Spain, Poland and the United States has not threatened or diminished democratic structures; religion has often contributed to the formation of democratic structures.[4] In fact, the

---

such authoritarian and oppressive regimes. The fact, however, that the public life is always in some measure a lie in such regimes also means that the private is not disconnected from the public, especially if the public is recognized as a relation of individuals often forced to wear masks that constantly evoke the question of truth or falsity. Totalitarian regimes may intensify one's interior life, but interiority is never private in relation to public life.

[4]José Casanova, *Public Religion in the Modern World* (University of Chicago Press, 1994).

momentum in Western political philosophy has shifted in such a way that most would not advocate for such a high wall of separation, including Charles Taylor and Jeffrey Stout.[5] Even John Rawls and Richard Rorty have modified their positions in relation to the role of the institutionalized and cultural presence of religion in the public political space.[6] Most would see the situation in France as a manifestation of 'secular*ism*' in its ideological form, while still affirming the need for secularity, the meaning of which is at the centre of the current debate, but has something to do with fostering a political space that is pluralistic.

The meaning of the 'secular' is a highly contested term, and even those who recognize its Western origins would still argue for its relevancy for understanding globally the repositioning of religion within the public political space. Charles Taylor, for example, rejects understanding the secular in terms of the church–state relation and sees it as a configuration of the public political space in terms of pluralism and differentiation. There are those who like to pronounce that we are living in a post-secular world, but that depends on what one means by secular. If one means the elimination of religion from the public political space, then, indeed, we are living in a post-secular society insofar as religion has not been eliminated as a result of modern processes of differentiation, and there are no longer predictions that it will be eliminated. If, however, one means a differentiated public and legal order based on religious freedom and democratic regimes that, according to Taylor, 'protect people in their practice of whatever religion or outlook they choose . . . treat people equally . . . give all people a hearing',[7] then we are *not* in a post-secular situation, as the secular is the political space marked by the democratic commitment that allows for pluralism. What Taylor is arguing is that democratic secularity is marked by the pluralization of all voices, including religious voices, regardless of the cultural situation or history. This is really the challenge for the Orthodox churches: Can they accept an understanding of a secular democratic liberal space defined *not* in terms of a high wall of separation between religion and the public political space, or between the church and state, but in terms of a differentiated public and legal order that maximizes pluralism?

What Casanova makes clear is that what we mean by public political space is not necessarily uniform and depends on the cultural and historical facts of

---

[5]Jeffrey Stout, *Democracy and Tradition* (Princeton University Press, 2004).
[6]John Rawls, 'The Idea of Public Reason Revisited', in *The Law of Peoples* (Harvard University Press, 2001). Richard Rorty, 'Religion in Public Square: A Reconsideration', *Journal of Religious Ethics* 31, no. 1 (2003): 141–9. See also Nicholas Wolterstorff's 'An Engagement with Rorty', *Journal of Religious Ethics* 31, no. 1 (2003): 129–39.
[7]Charles Taylor, 'Religion Is Not the Problem: Secularism and Democracy', *Commonweal* (25 February 2011): 21.

particular public political spaces.⁸ He differentiates between 'mere secularity', in which religious belief is a normal viable option (one might call this the American model); self-sufficient and exclusive secularity, where living without religion is normal (one sees this especially in the Scandinavian countries); and secularist secularity, which is the condition of feeling liberated from religion, and where religion is seen as a threat to liberty (the French model). While we may say that what constitutes a public political space are the distinct publics that constitute such a space, that is, the lack of any common theological perspective, the role of the church in its institutionalized form in relation to this public political space would depend on the historical and cultural factors at play in a given public political space. What is not clear is whether the current Orthodox situation would fit into any of Casanova's three models: mere secularity, sufficient and exclusive secularity, or secularist secularity. This raises the question of whether we can speak meaningfully of secularity in the Orthodox countries, or whether we need to adjust Casonova's model. But the general point is valid: put more simply, the role of religion, and specifically, the church, in public political life depends on which public we are speaking about. To complicate matters further, in the Orthodox world, the role of the church in public political life might look different in the United States, Greece and Russia.

Let us briefly look at the situation of the churches in the United States, Greece and Russia. In the United States, the Orthodox constitute less than 0.34 per cent of the total population, which amounts to about 1 million people out of a total population of 316 million.⁹ Orthodox Christianity has no position of privilege in the United States, and the institutional churches, all of which, with the exception of the Orthodox Church of America, are connected to the so-called mother countries, have very little effect on American public life, either culturally or politically. In Greece, the Orthodox Church has had and continues to have a strong cultural presence with roughly 98 per cent of the population identifying as Orthodox Christians.¹⁰ In Greece, the religious and the ethnic identities are not so easily differentiated, as a Greek who is an atheist may still consider himself Orthodox. Although levels of participation do not match the numbers of those who identify as Orthodox Christians, and although there are

---

⁸See his more recent essay, 'The Secular, Secularizations, Secularisms', in *Rethinking Secularism*, ed. Craig Calhoun, Mark Juergensmeyer, and Jonathan Vanantwerpen (Oxford: Oxford University Press, 2011), 54–74. This volume contains excellent essays reflecting from a global perspective on how the relations between religion, the secular and the public are differently negotiated for distinctive cultural and historical reasons.
⁹http://hirr.hartsem.edu/research/orthodoxindex.html (last accessed 16 December 2014).
¹⁰http://www.religionfacts.com/religion_statistics/religion_statistics_by_country.htm (last accessed 16 December 2014).

constant debates about the role of the church in public life, the fact that the church does have such a role is indisputable, even at the level of legislation.

The situation in Russia is more complicated. The latest polls from the Pew Research Center indicate that nearly 72 per cent of Russians now identify as Orthodox Christians, while only 7 per cent actually attend the liturgies, a decline from 9 per cent in 1998.[11] What this indicates is that the communist attempt to separate religious and national identity – to be a Soviet Russian meant *not* to be an Orthodox Christian – has now been reversed and Russian national identity has been again fused with religious identity. What is also clear is that the theological East–West divide has been appropriated to re-establish a geopolitical East–West divide between Russia and the West. According to the emerging political rhetoric under President Vladimir Putin, it is not that Russia does not support democratic structures, it is just that its understanding of democracy includes 'morality' as a result of its Russian Orthodox past, and this inclusion of morality is what differentiates Russian democracy from the godless liberal kind in the West, with its 'perversions' and licentiousness.[12] In this sense, some Russians have made common cause with such ultra-conservatives in the West like Pat Buchanan and, ironically, American evangelical Christians, even if evangelical Christians in Russia endure restrictions under the 1997 law 'On Freedom of Conscience and on Religious Association'. What is unclear in Russia is to what degree this emerging consciousness that being 'Russian' means being 'Orthodox' has any real effect on the cultural and political life of present-day Russia; or to what extent the Russian Orthodox Church as an institution has any real political influence, or has contributed to laws affecting other religious traditions, religious education or the so-called gay propaganda.[13]

It is clear, then, that when speaking about public ecclesiology, or the church *as* public *in* the public political space, the public political space looks differently for the Orthodox churches in the United States, Russia and Greece. The Orthodox churches in the United States have little effect on public life, while the Church of Greece de facto has a strong public presence, even if disputed, in large part due to the intertwining of ethnic and religious identity in Greece. Things are still in flux in Russia, where the political rhetoric affecting public life is shaped by the geopolitical East–West divide, in a way that is not dominant

---

[11]http://www.pewforum.org/2014/02/10/russians-return-to-religion-but-not-to-church/ (last accessed 16 December 2014).

[12]For a nuanced reading of the Russian Orthodox Church's linking of human rights language with morality, see Kristina Stoeckl, *The Russian Orthodox Church and Human Rights* (London: Routledge, 2014). See also http://www.washingtontimes.com/news/2014/jan/28/whos-godless-now-russia-says-its-us/?page=all (last accessed 17 December 2014).

[13]For one view, see Irina Papkova, *The Orthodox Church and Russian Politics* (New York: Oxford University Press, 2011).

in Greece. Given this descriptive reality, it would seem inconceivable to think that the church in Greece would not have a public role, just as it would be inconceivable, as Casanova showed, for the Catholic Church not to have a public role in Brazil, Poland and Spain. The Orthodox Church may be allowed to have a public role in the United States, but it will be limited in comparison with either Roman Catholic or Protestant forms of Christianity. The church's role in Russia is growing, but the future of such a role is still in question. *The extent and degree* to which the church has a role in the public political space depend on 'which public'. The question is whether distinct contextual situations should determine *the way* in which the church attempts to influence the public political space.

If we focus this question on specific issues, the Orthodox churches have shown unanimity in relation to their response in the public sphere. In order to address this question further, I would like to use gay marriage as a case study. There does not exist an Orthodox Church in the world that would support the legalization of gay marriage. The particular public, thus, does not affect the Orthodox churches' response to this moral question. In the United States, the Orthodox churches have issued statements, but to little effect, as the 2015 Supreme Court ruling effectively made gay marriage a national right. The legalization of gay 'marriage' in Greece and Russia is inconceivable at this time, though in Greece, EU pressure forced Greece to pass legislation in 2015 legally recognizing same-sex union, in spite of the efforts of the church; in Russia, in addition to resistance to the legalization of gay marriage, the so-called 'gay propaganda' laws have been passed, which do not exist in Greece. The legislation against gays in Russia is at a level not seen in Greece, even before EU integration. We, thus, see a slight difference between the churches in Greece and Russia as churches in Greece or other Orthodox countries are not endorsing laws against 'gay propaganda'; but, in general, the churches are fairly uniform in relation to laws endorsing gay unions of any kind.

9.2 WHICH ECCLESIOLOGY?

Should, however, such resistance to the legalization of gay marriage be the response of the churches that are committed to democratic structures? The Orthodox churches in Russia and Greece have a power and presence in the public political space not given to the Orthodox churches in the United States because of the role of Orthodox Christianity in shaping the cultural, ethnic and even national identity of these peoples; but, does this mean that these churches should use this power to influence public morality in particular direction while seemingly supporting democratic structures? These questions move us from the descriptive to the normative and the relation between the two. In order to answer this question, we must turn to ecclesiology. Before doing so, however, one myth must be dispelled: that liberal democracy in the West has no 'morality' and that the type of democracy supported by Orthodox countries in the East is one that is infused with morality.[14]

This juxtaposition of East–Democracy–Morality versus West–Democracy–Immorality is rhetorical demonization of the worst kind, as it is simply false that Western liberal democracy has been bereft of morality. It may not be the morality of a specific religious tradition, but it is a morality described best by Hans Joas as 'the sacredness of the person', expressed in the language of human rights.[15] The meaning of the 'sacredness of the person' is not self-evident, nor is its implications for structuring the public political space. I would argue that the ongoing interpretation of the meaning of the sacredness of the person and its expression in human rights language is best characterized by the Rawlsian notion of 'overlapping consensus', in which what emerges as a public morality is not that of evangelical Christians (and thank God for that!), but one which is contested and shaped by many voices.[16] In the United States, for example, one witnesses a tradition of contestation of the meaning of freedom and equality where at one-time women were excluded from voting, but now such an exclusion is unthinkable. The same debate is occurring in the United States on gay marriage. It is interesting to notice in this debate that religious actors, while being religiously motivated when giving public reasons for their objection, often revert to the vague notion of 'family values'. Most Americans are not convinced by the idea that somehow the legalization of gay marriage is a threat to the common morality of allowing to all humans freedom of expression and equal treatment, even if they are still divided equally over the morality of abortion. In fact, the American people are actually affirming the value of such things as commitment, trust, intimacy, honesty, integrity, etc., that are integral to lifelong commitments. Thus, to highlight the legalization of gay marriage as

---

[14]This rhetoric on 'Western' liberal democracy is evident among Orthodox hierarchs and thinkers alike but forms part of the Western theological critique of democratic liberalism. See, Vigen Guroian, *Incarnate Love: Essays in Orthodox Ethics* (Notre Dame, IN: University of Notre Dame Press, 1987); William T. Cavanaugh, *Torture and Eucharist: Theology, Politics and the Body of Christ* (Oxford: Blackwell Publisher, 1998); John Milbank, *Theology and Social Theory: Beyond Secular Reason* (Cambridge, MA: Blackwell, 1990); and, of course, Stanley Hauerwas, *Toward a Community of Character: A Constructive Christian Social Ethics* (Notre Dame, IN: University of Notre Dame Press, 1991).
[15]Hans Joas, *The Sacred of the Person: A New Geneology of Human Rights* (Georgetown University Press, 2013).
[16]On 'overlapping consensus', see John Rawls, *Political Liberalism*, 2nd edn. (Columbia University Press, 2005). See also Ronald Thiemann, *Religion in Public Life: A Dilemma for Democracy* (Georgetown University Press, 1996).

an example of Western democracy being without morality is simply false and, again, an example of the worst kind of rhetoric of demonization.

Only a crude understanding of homosexuality as 'perversion' could see lifelong gay unions as without any value. Such a crude understanding was evident in the recent statement by the Assembly of Canonical Orthodox Bishops in the United States after the Supreme Court decision that effectively legalized gay marriage in the United States.[17] In the statement they linked their affirmation of traditional marriage to the so-called protection of children, without giving any empirical evidence at all linking of the danger of gay marriage to children (because there is no danger); such a link is also implied in the Pan-Orthodox Council's document on 'The Mission of the Orthodox Church in Today's World'.[18] The fact that the Orthodox Church makes such an empirically unverifiable claim only indicates that it really cannot find any good arguments *within the terms* of democratic liberalism. In other words, it somehow wants to affirm the principles of democratic liberalism, and yet argue against gay marriage and gay civil unions; in order to do so, it makes unverifiable claims that promotion of homosexuality harms children, which very few in the West find convincing. There are really no convincing grounds on the terms of democratic liberalism for rejecting something like gay civil unions, or, more generally, free and open expression of same-sex attraction. The churches should simply be honest that they want a public political space that is heavily saturated with Orthodox morality; but they cannot do so and still claim that they are promoting freedom of conscience, freedom of religion and freedom of expression; in other words, to forcefully demand a public morality that is aligned with the church's morality should question the Orthodox churches' public commitment to democratic liberalism.

The question now becomes whether because of culture and history, the morality of the shared public political space of an Orthodox country should reflect the Orthodox morality of the Orthodox tradition. Before we answer this question, we must first ask whether Orthodoxy is compatible with democracy; and, in order to ask that question, we must now ask the question of which ecclesiology. As is well known, I have written on this,[19] the ecclesiology I think that makes most sense for understanding what it means to be a 'church' is Eucharistic ecclesiology. Kallistos Ware has written that although Eucharistic ecclesiology 'has been extensively criticized . . . what its opponents have done is to suggest modifications on points of detail rather than to propose a

---

[17]https://www.assemblyofbishops.org/news/news-archive/2015/response-of-assembly-of-bishops-to-obergefell-v.-hodges (last accessed 3 December 2020).
[18]http://www.pravoslavie.ru/english/90425.htm (last accessed 3 December 2020).
[19]Aristotle Papanikolaou, *The Mystical as Political: Democracy and Non-Radical Orthodoxy* (University of Notre Dame Press, 2012).

fundamentally different alternative'.[20] This is a nice way of saying that no one has come up with a better solution, so this is the best we have with which to work. I have argued that Eucharistic ecclesiology leads to a qualified Orthodox endorsement of democratic liberalism. Some misunderstanding, however, must be addressed, both of Eucharistic ecclesiology and of my own position. First, it is inaccurate to say that Eucharistic ecclesiology leads to a passive role of the laity and an autocratic understanding of the bishop.[21] Eucharistic ecclesiology developed in the context of countering such clericalism, and the mutually constitutive relationship of the bishop in relation to the laity, of the one and the many, is a fundamental tenet of Eucharistic ecclesiology. The fundamental logic of the Eucharistic ecclesiology was to identify the nature and location of the church as sacramental; in other words, in response to the question 'where is the Church?', Eucharistic ecclesiology points to the sacrament of the Eucharist and not to any institutional structures. In this sense, Eucharistic ecclesiology was meant and continues to intend to answer the question of the nature and the location of the church in such a way that includes the laity and precludes any reduction to the bishop or even a council of bishops. It is for this reason that John Zizioulas refers to the laity as being 'ordained' in baptism, which assumes a particular active role within the Eucharistic assembly.[22] The bishop is, according to Zizioulas, the 'visible center of unity' of the Eucharistic assembly, but there is no bishop, no unity to be expressed and symbolized in the bishop without the active constitutive role of the laity who are ordained into particular roles in the Eucharistic assembly through baptism.[23] As Zizioulas argues, 'the multiplicity is not to be subjected to the oneness; it is constitutive of the oneness. . . . This principle is that the "one" – the bishop – cannot exist without the "many" – the community – and the "many" cannot exist without the "one."'[24] There are

---

[20]Kallistos Ware, '*Sobornost* and Eucharistic ecclesiology: Aleksei Khomiakov and His Successors', *International Journal for the Study of the Christian Church* 11, no. 203 (2011): 216–35 (231).
[21]See Andrey Shishkov's contribution to this volume.
[22]John Zizioulas, *Being as Communion* (St. Vladimir's Seminary Press, 1985), 216. Zizioulas was making this claim as early as 1972 in 'Ordination – A Sacrament? An Orthodox Reply', *Concilium* 4 (1972): 33–9. For Zizioulas, ordination is inherently relational and active, and there is no member in the Eucharistic assembly who is not ordained. In fact, ordination of all participants is constitutive of the Eucharistic assembly.
[23]John Zizioulas, *Being as Communion*, 236.
[24]Ibid., 136–7. On the interdependence of the ministries, see 'The Ecclesiology of the Orthodox Tradition', *Search* 7 (1984): 42–53. On the relational understanding of authority, see 'The Nature of the Unity We Seek – The Response of the Orthodox Observer', *One in Christ* 24 (1988): 342–8. On the perichoretic nature of ministries and a rejection of the idea that the ministry of the bishop 'stands above it [the community] as an authority in itself', see 'The Church as Communion', *St. Vladimir's Theological Quarterly* 38 (1994): 7–19. For his most concise and elegant discussion of the mutually constitutive relationship between the one and the many, see 'Communion and Otherness', *Sobornost* 16 (1994): 3–16.

weaknesses to Eucharistic ecclesiology as it has developed over time, but the passive role of the laity is not one of them.

According to Zizioulas's understanding of Eucharistic logic, the unity of this particular local community is expressed in relation to other bishops through councils, and globally through a universal primate; but, even as this Eucharistic logic is expressed institutionally in council, the role of the laity is assumed to be expressed through the unity in the bishop.[25] It is in the institutional conciliar structures that the role of the laity is noticeably absent in the Orthodox churches, and it is in his own understanding of conciliarity that Zizioulas's extension of the logic of Eucharistic ecclesiology could be criticized as affirming a passive role of the laity. The conciliar structure as it currently exists and as Zizioulas describes it does not include a role for the laity; thus, at the regional and global levels, the institutional structures of conciliarity fail to iconically reflect the mutually constitutive dynamic of the one and the many in the Eucharist. In spite of the best of intentions, hierarchical councils can often look like the House of Lords without the House of Commons. This does not mean, however, that Eucharistic ecclesiology per se leads to a passive role of the laity; in fact, it is Eucharistic ecclesiology as described earlier that can serve as a critique for any institutional structures that do not iconically reflect the mutually constitutive dynamic of communion and otherness in the Eucharist; it can also critique any Christian living in the world that does not actively attempt to realize this dynamic in non-Eucharistic forms of community.

One of the weaknesses of Eucharistic ecclesiology concerns not discerning exactly what happens after the Eucharist; how the Christian is to walk and live in the world in a Eucharistic mode of being, which is one of learning how to love such that what are fostered are relations among other humans that realize personal uniqueness that is simultaneously an *ekstasis*, or a freedom from the determinism of the given. To address this, I argued for the integration of the ascetical into the understanding of ecclesiology.[26] It may be true that the theologians responsible for Eucharistic ecclesiology have overemphasized the Eucharistic communal assembly at the expense of the ascetical, but it is simply wrong to argue that Eucharistic ecclesiology does not allow for such an integration. It must be clarified that when speaking of Eucharistic ecclesiology, the church is strictly identified with the liturgical event of the Eucharist and only by extension with institutional structures, such as metropolises, patriarchates and councils. The church is a happening, a realization, a manifestation and a

---

[25]Ibid., 133–6. See also 'The Development of Conciliar Structures to the Time of the First Ecumenical Council', in *Councils and the Ecumenical Movement* (World Council of Churches, 1968), 34–41.

[26]Aristotle Papanikolaou, 'Integrating the Ascetical and the Eucharistic', *International Journal for the Study of the Christian Church* 11, no. 2–3 (2011): 173–82.

constituting of the assembly as the Body of Christ, and this is a result of the post-Pentecostal activity of the Holy Spirit. While such a sacramental understanding of church as event may imply certain after-the-Eucharist conciliar structures, less clear is the role and mission of the individual Christian in the world. What is also absent is reflection on how Eucharistic celebrations in their lived realities do not feel like the manifestation of the type of communion that Zizioulas describes. The latter two weaknesses result from a lack of integration of the ascetical into the Eucharistic understanding of the church.

One could argue that the logic of Eucharistic ecclesiology does not allow for such an integration of the ascetical, but this is inaccurate. The logic of Eucharistic ecclesiology is that of the mutually constitutive dynamic of communion and otherness as event. It may be, as Zizioulas argues, that as event, the constitution of the assembly as the eschatological Body of Christ does not depend on the individual ascetical struggle of the participants but on the invocation of the Holy Spirit; however, just as ascetical struggle wires the body towards openness to the ubiquitous presence of God in the world, so does such a struggle make possible the experience of the Eucharistic assembly as communion. Ascetical struggle does not cause communion but opens one up to the communion that is already given in the assembly as gift. In that sense, asceticism is inherently relational and forms the individual to relate to oneself, others, the world and God in a Eucharistic mode of being. If Augustine is right that God is closer to us than we are to ourselves, then asceticism does not cause the presence of God but allows such a presence to be more fully manifested in our lives, the measure of which is our love for the neighbour, even the enemy and the imagined unlovable.

To argue that Eucharistic ecclesiology does not allow for such an integration of the ascetical is to create a false opposition between the Eucharist and the ascetical and fails to see that the ascetical aims towards a Eucharistic mode of being, and that the Eucharist as an event of communion depends on the ascetical.[27] After the Eucharist, the Christian must enter the world in such a way as to ascetically struggle to learn how to love in the face of an other that does not share her Orthodox presuppositions. This asceticism means that the faith is shared by persuasion and not by force, which means that the Orthodox Christian must inhabit a space with others who do not share her beliefs or presuppositions – a shared public political space.[28] It would be important to emphasize that the language of human rights does not adequately express all

---

[27]Such a mutual interdependence is actually evident in the daily structure of services and prayers in the Eastern Orthodox tradition, all of which culminate in the morning and daily celebration of the Eucharist.
[28]For further development of this point, see Papanikolaou, *The Mystical as Political*.

that Orthodox theological anthropology asserts is possible for being human and all that Orthodoxy understands by the notion of 'sacredness of the person'. The political space is indeed distinct from the ecclesial, especially as it is one that would allow as one option among many the turn to belief in the non-existence of God; but, as seen through the perspective of practices of divine–human communion, or learning how to love, liberal democratic structures do not appear as foreign to an Orthodox understanding of the human person. Indeed, engaged in practices of divine–human communion, Christians would be actively shaping a political space structured around a minimal set of under-determined normative principles that include freedom and equality, guaranteed through human rights language that is not linked to a specific religious morality, all the while being aware that the ecclesial is not the political, even if, as I would argue, the mystical is the political.

9.3 ORTHODOXY, DEMOCRACY AND GAY MARRIAGE

With the recognition of a shared public political space that is distinct from the public space of the ecclesial community, the Orthodox Christian must live and act so as to create structures that would guarantee that all humans are treated as unique and irreducible; such structures would look something like those that we call today liberal democratic, and, in fact, all Orthodox churches throughout the world have indicated support for democratic political structures. This situation is very much unlike the Roman Catholic situation of the past century, when the debate was really about whether, in fact, the Roman Catholic Church could embrace democratic liberalism, and, in particular, the reality of church/state separation. It is also what differentiates Orthodoxy from the debate within Islam, where the question really is about the compatibility of Islamic beliefs and democratic liberalism. Now there may be non-Orthodox who raise this question, as Huntington did, among others, but among the Orthodox themselves, the debate seems to be not about the compatibility between democratic liberalism and Orthodoxy but about the role of religion within a democratic polity that affirms liberal values, such as freedom of conscience, freedom of religion and even, in some cases, church/state separation, which exists, for example, technically in Russia but not in Greece

To support, however, liberal democratic structures would mean to accept that the morality of the public political space would not be identical to that of the ecclesial public space, since the goal of the public political space is distinct from analogous to that of the church as a shared communal space of worship. In order to create structures that would guarantee that all humans are treated as unique and irreducible, the Christian would work towards maximizing pluralism such that the public political space could not be such that it endorses the morality of a single religious tradition, *no matter the cultural history of that shared public political space*. In working towards securing structures that guarantee that all humans are treated as unique and irreducible, the ascetical Christian – who is not simply the monk – is not accepting a public political space without morality but is working towards a public political space that is shaped by a morality that exists as an overlapping consensus. Given this theological point, the Orthodox churches in the mother countries should not use the privilege of history or culture as a means to enforce legally particular moral positions of the Orthodox Church, especially if they publically proclaim support for democratic structures. The churches should use the power of its public presence towards promoting, furthering and deepening the kinds of political structures that are most consistent with its own ecclesiological principles, or what should result when the 'Church is a social ethic'.[29] One may call such structures democratic, but that is irrelevant to the point. The church simply cannot use the privilege of its cultural and historical position to impose its morality on a shared, pluralistic, public political space. If it wishes to do so, then it must do so consistently: it should ask for laws against premarital sex, against lying, against divorce, etc. Why simply stop at one particular moral situation? Moreover, where is the church's opposition to the violence against the gay population, violence that even its own clergy incites at gay people? Why does not the church support laws against such violence? Where is the church's outcry at the growing income inequality that exists globally? Where is the church's outcry at the recent report of the *Economist* that states how only 110 people in Russia out of a population of 140 million control 35 per cent of the wealth? Why does the church care so much about gay sex and not about this massive income inequality, which also exists, albeit to a lesser degree, in Greece and the United States? Why are the Orthodox churches globally so silent about the rampant corruption in their countries? Why is it so difficult for the Church of Greece, in order to fight political corruption, to speak against laws granting immunity to elected officials? Given these arguments that I have proposed, the church should *not* oppose the legalization of gay 'marriage' in the public political sphere, nor anything remotely similar to laws against 'gay propaganda', whether it be in the United States, Greece or Russia. I write 'marriage' in scare quotes, as the Orthodox churches need not recognize such politically contracted unions as 'marriage', thus arguing that committed heterosexual unions are in some way distinct from committed union of the same sex;[30] but, politically contracted gay

---

[29]Stanley Hauerwas, *The Peaceable Kingdom* (University of Notre Dame Press, 1991), 99.
[30]Even here Orthodox must ask the kind of question posed by a draft of the recent Synod on the Family in the Roman Catholic Church – Is there really nothing of value that the church cannot recognize by committed, lifelong unions, whatever the sex of those involved in such unions?

unions do not threaten but, in fact, contribute to the morality of the democratic public political space, to which the church should use whatever power and influence it has to improving, extending and deepening. This is the church's ecclesiological imperative – its public ecclesiology.

9.4 CONCLUSION

I have described a situation where public ecclesiology depends on the particular public of which one speaks. It is clear that the churches in Russia and Greece have a public presence that is simply not available to the Orthodox Church in the United States. And, yet, the power of this public presence should not be used to advance the particular morality of the Orthodox Church, or particular moral points; it should be used to shape a public political space informed by its own ecclesiology and its own understanding of the ascetical call to live a Eucharistic mode of being in the world. Such structures involve the maximization of plural voices and a commitment to a public morality forged through an overlapping consensus. It is not necessary to call such structures democratic or liberal; in fact, since they are based on sound theological arguments and Orthodox ecclesiological principles, I would call such political structural principles Orthodox.

I want to end by saying that if the best response to my argument is simply to say that what I am proposing works in the United States but not in Russia or Greece, then such a statement is not a theological argument. It is an empirical claim without any support. If one were to argue that theological thinking in the West was not as credible as what emerges from the pure space of the so-called mother countries, one could counter-argue that the Orthodox theologians in the diaspora are forced to discuss Orthodox theology in such a way that mirrors the early Christian situation even up to the seventh century, when Christianity was not necessarily taken for granted philosophically, culturally or politically. It is during this time period that we see the development of theology that has become foundational for the Orthodox tradition; and it may very well be that we see in the diaspora, ironically, the development of an Orthodox political theology that is more authentically Orthodox than what see in the so-called mother countries.

CHAPTER 10

Post-liberal positions in public theology

BEN FULFORD

10.1 INTRODUCTION

In this chapter, I seek to show that, contrary to widespread caricatures of them as fideists eschewing publicly intelligible critical scrutiny, or sectarians advocating Christian disengagement from the public realm, post-liberal theologians have a deep commitment to publicness in both respects, which arises from their commitment to the irreducible particularity of Christian beliefs, practices and the stories which norm them. It is, I argue first, because of this commitment to Christian particularity and the orientation to the public it entails that they are critical of attempts to establish the public status of Christian belief and practice on a putatively universalist foundation or general theory of human existence or religion. They pursue this critique in order to preserve the public character of Christian faith. Second, to different degrees, they seek to mobilize what they take to be core resources of Christian tradition, not least its central scriptural narratives, in order to frame, orient and exemplify constructive Christian engagement with public issues and events. Third, they have sought to find ways to articulate the modes and terms of critical public accountability for Christian beliefs and practices without lapsing back into the very modes of theological and ethical argument against which they protest. These tend to liken the public intelligibility of Christian meanings to those of the culture of a community, and to combine realist, coherentist and pragmatic understandings to describe what it means to call Christianity 'true', which admit of a range of public ways of assessing Christian discourse without subordinating it to a distorting set of criteria.

The theologians most commonly described as 'post-liberal' are the Protestant theologians Hans W. Frei, George A. Lindbeck and Stanley Hauerwas, though several of their other colleagues and students are also often associated with the label and their contemporary influence runs much wider than this group.[1] Frei, Lindbeck and Hauerwas did not articulate a common project or platform.[2] What they share is a concern for renewing approaches to Christian theology and ethics that are rooted in the irreducibly specific practices, beliefs and virtues of Christian communities. Integral to that vision is the normative and formative role of biblical narratives in Christian practice and theology.[3] This common concern gives rise to a broadly similar orientation to public theology in each thinker that is both critical and constructive, but there are also some subtle but significant differences between them, which the common label can obscure. In respect of each aspect of their public theology, I argue that it is Frei who offers the most promising and coherent approach which helps make sense of the strengths, and resolve some of the problems, in the accounts of Hauerwas and Lindbeck.

10.2 AGAINST THE PUBLICNESS OF APOLOGETIC THEOLOGY

Frei, Lindbeck and Hauerwas all articulate critiques of what they took to be dominant ways in modern theology of securing the public status of Christian beliefs, practices and moral positions in terms of their conformity or correlation with some putatively universal account of human existence, religion or morality. They do so broadly in two ways.

On the one hand, they seek to show how such accounts ended up being reductive of the specific forms and logics of Christian belief, practice and

---

[1] Others associated with the term 'post-liberal' and what it names include Frei and Kelsey's Yale colleagues, David Kelsey, Paul Holmer and their students Garrett Green, George Hunsinger, Bruce D. Marshall, William C. Placher, Kathryn Tanner, Ronald Thiemann and Charles Wood.

[2] I follow DeHart, Higton and Springs in seeing Frei and Lindbeck's projects as significantly different from one another and would extend the same judgement to Hauerwas in comparison with them both. See Paul J. DeHart, *The Trial of Witnesses. The Rise and Decline of Postliberal Theology* (Malden: Blackwell Publishing, 2006); Mike Higton, *Christ, Providence and History. Hans W. Frei's Public Theology* (London: T&T Clark International, 2004); Jason A. Springs, *Toward A Generous Orthodoxy. Prospects for Hans Frei's Postliberal Theology* (New York: Oxford University Press, 2010).

[3] They also share a common regard for Karl Barth as exemplifying the attempt to realize this concern, especially in his *Church Dogmatics*.

character. Thus, Lindbeck recognizes the attractiveness, in a modern context, of apologetic theological strategies that understand Christianity in terms of a system of propositions or a symbolic expression of a core experience common to all major religions.[4] However, such accounts fail to do justice to the significant degree to which religions are constituted by a system of symbols and the grammar of their use, and the form of life correlated with it, and the way such systems and forms of life shape religious experience. They tend to abstract key terms from the systemic and pragmatic contexts which their meaning is bound up, by locating their meaning beyond that semiotic system in objective reality or experience.[5] Similarly, Hauerwas argues that the pursuit of an 'unqualified' or universalistic Christian ethic, in the mode of universalistic modern Western paradigms like utilitarian or Kantian ethics, makes convictions essential to the Christian life and identity secondary or irrelevant, abstracting the Christian ethic from its rationale and so distorting it.[6]

On the other, they argue that there are specific intellectual weaknesses to this strategy. Lindbeck finds grounds in his cultural–linguistic approach to religion for scepticism about the attempt of liberal theology to identify a foundational scheme for translating religious claims and showing their plausibility with reference to universal principles or structures.[7] For, like languages, religions can only be fully learnt and understood on their own terms, through acquiring the relevant skills of practice, and not by translation into another putatively universal idiom. Hauerwas makes similar anti-foundationalist and particularist claims. All accounts of the moral life, he argues, depend on communities and the stories which inform their basic purpose and make the virtues and rules they uphold intelligible.[8] Hence the possibility of an unqualified, universal ethic is highly implausible[9] and is essentially coercive.[10]

Hans Frei was sceptical of the prospects for a sufficient consensus in epistemology[11] that might provide a foundation for theology apart from the task of interpreting biblical narrative, though he was not strongly committed to an anti-foundationalist position as a general theory either.[12] In any case,

---

[4] George A. Lindbeck, *The Nature of Doctrine: Religion and Theology in a Postliberal Age* (Philadelphia: Westminster Press, 1984), 15–16, 31–3, 126–7.
[5] Ibid., 113–14.
[6] Stanley Hauerwas, *The Peaceable Kingdom: A Primer in Christian Ethics* (Notre Dame: University of Notre Dame Press, 1991), 10–11, 22–3.
[7] Ibid., 129.
[8] Hauerwas, *The Peaceable Kingdom*, 61, 118–19.
[9] Ibid., 59.
[10] Ibid., 12.
[11] Hans Wilhelm Frei, *Theology and Narrative. Selected Essays* (New York: Oxford University Press, 1993), 209–10.
[12] Hans Wilhelm Frei, *Reading Faithfully Volume 1. Writings from the Archive: Theology and Hermeneutics* (Eugene, OR: Cascade Books, 2015), 36–7.

Frei agreed with Karl Barth that nothing can establish the possibility of the gospel save the actuality of the Incarnation.[13] Frei also offers the most developed and sophisticated version of the first kind of critique, one which has two further advantages which justify examining it in greater detail. First, he applies that critique to a representative of the tradition of liberal theology who has sought to take on board the importance of Christian narratives and the particularities of Christian belief in the course of producing a defining work on public theology, namely, David Tracy. Second, Frei's arguments here bring out more fully how his critique is motivated by his own concern for the publicness of Christian faith, something which Lindbeck and Hauerwas' versions communicate less clearly.

David Tracy's *The Analogical Imagination* is one of a few books in public theology which are almost always cited in genealogies of the field.[14] Frei treats Tracy as exemplifying an approach which, in the quest for publicness, subverts the central Christian focus on the narrated person of Jesus Christ and undermines the focus on Christian life in a public social setting which flows from his story.

Frei's concerns for the public world of the gospel narratives, for the public of the church as a reading community and for the public discipleship of their Christian readers go back to his analysis of modern theological hermeneutics: *The Eclipse of Biblical Narrative*. There Frei's starting point was the 'history-likeness' or realism of biblical narratives prioritized in Western Christianity. They depicted characters 'firmly and significantly set in the context of the external environment, natural but more particularly social',[15] and rendered both characters and their circumstances through their interaction in a chronological sequence, mixing serious effect with the casual and everyday.

These stories, moreover, manifested a sense of providential design in the way the pattern of events and persons in earlier stories prefigured the climactic stories about Jesus Christ and the church, without losing the integrity of their own meaning. Premodern Western Christian readers, Frei argued, took this sequence of history-like stories to be the history of the world into which they must fit their own times, lives, experiences and circumstances through reading contemporary events and persons as figures

---

[13]Hans Wilhelm Frei, *Theology and Narrative*, 30.
[14]See, for example, Harold Breitenberg, 'To Tell the Truth: Will the Real Public Theology Please Stand Up?', *Journal of the Society of Christian Ethics* 23 no. 2 (2003): 55–96; Katie Day and Sebastian Kim, 'Introduction', in *Companion to Public Theology*, ed. Katie Day and Sebastian Kim (Leiden: Brill, 2017), 3–4, 11–12; Elaine Graham, *Between a Rock and a Hard Place: Public Theology in a Post-Secular Age* (London: SCM Press, 2013), 5–6.
[15]Hans Wilhelm Frei, *The Eclipse of Biblical Narrative: A Study in Eighteenth and Nineteenth Century Hermeneutics* (New Haven: Yale University Press, 1974), 13–14.

of the biblical world.[16] These readers' attention to the social worlds and events of biblical stories shaped an imagination in which faith was enacted publicly within a providentially ordered social and historical world. As Mike Higton[17] and Daniel Shin[18] have highlighted, what Frei values in these modes of reading is the attention to the public temporal world depicted in biblical narrative and the way it shaped and promoted engagement with the public world of historical human societies, where publicness has to do with life and engagement in shared social contexts.

In the rest of the book, Frei shows how this focus was lost in various forms of modern biblical hermeneutics which construed the meaning of these stories in terms of their possible reference to historical events, rational ideas or permanent features of human existence, judged by general canons of meaning and factual probability,[19] often in order to try to commend the public reasonableness and meaningfulness of Christianity. These developments led to hermeneutical procedures which overlooked the narrative meaning of the biblical stories and mitigated against the practice of learning to imagine ourselves and our social settings and circumstances as similarly ordered by God's providence. Frei's critique of Tracy should be understood in light of that argument.

That critique features as part of a wider reformulation of Frei's project in the 1980s, in which he explores how modern theologians navigated the ambiguity in Christian theology between theology as an academic discipline akin to philosophy and theology as the self-description of Christianity. In the second of these, theology is concerned with Christianity as a 'complex, various, loosely held, yet really discernible community with varying features', such as a sacred text focused around a central story, which is the subject of the community's interpretive tradition.[20]

Christianity so understood is like a culture in Clifford Geertz's sense of socially established structures of meaning.[21] It has flexible, informal, practically acquired basic rules for the interpretation of its sacred texts, rules which make possible a great deal of hermeneutical and exegetical variety and disagreement.[22] They are contingent in the sense that they develop historically. Over the centuries, he claims, there has been a minimal but broad, flexible consensus – one that makes meaningful disagreement possible – around the hermeneutical

---

[16]Ibid., 3.
[17]Highton, *Christ, Providence and History*, 99, 141, 143, 1490.
[18]Daniel D. Shin, *Theology and the Public: Reflections on Hans W. Frei on Hermeneutics, Christology, and Theological Methods* (Lanham: Lexington Books, 2019), 27–33.
[19]Frei, *The Eclipse of Biblical Narrative*, 10–12.
[20]Hans Wilhelm Frei, *Types of Christian Theology* (New Haven: Yale University Press, 1992), 12.
[21]See Geertz, *The Interpretation of Cultures* (New York: Basic Books, 1973).
[22]Frei, *Types of Christian Theology*, 13–14, 56–7.

priority of a set of such rules which came to be called the literal sense.[23] The most important of these took the person of Jesus of Nazareth to be the subject matter of the Christological stories in Scripture, and not some universal moral, existential or rational truth or disposition represented by him.[24] The effect of this basic continuity of rules in hermeneutical practice is to prioritize the textual rendering of Jesus' identity.

In *The Analogical Imagination*, Tracy offered a fully hermeneutical approach to correlating Christianity in its textual particularity and contemporary society, as a paradigm for public theology. Christian theology, he argued, would be public by offering interpretations of the visions of meaningful existence disclosed in religious symbols and their transformative possibilities for society.[25] Tracy does so by interpreting the New Testament as a religious classic.

Classics are about 'the fundamental questions posed to our common humanity'.[26] They combine a particular origin with a potentially universal disclosure of truth and meaning, a way of being in the world, in which lies their claim to publicness.[27] Religious classics focus on questions about the meaning of the whole and our relation to it, and how these connections bear on desire for human liberation and authentic existence.[28] They make a claim to public attention and truth as the disclosure and concealment of and from the power of the whole as a gracious mystery.[29] This claim depends on a correlation between the truth so disclosed and religious experiences: those which disclose the religious dimension of that existence.[30]

Tracy argues that Christian theologians recognize in present experiences of the event of Jesus Christ an event from and by the power of the whole, that is, of and from God. That event, he asserts, is intrinsically connected with the person of Jesus of Nazareth as remembered and experienced in Christian tradition as the person in whom the reality of the graced world is re-presented as the decisive event of the gift of God's own self, which is also a command.[31]

---

[23]Ibid., 14, 56. The minimal, flexible content of the rules Frei is concerned with here, and the way they permit wide disagreement among their adherents, makes his account less vulnerable to the criticisms of Geertz which Kathryn Tanner summarizes and applies to Christian theology than Lindbeck or Hauerwas. See Kathryn Tanner, *Theories of Culture: A New Agenda for Theology* (Minneapolis: Fortress Press, 1997).
[24]Hans Wilhelm Frei, *Theology and Narrative. Selected Essays* (New York: Oxford University Press, 1993), 15–16, 144–5.
[25]David Tracy, *The Analogical Imagination: Christian Theology and the Culture of Pluralism* (London: SCM Press, 1981), 6–13.
[26]Ibid., 105.
[27]Ibid., 110–11, 120–3, 132–3.
[28]Ibid., 157–63, 168.
[29]Ibid., 163, 168–9.
[30]Ibid., 160, 163, 194.
[31]Ibid., 232–6.

To this extent, he seems to uphold the literal sense. Yet Tracy's emphasis on the specificity and incarnational significance of the person of Jesus of Nazareth and the particularities of the textual witnesses to him is repeatedly in tension, Frei thought, with his concern to demonstrate the public significance of these stories by correlating it with the religious dimension of experience.[32] In consequence, the stories' Christological meaning is always focused on the possibilities disclosed and the event that takes place in front of the text.[33] In Frei's view, these aims are in conflict, and Tracy tends to resolve it by prioritizing the correlation of the story with present religious experience and its putatively universal significance over the particularity of the narrated figure of Jesus, and so tends towards allegorization.[34] Frei implies that in the end, despite Tracy's best intentions, he ends up subverting the literal sense. For Frei finds that by turning the stories of Jesus into allegory, Tracy effectively repeats the problem of his hermeneutic in his earlier book, *Blessed Rage for Order*. The meaning of the New Testament's realistic proclamatory stories of Jesus as the Christ comes to be a referent which transcends the plot, characters and world they describe, which Jesus merely displays, which identify him and of which his actions and sufferings are but a shadow.[35]

10.3 CHRIST, PROVIDENCE AND PUBLIC THEOLOGY

This critical concern for how the public world rendered by biblical faiths orients and frames Christians' engagements with their social contexts as spheres of meaningful interaction which are mysteriously governed by providence is also reflected in Hauerwas's work. For Hauerwas, the scriptural story the church tells and expounds, the story of Israel and Jesus, is key to the formation of its character as a community and the character of its members.[36] So formed, the church's function in God's purpose is as a radically alternative countersociety whose life witnesses to God's peaceable Kingdom, and so also reveals to the world its creatureliness and its violent distortedness under sin: a strategy embracing tactical engagement and affirmation, withdrawal and nonviolent resistance, depending on the circumstances. In all these modes it is to bear witness by its distinctive virtues and practices.[37]

---

[32]See, for example, Ibid., 248, 252, 254–8, 259–76.
[33]Ibid., 279–82, 308–9.
[34]Frei, *Theology and Narrative*, 130, n. 16.
[35]Ibid., 126–9.
[36]Hauerwas, *The Peaceable Kingdom*, 24–33.
[37]Stanley Hauerwas, and William H. Willimon, *Resident Aliens: Life in the Christian colony. A Provocative Christian Assessment of Culture and Ministry for People Who Know that Something Is Wrong* (Nashville: Abingdon Press, 2014).

Hauerwas's accounts of these virtues and how they speak to shared experiences and challenges in his society offer a kind of post-liberal publicly engaged theology, which is best exemplified by his writings on topics like peace-making, abortion, suicide and euthanasia, children, medicine, suffering, disability and being a patient.[38] Sometimes those arguments focus mainly on the contrastive ethos Christian communities should embody when formed by their story and the difference this story should make practically for Christians in respect of the issue at hand. For example, he argues that taking time to practice care for ordinary quotidian things (endangered species, sport, childrearing, universities) helps us learn how to be peaceful people, practising virtues which give unity and shape to our lives, and so embody the Christian conviction that God gives us the time and space to enjoy our creaturely existence in the face of nuclear war.[39] For only such a peaceful disposition will enable us to live without desperation, free of the sense of urgency created by that threat and the totalitarian power it lends to anti-nuclear initiatives, and so free to resist the forces that built the bomb.

In other cases, the implied public significance is clearer. In *Naming the Silences*, Hauerwas argues that Christians share a story, 'that we are creatures of a gracious God'[40] and can within that framework narrate their lives as a unity with a larger purpose, in such a way as to acknowledge and lament their inexplicable suffering, and their deaths, and learn to live meaningfully with them. In this way, he implies, the church has the resource that modern Western society lacks. It has a story that can reframe the practice of medicine that has been shaped by individualism focused on our autonomous choices and achievements, and the denial of death. This reframing, he implies, would allow medical treatment to serve people as the subjects of such stories, rather than have to function, to the detriment of patients and their families, as an end in itself. And it offers patients and their friends and families a way of living together with suffering and death. As a community living and embodying that story, the church has something profoundly important to offer to medicine.[41]

In both cases, Hauerwas commends a story-formed ethos enacted in the practices of Christian community as a way of embodying Christian convictions

---

[38]These observations at least significantly qualify James Gustafson's criticisms of Hauerwas. See James M. Gustafson, 'The Sectarian Temptation: Reflections on Theology, the Church and the University', *Proceedings of the Catholic Theological Society* 40 (1985): 83–94.
[39]Stanley Hauerwas, *Christian Existence Today: Essays on Church, World, and Living In Between* (Oregon: Wipf & Stock, 2010), 265.
[40]Stanley Hauerwas, *Naming the Silences: God, Medicine, and the Problem of Suffering* (Edinburgh: T & T Clark, 1993), 126.
[41]Hauerwas makes a similar case in 'Salvation and Health: Why Medicine Needs the Church', *Hauerwas* (2005): 539–55.

faithfully. He also implies that by doing so, Christians may exhibit to society an attractive alternative in face of wider existential challenges. In this ecclesiocentric apologetic mode, and especially in his more general formulations, Hauerwas's public theology is premised on the possibility of visibly distinctive Christian communities which are broadly united, coherent and homogenous in culture and ethos, so that they may offer a contrast to the world. That premise is questionable in terms both of theoretical developments in thinking about culture, as Kathryn Tanner shows,[42] and of ethnographic studies of actual Christian cultures, as Nicholas Healy argues.[43] Churches, like cultures, are more diverse in conviction and ethos between and within congregations, more porous to and less visibly different from the rest of society, more subject to the cumulative effect of individual negotiations of social, cultural and ecclesial circumstances, than Hauerwas seems to need them to be. Yet as proposals for life and constructive witness by congregations and their members, these arguments may be less vulnerable to that critique, without losing their significance as a kind of implicit public theology. For in these essays, Hauerwas also can be read as gesturing to the possibility that Christians may, by being faithfully present in these ways in institutions and movements, have some influence on their cultures and practices.

There are, however, limits to this kind of public theology in terms of the terms on which it imagines Christian making a difference in society in collaboration with others. For on Hauerwas' account the emphasis seems to be on non-Christians cooperating with Christians' modes of faithful living and the difference they make, when moved by their witness. The underlying logic requires that public theology makes a difference by persuading others to conform to distinctively Christian modes of practice. It is thus difficult to see how, on Hauerwas's terms, it might be possible for Christians to meet the challenge articulated by Ronald Thiemann's vision of a nonfoundationalist, Anselmian public theology: that of contributing to debate over, and cooperating with others to address, issues in society and public policy in fragmented, pluralistic societies, while remaining faithfully rooted in the scriptural narrative and Christian tradition.[44] Yet, Thiemann argues, such engagement is necessary to do justice to the calling to share and embody the gospel story, to think through its

---

[42]Tanner, *Theories of Culture*.
[43]Nickolas M. Healy, *Hauerwas: A (Very) Critical Introduction* (Grand Rapids: Eerdmans, 2014), 73–99.
[44]Ronald F. Thiemann, *Constructing a Public Theology: The Church in a Pluralistic Culture* (Louisville: Westminster/John Knox, 1991). Thiemann articulates this vision in contradistinction to Tracy's, which he thinks subverts Christians' capacities to engage in this task. See Thieman, *Constructing a Public Theology*, 19–22.

implications for our relations with society (faith seeking understanding) and to faith in God's enduring presence in the public realm.⁴⁵

Thiemann's argument in *Constructing a Public Theology* advances beyond Hauerwas in commending the idea of churches, suitably repentant for their own divisions and with reinvigorated catechesis, as models for pluralistic societies of unity in diversity, and beacons of a cruciform hope in the midst of their social engagements.⁴⁶ His argument is deeply and explicitly indebted to Frei, and it is Frei who offers further theological resources for such a project.

To understand how, we need to return to Frei's main dogmatic work, *The Identity of Jesus Christ*. That identity, Frei holds, is given normatively to us in the narrative witness of the New Testament, and primarily the Synoptic Gospels, above all their more realistic narrative sequences, culminating in those of the passion and resurrection. By tracing the logic of the scriptural witness to Jesus, of his identity as rendered in the patterns of its narratives, Frei held that it is possible to trace, even if only partially, the rational of affirming his presence in Scripture, sacrament, Christian community and, providentially, history. At the heart of Frei's argument is the claim that, as identified by the cumulative basic pattern common to the Synoptics' varied narratives, Jesus Christ cannot be thought not to live and is inseparable from the identity of God, as the embodied manifestation of God's presence.

So understood, Christ's identity clarifies the logic of ordinary Christian talk of Christ's freely sharing his presence in Word, Sacrament, community and history in light of his narratively rendered identity: it is 'the full focusing of his full identity in the resurrection' which enables him to do that and which accounts for our experience.⁴⁷ Since Christ's focused identity in the resurrection is inseparable from God's presence and action, he lives to God, in a mode of life that transcends ours and is veiled from us.⁴⁸

This presence is experienced indirectly in the church, a frail human instrument constituted by Christ's indirect presence in Word, Sacrament and human history and their unity in him.⁴⁹ But it is not confined to the church. Frei argues that Christ is also 'the ultimate presence in and to the world in its mysterious passage from event to event in public history'.⁵⁰ This claim leads Frei to develop an account of the relationship between church and world in history. Frei's statement of this relationship has a partially dialectical character

---

⁴⁵Ibid., 24, 119.
⁴⁶Ibid., 122–4.
⁴⁷Hans Wilhelm Frei, *The Identity of Jesus Christ: The Hermeneutical Bases of Dogmatic Theology* (Philadelphia: Fortress Press, 1975), 49.
⁴⁸Ibid., 172.
⁴⁹Ibid., 158.
⁵⁰Ibid., 158–9.

on account of the inseparable relatedness and abiding distinctness of the modes of Christ's presence in the church and to the world. On the one hand, Christ's identity as one who is identified with human beings and acts on their behalf means that his presence in the church makes it a community for the world. At the same time, because of Christ's presence in the world in public history, the church's orientation towards the world has the character of a witness to his presence in and to human history,[51] rather than its decisive manifestation. For the church exists as its unfinished public history in its interaction with that of humanity at large, which is providentially ordered in Christ's life, death and resurrection, in virtue of his presence to it (1975, 158).[52]

History, therefore, has a mysterious pattern, to be disclosed eschatologically, of which something may be discerned dimly with the heuristic aid of parables, such as the fitness of God's election of the Gentiles through his rejection of Israel in order to save Israel (Rom. 11.29-32) and Jesus Christ himself in his atoning work.[53] The former may help Christians recognize, by analogy, the enrichment the church receives from its neighbour, humanity at large and so the possibility that Christ's presence may be figured forth in history beyond the church. The latter may guide us to recognize figural hints of the 'pattern of union through the agonized exchange of radical opposites', in which the pattern in its incompleteness in a given historical event looks forward to eschatological reconciliation, redemption and resurrection.[54]

This account of Christ's presence gives Frei the basis and beginnings of a framework for Christian theologians to examine and speak into the history of church and world in any historical context, including modern national contexts. In *The Identity of Jesus Christ*, for example, he suggests that the second parable, of the Christological pattern of the sacrificial reconciliation of opposites, may illumine the Civil War and Civil Rights struggle in US history against the background of the history of slavery and segregation there and give cause for hope about the eventual pattern of history in relation to the suffering inflicted on Vietnam by the 'defensive provinciality' of the United States.[55] This approach, then, offers a perspective at once deeply sober, progressive, realist and hopeful on the national history and present situation of the United States and the witness, service and receptivity of the churches in that context, rooted in this providential understanding of Christ's presence as read through his identity. In just this way, it orients Christians, carefully, towards speaking and collaborating constructively in public in respect of issues in society at every

---

[51] Ibid.
[52] Ibid., 158.
[53] Ibid., 161–2.
[54] Ibid., 162.
[55] Ibid., 162–3.

level, in the realist hope that Christ is present to it, configuring it mysteriously and that, as Frei also affirms, a great variety of human political and cultural projects may eschatologically be fulfilled in him.[56]

10.4 THE CRITICAL PUBLICNESS OF CHRISTIAN THEOLOGY

Tracy's demand for critical public accountability, however, is not easily evaded. For he makes it on two widely accepted theological grounds: the universality of the one God of Christian faith and the constructive, loving orientation of the church to the world loved by God.[57] Here we might distinguish two related sets of issues: intelligibility (the extent to which, and the terms on which, Christian meanings are intelligible to others); and truth (the sense in which they may be true, including their truth within a form of life commended to others, and how their truth may be assessed).

On intelligibility, Lindbeck's cultural–linguistic approach precludes interpreting Christianity in terms of a general theory of religious experience, or as a series of propositions only. Religions are more comprehensive than propositions, and religious experience is too far shaped by different interpretive schemes to be reducible to a common essence. Indeed, they may be so different that translation between them is impossible: their concepts will be too different in meaning or they may lack equivalents for key concepts.[58] Yet the fact that he thinks one could show that this incommensurability pertains between two religions; that he thinks dialogue between religions is still possible; that Christianity may benefit from the insights of other religions and help them become better speakers of their languages; and that religions provide frameworks for interpreting all reality and other conceptual schemes,[59] suggests that he thinks that significant mutual understanding between adherents of diverse religions – and presumably therefore also with inhabitants of other kinds of cultural systems – is possible.

The idea that religions are like languages offers a way to make sense of this claim: one may acquire skill to a greater or lesser extent in more than one language,[60] even where these languages are very different in structures and concepts, although Lindbeck is sceptical about the possibility of such learning

---

[56]Ibid., 163. I explore the ethical and political dimensions of Frei's theology further in my forthcoming, *God's Patience and Our Work*.
[57]Tracy, *The Analogical Imagination*, 48–9, 51, 63.
[58]Lindbeck, *The Nature of Doctrine*, 47–9, 129.
[59]Ibid., 54, 61–2, 82–3, 114–17.
[60]Ibid., 129, 132.

in the setting of contemporary Western culture.⁶¹ Lindbeck also affirms the possibility of describing the meaning of religious meaning in terms of its function within a cultural system (intratextually), like any rule-governed behaviour, which seems potentially public.⁶² However, Lindbeck holds that religious meanings are a function of their relationship to the whole interpretive scheme and its correlate form of life, and religious propositions are only determinate enough to make truth-claims in the context of religious practice, so those who do not practice the religion cannot understand its propositional claims, however well they understand its vocabulary and grammar.⁶³ It is not obvious why this conclusion follows from the premise. In any case, there appears to be a serious tension here which Lindbeck does not seem to resolve in *The Nature of Doctrine*.

Hauerwas holds similarly that the meaning of Christian convictions and moral notions, like those in other traditions, depend on the languages and stories of that tradition and so may be quite diverse.⁶⁴ He clearly thinks that those differences may be discussed and that particular Christian moral notions may be interpreted in that light to a wider audience.⁶⁵ But the chief condition of their intelligibility is the display of their meaning in the lives and deaths of those who take them to be true, of Christian witnesses.⁶⁶

Frei seems to avoid the tension we find in Lindbeck and helps explain Hauerwas's position. In his later writings, he appealed to the ready intelligibility of Christian community and its uses of Scripture and other signs on analogy with a culture constituted as a system of signs in use. For the outsider, he argues, learn to read and describe the specific meanings of cultural forms in use, by careful attention to their uses and connections, without the need for a conceptually freighted explanatory theory of human culture or religion.⁶⁷ In other words, unlike Lindbeck, Frei is unequivocal in arguing that intratextuality, in all its concrete specificity, is indeed public.⁶⁸ Similarly, the norm against which theologians evaluate the faithfulness of specific Christian practices in context

---

⁶¹Ibid., 133.
⁶²Ibid., 114.
⁶³Ibid., 67–8.
⁶⁴Stanley Hauerwas, *Truthfulness and Tragedy: Further Investigations in Christian Ethics*. (Notre Dame, London: University of Notre Dame Press, 1977), 21–2.
⁶⁵Ibid., 21–2; Stanley Hauerwas, *Christian Existence Today: Essays on Church, World, and Living In Between* (Oregon: Wipf & Stock, 2010), 67–87.
⁶⁶Stanley Hauerwas, *With the Grain of the Universe: The Church's Witness and Natural Theology* (Grand Rapids: Baker Academic, 2013), 214.
⁶⁷Frei, *Types of Christian Theology*, 12–13; Frei, *Theology and Narrative*, 146–7.
⁶⁸Gary Comstock objects that Frei's position, adopted to avoid the problems of fideism, is in conflict with his claim made in *Identity* to protect himself from the need for apologetics, that non-believers cannot understand the text because they do not experience Christ's presence: Gary Comstock, 'Truth or Meaning: Ricoeur versus Frei on Biblical Narrative', *Journal of Religion* 66 no. 2 (1986): 117–40 (126–8).

– the literal reading of biblical narratives – is a component of this culture and intelligible in the same way. The narrative meanings of the more realistic stories prioritized in that practice, moreover, are similarly readily intelligible for they depict a world sufficiently like the everyday world we inhabit, for our slant on the characters depicted is a public one by way of their interaction with one another and their circumstances.[69] It would be perfectly possible, therefore, to follow and understand the logic of the narrative depiction of Jesus Christ in the gospels, as a non-believer. Frei appears to hold that, so read, these stories articulate meanings which have sufficient determinativeness to make truth-claims in respect of their central figure, while being publicly intelligible.

On truth, Lindbeck articulates a complex account of the truth of religions, and of religious utterances, in his *The Nature of Doctrine*, in order to show that a cultural–linguistic view of religion can accommodate religious claims to being unsurpassable.[70] The truth of religions, as idioms for making sense of reality, expressing reality and ordering life, is a matter of the adequacy of their categories: how far you can use them in application to reality and use them to say, do and symbolize true things.[71] A religion may be unsurpassable considered in its totality, as cultural system and correlated form of life, as a massive proposition which is true when, and to the extent that, it shapes its adherents in such a way that they conform to the ultimately real, or in Christian terms, to God's being and will. Religious propositions may be true (or false) in this sense when uttered as part of the total performance of the true religion (ontological truth), provided they cohere with it (intrasystemic truth).

Lindbeck does not elaborate on what he means by the correspondence or conformity of the performed religion as a whole to God's being and will. However, two ways of testing Christianity as a total proposition and Christian propositions or actions do follow from his view, in the absence of any neutral, universal framework for assessing religions.[72] Individual propositions or actions may be assessed in terms of their coherence with the whole religion, as already

---

There is a passage in Frei which can be read that way in isolation, but in context and read carefully, Frei is not saying the text and its logic is unintelligible to non-believers, only it has no personal significance or rational compulsion for them, since they are not committed to belief in Christ's presence. See Frei, *The Identity of Jesus Christ*, 7–8. As he says elsewhere, it is the relationship between meaning and truth (and not a diversity of meaning) which distinguishes believers and unbelievers with respect to the gospel stories: Frei, *Theology and Narrative*, 43.
[69]Frei, *Theology and Narrative*, 36.
[70]Bruce Marshall offers a sophisticated post-liberal account of truth that seeks to build on Frei and Lindbeck, too complex to explore in the scope of this chapter: Bruce D. Marshall, *Trinity and Truth* (Cambridge: Cambridge University Press, 1999).
For a careful critical discussion of these issues, see Adonis Vidu, *Postliberal Theological Method: A Critical Study* (Bletchley: Paternoster, 2005), 116–56.
[71]Lindbeck, *The Nature of Doctrine*, 47.
[72]Lindbeck, *The Nature of Doctrine*, 49, 130.

implied. But religions as a whole may also be assessed as comprehensive interpretive schemes 'within which believers seek to live their lives and understand reality',[73] and which seek to incorporate and interpret features of the world and culture in that framework.[74] While it is not possible to refute them decisively, they can be assessed in terms of their ability to assimilate data and provide adherents with an 'intelligible interpretation in its own terms of the varied situations and realities adherents encounter'.[75] Religions are confirmed or disconfirmed, therefore, over the *longue durée*, 'through an accumulation of successes or failures in making practically and cognitively coherent sense of relevant data' and are not decisively confirmed or disconfirmed for as long as they have adherents.[76] Presumably Lindbeck thinks that such cumulative success or failure may amount to the justification or failure to justify religious truth-claims because he assumes that a religion which is ontologically true will be capable of making sustained sense of a changing world for its adherents.

Hauerwas's emphatic, but not exclusive, focus is on the pragmatic dimensions of truth. Even more than Lindbeck, Hauerwas is chiefly interested in what makes truthful speech and action possible: his focus is on the characters of truthful agents and the truthful stories that shape their perceptions and actions, and the truthful ways of inhabiting those stories. The truth of the Christian story and the convictions embedded in it is primarily a matter of how it forms our lives truly.[77] True stories offer us a way of being in the world that allows us to deal with it by changing ourselves – a way of going on with courage in unknown territory.[78] True stories help us develop skills of perception and understanding, including our relation to the world and how to relate our plans to it.[79] They help us overcome our self-deception and tell us how to live, and know the world, in light of its vision of how the world should be.[80] Knowledge of God is self-involving.[81]

Learning to live and understand by the Christian story requires we learn from a community of witnesses, whose lives interpret the story to us[82] and

---

[73] Ibid., 117.
[74] Ibid., 117–18.
[75] Ibid., 131.
[76] Ibid.
[77] Stanley Hauerwas, *Truthfulness and Tragedy: Further Investigations in Christian Ethics*. (Notre Dame, London: University of Notre Dame Press, 1977), 73.
[78] Ibid., 73, 80.
[79] Ibid., 36–7, 74.
[80] Ibid., 80.
[81] Hauerwas, *With the Grain of the Universe*, 142,
[82] Hauerwas, *The Peaceable Kingdom*, 70.

display its truth.[83] For Hauerwas there is no other way of learning the truth of Christian convictions about God and the world, nor can Christians articulate the truth of their convictions apart from such lives, as the Holy Spirit works through them.[84] Nor can we accept them unless we are transformed by the same Spirit.[85] The rhetorical pragmatic role of witness in telling and learning the truth is necessary because of the fall, and because it is non-coercive and so reflects the gratuitous, nonviolent character of the divine economy and the peaceableness of God's triune life.[86]

An expansive but often implicit realism runs through his account, whose logic Hauerwas does little to explicate. The true story and the pedagogy of truthful witnesses teach us to understand ourselves and live gratefully as the creatures of God we actually are.[87] The positive transformative effects (such as peace) which follow are a function of that realism.[88] The lives of witnesses make claims about the way the world is.[89] There is some resemblance to Lindbeck's account of ontological religious truth here.

Like Lindbeck, Hauerwas's position assumes that the world is never available to us in neutral terms and that the terms in which we otherwise see it and ourselves are deeply deceptive, so there is no neutral basis for assessing the realist claims of Christianity. Coherence plays a part, implicitly, in the justification of Christian beliefs for Hauerwas. The truthful character of Christian convictions is a function of their part in the Christian story[90] and its function. The truthfulness of the testimony of witnesses has to do with how they embody the totality of their beliefs, a way of structuring the whole of the faith.[91] Christian witness coheres with the nature and economy of the God identified in the story, as we have seen. So it would be consistent with Hauerwas to assess the truth of Christian witness in terms of its coherence. Hauerwas also has room for the ad hoc apologetic refutation of challenges to this witness.[92]

However, Hauerwas's explicit emphasis, like Lindbeck's, is on the pragmatic testing of the truthfulness of Christian witness. 'The test of each story is the sort of person it shapes.'[93] Stories may be assessed in terms of their pragmatic fruitfulness, especially in freeing us from destructive and distorted ways of living

---

[83]Hauerwas, *With the Grain of the Universe*, 39, 199.
[84]Ibid., 207–11, 214.
[85]Ibid., 214.
[86]Ibid., 192, 207, 211.
[87]Ibid., 184.
[88]See, for example, Hauerwas, *The Peaceable Kingdom*, 44.
[89]Hauerwas, *With the Grain of the Universe*, 214.
[90]Hauerwas, *Truthfulness and Tragedy*, 77.
[91]Hauerwas, *With the Grain of the Universe*, 214.
[92]Ibid., 240–1.
[93]Ibid., 35.

and seeing, keeping us from violence, and helping us live, non-violently, with tragedy.[94] Similarly, the visible habitability of Christian convictions, embodied in witnesses, is crucial to their epistemic justification.[95] Many of Hauerwas's ethical writings are apologetic in commending this habitability, as we have seen. Yet we learn whose lives to attend to from the story-formed Christian community: the publicness of this testing is a qualified one, and it requires close familiarity, learning and attention.[96]

Lindbeck and Hauerwas' emphases on the pragmatic testing of Christianity's claim to ontological truth require a great deal of Christian churches and their members: the fully coherent, consistent performance of the meaning of one overarching biblical narrative, across lifetimes and eras. They are clearly aware of the failures of actual Christian churches, and Hauerwas at times acknowledges the dependence of the performance and its suasive efficacy on the work of the Holy Spirit. Yet the apologetic demands of their pragmatic understandings of truth do not seem to be able to accommodate the complexity, fallibility, ordinariness and diversity of actual churches.[97] And to place such an emphasis on performance for the display of the meaning and truth of the story risks its clarity and the possibility of the story's function as a publicly intelligible norm of practice.[98]

Such problems do not seem to attend Hans Frei's account of truth. He, too, combines realism with coherentist and pragmatic elements, but in a way which is much more focused on, and deeply shaped by, his Christology. For Frei, the gospel narratives make a cumulative and unique truth claim. Their narrative rendering of the identity of Jesus Christ, he argues, culminating in his resurrection, is such that his identity is inseparable from his being alive as the embodied presence of God. His presence, now, therefore, is the logical entailment of his identity, something that is true only of God (Ex. 3.14). The narrative continuity of Jesus' embodied identity from cross to resurrection makes this claim vulnerable to empirical falsification by the discovery of the corpse of Jesus of Nazareth.[99] However, no empirical or historical argument can be made for its truth, for his presence as one who lives to God is indirect, and the unity of identity and living presence the narratives ascribe to him is without analogy in creaturely experience. The claim rests on the coherence of the logic of the story.

---

[94] Hauerwas, *Truthfulness and Tragedy*, 35–7.
[95] Hauerwas, *With the Grain of the Universe*, 213–14.
[96] Stanley Hauerwas, *The Peaceable Kingdom*, 71.
[97] So Healy on Hauerwas, Healy, *Hauerwas*, 97–8.
[98] Ibid., 114–16.
[99] Frei, *The Identity of Jesus Christ*, 151.

Nevertheless, there are limits to our understanding of that coherence. We cannot explain how it is possible for identity and presence to coincide in someone. We can only seek to think after the reality, by describing the logic that leads to that conclusion and adapting to the purpose concepts that do not overdetermine the meaning of the story, like identity, enacted intention and the self-in-manifestation. But eventually, the logic transcends our ability to describe it conceptually, and we can only narrate the coincidence of identity and presence in this person.[100] Frei extends this approach to the logic of faith in general: one can describe that logic, up to a point, by borrowing concepts ad hoc, and in odd combinations, from other discourses and subordinating and bending them to the partial description of that logic of 'a mystery indefinitely penetrable by reason'.[101] The fragmentary rational grasp of the coherence of their use available to us now may be stated most adequately in negative rules about their combinations.[102]

There are many routes by which people come to affirm such a way of thinking, Frei asserts, and they are quite different from the logic of the story itself. What it means to affirm it as true is to make something which bears remote analogy to a factual claim on the basis of the coherence of this claim with the logic of the story, which one can only partly describe in other terms. It involves something like belief in the inspiration of the stories: that they are, by the gracious condescension of the one to whom they witness, sufficient for that witness. To a considerable extent, the logic of belief thus involves warranting relationships between beliefs, in respect of which an intelligible if partial degree of coherence can be articulated. Finally, the church's basic trust in the story, articulated in such terms, is warranted by its experience of 'the actual, fruitful use religious people make of it in ways that enhance their own and other people's lives'.[103] Frei infers a basic, but complex, long-term pragmatic justification for the church's central use of the story of Jesus in the experience of the church.

The content of this truth claim means that Frei also thinks it is self-involving. For the one whose living presence it affirms makes a claim on every human being, to identify themselves in relation to him, to follow him and pattern our lives after him[104], which is how the story becomes meaningful.[105] Hence, to

---

[100]Frei, *Theology and Narrative*, 36–7.
[101]Ibid., 32–7; Frei, *Types of Christian Theology*, 80–90.
[102]Frei, *Theology and Narrative*, 142.
[103]Ibid., 119. Jason Springs offers one way to defend such an account drawing on the pragmatic inferentialism of Wilfrid Sellars and Robert Brandom. See Springs, *Toward a Generous Orthodoxy*.
[104]Frei, *The Identity of Jesus Christ*, 149.
[105]Ibid., 170–1.

affirm the truth of the story, therefore, involves committing oneself entirely to the grateful love of God and neighbour.[106] Yet this effect, too, is a matter of the work of the Holy Spirit, by which the story is true in our experience, 'by being true to the way it works in one's life'.[107] And it is true, he adds, as an effective measure of human society: 'by holding the world, including the political, economic and social world, to account by the gauge of its truthfulness'.[108] There is thus a cognitive, descriptive sense in which the story is true, and a practical one. But in contrast to Lindbeck and Hauerwas, Frei does not tend to make the former contingent on the latter. Instead, he appeals to the doctrine of the Trinity as a ruled way of articulating their inseparable unity and abiding distinction as the truth of the one God.[109]

As David Tracy argues in *Plurality and Ambiguity*, traditions live by the quality of their conversations, not least, we might infer, across differences.[110] It is possible to see several ways in which Frei's account is open to such conversations, and the critical publicness they afford, without a general account of meaning and truth. The public intelligibility and rationality of literal reading, of the partially describable coherence of Christian belief, makes such conversation possible and invites critical challenges to interpretations of text and the fit between beliefs and between beliefs and practices.

The same applies to the ad hoc use of borrowed concepts to describe the logic of belief. Between the original uses and senses of these concepts and their adapted uses, we may also infer that there would be ad hoc analogies and correlations[111] making the new uses, and their new (if incomplete) coherence, publicly intelligible and comparable with other uses and applications. Such comparisons could inform the kind of critical scrutiny just discussed, and the possibility of making ad hoc arguments to the effect that Christianity can better account for analogous practical commitments and modes of interpretation and judgement pursued in other traditions.[112]

Frei's notion of figural reading of historical events and circumstances also involves a kind of publicly intelligible analogical thinking. For such figural reading involves imagining and understanding persons, situations, events and

---

[106]Ibid., 146.
[107]Frei, *Theology and Narrative*, 210.
[108]Ibid., 2010.
[109]Ibid.
[110]David Tracy, *Plurality and Ambiguity: Hermeneutics, Religion, Hope* (Chicago: University of Chicago Press, 1994), ix, 20.
[111]Springs, *Toward a Generous Orthodoxy*, 135.
[112]See William Werpehowski, 'Ad Hoc Apologetics', *Journal of Religion* 66 no. 3 (1986): 282–301. In drawing on Werpehowski in this way I am following Shin: Daniel D. Shin, *Theology and the Public: Reflections on Hans W. Frei on Hermeneutics, Christology, and Theological Methods* (Lanham: Lexington Books, 2019), 40–4.

experiences of the shared public world in terms of a relationship between the patterns of their describable public features and the patterns of the stories of Jesus Christ. The description of historical events and the judgement of a figural relationship between those patterns at least may be critiqued in terms of how well they fit the data, how far they make sense of all of it.

Frei was clear, in an essay comparing Barth and Schleiermacher, that theologians may be committed both to the integrity of the description of Christian meanings and their truth-claims, and to their public intelligibility and critical scrutiny. One must choose which one prioritizes in a given context, however, and there are costs to either choice.[113] Frei's overall sympathy in his context was with Barth's choice of prioritizing the former over the latter, and borrowing and bending concepts ad hoc to descriptive Christian uses rather than seeking to correlate, unsystematically, Christian meanings with conceptual schemes or academic critical methods from other disciplines. Nevertheless, both choices seek to uphold both sides of the equation as far as they can: it is by no means an either–or. In principle anyone with the skill and sensitivity to learn Christian semiotic uses and trace their internal logic, and compare them with the lived performance of the faith, and its application to interpret and evaluate the world, can judge for themselves whether they find that way of living in and understanding our common world compelling enough to enter upon it and discover its meaningfulness for themselves.

10.5 CONCLUSION

Post-liberal theologians, at least those examined here, are far from being fideistic advocates of a retreat from publicness. Their critiques of forms of public theology premised on putatively universal foundations or general theories of religious experience arise precisely from their commitment to the public engagement of Christian communities and their practices and beliefs: the approaches they critique subvert that engagement precisely by subverting both the integrity of Christian meanings and the specific ways by which they are oriented towards the public realm. Similarly (though less clearly and unambiguously in Lindbeck's case), they aim to recover and exemplify the possibility of speaking constructively into issues of public concern from particularly Christian perspectives and practices, understood in light of Christian readings of their Scriptures. They also articulate accounts of the public intelligibility and truth

---

[113]Frei, *Theology and Narrative*, 197. David Kamitsuka also appeals to this passage in defence of Frei's commitment to 'the importance of validating the theoretical credibility of Christian claims with some kind of accountability to public criteria of intelligibility' (1999, 23–5).

of Christian faith and practice which mix coherentist, correspondence and pragmatist elements. As I have sought to show, there are some significant differences between Lindbeck, Hauerwas and Frei on these issues, and of the three it is Frei's account which, by and large, is most successful in articulating the basis for a post-liberal approach to public theology.

CHAPTER 11

Ecumenical collaboration in public theology

FLORIAN HÖHNE

11.1 INTRODUCTION

Public theology has already been the topic of innumerable books and articles, conferences and workshops.[1] In many of these events and publications, theologians from different denominations have come together. Hence, one might argue that public theology is and always has been a project of ecumenical collaboration. The denominational affiliation of certain approaches to public theology has been made explicit, but public theologians have discussed public theology as ecumenical collaboration not as explicitly and extensively as one might think.[2] On this background, the aim of this chapter is to describe the different denominational origins of public theology (11.3.1 and 11.3.2) and their theoretical (11.3.3) and practical collaboration (11.4). Based on this, I will summarize reasons for understanding public theology as ecumenical theology (11.5). First, it seems necessary to clarify what the terms 'public theology' and 'ecumenical' mean (11.2).

---

[1] Cf. E. Harold Breitenberg Jr., 'To Tell the Truth: Will the Real Public Theology Please Stand Up?', *Journal of the Society of Christian Ethics* 23, no. 2 (2003): 55–96.
[2] Duncan Forrester narrates the story of public theology as ecumenical story: Duncan B. Forrester, 'The Scope of Public Theology', *Studies in Christian Ethics* 17 (2004): 5–19.

11.2 WHAT IS PUBLIC THEOLOGY? WHAT DOES 'ECUMENICAL' MEAN?

11.2.1 Public theology

The term 'public theology' has clearly more than one meaning.[3] It refers at least to an academic discourse, to certain traditions of theological thinking, to religious phenomena in the public sphere or to a programme for leading, representing or reforming the church:[4] Parts of the critique of public theology in Germany have understood it as a programme, namely as a label for the way the representatives of the Protestant Church in Germany participate in societal discourse on political issues.[5] Other works have used the term 'public theology' to discuss religious phenomena in public; in particular prominent figures such as Reinhold Niebuhr, Dietrich Bonhoeffer and Abraham Lincoln were called 'public theologians'.[6] Especially around 1990, a number of books were published that conceptualized public theology as a certain tradition of theological thinking.[7] David Tracy, Breitenberg, and Torsten Meireis, Frederike van Oorschot and myself have suggested seeing public theology as a discourse.[8]

---

[3] Cf. Breitenberg Jr., 'To Tell the Truth', 55f.
[4] See also Ibid., 63–5; Florian Höhne, *Öffentliche Theologie: Begriffsgeschichte und Grundfragen* (Leipzig: Evangelische Verlagsanstalt, 2015); Thomas Wabel, Florian Höhne and Torben Stamer, 'Klingende öffentliche Theologie: Plädoyer für eine methodische Weitung', in *Offentliche Theologie zwischen Klang und Sprache: Hymnen als eine Verkorperungsform von Religion*, ed. Thomas Wabel, Florian Höhne and Torben Stamer (Leipzig: Evangelische Verlagsanstal, 2017), 9–40.
[5] Cf. Johannes Fischer, 'Gefahr der Unduldsamkeit: Die "Öffentliche Theologie" der EKD ist problematisch', *zeitzeichen* (2016): 43–5; Wilhelm Gräb, 'Lebenssinndeutung als Aufgabe der Theologie', *Zeitschrift für Theologie und Kirche* 113, no. 4 (2016): 366–83.
[6] Cf. Martin E. Marty, 'Two Kinds of Two Kinds of Civil Religion', in *American Civil Religion*, ed. Russell E. Richey and Donald G. Jones (New York: Harper & Row, 1974), 139–57; Martin E. Marty, 'Reinhold Niebuhr: Public Theology and the American Experience', *The Journal of Religion* 54, no. 4 (1974): 332–59; Heinrich Bedford-Strohm, 'Dietrich Bonhoeffer als öffentlicher Theologe: Vortrag auf der Jahrestagung 2008 in Eisenach', *igb Bonhoeffer Rundbrief* 87 (2008): 26–40. For this kind of public theological literature see also Breitenberg Jr., 'To Tell the Truth', 63.
[7] I.e. particularly Max L. Stackhouse, *Public Theology and Political Economy: Christian Stewardship in Modern Society* (Grand Rapids, MI: W.B. Eerdmans Publisching Co., 1987); Robert W. McElroy, *The Search for An American Public Theology: The Contribution of John Courtney Murray* (New York: Paulist Press, 1989); Ronald F Thiemann, *Constructing a Public Theology: The Church in a Pluralistic Culture* (Louisville, KY: Westminster/John Knox Press, 1991); Robert Benne, *The Paradoxical Vision: A Public Theology for the Twenty-first Century* (Minneapolis: Fortress Press, 1995).
[8] Cf. David Tracy, 'Theology as Public Discourse', *The Christian Century* (1975): 280–4; Breitenberg Jr., 'To Tell the Truth'; Frederike van Oorschot, 'Public Theology Facing Globalization', in *Contextuality and Intercontextuality in Public Theology: Proceedings from the Bamberg Conference 23.-25.06.2011*, Theology in the Public Square/Theologie in Der Öffentlichkeit Band 4 (Zürich; Berlin: Lit, 2013), 225–31; Florian Höhne, 'Kinship in Time? Exploring the Relation of Public Theologies and Moltmann's Early Political Theology', in *Contextuality and Intercontextuality in Public Theology: Proceedings from the Bamberg Conference 23.-25.06.2011* (Zürich; Berlin: Lit,

Breitenberg defines: 'Public theology is thus theologically informed public discourse about public issues, addressed to the church, synagogue, mosque, temple, or other religious body, as well as the larger public or publics, argued in ways that can be evaluated and judged by publicly available warrants and criteria.'[9]

Understood as a headline for a discourse, public theology does not refer to one specific tradition of theological thinking that differs from others in method or claims. Rather, it signifies a discourse that is inherently diverse and collaborative. It is essential to a discursive understanding of public theology that it combines voices from different religious, denominational and cultural traditions. Hence, public theology as a discourse claims to be inherently ecumenically collaborative.

Public theology can be 'understood as theologically informed interdisciplinary discourse on public issues and the scholarly reflection thereof'.[10] According to this definition, it is the common topic that brings different theologians, perspectives and positions together in a discourse called 'public theology': the discourse is about 'public issues'. While public theologians have often seen these issues to be 'ethical in nature',[11] the scope of public theology includes all issues of public relevance. This definition implies that public theology involves a scholarly (self-)reflection of the public praxis. Public theology often wavered between a public and religious praxis itself and the scholarly reflection thereof.[12] This points to the indissoluble connection between public praxis and academic reflections:[13] On the one hand, academic discourse has a public dimension itself, insofar as it is more or less publically accessible and deals more or less with topics of public relevance. On the other hand, those who raise religious voices in the public sphere – representatives of churches for instance – often are involved in discourses of theological self-reflection as well.

The scholarly dimension of public practices and discourses and the public dimension of academic discourse need to be kept in mind where this chapter distinguishes between academic discourse and public practices in order to ask for ecumenical collaboration in both fields.

2013), 53–70; Torsten Meireis, 'Politischer Gottesdienst als öffentliche Theologie – Bedeutung, Rahmen und theologische Bedingungen', in *Politischer Gottesdienst?! Praktische Theologie im reformierten Kontext*, ed. Katrin Kusmierz and David Plüss, Vol. 8 (Zürich: Theologischer Verlag Zürich, 2013), 153–75.
[9]Breitenberg Jr., 'To Tell the Truth', 66.
[10]Cf. Berlin Institute for Public Theology, 'Mission Statement', https://www.theologie.hu-berlin.de/de/professuren/institute/bipt (last accessed 16 January 2020).
[11]Stackhouse, *Public Theology and Political Economy*, xi.
[12]Cf. Höhne, *Öffentliche Theologie*, 37f; Wabel, Höhne and Stamer, 'Klingende öffentliche Theologie', 14.
[13]Cf. Höhne, *Öffentliche Theologie*, 37f.

11.2.2 Ecumenism

The question of how to define the term 'ecumenical' is itself a contested issue between different Christian traditions.[14] While Roman Catholic positions see the ecumenical task in making the 'unity of the church in the world visible',[15] the 'Leuenberg Agreement' between 'Reformation churches in Europe' focuses on 'church fellowship' between different denominations including 'table and pulpit fellowship';[16] the Protestant churches in Germany have adopted this model of 'reconciled diversity'.[17]

For the purpose of this chapter, it makes sense to distinguish two senses of 'ecumenical'. The Greek origins of the term simply refer to the entirety of the 'inhabited world'.[18] Following such a broad understanding, the term 'ecumenical' points to the global, international and intercontextual horizon of Christian theologies, practices and institutions. In this broad sense, ecumenical collaboration means intercontextual collaboration. Public theology is ecumenical in this sense, insofar as it reflects on its topics on a global horizon.[19]

In a more narrow sense, 'ecumenical' refers to the practical and theological ways of dealing with the denominational diversity of Christianity. Ulrich H. J. Körtner has defined ecumenism as signifying the 'problem of diversity and unity of Christianity'.[20] In this narrow sense, public theology is ecumenically collaborative insofar as its discourse and practices bring different Christian denominations together.

---

[14]Cf. for example Ulrich H. J. Körtner, *Wohin steuert die Ökumene?*: *Vom Konsens- zum Differenzmodell* (Göttingen: Vandenhoeck & Ruprecht, 2005); Ulrich H. J. Körtner, *Ökumenische Kirchenkunde*, Bd. 9. (Leipzig: Evangelische Verlagsanstalt, 2018).

[15]Birgitta Kleinschwärzer-Meister, 'Ökumene I. Dogmatisch 1. Katholisches Verständnis', in *Religion in Geschichte und Gegenwart*, fourth edn., Bd. 6 (Tübingen: Mohr Siebeck, 2003), cols. 507–8. My translation of the quote: 'Ö. hat die Aufgabe, die in Christus gegebene Einheit wieder als Einheit der Kirche in der Welt sichtbar werden zu lassen.' See also UR (Unitatis Redintegratio), http://www.vatican.va/archive/hist_councils/ii_vatican_council/documents/vat-ii_decree_19641121_unitatis-redintegratio_en.html (last accessed 31 January 2020).

[16]Community of Protestant Churches in Europe, 'Agreement between Reformation Churches in Europe (The Leuenberg Agreement)', 1973, https://www.leuenberg.eu/documents/ (last accessed 13 February 2021).

[17]Ulrich H. J. Körtner, *Wohin steuert die Ökumene?*: *Vom Konsens- zum Differenzmodell* (Göttingen: Vandenhoeck & Ruprecht, 2005); Körtner, *Kirchenkunde*, 21, my translation of 'versöhnte Verschiedenheit', with reference to Rat der EKD, *Kirchengemeinschaft nach evangelischem Verständnis*: *Ein Votum zum geordneten Miteinander bekenntnisverschiedener Kirchen*. Hannover, 2001, https://www.ekd.de/22741.htm (last accessed 13 February 2021).

[18]Birgitta Kleinschwärzer-Meister, 'Ökumene I. Dogmatisch 1. Katholisches Verständnis'; Jutta Koslowski, 'Ökumene im Aufbruch – Die Entwicklung der ökumenischen Bewegung im 20. Jahrhundert' (2017): 17–36.

[19]Cf. van Oorschot, 'Public Theology Facing Globalization', 225f.

[20]My translation of: 'Der Begriff der Ökumene bezeichnet also das Problem von Vielfalt und Einheit der Christenheit'; Körtner, *Wohin steuert die Ökumene?*, 26.

The narrow and the wider sense of 'ecumenical' are interconnected, because denominational traditions are deeply intertwined with the context in which they are.[21] Different contexts with different relations of church and state, different constellations of power and different political cultures have led to different contextual and denominational approaches to public theology. The history of denominations and their distribution over the world is deeply intertwined with the history of colonialization and power.[22] Hence, the quest for ecumenical collaboration is also the quest for the cooperation of different contextual traditions whose power relations are asymmetrical.

11.3 THE ACADEMIC DISCOURSE OF PUBLIC THEOLOGY

11.3.1 Denominational diversity of origins

The discourse 'public theology' is fundamentally diverse, insofar as it is rooted in different denominational traditions. Public theology did not originate in one denominational tradition from where it spread to others; rather, it has its roots in different traditions and inherits different features from there.[23] The six stories of public theology Dirk Smit has summarized implicitly illustrate this denominational diversity.[24] Indebted to Smit's work, the following stories can be distinguished and connected with certain denominational heritages.[25]

11.3.1.1 Civil religion in the United States and a Lutheran story The *dominant story* traces the use of the term back to the Lutheran church historian and religious scholar Martin E. Marty who introduced the term 'public theologians' in the debate on American civil religion in the early 1970s:[26] Robert N. Bellah had introduced the notion of 'civil religion' to reflect the

---

[21]For the connection of context and denomination, see also Körtner, *Kirchenkunde*, 19.
[22]Cf. Ulrike Link-Wieczorek, 'Die Gestalt der Konfessionen in interkultureller Vielfalt', in *Basiswissen Ökumene, Band 1: Ökumenische Entwicklungen – Brennpunkte*, ed. Michael Kappes, Sabine Pemsel-Maier, Ulrike Link-Wieczorek, and Oliver Schuegraf (Leipzig Evangelische Verlagsanstalt, 2017), 87–105.
[23]See a similar thesis about the contextual nature of public theology: Dirk J. Smit, 'The Paradigm of Public Theology – Origins and Development', in *Contextuality and Intercontextuality in Public Theology: Proceedings from the Bamberg Conference 23.-25.06.2011*, ed. Heinrich Bedford-Strohm, Florian Höhne and Tobias Reitmeier (Zürich; Berlin: Lit, 2013), 11–23.
[24]Cf. Ibid.
[25]The first five of the following stories are described by Smit. The following description is indebted to Smit's narration of these story. Cf. Ibid.
[26]Cf. for this and the following description Ibid., 11–13, Quote on 11. Cf. also Breitenberg, Jr., 'To Tell The Truth', 56f.

'religious dimension of American democracy',[27] and Marty suggested to clarify this notion by distinguishing 'two kinds of two kinds of civil religion'.[28] For one kind that works with reference to God and uses religious references to criticize society in what Marty calls 'prophetic mode', he introduces the term 'public theologians' that qualifies the public role of people as diverse as Abraham Lincoln and Reinhold Niebuhr.[29] Thereby, Marty uses the category 'public theology' to reflect the public and religious witness of certain persons. This can be seen as the expression of a genuinely Lutheran mindset, insofar as Lutheran traditions of social thinking tend to focus on what the individual Christians do in their offices. Paradigmatically, Robert Benne later sketched such a genuinely Lutheran nudge to public theology. He sees the most important public role of the church in its indirect influence on society: the 'inward formation of the heart' of individual believers in congregations makes them as individuals engage in the public sphere.[30] Similarly, the liberal theology of 'Öffentlicher Protestantismus' in Germany actualizes this part of Lutheran traditions in its focus on the individual freedom and witness in public.[31]

11.3.1.2 Public discourse and a Catholic story in the United States The second story Smit narrates also takes place in Chicago but is 'a totally different story'.[32] In an article, published in 1975 in *The Christian Century*, the Catholic theologian David Tracy suggested to understand 'theology as public discourse'.[33] It is a 'totally different story' because it is not about the public role of prominent Christian thinkers and politicians but about 'the very character of the discipline itself',[34] as Tracy puts it right in the first paragraph of his famous article: 'The central question becomes the very character of the discipline itself: What modes of argumentation, which methods, what warrants, backings, evidence can count for or against a public statement by a physicist, a historian, a philosopher, a theologian?'[35] Smit suggests to interpret 'Tracy's own theological biography as

---

[27]Robert N. Bellah, 'American Civil Religion in the 1970s', in *American Civil Religion*, ed. Russell E. Richey and Douglas G. Jones (New York, 1974), 255–71. Rolf Schieder, *Civil Religion: Die religiöse Dimension der politischen Kultur* (Gütersloh: Gütersloher Verlagshaus Mohn, 1987).
[28]Cf. Marty, 'Two Kinds of Two Kinds of Civil Religion'.
[29]Cf. Ibid., 147–9.
[30]Cf. Benne, *The Paradoxical Vision*, 184f (quote on 185).
[31]Cf. Christian Albrecht and Reiner Anselm, *Öffentlicher Protestantismus: Zur aktuellen Debatte um gesellschaftliche Präsenz und politische Aufgaben des evangelischen Christentums* (Zürich: Theologischer Verlag Zürich, 2017).
[32]Cf. Smit, 'The Paradigm of Public Theology', 13–15 (Quote on 13).
[33]Cf. Tracy, 'Theology as Public Discourse'; Smit, 'The Paradigm of Public Theology', 13.
[34]Ibid., 11–23.
[35]Tracy, 'Theology as Public Discourse'. Also quoted by Smit, 'The Paradigm of Public Theology', 13. Similarly, Linell E. Cady focuses on the role of the academic theologian: 'In large part it reflects my effort to work out a satisfactory identity as a theologian within the context of a religious studies

the gradual fulfillment of this programmatic essay', because he published on Jürgen Habermas's work and because his famous distinction between the three publics of theology – church, academy and society – is about different modes of argumentation, warrants and methods.[36] Public theology in this sense of a Catholic theologian centres less on ethics than Marty's sense of public theology and is more about the hermeneutics of central Christian doctrines or 'classics'.[37]

11.3.1.3 The public church and a Protestant story in Germany Smit exemplifies his third story with the life and work of the German theologian Wolfgang Huber.[38] Already in his habilitation 'Kirche und Öffentlichkeit', which was published in 1973, Huber discussed the term 'public theology':[39] he was looking for an alternative term for 'political theology', a term used by Jürgen Moltmann, Johann Baptist Metz and others, to discuss the political role of the church, theology and Christianity.[40] According to Huber 'public theology' could emphasize the role of society and the interconnection between individual existence and societal processes.[41] Nevertheless, in 1972–3, Huber decides not to use the term 'public theology' because it is too vague.[42] But twenty years later, Huber starts to co-edit a book series called 'Öffentliche Theologie',[43] that is, 'public theology' and the term begins to gain a certain popularity in the German context. The reason for that is – to my view – the historical context: in the last years of the German Democratic Republic (GDR), certain Christian groups and congregations had played a role in organizing public spheres in the society. This experience of societal relevance of Christian groups makes it plausible to widen the focus on the churches' role in society. This is precisely what the term 'public theology' could emphasize.

---

department of a large public university.' Linell E. Cady, *Religion, Theology, and American Public Life* (Albany: State University of New York Press, 1993).

[36]Smit, 'The Paradigm of Public Theology', 14. See Ibid. for the reference to the following works of Tracy on Habermas: David Tracy, 'Theology, Critical Social Theory, and the Public Realm', in *Habermas, Modernity, and Public Theology*, ed. Don S. Browning and Francis Schüssler Fiorenza (New York: Crossroad, 1992), 19–42. On the three publics see David Tracy, *The Analogical Imagination: Christian Theology and the Culture of Pluralism* (London: SCM Press, 1981); David Tracy, 'Three Kinds of Publicness in Public Theology', *International Journal of Public Theology* 8, no. 3 (2014): 330–4.

[37]For the term, see Tracy himself: Tracy, *The Analogical imagination*, 99–115.

[38]For Smit's narration of this story, see Smit, 'The Paradigm of Public Theology', 15f.

[39]Cf. Wolfgang Huber, *Kirche und Öffentlichkeit* (Stuttgart: Ernst Klett, 1973); Wolfgang Vögele, *Zivilreligion in der Bundesrepublik Deutschland* (Gütersloh: Chr. Kaiser/ Gütersloher Verlagshaus, 1994).

[40]Huber, *Kirche und Öffentlichkeit*, 477f.

[41]Cf. Ibid., 478.

[42]Cf. Ibid.; Vögele, *Zivilreligion in der Bundesrepublik Deutschland*, 421.

[43]Cf. Wolfgang Vögele, *Zivilreligion in der Bundesrepublik Deutschland* (Gütersloh: Chr. Kaiser/ Gütersloher Verlagshaus, 1994).

This is a story centred on a Protestant theologian in Germany, Wolfgang Huber. It focuses on the responsibility of the church, and it understands this responsibility not only as political but also as societal.

11.3.1.4 Stories in transformation societies Despite their denominational difference, these three stories took place in contexts of the Global North, in more or less democratic societies.[44] Issues around the public and political relevance of Christian traditions also played and play a role in 'transformation societies'.[45] Dirk Smit identifies a fourth narrative in these contexts, where the term 'public theology' is often deliberatively[46] not used.[47] These stories are less about the civil contribution of theology to a public discourse and more about struggles: 'struggles for liberation, freedom and freedoms; struggles for justice, dignity and rights; struggles for acknowledgment, equity and equality; struggles for peace and for overcoming oppression and violence'.[48] Smit lists different names given to these theologies: 'liberation, black, contextual, prophetic, kairos'-theologies.[49] Smit does not tie them to any particular denominational tradition. Rather, they form an own theological tradition or practice that is often trans-denominational.[50] Smit discusses whether it is legitimate to call these theologies public theologies although they often criticize the term themselves. Independent of this issue, some of these traditions have strongly influenced or even led into public theology: the South African theologian John de Gruchy, for example, describes a 'significant theological event' in Cape Town in 1999 under the headline 'Public Theologies and Christian Conviction in a Democratic Society' as follows:[51] 'Secondly, whereas previously the liberation struggle was the core around which everything else was debated, now the focal point is democratic transformation, and within that the enormous challenge of inequality and poverty.'[52] Heinrich Bedford-Strohm, public theologian and

---

[44]Cf. Smit, 'The Paradigm of Public Theology', 16f.
[45]Ibid., 17.
[46]As quoted also by Smit, the South African Theologian Tinyiko Maluleke has criticized public theology for being too exclusivist, too harmonious and too civil for a context with so many angry people as South Africa was. Tinyiko S. Maluleke, 'Reflections and Resources the Elusive Public of Public Theology: A Response to William Storrar', *International Journal of Public Theology* 5, no. 1 (2011): 79–89; Smit, 'The Paradigm of Public Theology', 17f.
[47]Cf. Smit, 'The Paradigm of Public Theology', 11–23.
[48]Ibid., 17.
[49]Ibid.
[50]See for example John de Gruchy's reference to the 'South African Council of Churches': John W. de Gruchy, 'From Political to Public Theologies: The Role of Theology in Public Life in South Africa', in *Public Theology for the 21st Century: Essays in Honour of Duncan B. Forrester*, ed. Duncan B. Forrester, William Storrar, and Andrew Morton (London: T&T Clark, 2004), 45–62.
[51]Ibid., partly in bold types in the original.
[52]Ibid., 54.

Protestant bishop in Germany, has made this connection explicit by prominently writing about 'liberation theology for a democratic society'.[53] Hence, the traditions of liberation theologies have directly and indirectly, explicitly and implicitly contributed to the wideness of denominational plurality in the roots of public theological thought and action.

11.3.1.5 Ecumenical Movement as a story of public theology Smit describes another story of public theology in which 'the term public theology was not used' but whose 'programs were ecumenical attempts to deal with the questions of public theology but under global conditions' – namely the Ecumenical Movement.[54] While there had been more 'episodic' and person-bound attempts to reconcile the Christian denominations and enable more unity earlier, the attempts in the twentieth century had a 'new quality' and more continuity.[55] In 1910, the World Missionary Conference in Edinburgh laid grounds for the Ecumenical Movement which took particularly two forms, the Life and Work Movement and the Faith and Order Movement, one seeking practical collaboration and one doctrinal communication.[56] After the Second World War, both movements came together in the World Council of Churches (WCC), founded in 1948 in Amsterdam.[57] Its 'most important institution' is 'the General Assembly, which gathers approximately every seven years'.[58] From its beginning, issues of public theology, of publically relevant social thought, of justice and peace[59] have been an important part of the discussions and resolutions. The Section III of the founding conference in Amsterdam (1948) already worked on the topic 'The Church and the Disorder of Society'.[60] There and seven years later in Evanston the term 'Responsible Society' was discussed as orientation for social thought and reform.[61] In later debates about the 'revolutionary social change' and the 'solidarity with the victims of oppression', the term 'responsible society' gave 'way in favor of biblical themes available

---

[53] Heinrich Bedford-Strohm, *Liberation Theology for a Democratic Society: Essays in Public Theology*, Band 7 (Zürich: LIT, 2018).
[54] Smit, 'The Paradigm of Public Theology', 19. For this and the following, see also Ibid., 18f.
[55] Cf. Koslowski, 'Ökumene im Aufbruch', 19f. My translation of quotes.
[56] Cf. Ibid., 20f.
[57] Cf. Ibid., 22f.
[58] Ibid., 24, my translation.
[59] Cf. Ibid., 25.
[60] W. A. Visser 't Hooft and The Assembly of the World Council of Churches, *The First Assembly of the World Council of Churches Held at Amsterdam, August 22nd to September 4th, 1948: (Official Report) 1948* (London: SCM Press, 1949).
[61] Cf. Ibid., 77f; H. W. A. Visser 't Hooft, ed., *The Evanston Report: The Second Assembly of the World Council of Churches 1954* (London: SCM Press, 1955). See also Smit, 'The Paradigm of Public Theology', 18f.

to everyone'.⁶² At least from '1948 to 1974 the WCC had placed emphasis on the problem of "poverty"'.⁶³ Until the Nairobi-Assembly in 1975, ecumenical thinking about development moved (further) 'away from Western paradigms towards participatory postures'.⁶⁴ The new programme from Nairobi was called 'Towards a Just, Participatory and Sustainable Society (JPSS)'.⁶⁵ The sixth Assembly in Vancouver (1983) led to 'a conciliar process of mutual commitment to justice, peace and the integrity of creation (JPIC)'.⁶⁶

Of course, the term 'public theology' is not used programmatically.⁶⁷ However, with these topics discussed, the story of the Ecumenical Movement and of the WCC is clearly a story of public theology. Accordingly, Duncan Forrester described the emergence and development of an 'Ecumenical Public Theology' and 'Ecumenical Social Ethics' in connection with the history of the Ecumenical Movement.⁶⁸ The WCC is even part of the story of academic public theology, because the Assemblies and Sections provided a forum for the discussion of academic theologians. At least implicitly, present public theology has its roots also in the Ecumenical Movement, particularly because the international and global horizon of ecumenical meetings has a substantial impact on public theology: when theologians from the Global South and the Global North come together, contextual problems are seen in a wider, intercontextual horizon. According to Smit, the 'ecumenical attempts' were 'taking the complexity of many contexts into account, contexts often ignored by those doing public theology in the more homogenous situations of particular nation-states'.⁶⁹

Simultaneously, it needs to be said that the Ecumenical Movements and the WCC do not incorporate all Christian denominations: they are multilateral but not universal movements in Christianity – particularly the denomination with most members, the Roman Catholic Church, is not a (full) member.⁷⁰

---

⁶²Lewis S. Mudge, 'Ecumenical Social Thought', in *A History of the Ecumenical Movement*, ed. John Briggs, Mercy Amba Oduyoye, and Georges Tsetsis, Vol. 3 (Geneva: WCC Publications, 2004), 279–321; Torsten Meireis, 'Schöpfung und Transformation: Nachhaltigkeit in protestantischer Perspektive', *Nachhaltigkeit* (2016): 15–50.
⁶³Mudge, 'Ecumenical Social Thought', 287.
⁶⁴Ibid., 290.
⁶⁵Ibid., 291. For all these programmes see also Smit, 'The Paradigm of Public Theology', 18f; and Meireis, 'Schöpfung und Transformation', 20f.
⁶⁶Mudge, 'Ecumenical Social Thought', 296.
⁶⁷Cf. Smit, 'The Paradigm of Public Theology', 19.
⁶⁸Cf. Forrester, 'The Scope of Public Theology'.
⁶⁹Smit, 'The Paradigm of Public Theology', 19.
⁷⁰Cf. Koslowski, 'Ökumene im Aufbruch', 23, 27–32.

11.3.1.6 Evangelical stories into public theology In addition to the stories of public theology Dirk Smit narrated in 2013, there is another storyline that needs to be added, particularly because it might be of more importance in the future. It is the story of theologians from an evangelical, Pentecostal or Charismatic background who seek to develop a public theology and engage in research and education in public theology. Vincent E. Bacote's work serves as an example of that. In the preface to his book on 'The Spirit *in* Public Theology', published in 2005, he mentions his early 'experience with the parachurch organization the Navigators and the subculture of American evangelicalism' and identifies 'Pentecostalism' and 'the charismatic movement' with the 'evangelical circles with which I am familiar'.[71] He describes the starting point of his own theological development, which can be seen as a starting point for an evangelical development into public theology as follows:

> I had been exposed to approaches to Christian living that strongly emphasized the distinction between Christians and 'the world.' In this approach to Christian living, engagement in cultural activity was encouraged only if the public activity was distinctly Christian. This meant that the activity had to have objectives that were either evangelistic or aimed at spiritual edification. In addition, there was a skeptical attitude toward the value of endeavors such as political action and other forms of societal engagement.[72]

Drawing on the problematic work of the Dutch Calvinist theologian and politician Abraham Kuyper, Bacote finds a doctrinal way out of this situation in the 'connection between pneumatology and common grace'.[73] For him, it is the 'work of the Spirit in creation in a manner that is not explicitly redemptive [. . .] that provides a reason for Christian engagement in society'.[74] While one might want to discuss this dogmatic claim, the story of theological development Bacote tells his readers clearly is a story of public theology: the evangelical story of public theology starts with a sharp distinction between Christians and the world and leads to a public theology that develops doctrinal reasons for public engagement. With stories like this, public theology has not only Reformed, Lutheran and Catholic origins but also roots in Evangelicalism. As evangelical and Pentecostal movements gain members and relevance in global Christianity,[75] this story might become more important.

---

[71]Vincent E. Bacote, *The Spirit in Public Theology: Appropriating the Legacy of Abraham Kuyper* (Grand Rapids, MI: Baker Academic, 2005).
[72]Ibid., 7.
[73]Ibid., 8.
[74]Ibid., 9.
[75]Cf. Koslowski, 'Ökumene im Aufbruch', 34.

11.3.2 Denomination diversity of contents

These different stories show the diverse denominational origins of the academic discourse 'public theology'. The late 1980s and early 1990s saw some programmatic books being published on public theology, particularly in the United States. These concepts of public theology were written by theologians from different denominational traditions as well: Robert Benne has and Ronald F. Thiemann had a Lutheran background, Robert W. McElroy, Michael J. Himes and Kenneth R. Himes, O.F.M, wrote Catholic public theologies and the work of Max L. Stackhouse and others stand in United Church of Christ-traditions and Reformed traditions.[76] These works show how different denominational traditions provide different theological frameworks for thinking of theology, the church and religious traditions as (inherently) public.[77]

In the Roman Catholic tradition, natural law thinking has provided such a framework and basis for public theology. Robert McElroy has suggested seeing the work of John Courtney Murray as 'most compelling and comprehensive foundation for public theology in the United States today. Murray's natural law methodology, with its ability to project spiritual themes in a non-sectarian way, remains the most promising basis for public discourse on the role of religious values in American society'.[78] According to this, natural law is 'a valid description of the moral experience of all humankind' and hence accessible to 'all people'.[79]

Theologians in Lutheran traditions have worked with the Two-Kingdoms-Doctrine and the distinction between the Law and the Gospel, which leads to a partly similar outcome. Robert Benne, for example, distinguished two different kinds of God's rule and paralleled these with the distinction between the Law and the Gospel: 'God governs the "kingdom on the left" with his law and the "kingdom on the right" with his gospel. God's aim in both modes of rule is the same, to overcome evil and recall the disobedient creation to himself, but God uses very different means in each "kingdom".'[80] The Law provides a 'moral guidance system'; following this guidance is 'nonredemptive'.[81] The Gospel is 'God's saving Word', received by individuals

---

[76] Cf. Benne, *The Paradoxical Vision*; Thiemann, *Constructing a Public Theology*; McElroy, *The Search for An American Public Theology*; Michael J. Himes and Kenneth R. Himes, *Fullness of Faith: The Public Significance of Theology* (New York: Paulist Press, 1993). Stackhouse, *Public Theology and Political Economy*.
[77] For a more extensive elaboration of the following traditions, see Höhne, *Öffentliche Theologie*.
[78] McElroy, *The Search for An American Public Theology*, 183. See also Höhne, *Öffentliche Theologie*, 50.
[79] McElroy, *The Search for An American Public Theology*, 55.
[80] Benne, *The Paradoxical Vision*, 82; Höhne, *Öffentliche Theologie*, 58.
[81] Benne, *The Paradoxical Vision*, 82, 85.

'through the power of the Holy Spirit'.[82] While Benne also emphasizes the (indirect) public relevance of the Gospel, he warns theology of confusing the two:[83] 'The extravagant love revealed in the gospel cannot become the guiding principle for ordering life in the rough and tumble of this world.'[84] Thereby, the framework for public theology is the ordering law, in 'constant judgment' and 'lure' of the gospel and the indirect influence of the gospel through individual believers.[85]

Reformed traditions contributed the contested concepts of 'common grace' and 'sphere sovereignty' and particularly the Barthian notion of Christ's (kingly) reign to the debate.[86] In opposition to sharp separations of the two rules of God, the doctrine on Christ's reign emphasized that Christ is the ruler in all spheres of life, including the state.[87] This idea lays ground for a public relevance of the gospel and 'extravagant love'; Barth sees analogies to the Kingdom of God as guiding images for political engagement.[88]

This brief overview shows that different denominations have different reasons and different frameworks for conceptualizing public theology and entering the public discourse.

11.3.3 Ecumenical collaboration

The last paragraphs have shown the denominational diversity in public theology. The different traditions and theologians associate on different levels: ideas and theological works from one denomination are observed by and sometimes even adopted in other denominational theologies. There is ecumenical collaboration between individual scholars and inside institutes for public theology. The 'Companion to Public Theology' (2017), edited by Sebastian Kim and Katie Day, illustrates the former:[89] while Kim teaches at Fuller Theological Seminary – an 'evangelical, multidenominational' school – Katie Day, being a Presbyterian herself, was a professor at the United Lutheran Seminary.[90] Many other edited volumes published on public theology are not only international and interdisciplinary but multidenominational, bringing together authors of different denominational traditions. The team of the 'Berlin Institute for Public

---

[82]Ibid., 86.
[83]Ibid., 87f.
[84]Ibid., 87.
[85]Ibid., 87–9, 184f. Quote on 88.
[86]Cf. the summary in Höhne, *Öffentliche Theologie*, 52–7.
[87]Cf. Huber, *Kirche und Öffentlichkeit*, 453–65, part. 453f, 461.
[88]Cf. Karl Barth, *Christengemeinde und Bürgergemeinde*, 7 (Stuttgart: Kohlhammer, 1946); Huber, *Kirche und Öffentlichkeit*, 461.
[89]Sebastian Kim, and Katie Day, *A Companion to Public Theology* (Leiden: Brill, 2017).
[90]See: https://www.fuller.edu/about/mission-and-values/ and https://www.unitedlutheranseminary.edu/faculty-staff/katie-day (last accessed 3 February 2020).

Theology' illustrates the ecumenical collaboration within institutes: it consists of Reformed, Methodist, Lutheran, Roman Catholic, Jewish and Islamic scholars.[91]

One important institution of ecumenical collaboration on a global level is the Global Network for Public Theology (GNPT). The network was founded in May 2007 at Princeton:[92] it connects research 'institutions from all continents', from different contexts and different denominational traditions; its self-declared task is to 'foster scholarly exchange about the contribution of Christianity to public discourse in such diverse fields as social ethics, environmental ethics, and political ethics'.[93] While the work of the GNPT in itself can be seen as ecumenical collaboration, it also allows for further ecumenical collaboration and networking, particularly by two means: since 2007, the triennial consultation brings theologians from all over the world together to discuss topics of public theology. The Consultation in 2013 at the University of Chester focused on 'Public Theology in an Age of Global Media', in 2016 the network met in South Africa at Stellenbosch University and in 2019 in Bamberg.[94] The topic in Bamberg was 'Place and Space: Theological perspectives on living in the world'.[95] Second, the 'International Journal of Public Theology', 'affiliated with the Global Network for Public Theology',[96] provides a medium to publish and discuss articles on issues of public theology. While the authors of the articles published in this journal come from different denominations and even religions, ecumenical collaboration itself has been astonishingly little an explicit topic of the publications.

The list of member institutions of the GNPT contains Presbyterian, Lutheran and Baptist as well as Roman Catholic centres, the Australian Catholic University, for example.[97] Nevertheless, one can perceive a certain overbalance of Protestant, particularly of Reformed or Presbyterian perspectives.

---

[91]Cf. https://www.theologie.hu-berlin.de/de/professuren/institute/bipt/members (last accessed 3 February 2020).
[92]For this and the following information, see Höhne, *Öffentliche Theologie*, 31. The literature quoted there and the homepage of the GNPT: https://gnpublictheology.wordpress.com (last accessed 3 February 2020).
[93]Cf. https://gnpublictheology.wordpress.com/about-gnpt/ (last accessed 3 February 2020).
[94]Cf. https://gnpublictheology.wordpress.com/previous-conferences/ (last accessed 3 February 2020).
[95]Cf. https://gnpublictheology.wordpress.com/2018/06/20/call-for-papers/ (last accessed 3 February 2020).
[96]Cf. https://brill.com/view/journals/ijpt/ijpt-overview.xml (last accessed 3 February 2020).
[97]Cf. https://www.chester.ac.uk/node/15322 (last accessed 3 February 2020).

11.4 THE SOCIETAL AND ECCLESIAL PRAXIS OF PUBLIC THEOLOGY

A description of public ecumenical collaboration in church and society remains all too easily limited to describing collaboration and dialogue on an institutional level: between official church representatives and appointed theologians. To get a broader picture, it is helpful to distinguish different levels of collaboration and dialogue. This causes theoretical problems, because any categories available for this distinction would be specific to a certain denominational and contextual tradition and thus contested. Two examples for that: first, the Protestant theologian Wolfgang Huber has criticized and modified a distinction of four forms of the church drawn from the Roman Catholic parlance: the universal church (*ecclesia universalis*), the particular church (*ecclesia particularis*), the congregation and the religious order.[98] Huber problematizes particularly the distinction between the first two terms: every universal church – including the Catholic world-church – would have particularities, while every congregation would represent 'the universality of the church'.[99] Hence, Huber suggests distinguishing between four forms of the church: the federation, the regional church, the congregation and the initiative-group.[100] Second, the German practical theologian Dietrich Rössler has prominently distinguished the forms of modern Christianity: the ecclesial form, the societal or public form, and the 'individual or private' form.[101] Rössler's distinction is specific to the context of Western modernity (in Germany) with 'cultural manifestations' of Christian traditions and individualized forms of religion.[102]

Inspired by these two examples, the following levels of ecumenical encounters and collaborations can be distinguished: institutional, congregational, (grassroots) initiative-based and societal collaborations in public practice. I will name examples for each level in the contextual perspective of a Protestant in Germany.

11.4.1 *Congregational collaboration*

First, and maybe most importantly, there are innumerable ecumenical collaborations of public relevance on the congregational level.[103] There are

---

[98]Wolfgang Huber, *Kirche*, 2nd edn. (München: Kaiser, 1988).
[99]Ibid., my translation.
[100]Cf. Ibid., 46.
[101]Dietrich Rössler, *Grundriß der praktischen Theologie*, 2nd edn. (Berlin: de Gruyter, 1994), my translation.
[102]Ibid., my translation.
[103]See also in similar German words: 'So bedeutsam solche offiziellen Übereinkünfte auch sein mögen – am wichtigsten für die ökumenische Bewegung sind wohl die unzähligen Initiativen, die

ecumenical groups with Protestant and Roman Catholic members that discuss doctrinal, ethical and political issues. Congregations of different denominations collaborate in organizing parts of the common life in their village or urban district: common initiatives and events, invitations to each other's events. Koslowski mentions diaconal and ecumenically collaborative projects to help the homeless, for example.[104]

11.4.2 Collaboration in (grassroots) initiatives

Second, there are initiatives, grassroots initiatives and groups in which people work together ecumenically and with public significance. This entails what has been called 'Basis-Ökumene' ('basis-ecumenism').[105] Johannes Oeldemann names, for example, the women's 'World Day of Prayer' and action-groups formed in the conciliar Process for Justice, Peace and the Integrity of Creation.[106] The 'World Day of Prayer' is an international and Ecumenical Movement of women that invites them to pray for peace and justice on an annual basis and thereby raises public awareness for justice and gender justice on a global horizon.[107]

11.4.3 Institutional collaboration in federations

Different denominations do not only collaborate publically on a congregational level and not only in (grassroots) initiatives but on the level of regional church organizations or even global organizations. Particularly on this level, it is helpful to distinguish between situational collaborations for a limited time span (see Section 11.4.4) and organizational collaboration by which a federation or a council is formed that is meant to last.

Based on the more narrow meaning of ecumenism which referred to 'the practical and theological ways of dealing with the denominational diversity of Christianity' (see above), the 'most important institution for worldwide ecumenism' is the WCC, founded in 1948 in Amsterdam.[108] As already mentioned, this institutionalized ecumenical collaboration has a focus on issues of public relevance, social justice, peace, participation and sustainability. This conciliar process 'for Justice, Peace and the Integrity of Creation' which was

---

von engagierten Gemeindegliedern und Pfarrern vor Ort getragen werden' (Koslowski, 'Ökumene im Aufbruch', 33).
[104]Cf. Ibid.
[105]Johannes Oeldemann, 'Ökumenische Arbeitsorgane/Verbände in Deutschland', in *Religion in Geschichte Und Gegenwart*, 4th edn, Bd. 6 (Tübingen: Mohr Siebeck, 2003), cols. 513–14.
[106]Ibid., 513f.
[107]Cf. https://weltgebetstag.de/ueber-uns/haeufige-fragen/ (last accessed 3 February 2020).
[108]Koslowski, 'Ökumene im Aufbruch', 22. My translation of quote.

initiated in Vancouver in 1983 exemplifies this.[109] Yet, it needs to be emphasized that the WCC does not represent all of Christianity and not even the whole Ecumenical Movement.[110] First, not all denominational churches are a member. Until the Second Vatican Council, the Roman Catholic Church prohibited its members and priests to participate in the Ecumenical Movement because it challenged the Catholic conviction that the Catholic Church were already the one church of Christ; while the documents of the Second Vatican Council changed that position, the Catholic Church is still not a member of the WCC but participates in the commission for Faith and Order.[111] In addition to that, some orthodox churches left the WCC after an escalation of a discussion during the general assembly in Canberra in 1991.[112]

All the more important is it to mention other bodies that are also part of the public relevance of Christianity in different contexts. First, there are regional ecumenical federations: the Conference of European Churches (CEC), the 'All Africa Conference of Churches (AACC)' and the 'Christian Conference of Asia (CCA)'.[113] The CEC, for example, 'emerged as a peacebuilding effort' between East and West in 1959.[114] Hence, it had a public and political meaning from its beginning. Today, the CEC is in 'Dialogue with European Political Institutions' and deals with many topics of social ethics: migration, social justice, ecological justice, human rights or EU legislation.[115] Therewith, it can be seen as an example of an institutionalized and ecumenically collaborative praxis of public theology in the region of Europe.

In addition to that, there are institutionalized ecumenical federations with public significance on national level. In Germany, for example, seventeen churches are organized in the 'Arbeitsgemeinschaft christlicher Kirchen' (ACK).[116] If inner denominational plurality is the criterion, the Protestant Church in Germany (Evangelische Kirche in Deutschland, EKD) will have to be seen as an ecumenical federation in itself because it comprises Lutheran, United and Reformed churches.[117] It has public relevance at least through the publication on issues of politics and social ethics.

---

[109]Cf. Ibid., 26.
[110]Cf. Ibid., 23, 32.
[111]Cf. Ibid., 27–32.
[112]Cf. Ibid., 26.
[113]Cf. Ibid., 32.
[114]Cf. https://www.ceceurope.org/who-we-are/introduction/ (last accessed 3 February 2020).
[115]Cf. https://www.ceceurope.org/what-we-do/dialogue-with-the-eu-institutions/ (last accessed 3 February 2020).
[116]Cf. https://www.oekumene-ack.de/ueber-uns/mitglieder/ (last accessed 3 February 2020). See also Koslowski, Jutta. 'Ökumene im Aufbruch', 17–36.
[117]https://www.ekd.de/evangelische-kirche-in-deutschland-14272.htm (last accessed 3 February 2020).

On the background of the wider sense of the 'ecumenical' (meaning the inhabited world) other organizations come into view, which are less denominationally diverse but internationally collaborative, for example, the Lutheran World Federation, the World Communion of Reformed Churches (WCRC) and the Roman Catholic Church.

11.4.4 Institutional collaboration in initiatives

Different churches also collaborate in initiatives and projects with public relevance. The common utterances on social issues from the Catholic German Bishops Conference (Deutsche Bischofskonferenz, DBK) and the Protestant Church in Germany (Evangelische Kirche in Deutschland, EKD) are examples for such common public initiatives: in 1997, the DBK and the council of the EKD had already published a common document on the ecumenical and social situation in Germany.[118] Following up on this, they published a new document in 2014 which was meant to be participatory, to initiate and to include a public discourse on issues of solidarity, social justice and sustainability.[119] The text was released publically in February 2014 on an internet page where everybody – individual persons as well as groups – could leave comments and discuss the orientations and appeals of the paper.[120] After different economic crises, the ecumenical initiative stated what the 'common responsibility for a just society' would imply: ecological sustainability as well as inclusion and participation in the labour market, for example.[121]

Independently of the critique of the content of the paper, the whole initiative can serve as an example for ecumenical collaboration in public theology on an institutional level: protestant and Catholic Church organizations published a text together on matters of public relevance and had this text discussed publically. An outspokenly ecumenical initiative contributed to debating Christian orientations in a public discourse on the future of society, economy and state.

11.4.5 Societal collaboration

Among others, Dietrich Rössler has emphasized that Christianity takes not only the form of an ecclesial existence but is also present in the society, in the

---

[118]Kirchenamt der Evangelischen Kirche in Deutschland and Sekretariat der Deutsche Bischofskonferenz, 'Für eine Zukunft in Solidarität und Gerechtigkeit: Wort des Rates der Evangelischen Kirche in Deutschland und der Deutschen Bischofskonferenz zur wirtschaftlichen und sozialen Lage in Deutschland. Hannover/ Bonn, 1997', https://www.ekd.de/24153.htm (last accessed 16 February 2021).
[119]See https://www.ekd.de/pm29_2014_oekumenische_sozialinitiative.htm (last accessed 20 January 2020).
[120]Cf. http://www.sozialinitiative-kirchen.de/ (last accessed 20 January 2020).
[121]Ibid.

public sphere and in 'cultural manifestations'.[122] On this level, ideas, symbols, songs and rituals from different denominational traditions have left their traces in the public sphere – often interconnected or mixed. People of different denominations alike listen publically to Johann Sebastian Bach's St. Matthew Passion, for example.

In Germany, religious lessons at public schools are one way the state cooperates with the churches to take care of this public or societal form of religion.[123] These religious lessons are taught 'in accordance with the principles of the religious communities' ('in Übereinstimmung mit den Grundsätzen der Religionsgemeinschaften' (Art. 7, Abs. 3 GG)). This regulation has led to a religious plurality of religious lessons: in most places, there are at least Protestant and Roman Catholic religious lessons in school. Collaboration on this level is a publically relevant praxis of religious education: concepts for the cooperation of at least Protestant and Catholic approaches to religious education are discussed between Protestant and Catholic theologians as well.[124]

11.5 TO SUM UP: WHY COLLABORATE ECUMENICALLY IN PUBLIC THEOLOGY?

This chapter has tried to describe where ecumenical collaboration in public theology is already happening. While I leave it to the benevolent reader to evaluate whether this is enough or much more ecumenical collaboration could happen, I will finish this chapter by naming reasons for public theology to be and to understand itself as an ecumenical endeavour.

The Reception–Aesthetical Reason: At least in Germany, newspaper articles and news reports about scandals, public utterances or just stories of the church often speak about 'the church', without identifying the denomination of the institution or the people acting.[125] What applies to journalists holds true for other people as well. In 2013, during the scandal around the Catholic bishop of Limburg, Franz-Peter Tebartz-van Elst, who had spent a lot of money on

---

[122]Rössler, *Grundriß der praktischen Theologie*, 93.
[123]Cf. Ibid.
[124]Cf. Jan Woppowa, Tuba Işik, Katharina Kammeyer and Bergit Peters, eds, *Kooperativer Religionsunterricht: Fragen – Optionen – Wege*, Band 20 (Stuttgart: Kohlhammer, 2017); and particularly Bernhard Grümmes contribution: Bernhard Grümme, 'Konfessionell-kooperativer Religionsunterricht: eine verheißungsvolle Alternative', 12–25.
[125]Cf.: 'Berücksichtigt man den hohen Anteil fehlender Konfessionalität in den Beiträgen, könnte die journalistische Wahrnehmung das Selbstverständnis einer Mehrheit von Lesern widerspiegeln, die sich primär als kirchlich oder unkirchlich, sekundär als evangelisch oder katholisch und nur sehr selten als Mitglied einer bestimmten Landeskirche oder der Institution EKD identifizieren.' Daniel Meier, *Kirche in der Tagespresse: Empirische Analyse der journalistischen Wahrnehmung von Kirche anhand ausgewählter Zeitungen* (Erlangen: CPV Christlicher Publizistik-Verl, 2006).

his vicarage, the number of people leaving the church rose; but it was not only Catholic Christians who dropped out of their church; the Protestant churches were affected as well.[126] Hence, it seems safe to say: in the common public perception of many people, ecumenical unity is already a reality. People involved in the practices of public Christianity – be it in academic theology, be it in grassroots initiatives, congregations or as official representatives of an institution – need to deal with this public perception: what they are doing and saying is often perceived on the background of the public appearance not only of their own denomination but of all Christian churches. This provides a strong incentive for the theory and practice of public theology of one denomination to collaborate with others and to make their difference and unity publically visible.

The Social-Ethical Reason. In the course of this chapter, a couple of topics have been mentioned which public theology deals with in theory and praxis: civil religion, liberation, justice, peace, sustainability. Heinrich Bedford-Strohm has listed the following topics: social justice, challenges of globalization, ecological justice, ethics of biotechnologies, military force and peace-ethics and the public role of religion.[127] Bedford-Strohm then describes guidelines for the public expression of churches; the fifth guideline is 'the meaning of ecumenism', also in the wider sense of the word:[128] all these topics should be dealt with in a global horizon.[129] Bedford-Strohm emphasizes that the Christian commandment to love is not limited to national borders.[130] Hence, the discourse about countermeasures and consequences of climate change, for example, should not be restrained to national or even continental consequences. To situate this discourse on a global horizon, and to discuss the issues together with people from the Global South and from Pacific Islands as the GNPT makes it possible, gives public theology a necessary deeper and wider understanding of those consequences. The debate on social justice must deal with inequalities in Western societies but must also situate these issues on a global horizon. That is the social-ethical reason why public theology needs to be an ecumenically collaborative discourse and praxis.

The Theological Reason. The Niceno-Constantinopolitan creed professes faith in 'one holy catholic and apostolic Church'. Hence, the unity of the church

---

[126]Cf. https://www.spiegel.de/panorama/mehr-kirchenaustritte-nach-affaere-um-tebartz-van-elst-a-932269.html (last accessed 21 January 2020).
[127]Cf. Bedford-Strohm, Heinrich. 'Öffentliche Theologie in der Zivilgesellschaft', in Grundtexte Öffentliche Theologie, ed. Florian Höhne and Frederike van Oorschot (Leipzig: Evangelische Verlagsanstalt, 2015), 211–26.
[128]Ibid., 221, my translation.
[129]Cf.: 'Das öffentliche Reden der Kirche kann deswegen nie von seinem universalen Horizont abstrahieren' (Ibid.)
[130]Cf. Ibid.

is part of the Christian faith as shared by most denominations. Simultaneously, the denominational diversity and a multitude of organizations called 'church' all around the globe is a given. This poses the question of how to deal with this diversity, how to strive for reconciliation between denominations. Where is it that the unity of the church can be experienced? It is this tension between given plurality and professed unity that makes ecumenical debate and collaboration necessary – for a genuinely theological reason and in public.

CHAPTER 12

Relations to other religions

MANFRED L. PIRNER

INTRODUCTION

The question of how public theology relates to other religions embraces two fundamental aspects. First, it implies the question of how public theology as an originally Christian concept relates, or should relate, to other religions – to put it more precisely: how in the discourse and diverse concepts of Christian public theology other religions are considered; this will be the focus of Section 12.1. Second, it includes the question of whether and in what way other religions refer to the concept and intentions of public theology; this will be dealt with in Section 12.2. In Section 12.3, basic insights from the analyses of the two preceding sections will be summarized and commented from my own perspective.

Methodologically, I will concentrate on texts and approaches that explicitly and programmatically use the term 'public theology', because including publications that follow the theological rationale and objectives of public theology without using the term would make the research boundless.[1]

As to definitions, I will deliberately refrain from narrowing down 'public theology' to a distinct approach. I will, however, narrow down the notion of 'other religions' to focusing on Judaism and Islam (in Section 12.2) – while

---

[1] This, of course, means excluding important contributions in the area of inter-religious theological dialogue and collaboration such as the Global Ethics Initiative (https://www.global-ethic.org), the NGO Religions for Peace (https://www.rfp.org/) and many others.

Buddhism and Hinduism will receive strong references in the report on Asian public theology in Section 12.1.3.3.

It is good academic practice for researchers to disclose their own background. Mine is that of a Protestant German theologian, basically rooted in the Lutheran tradition, mainly occupied with the education of teachers of Religious Education, which in Germany is an ordinary school subject with a denominational, theological profile at all public schools, yet with the goal of promoting students' open, critical thinking and self-determined judgement in matters of religion and ethics. Convinced that for this context specifically, public theology is the ideal theological basis, I founded the 'Research Unit for Public Religion and Education' (RUPRE)[2] in 2016 and in my academic work have focused on the links between public theology and inter-religious dialogue, human rights as well as education.[3]

12.1 THE REFERENCE TO OTHER RELIGIONS IN CHRISTIAN PUBLIC THEOLOGY

12.1.1 The neglect of other religions in public theology classics

Given that one of the basic tenets of public theology is the awareness of Christianity's particularity in an ever more diverse and secular world, it is surprising to realize that – as far as I can see – none of the classic approaches of public theology reflected systematically on Christianity's relation to other religions. The focus of authors such as those assembled in the book *Basic Texts of Public Theology*[4] was primarily on defining the role and perspectives for theology in the context of a secular state and of public discourse in a society that is not Christian any longer.

At the beginning of the twenty-first century, religion was so vigorously and violently thrust into the spotlight of the public sphere that the whole world held its breath: 9/11 and the ensuing increase of Islamic terrorism worldwide marked a turning point also for public theology, definitely robbing it of its innocence

---

[2] See http://www.rupre.phil.fau.eu/.
[3] See, for example, Manfred L. Pirner, Johannes Lähnemann and Heiner Bielefeldt, eds, *Human Rights and Religion in Educational Contexts* (Cham: Springer International Publishing, 2016); Manfred L. Pirner et al., eds, *Public Theology, Religious Diversity and Interreligious Learning: Contributing to the Common Good through Religious Education* (New York: Routledge, 2018); Manfred L. Pirner et al., eds, *Public Theology Perspectives on Religion and Education* (New York: Routledge, 2019); Manfred L. Pirner, Guest-Editor of the Special Issue 'Public Theology – Religion(s) – Education', *IJPT* 11, no. 3 (2017); Manfred L. Pirner, 'Public Religious Pedagogy: Linking Public Theology, Social Theory and Educational Theory', *IJPT* 11, no. 3 (2017): 328–50.
[4] Florian Höhne and Frederike van Oorschot, eds, *Grundtexte Öffentliche Theologie* (Leipzig: Ev. Verlagsanstalt, 2015).

and – at least in Western democratic countries – often harmonizing visions of the peaceful coexistence of people with diverse religions. In particular, the issue of Islam and other religions was set on the agenda of public theological discourse. In this context, William Storrar's comments on the Festschrift for Duncan Forrester that he had prepared only days before 9/11, and that – he felt – was already outdated at its publication, were significant:

> [T]his timing means that the book maps public theology at the very end of the pre-9/11 world; it focuses on the contested western intellectual and political legacy of modernity, while recognizing the growing importance of economic globalization. [. . .] The volume does not offer any substantial Christian theological engagement with [. . .] the inter-religious dimension of global public affairs that have received so much attention from politicians, policymakers and scholars in the years since 2001. Such inter-religious thinking on public affairs must now constitute an essential component in doing public theology in the twenty-first century.[5]

It may be seen as indicative of (Christian) public theologians' risen awareness of the importance of inter-religious perspectives that E. Harold Breitenberg included them in his definition of public theology in his famous essay from 2003:

> Public theology is thus theologically informed public discourse about public issues, addressed to the church, synagogue, mosque, temple or other religious body, as well as the larger public or publics, argued in ways that can be evaluated and judged by publicly available warrants and criteria.[6]

Obviously, Breitenberg assumed that public theology was not just a Christian endeavour, but also one present in and relevant for Judaism, Islam and other religions.

12.1.2 The inter-religious dimension of public theology in the context of the GNPT

The first issue of the *International Journal of Public Theology* (*IJPT*), published in 2007, bears witness that religious diversity and inter-religious aspects have from the beginning belonged to the kind of public theology favoured by the Global Network of Public Theology (GNPT) in its diverse multi-continental

---

[5] William F. Storrar, 'The Oscillating Public Sphere', *IJPT* 3 (2009): 245–50.
[6] E. Harold Breitenberg Jr., 'To Tell the Truth: Will the Real Public Theology Please Stand Up', *Journal of the Society of Christian Ethics* 23, no. 2 (2003): 55–96 (66).

and multinational perspectives. In his opening essay on the 'Kairos Moment for Public Theology' that for him was represented by the establishment of the Global Network and the journal, William Storrar contended 'that only the ecumenical fullness and global breadth of the Christian tradition, *in dialogue with the other great religious traditions*, can enable a faithful theological engagement with contemporary public issues'.[7] He reported how the Edinburgh Centre for Theology and Public Issues (CTPI) after 9/11 had increasingly sought exchange with Islamic studies and was involved in several research projects on the beliefs, political attitudes and civic engagement of diverse faith communities, for example, Muslim, Hindu, Sikh and Jewish.

From his South African perspective John W. de Gruchy, in his essay in the first issue of the *IJPT*, emphasized that in general 'good practice in public theology requires that secularity *and religious diversity* are taken seriously'[8] and that especially for the South African context, even though Christianity is by far the predominant religion, 'no one faith should be elevated above others'.[9]

As Christian theologian and as director of the Cambridge Inter-Faith Program, David Ford, in his article in the issue, elaborated on the 'scriptural wisdom' of the three major religions Judaism, Christianity and Islam as valuable contributions to public life.[10]

And from an Asian perspective, Peter Tze Ming Ng from the Chinese University of Hong Kong presented the views of Dr Francis C. M. Wei (1888–1976), the first Chinese president of the University of Central China, as a model for a Christian theology that does not claim that the treasures of the Christian faith will 'supersede the ethical and religious traditions of the Chinese, but they will enhance them'.[11]

Despite this evidence that inter-religious aspects played a role right from the beginning of the *IJPT* and thus of the GNPT, the critical question can be raised, in how far these aspects were and are understood as an 'essential component in doing public theology' (Storrar, see 12.1.1). In his programmatic editorial to the first edition, Sebastian Kim stated that 'public theology results from a growing perception of the need for theology to interact with public issues of contemporary society. It seeks to engage in dialogue with different academic

---

[7]William F. Storrar, 'A Kairos Moment for Public Theology', *IJPT* 1 (2007): 5–25 (25) (my emphasis).
[8]John W. de Gruchy, 'Public Theology as Christian Witness: Exploring the Genre', *IJPT* 1 (2007): 26–41 (26) (my emphasis).
[9] (ibid., p. 29).
[10]David F. Ford, 'God and Our Public Life: A Scriptural Wisdom', *IJPT* 1 (2007): 63–81.
[11]Peter Tze Ming Ng, '"Glocalization" as a Key to the Interplay between Christianity and Asian Cultures: The Vision of Francis Wei in Early Twentieth Century China', *IJPT* 1 (2007): 101–11 (109).

disciplines, such as politics, economics, cultural studies and religious studies, as well as with spirituality, globalization and society in general'.[12] Other religions are not mentioned as dialogue partners here. Nor are they included in the 'Seven Theses on Public Theological Praxis' put forward by de Gruchy in his essay.[13]

In order to get a more valid general picture of the significance of interfaith perspectives in the context of the GNPT, I conducted a comprehensive content analysis of the fourteen volumes of the *IJPT* from 2007 to 2020. It reveals that among the about 400 articles there are 25 that either focus on inter-religious aspects or were written from a non-Christian religious perspective. References to other religions are by far outnumbered by references to the secular. What is also quite typical of the public theology discourse mirrored in the *IJPT* is that the term 'religion' tends to be used in the singular rather than in the plural, and that the frequent reference to 'religious pluralism' mostly remains abstract and belongs to a *via negationis* of argumentation: Christianity does *not* or *no longer* claim to be in a dominant or superior position but affirms that it is one religion among others in a society whose public 'is inescapably pluralistic'.[14] The consequence most often drawn is that Christian theology has to make its contributions to public discourse with the appropriate mixture of 'boldness and humility';[15] only rarely is the idea developed that religious pluralism requires Christian theology to engage in exchange with other religions (exceptions will be reported section 12.1.3). In particular, inter-religious dialogue and discourse do not seem to belong to the general concept of public theology as it is repeatedly outlined and discussed with varying accentuations in *IJPT* articles. This impression that interfaith communication is not perceived as 'constituting an essential component in doing public theology' (Storrar) within the GNPT context is reinforced by the fact that inter-religious perspectives have not received a separate chapter or any special attention in the otherwise comprehensive and substantial *Companion to Public Theology*[16] whose editors and authors widely represent the GNPT.

However, as indicated earlier, there are *IJPT* articles – and publications beyond the *IJPT* – that focus on interfaith aspects. In the following section, I will try to categorize them according to typical ways in which they relate public theology and inter-religious thinking.

---

[12]Sebastian Kim, 'Editorial', 1 (2007): *IJPT* 1–6 (1).
[13]De Gruchy, 'Public Theology as Christian Witness', 39–40.
[14]Scott Paeth, 'Whose Public? Which Theology? Signposts on the Way to a 21st Century Public Theology', *IJPT* 10 (2016): 461–85 (470).
[15]James Eglinton, 'Vox Theologiae: Boldness and Humility in Public Theological Speech', *IJPT* 9 (2015): 5–28.
[16]Sebastian Kim and Katie Day, eds, *A Companion to Public Theology* (Leiden/Boston: Brill 2017). This was rightly criticized by David Thang Moe in his review of the book in vol. 11 (2017) of the *IJPT*, 501–5.

12.1.3 The inter-religious dimension of public theology – a typology of approaches

In the following, three basic sets of approaches will be distinguished that represent three different fundamental perspectives. According to the first perspective, the presence of diverse religions and world views in pluralistic societies poses a challenge for peaceful coexistence, because they imply strong truth-claims that are in tension or even in contradiction to each other and have generated conflicts in past and present. In this view, understanding, channelling and shaping religious plurality are essential tasks of public theology in its endeavour to promote the common good and social cohesion. While this perspective concentrates on the diversity of religions as a problem that needs to be addressed, the second perspective focuses more on the positive potential of the diversity of religious traditions and communities to contribute to the common good, to solving ethical problems or practical challenges such as digitalization, refugee migration and climate change. In this perspective, interfaith communication primarily aims at interfaith cooperation. From a systematic-theological point of view, the constructive development of the first perspective can be seen as a precondition for a beneficial second perspective, although in practice – as we will see – it may be possible to start with pragmatic and goal-oriented collaboration without prior clarification of the relationship between two religions, which instead may be stimulated (more or less) and come about on the way. The third perspective emphasizes the self-reflective and self-critical reconceptualization of public theology in the light of (the neglect of) religious diversity. While the first perspective focuses on religious diversity as a problem and the second perspective on problems of social ethics, this perspective, one might say, addresses public theology itself as a problem in the way it has tended to be dominated by Western Christian theology and to marginalize theological insights from other parts of the world and from other religions.

12.1.3.1 The first perspective: Interfaith dialogue as a cornerstone of democratic citizenship Interestingly, in the *IJPT*, this approach is often represented by contributions from Indonesia, a context that is characterized by the official acknowledgement of six religions (Islam, Protestantism, Catholicism, Hinduism, Confucianism and Buddhism), in which Christianity finds itself in a minority situation while about 87 per cent of the population are Muslims, and Buddhism is very influential.[17]

---

[17] See, for example, Jeremy Menchink, *Islam and Democracy in Indonesia: Tolerance Without Liberalism* (New York: Cambridge University Press, 2017).

For instance, in his article 'Religion in a Democratic and Pluralistic Society' from 2018, Adrianus Sunarko starts with the basic insight that religions must develop a certain rationality of faith, if religions are not to become a source of conflict in a pluralistic democratic society like Indonesia. 'That rationality is related to the attitude towards other religions and beliefs, to the autonomy of science, and to the procedures inherent in the democratic system.'[18] He emphasizes, in accordance with Jürgen Habermas, that for religions the development of constructive attitudes in these fields without denying their religious identity can only be the result of a learning process that comes from within the religious community itself and can thus be conceptualized as the development of a public theology. If this learning and developing process is successful, the author concludes, the adherents of religions can make 'an important contribution to the development of democracy in Indonesia'. Thus, it is quite clear that for Sunarko, clarification of inter-religious relationships is the precondition for religions' contribution to the public good.

Two other *IJPT* articles function as apt complements of Sunarko's perspective. In a survey article, Emanuel Gerrit Singgih gives an overview of 'contemporary Christian and Muslim Public Theologies' in Indonesia.[19] Fransisco Budi Hardiman, in his article, provides a Christian example of the kind of public theology that is needed in the Indonesian context. He introduces the Jesuit Franz Magnis-Suseno (born 1936) as an important etichian and interfaith figure in Indonesia. 'Through his publications, he [Magnis-Suseno] seeks to assist Muslims and Christians to build an ethics of citizenship in a pluralistic democracy with the second Vatican theology of religions as his intellectual foundation.'[20] Hardiman comments that Magnis-Suseno demands more of religions than do Rawls and Habermas in terms of moderating their doctrinal positions vis-à-vis other religions.

12.1.3.2 The second perspective: Public theology as interfaith collaboration for the common good

Probably the best example of this type of approach is the special issue of the *IJPT* (2012, issue 4) on 'Faith-Based Organizing in the USA', edited by Katie Day. In her introduction, she makes clear that community organizing has a long tradition in the United States and has gained increased importance over the past decades. Community organizing means that people from a common neighbourhood engage voluntarily in collaborative action to

---

[18] Adrianus Sunarko, 'Religion in a Democratic and Pluralistic Society (The Experience of Indonesia)', *IJPT* 12 (2018): 440–54 (440).
[19] Emanuel Gerrit Singgih, 'What Has Ahok to Do with Santa? Contemporary Christian and Muslim Public Theologies in Indonesia', *IJPT* 13 (2019): 25–39.
[20] Fransisco Budi Hardiman, 'Franz Magnis-Suseno, Dialogue Ethics and Public Reasoning of Religions', *IJPT* 14 (2020): 187–205 (187).

improve the situation and tackle practical problems in their city district, for example, when it comes to bad housing or health conditions of poor people, lacking security of industrial workers or decaying schools. In Chicago, in the 1940s, the secular Jew Saul Alinsky started to organize such people who actively contributed to the common good in bigger networks that developed into the Industrial Areas Foundation (IAF). Today, there are several such networks of national or regional importance, most of them started in Chicago, and one of their characteristics is that they are mainly supported by and closely tied to faith communities and their religious leaders. Faith-based community organizing can thus be seen as practical public theology, namely believers who are actively committed to the common good out of their religious motivation.

Today, the major networks are multi-faith bodies that embrace a diversity of Christian denominations – mainly urban Catholic, mainline Protestant and historic Black Protestant churches – as well as Jewish and Muslim congregations. In their contribution to the special issue, Brad Fulton and Richard L. Wood speak of '*Interfaith* Community Organizing' (my emphasis). In their report on an empirical survey from 2011 of institution-based community organizations (IBCOs), they show that more than 80 per cent of IBCO member institutions are religious congregations or faith-based organizations, among them 5 per cent Jewish and 1 per cent Muslim.[21] Interestingly and surprisingly, it is reported that participants rarely focus on their religious differences, and that religious differences have a minimal effect on the planning of their meetings.

> Furthermore, the directors of religiously diverse IBCOs did not report it to be any more difficult to accommodate different faith traditions in their organizing work than did directors of less diverse IBCOs. As IBCO members from diverse faith traditions work together to improve their communities, they appear to navigate their religious differences by downplaying them. [. . .] In an increasingly polarized political culture, in which religious differences are often used to amplify political disagreements, IBCOs are strikingly counter-cultural.[22]

This is all the more astonishing as religious practices and references continue to be an integral part of the faith-based networks. For instance, over 90 per cent of IBCOs are reported to open and close their meetings with a prayer, and more than 70 per cent often have discussions about the connection between faith and

---

[21] Brad Fulton and Richard L. Wood, 'Interfaith Community Organizing. Emerging Theological and Organizational Challenges', *IJPT* 6 (2012): 398–420 (407. 409).
[22] Ibid., 413.

organizing.[23] Also, 'increasing the religious diversity of an IBCO does not seem to dampen the influence of religious faith in the organization'. On the contrary, 'religiously diverse IBCOs are more likely to incorporate religious practices into their organizing activities, and the directors of religiously diverse IBCOs reported being more comfortable with this'.[24] Many of them even indicated that religious differences enhanced their organization's planning meetings. Fulton and Wood conclude that this finding 'reflects significant comfort with the role of religion in the public arena' that 'contrasts sharply with both radical secularism and religious intolerance'.[25]

> While many IBCOs tend to ignore religious differences, they do not ignore religion altogether; rather than being venues for interfaith dialogue, IBCOs are vehicles for interfaith action. In addition to employing nonreligious principles rooted in the American democratic tradition, IBCOs incorporate faith into their organizing efforts, by drawing on various religious teachings, narratives, prayers and symbols. Such practices serve to motivate and mobilize the faith-oriented members around issues of common concern, while building relationships between leaders of differing faiths.[26]

Yet, the authors also contend that the growing religious diversity among the IBCOs will demand theological work within and across traditions. Such theological work is challenged primarily by practical questions such as

> how to handle cultural elements and theological beliefs from differing traditions that are not mutually acceptable (for example, praying in the name of Jesus when non-Christians are in the room, asking for the protection of Mother Earth among monotheists, invoking mitzvoth when non-Jews are present, invoking Mary's intervention among non-Catholics, or asking the audience's submission to Allah when many non-Muslims are in attendance).[27]

Possible solutions are either to ask speakers to choose religious references that are acceptable to all or to let them go on using their own tradition freely. 'The latter approach demands a significant level of trust between individuals across traditions: trust that is not always in existence, but which instead must be built. Meanwhile, the former approach risks a "thinning out" of theological

---

[23]Ibid., 414.
[24]Ibid., 415.
[25]Ibid.
[26]Ibid., 416.
[27]Ibid., 417.

depth that, in the name of acceptability, ultimately fails to sufficiently motivate anyone to be effective in the public arena.'[28]

Another problem with theological implications Fulton and Wood point to is the underrepresentation of Evangelical and Pentecostal congregations and other conservative (e.g. Jewish and Muslim) groups in the IBCOs. Efforts to include more of them might 'preclude or at least inhibit IBCOs from addressing some issues (such as same-sex marriage or other gay rights, prochoice issues and possibly even immigrant rights)'.[29]

12.1.3.3 Interfaith dialogue as constitutive for public theology in a postcolonial perspective The probably most (self-)reflective, substantial and consistent attempts to integrate inter-religious thinking into public theology have recently come from the Asian context. In particular, three authors can be named who have advanced innovative approaches that are clearly linked to religious diversity and to the problematic colonial history of Christianity on the Asian continent.

Paul S. Chung is associate professor at the Lutheran School of Theology at Chicago with roots in and connections to South Korea. Chung has consistently been engaged in dialogue between Asian and Western theology, as well as between Christian theology and Buddhism,[30] but also in issues of social ethics.[31] In his book *Postcolonial Public Theology* of 2016[32] the major threads of his theological thinking are woven together and are at the same time integrated into the two intertwined frameworks of postcolonial theory and public theology. Chung sees the potential of the postcolonial perspective for public theology in its 'critical and analytical epistemology that enables us to overcome the limitations of the Western project of Enlightenment embedded within the nexus between knowledge and power'.[33] As to Christian theology, this means that 'a new geography of Christianity is of polycentric character'.[34] It also implies that in the context of what he calls an 'analectical' hermeneutic – that draws on Karl Barth's dialectical and David Tracy's analogical thinking –

---

[28]Ibid.
[29]Ibid., 419.
[30]See, for example, Paul S. Chung, *Martin Luther and Buddhism: Aesthetics of Suffering* (Eugene, OR: Pickwick Publications, 2nd edn., 2008); Paul S. Chung et al., eds, *Asian Contextual Theology for the Third Millenium: Theology of Minjung in Fourth-Eye Formation* (Eugene, OR: Pickwick Publications, 2007).
[31]For example, in Paul S. Chung, *Church and Ethic Responsibility in the Midst of World Economy: Greed, Dominion, and Justice* (Eugene, OR: Cascade, 2013).
[32]Paul S. Chung, *Postcolonial Public Theology: Faith, Scientific Rationality, and Prophetic Dialogue* (Eugene, OR: Cascade 2016).
[33]Ibid., 5–6.
[34]Ibid., 6.

'public religious theology' is conceptualized 'in critical-constructive correlation of one religious tradition with another religion'.[35] Taking up approaches of a 'comparative theology' (Francis Clooney[36]) and adapting concepts of Ernst Troeltsch, he advocates 'the comparative study of religions in the framework of interreligious dialogue'[37] and a 'Comparative Public Theology'.[38] As the theological basis for this endeavour, he points to creation and reconciliation theology. 'Seen in the light of *creatio continua* creation is the world with which God is reconciled in Christ. God's act of speech in the fashion of Infinite Saying assumes plural and multiple horizons in the reconciled world through the world of other religions.'[39]

With this sophisticated theological concept, Chung on the one hand reinterprets classic theologians such as Martin Luther, Dietrich Bonhoeffer and Karl Barth through the postcolonial and inter-religious lens and on the other hand applies this lens also when he theologically addresses burning ethical issues of today. In this context, he makes it quite clear that for him, inter-religious perspectives are constitutive for public theology.

> Accordingly, I focus public religious theology on respecting the integrity of life, ethical maturity and responsibility, as well as recognizing the moral source and dignity of the Other in different religious traditions. Without intentional learning and appropriate understanding of the culture, religion, and spiritual experiences of those in other contexts, Christian public theology cannot be developed as a viable project.[40]

As one example of how such comparative or inter-religiously informed public theology can work, Chung discusses the problem of global economic justice in the light of Christian and Buddhist perspectives, shows how they can complement each other and to this end offers insights from a 'trans-scriptural reading'. For instance, the understanding of compassion in Mahayana Buddhism can widen the Christian understanding of compassion by emphasizing the significance of an appropriate notion of loving yourself (as your neighbour) and by encompassing ecological, cosmological dimensions 'in the face of the

---

[35] Ibid., 14.
[36] Francis X. Clooney, ed., *The New Comparative Theology: Interreligious Insights from the Next Generation* (New York: T&T Clark, 2010).
[37] Chung, *Postcolonial Public Theology*, 14.
[38] Chung has developed this comparative concept also in an essay in the *IJPT*: Paul S. Chung, 'Constructing a Public Comparative Theology: Examining Ernst Troeltsch through a Critical Hermeneutic Lens', *IJPT* 12 (1018): 218–35.
[39] Chung, *Postcolonial Public Theology*, 14.
[40] Ibid., 168.

reality of all living beings'.[41] This example can provide evidence for Chung's contention that inter-religious learning can generate 'fresh theological insights into the newly encountered traditions as well as the home tradition. Thus, public religious theology is a theological, practical response to religious diversity by interpreting the world in light of engaged faith traditions'.[42]

While Chung still seems to be strongly rooted in the Western theological context, Indian Catholic theologian Felix Wilfred clearly draws mainly on his experience and wide knowledge of theological thinking from the Asian context. From 1993 to 2008, Wilfred was professor of theology at the University of Madras, India; thereafter up to now he has been founder-director of the Asian Centre for Cross-Cultural Studies (ACCS) in Madras.[43] He has recently edited the *Oxford Handbook on Christianity in Asia* (2014). In his book *Asian Public Theology. Critical Concerns in Challenging Times*, from the start Wilfred makes clear that 'Asian Public Theology is one in which the accent will be stronger on the "public" than on theology. The focus will be the issues and questions that affect the people and societies in Asia and which need to be addressed urgently'.[44] In the process of addressing the public concerns, this kind of theology 'constitutes itself as interreligious'; it 'ceases to be sectarian, and becomes inclusive'.[45] Similar to Chung, Wilfred develops his view of Asian public theology in contrast to the Western mode of public theology that is dominated by a Christian majority-perspective, while in India and several other Asian countries the minority position of Christians among a diversity of religions requires inter-religious collaboration and suggests a focus on advocating for the subalterns, on overcoming exclusion and critically engaging for social justice and a good, democratic government. The theological basis of inter-religious discourse and collaboration is for Wilfred the insight that God is mysterious and beyond Christian comprehension and that, therefore, God's voice can also be heard through the dialogue with other religions.[46] In his reflections on the 'post-metaphysical God in a post-secular society', Wilfred contends that only if religions 'revise critically the metaphysical foundations of their narrations of God' will their presence and engagement in life be 'promising and constructive'.[47] How urgently needed such engagement is, is finally demonstrated by Wilfred in his last-but-one chapter 'Towards an Interreligious Eco-theology'.

---

[41]Ibid., 174.
[42]Ibid., 177.
[43]See http://accschennai.com/founder-director/.
[44]Felix Wilfred, *Asian Public Theology: Critical Concerns in Challenging Times* (Delhi: ISPCK, 2010), xi.
[45]Ibid., xix.
[46]See Ibid., 303–4.
[47]Ibid., 302.

Even more provocative in its title than Wilfred's volume, while developing similar perspectives, is D. Preman Niles's book *Is God Christian? Christian Identity in Public Theology: An Asian Contribution*,[48] a book title that reminds one of the book, *God Is Not a Christian*, by Desmond Tutu, South Africa's probably most prominent public theologian.[49] Niles is a Protestant theologian (United Reformed Church), was director of a 'Programme on Justice, Peace and the Integrity of Creation' with the World Council of Churches in Geneva and is now general secretary of the Council for World Mission in London. One central claim of Niles's book that he shares with his colleague and friend Felix Wilfred is that Asian public theology 'will be inherently interreligious in nature', if it wants to address the challenges posed in the wider arena of social and political life in Asia. As a basis for a 'cross-textual hermeneutics as counter-colonial approach', he offers three illuminating examples of cross-textual reading: Mohandas Gandhi (1869–1948) of India, who read the Bible and the Qur'an together with the Bhagavad Gita on a daily basis; Lakshman Wickremesinghe (1927–83) of Sri Lanka, who used his cross-textual reading of Hindu scriptures and the Bible to promote the inter-religious dialogue on human rights; and Ahn Byung-mu (1922–96) of Korea, who as a New Testament scholar joined the *minjung* theologians in their struggle for democracy and human rights in Korea. Different from Chung, Niles is more critical of Clooney's *Comparative Theology* that he regards as quite academic or even elitist and in its tendencies rather harmonistic. He combines his cross-textual hermeneutic with a postcolonial hermeneutic (in chapters 3 and 4) and finally a subaltern, counter-theological hermeneutic (in chapter 5) that advocates a preference for stories (in the understanding of the socially disadvantaged and oppressed) in contrast to theological ideas (that have mainly been developed by academic, powerful elites).

12.2 THE REFERENCE TO PUBLIC THEOLOGY IN OTHER RELIGIONS

12.2.1 Judaism

In her contribution to our Nuremberg conference on public theology in 2016 and her subsequent book chapter, Sabrina Worch contended that a 'striving for the salvation, preservation and well-being of the world itself and all its inhabitants

---

[48] D. Preman Niles, *Is God Christian? Christian Identity in Public Theology: An Asian Contribution* (Minneapolis, MN: Fortress Press, 2017).
[49] Desmond M. Tutu, *God Is Not a Christian: Speaking Truth in Times of Crisis* (Johannesburg: Rider 2011).

is ingrained in Judaism'.[50] She focused on the traditional notion of *Tikkun Olam* – that literally means 'repairing' or 'mending of the world' – that since the 1970s has increasingly been invoked by reflections on Jewish contributions to the common good, although its origin is not quite clear. It seems that Jewish publications on 'Tikkun Olam' can be seen as widely corresponding with the idea of public theology.[51]

As for the context of the post-9/11 upsurge of academic discourse on the public role of religion, Jewish contributions were soon actively involved, especially in the United States. Two volumes edited by Alan Mittleman et al. in 2002 offer informative insights on the active public role and political influence of Jewish communities and thinkers in the United States.[52] One example of the fact that Jewish engagement with democratic, pluralistic society has also been subject to deepened theological reflection is David Novak's book *The Jewish Social Contract: An Essay in Political Theology* of 2005. Novak, rabbi and professor of the study of religion and philosophy at the University of Toronto, prefers the notion of 'political theology' to 'public theology'; his intention, however, reveals the equivalence of both terms. Building on previous studies,[53] Novak aims to answer the question of 'How can anyone participate actively and intelligently in a democratic polity in good faith?'[54] And he explicitly claims that, today, 'Jews and Christians have a unique opportunity now to develop parallel political theologies that move beyond the usual political distinctions between "liberals" and "conservatives"'.[55] Basically, Novak argues and demonstrates that for Jews their commitment to the biblical covenant and the Torah is not only compatible with the democratic social contract but can be viewed as one

---

[50]Sabrina Worch, 'The Contribution of Religions to the Common Good in Pluralistic Societies: A Jewish Perspective, Exemplified by the Concept of *Tikkun Olam*', in Manfred L. Pirner et al., eds., *Public Theology, Religious Diversity, and Interreligious Learning* (New York: Routledge, 2018), 22–6.

[51]See, for example, Elliot N. Dorff and Cory Willson, *The Jewish Approach to Repairing the World (Tikkun Olam): A Brief Introduction for Christians* (Woodstock, VT: Jewish Lights, 2008); Jason A. Goroncy and Alfonse Borysewicz, *'Tikkun Olam' To Mend the World: A Confluence of Theology and the Arts* (Eugene, OR: Wipf & Stock Publishers, 2014); David Shatz, Chaim I. Waxman and Nathan J. Diament, eds, *Tikkun Olam: Social Responsibility in Jewish Thought and Law* (London: Jason Aronson, 1997).

[52]Alan Mittleman, Jonathan D. Sarna, and Robert Licht, eds, *Jews and the American Public Square: Debating Religion and Republic* (Lanham, MD: Rowman & Littlefield Publishers, 2002); Alan Mittleman, Jonathan D. Sarna, and Robert Licht, eds, *Jewish Polity and American Civil Society: Communal Agencies and Religious Movements in the American Public Square* (Lanham, Maryland: Rowman & Littlefield Publishers, 2002).

[53]See, for example, David Novak, *Covenantal Rights: A Study in Jewish Political Theory* (Princeton, NJ: Princeton University Press, 2000).

[54]David Novak, *The Jewish Social Contract: An Essay in Political Theology* (Princeton, NJ: Princeton University Press, 2005), xi.

[55]Ibid., xix.

root of it. On the other hand, he emphasizes the deliberate limitations of the kind of commitment that democratic polity requires compared to religious commitment. On this basis, he contends, Jews have made and can further make valuable contributions to a democratic pluralistic society.

Such contributions in the sense of public theology can, for instance, be seen in publications like Aryeh Cohen's *Justice in the City: An Argument from the Sources of Rabbinic Judaism*.[56] In the British context very prominent and influential book contributions have come especially from the late Rabbi Jonathan Sacks who can doubtlessly be called a Jewish public theologian par excellence, although he does not seem to have used the term in his numerous publications.[57]

As indicated earlier, the *IJPT* published a special issue in 2013 titled *Jewish Public Theology* with four articles on diverse topics (popular culture, murder, the peace process in Israel, the Holocaust). The probably most explicit and comprehensive concept of a 'Jewish Public Theology', however, has been developed recently by Abraham Unger in his book of the same title, *A Jewish Public Theology: God and the Global City*.[58] In it, Unger correlates the major problems of the 'global city' – such as the gap between the rich and the poor, ethnic and religious conflict, sustainability, immigration and healthcare – with the central topoi of Jewish theology – revelation, covenant, law and community. In the second chapter he explicates the Jewish perspective of the concept of justice and which aspects of it can be beneficial for addressing the injustices in this world. In particular, he emphasizes the orienting power of a Messianic ethic that offers the vision of 'an ideal state of social justice'.[59] Unger does not stop short with theological visions but goes on to make concrete suggestions for policy development and strategic urban planning, for example, when he brings together immigration issues with Jewish covenantal ethic and applies Halakhic wisdom to economic dilemmas. In his review of Unger's book, Matthew Eaton understandably expresses his jealousy 'as a Christian ecological theologian who desires a better grasp of precisely what Unger excels at – integrating the wisdom of a faith tradition with the actual legislative and policy structures that determine the shape of contemporary life'.[60]

---

[56] Aryeh Cohen, *Justice in the City: An Argument from the Sources of Rabbinic Judaism* (Boston, MA: Academic Studies Press, 2013).
[57] See, for example, Jonathan Sacks, *The Dignity of Difference: How to Avoid the Clash of Civilizations* (London: Continuum, 2002); Jonathan Sacks, *To Heal a Fractured World: The Ethics of Responsibility* (London: Knopf Doubleday, 2007); Jonathan Sacks, *Morality: Restoring the Common Good in Divided Times* (London: Hodder & Stoughton, 2020); and many others.
[58] Abraham Unger, *A Jewish Public Theology: God and the Global City* (Lanham, MD: Lexington Books, 2019).
[59] Ibid., 21.
[60] Matthew Eaton, '*A Jewish Public Theology: God and the Global City, written by Abraham Unger*', *IJPT* 14 (2020): 377–9 (378).

12.2.2 Islam

As a consequence of the 9/11 attacks and the subsequent rise of Islamistic terror, Muslims in Western democracies worldwide have found themselves on the defensive, often being identified with 'the' Islam that appeared to be the source of intolerance, aggression and terrorism. In the context of this predominant mood there was obviously little willingness to expect and listen to Muslim contributions to the common good in pluralistic societies. Yet, as, for example, Terry Lovat has argued, it is precisely a better and deeper understanding of Islam in its theological dimensions – and thus overcoming a neglect of public theology – that may help to address extremism and appreciate, as well as promote, the humanizing potentials of this religion.[61] On the other hand, it seems that controversial disputes among Muslim theologians on the relationship between the Islamic tradition and basic principles of modern societies like human rights, democracy, rule of law, civil society, and religious and world view pluralism have not yet resulted in consensual positions that find wide approval among substantial numbers of Muslims. However, there are more and more insightful and innovative contributions by Islamic theologians that do not only prove the compatibility of Islam with the modern principles mentioned earlier but claim that Islamic theology and discourse can make valuable and also critical contributions to a democratic, human rights-based culture. In the following I will only highlight a few of them who have linked themselves closely with the term and concept of public theology.

Probably the earliest reflection of an Islamic theologian on the concept of public theology is the essay by Pakistani scholar Ausaf Ali from 1995.[62] He admits that the term is quite new to him and is little known in the Islamic world, but that it has 'captured' his 'imagination' and made him think that he has 'always been a public theologian' himself.[63] With remarkable knowledge of the public theology discourse in the United States, he perceives one basic potential of public theology in constituting a meaningful counterweight against an increasingly secularized and thus 'naked' public space. His approach is in general appreciative, especially of the Catholic theologian John Courtney Murray that he discusses at greater length, but also implies critical views of Western culture with apologetic Islamic overtones, for instance when he refers to Alasdair MacIntyre's and others' analysis of the moral deficits of Western secular and pluralistic societies, the Western 'propensity to be violent, overbearing, aggressive, domineering, and imperialistic' and the failure of

---

[61] See, for example, Terry Lovat, 'Securing Security in Education: The Role of Public Theology and a Case Study in Global Jihadism', *Religions* (2018): 9, 244, 1–14.
[62] Ausaf Ali, 'An Essay on Public Theology', *Islamic Studies* 34, no. 1 (Spring 1995): 67–89.
[63] Ibid., 67.

Christianity to 'soften' such tendencies,[64] or when he claims the advantage of Islam over modern thinking.

> Consensus is at the heart of public theology. But the consensus for which it strives is to be arrived at through reflection, discourse, and communication. It is interesting to note that the modern or the postmodern world has arrived, at long last, at an institution which is a standard part of the basic methodology of Islamic sources of knowledge in Islam, viz. Ijma' (consensus). Other sources are the Qur'an (holy scripture), Sunnah (life of the Prophet Muhammad), Qiyas (analogical reasoning), and Ijtihad (analogical reasoning).

Ali ends with the ambivalent estimation that in face of the numerous social crises the United States is caught up in, public theologians of diverse religions will have 'no shortage of productive, constructive, and creative work'.[65]

In contrast to Ali's self-assured stance, Islamic discourse on the question of whether Islamic perspectives can contribute to the common good in democratic, pluralistic societies is mostly tied to a self-critical perception of the present mainstream Islam and to the demand of reforms. For instance, in a journal article titled 'Public Theology in Islam: A New Approach?', Indonesian law scholar Nadirsyah Hosen introduces a number of reformist Islamic theologians, from Muhammad Abduh, Nurcholish Majid and Hassan Hanafi to Asghar Ali Engineer and his Islamic Liberation Theology.[66] For Hosen, such reforms and modernization of Islam are the precondition for it to be able to 'provide ethical and spiritual considerations in contemporary issues and public debates'.[67] As one example of such Islamic contributions, he points to the global financial crisis and the alternative financial strategies of Islamic economists who have experiences with banking systems that work without interest rates. Referring to the Qur'anic tradition of the *Shura* (consultation), he advocates that this 'new approach of Islamic public theology requires collaboration of religious leaders with scholars from related disciplines'.[68]

In a document titled 'Religious Plurality and the Public Space. Joint Christian–Muslim Theological Reflections' published by the Lutheran World Council, Mouhanad Khorchide – who is professor of Islamic religious education at the University of Münster, Germany – draws attention to another controversial fundamental issue within Islamic discourse. The question of whether there is

---

[64]Ibid., 81.
[65]Ibid., 88.
[66]Nadirsyah Hosen, 'Public Theology in Islam: A New Approach?', *Interface* 15, no. 1&2 (2012): 59–72.
[67]Ibid., 67.
[68]Ibid., 69.

an actual need for political values and principles such as democracy and human rights to be underpinned by religious faith perspectives can find different answers. In his contribution, Khorchide advances the proposition that 'the question of whether or not Islam is compatible with democracy is not to be resolved by means of a theological discourse. On the contrary, this question depends on cultural, societal, political and economic frameworks'.[69] In this line, Khorchide argues that it is precisely the widely shared view that in Islam the order of society is provided and prescribed by God that should be challenged, primarily by distinguishing between Muhammad as a prophet (in which role he can rightly claim religious authority) and as a political leader (in which role he cannot claim authority),[70] and by distinguishing within the Qur'anic tradition between concrete legal regulations that addressed specific historical situations and the principles behind them that can still provide guidance for today. As such principles Khorchide elaborates the following five:

- Justice
- Inviolability of human dignity
- Freedom of all people
- Equality of all people
- Social and ethical responsibility of humanity[71]

Khorchide argues that a Qur'anic justification of democratic values beyond these principles is not necessary. He points to the role of reason in the Mu'tazilite concept of Islam (as opposed to the Ash'arites' view).[72]

> This Mu'tazilite position allows for revelation and reason not to be played off against each other. [. . .] To take the thought even further, we could say that reason is a medium of revelation. While according to Islam the Qur'an is God's ultimate Word, God still reveals Godself through human reasoning. Following this thought, we do not need to find a Qur'anic foundation for achievements through reasoning in order to find legitimacy in an Islamic context as long as nothing is at odds with Qur'anic principles. It would then be revelation's duty to call people to reflect, to remind them of their

---

[69]Mouhanad Khorchide, 'State and Religion in Islam – Islam's Contribution to the Political Culture of Democracy', in *Religious Plurality and the Public Space: Joint Christian–Muslim Theological Reflections*, ed. Simone Sinn, Mouhanad Khorchide and Dina El Omari (Leipzig: Ev. Verlagsanstalt), 11–26 (14).
[70]Ibid., 18. Khorchide refers here to Ali Abdarraziq as well as a number of modern Muslim scholars who picked up on him such as Muhammad Said al-Ashmawy, Nasr Hamid Abu Zaid and Fuad Zakariya.
[71]Khorchide, 'State and Religion in Islam', 20.
[72]The Mu'tazilites and the Ash'arites were important theological schools in early Islamic history.

ethical and social responsibility and to allow for them to experience God in a spiritual manner.[73]

It should be clear that this kind of argumentation assigns (public) theological reasoning an important but also limited role when it comes to defining the relationship between Islam and democratic, pluralistic societies and motivating possible contributions of Muslims to the common good.

Concluding this section, it can be said that within Islamic discourse the notion of public theology does not seem to have been significant up to now, but contributions from Muslim theologians to social and ethical issues have partly been categorized as 'public theology'. This applies to the Indonesian,[74] South African,[75] US American,[76] German-speaking[77] and British[78] contexts.[79]

12.3 PUBLIC THEOLOGY AND RELIGIOUS DIVERSITY – CONCLUDING PERSPECTIVES

12.3.1 Present chances and challenges

The analyses presented in Section 12.1 have shown that religious diversity has in many ways become increasingly relevant for public theology discourse: According to the first perspective outlined, the tensions between adherents of different religions and worldviews, as well as extremist forms of various religious or anti-religious groups, can cause or aggravate conflicts on the micro, meso and macro levels of the public sphere. Therefore, public theology's aim to contribute to a peaceful, humane and flourishing society requires it to provide models of thought, faith and practice that enhance constructive

---

[73] Khorchide, 'State and Religion in Islam', 24.
[74] See, for instance, Emanuel G. Singgih, 'What Has Ahok to Do with Santa? Contemporary Christian and Muslim Public Theologies in Indonesia', *IJPT* 13 (2019): 25–39.
[75] Aaslam Fataar, *Searching for Islamic Ethical Agency in Post-Apartheid Cape Town: An Anthology* (Beyers Naudé Centre Series on Public Theology, Book 13) (Cape Town: African Sun Media, 2019).
[76] John L. Esposito, 'Islam in the Public Sphere', *Journal of the American Academy of Religion* 82 (2014): 291–306.
[77] See beside Mouhanad Khorchide for instance Ednan Aslan, Mohammed Nekroumi, Fahimah Ulfat and Zekirija Sejdini.
[78] See, for example, Abdullah Sahin, 'The Contribution of Religions to the Common Good in Pluralistic Societies: An Islamic Perspective', in *Public Theology, Religious Diversity, and Interreligious Learning*, ed. Manfred L. Pirner et al. (New York: Routledge), 27–39.
[79] In his doctoral thesis *Public Theology in a Foreign Land* Gonzalo Villagran has made the interesting attempt of bringing public theology to the Spanish context by integrating in his mainly Catholic perspective the position of unbelief as well as the Islamic tradition. As Islamic conversation partners he names Abdulaziz Sachedina, Nurcolish Majid, Adullahi An-Naim, Tariq Ramadan and Alli Allawi. See Gonzalo Villagran, *Public Theology in a Foreign Land* (Boston College, 2012), http://hdl.handle.net/2345/bc-ir:104416.

ways of dealing with religious and world view differences. The second perspective illuminated that the crises, problems and ethical challenges of life affect all people with different religious or non-religious beliefs, and their solution benefits from collaboration on the basis of all creativity, motivation, commitment, virtue and hope available in the diverse traditions, religions and world views. However, as could be evidenced by a closer look at the *IJPT*, inter-religious thinking still does not seem to 'constitute an essential component in doing public theology', as William Storrar demanded after the terrorist attacks of 9/11 (see section 12.1.1). The examples from Indonesia showed promising approaches of promoting mutual understanding between religions, and the example of faith-based community organizing in the United States demonstrated impressive collaborative practice, but in both contexts a need for deeper theological reflection on inter-religious issues seems to be felt. It is this deficit of mainstream (Western) public theology that is criticized and constructively addressed by those Asian authors who were introduced under the third perspective. In their concepts of Asian public theology inter-religious thinking *is* essential, precisely because they have become aware of the limits and shortcomings of the Christian faith in this postcolonial setting and at the same time have come to appreciate the treasures and potentials of other religions and world views. These treasures and potentials have also become visible when links to the concept and basic intention of public theology were explored in Section 12.2. In both Judaism and Islam, the striving to contribute to the well-being of the whole community and humanity in general is ingrained in their traditions and their present mainstream self-understanding. The exemplary publications that were introduced bear witness to the fact that vice versa Jewish and Muslim scholars have benefitted from grappling with secular and Christian ideas.

I conclude with three observations and comments from my own perspective.

12.3.2 Concluding observations and comments

12.3.2.1 Inter-religious public theology needs to take account of the double secularity in democratic, pluralistic societies While in the Western context, for a long time, public theology was more occupied with addressing the secularized political public sphere than relations to other religions, it seems to me that in the welcome upsurge of inter-religious discourses and collaborations the reflection of their relationship to the secular tends to be neglected in a double sense. On the one hand, as the term 'inter-religious' signifies, people with non-religious positions and world views (positional secularity) run the risk of being marginalized, especially as they may not be represented by community associations like religious congregations and churches. On the other hand, it is important to clarify the relationship between inter-religious perspectives and overarching secular principles and values such as human dignity and human rights (neutral secularity). For instance, in democratic, human rights-based countries even very unconditional and direct forms of inter-religious discourse or collaboration are already – subcutaneously so to speak – facilitated by such common basic political values, because they form the foundation of the culture and the communicative atmosphere of a country. It is sensible and may be helpful to explicitly address and reflect this rather trialogical character of the dialogue between two religions.[80] In my view, John Rawls's philosophical model of 'public reason' and 'overlapping consensus' (in its revised form) is still beneficial in this respect.[81] In addition, Rawls's model may be supportive in clarifying the relationship between reason and revelation or mysticism *within* one religion or certain variants of it, which may also have repercussions on its attitude towards 'public reason' (remember, e.g., the dominant role of reason in the Mu'tazilite school of Islam, or in the natural law concept of Catholicism).

12.3.2.2 Inter-religious public theology will build on the historical and epistemological awareness of the discursive nature and the limitations of one's religion Postcolonial public theology is one important example of public theology's general necessity to address the Christian history of guilt in its various forms. This history of guilt often affected other religions or beliefs, from the Inquisition, the witch hunts and the justification of slavery to the persecution of Jews and, in Germany, the provision of the religious background for the Shoah. D. Preman Niles reports a discussion with Jewish theologians after they had listened to presentations of the history of Christianity in Asia, in which they asked the following questions:

> If Christianity is foreign to Asian religious tradition, why do you still remain Christian? Why bother with Christianity after all? Is it not the aim of Asian Christians to get rid of the Christian faith rather than try to come to terms with it when it has caused so much suffering and pain as well as carving so deep a scar on the soul of the people?[82]

---

[80]This is, for instance, the approach of the extensive project 'Key Concepts in Interreligious Discourses', conducted by the Bavarian Research Center for Interreligious Discourses (https://www.bafid.fau.eu/).
[81]Rawls revised especially his initially rather restrictive view of the role of religions and religious contributions to the public sphere in later editions of *Political Liberalism* (e.g. Expanded Edition, New York: Columbia University, 2005) and in particular in his essay 'The Idea of Public Reason Revisited', in Idid., *Collected Papers* (Cambridge, MA: Harvard University Press, 1999), 573–615. See also Pirner, 'Public Religious Pedagogy', 340–6.
[82]Niles, *Is God Christian?*, 28.

It is crucial for public theology to find answers to questions like these. As one aspect, public confessions of guilt, such as the Stuttgart Confession of the Protestant Churches in Germany after the Second World War and the Mea Culpa prayer of Pope John Paul II in 2000, are an important element of public theology – and one that in my view could be practised more widely. It is even more important to work on the consequences as well as to become more modest and aware of the limitations of the Christian faith and of possible failures today. It is just as significant, however, to realize and elaborate the stimulating interactions and mutual enrichments between religions in history and present and thus become aware of the fundamentally discursive nature of all religions.[83]

Such insights and the epistemological understanding that humans will never be able to fully grasp the divine, the true and the good can mutually reinforce each other and lead to the willingness to open up to the wisdom of other religions, world views and philosophies while re-appreciating one's own.

12.3.2.3 Inter-religious public theology needs a theology of religions As we have seen, dialogue and collaboration with other religions can in public theology be justified and motivated in different ways. It can be regarded as a reasonable way to contribute to peace and social cohesion by reducing the tensions and possible conflicts between believers of different religions. It can also be seen as a pragmatic necessity in order to tackle more successfully the social problems and ethical challenges in society. Although the urgency of common public action may often be more important than reflecting on the relationship between different religions, in my view, both options will benefit from such a deepened, genuinely theological deliberation.

On the basis of an evaluation of existing approaches and publications,[84] including those introduced in this chapter, I suggest to distinguish four different theological thought patterns in a kind of stage model:

At the first stage, we recognize that our own faith can be better understood in comparison with other religions.

At a second stage, we grant the possibility that God also works in other religions and speaks to us through them. This view can also take effect if the possibility of salvation is fundamentally denied to the other religions.

---

[83]See, for example, Jay Johnston and Kocku von Stuckrad, eds, *Discourse Research and Religion. Disciplinary Use and Interdisciplinary Dialogues* (Berlin: DeGruyter, 2021); Frank Neubert, *Die diskursive Konstitution der Religion* [The Discursive Constitution of Religion] (Wiesbaden: Springer, 2016).
[84]See Manfred L. Pirner, 'Interreligiöse Diskurse – evangelisch-theologische Perspektiven', *Erlanger Jahrbuch für Interreligiöse Diskurse* 1 (Würzburg: Ergon-Verlag, 2022, in press).

At the third stage, we concede the general possibility of salvation in other religions, and consequently the possible presence of God in other religions is valued even more highly so that the willingness to learn from them is increased.

A fourth and final stage is reached if we do not only reckon with the possible enrichment of our own faith by the encounter with the divine in the other religion but we regard the criticism, supplementation and correction from outside our own religion as a necessity provided for or at least permitted by God and as part of his salvific history with humankind. Clearly, it is this last option that implies the best prospects for beneficial relationships between religions and provides the best foundation for their collaborative efforts to improve peace, justice and well-being in this world.

PART III

Theological tenets in public theology

CHAPTER 13

Public theology and social ethics

HAK JOON LEE

The topic of this chapter is the relationship of public theology to (social) ethics. A great deal of confusion and ambiguity exists in distinguishing the two and understanding their relationship because both are closely related.[1] For example, Reinhold Niebuhr, Dietrich Bonhoeffer and others are regarded as public theologians, as well as ethicists, without much explanation on such distinctions. For some scholars, public theology is treated as a sub-discipline of social ethics, while for others 'public theology' is a broad umbrella term that includes social ethics.

However, more significantly, the confusion between public theology and (social) ethics is based on the fact there is no generally accepted disciplinary definition of public theology. As a relatively young theological genre, public theology suffers from methodological opaqueness; the term 'public theology' has been used without clear definitions, methodological clarity and shared meanings. A number of scholars use the term 'public theology' in very loose and manifold ways exchangeable with public ethics, (social) ethics, public religion, political philosophy, public philosophy or social philosophy.[2]

---

[1] E. Harold Breitenberg, Jr. 'To Tell the Truth: Will the Real Public Theology Please Stand Up?', *The Journal of the Society of Christian Ethics* 23, no. 2 (2003): 55–96 (62).
[2] Harold Breitenberg notes that confusion, ambiguity and nebulousness in literature on public theology results from 'in large measure on how a writer understands the other terms and concepts

The nebulousness of public theology partly results from the fact that the very term 'public' was adopted without a clear distinction from its use by secular liberal counterparts.[3] This liberal definition of public is cerebral, male-oriented and opposed to the private, and its narrow scope has been rightly criticized by feminist thinkers. Without a conscious endeavour to distinguish itself from its secular liberal counterpart, public theology is suspected of a narrow scope, androcentrism and assimilationist tendency. There have been extensive attempts among theologians to define 'public' in distinction from a liberal (secular) definition and to address the criticism raised by feminist theologians.

This chapter begins with my working definition of public theology and (social) ethics, and then compare them – their similarities and differences, overlapping concerns and distinctiveness, by asking: Are they synonymous or different? Do they deal with the same subject matter or different ones? What are their mutual relationships? I claim that just as theology and ethics, while interrelated, are different, so are public theology and social ethics; they overlap but are distinctive. I also argue that the biblical idea of covenant helps bring a methodological coherence and clarity to public theology and its relationship with (social) ethics. In particular, the covenantal idea of social spheres, a complex and differentiated view of a society, is helpful in understanding the similarities and differences between public theology and (social) ethics. When located in a covenantal framework, public theology and (social) ethics gain better disciplinary identity and clarity on their mutual relationship.

13.1 PUBLIC THEOLOGY

As mentioned earlier, despite growing literature and a wide usage of the term among theologians, public theology is still a highly contested, nebulous concept. What is public theology? How is it different from other forms of theology, such as systematic theology, practical theology, moral theology and liberation theology? How should we understand the public nature of theology? What does 'public' exactly mean? Does it refer to the public square or a particular method of theology? These questions typically accompany or are implied in the discussion of public theology.

---

and the relationships among them, as well as the academic and ecclesiastical perspective from which he or she approaches them' (Breitenberg, 'To Tell the Truth', 57). The problem of definitional looseness is often found in social ethics as well, which has often been used exchangeable with social philosophy or political philosophy; however, with its long disciplinary history, social ethics does not face the same degree of confusion and ambiguity with regard to disciplinary boundary and method, as public theology does.

[3]This suspicion is aggravated by the fact that public theology's early advocates were mostly white male European theologians, who engaged public theology in a close conversation with liberal political theorists, such as John Locke, John Rawls and Jürgen Habermas.

This chapter defines public theology as a genre of theological discourse that communicates specific visions, claims and convictions of a particular religious community to its own members as well as to the wider audience in diverse publics. Hence, it is a misunderstanding to dismiss public theology as uncritical assimilation, or even a theological selling out, to liberal democracy in order for a religious community to gain or maintain political influence, as some critics assert. Unlike public philosophy, public ethics or public religion, public theology is rooted in a particular faith tradition. Importantly, 'public' in public theology refers to more than a locale; it is 'a posture of doing theology',[4] namely a critical dialogical openness to others in seeking mutual understanding and the enhancement of truth, justice and the common good. Because of its commitment to the common good, justice and care for family and the marginalized, 'public' is not opposed to 'private'.

Public theology has the following characteristics:

(1) 'Public' in public theology is not just descriptive but also normative in the sense that 'public' indicates the commitment to the common well-being of a society. Public theology concerns not only the mission of religious institutions but also the shape, direction and moral quality of our common life, whether the nation or the global community.

Such a disposition is grounded in the theological conviction and missiological nature of the Gospel – a belief that God cares for God's creation and wants to redeem it from sin and evil. God's purpose is to build the shalom community that is characterized by love, justice, peace and common flourishing. In other words, a public disposition, which reflects God's moral character, is the manifestation of *missio Dei*. God's mission is cosmic in its scope and horizon and ethical in its intent and nature. God governs the universe with love and justice.

The proponents of public theology point out that in spite of its relatively recent introduction, public theology has a long historical root in Judaism and Christianity. From the Exodus event, the reception of the Law at Mt. Sinai, the Prophets' criticism of corrupt powers and unjust systems, to Jesus' confrontation with religious and political authorities, the commitment to justice, common good and care for the poor runs throughout the Bible.

Historically, Christians have actively engaged in various political and social issues through their prophetic ministry and social advocacy work and have made significant contributions to social justice and human rights, as we see in their participation in various liberation, abolitionist, human rights, peace movements and so on.

---

[4]Hak Joon Lee, 'Public Theology', in *The Cambridge Companion to Christian Political Theology*, ed. Craig Hovey and Elizabeth Phillips (New York: Cambridge University Press, 2015), 44–65 (44).

The Christian work for justice, love and peace is an indispensable aspect of their calling and mission to witness God's reign. The church is called to participate in a social life and contribute to the common good and justice. The task of public theology is to assist this ministry of the church.

(2) Public theology is polemical in its nature, birthed out of its concern over the spread of individualistic spirituality and Christocentric theology that distrusts the full-fledged public engagement of the church. Public theology is highly critical of the privatization of religion, privileged or fideistic claims of theology and practices that reject the active social role of the church in the public realms and/or refuse to validate Christian truth and moral claims with relevant warrants and evidences. The advocates of public theology have engaged in extensive polemical debates with Christians holding sectarian beliefs with authoritarian or individualistic orientations.

Public theology is equally critical of secular enlightenment philosophies and political ideologies that have attempted to relegate religion to the private realm and organizes a collective life that excludes religion (e.g., the French Revolution, atheism, communism). Since the Enlightenment, constant efforts have been made by secular intellectuals and politicians to provide a foundation for politics and morality without any resources in religion. Public theology is critical of this truncated notion of the public, its thin universalism and narrow proceduralism. Max Stackhouse's critique deserves our attention.

Those of us who today claim the legacy of public theology point out that the 'logos' (the logic/living word) of philosophical thought, social analysis, and moral judgment is unstable by itself. It bends easily to the unscrupulous interests that lurk in the very heart of the best of us, if it is not rooted in a holy, true, just creativity that is greater than we humans can achieve in our subjectivity. Indeed, it tends always to be distorted, if it is not ultimately grounded in God, for the human wisdom of philosophy, the ordering systems of societies, and the ethical judgments of individuals may express the irrational elements of human fantasy no less than does private religion; and all of them need to be seen as subject to standards, purposes, and an unconditioned reality greater than our wisdoms, systems, judgments, and religions can generate or discover alone. 'Logos' requires 'theos'.[5]

---

[5] Max L. Stackhouse, 'Public Theology and Ethical Judgment', in *Shaping Public Theology*, ed. Scott Paeth, E. Harold Breitenberg, and Hak Joon Lee (Grand Rapids, MI: Eerdmans, 2014), 116–33 (121).

Refusing to be relegated to the private realm, public theology asserts a rightful place of religion in the public life. Rejecting the dichotomy of fact and value, the religious and the civic, public theology advocates a constructive role of religious discourses for the common good of a society.

(3) Closely related to the above-mentioned two tasks is the apologetic task of public theology. The proponents of public theology claim that truth-claims of Christianity are not only publicly communicable but also defensible. Public theology is rooted in a very simple but powerful desire of religious people – to offer a reasonable account of why they believe what they believe.[6] Also, this disposition is not something new for Christians. From the beginning of their history, Christians faced this question from within and without, not only by Jews and Romans and other peoples (both learned and ordinary) but also by new converts: Who is Jesus and why do you believe in him as the Lord and the messiah? Early Christian writings, especially the Gospel of Luke, were written to answer those questions. Over the two millennia, an apologetical task was presumed in the variety of activities of the church and its members.[7]

Apologetics in public theology takes various forms. In the area of systematic theology, David Tracy offers a sophisticated and creative understanding of public theology, especially as he engages it with the question of theological method. Tracy contends that the public nature of theology is the very heart of Christian theology. He declares, 'all theology is public discourse'.[8] Tracy builds his system of Christian theology on the premise of the publicness of theological claims; the truth-claims of Christianity either can be redeemed publicly or at least cannot be completely disputed, as they are reasonable and publicly communicable; Christian claims of truth and ethics are open to criticism and questions from the members of a society other than Christians. To be genuinely public, Christian claims, along with the criteria and process of their deliberation, cannot be private, esoteric or privileged because only through openness and public scrutiny does it gain public integrity and respect.

---

[6]Lee, 'Public Theology', 49.
[7]Ibid., 50.
[8]David Tracy, *The Analogical Imagination: Christian Theology and the Culture of Pluralism* (New York: Crossroad, 1998), 2.

In defending the public nature of theology, Tracy specifically draws upon the idea of a 'classic'. That is, he proposes that religious canons be treated as classics (like cherished work of art and literature) whose disclosive meaning and transformative power are enduring and transcultural – thus *public*.[9] Tracy notes:

> The notion of the public character of all symbols (warranted by both a theory of symbol and the hermeneutical notion of truth as manifestation of possibility) renders the classic works of art and religion available to the public realm for dialogue and argument and not merely for the private states of the religious or aesthetic subject. The technicization of the public realm, so well analyzed by Habermas under the rubric or the colonization of the lifeworld, is linked in modernity to the marginalization of art and the privatization of religion. To ignore the claims of religion and to narrow the claims of art to claims of personal sincerity can only, I fear, increase the colonization of the lifeworld that Habermas so forcefully wants to overcome. The vestiges of reason in our lifeworld include the vestiges of possibility for individual happiness and communal good in the great classics of art and religion.[10]

Tracy proposes the three publics, church, society and academia, as the areas of theological investigation. Since each of these publics has its own distinctive concern, criterion and the audience, Christians need to engage them accordingly, with proper attention to their distinctive characteristics. In particular, Tracy differentiates the genres of Christian theology and their disciplinary partners of theology corresponding to these three publics: fundamental theology with philosophy in academia, systematic theology with hermeneutics in the church and practical theology with hermeneutics and critical social theory in society.[11] In each public, public theology performs its distinctive function.

For example, in the church, Christian identity and faithfulness are the central concerns, and public theology carries out a discerning and rule-making function to avoid arbitrary interpretations of Scripture, doctrines and creeds. In academia, the primary audience of public

---

[9]Ibid., 108.
[10]David Tracy, *Habermas, Modernity, and Public Theology*, ed. Don S. Browning and Francis Schüssler Fiorenza (New York: Crossroad, 1992), 38.
[11]Gaspar Martinez, *Confronting the Mystery of God: Political, Liberation, and Public Theologies* (New York: Continuum, 2001), 199.

theology is other scholars. It asks: What are universally acceptable truths? What are justifiable bases of Christian truth-claims? Public theology seeks the universal validity of Christian truth-claims. In society, public theology engages with citizens in seeking justice and the common good. It asks: How can a society achieve rough justice and promote the common good? Tracy's pluralistic idea of the public, as will be further discussed later, is important to clarify the relationship between public theology and social ethics. In his framework, public theology and social ethics overlap in the public of society as both are concerned about social justice and the common good, but not in the other publics (church and academia) that focus on the redemption of truth-claims ecclesiastically or academically.

Public theology continues this impulse today. Living in a pluralistic society, this apologetic role is urgent because Christians find themselves challenged to defend their faith and practices in relation to public policies and other religious faiths and ideologies. Under the stricture of religious freedom, Christians cannot claim privilege but should seek to move public opinion and gain the support of other people with different values and convictions.

In summary, one sees that public theology has a broad swath of theological agendas, intellectual interests and commitments: care for the common good, commitment to justice, polemics (to defend the public nature and role of the church), apologetics (defend the validity of the Gospel). Not all advocates of public theology equally commit to or address all these agendas and concerns; they build their version of public theology upon one or a few of them, often without clarifying its (their) relationship to the rest, which is another source of confusion around public theology. That is, some advocates focus on justice and social responsibility of Christians, while others are interested in the apologetic or polemical purpose.[12]

Having discussed public theology, we now turn to social ethics.

---

[12]These three tasks closely reflect the historical background and ethos around its genesis. The birth of public theology in the United States was informed by the liberal democratic ethos of the West – the role that Christianity (theology) has played in the public life in Western history in general, the modern democratic society in particular. Furthermore, public theology, in its genesis, carries in it a unique American political and moral sensibility and political tradition, such as the idea of religious freedom, the separation of church and state, cultural–religious pluralism, as well as a strong Christian tradition of civic participation and advocacy in civil society. Churches are compelled to defend the truth-claims of the Christian faith and constantly engage polemics of its critiques within and without, carrying out its strong tradition of social justice and public responsibility through advocacy and prophetic engagements.

13.2 SOCIAL ETHICS

Ethics is a discipline that studies the foundation and nature of morality and the validity and method of moral decisions and actions. Ethics asks what we ought to do and how we make good decisions and actions. It is typically framed by the categories of right, good or fit, or their combinations,[13] which constitute the ground of moral obligations and the standards to measure the normativity of our decisions and actions. These normative grounds are important because they render legitimacy and moral authority to our decisions and actions.

The ideas of right, good or fit come from various sources: religion, metaphysics, philosophy, cultural traditions and customs, reason, experiences. Different people claim different sources as the normative ground of their ethics. For example, for postmodernists, right, good and fit are the products of a social construct, mostly a dominant group (class, gender, race), while for secular liberals, they are the work of human reason; for naturalists, the ideas of right, good and fit are the results of a long evolutionary process of the human species.

Ethics is practised in various levels of human life: personal, institutional, societal and international or global. Social ethics is a sub-discipline of ethics that is practised at the societal level. The idea of social justice is at the heart of social ethics, and social ethics investigates the normative grounds and procedures in organizing a society, its institutions and coordinating communal activities/practices, according to the principles of justice. These principles guide public policy decisions, legislation and the implementation of policies and laws. The ongoing task of social ethics is how to discern and establish proper principles and criteria of justice accepted by the members of a society.

Gibson Winter identifies three essential elements of social ethics: the factual situation (or social conditions), the evaluative norms (or ethical order) and 'the ultimate or comprehensive order' (or a religious vision).[14] Here, social conditions refer to the state of society or a particular social context where moral decisions are made (which is typically the object of social analysis); evaluative norms denote the demands of the right, good or fit which serve as the authoritative basis of moral decisions; finally, a religious vision describes the ultimate or comprehensive order that the members of a society broadly share, which influences the overall direction and moral ethos of a society. Human

---

[13]Max Stackhouse, 'Ethics: Social and Christian', *Shaping Public Theology*, 133–53 (136). The categories of right, good or fit are phrased in different terms and languages, such as rule or duty (right), goal or consequence (good) and responsiveness or appropriateness (fit). Virtue ethics is a genre of ethics that is typically associated with the category of good. Describing morally excellent or praiseworthy traits, virtues are shaped through repeated practices (habits) as a moral agent desires and pursues a certain good (*telos*).

[14]Gibson Winter, 'Introduction: Religion, Ethics, and Society', in *Social Ethics: Issues in Ethics and Society*, ed. Gibson Winter (New York: Harper & Row, 1968), 15.

moral decisions and actions are inevitably informed by a certain sense of the ultimate (typically taking a religious or metaphysical form) because humans justify their ethical decisions and action by appealing to the highest authority. The vision, values and norms of social ethics are usually inherited from the past in the form of religious cultural traditions, ideologies, shared moral ethos and customs.

Social ethics relies on social science to carry out its descriptive task – to understand the social conditions and changing social realities (e.g. technology, globalization, capitalism and religious cultural pluralism) that affect collective lives. Through the empirical study of social behaviours of institutions and individuals, social ethics studies what is going on in a society and people's lives.

Social ethics is evaluative in assessing and judging the decisions and actions of social institutions, the government and communities in light of a society's vision, moral norms and values. It asks whether what is going on should go on or should be changed; what is the right, good or fit that a society relies on, and which norms, ideals and values should be prioritized in making decisions on a particular social issue, and why.

Finally, social ethics is prescriptive in offering concrete directives, public policy proposals and legislative options to improve or correct the situation. One major challenge in a pluralistic society is that it is increasingly difficult to find shared norms and a vision.

Social ethics presupposes the sociality (interdependence) of human existence. Ethics is essentially a social enterprise; it presupposes the sociality (symbiosis) of human life; hence the study of social ethics requires the study of how sociality is embodied, exercised and what its contours and dynamics are. As it is normative and prescriptive by nature, social ethics is intentional; it presupposes human freedom and agency that are exercised in choosing various moral decisions and the course of actions. Social ethics is deliberative, as it seeks the best possible course of action among available options and limited time and resources. Both sociality and intentionality are informed by a certain account of the origin and destiny of humanity, the nature of human freedom and purpose, and the content and meaning of human fulfilment.

These three essential components of social ethics are interrelated. Winter's concise summary is apt and helpful in understanding what social ethics is. Social ethics is 'the expression of ultimate commitment in the shaping of man's future, embodying a view of man and his fulfilment in concrete recommendations for public policy'.[15]

---

[15]Ibid., 17.

13.3 PUBLIC THEOLOGY AND SOCIAL ETHICS: SIMILARITIES AND DIFFERENCES

13.3.1 Similarities

Public theology and social ethics (except Christian ethics of sectarian traditions) are concerned with the well-being of a society and its common life.[16] They deal with the issues and concerns that are social or public in nature, which are larger than personal concerns and individual interests. Public theology and social ethics share a normative concern; justice is central to both disciplines.[17] In particular, public theology and social ethics share their critique of selfish utilitarianism, the spiritualization or individualization of Christian faith and its sectarian retreat from a society. Distancing themselves from a narrow Christocentrism in theology and ethics,[18] public theology and Christian social ethics respect the importance of the general revelation of God (common grace, natural law) operating in history, and uphold justice and Christian responsibility in a society as the integral aspect of Christian vocation, mission and discipleship.

Public theology and (social) ethics respect publicity. Like public theology, social ethics also cannot avoid public scrutiny because moral decisions are not always free from the influences of ideologies, vested self-interests and social mores rather than guided by the professed moral values and standards of justice. For these reasons, ethical decisions are potentially fallible, thus requiring public scrutiny.

Public theology and social ethics are interdisciplinary, as they use and engage with other disciplines (either as allies or as polemical opponents). Public theology engages with the variety of other disciplines (e.g. philosophies, sociology, aesthetics and literatures), depending on its specific public, to communicate and defend the truth-claims of Christian faith, while social ethics relies on social sciences in conducting a social analysis; it is interdisciplinary but its scope is not as extensive as public theology.

Both public theology and social ethics are contextual in attending to the current affairs of the public or a society. They equally engage in a descriptive

---

[16]Not every Christian social ethicist believes that public responsibility is integral to Christian discipleship. Some are in fact very critical of public theology and its agenda. They claim that Christian social ethics is possible without being publicly oriented. For example, Stanley Hauerwas claims that to be the church is Christian social ethics – to live out the narrative of the Cross faithfully in a pluralistic society. For them Christian social ethics is identical, co-extends with the church and a Christian community; its focus is solely the witness to the world than engagement.

[17]This shared concern and commitment to the well-being of the common life and justice contributes to the great deal of confusion when compared with social ethics.

[18]For the detailed discussion on the limitation of Christocentrism for social ethics, see E. Clinton Gardner, *Christocentrism in Christian Social Ethics: A Depth Study of Eight Modern Protestants* (Washing, DC: University Press of America, 1983).

task in studying social realities and historical changes. Discussions of public theology and social ethics do not take place in a cultural vacuum. They are self-conscious of the influences of culture, historical experiences and religious traditions of a particular society on their normative understanding of a social issue or public discourse.

13.3.2 *Differences*

Public theology and social ethics, despite common concerns and similarities, are different in their respective subject matters, emphasis and scope. Social ethics is not necessarily theological, and public theology is not inevitably ethical. Not every issue and topic that public theology addresses are immediately ethical, while ethical implications may be implicitly involved. For example, in Tracy's public theology, the two publics of church and academia are not primarily ethical, but theological (dogmatic) and fundamental-philosophical, respectively.

Public theology differs from social ethics in its apologetic and polemical nature because it explicates and defends the validity and plausibility of Christian perspectives. While apologetic and polemical interests could be involved, they are not the primary tasks of social ethics. Its focus is normative in formulating and clarifying the ground and nature of moral good, right, duties and purposes.[19]

This means that the scope of public theology is broader than social ethics. While public theology is rooted in a particular religious tradition, social ethics does not have to be.[20] There are a number of social ethics that rely on (social) philosophies of reason, science and collective experiences as their authoritative moral sources (libertarian, utilitarian, social contractarian, Marxist, postmodern, liberal, Aristotelian). However, public theology, by definition, is purposely theological. God and God's relationship to humanity are the starting point of public theology. This difference manifests in their respective interdisciplinary scopes, as mentioned earlier. While social ethics relies on social science more than any other discipline,[21] this is not necessarily the case for public theology. Public theology engages with far more diverse disciplines in communicating the public meaning and implications of theology.

---

[19]Breitenberg, 'To Tell the Truth', 61. In fact, a considerable number of Christians belong to theological traditions that are highly suspicious of such efforts. They consider apologetics as a major source of the corruption and erosion of Christian identity and conviction.

[20]Civil religion, which played an instrumental role in the rise of public theology, also does not rely on a particular religion.

[21]However, this does not imply that social ethics is neutral or objective because it inevitably relies on certain symbols and narratives in its explications and expositions, although it, in general, seeks and relies on shared or common morality (natural law), moral vision, rational principle and moral epistemology (reason, conscience, social experiences) found across different cultures and religions.

While they share a broad normative concern, public theology and social ethics are slightly different in their respective focus and emphasis. The focus and emphasis of public theology is God and God's actions, while social ethics focuses on human decisions and actions. Public theology is still God-talk – who God is, what God does and how God relates to humanity and the world; social ethics is normative in essence, which has to do with human responsibility and obligations in relationship to God and others. Public theology attends to the divine will, purpose and the worth of human existence that bear upon the common good and justice, social ethics concerns the questions of the right, good or fit in organizing a society and its institutions, and establishing regulatory authorities and public policies.

For example, love, justice and truth-telling are moral norms and values found in every religion and culture, which are indispensable in guiding human moral decisions. Public theology explicates the theological ground and meaning of these norms in light of religious symbols (the Cross, the Lord's Supper) and narratives (the story of the Incarnation, passion), while social ethics studies their normative meaning and binding nature (informed by theology) in making decisions. The prohibition of murder ('Thou shall not murder') is a normative demand found in every society. In ancient societies, the authority behind this prohibition was religious, not just ethical. For example, in Christianity, this commandment was given by God to all humans through Noah, and later to the Israelites through Moses; human life should be protected because it is created in the image of God. Public theology offers a theological justification for why this obligation is necessary (whence of this obligation), while social ethics discusses not only the foundation of this obligation but also its policy and legal implications and scope (e.g. killing in a just war).

When compared, public theology aims at persuasion (thus, it tends to be discursive, rhetorical and apologetic), and social ethics, in the final analysis, is prescriptive to the extent it makes specific public policy proposals and calls for concrete corresponding actions. Social ethics inevitably accounts proportionality and practical wisdom in deliberation (thus, more reality bound than public theology); it asks not only about duty and obligation but also what is practically possible in a given social situation and social condition, especially in terms of power dynamics and resources. That is, social ethics considers that our moral decisions are always made within the bounds of limited time, material resources and capabilities, which makes our decisions less than ideal. In short, public theology is perspectival or orienting in engaging with public issues, social ethics is concrete and actional.

In the final analysis, public theology and social ethics, while overlapping, are distinctive and complementary. As Herman Bavinck says, 'The two disciplines, far from facing each other as two independent entities, together form a single system; they are related members of a single organism.'[22] While dogmatics precedes ethics, dogmatics is incomplete without ethics, just as ethics is insufficient without dogmatics. Metaphorically speaking, if dogmatics is the root, ethics is its fruit. Without theology, ethics loses its distinctive identity and foundation, while without ethics, theology becomes speculative and abstract, losing its social relevance and transformative power.

We see in Martin Luther King, Jr. and Dietrich Bonhoeffer's speeches a creative, complementary synthesis of public theology and social ethics. They relied on public theology in their critique of Adolf Hitler and white racism, and their defence of the rights of Jews and African Americans. However, Bonhoeffer's participation in the conspiracy to assassinate Hitler and King's strategy to boycott and target Bull Connor in the Birmingham Campaign were more social-ethical than public theological.

One sees a similar example in Reinhold Niebuhr. His idea of justice as the balance of power is ethical; he claims that the balance is necessary to achieve a rough social justice in a society; however, his justification is based on his profound theological anthropology informed by the doctrine of human freedom and sin (how human sinful desires are amplified at a collective level).

Public theology and social ethics need each other. Theology answers why something is moral in the deepest sense; the whence of 'ought-ness' (where moral obligation comes from?), while ethics asks, by what authority? Public theology serves as meta-social ethics for Christians, as it helps examine a society, its institutions and social issues from the perspective of faith.[23] Most Christian social ethics presupposes some form of public theology (the first principles grounded in or derived from Christian theology), although not every public theology is social-ethical.

13.4 A CONSTRUCTIVE PROPOSAL: COVENANT, PUBLIC THEOLOGY, SOCIAL ETHICS

I introduce covenant as a key biblical idea that links and mediates public theology and Christian social ethics. Better than any other biblical concept, covenant clarifies their mutual relationship – distinct as well as complementary

---

[22]Herman Bavinck, *Reformed Dogmatics: Prolegomena* (Grand Rapids: Baker Academic, 2003), 58. Similarly, Barth declares: 'There is no grace without the lordship and claim of grace. There is no dogmatics which is not also and necessarily ethics.' Karl Barth, *Church Dogmatics*, II/2, *The Doctrine of God* (Edinburgh: T&T Clark, 1957), 12. Likewise, one may say that there is no social ethics without public theology; conversely there is no public theology without social ethics.
[23]Cf. Nicholas Wolterstorff, *Hearing the Call: Liturgy, Justice, Church, and World*, ed. Mark R. Gornik and Gregory Thompson (Grand Rapids: Eerdmans, 2011), 432.

nature. Further expanding the methodological insight of Tracy on the plurality of public, a covenantal idea of social spheres helps to see how public theology and social ethics operate relatedly and distinctively in various spheres of a society.

Covenant, in general, refers to a method by which different parties freely reach an agreement around certain terms with God as its partner or its guarantor. The terms specify the stipulations that the parties should perform towards each other based on their free and mutual commitments and promises. Covenant, unlike contract, carries in it a public disposition; various covenants in the Bible (Creation Covenant, Noahic covenant, Sinai Covenant, the Covenant of Jesus) aim to achieve God's public purpose and concern. These major covenants are public in their nature and disposition and universal in their scope.

In the covenant, we see the collaboration between God and humans. Covenant is communicative; God's self-communication takes place in covenant and God Himself becomes the communicative partner of humanity. The covenant is open to renewal, correction, respect truthfulness and transparency. Covenant is established and sustained by ongoing communications between the parties. Covenant is the method God Himself chooses to advance the common good, and God transforms humans into public agents through His covenant (Gen. 12.1-3). Covenant is the vehicle through which God's moral purpose and character are translated into human obligations of justice and law in the form of agreement (covenantal stipulations). Covenant is apt and fruitful in describing God's being and action and God's moral character, in particular, God's public concern for common flourishing. Covenant best communicates God's creational design and public intent for humanity. Through covenant, humans know who God is and what God demands, and God holds humans accountable for their actions. Hence, covenant naturally mediates theology and ethics.

Covenant carries democratic values and sensibilities. It is liberative, egalitarian and reciprocal; it rejects a hierarchical or atomistic form of society. Although many secular theorists refuse to acknowledge it, covenant theology and ethics have substantially contributed to the rise of modern democracy, human rights, constitutionalism, rule of law, separation of power and civil society; these values and institutions, in their secular forms, have spread in the world without acknowledgement of their theological origins. In the aftermath of the Second World War, the shaping of the transnational order and structures, such as the United Nations, was also covenantally informed.

13.4.1 Covenant and spheres

A covenantal approach has another benefit. Covenant is a theological idea that envisions a pluriform of social spheres/publics.

Covenant serves as a formative organizing principle of society in the Bible.[24] It is a structural device that God uses to organize a society according to justice. In ancient Israel, covenant was the source of their sociological imagination in organizing the society. Israelites imagined social relationships and institutions in terms of God's covenant; the Torah discusses the law in different social relationships and institutions.

A covenantal social vision, germane to the Bible, was further developed by early Reformed theorists, such as Johannes Althusius and the Puritans, which was later refined by Abraham Kuyper and Herman Dooyeweerd. These theologians claim that the plurality of social spheres is God's design from the beginning; it shows that God's reign is not monolithic but differentiated and accommodating to the needs of humanity.

Stackhouse was a theological ethicist who elaborated covenant in a globalizing social context by engaging social science and comparative religious ethics. According to him, across all different cultures and times, human societies share five core social spheres: economy, politics, family, media and religion. Despite cultural and historical variations (and despite different ideologies and material-technological levels), these five spheres meet the enduring needs of humanity: eat and find shelter, adjudicate conflicts, have sex and procreate, share information and feelings, pursue the ultimate meaning.[25] Stackhouse's idea of spheres shows that human social activities are covenantally organized around several moral authorities, as designed by God, in order to meet key biological and social needs under God's rule.

Covenant offers a theological ground of spheres/publics. Covenant envisions a complex, organic and associational form of society. As the art of organizing, covenant imagines a society consisting of multiple spheres (politics, family, economy, criminal justice, education, law, school, church, hospital, etc.) that are interrelated with each other, while maintaining their relative autonomies.

A sphere is a socio-ethical as well as public entity. Socially, each sphere performs a certain public function requisite for a society, but theologically, it performs a specific mandate from God. Each sphere has its own distinctive purpose (mandate or mission), rules and practices. It functions as a public because every sphere has public responsibility towards the common good and requires transparency and openness to its members and beyond. For Christians, social spheres are important because they are domains where Christian vocation and discipleship are exercised. Closely associated with the Protestant doctrine

---

[24]Stackhouse writes that 'the structures of covenantal justice are both internal to ethics and external in the organizational life of society' (Max L. Stackhouse, 'Covenantal Justice in a Global Era', *Shaping Public Theology*, 204–19 (214).
[25]Max L. Stackhouse, 'General Introduction', in *God and Globalization, vol. 1. Religion and the Powers of the Common Life*, ed. Max L. Stackhouse and Peter J. Paris (Harrisburg: Trinity Press International, 2000), 1–52 (36).

of vocation, each sphere (and institutions) is a social locus where Christians live out God's calling.

13.4.2 Publics and spheres

Various social spheres serve as distinctive 'publics' in a society. Public discourses occur in the contexts of these spheres as well as in a broad society. Ethical deliberations of social ethics (especially distributive justice) are sphere-based. The nature and content of the apologetic-polemical task of public theology and the evaluative and prescriptive tasks of social ethics vary depending on social spheres. That is, the specific contours and contents of these tasks, criteria of adjudication in theological critique and ethical deliberation depend on particular spheres.

'Publics' and 'spheres' are not exactly identical, but they mostly overlap in a modern democratic society. Despite their potential, spheres did not perform as 'public' (nor fully differentiated) in a pre-modern society. Through a series of political social transformations after the Reformation and the Enlightenment, social spheres began to operate as 'public' in a modern sense. And covenant has played a pivotal role in this transformation. Specifically, the structure and configuration of modern spheres have covenantal origins, which are still found in the mission statements and organizational structures of modern spheres and institutions (e.g. a board of trustees and its by-law).

Spheres do not exhaust the breadth of public, but public operates significantly along with spheres. Public and social spheres overlap, if not exactly coincide. Social spheres serve as a kind of public; however, the communities of race, gender and sex also serve as important subaltern publics. Women, diverse racial-ethnic and gender communities serve as important subaltern publics of a society. Since these communities are justice-oriented (to overcome systemic forms of exclusion and discrimination), their public discourses (including theology) and social practices cannot exclude the knowledge of spherical mandates and boundaries in order to achieve their goals (e.g. political-legal sphere for legal protection of their human rights, economic sphere for fair distribution of resources, etc.).[26]

Conversely, as Tracy noted, not every public takes social justice as its primary concern. For example, in academia, social justice is not the primary concern (although the idea of justice is implied in the academic rules, standards and the policies of professional societies). Rather, public theology's apologetic and polemical interests are most prominent in this public.

---

[26]It is another question that deserves an extensive discussion: whether these communities can operate as covenantal communities. My view is that we may safely assume that they operate as quasi covenantal communities.

Each sphere has a distinctive purpose, and public theology and social ethics need to perform their tasks according to it. It is one of the important tasks of public theology to explicate the theological grounds and accounts of the divine mandate of each sphere (public) and its ethical implications.

13.5 CONCLUSION

This chapter studied the relationship between public theology and (social) ethics. Public theology and social ethics, while overlapping, are not identical; their disciplinary foci and emphases are different. While the task of public theology is normative, apologetic and polemical, that of (social) ethics is essentially normative. When pressed, public theology's concern is theological, while social ethics is ethical. Public theology seeks to elaborate and defend the public relevance and significance of Christian symbols, narratives and practices, while social ethics explicates the ground and nature of moral obligations that bear on public policies, social institutions and particular social issues.

The chapter also discussed a constructive possibility of covenant for public theology and social ethics based on its imaginative fertility and theoretical capaciousness. A covenantal approach is helpful not only in clarifying the difference/similarity between public theology and social ethics but also in offering a more sophisticated understanding of public theology and social ethics. In covenant, both are complementary. One may say that public theology is a theological aspect of divine covenant, while Christian social ethics is the ethical aspect of covenant. Authentic Christian witness, discipleship and social engagement require the balanced and well-integrated combination of public theology and social ethics.

The covenantal idea of social sphere, which conceives a society as the ensemble of multiple publics, is crucial in clarifying how and where the tasks of public theology and social ethics overlap and diverge. A covenantal approach reframes and expands David Tracy's three publics and corrects the mistakes of many proponents of public theology who have not given proper attention to the idea of diverse spheres/publics and only create unnecessary confusion and misunderstanding.

The covenantal idea of public addresses the feminist critique of the dualistic/binary concept of a liberal democratic public. In this covenantal framework, family is a sphere which is crucial to enhance the common good and shalom. It is equally a public domain that deserves extensive public attention and democratic debates in promoting women's welfare and children's rights. Like other spheres, family is obliged to fulfil its distinctive mandate and to promote justice and the common good.

The need for public theology grows today. In a pluralistic society, Christians face the growing gap or dissonance between the Christian world view and secular liberalism and other religious views. Many Christians are struggling to bridge the gap between their faith convictions and the current vision and arrangements of society. Unfortunately, tension and conflicts are aggravating as seen in the deepening polarization in the United States and other countries.

The idea of covenant is certainly convincing, especially in today's pluralistic society in the global era. Covenant is 'biblically based and theologically rooted, but broadly ecumenical social ethic, one intentionally open to interfaith influences and able to give guidance in and to the emerging global civilization'.[27] Covenant is capacious to the extent it 'is able to reach across barriers of culture, civilization and context and call people to conviction, will be compelling'.[28] Every society needs to have a certain social covenant that serves as a shared framework within which people engage public realms with shared moral goal, principles and expectations.

I anticipate further fruitful conversations between public theology and social ethics around the idea of covenant.

---

[27]Stackhouse, 'The Fifth Gospel and the Global Mission of the Church', *Shaping Public Theology*, 185.
[28]Stackhouse, 'The Task of Theological Ethics', *Shaping Public Theology*, 93–103 (103).

CHAPTER 14

Public theology and the doctrine of God

ANNE SIEBESMA

Over the past century, theologians and churches have concerned themselves extensively with society at large. Both Catholic and Protestant churches and theologians show awareness that theology is about more than the life and well-being of the church alone and that theological views have consequences for and are influenced by public and political issues and contexts.[1] At the same time, widespread secularization and increasing pluralism have problematized this connection of theology and society in Western contexts. Public theology originated in the United States as a response to this marginalized public role of church and theology in society.[2] Public theologians defend the claim that theology is still relevant for society and has a right to speak in the public sphere. Speaking from a Christian theological background, but in a way that is also accessible to non-believers, public theologians attempt to enter into dialogue with others in society and offer theological contributions in order to support a

---

*This chapter was originally published in Dutch as: Anne Siebesma, 'De maat van alle dingen: publieke theologie en particulariteit', *Tijdschrift Voor Theologie* 59 (2019): 138–55. Small clarifying corrections have been made in the translation.

[1] Awareness of such a mutual influence is expressed, for instance, in Francis Schüssler Fiorenza, 'Political Theology as Foundational Theology', *Proceedings of the Catholic Theological Society of America* 32 (1977): 142–77.

[2] Hak Joon Lee, 'Public Theology', in *The Cambridge Companion to Christian Political Theology*, ed. Craig Hovey and Elizabeth Phillips (New York: Cambridge University Press, 2015), 45.

society in which the common good is upheld. Furthermore, public theologians reflect on the criteria for 'public' contributions and seek to demonstrate that theology can meet these criteria.

However, such a dialogical approach and the idea that it is the task of theology to contribute to the organization and well-being of society are contested. This is especially visible in the various typologies of public theology that have appeared in recent years. Stephan van Erp,[3] Eneida Jacobsen[4] and Gerard Mannion[5] have all identified alternative ways of thinking about the relationship between church and society or theology and society, besides the approach described earlier. What is important in light of this chapter is that all three authors distinguish a type that starts from the contrast between Christianity and the secular society.[6] Several theologians who write about the relationship between theology and society emphasize that the church and Christian faith present an alternative form of public life that provides a correction to the assumptions, values and aims of secular society.[7] Moreover, they speak from within a Christian narrative and reject the notion that public contributions must be translated into a 'shared language'.[8]

The aim of this chapter is to offer a contribution to the debate surrounding particularity and public theology by shifting the focus from questions about relevance and language to the question of the particular nature of theology and what it means to speak about God. After discussing public theology and the critiques raised by those who stress the particularity of the Christian language of faith and ecclesial praxis, I ask what is specific about theology and what the emphasis on this form of particularity could mean for public theology. This particularity lies in treating God, not as concept but as reality and agent or other, as the ultimate standard for its claims. Consequently, public theology should not in the first place be concerned with demonstrating the public relevance of theology but should describe public life within the greater but not fully delineated framework of God's salvific involvement with the world. With

---

[3]Stephan Van Erp, 'The Sacrament of the World: Thinking God's Presence Beyond Public Theology', *ET Studies* 6 (2015): 119–34.
[4]Eneida Jacobsen, 'Models of Public Theology', *International Journal of Public Theology* 6 (2012): 7–22.
[5]Gerard Mannion, 'A Brief Genealogy of Public Theology, or, Doing Theology When It Seems Nobody is Listening', *Annali Di Studi Religiosi* 10 (2009): 121–54.
[6]Van Erp, 'The Sacrament of the World', 124–6; Jacobsen, 'Models of Public Theology', 20; Mannion, 'A Brief Genealogy of Public Theology', 145.
[7]e.g. William Cavanaugh, *Theopolitical Imagination: Discovering The Liturgy as a Political Act in an Age of Global Consumerism* (London/New York: T&T Clark, 2002); James K. A. Smith, *Awaiting The King: Reforming Public Theology* (Grand Rapids: Baker Academic, 2017).
[8]e.g. Daniel Strange, 'What on Earth? Why on Earth? Evangelicals and Public Theology', *Foundations* 56 (2006): 6–17; Graham Ward, *The Politics of Discipleship: Becoming Postmaterial Citizens* (Grand Rapids: Baker Academic, 2009).

this perspective in mind, I turn to the discussion about the particularity of the language of faith and the discussion about the relationship between church and society. I argue that theological particularity does not necessarily entail an emphasis on faith at the expense of reason, nor an exclusive reflection on the church as an own form of public life over and against that of society.

14.1 PUBLIC THEOLOGY UNDER ATTACK

14.1.1 *Public theology as a defence of theology's societal relevance*

Public theology, as it is usually understood, seeks to offer relevant contributions to society and to simultaneously convince society of the relevance of these contributions. In doing so, public theology rejects both fundamentalist views on faith and society that deny the possibility of mutual understanding between believers and secularized society, and secularism, which tries to keep religious voices out of the public debate.[9] One important societal contribution public theology seeks to make lies exactly in its reflection on and support of a public sphere in which various domains of society (including churches and religious communities) can enter into dialogue.[10] This dialogue requires its participants to speak in a language that is accessible to all. Although public theologians make use of Christian sources in developing their contributions, and although recent authors in this field search for holistic forms of rationality,[11] public theologians seek to defend their stance in a shared language and according to shared criteria for what makes a convincing contribution.[12]

The American, Protestant theologian Max Stackhouse has been closely involved in the early development of public theology in the United States and can serve as an example here. His last book on public theology before his death concerns globalization.[13] According to Stackhouse, public theology can contribute to a better understanding of the global society by analysing the way in which

---

[9]Lee, 'Public Theology', 50; Gaspar Martinez, *Confronting the Mystery of God: Political, Liberation, and Public Theologies* (New York/London: Continuum, 2001), 217–18.
[10]e.g. Sebastian Kim, *Theology in the Public Sphere: Public Theology as a Catalyst for Open Debate* (London: SCM Press, 2011). A collection of publications like Sebastian Kim And Katie Day, eds, *A Companion to Public Theology* (Leiden: Brill, 2017), shows the great variety of other concrete issues that public theologians respond to: for example, globalization, health care, modern slavery and ecology.
[11]e.g. Mary Doak, *Reclaiming Narrative for Public Theology* (Ithaca: SUNY Press, 2004), 11; Elaine Graham, *Between a Rock and a Hard Place: Public Theology in a Post-Secular Age* (London: SCM Press, 2013), 205–9; Heather Walton, 'You Have to Say You Cannot Speak: Feminist Reflections upon Public Theology', *International Journal of Public Theology* 4 (2010): 21–36.
[12]Doak, *Reclaiming Narrative*, 4–5.
[13]Max L. Stackhouse, *God and Globalization Volume 4: Globalization and Grace*, series Theology for the twenty-first century (New York/London: T&T Clark, 2007).

Christianity has shaped globalization historically. What is more, Stackhouse believes theology can still provide global society with guidance and correction because a global society requires an underlying, shared and all-encompassing metaphysics and moral law. Such a metaphysics and moral law can offer societal models that can integrate the various aspects and institutions belonging to the global society into an organized whole.[14] According to Stackhouse, a Christian theology can provide such an all-encompassing vision, because the Christian God is not solely concerned with the church but with all aspects of life, and because such a vision can be communicated in a way that is accessible to all. In order to reach such a metaphysical moral framework that is truly universal and that can therefore support such a global society, theologians must enter into dialogue with others in society. In this dialogue, they must discern which aspects of the Christian tradition refer to 'what should be believed and lived out according to the highest, widest, deepest and most comprehending reality that we humans can discern' and read public life accordingly.[15] According to Stackhouse, theological contributions must be intelligible to all and must be tested for their compatibility with faith in a universal God and for their capacity to be internalized by society and offer guidance.[16]

The British, Anglican public theologian Elaine Graham can serve as an example of a more recent form of public theology. Graham writes that contemporary society is characterized by secularism on the one hand and the return of public expressions of religion that are more pluralistic than before on the other hand. In this context, Christian theological language is less and less accessible to the wider public.[17] Consequently, in Graham's view, public theology should not only demonstrate that theology can contribute to a good society but should also translate such theological contributions in order to make them intelligible once again.[18] Public theology is apologetic, but what is defended is not a truth claim but the relevance of religion to society and the right of religious people and religious communities to let their voices be heard in the public realm.[19] Graham is more critical than Stackhouse about the notion of universal reason. She explores alternative forms of witness such as speaking to the imagination and practices of good citizenship.[20] Also, her public theology is formulated partly in response to recent theological movements such as Postliberalism and

---

[14]Ibid., 32–6, 84–5.
[15]Ibid., 84.
[16]Ibid., 84, 112–13.
[17]Graham, *Between a Rock and a Hard Place*, xiv–xviii.
[18]Ibid., 97, 179.
[19]Ibid., 180–1, 213–15.
[20]Ibid., 213–15.

Radical Orthodoxy, which stress the particularity of church and theology. It is to this critique on public theology that we now turn.

14.1.2 A greater emphasis on particularity?

In her discussions of several criticisms to public theology, Graham explicitly engages with Postliberalism and Evangelical positions that stress the contrast between Christian identity and morality on the one hand and the culture of the wider society on the other hand. Under the umbrella of Postliberalism, Graham also treats authors associated with Radical Orthodoxy. Rather than seeing Christian sources and doctrines as a potential source of values that support culture, Postliberalism claims that these function as an own language game. The church narrates and lives out an alternative story, based on biblical events. Postliberalism is therefore critical of the liberal society and its claim to neutrality and allows a reading of the church's life as political. Radical Orthodoxy shares many of these concerns but pays more attention to the underlying ontology. It defends an ontology of participation according to which there is no natural, autonomous, secular sphere separate from God.[21]

Over and against public theology, authors belonging to the abovementioned movements stress Christian particularity in at least two ways. First, some authors pose that the church itself presents a form of public or political common life, which can contrast with that of the secularized society to which public theologians seek to contribute. James Smith, a theologian of Calvinistic orientation who sympathizes with Radical Orthodoxy, for example, draws on Augustine's description of the earthly and divine city in order to find the proper public theological stance of the church. Although he writes that Christians must work to sustain those aspects of society that support the well-being of one's 'neighbours', he points out that the earthly city constantly promotes the egoistical love of self through all kinds of secular 'liturgy'. It is in the church and its liturgy, he argues, that Christians are trained in an alternative kind of politics, based on the love of God, which they then live out in the world.[22]

The Catholic political theologian, William Cavanaugh, criticizes public theology for uncritically accepting the underlying imaginary of modern secular politics. The state and civil society, for example, are treated as objective spaces within which Christians can participate only as individuals, and only as such are seen as acting politically.[23] As a result, Cavanaugh argues, public theology

---

[21] C. F. Daniel M. Bell Jr., 'Postliberalism and Radical Orthodoxy', in *The Cambridge Companion to Christian Political Theology*, ed. Craig Hovey and Elizabeth Phillips (New York: Cambridge University Press, 2015), 112–26.; c.f. Elizabeth Phillips, *Political Theology: A Guide for the Perplexed* (London/New York: T&T Clark, 2012), 52–3.
[22] Smith, *Awaiting the King*.
[23] Cavanaugh, *Theopolitical Imagination*, 84.

overlooks the fact that the church itself is a political community, shaped by the Eucharist, which offers a very different political imaginary.[24]

A second way in which some critics of public theology stress Christian particularity is by pointing out the particularity of revelation and faith as epistemological sources, which problematizes the notion of a universal language or translation. Smith writes that Radical Orthodoxy rejects apologetic approaches, because human reason has been radically impaired by sin, which means reason is no longer able to discern God in creation. Revelation is therefore necessary. For those who do not accept it, the Gospel is 'foolishness'. Because Radical Orthodoxy does not accept the existence of universal language, it holds that one can only place one's own narrative about reality over and against other secular narratives. Apologetics is therefore useless.[25] Speaking from an Evangelical background, Daniel Strange too criticizes public theology for its premise that there is a universally shared basic vision about reality and for demanding that one enters into dialogue with others in a shared language. He too mentions the consequences of the Fall for the human intellect.[26] He agrees with public theology that Christians should engage with societal issues but writes that if Christians 'don't speak God's way', the public sphere is left to others who 'speak in their godless ways'.[27]

The authors discussed in this subsection belong to varied movements and denominations and place different emphases, but what they have in common is that they understand the relationship between faith and society differently from public theology. Graham responds to such perspectives that stress particularity, by claiming that reason and human culture can be channels of God's grace and revelation, and that public theologians should concern themselves with 'the salvation of the world, and not the survival of the Church'.[28] This suggests that at a deeper level, the different views on public theology have to do with how one understands the relationship between the church, the world and God, as well as the relationship between nature, sin and grace.

14.2 THEOLOGICAL PARTICULARITY

However, these deeper, theological concerns receive varying amounts of attention and can be approached in different ways. Instead of pointing out the particularity of the language of faith over and against the insistence on a

---

[24]Ibid.
[25]James K. A. Smith, *Introducing Radical Orthodoxy: Mapping A Post-Secular Theology* (Grand Rapids: Baker Academic, 2004), 179–81.
[26]Strange, 'What on Earth?', 6–7.
[27]Ibid., 13.
[28]Graham, *Between a Rock and a Hard Place*, 223.

universal language, and the particularity of the ecclesial public praxis over and against the public life of society, one could ask what is the particular nature of theology. This theological particularity can be seen to lie in God, as reality about which one tries to know the truth rather than a human concept, being the standard for theology. Public theology should do more justice especially to this kind of particularity.

To varying degrees, public theology's aim to offer a public contribution limits the way one can speak about God in advance. The public theology of Neil Ormerod, which starts explicitly from a reflection on what can count as 'public', can clarify this tension. This Australian Catholic theologian has written about doctrines like the Trinity, salvation and the church. However, when one does public theology, he argues, one must limit oneself to what can be known through natural reason. Ormerod criticizes public theologians who start from Christian sources, because according to him they do not speak in a truly public manner.[29] In his own public theology he tries to show that one can demonstrate the existence of God with natural reason alone, and thus in a public manner. He points out, among other things, that although science presupposes a correspondence between reality and the human intellect, this correspondence cannot itself be demonstrated through scientific methods, which can examine only contingent phenomena.[30] The correspondence between intellect and reality is a metaphysical claim which can only be considered necessary if both intellect and reality find their origin in a non-contingent being: 'God'.[31]

Ormerod argues that because the existence of God can be demonstrated with natural and therefore public reason, the implications of this existence deserve consideration in public debate and political decision making. In other words, Ormerod's public theology is built on a doctrine of God. Yet this doctrine of God is limited beforehand by a concern to meet the criteria for a 'public' contribution. A consideration of God's action within history, eschatology and other potential aspects of a faith perspective on public life has no place in a public theology according to Ormerod, because they cannot be defended on the basis of natural reason alone. In Ormerod's perspective, public life is something about which one can speak in a neutral language and to which one can relate a part of God, namely that part that can be known by natural reason. Public life can be approached as a delineated whole without interpreting it in the framework of salvation history.

---

[29] Neil Ormerod, *A Public God: Natural Theology Reconsidered* (Minneapolis: Fortress Press, 2015), viii.
[30] Ibid., 48–57.
[31] Ibid., 102–3.

Unlike Ormerod, Stackhouse and Graham do choose to start from Christian sources and reject a sharp contrast between faith and reason. They do try to create room for a specifically Christian contribution. Nevertheless, their public theology is governed by a concern for societal relevance and acceptability, and this restricts the manner in which they can speak about God beforehand. In order to defend its right to speak, public theology seeks to show that there are societal needs and questions that theology can provide answers to. In developing such contributions, public theologians of this branch make use of Christian sources.

However, making use of Christian sources in itself is not necessarily a theological activity. Literary and social sciences too may study the Bible and take from it values, norms and inspiration that are 'relevant' for advancing a good society. The particularity of theology therefore lies not in its sources but in its use of these sources. Theology is in the first place the study of God and all of reality in its relation to God.[32] What is particular to theology is that it does not see God and everything in relation to God as human concepts (or even symbols or tools) that can be applied and that can, in principle at least, be substituted by other useful concepts, but as reality and therefore Other, which one is trying to come to understand better and to which one is trying to do justice in one's claims. This reality as reality itself is thereby the ultimate standard to which this understanding (and resulting interpretations of public life and other contributions) is subject. This does not preclude the possibility that certain values or theological interpretations of public life can be relevant to society, but in a theological contribution these should flow from a concern to do justice to who God is and how God relates to the world (and therefore society).

Graham and Stackhouse do speak about God, but the theological concern for doing justice to the reality of God and everything in relation to God is at risk of becoming secondary to or being restricted by the concern for public relevance and accessibility. Although Graham does take from Postliberalism the notion that public theologians must take their starting point in Jesus Christ,[33] she barely mentions Christ or God. This could be because of her strong emphasis on Christian practices as a form of public witness. This does show that Graham takes God seriously as a reality, since it is the believer's active relationship with God, rather than God as a useful concept or model, that is the basis for public engagement. Important as this is, however, such practices in themselves are not yet theology. Stackhouse speaks more about God in his vision of public life. However, because of his concern for public relevance, speaking about

---

[32] Cf. Thomas Aquinas, *Summa Theologiae* I, 1, 3 Ad 1.
[33] Graham, *Between A Rock and a Hard Place*, 139.

God must meet the criteria of universality and public acceptability. Stackhouse writes about God as creator and as source of shared moral principles that have been preserved after the Fall, by which a flourishing society continues to be possible. With regard to Christ and salvation, Stackhouse speaks in terms of the birth of a hope for an eschatological vision that Christians believe is already inaugurated. This vision has inspired globalization and can still inspire a flourishing global society and offer hope through which one can work towards a good society despite adversities.[34] The hope that such a vision can offer and Graham's attention to Christian practices of discipleship are both important contributions. But these both concern the Christian's action or inspiration. There is hardly any attention to how God is already at work, for instance through Christ's connectedness with the church, and the Holy Spirit and what this means for a theological view on public life.

In speaking about God and everything in relation to God, (public) theology must indeed always account for its contributions. The question is: By whose standards? Those authors who place a greater emphasis on particularity rightly point out that it is naive to assume a neutral public space with neutral criteria for communication as one's starting point and standard. When one demands that religious and theological principles and notions must be translated to what can count as a relevant contribution according to the criteria of the public domain, one overlooks the fact that public life itself can be understood theologically in relation to God.[35]

A public theology that seeks to do justice to who God is could offer its own particular contribution exactly in such a theological vision. In a discussion about the political significance of the Christian faith, Edward Schillebeeckx states that this faith actually fails to be relevant for society if it is not taken seriously *as faith* with its own ends. Hence, the particular relevance of theology lies not so much in specific ethical proposals or social analyses, for which one does not need faith and consequently theology but lies rather in the way in which reality in its totality is understood as a reality sustained by God. Its significance for society does not arise from concrete political proposals but from the fact that faith is concerned with salvation.[36]

---

[34] Stackhouse, *Globalization and Grace*, 197–201, 228–9.

[35] This point is made, for instance, by Stephan van Erp, who writes that public theology rejects a large gap between church and world, in order to defend over and against secularism that theologians can make public contributions to the well-being of society. Van Erp criticizes public theology because the gap between the church and world is merely rejected for pragmatic reasons. Van Erp believes that one should rather reject this gap on theological grounds. Basing himself on the theology of Edward Schillebeeckx, he offers an interpretation of the world as the domain of god's activity within which the church has a place. Van Erp, 'The Sacrament of the World'.

[36] Edward Schillebeeckx, *Gerechtigheid En Liefde: Genade En Bevrijding* (Bloemendaal: Nelissen, 1977), 714–15.

In a similar way, public theology's unique contribution lies in its theological task to do justice to God as a reality. God as God (rather than concept) and God as God actually relates to the world is then the ultimate standard for theology's reflections on public life. This does not imply that theologians, as opposed to others, can fully comprehend this standard and can measure everything by it, as I will argue later in the chapter. The point is rather that in this perspective, God and salvation history are not 'concepts' that can be applied to a neutral public realm, but rather, one tries to understand how everything, including public life, already relates to God.

Two examples can clarify this. Kathryn Tanner, an American Anglican theologian who has written on theology and society extensively, criticizes attempts to apply the inter-trinitarian relations as a model for human coexistence. According to her, this very Trinitarian God is already involved in the economy of salvation and therefore, rather than being a model that can be applied to another reality, the Trinity is already related to humanity's common life.[37] Referring to this reasoning, William Cavanaugh argues that the Eucharist does not inspire or add meaning to political action or society, but that the Eucharist itself contributes to a relationship of participation in Christ and the action of Christ through the Spirit, in which Christians continue to participate in their political and social action.[38] These examples show an approach in which the attempt to understand God as reality and everything in relation to God forms the basis for a vision of public life. In the next two paragraphs I will work out what this type of theological 'particularity' could mean for public theology with regard to the debate on the particularity of faith versus shared reason and the focus on the particularity of the church's public life versus the public life of society.

14.3 PRESENCE AND CONCEALMENT: SHARED CAPACITIES AND THE LANGUAGE OF FAITH

We have seen that one way in which some authors stress particularity is by pointing at faith and revelation as unique and untranslatable epistemological sources over and against public theology's demand of speaking in a shared language and by universal standards. If one focuses on the particular nature of theology as described earlier, one must agree with these authors that the notion of pre-established 'universal' norms for what is 'public' is problematic indeed, and that public theology must take revelation seriously in its understanding of public life. If God has acted and has revealed Godself in history and is

---

[37]Kathryn Tanner, 'Trinity', in *The Blackwell Companion to Political Theology*, ed. Peter Scott and William Cavanaugh (Malden: Blackwell Publishing, 2004), 328–31.
[38]William Cavanaugh. 'The Church in the Streets: Eucharist and Politics', *Modern Theology* 30 (2014): 391–2.

bringing history to a certain eschatological fulfilment, then this co-determines the ultimate meaning of history and therefore of public life.[39] Although one can interpret this public life in different ways, from a theological perspective one cannot understand it as an otherwise neutral and separate reality to which speaking about Christ and other aspects of salvation history are an optional addition. This would be to treat them as concepts or models, or otherwise as an alternative reality, rather than in relation to God as ultimate reality.

This does not imply a rejection of reason. Nor are faith and revelation absolute and pure sources for a public theology. An example of such a strong suspicion towards reason and a presentation of faith and revelation as alternative can be found in an article by Andrew Moore in which he criticizes natural theology. Though he does not refer to public theology, Moore too believes that excluding revelation in speaking about God cannot do enough justice to God. Moore writes that natural theology results in the description of an idol, not in a relationship to and worship of God. Even if in principle one could come to know that God exists via creation, this would only concern the acknowledgement of an impersonal power, not of the biblical God. But Moore goes further. His rejection of natural theology relies on a specific perspective on the relationship between faith and reason. He argues that the tendency towards idolatry is in part the result of our fallen state, which compromises and misdirects our intellectual capacities. Moreover, he writes that natural theology distracts from the revelation that has in fact been given and thus from the only source of redemption.[40]

Moore's critique on natural theology is similar to that of Strange and Smith on public theology and apologetics. They share a negative perspective of the human intellectual capacities and suggest that revelation and faith are a distinct, (more) reliable source of knowledge of God. But such a sharp distinction between faith and reason and devaluing of reason is problematic. Revelation takes place within history and requires interpretation and therefore reason. One could therefore argue that in a sense 'all theology is natural theology'.[41] Revelation happens in and through the world and can only be expressed from

---

[39] This might be seen differently by those who believe that the incarnation, life, death and resurrection of Christ have not changed the world but have made grace available only to individuals, and that the Kingdom belongs entirely to the end of history. If one starts from a greater distinction between the present world and the Kingdom and between nature and grace, one can more easily consider public life as a closed whole to which Christians could bring inspiration.

[40] Andrew Moore, 'Should Christians Do Natural Theology?', *Scottish Journal of Theology* 63 (2010): 131–6.

[41] Ernst Conradie, 'All Theology Is Natural Theology: The Hermeneutic Necessity of Natural Theology?', *Nederduitse Gereformeerde Teologiese Tydskriff* 52 (2011): 58–65. 'In a sense', because revelation does not ultimately come from the world even though it can only come about through and within it. It is not *only* natural.

within one's world, and hence with the understanding and language from within the world.⁴² If reason has been affected by sin, then this applies to revealed knowledge as well. The biblical God would then be an 'idol' as well. Moreover, if reason had indeed been compromised as much as Moore suggests, then one can wonder about the status of Moore's own argument.

That is not to deny that human understanding is always limited regarding what it can grasp of God and everything in relation to God. We have seen that in Ormerod's natural theology, the existence of God must be affirmed in order to ground the human knowledge and scientific knowledge in particular. Although the existence of God is presented as a 'solution' to a metaphysical problem here, all that is really affirmed is that the human intellect cannot ground itself and hence continues to maintain at its core an element of mystery. In that perspective, 'God' is the expression of the awareness that something in our reason and judgements remains unfounded or unexplained. This is Denys Turner's reading of Aquinas' arguments for the existence of God, the same arguments that Ormerod builds on. In this reading, although reason can be brought to the necessary affirmation of God's existence, it is at the same time unable to understand what it affirms.⁴³ Reason can then be seen as a form of faith when it trusts that its understanding and judgement about reality are not without truth, because it has a foundation. This foundation, because it grounds reason, cannot itself be comprehended by reason. Turner writes that if one questions reality all the way to its ultimate foundations, one does not reach an answer that does away with the need for all further questions but a question that allows for no further intelligible answers. And this is referred to as 'God'.⁴⁴

To affirm God, then, is to affirm that human reason cannot fathom all, but that it is marked by God as unfathomable foundation. This affects all speaking about God, including faith claims. In his Gifford lectures on natural theology, Rowan Williams states that critics of natural theology are right to point out that natural theology cannot do justice to the triune God as confessed by Christians. However, he goes on to argue that those who start with the particularity of revelation sometimes tend to not account for their way of speaking about God at all, with the risk of simplifying God into an agent *within* history.⁴⁵ For this reason, Williams sees a specific use for natural theology in reflecting on how we speak about God. Such a natural theology would especially focus on those moments at which it becomes clear that reality eludes our description:

---

⁴²Ibid., 62.
⁴³Denys Turner, *Thomas Aquinas: A Portrait* (New Haven/London: Yale University Press, 2013), 139–43.
⁴⁴Ibid., 143.
⁴⁵Rowan Williams, *The Edge of Words: God and the Habits of Language* (London: Bloomsbury Continuum, 2014), 2–5.

those moments at which language has reached its limits and has 'failed to exhaust what "needed to be said"'.[46] Such a natural theology makes speaking about God seem less strange, but only by showing how elusive reality itself is in relation to our language, and how strange our language is as a result.[47] Such a natural theology can therefore remind revealed theology that it must do justice to the fact that it speaks and thinks about something that simultaneously eludes human language and thought. When one speaks about a present and active God on the basis of revelation, the meaning of this presence and activity cannot be fully comprehended and expressed. Hence, a public theology that takes revelation seriously cannot thereby pretend to be able to make absolutely certain or adequate claims about public life or even fully grasp what its claims mean.

In fact, if one acknowledges that God acts within history and one sees public life within this framework, this leads to the acknowledgement that even public life itself cannot be fully grasped. This is evident in the 'public theology' of Graham Ward. This Anglican theologian is sometimes counted under Radical Orthodoxy, but his theology is very different from Smith's. According to Ward, the church cannot be clearly demarcated, church and society influence one another, and signs of God's Kingdom are present within society. Yet he tries to place public life and Christian public praxis within an alternative Christian metaphysics so as to question certain developments within society and the self-evidence of its underlying assumptions.[48]

Because Ward considers public life and the public actions of Christians in relation to God's acting within history, however, this metaphysics is not a closed framework of meaning but is fundamentally marked by what he calls 'the eschatological remainder'.[49] By this he means that the ultimate meaning and fulfilment of history lie in a world towards which God is still leading the world and of which only God knows the ultimate shape, while at the same time there is already a certain continuity between contemporary forms of public life and the Kingdom. Because God has already worked and is working within history to bring it to a specific fulfilment, people can participate in this work of God through their political desires and ways of public life. As such, they can foreshadow this eschatological fulfilment. The final meaning of history and

---

[46]Ibid., 8.
[47]Ibid., xii–xiii.
[48]Ward, *The Politics of Discipleship*, 163–7.
[49]Ibid., 167. Ward bases this notion on Johann Baptist Metz's 'Eschatological Proviso', but by speaking of a 'remainder', he indicates that the Kingdom is already present, and that there is no break between this and the Kingdom yet to come, but that the Kingdom yet to come is its fulfilment. Ward, *The Politics of Discipleship*, 169–70; Johann Baptist Metz, *Zur Theologie Der Welt* (Mainz/München: Grünewald Verlag/ Kaiser Verlag, 1986), 110.

therefore of public life lies in the future and can therefore not be fully grasped but is at the same time not completely alien to us.[50]

Although Ward focuses especially on how the church participates in Christ's activity, he holds that both the church and secular forms of common life are part of a world in which the Kingdom is in the making. This has consequences for how one should speak about the world, according to Ward. Within the tension of participation and continuity on the one hand and the 'not yet' of the eschatological Kingdom on the other hand, the church with its own eschatologically oriented metaphysic speaks from a position *within* the world, while simultaneously trying to speak eschatologically, 'from *beyond*' the world.[51] Though Ward considers it necessary to speak about public life from an eschatological viewpoint, this speaking always remains provisional. The church, too, can only *participate* in God's work and cannot be identified with, nor fully grasp, God's activity and God's coming Kingdom.[52]

Therefore, although a theological vision of public life requires doing justice to God's action within salvation history and therefore to revelation, such a vision does not exclude reason and acknowledges its own provisional nature. Here, public life is understood as part of a history which is still unfolding, the final meaning of which lies in the future. Stackhouse seeks to defend that a Christian metaphysics is the most universal framework and that it can therefore function as the foundation of a global society. Although it is fair to assume that what is most universal lies in the relation of all things to God, such a comprehensive vision of how all things relate to God is exactly what is missing from our side. This applies equally to a fully Christian perspective that integrates particular faith claims. This does not mean that Christians should not speak about public life, but it does mean that this speaking is subject to a standard which cannot be fully grasped. Thus, a Christian metaphysic and resulting public theology cannot be a closed, universal framework.

14.4 PUBLIC LIFE AND GRACE

The other concern for particularity described earlier in response to public theology concerns content rather than language or epistemology. Rather than defending Christianity's relevance to secular society, authors who defend this type of particularity present the public life of the church under God as an alternative over and against secular society. Smith is a clear example of this. Although he states that Christians must discern where and how they can help

---

[50]Ward, *The Politics of Discipleship*, 167–80.
[51]Ibid., 24.
[52]Ibid., 24–5, 170–80, 288.

build up society and orient it more towards God's Kingdom, he identifies the politics of society, especially in the form of liberal democracy with Augustine's earthly city, and the political-liturgical life of the church with Augustine's heavenly city. According to Smith, the positive developments within society to which Christians should contribute are themselves the result of the historical influence of Christianity on society.[53] As such, Smith upholds a dichotomy between church and society and focuses on a one-sided movement *from the church* to society. Other authors who stress particularity also tend to focus on God's work within and through the church.[54]

Graham criticizes both this one-sided emphasis on the church and the dichotomy between the church and the world. In such perspectives, the church can correct society but has nothing to learn from this exchange with the world.[55] According to Graham, God can also be found in ordinary day to day life[56] and the world already carries within it 'the seeds of its own redemption'.[57] Part of this discussion therefore concerns where God works and how nature, grace and human freedom relate to one another. If one takes seriously the particular nature of theology as described earlier and takes as one's standard God and the way all things relate to God, a public theology must give these considerations central place.

Although Graham mentions salvation in society, she does so sporadically, in order to defend the dialogical method, and does not work out what she means by it. Graham and Stackhouse mostly point to the created, shared human capacities. In doing so, they seem to speak of God's relation to the world especially in terms of what is often called 'common grace'. This concept does not refer to the concrete history of humanity's redemption but to the notion that God has preserved the common moral law and other aspects of creation, despite the Fall. This makes the formation of a stable society possible.[58] Smith, on the other hand, refuses to ground the participation of Christians in society on the acknowledgement of common grace. According to him, this concept is too ahistorical and does not actually help say anything about concrete situations in society and how Christians should deal with these. Furthermore, he argues, what is good in society should not be ascribed to common grace but to special grace, which he refers to as 'providence' and which, he claims, has left its mark on society as a whole in a concrete and historical manner via the church.[59]

---

[53]Smith, *Awaiting the King*, 92–124.
[54]E. G. Ward, *The Politics of Discipleship*; Cavanaugh, *Theopolitical Imagination*.
[55]Graham, *Between a Rock and a Hard Place*, 30, 137–8.
[56]Ibid., 136–7.
[57]Ibid., 130.
[58]Cf. Smith, *Awaiting The King*, 123.
[59]Ibid., 123–4.

Smith focuses on the church as locus of God's grace too one-sidedly. If history in its entirety is ultimately sustained by God, and if God's activity and God's Kingdom are not the church's possession, theological particularity requires that public theology considers the public life of society as a whole in the light of God's involvement with the world. Nevertheless, Smith's discussion of common and special grace is relevant, because it draws attention to public theology's tendency to speak about public life solely in the context of creation as a finished and sustained entity, rather than in the context of God's salvific activity.

A public theology that takes God and God's relationship to the world as measure for its claims should allow God's salvific activity to play a role in how one speaks about public life. When Ward describes what it means to be a disciple of Christ, he states that this is not about adhering to a specific teaching (or a set of rules) but about a transformative relationship, in which Christ is in the disciple and the disciple is in Christ.[60] A public theology that seeks to do justice to God, not merely as a concept but as a reality and other, then, should not search for general norms or inspiration for society or a closed metaphysics. In the first place, it should seek to point towards God's activity and the acknowledgement that this transcends the human organization of a good society. This vision is in line with the acknowledgement of God as hidden ground of our knowledge rather than as delineable object within it. Here too it is God and God's action that are the standard, even if elusive to us. Thus, the particular theological contribution of a public theology lies in placing public life in the larger but not delineable framework of a God who is engaged in the world, and therefore in that public life. In this view, public life is not only a human reality, subject to human planning and organization that may or may not be based on a divine moral law but is subject to God's salvific, gracious presence.

Erik Borgman might serve as an example of what such a more theological public theology could mean. Inspired by Edward Schillebeeckx, his public theology is built on the notion that God is relevant to all people in society, because the world in which public life takes place has been given and is sustained by God. Public theology interprets society from this perspective.[61] The Catholic reflection on society that Borgman proposes therefore radically presupposes grace. It acknowledges that society is constantly changing and that as such, a new world is already coming into existence. Borgman speaks here of a 'loving gift'.[62] A

---

[60]Ward, *The Politics of Discipleship*, 276–7.
[61]Erik Borgman, *Overlopen Naar De Barbaren: Het Publieke Belang Van Religie En Christendom* (Kampen/Kapellen: Klement/Pelckmans, 2009), 7–19.
[62]Erik Borgman, *Leven Van Wat Komt: Een Katholiek Uitzicht Op De Samenleving* (Utrecht: Meinema, 2017), 15. Own Translation: 'liefdevol geschenk'.

Catholic response to society is not primarily the offering of specific ideals, norms or solutions for societal problems but, rather, involves acknowledging this gift and nurturing and working under it.[63] Here too public theology acknowledges and stands in service of a standard outside of itself. Borgman writes that acknowledging this grace and this holiness within human society is a *response* to something that 'appears from our conversations and confrontations as clothed with authority'.[64] Therefore, although one can make wrong judgements about this, it concerns something that is first of all given to us.[65]

Of course, one cannot simply identify salvation or God's salvific activity with the public life of society, nor with that of the church. If God works through the human world and human actions, there is human finitude and freedom to consider. Christoph Hübenthal in a response to Borgman also refers to Schillebeeckx, but in order to point out that salvation requires acceptance of this salvation.[66] Offering a genealogy of the secular, Hübenthal argues that the value and essentially Christian nature of the secular lies in its acknowledgement of the autonomy of the human being who can shape society freely and therefore has the choice to freely answer God's invitation to mutual love in doing so. Here human acceptance of God's influence is a condition for the bringing about of God's transformation of society.[67] One can wonder whether such a strong emphasis on free will and sharp distinction between offer and response do not place God's action and human action too much on the same level. It would require another chapter to work out this debate. What is clear is that the way in which one configures the relationship between God's action and human freedom will matter for the exact relationship between church and world and the concrete vision on God's acting in public life. A public theology that wishes to take seriously God as a reality will have to consider the relationship between God's action and human action.

To sum up, the particularity of a theological response to society lies not in offering a universally acceptable framework that can underpin society or in models for the organization of society, nor in the first place in supporting certain moral values. But neither should theological particularity be sought in faith as an alternative, absolute view of reality, within which all aspects of society can be understood and organized. Taking God seriously as reality and therefore as standard for truth actually undermines such an absolute vision.

---

[63] Ibid., 13–15.
[64] Ibid., 206. Own translation: 'Uit onze conversaties en confrontaties tevoorschijn komt als bekleed met autoriteit'.
[65] Ibid., 206-7.
[66] Christoph Hübenthal, 'Naar Een Ontologie Van De Liefde: Publieke Theologie Als Verlichting Van Het Seculiere', *Tijdschrift Voor Theologie* 58 (2018): 69–70.
[67] Ibid.

Nor can one only focus on the theological significance of the public life of the church at the expense of a theological reflection on society at large. The particularity of a theological approach to society lies in the way one looks at society. According to Borgman, God is transforming the whole world, not just the church 'but the person who knows this, lives differently because she or he sees other possibilities, or, if these remain invisible for her or him, [he or she] knows that he or she must look more carefully or persist longer in looking'.[68]

In a specifically theological approach, God is the final measure of all things. This means, for example, that although one speaks critically of those developments that lead to oppression and those who contribute to such developments, one does not consider these situations or the persons involved as lost. Even where human failure and sin promote destruction rather than salvation, a theological contribution must reject despair and the full demonization of the perpetrators, because even in fallen and damaged public life, God's offer of grace remains present. That God is the standard for understanding public life cannot lead to indifference towards harmful developments. But it does mean that one tries to recognize God's continuing involvement and mercy and acknowledges that what is impossible for human beings is possible for God (Lk. 18.27).

---

[68]Borgman, *Leven Van Wat Komt*, 19. My translation: 'Maar wie dit weet, leeft anders omdat zij of hij andere mogelijkheden ziet, of, als deze voor haar of hem onzichtbaar blijven, weet dat zij of hij beter moet kijken of het kijken langer vol moet houden.'

CHAPTER 15

A Black soteriological dialogue with public theology

REGGIE NEL

Public theology is more than simply 'making theology relevant' for the public sphere. It is rather about doing good theology[1] – conscious of your public. It is about 'theology that addresses the world as a whole'[2] – the real world. In the southern African context, while producing key contributors to the emergence of public theology or better, public theologies globally, this quest was not without an ongoing struggle and controversy – it bears the marks of a cross. This contribution hopes to remain conscious of, what I would prefer to call, this ongoing dialogue, while doing it within a global context. In this Black soteriological dialogue, I hope to contribute to transcending historical faultlines.

---

[1] Piet J. Naudé, '"Public Theology" from Within the Church?', in *Pathways in Theology: Ecumenical, African and Reformed*, ed. Henco van der Westhuizen (Stellenbosch: Sun Press, 2015), 295–309 (297); Dion A. Forster, 'The Nature of Public Theology', in *African Public Theology*, ed. Sunday Bobai Agang, H. Jurgens Hendriks and Dion A. Forster (Bukuru, Plateau State, Nigeria: HippoBooks, 2020), 15–26.
[2] Heinrich Bedford-Strohm, *Liberation Theology for a Democratic Society: Essays in Public Theology* (Lit Verlag: Zürich, 2015), 5.

At least within southern Africa, and there could be resonances in other contexts, these historical faultlines relate to the tension between, on the one hand, those who argue that public theology is a continuation of liberal Western political theologies and, on the other, those who remain committed to liberation theologies emerging from doing theology from the underside of history,[3] and therefore, who remain engaged in a praxis of transformation. In this regard in southern Africa, public theology has even been projected as the fulfilment (end) of liberation theology and therefore for some, an assault on Black Theology of Liberation. The late Vuyani Vellem, former director of the Centre for Public Theology at the University of Pretoria, addresses this struggle and controversy, as he reflects on what he terms the Black Public Theology of Allan Boesak.[4] Vellem refers to this view that when public theology emerged in South Africa, it was seen as the replacement of Black Theology of Liberation and 'being propelled as a model for theology and the "midwifery" of democracy in South Africa'.[5] This was experienced as an 'assault' on Black Theology of Liberation (BT). While Vellem didn't go so far as to suggest that this assault came directly from proponents of this relatively new field within theology, he, however, refers to one of the key proponents of BT at the time, Tinyiko Maluleke's perspective. Maluleke's critical assessment is that public theology was largely driven by higher education institutions in Europe, and in South Africa, by institutions mainly attached to the Dutch Reformed tradition. It was indeed seen as 'either a successor of liberation or a fulfilment of liberation theology'.[6] For Vellem, there was a healthy internal debate among proponents of BT during the 1990s on its future and the need for ongoing revision. However, as Vellem (and Malukeke) argues and demonstrated in the work and affirmation of Boesak, the issue for BT was never the need for another white saviour – it was public by definition and intent. Black public theology, they argued, is therefore about doing sound theology yet remaining open about the specific public (among many other publics), from which this theology emerges and to which public it intends to speak. The different publics relate directly to each other and need each other. There is therefore a need to dig a little deeper into the heart of doing good theology for our times in order to make these connections – that heart, I would argue, is the gospel of Jesus Christ.

---

[3]Sergio Torres and Virginia Fabella, eds, *The Emergent Gospel: Theology from the Underside of History: Papers from the Ecumenical Dialogue of Third World Theologians, Dar Es Salaam, August 5–12, 1976* (Maryknoll, NY: Orbis Books, 1978).
[4]Vuyani Vellem, 'Allan Aubrey Boesak: A Black Public Theologian from the Belly of a Kgodumodumo', in *Prophet from the South: Essays in honour of Allan Aubrey Boesak*, ed. Prince Dibeela, Puleng Lenka-Bula and Vuyani Vellem (Johannesburg: UCCSA Publications, 2012), 404–16.
[5]Ibid., 406.
[6]Maluleke in Ibid., 409.

In this contribution, I argue that at the heart of the gospel of Jesus Christ is not merely an anguish over the relevance of the church and theology in current times – at the heart of the gospel is the triune God's love for this whole world.[7] This is a saving, healing, liberating and transforming love – expressed publically as compassionate justice. A theological examination of the soteriological heart of the gospel is meant to discern this saving, healing, liberating and transforming love, that is, how compassionate justice is rooted theologically and embodied in specific publics. Doing good theology, and for this chapter, doing good soteriology, is public by intent.

It is not possible in one chapter to say everything about all the soteriological developments over the last few decades, let alone over the entire church history and how it relates and impacts on all the publics of our time and its relevance for this publication. In this contribution, therefore, I made a choice to introduce a case study of what I consider such good soteriology for public theology for our times, through the brilliant analysis of James Cone in his publication entitled *The Cross and the Lynching Tree*.[8] This book can be seen as perhaps a concentration point of Cone's work on BT, over the last fifty years, or so. Cone explains,

> This work is a continuation and culmination of all my previous books, each of them, in different ways motivated by a central question: how to reconcile the gospel message of liberation with the reality of black oppression. [. . .] I do not write this book as the last word about the cross and the lynching tree. I write it in order to start a conversation so we can explore the many ways to heal the deep wounds lynching has inflicted upon us. The cross can heal and hurt; it can be empowering and liberating but also enslaving and oppressive. There is no one way in which the cross can be interpreted.[9]

I therefore address the theme, through a dialogue with Cone, on his Black soteriology, but also some of the critics of Cone. Cone is chosen as representing a particular challenge to the dominant (classic) expressions of theology and therefore also its soteriology, namely the challenge from BT. In agreement with Vellem and Maluleke, I would hold that BT, as a liberation theology, did have a profound influence on the emergence of what is now referred to as public

---

[7] Nico Koopman, 'In Search of a Transforming Public Theology: Drinking from the Wells of Black Theology', in *Contesting Post-Racialism: Conflicted Churches in the United States and South Africa*, ed. R. Drew Smith, William Ackah, Anthony G. Reddie (Jackson: University Press of Mississippi, 2015), 211–25 (211–13).
[8] James H. Cone, *The Cross and the Lynching Tree* (Maryknoll: Orbis Books, 2011).
[9] Ibid., 273.

theology.[10] Public Theology is, however, not its fulfilment; it remains to be challenged by BT. As a case in point, in rooting his exposition of public theology, Koopman writes, 'My own involvement with public theology was nurtured by decades of drinking from the wells of black theology.'[11] He continues, 'To develop an adequate public theology in our contemporary context, I need to drink from the wells of black theology afresh.' Referring then, like Vellem, specifically to the influence of the BT of Boesak for his theological articulation of public theology and in particular Boesak's emphasis on the lordship of Jesus Christ,[12] Koopman continues and illustrates this drinking and nurturing through the following narrative, which incidentally also brings the argument on soteriology into focus. Koopman explains,

> As a member of the student congregation that Boesak ministered to in the apartheid years, I remember how this notion of the lordship of Christ enabled us to overcome the theological dualisms to which some strands of so-called reformed preaching wanted us to adhere. One of these was that salvation is only a spiritual matter, it is only for the soul. [. . .] We suddenly found clear theological articulation for the public theology we were taught at home when our struggling parents told us about a God who does not view us as inferior, although apartheid ideology does. . . .
>
> Yes this notion of the comprehensive lordship of Christ broadened our understanding of Christian salvation it opened our eyes to see that God is at work in all walks of life. It challenged us to develop broader understanding of obedience, faithfulness, social ethics, public theology and public witness.[13]

In pinpointing Boesak's Black soteriology in his own formation, Koopman is in the same spirit with Cone's concern. Cone was also discerning what would be the call of theology for this time and for his generation. This happened at the same time as Boesak, yet across the Atlantic and also in the midst of Black trauma, or what one can name the overbearing power and resilience of sin and death through racist oppression. Cone also does it so, with an unwavering commitment to the cross of Jesus Christ. He writes,

> African Americans embraced the story of Jesus, the crucified Christ, whose death they claimed paradoxically gave them life, just as God resurrected

---

[10]Koopman, 'In Search of a Transforming Public Theology'; Heinrich Bedford-Strohm, *Liberation Theology for a Democratic Society: Essays in Public Theology*, collected by Michael Mädler and Andrea Wagner-Pinggéra (Zürich: Lit Verlag, 2018), 20–1.
[11]Koopman, 'In Search of a Transforming Public Theology', 213.
[12]See also Vellem, 'Allan Aubrey Boesak', 407–8.
[13]Koopman, 'In Search of a Transforming Public Theology', 215.

him in the life of the earliest Christian community. While the lynching tree symbolized white power and 'black death,' the cross symbolized divine power and 'black life' – God overcoming the power of sin and death.[14]

What I would also argue is, in shorthand, perhaps the contribution of a Black soteriology for a public theology for today and the future. It is, however, not enough to say this.

While in this contribution, I invoke Cone, he and therefore the legacy of BT have also been challenged. I will therefore also contrast his soteriology with what is often referred to as the classic analysis. In this regard, I use Willie Jonker, in particular, a South African Dutch Reformed theologian. Cone and Jonker, I concede, perhaps never met in real life. I choose Jonker because, while his theology remained largely and self-consciously Eurocentric[15] and Dutch Reformed,[16] he shaped the thinking of many other contemporary South African exponents of public theology, like Dirk Smit,[17] Piet Naudé[18] and also Nico Koopman.[19] Jonker is also a key contemporary of perhaps one of the most well-known white public theologians of colonial times in South Africa, the late Beyers Naudé. In his autobiography, Naudé[20] shares many anecdotes of his journey with Jonker, but in particular, working together on *Pro Veritate*, an ecumenical publication by the Christian Institute, which addressed public issues at the time and was later banned by the South African government. While Naudé was opting to work 'outside' the white establishment, Jonker remained a theologian and sought-after preacher within the white Dutch Reformed Church, growing the next layer of ministers and scholars. With the establishment of the Global Network for Public Theology in 2007, there has been a fruitful engagement between these South African scholars with the various centres around the globe.

---

[14]Cone, *The Cross and the Lynching Tree*, loc. 607.
[15]Willem Daniel Jonker, 1991. 'Reaksie op Naudé en Fürstenberg se bespreking van Uit vrye guns alleen', *Ned Geref Teologiese Tydskrif* 32 no. 1 (1991): 119–23 (120–1).
[16]Piet Naudé, 'Uit vrye guns alleen: grondlyne vir 'n pastorale dogmatiek', *Ned Geref Teologiese Tydskrif* 32 no. 1, 110–18 (117); Naudé, '"Public Theology" from Within the Church?', 304.
[17]Dirkie Smit, 'Voorwoord', in *Die relevansie van die kerk: teologiese reaksies op die vraag na die betekenis van die kerk in die wêreld*, ed. Willem Daniel Jonker, Nico Koopman, Christo Lombard and Piet Naudé (Wellington: Bybel-Media, 2009), vii–xxii (xix); Dirkie Smit, 'On Reading Karl Barth in South Africa – Today?', in *Essays on Being Reformed: Collected Essays 3*, ed. Robert Vosloo (Stellenbosch: SUN Press, 2009), 275–92 (275).
[18]Naudé, *Pathways in Theology*.
[19]Nico Koopman, 'Suid-Afrikaanse kerke en die openbare lewe. Enkele lesse uit die teologie van Willie Jonker', in *Die relevansie van die kerk*, ed. Jonker, 165–88.
[20]Beyers Naudé, *My Land Van Hoop: Die lewe van Beyers Naudé* (Cape Town: Human & Rousseau, 1995).

It needs to be said though that his necessary delimitation and therefore my analysis, from a southern African context, will be skewed and inadequate. However, this delimitation does indicate what has shaped thinking and the creative tensions at least at the difficult birth of public theology in this part of the African context. Also, I hope, this limited engagement here could spur us all on to continue taking up the prophetic challenge from Cone and his soulmates (again), in continuing the calling in decolonizing the hegemony of Western theology today still. It can be a corrective to what Maluleke correctly indicates the overwhelmingly white European influence on the emergence of public theology over the last two decades or more. This, I hope, is also taking up the call from Koopman, for drinking from our respective wells (again), in order to develop theologies for our publics.

After this engagement with Cone and Jonker, I will conclude with painting two narratives from the African context of doing (public) theology for our time. What can this dialogue between Cone and Jonker teach us about how God love and redeems the world?

15.1 JAMES CONE – DOING LIBERATION THEOLOGY ROOTED IN THE CROSS

James Cone passed away in 2018, yet, since the late 1960s with the publication of his work, *Black Theology and Black Power*,[21] he is leaving behind a paradigm par excellence for doing liberation theology for many years to come. In *The Cross and the Lynching Tree*, Cone grapples more extensively with the meaning of the cross of Jesus Christ, also, in the light of his many critics. He maintains the centrality of the cross for contemporary Black communities at large.

Cone discerned, for at least the last five decades, one of the key signs of our times – systemic racism and its direct link to global and national inequalities. This, he argues passionately, impacts directly on doing good theology, unlike how (bad) theology was done in the past. His concern, or better, his anger, was however not myopically channelled to 'save' (white) theology. That, he considered not to be his call, or even chastising white theology for not 'saving' Black Theology. This, he argued, was not possible. He does argue, though, that the gospel is available to all, including white people; that it calls all people to a *metanoia*,[22] and that in him, in bringing the two symbols, the cross and the lynching tree, together, he addresses the key issues of the times, because indeed,

---

[21] James Cone, *Black Theology and Black Power* (Maryknoll: Orbis Books 1969).
[22] James Cone, *My Soul Looks Back* (Nashville: Abington, 1982), 16.

what is at stake is the credibility and promise of the Christian gospel and the hope that we may heal the wounds of racial violence that continue to divide our churches and society.[23]

He continues in terms of his North American public to explain,

> To forget this atrocity [the racism as symbolized by the lynching tree-RWN] leaves us with a fraudulent perspective of this society and of the meaning of the Christian gospel for this nation[24]

This atrocity continues – not just in the United States. It can be seen from the global resonance of the #BlackLivesMatters movement and the anguish of migrants today, in the Americas, Europe, but also in South Africa. Put differently, the public edge, but more so, the continued relevance of BT, is currently demonstrated in a pronounced way with the public upsurge of white supremacy under the devastation caused by what is often referred to as Trumpism, but also in various European countries under the rubric of populist nationalism (against migrants). These atrocities are upheld by Christian fundamentalism and perpetrated by religious fanaticists, who goes through as 'evangelical'. The inequalities amplified by the Covid-19 global pandemic and the roll-out of vaccines are direct consequences of this 'fraudulent perspective of this society'. The credibility of the Christian gospel remains still at stake globally – publicly.

For Cone then, while the cross is arguably one of the most recognized and powerful symbols of the Christian gospel and specifically for its theology of salvation, this symbol has been transformed into a 'harmless, non-offensive ornament that Christians wear around their necks'.[25] This, he contrasts with what happens in Black churches (and communities) where the Christian gospel is preached with the cross being a source of resilience and activism – from his own early experiences, which became the driving force for his theology. This, he deems to be the only message to the world. How did Cone come to this interpretation?

In his work, Cone wanted to consciously reconcile the message of the Christian gospel with the reality of Black oppression. In this struggle the cross was central, and he explains, 'The cross helped me to deal with the brutal legacy of the lynching tree, and the lynching tree helped me to understand the tragic meaning of the cross.'[26] The cross, for him, was God's critique of (white)

---

[23]Ibid., 180.
[24]Ibid., 187.
[25]Ibid., 194.
[26]Ibid., 257.

oppressive power. Its meaning can only make sense for oppressed people – people who live under suffering and trauma. He illustrates this resonance by showing how Black Christians sang, as well as preached and witnessed about the cross more than any other aspect of Jesus' ministry. The life and identification with the poor and oppressed people of Jesus' day, under the heel of the Roman Empire, as well as the resurrection, demonstrating the victory over death gave meaning, but for Cone, it was the cross which touched a deep nerve among oppressed Black people. He explains this resonance by stating, 'The cross places God in the midst of crucified people, in the midst of people who are hung, shot, buried and tortured.'[27]

However, this resonance was not a simplistic naive acceptance of its contradictions – merely as an opium, soothing or worse, justifying the paradox of protracted systemic trauma experienced for generations through slavery, segregation and lynching. Cone shows the struggles with cross led to an ongoing struggle and questioning of easy answers, but also the rejection of white theology and its churches, the white god, but more importantly, and creatively, it became the heart of a spirituality which gave birth to the freedom movements in the streets. Cone declares, 'it was Jesus' cross that sent people protesting in the streets, seeking to change the social structures of racial oppression'.[28]

What has been said so far is nothing new. Boesak himself took up this challenge in his own doctoral work in the 1970s, and he shares his earliest engagements with Cone.[29] Within a southern African context, Takatso Mofokeng wrote a doctoral thesis on forming a Black Christology, entitled *The Crucified amongst the Crossbearers*.[30] Mofokeng refers to the cross as 'a theological culmination and starting point of the history of liberation'.[31][32] Many a white theologian in South Africa aimed at either ignoring or dismissing Cone's work, without any serious theological engagement;[33] however, his work sparked heated theological engagement and inspiration from Black theologians. However, for Cone, it was his own students, in particular womanist theologians, like Jacqueline Grant and Delores Williams, who found the interpretation of the substitutionary meaning of the cross offensive as a symbol of hope or redemption. Cone (2018)

---

[27]Ibid., 767.
[28]Ibid., 810.
[29]Allan Boesak, *Farewell to Innocence: A Socio-Ethical Study on Black Theology and Black Power* (Maryknoll: Orbis Books, 1977), 12–16, 97, 123–52.
[30]Takatso Mofokeng, *The Crucified amongst the Crossbearers: Towards a Black Christology* (Kampen: J.H. Kok, 1983).
[31]Ibid., 92.
[32]Mofokeng's dialogue partners are not Cone but Jon Sobrino and Karl Barth.
[33]Here we need to note the exceptions of serious engagements from Bosch (1974), Durand (1987), Kritzinger (1988) as well as CBF Naudé during his work in the Christian Institute and later, as the general secretary of the South African Council of Churches (SACC).

concedes that Williams is correct in arguing that the idea of Jesus being a surrogate (in terms of the Black women's experience) must be rejected.[34] It would be important to give background to Williams's argument.

For Williams, in particular, Jesus did not die on the cross in humanity's place in order to accomplish salvation or liberation. Williams engages BT in three areas, namely its theological method, on specific Christian doctrinal and lastly on ethical matters.[35] She takes male proponents like Cone on with regard to their usage of the biblical text, but here, I will narrow my engagement down to her critique on the Christian doctrine of surrogacy and redemption. Her starting point is the theology in mainline churches on the sinfulness of humanity and Jesus' substitutory death on the cross. Jesus, in this theology, is considered the ultimate (and sacred) example of surrogacy in the context of salvation.[36] Williams acknowledges that the language and imagery of the doctrine on atonement and its development whether it be Origen, Anselm, Abelard, the Reformers, etc. resemble the time and cultural context. Hence, for her, it is indeed reasonable to 'use the language and sociopolitical thought of the time to render Christian ideas and principles understandable'.[37] She explains the implications as follows:

> So, the womanist theologian uses the sociopolitical thought and action of the African-American woman's world to show Black women their salvation does not depend upon any form of surrogacy made sacred by traditional and orthodox understandings of Jesus's life and death. Rather their salvation is assured by Jesus's life of resistance and by the survival strategies he used to help people survive the death of identity caused by their exchange of inherited cultural meanings for a new identity shaped by the gospel ethics and world view. . . .
>
> This kind of account of Jesus' salvific value – made compatible and understandable by use of African-American women's sociopolitical patterns – frees redemption from the cross and frees the cross from the 'sacred aura' put around it by existing patriarchal responses to the question what Jesus' death represents.[38]

---

[34] James Cone, *Said I Wasn't Gonna Tell Nobody: The Making of a Black Theologian* (Maryknoll: Orbis Books, 2018).
[35] Delores S. Williams, *Sisters in the Wilderness: The Challenge of Womanist God-talk* (Maryknoll: Orbis Books, 1993), 127.
[36] Ibid., 143.
[37] Ibid., 145.
[38] Ibid.

For Williams, the cross is freed (liberated) and the resurrection doesn't depend on the cross for life. Rather, redemption is about God

> giving humankind the ethical thought and practice upon which to build positive, productive quality of life. Hence, the kingdom of God theme in the ministerial vision of Jesus does not point to death; it is not something one has to die to reach. Rather, the kingdom of God is a metaphor of hope God gives those attempting to right the relation between self and self, between self and others, between self and God as prescribed in the sermon on the mount, in the golden rule and in the commandment to show love above all else.[39]

In this understanding the cross of Jesus is rather an image of 'defilement, a gross manifestation of collective human sin'.[40] This notion of defilement becomes the point of resonance in the experience of Black women raped in wanton desecration, as well as how it happens with nature, cultures and indigenous peoples.[41] Williams would hold that while there is nothing sacred about the cross and the blood of Jesus, and they cannot worship it, yet they cannot forget. It is on this basis that Williams states that Black Theology's Christology holds little promise for Black women.[42]

As indicated earlier, Cone accepted that Williams is correct, because if not, it provides support for Black women accepting their own surrogate role in suffering – like Jesus did. Cone explains,

> I accept Delores Williams's rejection of theories of atonement as found in the Western theological tradition and in the uncritical proclamation of the cross in many black churches. I find nothing redemptive about suffering in itself. The gospel of Jesus is not a rational attempt to be explained by a theory of salvation, but a story about God's presence in Jesus' solidarity with the oppressed, which led to his death on the cross. What is redemptive is the faith that God snatches victory out of defeat, life out of death, and hope out of despair, as revealed in the biblical and black proclamation of Jesus' resurrection.[43]

He continues,

---

[39]Ibid., 146.
[40]Ibid., 147.
[41]Ibid., 146–7.
[42]Ibid., 150.
[43]Cone, *The Cross and the Lynching Tree*, loc. 4067.

> But in the end, I am in closer agreement with other womanist theologians ... who view the cross as central to the Christian faith, especially in African American communities. ...
>
> The cross is the burden we must bear in order to attain freedom.
>
> We cannot separate the cross from the Christian gospel as found in the story of Jesus as lived and understood in the African American Christian community. The resurrected Lord was the crucified Lord. Whatever we think about the meaning of the cross for black women should arise from their experience of fighting for justice, especially as seen in their collective lives and struggles in the civil rights movement. God's salvation is a liberating event in the lives of all who are struggling for survival and dignity in a world bent in denying their humanity.

It would seem that Cone held onto his particular soteriology rooted in the cross of Jesus Christ, while not excluding, at least theoretically, the possibility of other expressions and corrections to his limitations. With this in mind, I will now turn to the challenge from Jonker.

15.2 WILLIE JONKER ON BT AS AN EXPRESSION OF MODERN THEOLOGICAL DEVELOPMENTS

When BT burst onto the scene in the late 1960s and 1970s in South Africa, one of the key critiques against it was that it represented a functional Christology and soteriology; to put it crudely, it was merely just another expression (logical extension) of modern (Western) liberal theology. I will now explain this critique through the work of South African theologian Willie Jonker on how it developed.

For Jonker this functionality meant that the value of the person of Christ is exclusively dependent on and reduced to the specific function that he had to fulfil.[44] While this functional soteriology had some earlier expressions, Jonker explains the modern (post-*Aufklärung*) variants by referring among others to the work of Friedrich Schleiermacher. According to Jonker, Schleiermacher starts true to the general thinking of the time with the experience.[45] Hence, by establishing what Christ did and still does to the community called the church (within a modern Western context), conclusions can be drawn in terms of who Christ is supposed to be. Schleiermacher, for Jonker, remained a child of his time, with a specific (modern) understanding of rationality, and thus he steers clear of

---

[44]Willie Jonker, *Christus, die Middelaar* (Transvaal: N.G. Kerkboekhandel, 1977), 80.
[45]Ibid.

speculative Christologies. Salvation, Jonker shows, is defined in this context, as the 'influence' which goes out to humanity. This strengthens humanity's 'God consciousness' against a worldly consciousness, and this God consciousness becomes the principle to live by. Salvation does not have anything to do with a supernatural event in the suffering and death on the cross and resurrection and ascension of Jesus Christ; these events do not necessarily strengthen the God consciousness and are therefore in essence irrelevant. Salvation is about the influence of the example of Christ, with his complete God consciousness, on humanity. This salvation is a psychological and historical process which unfolds in the congregation. The congregation was established through this influence of Christ and carries this influence through history. In this, the Holy Spirit, as the community spirit of the church, is the secret to this influence. To repeat, in referring to Schleiermacher as example, according to Jonker, salvation is not understood theologically, as relating to Christ's divine nature as well as human nature, and therefore having an objective and subjective character, but more in terms of the function (effect) that emanates from Christ.[46] Here a specific modern understanding of salvation is decisive for the Christology. Not the other way around. It is also not necessarily derived from Scripture but, rather, derived from Scheiermacher's definition of religion in terms of his philosophy of religion at the time. Depending on how the individual's religious need is understood, salvation is defined; depending on the starting points of the theologian, the function of Christ is described in a particular way and specific conclusions on his person are drawn.[47]

Jonker then continues to explain this functional soteriology, by also referring to Albrecht Ritschl, where salvation is the experience of emancipation out of humanity's moral weakness – the emancipation from the sense (feeling of guilt) and the ability to answer to the moral call. Christ's function is to exercise a powerful virtuous influence on people. Christ, in this understanding, is seen as the founder (originator) of the reign of God on earth. Jonker shows that this means for Ritschl that those under His influence and message are enabled to live under a particular moral code. Ritschl, in turn, was influenced by Immanuel Kant's philosophy; however, he used the traditional terms like 'justification' and 'reconciliation', filling it with a particular philosophical meaning. Justification is where Christ in his message reveals God's love and gives everyone the assurance that God does not ascribe to the people their moral transgressions. When one truly hears and accepts this message, reconciliation is established in you as a person. With a view of Christ and his faithfulness to his call and moral ideal, there is also a courage that is formed within an individual to change

---

[46]Ibid., 81.
[47]Ibid.

the self internally and commit oneself to this moral ideal. For Jonker this is simply another variant of the same functionalism, which echoes the Western philosophical developments after the Enlightenment period; it is a liberal theological response to modernism. Jonker concludes that with these thinkers, it is evident: where the Christology is approached from the perspective of what salvation means for the specific Western person, this will shift all the time, and hence the Christology will shift, depending on how salvation is understood. Every time and every theologian create a different Jesus.[48] He explains,

> not only because the New Testament scholarship came to the conclusion that in the Bible there is not just one image of Jesus, but also, that a whole number of these would differ from each other; also the hermeneutical shift in theology in our time contributed to the fact that it is seen as legitimate that every time on its own way will speak of Christ.[49]

In this regard it follows that Dietrich Bonhoeffer also asked the question from prison about Christ as the lord of the secular person: 'Who is Christ for us today?' He started to grapple with the idea of the human for others, and as such, he argued that Jesus would still have meaning for humanity in his day and personify (embody) salvation.

While most of these considerations seem familiar today and can be discerned in various expressions of contemporary theology, Jonker's critique is that these developments were not necessarily taking serious the biblical witness on Jesus or the historical scholarship, but rather, what mattered in these Eurocentric modern variants was the common trait that the cultural situation or context was the starting point within which salvation is defined. Therefore, it is not surprising for Jonker that, during his time, the attempts to develop 'contextual theologies' also brought a number of different Christological themes to make it possible for people to see that Jesus can have meaning for different people in different circumstances. He then refers to the theologies of the revolution, of liberation theology, and refers in particular to what he calls specific forms of Black Theology where Christ is brought into play in a new way, as revolutionary or liberator, the follower (adherent) of the poor and the oppressed, the one who opens the future or even the political Messiah, diametrically opposed to the existing status quo.[50] In all of these expressions, Jonker argues, the fundamental idea is that the relevance of Jesus is made dependent on his functionality as a provider of a particular expression of the salvation asked for. Jonker concedes

---

[48] Ibid., 83.
[49] Ibid.
[50] Ibid., 84.

that these expressions do refer to a 'divine' salvation. However, for him it is done in such a way that Christ does not need to be a real (historical) human anymore to be instrumental in the mediation of the salvation. The biblical titles are being used, but this does not necessarily mean that Christ's full divinity is acknowledged in functional Christologies. Christ as Saviour is rather dependent on his unique function and an exceptional empowerment towards this. In different ways, Christ is pictured as a supreme example, and as such as the revelation/expression of God, as human representative of God.[51] Under the notion of Christ as human representative of God, Jonker refers among others to the work of Dorothee Sölle, Hans Küng and others.[52] In this appropriation, Christ is not just the representative of humanity, the *plaasbekleder* (place-keeper), but also, especially in the work of Sölle, vicariously, the place-keeper of God for modern humanity. In the context of the absence of God in the (modern) secular world, experienced by modern humanity as the death of God, or at least the absence of a realization of the givenness of God in the world, God needs a place-keeper who keeps his space open, until a new revelation of God steps in.[53] Jesus identifies himself with God and represents God's interest in the world. He is not identical to humanity nor to God. He makes visible divine love in the world, and he demonstrates the self-emptying of God in his identification with suffering humanity to the ultimate sacrifice – his death on the cross. In the crucifixion of Christ, the world sees the true identity of humanity as a self-giving (sacrifice) of self, for the sake of the other. This is the ultimate expression of human love. At the same time, the love of God is revealed as a love that is willing to suffer for the sake of the other.[54] We are therefore called, through the example of the cross, to follow Christ and suffer with the other, the suffering of God in and for this world.[55] In this, there is no need to hold on to the confession that Christ is fully God. He is a metaphor which gives humanity courage to hope that the world is not fully godless but that God will after the times return after a season of self-emptying and absence. Christ plays the role of God for us (humanity), but we all are called to play that role for our fellow-humanity. Christ is the leader in this regard. For Küng, as a case in point, it is crucial to speak of Christ so that the modern person can understand within their own world view. This means that one must abandon all mythological representations. Küng still wants to hold on to the intention of the biblical authors, but he wants to abandon metaphysical categories. Jesus is the representative of God – the last revelation of God. This last representative

---

[51] Ibid., 85.
[52] Ibid., 85–9.
[53] Ibid., 92.
[54] Ibid., 93.
[55] Ibid.

has the power to call humanity to change. He sets the norm for other human beings. God works in and through Him – as a human being, on behalf of all humanity.

In Jonker's critique of these developments, as well as the specific expressions of a Black soteriology (which he does not specify), Jonker returns to and upholds largely what he calls classic soteriology as well as period up to the Reformation.[56] In this the doctrine of the two natures of Christ played a key role. However, for him, in the shift to the new (modern) era there is more emphasis on the understanding of Abelard – who was critical of the objective soteriology, where God was the actor and arbiter. Abelard, Jonker argues, was against the idea that there must be a satisfactory offer to God as a condition for His forgiveness of sin. He argued that God can forgive sins without the cross of Jesus Christ. The symbolism of the cross is cruel and unfair. Christ does not carry the world's sins substitutionally through the cross; rather, Christ reveals God's love. Out of love he took our human nature upon himself, lived the life of a moral teacher and an example unto death, and this example quickens love in the human person. There is here a stronger emphasis on the subjectivity of humanity. Again, Jonker concludes, the influence of the *Aufklärung* on the modern liberal Christologies and soteriologies is evident, namely the specific expression of rationalism. Christianity is viewed as teaching the uprightness of humanity; atonement is seen as bringing humanity, through the teaching and example of Jesus, to improve their lives and thus become pleasing to God. Redemption and atonement remain subjective events within the human person, and therefore BT (and other political theologies) is merely an extension of Western liberal theologies. For Jonker, this is a deviation from the classic soteriologies of ecumenical theology.

It therefore remains a question if this critique from Jonker on the soteriology of liberation theologies like BT can be sustained against how, I have shown, Cone deals with the place of the cross in his soteriology. Answering this question will start to assist in doing good theology for the publics of our time and for the future. It seems to me that Cone, specifically in his response to the critique as represented by Williams earlier, aimed at upholding the centrality of the cross of Jesus Christ in redemption. His theology cannot simply be dismissed as merely an extension of modernist Western theologies – theologies that uphold a functionalist soteriology. Cone is correct in his critique that the position of Williams is influenced by the modernist versions presented by Jonker. Cone, however, concedes that he remains influenced by twentieth-century theological developments, but he does not necessarily uphold their total allegiance to Western philosophical categories. His soteriology, he would hold, relates closer to his own deep participation in the religious life in the Black churches in Bearden,

---

[56] Ibid., 128.

Arkansas and the embodiment of rituals of lament and defiance, performing the spirituals and the blues, but also protest marches in the face of the lynching tree. These practices are rooted in his soteriology of the cross. It is embodied and performed. For Cone, this Black soteriology is not merely living in (or being experimented with) the pages of theological treatises. It is embodied in the vulnerability (of the cross) performed in public spaces, defying and challenging the dominant expressions of powers that be. It was only much later in their own development, but perhaps more so from the challenge by scholars like Cone and others, where scholars (like Jonker) conceded that their own theological work was also contextual, speaking in forms, categories and language that is foreign to the southern African publics of our time. Indeed, with these expressions being contextual, embodied, it would also be proper to also affirm that soteriologies remain human endeavours – flawed and therefore bearing our own shortcomings and vulnerabilities. What the contributions and contestations between Cone, Williams and Jonker show is the importance of doing good theology, with each other – in dialogue, but also, being open about our public and vulnerabilities.

In the last section, I will, therefore, illustrate this expression as a soteriology of the cross, within the contemporary African context.

15.3 EMBODYING PUBLICLY THE SOTERIOLOGY OF THE CROSS – TODAY

As a synthesis of sorts, I will now introduce the very creative narratives by Emmanuel Katongole as expressions of taking the challenge of Cone's soteriology of the cross further. Katongole doesn't refer directly to Cone in his work, but like those of Cone, his soteriology emerge from his agony over the reality of protracted trauma, symbolized in the lynching tree, while hoping to still hold onto the triune God's redemptive reality historically, through the cross of Jesus Christ. Katongole participates in, listens to and studies the songs (prayers) of public lament that emerged in the wake of the genocide in Rwanda and its devastating impact on East Africa. He, like Cone, relates it as follows:

> the East African laments are not much different from the Negro spirituals. However, while the Negro spirituals are very explicit in connecting slaves' suffering to God's (Jesus's) suffering, the connection between the cries of lament from East Africa and God's own is not as explicit. It is this connection that we need to make explicitly in order to bring to the fore the rich theological – but also the immense social, political, and ethical – significance of a crucified God in Africa.[57]

---

[57]Emmanuel Katongole, *Born from Lament: The Theology and Politics of Hope in Africa* (Grand Rapids, MI: William B. Eerdmans Publishing Company, 2017), Loc. 2649.

He goes on to share narratives on the pastoral, practical and public responses to the reality of what he also calls this 'crucified' or 'suffering' God. In this, he shares the narrative of Archbishop Emmanuel Kataliko from Bukavu (Democratic Republic of the Congo) and of Sr Rosemary Nyirumbe from Gulu (Uganda). As background and connection, he grounds their public ministry in the 'excessive love of God which was manifested on the cross'.[58] For Archbishop Kataliko, in his public ministry, even in exile, God conquers the violence of the world through an excess of love, through suffering – God's own suffering. Katangole continues to explain this understanding, God's agency in human history, especially God's solidarity with humanity, is revealed in the incarnation and in Jesus' suffering and death on the cross and opens up the possibility of a 'new form of transformed agency, a nonviolent alternative in the midst of violence'.[59]

A second narrative of Sr Rosemary Nyirumbe commences in the wake of the horrific civil war, in northern Uganda, with children being abducted and raped by what is known as the Lord's Resistance Army (LRA), but also an Ebola outbreak. Here Sr Nyirumbe founded her vocation through the St Monica's Girl's Vocation School to help young girls abducted by the LRA rebels to experience the restorative love and forgiveness in practical ways.[60] These girls, Katongole notes, were deeply scarred. They then developed practical training programmes, counselling and job opportunities, but on a deeper level, it was about being loved. Katongole quotes Sr Nyirumbe:

> I think what we should do is love and accept these girls and walk with them, in their shoes. Let us accept them as they are and not judge them for what they have done. We must treat them as normal people and not as people who have done terrible things. This is not about giving them training. It is about giving them love.[61]

In his reflection on this remarkable narrative, Katongole explains what he calls the theological logic behind it. For him, Sr Nyirumbe offers to the girls the same selfless love she has found in the Sacred Heart of Jesus – a symbol and expression of God's infinitive love for humanity made manifest in Jesus' suffering and death on the cross. This odd logic is also the case for the work of Archbishop Kataliko. While this logic for Katongole is opaque, it is unmistakable and embedded in their theology. He states, 'at the basis of their life and work is

---

[58] Ibid., loc. 2702.
[59] Ibid., loc. 2831.
[60] Ibid., loc. 2901
[61] Ibid., loc. 2919.

the Christological reality of the crucified God'.[62] In any event, by turning to the crucified love of God, both Kataliko and Nyirumbe are able to discover forms of passionate, pastoral and practical engagements on behalf of the crucified peoples in Bukavu and Northern Uganda, respectively. Their public witness embodies beyond words, beyond a neat system, a glimpse of God's redemption.

Good theology is indeed theology that finds resonance in the passionate, practical and public lives of people, in particular among the cross-bearers today. God is the author and the finisher and ultimately remains God, beyond our human estimations, formulations and yearnings. Cone showed us through his work that our expressions remain flawed and inadequate in fully capturing the breadth, length and depth of the triune God's love for the world – this world in the shadow of the cross. However, in living this out, also in doing our theologies, goodness becomes visible – public.

---

[62]Ibid., 141.

CHAPTER 16

Public theology and ecclesiology

AL BARRETT

16.1 INTRODUCTION

While the 'public' in public theology has focused the spotlight on whom the theological sub-discipline is speaking *to*, what public theology has often lacked is equal attention to whom it is speaking *for* – and where it is speaking *from*. These latter concerns are commonplace among the more explicitly contextually aware 'theologies of liberation', situated as they are within the multiple edges of power and recognition in our societies and our world. But they are also the concerns of another theological sub-discipline, *ecclesiology*, that seeks to describe – and often prescribe – the purpose, shape and structures of the Christian church, that body which, among other vocations, is called to bear witness, truthfully and faithfully, in the world.

At the point of convergence between these three trajectories (public theology, theologies of liberation and ecclesiology), we might ask the following questions:

- What (imagined) 'public' is being *addressed*? Who is actually *listening*?
- In what ways is public theology speaking to the *church*? And who, in the church, might hear it?
- Which 'publics' (or sub-sections of a 'public') are being spoken *from*? Who is doing the *speaking*, and what is their location within – or beyond – the church?

- Who is – and isn't – being *spoken for*, and what is the relationship between them and those who speak?
- Who, in the crafting of public theology, is being *heard* – both within and beyond the church? And whose voices go *unheard*?

This chapter, while seeking to address some of the *general* questions that connect public theology and ecclesiology, is written amid the concerns emerging from a very *specific* context: that of an urban, multi-ethnic neighbourhood on the edge of the city of Birmingham, England; its local church, which is denominationally part of the Church of England; and my own location and identity as priest and theologian, but also a multiply privileged, middle-class, white male. My argument here, for a re-formed, repentant and radically receptive, ecclesially rooted public theology, is developed through tracing the initial articulation of, and subsequent 'ripples' from, a defining moment in the tradition of public theology within the Church of England: the *Faith in the City* report of 1985, which aimed to address and critically challenge both 'Church and Nation' on the injustice of urban deprivation. In exploring the ways in which *Faith in the City* was (negatively) received by both the theological academy and the Church of England's internal structures, however, I highlight two of public theology's critical limitations: first, its resistance to articulating a distinctively Christian, and distinctively *ecclesial*, theology; and second, its reliance on assumptions which are implicitly – if not explicitly – rooted in *white racial privilege*.

To address these limitations, I turn to two of public theology's sister sub-disciplines: to ecclesial political theology first, and then to Black (liberation) Theology. While the former insists on speaking from within the church, but a church that turns out to have tendencies towards both eschatological idealism and cultural imperialism, the latter, conversely, is agreed on the church's flawed – and, more specifically, white supremacist – reality, but is internally divided between those who seek to reform that church from within, and those who want to critically distance themselves from any kind of 'church'. Rather than concluding with a universal prescription for 'public theology' in the abstract, I return to the (white majority) Church of England's most recent attempts to challenge institutional racism – both in British society and within its own structures – and offer a modest proposal, in this specific context, for ecclesial repentance as public theology.

16.2 *FAITH IN THE CITY*: ADDRESSING CHURCH AND NATION

1985 was a defining moment for the Church of England – but a moment that is still in the process of arriving. That year marks the publication of the report of the archbishop of Canterbury's Commission on Urban Priority Areas, *Faith in the City: A Call for Action by Church and Nation*. The Commission, which included bishops and clergy, academics, union leaders, CEOs and directors of voluntary organizations, was given the task of inquiring into the life of the Church of England in 'urban priority areas' (UPAs), and 'the social and economic conditions which characterize[d]' those areas.[1] The Commission's members listened to the 'accounts and experiences' of local people living in UPAs and representatives of UPA churches and other organizations, they gathered sociological statistics, they reflected on the 'theological priorities' and they called on '*Christians throughout the country*' to 'listen to the voices of our neighbours who live in the UPAs, to receive the distinctive contribution that they (not least the Black people among them) can make to our common life and *to set an example to the nation* by making our support and solidarity with them a high priority in our policies, our actions and our prayers' (xvi, my emphasis).

One recurring theme running through *Faith in the City* is that of the experience of *alienation*, through which people are made 'to feel themselves to be "outsiders" . . . [by] a particular *order* that is felt to be unresponsive and uncaring' (316). Emerging from its careful work of listening, the Commission highlights multiple alienations in British society, including

- 'the sense of alienation and powerlessness' of millions on low incomes who are unable to participate fully in a consumption-driven economic system (55);
- the sense of alienation and 'estrangement', among many who live in UPAs, 'from their neighbours, from social institutions and indeed from the rest of the country' (59), including a 'widespread alienation from the present systems of democratic government' (174);
- the 'profound sense of alienation experienced by young people today' (59), an alienation 'from adult ideas of how young people should behave; from their peers of different social classes; from agencies they think of as acting on adults' behalf and not usually in the interest of young people, e.g. from the police; from school; and from the Church' (315).

This last point, turning to the church's own complicity in social alienation, is a recurring theme in the report, highlighting alienations not just between the Church of England and young people but between the church 'and the majority of working-class people' (75) and 'UPA communities' more generally (113), and also 'the alienation, hurt and rejection experienced by many black people in relation to the Church of England' (96).

---

[1] ACUPA, *Faith in the City: A Call for Action by Church and Nation* (London: Church House Publishing, 1985), v–xiv. Further page numbers are given in the text.

After eleven chapters of structural and policy recommendations for both 'church' (four chapters) and 'nation' (seven chapters), on the report's final page the Commissioners issued a challenge to the neoliberal government of the day (led by Conservative prime minister Margaret Thatcher), which would make headlines when the report was launched. '"The exclusion of the poor is pervasive and not accidental,"' they argued, quoting one submission to the Commission. '"It is organized and imposed by powerful institutions which represent the rest of us." The critical issue to be faced', the report-writers concluded, 'is whether there is any serious political will to set in motion a process which will enable those who are at present in poverty and powerless to rejoin the life of the nation' (360).

16.3 THE DISTINCTIVE CHARISMS OF PUBLIC THEOLOGY

Faith in the City is an example of public theology with its threefold understanding of 'publicness'. First, public theology assumes that religious belief and practice have innately 'corporate, political and societal meanings' (rather than being purely 'private and pietist'). Second, it assumes that debates around those 'public trajectories of faith' should be conducted 'in ways that are transparent and publicly accessible and defensible', requiring theological speakers to 'translate' their key concepts into the terms of a commonly accepted 'public' language.[2] These together contribute to a third understanding of publicness, in the specific commitment of public theology to 'a shared realm of political and civic action' (Elaine Graham),[3] to 'maintaining the quality of our public life and to pursuing a common good' (Mary Doak)[4] or, in William Storrar's words, to 'participating in creating and sustaining an inclusive public sphere' – the latter understood as 'a domain of our social life in which public opinion can be formed, where any and all citizens can gather freely and without coercion to consider matters of general interest'.[5] For *Faith in the City*, this 'shared realm' or 'public sphere' was synonymous with 'the life of the nation'.

The discipline of public theology has evolved significantly in the thirty-five years since *Faith in the City* – and since David Tracy's influential text, *The Analogical Imagination*, which preceded the Church of England's report

---

[2]Elaine Graham, *Between a Rock and a Hard Place: Public Theology in a Post-Secular Age* (London: SCM Press, 2013), xx, 48.
[3]Graham, *Between*, 98.
[4]Mary Doak, *Reclaiming Narrative for Public Theology* (Albany, NY: State University of New York Press, 2004), 9.
[5]William Storrar, 'The Naming of Parts: Doing Public Theology in a Global Era', *International Journal of Public Theology* 5, no. 1 (2011): 23–43 (28).

by four years[6] – as have the increasingly multiple, fluid and contested nature of the space(s) we call 'public'. But central to public theology's distinctive 'charism' remains a commitment to what we might call either *expansiveness* or *inclusivity*. Three decades on from Tracy's book, for example, Sebastian Kim identified 'the main players in the public sphere' as including 'the state', 'the media', 'the market', 'religious bodies', 'the academy' and 'civil society' (including voluntary and community organizations, both 'secular' and 'faith-based'), recognizing that 'the relative power of each and the interrelations between them may vary from one society to another'. Noting that theology has its feet planted primarily in the two camps of the academy and religious communities, Kim argues that public theology *'deliberately expands its sources, audience and applications in the public sphere* in association with the other four players', depending on the particular issue in focus.[7]

Public theology's claim to expansive inclusivity is its greatest gift, but also its greatest danger – if not accompanied by a deliberate *humility*. One aspect of this necessary humility is to be found in the way public theologians frequently engage in spaces they do not control and seek to open themselves to the insights and challenges, the concerns and questions, of non-theological speakers. As Duncan Forrester puts it, public theology 'seeks the welfare of the city before protecting the interests of the Church' and 'often takes "the world's agenda", or parts of it, as its own agenda'.[8] For some of public theologians' (admittedly critical) 'close family' in what I will call *ecclesial political theology*, this apparent humility is, rather, a dangerous capitulation – a criticism we shall return to shortly. But first we will consider a critique of public theology from a different direction, which urges a second kind of humility on the discipline: a recognition of the *limits* of public theology's inclusivity and of what and whom it might fail to include in its claims to 'publicness'.

16.4 PUBLIC THEOLOGY AND WHITENESS

As Hannah Arendt highlighted of ancient Greece, the very notion of 'the public' draws lines of exclusion (women, children and slaves were consigned to the *oikos*[9]), just as it seeks to delineate a shared space. In so-called 'public' spaces, as Stephen Burns and Anita Monro observe, '[t]here are always limitations on

---

[6]David Tracy, *The Analogical Imagination: Christian Theology and the Culture of Pluralism* (London: SCM Press, 1981).
[7]Sebastian Kim, *Theology in the Public Sphere: Public Theology as a Catalyst for Open Debate* (London: SCM Press, 2011), 11–13 (my emphasis).
[8]Duncan Forrester, 'The Scope of Public Theology', *Studies in Christian Ethics* 17, no. 2 (2004): 5–19 (6).
[9]Graham, *Between*, 87.

the "public" who may enter, speak, act, and the roles that they are allowed to play' there, and 'public theology' is no exception: assertions of 'publicness' risk either dismissing certain activities as 'not public' (as has often been the case for 'women, non-Anglo-Europeans and other marginalized people groups') or 'claim[ing] for itself a privileged position' precisely in its claim to 'speak *for* the marginalized'.[10]

As South African theologian Cobus van Wyngaard has observed, 'if public theology is by definition possible only where certain ideal conditions of participation are already met, then not only do we not actually find many such examples, but this very approach also remains the privilege of a few, indeed of only certain classes of people'.[11] Van Wyngaard is particularly interested in the ways in which the concept of 'the public' is *racialized*, noting that 'in the public sphere . . . whiteness continues to confer excessive resources for public opinion formation': '[i]n the process of racialisation, those who are white have been taught that we are more likely to have the truth, while others have been taught the opposite, and this impacts on how we speak and to whom we listen on issues of public concern'. Drawing on the work of Linda Martin Alcoff, van Wyngaard presents some critical questions that need to be asked of so-called 'public' discourse: '"who has the right to speak in public debates conducted in the square? Are white or black people more likely to be interrupted with greater frequency? Are white or black people more likely to be referred to as having had a good idea in these discussions?"'[12]

Having highlighted the whiteness of 'public' discourse in general, van Wyngaard then goes on to point to the whiteness embedded in public theology's own foundations: the assumption 'that theologians and churches may participate in discussions on the common good and the formation of public opinion' is, he argues, 'characteristic of how whiteness functions in a racialised world: having a particular history of insisting on its right to determine public opinion and policy, and in a racist society having the belief in its authority to enter any public space freely, a freedom denied to black people'. White theologians, he concludes, 'need to become aware of how their social location contributes to both motivation and opportunity for participating in the public sphere. In short: how public theology is intertwined with the historical relations of power which

---

[10]Stephen Burns and Anita Monro, 'Which Public? Inspecting the House of Public Theology', in *Public Theology and the Challenge of Feminism*, ed. Anita Monro and Stephen Burns (Abingdon: Routledge, 2015), 1–14 (1. 8.). (emphasis mine).
[11]Cobus van Wyngaard, 'Whiteness and Public Theology: An Exploration of Listening', *Missionalia* 43, no. 3 (2015): 478–92 (484).
[12]Ibid., 480–1.

are tied to the visible bodies with which we live and the meaning attached to these bodies in a racialised world'.[13]

Van Wyngaard's exposure of the gap between the 'ideal conditions of participation' to which public theology aspires and the racialized reality suggests that what Storrar names the 'inclusive public sphere' describes less a present reality and more something to be sought after – an *eschatological* goal, even. As feminist public theologian Rosemary Carbine has put it, public theology seeks to 'act on a *convocative* or community-building imperative' to 'theologically envision and enliven a common political order' which 'conjoin[s] disparate groups' into an 'ultimate public'.[14] For Carbine and others, however, it is not coincidental that an imperative towards 'convocation', within an eschatological horizon, has decidedly *ecclesial* overtones. Might 'church' in some form, then, transcend the lines of exclusion highlighted by Burns and Monro, and van Wyngaard? It is to those who would answer 'yes' to that question that we now turn.

16.5 ECCLESIAL POLITICAL THEOLOGIES: ECCLESIOLOGY AS PUBLIC THEOLOGY

Democracy, argues Graham Ward, 'is always in *search* of a body' – the 'body politic' – 'a body that continually is absent'.[15] For what I am calling 'ecclesial political theologians' (of which Ward has been a prominent representative),[16] public theology is on a similar fruitless search, but the body they are searching for is right under their noses: the body of Christ, the church. From the perspective of ecclesial political theology (EPT), then, 'public theology is simply *not public enough*': it loses out on the vital possibility 'of challenging ... the dreary calculus of state and individual' with the 'truly free alternative space' that Augustine named 'the City of God'.[17] Within its dialogical engagements public theology might strive, as Forrester puts it, to 'offer' into the public sphere 'something that is distinctive, and that is gospel, rather than simply adding the voice of theology

---

[13]Ibid., 481.
[14]Rosemary Carbine, 'Ekklesial Work: Toward a Feminist Public Theology', *Harvard Theological Review* 99, no. 4 (2006): 433–55 (436).
[15]Graham Ward, *The Politics of Discipleship: Becoming Postmaterial Citizens* (London: SCM Press, 2009), 56. Following the argument of French political theorist Claude Lefort.
[16]In addition to those cited here, much of this 'school' of political theology can be traced back to the work of either John Milbank (and 'Radical Orthodoxy') or Stanley Hauerwas – or, as in James K. A. Smith's work, both. See, for example, James K. A. Smith, *Awaiting the King: Reforming Public Theology* (Grand Rapids, MI: Baker Academic, 2017).
[17]William Cavanaugh, *Theopolitical Imagination: Christian Practices of Space and Time* (London: T&T Clark, 2001), 117 (my emphasis).

to what everyone is saying already'.[18] But EPT worries that such theological 'offers' inevitably end up being 'shaped by conceptualizations and forces external to Christian belief and practice' which, as Luke Bretherton argues, tend towards *'co-option'* ('where the state sets the terms and conditions of, and thence controls, the relationship'), *'competition'* (where the church becomes 'just another minority identity group demanding recognition for its way of life') and *'commodification'* (where Christianity becomes 'simply another privatized lifestyle choice', 'a product to be consumed or commodity to be bought and sold').[19] Just as van Wyngaard questioned the neutrality of the so-called public sphere with regard to *race*, so EPT seeks to expose its 'true nature' as a 'vassal of the capitalist order' which 'exercises dominion by capturing and distorting desire'.[20] Here is EPT's vital contribution to political theology: an in-depth analysis of human *desires*, their formation (and deformation) by the 'earthly city' and their possibility of transformation within the body of Christ.

Theological resistance, as Daniel Bell argues, must therefore go deeper than looking to the church at best to *'inspire* or *motivate'* Christians to move into the supposed 'real world' of politics in the public sphere but must instead reject both 'the desacralization of politics' and the depoliticization of the church and rediscover the latter as *'an immediately political agent'*: not just 'another interest group in civil society' but *'a public in its own right'*, an 'uncivil society', a community which practises 'an alternative way of life', a 'certain [kind of] performance' that 'counters capitalism by liberating and healing desire'.[21] Where public theology desires maximal inclusivity for the 'public sphere', EPT boldly asserts such inclusivity as a fact of *the life of the church itself*. The church should be understood as 'the *true* polis', 'an assembly of the *whole*' where, from the very earliest days of Christianity, 'those who are by definition excluded from being citizens of the polis and consigned to the *oikos* – women, children, slaves – are given full membership through baptism'.[22]

The danger, of course, is that such a claim is as much an eschatological ideal, rather than a present-day reality, as the claims of public theology that EPT disputes. It is telling that even Graham Ward, who is unusual within EPT in seeking explicitly to be 'engaged' with non-theological voices, subtly modifies Johann Baptist Metz's language of 'eschatological *reserve*' into an

---

[18]Forrester, 'Scope', 6.
[19]Luke Bretherton, *Christianity and Contemporary Politics: The Conditions and Possibilities of Faithful Witness* (Chichester: Wiley-Blackwell, 2010), 1–2.
[20]Daniel M. Bell, Jr., *Liberation Theology after the End of History: The Refusal to Cease Suffering* (London: Routledge, 2001), 74.
[21]Ibid., 71–2.
[22]Cavanaugh, *Theopolitical Imagination*, 117–18 (my emphasis). See also Arne Rasmusson, *The Church as Polis: From Political Theology to Theological Politics as Exemplified by Jürgen Moltmann and Stanley Hauerwas* (Notre Dame: University of Notre Dame Press, 1995).

'eschatological *remainder*' which, while seeking to remain conscious of a present 'incompleteness' – the gap between the 'now' and the 'not yet' – nevertheless centres his writing on the ways in which the church enables participation in the 'fullness of Christ', in the present.[23]

What Ward *does* offer, however, is a diagnosis of 'alienation' with a theological depth that *Faith in the City* lacks: the divisions and depoliticization of 'the postmodern city' are rooted in a profoundly individualistic desire to consume, which has produced a 'dismemberment', a 'social atomism' at the core of Western culture, that both effects and depends on a 'disembodiment', not just of social bodies but of physical human bodies too.[24] In response, it is the task of the theologian to re-interpret the world, 're-school the cultural imaginary',[25] through an 'analogical worldview' which understands all bodies (both physical human bodies and metaphorical social 'bodies') to find their meaning, their very existence, in their participation in the (eucharistic) body of Christ.[26] There is a passionate, outward-moving dynamic at work here, with the whole city as its horizon: in Ward's vision, the eucharistically formed 'erotic communities' of the church 'function first locally, and then expand ever outward'. It is in the daily life and service of the Christian layperson especially that Ward locates the work of 'enacting the incarnation', 'performing Christ', as 'alternative forms of sociality, community and relation are fashioned, imagined, and to some extent embodied', beginning with the eucharistic gathering but venturing out into the city, embracing – and 'disseminating' themselves through – 'the civic and social bodies within which they dwell'.[27]

Ward's EPT shows signs of ecclesial humility. He recognizes that 'the operations of grace are not limited to the *ecclesia*'; that the worldly church is – in Augustine's terms – a 'corpus permixtum', a body whose members are subject to desires both holy and sinful, with an ongoing need for 'correction, repentance, and reconciliation'; and that 'the church's address to the world' issues from 'an internal struggle to discern the truth of its own vision and mission'.[28] At least implicitly, when he confesses that '[t]he ghettoisations and the segregations of racism, sexism, class, and ageism done in my name, condoned by my silence, injure me', he at least hints at the possibility that these segregations happen within the church as well as within the wider

---

[23] Ward, *Politics*, 279–83.
[24] Ibid., 69–70, 221ff.
[25] Graham Ward, *Cultural Transformation and Religious Practice* (Cambridge: Cambridge University Press, 2005), 152.
[26] Graham Ward, *Cities of God* (London: Routledge, 2000), 75.
[27] Ward, *Cultural Transformation*, 172, 59; *Cities*, 77, 92.
[28] Ward, *Cities*, 229; *Politics*, 24, 203.

world.²⁹ However, as the eschatological tension in Ward's work tends to collapse, so the opposition between 'church' and wider society tends to deepen. The Christian theologian, Ward claims, stands just inside the church's door, looking in two directions but with unequal affection: on the one hand, they look 'back into the church [where] *the order of life is presented*'; on the other, looking outwards into the world they see 'the serried ranks of city life . . . so many high points and squalid allies, neon-lights, plasma-screens, crowded tenements, seductions, excitements and destitutions'.³⁰ As Elaine Graham observes, there is a clear 'one-way' flow; the church's role is 'to bestow peace and reconciliation on a degenerate culture' – a 'contradictory and disordered' world – 'whilst never appearing to require words of insight, healing or forgiveness in return'.³¹

As I have argued at length elsewhere, this 'monological' or 'centrifugal' dynamic in Ward's work, characteristic also of EPT more widely, inevitably resists being radically receptive not just to the church's non-Christian 'others' but also to those who are 'othered' by dominant groups within the church's own structures.³² Ward's framing of the church as an 'erotic community' is helpful, however – whether intentionally or otherwise – to expose the gendered, racialized and colonialist undercurrents of ecclesial expansiveness, especially when unchecked by a careful analysis of where power is concentrated: Ward describes the church, for example, as 'overspill[ing] defined places', 'disseminat[ing]' itself 'through a myriad of other bodies', entering 'into the "deepest, darkest immanence"', and 'penetrat[ing]' the barren wastelands and violent 'ghettos' and 'no-go zones' of the city.³³ As van Wyngaard has identified public theology, so also in EPT we see the 'belief in its authority to enter any public space freely' that is characteristic of privilege in general and whiteness in particular. Furthermore, when Ward confesses to an anxiety about the 'risks' of the church's action-in-dispersal being 'vulnerable' to the possibility of 'making mistakes, making compromises, being blemished', the further such action is located from the institution's 'chancels and cloisters',³⁴ he betrays an apparent obliviousness of the long history of the often-abusive machinations of ecclesial 'centres'. We now explore one concrete example of such ecclesial machinations, as we return to the story of *Faith in the City* and its reception.

---

²⁹Ibid., 92.
³⁰Ward, *Cultural Transformation*, 59.
³¹Graham, *Between*, 129–30.
³²Al Barrett, *Interrupting the Church's Flow: Developing a Radically Receptive Political Theology in the Urban Margins* (London: SCM Press, 2020).
³³Ward, *Cities*, 176–80, 77; *Politics*, 219–20; *Cultural Transformation*, 55–6.
³⁴Ward, *Politics*, 203.

16.6 *FAITH IN THE CITY* AND INSTITUTIONAL RACISM IN THE CHURCH

While *Faith in the City*'s perceived criticism of the neoliberal ideology of Margaret Thatcher's government lent it a frisson of public controversy, apparently setting 'church' against 'state', the report nevertheless determinedly held together its *external* critique of national institutions with its self-critique of the church's *internal* life: the possibility of healing social alienations that is at the heart of the Christian gospel, it argued,

> must be witnessed to by the corporate life of the church. It is only when the church itself is sensed to be a community in which all alienation caused by age, gender, race and class is decisively overcome that its mission can begin to be authentic among the millions who feel themselves alienated, not only from the church, but from society as a whole.[35]

Within the church, however, the Commission identified profound divisions and obliviousnesses, not only in relation to *poverty* but also in relation to *race*:

> 5.55 Although our survey indicated that 'race and community relations' was not seen by (mainly white) clergy as a major problem in UPAs, this was not the view expressed by the black people (including black clergy) who gave us evidence. . . .
>
> 5.56 The Church of England certainly has an unrivalled network of local organisations uniquely placed to take a strong lead in spelling out the message of racial equality. Yet the Commission for Racial Equality said in their submission to us that members of minority ethnic groups who, for the most part, feel left out of the mainstream of British society, feel equally ignored and relegated to the peripheries of church life. Many black Christians told us that they have felt 'frozen out' of the Church of England by patrician attitudes. Some had left the Church, yet others were still solid Anglicans. We have heard repeated calls for the Church of England to 'make space' for – and so better receive the gifts of black Christians.
>
> 5.58 . . . We believe that the Church must make a clear response not only to racial discrimination and disadvantage, but also to the alienation, hurt and rejection experienced by many black people in relation to the Church of England.[36]

---

[35] ACUPA, *Faith in the City*, 60.
[36] Ibid., 96.

As Black Anglican theologian Azariah France-Williams outlines in detail, when *Faith in the City* was presented to General Synod in 1985, all but one of its sixty-one recommendations were accepted enthusiastically. The sole recommendation which Synod did *not* accept – because the Standing Committee refused to put it forward – was related to race: a proposal to create a Commission for Black Anglican Concerns. 'This would have been groundbreaking', France-Williams explains: creating a place for 'the concerns and needs of black and brown communities' to be heard and 'empowered by the church, reformatting our colleges, our training, our theology, our teams, and therefore transforming our congregations'. The blocked proposal was 'intended to help the church recognise that *as well as holding up a mirror to communities, [it] needed to do the same for itself*'.[37] But it was not to be. As Canon Clarence Hendrickse (a priest born and raised in South Africa) observed of the behind-the-scenes machinations at General Synod, '[t]here was an underlying feeling within the Standing Committee that groups of black people meeting together might become subversive . . . the fear in Synod flowed from the idea of groups of black people . . . having the power to officially criticise the values, attitudes, and modus operandi of Boards or Committees'.[38]

16.7 BLACK THEOLOGY, 'COMMUNITIES OF RESISTANCE' AND THE CHURCH

Of course, Black Christians have been 'meeting together', 'stealing away' beyond the reach of white eyes and ears, for centuries. White voices have no monopoly on spaces for conversation, even when we (I write as one of those white people) imagine we do by naming some spaces 'public'. While the 'Black' of Black theology is, as two of its leading exponents acknowledge, 'a contested and even controversial notion', it nevertheless names an ambivalent, twofold reality. On the one hand, 'Black' names the space of an 'alternative public', the site of a 'counter-performance', forged amid slavery and developed politically and theologically in the crucible of the American Civil Rights and Black Power movements in the 1960s. On the other hand, 'Black' names also the 'doctrine of racial inferiority ascribed to people of African descent'[39] which, as Willie Jennings has comprehensively argued, was 'invented' within the deadly nexus of the European missionary-imperialist enterprise, transatlantic slave trade,

---

[37]A. D. A. France-Williams, *Ghost Ship: Institutional Racism and the Church of England* (London: SCM Press, 2020), 98–100.
[38]Ibid., 102.
[39]Michael Jagessar and Anthony Reddie, eds, *Black Theology in Britain: A Reader* (London: Equinox, 2007), 2.

Christian 'missions' to the Americas and the so-called Enlightenment.[40] The roots of Black Christianity in the Americas, the Caribbean and Britain are to be found, then, in what Anthony Pinn has called the 'quest for complex subjectivity': the efforts by Black people of the African Diaspora 'to construct notions of their own humanity on terms that are more amplified and nuanced' than the 'fixed objectification' imposed on them by the white supremacist structures within which they lived – including, critically, *ecclesial* structures.[41]

For Michael Jagessar and Anthony Reddie, therefore, there is a vital distinction to be drawn between theology which articulates 'Black Christian religious experience' and *Black Theology*. While the former does 'not necessarily have a political or explicitly transformative agenda' – often embodying at best what Valentina Alexander has labelled '*passive* radicalism', an internalized, spiritualized resistance that enables Black people to at least *survive* in a hostile world – the latter intentionally pursues an '*active* radicalism' which seeks to *confront* and *transform* the structures of oppression.[42] Black theologians, beginning from 'the material reality of Black experience', seek to confront not only 'the systemic violence against Black people within the body politic' – such as the deaths of Black people in police custody – but also the multiple ways in which, historically, 'the inhuman institution of slavery found a willing accomplice in the allegedly egalitarian doctrines and practice of Christianity and the Christian church', and in the present, the church continues to be entangled in the workings of white supremacy. One of the primary goals of Black theology, therefore – at least in a British context – says Reddie, 'is the desire to rid Black people of the stultifying effects of polite, White middle-class, establishment-friendly forms of religious rhetoric', and to see 'Blackness as a primary hermeneutical lens for re-interpreting the Christian faith'. And this is true not just for Black people who worship in white-majority churches but also for those who worship in Black churches which can, as Reddie argues, through 'the residual stains of internalized racism', 'be as "unsafe" to "some" Black people who are not considered "respectable enough", as the White ones!'[43]

What might seem like an extended detour, then, returns us to our central cluster of questions. Where public theologies have often sought to advocate *for* those excluded from a supposedly 'public' sphere, Black theologies (in common with other theologies of liberation) insist that those 'others' need

---

[40] Willie James Jennings, *The Christian Imagination: Theology and the Origins of Race* (New Haven, CT: Yale University Press, 2010).
[41] Jagessar and Reddie, *Black Theology in Britain*, 2–3.
[42] Anthony Reddie, *Black Theology* (London: SCM Press, 2013), 18–19. (cf. Valentina Alexander, 'Passive and Active Radicalism in Black Led Churches', in *Black Theology in Britain*, ed. Jagessar and Reddie, 52–69).
[43] Jagessar and Reddie, *Black Theology in Britain*, 5, 11–12; Reddie, *Black Theology*, 80, 110–12.

to be able to inhabit spaces in which, and find voices with which, they can speak for themselves. Where public theologies and ecclesial political theologies claim, in differing ways, to be committed to the idea of a 'shared realm of political and civic action' or an 'assembly of the whole', Black theologies (and other liberation theologies) are unashamedly *partial*: not just in the sense of rejecting any and all pretensions to speak of or for 'the whole' but also in the sense of *taking sides*, living and speaking from among the oppressed, excluded and alienated, with the aim of their liberation from, and/or transformation of, the prevailing political order. And where ecclesial political theologies turn away from 'the public sphere' and towards the church as 'the true *polis*', Black theologies respond firmly that the politics of the latter is far from innocent: Black Christians need liberating from, and the transformation of, the church too.

But within Black theology, theologians disagree about whether that work of liberation and transformation happens best from the 'inside looking out' (as Anthony Reddie describes his own work) or from the 'outside looking in' (as Reddie locates the work of fellow Black theologian Robert Beckford). Beckford describes his work of 'documentary [film-making] as exorcism' as having the potential 'to remake the world': using the power of visual storytelling to contest dominant, non-liberative representations (both within and beyond the Christian church) of Black Christianity, and to expose and exorcise not just 'the deep suffering of the past' but also 'the underside of Christianity, its collusion with the empire's occult [practices]'. Beckford seeks to speak particularly to Black Pentecostal Christians who, he argues, need 'to undergo an internal exorcism, in order to "destroy the yoke" of colonial Christianity'. But his films, broadcast on 'mainstream' British TV channels (the BBC and Channel 4), have not only reached far wider audiences but also at times contributed to changes in policy (e.g. pushing Cadbury's towards fair trade) and wider public debates (around reparations for slavery).[44] Beckford addresses himself to Black churches but, as Reddie observes, largely from the 'outside'. His work of 'Dread Pentecostal Theology' often comes across as a rather solitary activity. Although he does acknowledge the need to develop 'communities of resistance', where 'liberative theological praxis' is taken seriously, such communities appear in his writing more of an eschatological dream than a lived reality. He remains 'in search of a body'.[45]

---

[44]Robert Beckford, *Documentary as Exorcism: Resisting the Bewitchment of Colonial Christianity* (London: Bloomsbury, 2014), 200, 202, 159–72.
[45]Robert Beckford, *Dread and Pentecostal: A Political Theology for the Black Church in Britain* (London: SPCK, 2000), 210–17.

Reddie, too, is interested in 'liberative theological praxis' and similarly insists on a twofold focus for Black theology: on 'the need to challenge the broader society' on issues that 'prevent human flourishing', alongside critiquing 'the meaning and intent of Christianity as the "religion of empire"'. But unlike Beckford he is, we might say, a self-confessedly *ecclesial* Black liberation theologian, even while he is clear that his work is 'an attempt to deconstruct' and 'remake' some of the 'building blocks' of the church that 'have been circumscribed for some 2000 years'. Reddie deliberately commits to working *'within the self-defined world of the Church* and the perceptions and attitudes of Black Christians themselves' to *'re-imagine . . . church as a site for liberative praxis and transformative change'*. And he does so as a 'religious educator', rooted in Paulo Freire's understanding of 'conscientization', working primarily with groups of Christians (both Black and white) using participative, dramatic exercises as a facilitative tool – a 'performance' that is much more *ecclesial* in nature than Beckford's 'documentary' approach. Reddie is not 'in search of a body' – he is seeking to make the best of the 'body' within which he already finds himself.[46]

16.8 THE 'WINDRUSH SCANDAL' AND AN APOLOGETIC CHURCH OF ENGLAND

In February 2020, the General Synod of the Church of England discussed a private member's motion from the Reverend Andrew Moughtin-Mumby. The motion highlighted what has become known as the 'Windrush Scandal': the attempt by the UK government to remove the rights of citizenship from, or even deport, thousands of British Commonwealth citizens who had arrived in the UK, mostly from the Caribbean, on the *Empire Windrush* ship in June 1948 and subsequent years. These people had been summoned to Britain, as British subjects, to help rebuild the country after the Second World War and had faced racism in British society, at both personal and structural levels, over the seventy years since. The deportations and attempted deportations represented the latest chapter in that long history, as part of the current government's 'hostile environment' immigration policy.

Moughtin-Mumby's motion noted that the Windrush Scandal coincided, ironically, with the celebrations of the seventieth anniversary of the arrival of 'the Windrush generation', and that Church of England bishops had 'spoke[n] out about this terrible injustice in Parliament and in the press'. He went on to note, however, the ways in which, as in wider UK society, the Church of England has profoundly benefitted from the Windrush generation and their

---

[46]Reddie, *Black Theology*, 141–4, 74–80.

descendants and successors but has also subjected 'countless Black, Asian and minority ethnic (BAME) Anglicans' to 'conscious and unconscious racism' in 1948 and subsequent years. His motion called on the General Synod to 'lament' this, to 'express gratitude to God' for BAME Anglicans' 'indispensable contribution to the mission, ministry, prayer and worship of Christ's Church' and in wider society, and to 'resolve to continue, with great effort and urgency, to stamp out all forms of . . . racism' in the Church of England.[47]

In an impromptu speech during the debate, the Archbishop of Canterbury Justin Welby confessed to being 'sorry and ashamed. I'm ashamed of our history, and I'm ashamed of our failure . . . I'm ashamed at my lack of urgent voice to the Church. . . . There is no doubt when we look at our own church that we are still deeply institutionally racist'. In the final motion that was carried unanimously, a request was added for research to be commissioned 'to assess the impact of this [racism] on the Church of England in terms of church members lost, churches declining into closure, and vocations . . . missed'. The words 'apologises for' were also added alongside the call to 'lament' the church's racism, with the bishop of Leicester, who proposed the amendment, insisting that 'we're taking our first steps into a new culture defined by humility'.[48]

The Synod vote, and Welby's apology, was covered widely in the national press at the time. Fifteen weeks later, in the aftermath of 46-year-old Black man George Floyd's murder (on 25 May 2020) by white police in Minneapolis, Church of England bishops (almost all of them white) were among the more prominent British public figures 'taking the knee' – as part of the 'Black Lives Matter' movement that had suddenly exploded into public visibility across the world – in grief, solidarity and resistance to white supremacy and racism. Accompanying statements made it clear that this action was a visible embodiment of that 'new culture [of] humility' of which the bishop of Leicester had spoken in February.[49]

16.9 CONCLUSIONS: RE-FORMING AN ECCLESIAL PUBLIC THEOLOGY?

Is it just possible that an ecclesial *apology* might be a small but significant step towards the kind of re-formed public theology that Elaine Graham calls

---

[47] 'Windrush Commitment & Legacy', paper for Church of England General Synod February 2020, GS 2156A.

[48] Adam Becket, 'Synod Apologies to Windrush Generation for CofE Racism', *Church Times*, 11 February 2020, https://www.churchtimes.co.uk/articles/2020/14-february/news/uk/synod-apologises-to-windrush-generation-for-c-of-e-racism (last accessed 30 July 2020).

[49] 'Bishops Take the Knee', Diocese of Leicester website, 8 June 2020, https://leicester.anglican.org/news/bishops-take-the-knee.php (last accessed 16 August 2020).

an '*apologetics* of presence'? Through receptive engagements with both the liberationist and EPT traditions, Graham identifies four dimensions to such an apologetics: (1) 'nurtur[ing] a [single] pluralist, deliberative space of civil discourse'; (2) 'speaking truth to power' on behalf of 'those who have been marginalized and disempowered by global economic and political forces'; (3) 'seeking the welfare of the city', through faithful 'Christian performance'; and (4) 'bring[ing] to the forefront' the vital 'secular' (i.e. *worldly*) 'vocation . . . of the [church's] laity'.[50]

The argument that I have made in this chapter, however, has raised either substantial criticisms, or at least significant qualifications, of each of these, particularly seen from the perspective of a white theologian in a church and a wider society infected by white supremacist habits of thought and action. The idea of a single, inclusive 'public sphere' (1) is, we have seen, both an unrealistic expectation and an exclusionary illusion, as is the desire to 'speak for' others (2) who have been 'marginalized and disempowered' by precisely the societal and ecclesial dynamics which privilege me and other white people. Such a desire, to 'speak truth to power', both imagines an all-too-easy, undistorted access to the 'truth' (of the ways in which the dynamics of injustice work) and reinforces the injustice of an already-skewed access to 'power'. While broadly affirmative of the intention towards faithful 'Christian performance' (3), expressed through the discipleship of the whole people of God (4), I have also laid out here various evidence to suggest we should not simply be *cautious* about the 'faithfulness' of the church's 'performance', but profoundly *penitent*. As Allison Fenton comments bitingly of Graham's writings, and of public theology more widely, the church 'is not yet in a position to "dismantle systems of domination and hierarchy"' when it is 'still asking to join in'.[51]

Public theology is, as Graham Ward puts it, 'in search of a body' – the 'body politic' – that turns out to be an elusive eschatological ideal. While EPT responds that the body in question is in fact the church, Black theology insists that that body is riddled with the disease of colonialist and institutional racism. As Katie Walker Grimes puts it, there is a vital theological task in critically 'discerning the [actually existing] body' – both the 'body politic' and the ecclesial body – with all those bodies' segregations and exclusions, but also with their possibilities for redemption. To the analytical and theological tools of public theology for 'discerning the body *politic*', then, I argue for adding the critical tools of Black theology that I have all-too-briefly touched on here, and also the complementary tools of what Nicholas Healy has called 'practical-prophetic ecclesiology'. In contrast to the excessively

---

[50]Graham, *Between*, 212–13.
[51]Allison Fenton, 'Elaine Graham and the "Good City"', in *Public Theology and the Challenge of Feminism*, ed. Monro and Burns, 124.

realized eschatologies of what he names 'blueprint ecclesiologies', Healy proposes drawing on the analytic tools of ethnography so that 'ecclesiology become[s] a church-wide social practice of communal self-critical analysis'.[52] Ecclesial ethnography, developing 'thick descriptions' of the 'concrete church' in all its mixed-up faithfulness and sinfulness, enables the church to present a more faithful witness to the world, Healy argues: '[b]y talking about the Church in ways that acknowledge its failings, even drawing attention to them, what we say about God becomes less easily confused with what we say about ourselves.'[53]

Such 'thick descriptions' would seek to describe the culture of local churches with a careful attention to what Mary McClintock Fulkerson identifies as embodied habits of 'obliviousness' – the 'power-related willing[ness]-not-to-see' – as well as their opposite: practices which create 'shared space[s] of appearance' in which those who have been 'othered' are seen, heard, acknowledged, recognized.[54] Also included within this field of 'practical-prophetic ecclesiology' would be France-Williams's careful documenting of the workings of the Church of England's General Synod, and Grimes's attention to the racially segregated geographies of eucharistic sharing (and non-sharing) of Detroit's Roman Catholics which, as Grimes suggests, 'would at least enable the church to feel the weight of its sin across every inch of its corporate body' and present it with 'the unsettling possibility that we may never be able to fully receive Christ while residing this side of the eschaton'. What would result from such analytical work would be not just, as Grimes hypothesizes, the energy to 'agitate' for wider social change (modestly, Grimes proposes 'the expansion of public transit between inner city and outer suburb' as an example of this)[55] but also, as Healy hints, and as Jennifer McBride teases out at length, communal practices of ecclesial penitence and commitments to reformation and reparation, themselves understood *as* acts of public witness.[56]

But Grimes's proposals, as with much of my wider argument here, stand or fall on the capacity of those of us who are multiply privileged – and therefore most directly afflicted by multiple obliviousnesses – to be radically receptive to both the

---

[52]Nicholas Healy, *Church, World and the Christian Life: Practical-Prophetic Ecclesiology* (Cambridge: Cambridge University Press), 178.
[53]Healy, *Church*, 13.
[54]Mary McClintock Fulkerson, *Places of Redemption: Theology for a Worldly Church* (Oxford: Oxford University Press, 2007), 15–21. Even in this chapter, I need to acknowledge that questions of *gender*, and the voices of feminist and womanist theologians, have been pushed to the edges as I have sought to bring other concerns (e.g. race) to visibility. The search for genuinely 'shared spaces of appearance' goes on!
[55]Katie Walker Grimes, *Christ Divided: Antiblackness as Corporate Vice* (Minneapolis: Fortress Press, 2017), 234–5.
[56]Jennifer McBride, *The Church for the World: A Theology of Public Witness* (Oxford: Oxford University Press, 2012).

gifts and the challenges of our 'othered' siblings, both within the body of Christ and beyond the ecclesial body's porous boundaries. To be even involved in the work of discerning the truth, let alone speaking it, we need the kind of exorcism that Robert Beckford prescribes: a 'shaking to the core' (as Jim Perkinson puts it) of those habits of whiteness that have engrained 'social superiority and cultural normativity as . . . unthought birthright[s]'.[57] In conclusion, then, I offer Cobus van Wyngaard's 'guidelines' for white engagement in the profoundly racialized 'public sphere' in South Africa, with the understanding that they should also apply to white Christians' engagement in *internal* conversations within the embodiments of the *ecclesia* wherever we might be located:

- 'Analysing the impetus to speak and fighting against it', particularly where we are more prone to 'speaking for' others than listening to them.
- A willingness to be silent, not to withdraw but to 'signal one's willingness to receive the other's struggle to find words . . . for his or her experiences' and to 'open up the space for those excluded from the public sphere [to] become voices in the formation of public opinion, including my own opinion'.
- Listening to Black voices, not to 'learn what "they" want' but so that 'we learn about the world we are in and how we have been shaped' by racist histories, structures and assumptions, 'refusing to deny [their] continuing impact'.
- Listening seriously to the voices which 'scandalise' us, which defy white norms of 'acceptability' and 'respectability' – whether through anger and protest, or ways of expression that feel 'alien' to us – that call us to conversion.
- When we do speak, interrogating the 'possible connections between our social location and what we are saying', 'tak[ing] responsibility for what we are saying, and commit[ting] to being held accountable', including being open to criticism, and being wary 'where we note a quick rejection of criticism in ourselves'.
- At the same time as listening attentively to Black voices as 'our primary influence concerning matters of race', directing our speech primarily towards 'the white public as our primary audience, calling members of this particular group, as part of this group, into active work on the disorder associated with [our] position, and a struggle against its unearned privilege'.[58]

---

[57]James Perkinson, *White Theology: Outing Supremacy in Modernity* (New York: Palgrave Macmillan, 2004), 215.
[58]Van Wyngaard, 'Whiteness', 485–91. Drawing on the work of Alcoff, Samantha Vice, Klippies Kritzinger and James Perkinson.

CHAPTER 17

Liturgy and public theology

CATHERINE PICKSTOCK

In the preface to his translation of Jean-Louis Chrétien's *The Unforgettable and the Unhoped For*, Jeffrey Bloechl asks whether the structures which we have contrived to describe reality are sufficiently sensitive to the way reality actually is. This question may be turned upon the nature of our theological structures: Are they reflective of the transcendent God and our human embodied and speculative approach, and do they allow us to negotiate the world around us in such a way that is not inimical to theological purpose?

The increasing interest in theology as a way of life, as opposed to rarefied doctrine, can occasion an examination of the implications of liturgy as public theology, or manifest theology, and of liturgy as a means by which we may attempt to align our lives visibly with the highest reality. One can extend the notion that speculative metaphysics must be as much performed as theorized beyond language and poetics into a consideration of liturgy, especially with regard to its links with integrated, 'synaesthesic' bodily sensation and spiritual formation.

The emphasis on the publicness of theology is not new; indeed, truth is to be regarded as a matter of all-encompassing witness and realization, in accordance with a specifically Christian Patristic and Medieval realization of the inherently 'sensing' character of thought itself. But it is timely to revisit this emphasis on embodied testimony or on 'shewings', to use Julian of Norwich's word for revealed visions or theophanies, in the light of recent phenomenological interest in the body, and on the significance of performed or 'seen' and 'habituated' ritual enactment. This enactment is public in the sense of shared and inclusive, but also as appealing publicly to the bodily senses.

In terms of the poetic 'qualification' of traditional realism, a theoretical exposition of metaphysics yields equal space to its poetic performance. This performance is not just verbal, lexical or aesthetic but shown in the expressive dilation of a human culture, insofar as it can be taken as 'liturgically' gesturing towards transcendence.

So it is to the plausibility of this gestural theology that we turn in this chapter. What are its prime features? Is an inhabited or shown theology newly disclosive? What are the implications of such an appreciation of the role of the body – of language, gesture, posture, sound, variations of light and space, the passage of time – for theological understanding? An attentiveness to physical and temporal mediations and embodiments of theological truth goes hand in hand with the appreciation of participatory metaphysical frameworks, and a renewed interest in pre-modern resources in which the modes of embodied and postural contemplation and devotion are not held in a hostile relation to theoretical reasoning.

The requisite modes of enactment – contemplation, prayer and ritual – entail an integrative stance which brings together active and passive modes or dispositions, a fusion of subject with object, and a subversion of one's usual kinds of knowing and doing. They involve a perception of reality which is also conscious of its own part in that reality. In contemplation, one moves towards an object, and yet one already rests in it; human spiritual perception is realized not by a refusal of the body and time but by their drawing in through ritual bodily practice, a process which reaches its apotheosis in liturgical activity, which one might see as an outward and inward 'common-sensing', and the synaesthetic mingling of the different physical and spiritual senses which such activity involves.

Why do human beings need to repeat their liturgy? As fallen, the human person forgets that she is created, that in every moment of flourishing, she copies and draws near to God; she exults when she remembers this, and her mind is aligned with her created ontology, and that of her neighbours; and she despairs when she tends away from this, forgetting such an alignment. In liturgical enactment, the human person performs and then recollects forward or prospectively her spiritual and embodied unity with herself, with her neighbours and with God. Because human acts of worship fail to coincide with human nature, as they should, the gesture of worship must be explicitly repeated. Conscious and active repetition of liturgy is needed, and so liturgy itself is requisite for there to be liturgy.

It follows that within liturgical enactment, one might look for a theology and metaphysics of alignment: of the redeemed physical senses, of their co-ordination with spiritual counterparts, of their commingling and unification, as a prefigured restoration of the paradisal body.

We have so far mentioned different kinds of sensing: the bodily senses, and the crossing-over of these perceptual modes in synaesthesia; but there is also common sensing and spiritual sensing to consider. These modes of sensing are often separated in perceptual compass. Spiritual perception refers to a range of perceptual powers that conceive divine–human alignment. In a more specific fashion, the tradition of spiritual senses concerns the heightened psychic equivalents for physical sensations and even parts of the body, traceable to Origen. The *sensus communis* or central sense, for Aristotle, later developed by Aquinas, by contrast, refers to the *unification* of the primary sense-perceptions, *the perception of perception*, to judgements of comparison, contrast and discrimination of the deliverances of the senses and the residual sense images which compose imagination, together with the voluntary and involuntary reproduction of sensation through memory. The term 'synaesthesia', meanwhile, refers to the perceptual phenomenon whereby stimulation of one sensory or cognitive pathway leads to involuntary experiences in a second sensory or cognitive pathway. It is today taken to apply to a pathological phenomenon, but it can be argued that such 'pathology' heightens a sensory mingling and transference that occurs in all human beings, if a 'common sensing' and so the first emergence of *intelligible* 'sense', or meaning, is to be possible at all.

Although these terms are not usually taken together, the gestural and enacted nature of liturgy, its sensory complexity and its exorbitant fusion of high metaphysics and inhabited reality suggest that it would be instructive to allow for their connection for the purposes of a discussion of public or manifested theology.

The reality of the 'spiritual senses', since Origen, was thought to depend neither on a purely spiritual organ, or set of organs, nor a corporeal metaphor for spiritual apprehension. Rather, it was rooted in a classical ontology of the bodily senses which viewed them as already obtaining a pneumatic aspect. Spiritual sensing accordingly involved a heightening of this natural capacity in its being directed towards the angelic and the divine.

It would be more accurate, however, to say that ordinary sensing was rather a diminished exemplification of this supernatural scope, impaired since the Fall; and that in the liturgical fusing of the ideal and the real, one finds an aspiration to the unification of the senses, a partial realization of the anagogic marriage of sense with spirit, in which fallen reason is offset by the intensified alignment of bodily sense-perceptions, in such a way that, for example, although reason fails to discern the body and blood in the Eucharistic elements, nonetheless the senses are drawn by their sweetness and savour.[1] Given the marked physicality

---

[1] Thomas Aquinas, *ST* III Q. 74 a. 3 ad 1; a. 79; Q. 81 a. 1 ad 3.

of one's activity in the offering of liturgy, the human senses now take the lead over the human mind, guiding one's reason through a mimicry of its restoration, as if in aspiration an authentic realization will follow upon such momentary and repeated copying.

Indeed, this eventual realization is a true copying of the divine pattern of the *Logos* which is the very copy of the Paternal origin. Since Trinitarian doctrine teaches the paradox that this secondary copying is essential to the origin in which it inheres, one's normal inclination to instrumentalize ritual is reversed in the Christian case. If mimetic gesture is 'original', then liturgy remains even when it is completed as spiritual attitude. For liturgical offering as eternal 'movement' persists even in God as the eternal filial praise of the Father.

One can observe other related forms of liturgical alignment: between the individual and the collective, unity and diversity, body and spirit, word and sense. It is as if in the liturgical space, realized through enactment, an exteriorization of the *sensus communis* is dramatized, and the human participants become, as it were, personifications of sense. The link between the senses of the individual bodies in shared meaning is 'transubstantiated' into the link between all the sensing bodies into that shared cultural sensibility which was the earlier meaning of 'common sense' present in more judgemental daily usage.[2]

The space of the liturgy, the edifice of the church or the performed space of enactment become a dramatization and exteriorization of the mind, of unfallen reason which remembers that it is created and is now at one with the diversity of creation and with God, where knowing and unknowing coincide in illumination and the forgetting of isolated self.

However, liturgy concerns not just gesture and bodily comportment but also language and musical extension. This dimension constitutes a link between the verbal and the sensing. Thus, Plato adverted to the way in which one does not adequately understand the impact of language and representation upon one's spiritual estate: for example, the profound and sometimes dangerous spiritual interiorization of ideas through the senses of hearing and vision when the mimetic arts propound disordered or distorting representations of reality. The ancient audience, on witnessing the mimetic performances of the tragedians, would put on their sufferings, exult and despair along with the characters.[3] This was sustained in Origen's identification of the anagogical sense of scripture

---

[2]Hans-Georg Gadamer, *Truth and Method*, trans. William Glen-Doepel (London: Sheed and Ward, 1975), 19ff.
[3]Plato *Republic*, X 597 B; Eric A. Havelock, *Preface to Plato* (Cambridge, MA: Harvard University Press, 1963); Hans-Georg Gadamer, 'Plato and the Poets', in *Dialogue and Dialectic: Eight Hermeneutical Studies on Plato*, trans. P. Christopher Smith (New Haven: Yale University Press, 1983), 39–73.

whereby the reader puts on, or enters into, a scriptural passage so completely that she exceeds contemplation and knows the words with her whole being.[4]

Language can in these ways both confound and restore the human person, which prompts the observation that language does not keep pace with reality as though it were a transparency one lays over the real to archive its affairs. Rather, language is part of reality, and as such it can shape the human person's mind, lead her ahead of herself, or undo her. Sensation hurls reason ahead of itself from beneath, while chanted language draws reason beyond itself on a horizontal plane. Together, word and sensation compose the gestural and ritual act, which expresses a vertical inclination (in excess of the 'finished' products of reason) of the whole person.

This active fusion of the sensing and the linguistic was exemplified in Origen's connecting of mystical and hermeneutic doctrines, in such a way that defined the authentic later grammar of the Christian life.

Because of the Incarnational focus of Christianity, and the biblical derivation of full understanding from the operation of the 'heart', both corporeally and linguistically in excess of mere 'mind', spiritual perception was understood, in its cleaving to the bodily, as correspondingly diversified in terms of the five natural senses themselves. These 'sensings' were held to be involved in the discernment of the three, and eventually after him fourfold 'senses' of Scripture which were developed initially by Origen. At the core of his hermeneutic theory stood the Solomonic *Canticles* which for the Alexandrian Father had a directly allegorical meaning, concerning Christ and his Bride. It was also taken by Origen to be the prime and most sensuous source for the understanding of the spiritual senses.[5]

I have argued elsewhere that the hermeneutic priority over foundational 'givenness' in the Analytic sense, and its equal priority over the phenomenological sense of supposedly pure 'donation', can be saved from scepticism if interpretation goes to the distance of metaphysical speculation, which remains an affective reception of a gift which cannot be grasped or commanded.[6] The mode of metaphysics which Rowan Williams proposes in *The Edge of Words*[7] is of just such a kind. Yet it is a distinctively novel variant. From the presumed authenticity of one's own poetic additions to natural reality, the sphere of culture as such, Williams argues that this truthful 're-presentation' of the real is

---

[4]Henri de Lubac, *Medieval Exegesis: The Four Senses of Scripture*, trans. Marc Sebanc and E. M. Macierowski, 3 vols (Grand Rapids: Wm. B. Eerdmans and Co., 2009).

[5]Jean-Louis Chrétien, *Symbolique du Corps: La tradition chrétienne du Cantiques des Cantiques* (Paris: Presses Universitaires de France, 2005).

[6]Catherine Pickstock, 'The Phenomenological Given and the Hermeneutic Exchange: Which Holds Priority?', *Revista Portuguesa de Filosofia* 76, no. 2–3 (2020): 715–28.

[7]Rowan Williams, *The Edge of Words: God and the Habits of Language* (London: Bloomsbury, 2014).

neither a matter of mirroring nor an aleatory and self-authenticating patchwork. Its continuously attempted 'completion' of nature seems to indicate both an aiming towards and a participation in a truth which is eternally transcendent to both nature and culture. It must be this if our additions are neither an accidental upshot of evolution nor an arbitrary expression of human preference.

Yet for such a metaphysics, the elaboration of theory, though essential, is not sufficient, for all depends upon the authenticity of the poetic performance, and even the theoretical reflection on this performance, the 'argument to God' which Williams is making, must be performed well. And such a reflection must in turn help to inspire further 'poetic' performances in the future, since such performances serve to sustain a confirmation of the theoretical argument. This is not simply because one must be able to take poetic performances as authentic re-presentations of nature, but also because the distinction between the practical poetic and the philosophical theoretical levels is relative in nature. At the poetic level, existential perplexity, and reflection upon it, have already begun, and for this reason, the 'poetic' or cultural act emerges as a partially conscious attempt faithfully to re-present nature or to repeat her non-identically. The possibility of this enterprise is already seen to depend upon the reality of an overarching transcendent carapace, embracing both the natural and the cultural. In consequence, the poetic attempt truthfully to re-present is at one with the attempt to represent a greater and eternal cosmic order.

This is the primordial human claim to be in the truth, which is a matter of enactment as well as speculative vision. Such a claim is ineluctably public – ritual or liturgical – in character. Williams's proposal suggests that human beings can never be released from this fundamental arrangement: that successfully to speculate is also to perform or show well, according to an accepted human judgement, for which there are no extrinsic criteria. For this reason, the interpretation and re-shaping of form in nature, the sacred *mimesis* which one observes already in prehistoric cave paintings, is inseparable from one's corporeal negotiations of the world. Our corporeal engagement encounters and performs the 'truth' when it mediates pre-given natural form and mystically conveys the eternal 'forms', however these are understood, which are the archetypal and vertical source for both natural and cultural formations. In this way, we can combine an ancient sense of knowledge as the ethereal transmutation of material with a modern sense of the crucial role of the body in enabling such a mediation.

The new understanding of public theology lies not just in theoretical reflection upon poetic practice but in the furthering of this practice, and its assessment, insofar as it reaches the intensity of the liturgical. It holds together, as of equal importance, the ontological setting of presumed re-presentation of, and participation in, truth and the continuous event of the performance of this setting, which in turn modifies one's sense of it. It thereby combines the Aristotelian perspective of a stable hierarchy of actual, given essences, with a Neoplatonic invocation of a primal and unforeclosed power of creative inauguration and motion in which every essence participates and which every essence mediates. This is not finitely foreclosed, since there may be exemplifications and modifications to come, but neither is it infinitely foreclosed, since the 'infinite' exceeds the contrast of the bounded and the unbounded, or of the actually finished and the potentially prospective, as Nicholas of Cusa, who placed the poetic and the ritual at the heart of reality, enunciated.[8]

For such an outlook, then, ontology is not a transcendental carapace which the poetic extrinsically exemplifies. Rather, a poetic ontology specifically grants to 'poetry' an equality of truth alongside philosophy, if human truth-claims should negate themselves before the transcendent source of all order and all novelty, which sustains but revises order in unexpected ways. And, as I have argued earlier, this 'poetry' is already performing the poetic ontology.

17.1 WHAT IS LITURGY?

Recent study of pre-modern monastic and liturgical ritual has emphasized that such operations do not encode hidden messages at a remove from ordinary activity nor divide inner purpose from outer gesture. Rather, they seek to realign inner motive and outer shape via the formation of virtues through the exercise of certain disciplines which are embedded within and constitutive of a way of life. Indeed, rather than appending ritual activity to the normative instrumental activity of the everyday, it is implied that, if anything, one should approach the matter the other way around.

For this reason, some scholars argue that 'ritual' can be a misleading term when applied to the Middle Ages. Echoing in part John Milbank's argument that sociology is disguised theology, Philippe Buc has shown how, ironically, normative anthropological and sociological notions of 'ritual' are secularizations of post-medieval theological ones.[9]

In an elaboration of Buc's case, one can argue that after the disenchantment of the medieval symbolically saturated universe, sacramentality and ceremony came to be seen more in terms of an officially authorized exception, consciously construed as mediating divine will and power, and as vital for sustaining belief and political order – a move which in turn effectively privatized religion. After the French Revolution, reactionary Catholic thinkers emphasized the necessity

---

[8]Nicholas of Cusa, 'De Possest', in *Complete Philosophical and Theological Treatises of Nicholas of Cusa*, trans. Jasper Hopkins, vol. 2 (Minneapolis: Arthur J. Banning Press, 2001), 914–54. See Andrea Bellantone, *La Métaphysique Possible: Philosophies de l'Esprit et Modernité* (Paris: Hermann, 2012), *passim*.
[9]Philippe Buc, *The Dangers of Ritual: Between Early Medieval Texts and Social Scientific Theory* (Princeton: Princeton University Press, 2001), 230.

of a consecrated, monistic 'representation' at the centre of society, if order was to be secured. The unity of society was virtually equated with the presence of God, and it was from here but a small step for secular thinkers to invert this into the view that 'ritual' is functionally necessary for the securing of political peace.[10]

But such an outlook presupposes that a ritual dimension is other from, and exceptional to the everyday, and that its sacrality situates it beyond any rational debatability. It is hereby presented as something superimposed, and something to which ordinary people superstitiously submit.

However, as Buc suggests, even if one source of modern thinking about ritual might be Catholic in origin, its perspective scarcely applies to the Catholic Middle Ages.

This is for three main reasons: first, in that period, the pragmatic and the symbolic were bound together. Material things were seen as meaningful, and meaning was seen to reside as much in things as in signs. Every action accordingly tended towards the symbolically gestural.[11]

Second, ritual order in the Middle Ages was far from monistic in character: the division between *sacrum* and *regnum* ensured that there were degrees of ritual importance, and that there was an awareness that certain matters needed to be sequestered as relatively insignificant and instrumental, since they pertained to this life only and were subject to contestation. These tended to belong to the sphere of the *regnum*, though the difference remained relative.[12]

Third, there was nothing invariable about medieval liturgy and ceremonial: on the contrary, what was appropriate was constantly argued over, and many different interpretations of commonly shared ritual actions were given. The interpretations were as important as the original rituals themselves and in turn inflected their character. Thus, in the wake of Paul Ricoeur, Buc contends that one must not conflate an already hermeneutic era, such as the medieval period, with earlier, more static oral cultures.[13]

This does not, however, mean that the Middle Ages, up to the fourteenth century, were by comparison less ritual in character, or more given to unification by law than ceremonial performance, in accordance with an evolutionary

---

[10]Ibid., 235.
[11]Hans Henrik Lohfert Jørgensen, 'Into the Saturated Sensorium: Introducing the Principles of Perception and Mediation in the Middle Ages' and 'Sensorium: A Model for Medieval Perception', in *The Saturated Sensorium: Principles of Perception and Mediation in the Middle Ages*, ed. Hans Henrik Lohfert Jørgensen, Henning Laugerud and Laura Katrine Skinnebach (Aarhus: Aarhus University Press, 2015), 9–23, 35–70.
[12]This mere relativity is strongly emphasized with very detailed examples by Andrew Willard Jones in his *Before Church and State: A Study of Social Order in the Sacramental Kingdom of St. Louis IX* (Steubensville, OH: Emmaus Academic, 2017).
[13]Buc, *The Dangers of Ritual*, 247.

scheme common since the nineteenth century, as articulated by Fustel de Coulanges, and many others.[14] Rather, law and ritual existed alongside one another, reinforcing each other, in part because of the 'instructive' character of Christian liturgy. The latter tended to bring together thought and physicality to a paradigmatic degree, again in terms of a further enactment of the Incarnation and the mediation of a Trinitarian God who was internally as well as externally active, ordering, expressing, speaking, imaging and inspiring.[15]

As scholars have shown, this mediating integration was achieved by recourse to *synaesthesia*, or simultaneous appeal to all the bodily senses, in such a way as to transfigure the things perceived, and the subject perceiving them, uniting them through the 'immutation' of the senses which conforms them to, rather than extrinsically represents, the objects of perception.[16] This appeal concurred with the emphasis of Aristotelian-influenced theologians, such as Bonaventure and Aquinas, upon one's 'common sensing', whereby an 'inner sense' blends together the products of the five senses and perceives through them all, by way of a shared quantitative dimension (size, shape, position etc.), as the mediating threshold between body and mind and as essential to the thinking process of finite creatures.[17]

In this way, the medieval liturgy conspired to enchant matter, and to concretize spirit, in a manner that seems contradictory to post-Cartesian thinkers. The incarnated mystery was divine by virtue of its creative, transformative capacity, as already mentioned. For this reason, the miraculous was not seen as surprising or disruptive, the thaumaturgic being anticipated, as it were, and frequently recorded.

One can suppose that synaesthesia encouraged such a sense of enchanted openness, because illuminating sight came to be linked with the haptic, insight with movement, vision with alteration. Sensing was regarded as a mode of touch, which was seen as both passive and active and as more analogical in character than the other four, more exclusivist senses. This was because touch, following Aristotle, was regarded as inherently various, lacking in a common genus, such as 'vision' for the eye, and as united by its prodigious substantive location, which is the whole surface of the body. Since touch was regarded

---

[14]Ibid., 219–23.
[15]Agamben, *Opus Dei*, 17–86.
[16]Jørgensen, 'Into the Saturated Sensorium' and 'Sensorium: A Model for Medieval Perception'; Kristin Bliksrud Aavitsland, 'Incarnation; Paradoxes of Perception and Mediation in Medieval Liturgical Art'; Laura Katrine Skinnebach, 'Devotion: Perception as Practice and Body as Devotion in Late Medieval Piety'; Nils Holger Petersen, 'Ritual: Medieval Liturgy and the Senses', and Henning Laugerud, 'Memory: The Sensory Materiality of Belief and Understanding in Late Medieval Europe', in *The Saturated Sensorium*, ed. Jørgensen, Laugerud and Skinnebach, 9–23, 24–71, 72–90, 152–79, 180–205, 246–72, respectively.
[17]Thomas Aquinas, *ST* I q. 78 a. 4.

in these terms as the surface medium between mind and matter, all human knowing was seen as a kind of haptic circulation and real ontological exchange of spirit with corporeal things.[18]

One can observe a wide field of examples of pre-modern awareness of corporeally involved modes of direct encounter with the truth, which have been articulated in the post-epistemological phase of modern philosophy. The medieval coexistence of a fundamental realism of form, as shared between things and mind, with an already 'involved' realism of corporeal engagement, raises the question of whether, today, the revival of the latter sort of realism depends upon the former. For in this period, the body was taken to be a mediator of truth because it was a conveyer and modulator of *eidos*, grounded in a divine ordering of reality. Otherwise, one might be referring to a merely pragmatic negotiation of the world, or of aesthetic pleasures within the world which could be an accident of one's biological constitution. However, there would conversely be no mediation of form from matter to mind without this corporeal threshold, without the belonging of ensouled body to both realms at once. For this reason, one can argue that ancient realism depended upon both formal continuity and (more implicitly) a *zuhanden* corporeal engagement for there to be sharing in, and conveyance of, truth, which was taken to mean an eternal and abiding reality.

This combination suggests that the full metaphysical realism of this period was itself liturgical in character, if one attends not just to medieval theoretical texts but also to their ultimate setting within spiritual practices. Beyond the abstraction of ideas, and the inert givenness of lapidary things, reality was disclosed as radically operational and creatively mastering of matter alongside spirit, holding the active key to their integration.[19] It is in these terms that Giorgio Agamben has argued that Christianity, especially the religious orders, brought the ritual character of human life to a new pitch of intensity by seeking to make life coincide with the heightened activity of liturgy, just as Christ's perfectly restored humanity was a continuously unbroken broke-offering. One sees this in the unceasing round of Cluniac prayer, the Benedictine integration of labour into liturgy and the attempt of the orders of friars to extend this coincidence to everyday life. Being, life and prayer came almost aspiringly to coincide.[20] If the realisms of form and corporeal involvement coincide in liturgy, the attempt to ritualize all of life was also an attempt to render life truthful or, inversely, to ensure that truth was performed in order to be known, given that

---

[18] Aquinas, *In De Anima*, I, 54–82, II, 22; Jørgensen, 'Sensorium'; Petersen, 'Ritual'; John Milbank and Catherine Pickstock, *Truth in Aquinas* (London: Routledge, 2001), 60–87.
[19] Agamben, *Opus Dei*, loc. cit.
[20] Ibid.

complete truth was seen as an event that had arrived, as the Incarnation of God, in the course of human history.

17.2 'MIXED CREATURES'

This approach to an absolute fusion of life and liturgy reflects Christian anthropology. For the Christian tradition, human beings are mixed creatures, neither quite beast nor quite angel, as Blaise Pascal expressed it.[21] This apparently grotesque hybridity is one's miniature dignity. Unlike angels, as a human being one combines in one's own person every level of the created order, from the inorganic, through the organic and the animally psychic, to the angelically intellectual. God must communicate with human beings through their bodies and senses, as a tilting of his sublime intellection towards their particular mode of understanding. But this tilting denotes more than condescension and economic adaptation, however much these are necessarily involved. This is because human beings, unlike angels, have a privileged access to the mute language of physical reality.[22] The latter is an essential aspect of God's creation for a biblical outlook, part of the plenitude of divine self-expression, and so, in this respect, human beings enjoy a certain advantage, as compared with angelic spiritual confinement. For even if material reality is lower in metaphysical status than angelic or human rational being, it must, as part of the plenitude of creation as a whole, be an essential part and so reveal something of God hidden even from the angels, just as the angels could not comprehend the mystery of the Incarnation.[23] The dumb simplicity and lack of reflexivity in physical things, or the spontaneity of animals, suggest aspects of divine simplicity and spontaneity, which cannot be evident to the somewhat reflective, discursive and abstracting operation of limited human minds or to the abstract direct intuition of angels, that do not enjoy the full divine insight into particulars

This is one reason why sacramental signs have a heuristic function for Christian theology, vital for the instilling of truth; they are not just illustrative or metaphorical. Rather, they prompt human beings to new thought and provide guidance into deeper modes of meditation, because they contain a surplus which human thought can never anticipate or fathom. It is also the case, as Aquinas elaborates in his discussion of analogical language at *Summa* I, q.13, that when one hazards an analogy (or, one could add, a metaphor), one cannot comprehensively survey its meaning but, rather, tentatively live and move in the direction of its sense. For the source of its meaning lies pre-eminently in

---

[21]Blaise Pascal, *Pensées* (Paris: Delagrave, 1897), 329.
[22]St Thomas Aquinas, *ST* I, q 77, a 3 resp.
[23]Eph. 3: 9–10.

God, and only derivatively, by dint of participation, in the world to hand. From this, it follows that if such density of language applies especially to theological discourse, the latter intensifies what pertains in the case of language as such, since all words refer, as Aquinas indicates, primarily to material things, but these things themselves borrow their being and ultimate significance from divine pre-containment.

Liturgy is therefore not simply a public duty. Rather, it is the primary means by which the Christian, throughout her life, from baptism to extreme unction, is gradually inducted into the mystery of revelation and transformed by it.

In these three aspects detailed earlier, we can find a context for thinking about liturgy as public theology: sacraments are heuristic not metaphoric; the physical and sensorial liturgical enactment is itself a work of saving mystery; liturgy involves a redemptive heightening of the senses into the playing of the divine game.

17.3 'O TASTE AND SEE'

These aspects must be borne simultaneously in mind in our further reflection on the innate logic of Christian liturgy and its disclosive capacity.

Sensation, in a liturgical context, has both a passive and an active dimension, in accordance with the principle that liturgy is a divine–human work, because it is a Christological work. In liturgy, the participants undergo sensory experiences, but they – collectively – produce this sensory experience, along with the natural materials and instruments which they deploy.

In this process, sacramental elements, ornaments and 'technological' instruments, rather like Heidegger's 'tool-being', in order better to focus upon things – such as the *ciborium* – tend to merge into one another.[24] Equally, they work to alter the human subject who has yet, as both artist and immersed spectator, in some sense, herself contrived everything, even though she is herself, as a subject, re-shaped by this mediated inspiration.[25] She imagines and remembers what is sensorily encountered – memory being taken as more active than the imagination, for medieval thinkers – the liturgical subject is, in one sense, recomposed by things; yet in another, she is their 'alchemical' still, their re-composer, through re-memoration, and the repeated expressive utterance of *melisma* and *modulatio*. Her *musica humana*, harmonizing soul and body, are realized through corporeal musical utterance which conveys the *musica*

---

[24]Guilielmus Durandus, *The Rationale Divinorum Officiorum* (Louisville, KN: Fons Vitae, 2007), 'On the Mass', Rama Coomaraswamy tr, cap I, 12, 237; Jørgensen, 'Sensorium'; Aavitsland, 'Incarnation'.
[25]Aquinas, *ST* I q. 78, a. 4; Skinnebach, 'Devotion'; Laugerud, 'Memory'.

mundana of the cosmos. But again, this is synaesthesically construed: 'music' is in the dance of the spheres, in spoken as well as sung signs, and in human rhythms of movement and painting, just as the sung note is not without a word, and a word is never without an illustration which further incarnates it.[26]

Insofar as the sensory and aesthetic experience of the Mass is a manner of instruction adapted to the mode of humanity, as Thomas Aquinas emphasized, it incites the participants' spiritual desire to penetrate further into the mystery and worship ever more ardently: the 'inner chamber' is first of all situated as a fold within external and collective space, for it is archetypically the nuptial chamber, after Origen. And most primarily, one's own psychic 'inner chamber' is paradoxically external to one, because it is really the inner chamber of God himself, for Origen as for Augustine.[27] Were the smell of incense, the sight of the procession or the savour of the elements mere triggers for the recollection of extrinsic concepts, they might do their work on one single occasion. But that they must be repeated, and returned to, suggests that they are vehicles for the forward moving of human spiritual desire, which can never be disincarnate, or separated from these physical allurements.

17.4 THE SPIRITUAL SENSES

It can be argued that the senses, as they function within the liturgy, are harnessed as natural symbols for an inner attentiveness and responsiveness to divine meaning. However, as already stressed, the sacraments are *heuristic* rather than metaphorical. If sensations are essential lures for one's true thinking, and all the more so in the order of redemption after the Fall, can it be that the 'spiritual' sensations are all that really matter? Jean-Louis Chrétien has shown, in his discussion of the tradition of commentary upon the *Canticles*, why this is not the case. First, as we have seen, the idea of the 'spiritual senses', or the notion that there are psychic equivalents for physical sensations and even parts of the body, is traceable to Origen. This holds a biblical rather than Greek lineage, since the Bible spoke of 'the heart' of a human being in such a way that was both physical and spiritual and included thinking and willing, as well as suggesting a concentration of the whole human personality.[28] Such a sense is preserved today in the liturgical *sursum corda*: 'lift up your hearts'.

It is, however, the Christian reading of the *Canticles* as referring to one's love for Christ, who is God incarnate, which seems to have suggested a kind of

---

[26]Jørgensen, 'Into the Saturated Sensorium'.
[27]Jean-Louis Chrétien, *L'Espace Intérieur* (Paris: Minuit, 2014), 38–74.
[28]Heather Webb, 'Catherine of Siena's Heart', *Speculum* 80, no. 3 (2005): 802–17; Heather Webb, *The Medieval Heart* (New Haven: Yale University Press, 2010).

physicalization and diversification of the Biblical heart, which, for Origen, was more commonly construed in terms of the soul, or *anima*, though Augustine often reverts to heart or *cordis*. One should not read this nomenclature, Chrétien argues, as simply many analogues for the essential unity of the heart or soul: only in God is it the case that the diversity of the spiritual senses is mysteriously 'one' in pure simplicity. Rather, there is a real diversity in the human soul, on account of its close link with the body, of which it is the form, in Greek philosophical terms. The soul 'hears', for example, in its imaginative recollection or in its mental attention to God, because it is primarily conjoined with the hearing function of the physical body.[29]

However, as Chrétien implies, this point may be reversed. It is not that, via a secondary move, sensation is metaphorically transferred from body to soul; rather, it is the case that sensing has a double aspect, outer and inner, in accordance with the double biblical meaning of the term 'heart'.

In this way, liturgy can be seen as the best guide to the double aspect of sensation, as understood by Aristotle, referred to earlier, which it instantiates in an intensified manner. Christian liturgy points to the primacy for humanity of the history of ritual over both material utility and ideal intention. The core gesture of ritual is simultaneously externalizing and interiorizing. This is because the ritual object 'interrupts' and 'stands out', since a normally taken-for-granted exterior process is here stalled, through reflection, both as artefact and as mental awareness. Without this exterior and interior duality, it could not occur in the way that it does.

A related point is that if one sees from the very outset with the inner as well as with the outer eye, one relates one mode of sensation to another. The mental operation of synaesthesia is in play whenever just one of our physical senses is activated.[30] The Church Fathers sometimes spoke in the synaesthesic terms implied by ancient Christian liturgy when they suggested that our eyes should listen, our ears see or our lips attend like ears to the word of God through a spiritual kiss, implying that for our inner sense, contemplation is also active obedience and vice versa, while one's speaking to and of God must remain an active attention to his presence. But this kind of language does not remove one from one's actual body: rather, the inner and synaesthetic echo that is 'inner sensing' pervades one's bodily surface in the course of one's original sensitive responses, since were these purely physical, one would have no sensory awareness whatsoever.

---

[29] Jean-Louis Chrétien, *Symbolique du corps: La tradition chrétienne du Cantique des Cantique* (Paris: Presses Universitaires de France, 2005), 15–44.
[30] Ibid., 35.

What this implies for liturgical practice is that worshippers are regarded as making the response of incarnate souls – a response of the heart – to the incarnate God. This response is immediately inscribed in the body and requires no extrinsic interpretation. In liturgical terms, worshippers are invited to adopt diverse stances appropriate to the various phases of worship and the positions that should be assumed before God.[31]

Just as bodily postures are also inward, so inner sensation has an outward aspect. Because sensation has an interior dimension, it becomes possible for this interiority to be deepened, and so for the sight of material things to turn into the sight of spiritual things. However, the possibility of this deepening is paradoxically connected with the excess of material things over rational thought. The mind can exceed abstract reflection in the direction of mystical encounter, the inward absorption of the liturgical mysteries, through the constantly renewed prompting of corporeal sensing by the sacramental realities. The distance of material things from one is thereby a vehicle for conveying the infinite 'distance' of God from one. And because of the Incarnation, in the Eucharistic liturgy, which is its extension, these two distances become one and the same, a radical closeness.

17.5 SACRAMENT OF SACRAMENTS

The sensory aspect of the liturgy is not something passively received by the individual worshipper; it is actively and collectively produced. The participants pray, sing, process, look forward and exchange the *pax* through mutual touch. The resultant sensory experience can to some degree be received by an individual worshipper but is in a certain sense more purely received by an angelic and a divine gaze.

The collective body of the congregation is inevitably made up of individual bodies. It is the individual body which stands as the gatekeeper between the two different allegorical senses for the bodies of the lovers in the *Canticles* – by allusion to the soul, on the one hand, and to the church, on the other. Within the liturgy, this is perhaps most symbolized by the ceremony on Maundy Thursday, and at other times of the *mandatum* or the washing of the feet (in imitation at once of Christ and of Mary Magdalene)[32] of monks by fellow monks or of the congregation by the priest. This was described by Rupert of Deutz as 'a

---

[31] See, for example, Peter the Chanter, *The Christian at Prayer: An Illustrated Prayer Manual*, trans. Richard C. Trexler (Binghampton, NY: State University of New York Press, 1987), especially Part Two.

[32] As traditionally assumed, exegetes do not accept the identification of the woman ('sinful' in Luke), recorded in the four canonical gospels as anointing Jesus' head and feet, with Mary Magdalen.

sacrament of the sacraments', because of its kenotic blending of high and low, meaningful and sensory, spectacle and touch.[33]

The parts of these bodies and their sensations have spiritual aspects as the spiritual senses. Thereby, as we have seen, Christianity diversified the unity of the soul. Bodies and their sensations, following St Paul, represent offices in the church, since the latter, more emphatically than the soul, is taken to be the 'bride' of the Canticles. And so, Christianity unified the human social community in a very specific manner.[34]

The relationship between the inner soul and the collective body, as mediated by the individual body, is central to a deepened grasp of the liturgical action which dramatizes the relationship between Christ and his Bride. In doing so, it draws, like Christianity itself, upon a certain fluidity within the *Canticles*, a book which, as Chrétien shows, the church effectively raised to the status of a kind of 'Bible within the Bible', an hermeneutic key to the relationship between the two testaments.[35]

It was such a key despite or perhaps because of its own dense obscurity and intrinsic call for interpretation. Chrétien observes that one does not know who its protagonists are, at a literal level, and that their status as lover and beloved is not exhausted by any conceptual equivalence. They are God and Israel, Christ and the church, Christ and the soul, but also human marriage partners (given the Pauline signification of Christ and the church) as the supreme model of natural inter-human love, and so by extension, they represent any human loving relationship. One can see a pattern here: a sensory image elevates the participants' spiritual perceptions, but it does so because of, and not despite the fact that it is a sensory image. It can further elevate them if it is constantly returned to, just as the human worshipper can grow in love for God if she is constantly re-confronted with the challenge of her human neighbour.

17.6 THE MEDIATION OF LITURGY

In the liturgy, all these relationships are at stake. And the individual, sensing physical body is their pivot. How is one to understand its mediating role?

One can start with the earlier observation that while Christianity diversifies the soul, it also grants organic unity to the human collectivity. Instead of the *polis* being compared with the hierarchy of the soul, as for Plato, St Paul compares the church polity with the cooperation of the various functions of the human body. However, this is no more a metaphor than was the case with

---

[33]Petersen, 'Ritual', 202.
[34]Chrétien, *Symbolique du Corps*, 15–72.
[35]Ibid., 291–5.

the relationship of the physical with the spiritual senses. Metaphoricity runs rather from the collective to the individual body. Thus St Paul speaks of eye and hand, head and feet announcing their need for one another, like holders of different offices within the church (1 Cor. 12.21). This is to compare eye and hand with individual Christians, rather than the other way around.[36] Similarly, one might expect a metaphoric transference of the unity of the physical body to the unity of the Christian people. However, the 'bodiliness' of a social body is not a fiction; human beings physically and culturally depend upon one another, and one could argue that this is our primary source for one's understanding of embodied unity, since one's psychic unity arises as a reflex from social responses, as Jacques Lacan and others have shown.[37]

By contrast, outside the social and interpersonally linguistic context, the parts of the individual soul-body might remain just 'parts'. Alternatively, they might become aspects of a continuous blur and not really be distinguished at all. Thus, it is equally the case that diversification as well as unity are borrowed from the social organism and then applied to the individual, physical one. It is through the comparison of the eye and hand and other bodily parts to members of the community, in this case the church, that the blur of a (Deleuzian) 'body without organs'[38] is interpretatively avoided, and so the body and in consequence the soul are dramatically diversified. If the body is first of all the collective body, then equally, it is the parts of this body which possess distinct integrity. The collective body of the church possesses decisively distinct parts, since these are independent persons with independent wills, despite the circumstance that they are diversified according to specific, socially defined offices – priesthood, prophecy, the diaconate and so forth – rather than according to their biological individuality. For this reason, the church, as absolutely and eternally unified through the Holy Spirit, uniquely possesses an organic or bodily unity, a unification of genuinely independent parts which nonetheless exceeds their sum. Bodies and souls are to be conformed to the church more than the other way around. This is why Christian non-liturgical spirituality is problematic. For the rich potential of diversity specific to the Christian soul is opened up through participation in collective worship, just as the unity of individual character is given as a mirroring of the collective character of the church. When the participant loses herself in the liturgical process, she finds herself, whereas

---

[36]Ibid., 45–72.
[37]Jacques Lacan, 'The Mirror Stage as Formative of the Function of the I' in Jacques Lacan, *Ecrits: A Selection*, trans. Alan Sheridan (London: Routledge, 2001), 1–9.
[38]Gilles Deleuze and Félix Guattari, *A Thousand Plateaus: Capitalism and Schizophrenia*, trans. and forew. Brian Massumi (London: Athlone, 1988), 149–66.

when she cleaves to a supposedly natural unity of soul and body, she will find that this hysterically dissolves.[39]

At the same time, the individual is not absorbed into the congregation as though into a modern undifferentiated mass or 'crowd', which represents an anti-congregation.[40] Individual rumination within and upon the liturgy is important, and this is shown especially with respect to the traditional *Canticles* imagery of the teeth. Collectively speaking, the teeth guard the church, but they also allow entrance of the divine word and a mastication of this word by church doctors whereby they further utter, through their mouths, truths appropriate to time, place and circumstance. But this digestive process can only be consummated within the individual person, the organic unity of soul and body, who remains by nature most substantially one, even though her formal unity as also a psychic one must be 'borrowed' from the community.[41]

One can, in consequence, observe in Christian practice a liturgical tension between the priority of a congregational construction of sensation, on the one hand, and a private sensory meditation, on the other. This tension is benign and perhaps never resolved since it derives from the originally liminal character of ritual action.

17.7 THE BODY AS MEDIATOR

Christian liturgy exemplifies the logic of ritual process. But more specifically, it inflects this logic with an intensified emphasis upon the body as the mediator between inner and outer, which ritual experience must hold in balance. This insistence upon the body as a pivot helps to perfect this equilibrium.

Such a corporeal focus arises because of Christian incarnationalism, and the mediation of the sacred through an economy of the physical and the corporeal. Moreover, beyond the economic perspective, the doctrine of the resurrection exalts the body to an eternal finality. In consequence, as we have seen, the extreme focus upon bodily experience in Christian liturgy is often regarded as being in harmony with, and not opposed to a spiritual intensification. This vision accords with the logic of ritual, because the inherently ritual birth of language suggests that in this threshold of sense resides the very possibility of meaning. From this perspective, one can approach Christian liturgy not simply as the claimed worship of the triune God and of the *Logos* incarnate but as a complex and collective attempt performatively and publicly to meditate upon

---

[39]Chrétien, *Symbolique du Corps*, 45–72, 294–5.
[40]Elias Canetti, *Crowds and Power*, trans. Carol Stewart (New York: Farrar, Strauss and Giroux, 1984).
[41]Chrétien, *Symbolique du Corps*, 73–88.

the character of the pre-human *Logos* which calls one, within the dream of the body, out of one's merely corporeal state into a state of trust in a secure but partially concealed order, which human culture seeks to manifest and restore. The faith which informs Christian liturgy is the assertion of a coincidence of the liturgical with the ontological, and of worship with being. And it is such bodily gesture, coded and yet in excess of all codes, which secures and witnesses to this fusion.

The focus upon the liturgical dimension helps us to see that public theology is not to be contrasted with the most intimate, spiritual and theoretical. It is rather the consummation of all three. As such, theology manifests itself in public as the perfecting transformation of the public sphere itself. All that is seemingly complex is here simplified and resolved, yet without betrayal of perplexity. All that is ineffable is here made concrete, visible, soundable and touchable, and yet with an intensification of ineffability. All discords between individuals are here suspended, and yet in a collective gesture of poetic artifice that is more real than our awkward daily contrivances. The wonder is not that of fiction, or of suspension of disbelief, but of the realization that in the symbolic enactment of peace, one is glimpsing an abiding truth in the moment of its passage through time. Suspension rather recommences when the liturgy is over and we pass out of the doors. And yet the same moment also opens out the prospect of rendering all of our lives in time continuously liturgical, a continuous performance and reception of the theological.

CHAPTER 18

Public eschatology

Seeking hope in a world of despair

MARY DOAK

The world faces serious problems and so far is failing to rise to the challenge of resolving them. This failure may be due in part to the enormity of the issues: greenhouse gas emissions are causing a global climate change that is accelerating mass extinctions, spreading new diseases, disrupting agricultural patterns, triggering more frequent and severe natural disasters, and overall threatening the conditions of life on this planet.[1] At the same time, the global capitalist economy that is credited with lifting many out of desperate poverty has also increased inequality, undermined job security and contributed to the fracturing of societies as the economy's benefits are disproportionately enjoyed by an elite class with little understanding of how severely global market shifts have affected others.[2] Moreover, humanity is experiencing one of the largest migrations in human history as these economic and climate pressures force

---

[1] Current information on the causes and effects of global climate change is available from the United Nations' Intergovernmental Panel on Climate Change. In addition to more recent updates, see especially the IPCC report 'Global Warming of 1.5°C' (October 2018), https://www.ipcc.ch/sr15 (last accessed 15 January 2020).

[2] For informed discussion of the strengths and weaknesses of global capitalism, see especially 'Decline of Global Extreme Poverty Continues but has Slowed: World Bank', The World Bank website, https://www.worldbank.org/en/news/press-release/2018/09/19/decline-of-global-extreme-poverty-continues-but-has-slowed-world-bank (last accessed 15 January 2020); Deborah Hardoon, 'An Economy for the 99%', Oxfam website, https://www.oxfam.org/en/research/economy-99 (last

many to leave their homes in search of livelihoods elsewhere, where they are met with suspicion and a resurgence of ethno-nationalism protecting established privileges.[3] It is becoming apparent that the current path of environmental destruction, growing inequality and social polarization is not sustainable.

While the challenges are considerable, these problems are not unsolvable, given the available resources. Many of the world's brightest minds are developing solutions to climate change and economic dysfunctions, and structures exist that could facilitate the international cooperation needed to resolve the refugee and migration crises without overwhelming any country.[4] Although meeting these challenges will require much concerted effort, the greatest obstacle is not a lack of solutions but rather a lack of sufficient political will to make the requisite changes. Paralysis and despair are the norm instead of working together to solve our momentous problems.

There are undoubtedly multiple causes contributing to this pervasive failure of political will, but surely one key contributor is a loss of hope for the future. Instead of envisioning and working for a better world, many are projecting a dystopian future and are resigned to making the best of what seems likely to become a very bad situation – some are even preparing for a Darwinian competition for survival amid expected catastrophes and the anticipated breakdown of society.[5]

It is, of course, impossible to know whether people will rise to the demands of this historical moment, changing their personal habits and economic processes at least enough to ensure that a better future remains possible. But this change will certainly not come unless a sufficient number of people have enough hope to make the adaptations necessary to secure a viable future.

In this time of much despair and meagre hope, public theology has an important role to play. The recovery of hopeful action requires understanding the cultural shifts that are behind the diminished sense of possibility so widespread today. There is also a need for historical hopes that are truly credible and capable of inspiring appropriately transformative action. The expertise of

---

accessed 15 January 2020); and Paul Collier, *The Future of Capitalism: Facing the New Anxieties* (New York: HarperCollins, 2018).
[3]See especially 'Migration and Migrants: A Global Overview', chap. 2 of *World Migration Report 2018* (Geneva: IOM, 2018); and Elizabeth W. Collier and Charles R. Strain, *Global Migration: What's Happening, Why and a Just Response* (Winona, MN: Anselm Academic, 2017), 23.
[4]Inter alia, see Intergovernmental Panel on Climate Change, *Climate Change 2014: Mitigation of Climate Change*, IPCC website, https://www.ipcc.ch/site/assets/uploads/2018/02/ipcc_wg3_ar5_frontmatter.pdf (last accessed 15 January 2020); Robert B. Reich, *Saving Capitalism: For the Many, Not the Few* (New York: Penguin Random House, 2015); Collier, *The Future of Capitalism*.
[5]Stephen Marche, 'America's Midlife Crisis: Lessons from a Survivalist Summit', *The Guardian*, 2 August 2017, https://www.theguardian.com/us-news/2017/aug/02/preppers-survivalist-summit-constitution-americas-midlife-crisis (last accessed 15 January 2020).

theologians is vital to these conversations, given that theology is a discipline focused on identifying and analysing ultimate beliefs and values. Especially relevant here is the theological subfield of eschatology, with its attention to the credibility, coherence and adequacy of hopes for the 'last things' or the ultimate goals of human life and history.

I contend that public theology, especially theological eschatology, has three major contributions to make to the revitalization of an adequate and transformative common hope. First, public theology can and should contribute to the public discussion by identifying and evaluating the concepts of the future prevalent in society. Second, theological eschatology brings to the public discourse religious wisdom about the ultimate goals of human life and history, along with skill in identifying the strengths and weaknesses, the insights and deformations, of these religious perspectives. Thus clarifying a religion's eschatological hopes along with the implications of these hopes for contemporary public issues is not only a service to the religious community but also to the society that may benefit from the faith community's witness and work for a better future. More controversially, I maintain that the theological elucidation of the meaning of religious hopes may contribute as well to the broader society's conception of its proper hopes and goals insofar as religious hopes express a truth that is generally applicable and comprehensible. That is, religious beliefs are genuinely public claims that can and should be evaluated by all. Finally, a third contribution will be made by a public theology that avoids hubris and does not betray its deepest insights about human finitude. To the extent that theological arguments can be included in public life without attempting to silence other religious and non-religious options, theology will contribute to keeping open the space for diverse views and thus for a more capacious public reasoning, which is surely needed given the complex challenges we face.[6]

In accordance with the first contribution of public theology identified earlier, this chapter will begin with attention to the widely accepted postmodern rejection of metanarratives in the wake of the failure of Enlightenment optimism about human perfectibility. The refusal of grand narratives has not left a vacuum, of course, and the widespread ideologies of neoliberalism and of scientific-technocracy beg for a theological critique of their assumptions and implications. Perhaps most fundamental, however, is the obvious and crucial question of whether there can be any hope for history that does not replicate the deformations of the modern and colonial metanarratives of progress. This

---

[6]This account of the three contributions of theological eschatology is my own, but informed by the similar arguments of Christoph Hübenthal, 'Are the Last Things Exclusively Positive?: Schillebeeckx's Eschatology and Public Theology', in *Grace, Governance and Globalization*, ed. Stephan van Erp, Martin G. Poulsom and Lieven Boeve (London: T&T Clark, 2017), 143–58 (152–4).

question must be faced not only by religious traditions but by all who seek to live with hope amid the postmodern suspicion of metanarratives.

Turning to the second contribution of public eschatology outlined earlier, this chapter will then explore the particular hopes of the Christian tradition, especially as these hopes have been refined and clarified through the eschatological discussions of the twentieth century. As noted already, we will be concerned not only with providing an appropriately nuanced account of Christian hope to the church, important as this may be, but also with exploring what Christian eschatology might contribute to the public task of formulating a common hope that enables society to respond adequately to the current crises. Can Christian eschatology speak meaningfully even to those who do not accept foundational Christian beliefs about God, grace and an afterlife?

Although it is commonly assumed that theology cannot be publicly intelligible without losing its religious particularity, in fact there are numerous theologians and religious leaders who have effectively addressed the public while remaining firmly rooted in their specific religious traditions. Pope Francis is one current example of someone whose thoroughly Christian faith is the basis of insightful cultural criticism and of an alternative vision with appeal beyond the Christian community.[7]

The flip side of the belief that religious thinking is not publicly intelligible is the fear that religion in public life will inevitably seek a hegemony that silences other perspectives. Unfortunately, this fear is not baseless, as fervent religious believers have often asserted that commitment to the truth of their religion will not permit the toleration of other views. My own Catholic branch of Christianity did not officially accept religious freedom until 1965 because it equated religious freedom with an unacceptable relativism.[8] There are thus grounds for suspicion of the claim that public theology might contribute to safeguarding diversity in public life. Nevertheless, fundamental religious beliefs about the ineffability of the ultimate and the limits of human comprehension are in conflict with religious intolerance, as Reinhold Niebuhr and Orlando Espín have adeptly argued.[9] Their works suggest that any Christian public theology that recognizes the implications of its basic beliefs about God and humanity must strive to keep the public conversation open not only for Christian perspectives but for a genuine diversity of religious and non-religious views.

---

[7] See especially Pope Francis's widely discussed Apostolic Letter *Evangelii Gaudium* (24 November 2013), and his Encyclical *Laudato si'* (24 May 2015).

[8] Vatican Council II, *Dogmatic Constitution on Divine Revelation (Dei Verbum)*, http://www.vatican.va/archive/hist_councils/ii_vatican_council/documents/vat-ii_const_19651118_dei-verbum_en.html (last accessed 15 January 2021).

[9] Reinhold Niebuhr, *The Children of Light and the Children of Darkness: A Vindication of Democracy and a Critique of Its Traditional Defense*, intro. Gary Dorrien (Chicago: University of Chicago Press, 2011), especially 119–52; and Orlando O. Espín, *Idol and Grace: On Traditioning and Subversive Hope* (Maryknoll, NY: Orbis, 2014), 77–84.

It is, of course, beyond the scope of this chapter to provide a Christian eschatology adequate to the demands of public life today. My intention is rather to encourage theological eschatology to continue developing along the lines of these three signal contributions to the public task of constructing a coherent and credible hope sufficient to motivate transformative action in response to the serious crises humanity currently faces. My argument for the societal importance of theological eschatology is not intended to apply only to Christian theology but pertains to any inquiry into the meaning and truth of a particular religion's eschatological beliefs and practices. However, the examples discussed here will be drawn from Christian theology as this is the religion I know best and is one with considerable impact on public life in the global West. The review of major developments in clarifying and nuancing Christian eschatology is meant to promote more adequate expressions of hope in Christian theology as well as in public life.

18.1 PUBLIC ESCHATOLOGY: THE CRITIQUE OF SOCIETY'S INADEQUATE HOPES

Public eschatology's first contribution to be explored here involves identifying and evaluating socially operative – but often implicit – notions about the processes and goals of history.[10] For much of the twentieth century and thus far into the twenty-first century, cultural assumptions about history in the global West have been marked by the repudiation of Enlightenment optimism about historical progress. This modern hope for history was expressed in a variety of popular as well as philosophical forms, of which the two most influential may well be the projected global triumph of Western civilization and Marxism's envisioned resolution of all conflict in the achievement of the classless society. These influential hopes foundered on the horrors of the twentieth century, with its world wars, genocides (especially the Shoah), communist brutality and environmental disasters. As it became apparent that advances in reason and technology would not create the perfect society but might instead exacerbate the disasters of history, the dominant Western culture largely relinquished its belief that reason could lead to the achievement of the perfect or near perfect society.[11] Modernity, it is safe to say, lost confidence in itself.

---

[10]A similar approach is developed in Christoph Hübenthal, 'The Theological Significance of the Secular', *Studies in Christian Ethics* 32, no. 4 (2019): 455–69 (468); as well as in Hübenthal, 'Are the Last Things Exclusively Positive?', 152.

[11]Christoph Schwöbel, 'Last Things First? The Century of Eschatology in Retrospect', in *The Future as God's Gift: Explorations in Christian Eschatology*, ed. David Fergusson and Marcel Sarot (Edinburgh: T&T Clark, 2000), 217–41; and Richard Bauckham, 'Conclusion: Emerging Issues

This postmodern rejection of modernity's confidence in historical progress has been further developed as a philosophical critique of metanarratives. French philosopher Jean-François Lyotard denounced modern 'grand narratives' of the goal of history as totalizing theories that result in intellectual closure. Such grand or 'meta' narratives describe the outcome of history and so, Lyotard argued, cannot allow for the interruption of the genuinely new.[12] Metanarratives condemn history to repeat what is already known and so are judged to be intellectually and socially oppressive, a point reinforced by more recent studies of the colonial and racist dimensions of the Enlightenment ideal of advancing European civilization.

Postmodernism's renunciation of metanarratives has itself been criticized as relativistic insofar as it rejects truth as necessarily totalizing.[13] Indeed, postmodernism has been condemned as the hedonistic ideology of late capitalism rather than the politically liberating force it seems to be.[14] Certainly, the postmodern disavowal of efforts to discern history's goal is consistent with the general loss of a sense of participating in the unfolding of history towards a better future. While modernity's metanarratives may have led to intellectual closure, the rejection of these metanarratives has resulted in a temporal closure in which the present is cut off, unable to discern meaningful ties from the past to the future. Society thus seems to be between a rock and a hard place, and a pressing question for eschatology today is whether a credible account of the goal of history can be formulated that avoids the totalizing closure of modern metanarratives without falling into the aimless relativism of so much of the postmodern era.

Notwithstanding this explicit rejection of grand narratives, it nevertheless remains the case that orienting myths enabling people to make sense of history's unfolding continue to function in Euro-American societies, as Richard Bauckham has insightfully noted. One such myth is the neoliberal insistence that unregulated (or minimally regulated) markets will provide the best possible life for all.[15] Neoliberalism may present itself as simply an economic theory, but Francis Fukuyama revealed neoliberalism's role as an eschatological metanarrative when he argued that political-economic struggles had come to an end with the late twentieth-century victory of political democracy wed to free-

---

in Eschatology in the 21st Century', in *The Oxford Handbook of Eschatology*, ed. Jerry L. Walls (Oxford: Oxford University Press, 2008), 673–5.

[12]Jean-François Lyotard, *The Postmodern Condition: A Report on Knowledge* (Minneapolis: University of Minnesota Press, 1984). See also Bauckham, 'Conclusion', 678.

[13]Bauckham, 'Conclusion', 675.

[14]Fredric Jameson, *Postmodernism, or, The Cultural Logic of Late Capitalism* (Durham, NC: Duke University Press, 1991).

[15]Bauckham, 'Conclusion', 676–7.

market economics. Since, in his view, the ideal politico-economic system had been achieved, no further major developments were to be expected.[16]

Though the idea that humanity has achieved the 'end of history' is scarcely credible given the ongoing struggles and unforeseen crises that followed the fall of communism, resistance to imagining a better economic system remains widespread. Furthermore, market capitalism is often treated as a force that will resolve humanity's problems as long as people do not obstruct it. A theological critique is certainly in order here to point out that this belief in an unfettered market economy automatically achieving the best possible society for all is but a secular form (like Marxism) of belief in a providential force directing history to a pre-established goal.[17] Moreover, these secular ideologies of providence deny human freedom and responsibility for the outcome of history, since they maintain that history's goal will be inevitably attained through autonomous economic forces. From the perspective of neoliberalism, then, society bears no responsibility to rectify economic inequality other than to protect the market from being hampered, because the market itself will necessarily create the best possible outcome.[18]

As Pope Francis has further argued, neoliberal confidence in capitalism has placed the economy in the position of society's god, the idol to which we sacrifice everything in hopes of salvation from poverty.[19] A well-functioning economy is of course important. The problem is not that people value a robust economy but rather that the economy has become ultimate, the highest value in society. Both personal and public life are focused on serving the economy, rather than on ensuring that the economy serves human life and well-being. Hence, as Pope Francis has observed, anything without market value is then without social value and is unprotected from the savage demands of unrelenting economic competition. [20]

To be sure, there is much to be said for resisting the over-regulation that stifles economic creativity. Moreover, at this point and for the foreseeable future, some kind of profit-oriented market system is likely to be the most effective form of economic life. After all, the economy is, at least for now, too complex to be entirely planned and directed with efficiency. Nevertheless, hostility to nearly all government regulation of the economy goes too far and is based on an unwarranted confidence in the beneficent functioning of the

---

[16]Francis Fukuyama, *The End of History and the Last Man* (New York: Simon and Schuster, 1992).
[17]Bauckham makes a similar point in his 'Conclusion', 674.
[18]See Benedict XVI, Encyclical Letter *Spe Salvi* (30 November 2007), 21 for a critique of the lack of freedom in Marxism, and Francis, *Evangelii*, esp. 54 on the autonomous market economy.
[19]Francis, *Evangelii*, 55–8.
[20]Ibid., 56.

profit motive in a capitalist economy.[21] Too often, neoliberalism has further persuaded people that a flourishing economy is the most important, if not the only, concern of politics. As Pope Francis has suggested, whatever one thinks of the strengths and weaknesses of global capitalism as an economic system, the neoliberal belief in an unregulated economy as a providential force in history is neither true nor good. This unquestioned hegemony of the economy in contemporary society is diminishing human life, undermining solidarity and destroying the environment.[22]

The other metanarrative common today, as Bauckham has observed, is the scientific-technological myth of progress.[23] It is arguable that the unreflective acceptance of new technologies, which are dramatically transforming patterns of personal life and social relationships, is rooted in a confidence that scientific advancements and technological innovations are (like the dictates of the market in neoliberalism) inherently good and socially beneficent. Perhaps more to the point, the scientific-technological myth of progress is explicitly invoked in discussions of climate change. In this case especially, confidence in science is often combined with neoliberal trust in the market. People then look to the market to spur and spread technological developments that will resolve the climate crisis without any need for personal sacrifice or governmental action.

To be sure, suspicion of science has also become common given the ecological damage caused by many scientific and technological innovations, so there are dissenters from the myth of scientific-technological progress just as there are dissenters from the myth of neoliberalism. Additionally, there is considerable truth in the claim that science can help to improve human life, just as there is some truth in the neoliberal fear of over-regulating the economy. Scientific knowledge has contributed so much to the length and quality of life that few even of science's critics are willing to live without its benefits. Moreover, there can be no doubt that scientific advancements in energy conservation and in the development of sustainable energy sources are essential to any viable plan to lower greenhouse gas emissions today. Science is definitely necessary to improve human life and to solve the crises we face.

The problem is not science per se, but rather the belief that science (perhaps along with the economic forces of the free market) will inevitably solve humanity's problems. Science is a powerful tool that, like all such tools, can be used for good or ill, depending on human choice. Indeed, assumptions about the benefits of technological progress have already caused much ecological

---

[21]Reich, *Saving Capitalism*, esp. 81–6.
[22]See especially Pope Francis, *Evangelii Gaudium*, 50–60.
[23]Bauckham, 'Conclusion', 677. See also the discussion of Schillebeeckx's similar critique in Frederiek Depoortere, 'Schillebeeckx's View on Eschatology as Public Theology Today', in *Grace*, 181.

destruction, including climate change, which might have been avoided had there been more careful and critical scrutiny of the effects of these technologies.

The world's religions have deep wisdom about the human inclination to misuse freedom, and theology ought to serve public life by identifying and critiquing ideologies that deny the need to limit evil and to increase the good. I argued earlier that the postmodern refusal to have any positive hope for history is surely among the major obstacles to the necessary collective action to address the serious crises humanity faces. As Bauckham has further noted, where a viable hope for history is lacking, other myths are likely to fill the gap, providing people with a sense of historical meaning and direction. Hence the myths of neoliberalism and of scientific-technological progress have developed to give hope for history in the absence of a credible account of historical purpose.

While theologically informed critiques of common assumptions and myths about the direction of history might be proffered in sufficiently non-religious terms to be unobjectionable to the general public, it is another question whether the content of theological eschatology can contribute to a public hope appropriate to our postmodern context. Even if its specific religious content were tolerated, could theological eschatology avoid proposing some version of the grand narratives that postmodernism has rejected as incredible and pernicious? After the demise of the modern metanarrative, are we not all condemned to live in a present interpreted through the equivalent of short stories that cannot give meaning to the whole of public life?[24]

Even though we cannot resolve these questions fully in this chapter, I concur with those who hold that any worthwhile concept of the purpose of history must be able to provide a hope that is definitive enough to give a sense of direction without being so definitive as to close off the possibility of the new.[25] Many of the eschatological debates in Christian theology of the twentieth century, a period marked by a resurgence in theological eschatology, were concerned with just this challenge of how to maintain a hope that inspires transformative praxis without resulting in a totalizing certainty closed to anything genuinely new in the future. Turning now to the developments in Christian eschatology, we will explore how this theological conversation might illuminate the public implications of Christian hope as well as what Christianity might contribute to the effort to formulate a more adequate public hope.

---

[24]Schwöbel, 'Last Things First', 236.
[25]See especially Stephen H. Webb, 'Eschatology and Politics', in *Oxford Handbook*, 509–10, and Paul S. Fiddes, *The Promised End: Eschatology in Theology and Literature* (Oxford: Blackwell, 2000).

18.2 PUBLIC ESCHATOLOGY: THE CONTRIBUTIONS OF CHRISTIAN HOPE

Essential developments in Christian eschatology in the twentieth century can be appropriately discussed in terms of the four symbols emphasized by the Dutch theologian Edward Schillebeeckx. These four symbols, found in the Bible and throughout the Christian tradition, are the Kingdom (or reign) of God, the resurrection of the body, the new heaven and earth, and the Parousia (or Second Coming) of Jesus.[26] As this list suggests, hope for a personal afterlife is retained in contemporary Christian eschatology but broadened to incorporate the physical and social dimensions of life as well as the non-human world.

The first of these symbols, the reign of God, has been restored to a focal place in Christian eschatology due in large part to biblical scholarship's recovery of the significance of the coming reign of God in Jesus' preaching.[27] Rooted in the ancient Jewish hope for a state on earth in which all proceeds according to God's will for harmony between God and creation, the symbol of the reign of God anticipates the achievement of just and loving relations among a unified but diverse humanity. Because humanity is understood to be inherently communal, our salvation cannot pertain to the individual alone but includes the healthy and harmonious communities which are indispensable to human flourishing.

The communion of all in God has thus become a dominant image of the eschatological goal as expressed in ecclesial statements across Christian denominations. This is evident in the influential writings produced by the Catholic Church's Second Vatican Council. Drawing on the concept of *theosis* central to Orthodox theology, both of Vatican II's major documents on the church (*The Dogmatic Constitution on the Church* and *The Pastoral Constitution on the Church in the Modern World*) declared that the mission of the church is to be a sign and instrument of this goal of union with God and unity among humanity.[28] More recently, a World Council of Church's document similarly stated that the task of the church is to be an instrument within history of this divine purpose to

---

[26]Edward Schillebeeckx, *Church: The Human Story of God*, trans. J. Bowden (London: Bloomsbury, 2014). See also Hübenthal, 'Are the Last Things Exclusively Positive?', 155–7.

[27]Christopher Rowland, 'Scripture: New Testament', in *The Wiley Blackwell Companion to Political Theology*, ed. William T. Cavanaugh and Peter Manley Scott, 2nd ed. (Hoboken, NJ: Blackwell, 2019).

[28]'Dogmatic Constitution on the Church, *Lumen Gentium*, 21 November 1964', in *Vatican Council II: the Conciliar and Post Conciliar Documents*, ed. Austin Flannery (Collegeville, MN: Liturgical Press, 1975), 1. See also 'Pastoral Constitution on the Church in the Modern World, *Gaudium et spes*, 7 December 1965', in Flannery, *Vatican Council II*, 42.

bring humanity to a state of loving communion.[29] With the resurgence of attention to the doctrine of the Trinity in the late twentieth century, this eschatological goal of communion is now frequently described as the incorporation of the redeemed into the loving mutuality of the life of the triune God.

Although the reign of God is therefore a hope that transcends history, it is also a hope for history or, to be more precise, a hope for the positive resolution of all of history's struggles. This tension gives rise to a question that has dominated much of twentieth-century Christian eschatology: How to affirm that history matters as the one history of salvation, a point Gustavo Gutiérrez defended in his groundbreaking *A Theology of Liberation*, while at the same time maintaining history's openness to a transcendent goal beyond history?[30] Jürgen Moltmann's answer was to stress God's futurity, unconstrained by present and past.[31] But this open future must also have sufficient content to give meaning and direction to human action. As Michael Kirwan explains, Schillebeeckx's proposed solution to this dilemma is his concept of the 'negative contrast experience' in which the sufferings of this world are recognized and resisted as the negation of the coming reign of God.[32]

Among the most nuanced accounts of the relation of history to the eschatological future is the account provided by Reinhold Niebuhr. Niebuhr was adamant that the meaning of history can only be found beyond history, because any hope that can be realized within the limits of history is too narrow and impermanent to satisfy human longing. To uphold the value of historical efforts without constraining hope to what is possible in history, Niebuhr insisted that there is no limit to how much humans can build the reign of God in history – except that humans cannot build the Kingdom of God in history.[33] In other words, the world can always be improved, but perfection cannot be achieved in history.

This contention that no historical action will usher in the reign of God on earth has been helpfully described by Erik Peterson as 'the eschatological proviso'.[34] This concept resists the absolutization of any contingent historical project (and

---

[29] World Council of Churches, *The Church: Towards a Common Vision*, Faith and Order Paper No. 214 (Geneva; World Council of Churches Publications, 2013), esp. 15.

[30] Gustavo Gutiérrez, *A Theology of Liberation: History, Politics, and Salvation*, trans. and ed. Sister Caridad Inda and John Eagleson (Maryknoll, NY: Orbis, 1973).

[31] Jürgen Moltmann, *Theology of Hope: On the Grounds and Implications of a Christian Theology*, trans. James W. Leitch (Minneapolis: Fortress, 1993). See also Schwöbel, 'Last Things First?', 230–1.

[32] Michael Kirwan, '"Putting the Facts to Shame": Eschatology and the Discourse of Martyrdom', in *Grace*, 163–5.

[33] Reinhold Niebuhr, *Nature and Destiny of Man*, 2 vols. (New York: Scribner's Sons, 1941–43), II: 244, 286.

[34] Patrick Ryan Cooper, 'Poor Wayfaring Stranger: Erik Peterson's Apocalyptic and Public Witness Against Christin Embourgoisement', *Religions* (2017): 8, 45d.

historical projects are, by definition, contingent). What we can achieve in history, however important this may be, cannot end all suffering and in any case may well be reversed in the course of time. The eschatological proviso is intended to counteract the common human tendency to inflate the importance of political struggles – and also to inflate the means that are justified to achieve success. Instead of becoming ruthless in our efforts to make society fit our concept of the divine plan, Christians ought to remember that God's plan for history surpasses what can be imagined or achieved within history, even as we hope that what we achieve here will somehow contribute to that final goal that only God can bring in full.

The second symbol of Christian eschatology to receive renewed attention in the twentieth century is the resurrection of the body. This Christian tenet expresses a hope for the person, which has been and remains central to much Christian piety focused on achieving an afterlife for the soul in heaven and avoiding hell. Recovering the Christian doctrine of the resurrection of the body, however, expresses a hope for the salvation of the whole unique and embodied person. Moreover, since ancient Jewish thought and much of the Christian tradition envision the bodily resurrection of the dead occurring at the final establishment of God's reign, the symbol of the resurrection of the body suggests that even the long dead ought to enjoy the achievement of the goal of history they in some way contributed to. Indifference to the dead and to their sacrifices for a better world is an offence against basic justice.

Johann B. Metz, theologizing as a German as a German in the decades following the Shoah, has been especially eloquent in his defence of hope for the dead victims of history. Precisely because of the dominance of injustice throughout human history, Christian hope for God's reign must include also a hope for the future of those who, like Jesus, were unjustly slaughtered by the powers of their day. As Metz declares, God's resurrection of Jesus stands as an outstanding promise to restore those whose possibilities were cut off by the outrages of history. He further cautions that the contemporary neglect of the dead undermines the meaning of all human life: if the lives of the dead, with their particular hopes, dreams and sufferings, no longer matter, then all of our lives are lived in the shadow of the impending meaninglessness of death. An adequate hope for the reign of God consists not only in the positive resolution of history's struggles but also in the restoration of all those who died in the course of that history.[35]

The third of Schillebeeckx's symbols, the New Heaven and the New Earth, expands beyond human-centred concepts of redemption to include all of creation in the final salvation. The phrase 'new heaven and new earth' comes from Revelation

---

[35] Johann Baptist Metz, *Faith in History and Society: Toward a Practical Fundamental Theology* (New York: Seabury, 1980), esp. 74–6, 105–13.

21 and is a description of the renewal of the universe at the end of history. This symbol is increasingly examined in ecological theology, as environmental crises spur reconsideration of the value of non-human nature. It has become evident that an eschatological hope that has no room for the rest of creation is not consistent with biblical ideas or with the best insights of the Christian tradition.

To be sure, Christians have often asserted that human beings alone have intrinsic value due to their everlasting destiny with God. Christians have often presumed that the 'dominion' given to humanity in Gen. 1.28 indicates that non-human nature exists solely for the sake of humanity. Yet biblical depictions of the eschatological reign of God include nature in that ultimate harmony, as in Isaiah's description of the peaceable Kingdom wherein 'the wolf lives with the lamb' (Is. 11.6). Moreover, the Hebrew Bible commandments to care for nature and to avoid inflicting undue suffering on other creatures imply that non-human nature has value in itself and not only for its usefulness to humans. Of course, the unfathomable temporal and spatial extension of the universe further suggests that God's purposes are not as anthropocentric as Christians have assumed.

The inclusion of nature in the eschatological communion of the reign of God is also supported by the Christian doctrines of the Incarnation and the Resurrection. Since the Patristic era, the Christian tradition has maintained that God redeemed humanity by becoming fully human in Jesus of Nazareth, thus overcoming the sin that separated humanity from God. But as Denis Edwards argued (and Pope Francis similarly stated in his encyclical *Laudato si'*), in becoming incarnate with a fully human body, Jesus also united divinity with the elements of the universe that comprise bodily existence.[36] Furthermore, the resurrected Jesus has taken physical embodiment into the life of the Trinity. It follows then that just as humanity is saved through the union of God and humanity in Jesus, so also the physical universe is forever united to God – and thus saved – through the event of Jesus Christ.

The final eschatological symbol to be discussed here is the symbol of the Parousia, or the Second Coming of Jesus who rules (and judges) the world at the end of history. The life, death and resurrection of Jesus is then the standard by which our lives and all of history are to be judged. As Orlando Espín has pointed out, since God is revealed in Jesus, a peasant who died with confidence in a God who is compassionate to the oppressed, our lives and societies should (and will) be evaluated according to the extent to which they evince this divine compassion, especially to the vulnerable.[37]

---

[36]Denis Edwards, *Partaking of God: Trinity, Evolution, and Ecology* (Collegeville, MN: Liturgical Press, 2014), 60–4; *Laudato si'*, 99.
[37]Espín, *Idol*, 79–80.

Of course, the symbol of the Parousia is integrally related to apocalypticism, which is at best an ambiguous development in Christian history. Apocalyptic views of history can be supported biblically and are found especially in the book of Daniel, some of Paul's letters, the Gospel of Mark and the book of Revelation. However, there are other, non-apocalyptic, biblical views, such as the Gospel of John's realized eschatology and the Gospel of Luke's gradual eschatology. Most of the mainstream Christian tradition has resisted the literal interpretation of biblical apocalypticism, and Catherine Keller has astutely identified two main dangers of apocalyptic interpretations of history: (1) the danger that every political issue and project is liable to be seen as the ultimate apocalyptic struggle against evil; and (2) the danger that people will fail to be responsible in their care of this world and society because they look for God to end this mess and create a new reality for us.[38]

Nevertheless, there are important truths in the apocalyptic imagery of the Christian tradition. Metz has defended apocalyptic hope as a hope in God to interrupt history on behalf of history's victims.[39] Those who cannot bear their current conditions but are powerless to improve them often have recourse to an apocalyptic hope in which God will come very soon to defeat evil and rectify the situation for them. In other words, apocalypticism is the hope of the otherwise hopeless.

Niebuhr has further argued that the apocalyptic description of the ultimate conflict between Christ and the anti-Christ at the end of history represents an important truth about the mutually implicated growth of good and evil in history. Insofar as human knowledge increases in history, the power it makes possible also increases – and this power can be used for greater evil as well as for greater good. Hence, good and evil (Christ and anti-Christ) are likely to increase in impact as history unfolds, and humanity must be prepared for this reality.[40] Any naively optimistic anticipation of an uncontested progression of the good in history must be corrected by the realization that the parallel growth of evil is also to be expected.

This should serve as a caution against the myriad academic investigations looking for that point in Western intellectual history (nominalism? the Protestant Reformation? modernity?) where philosophical mistakes were made that led to the catastrophic violence of the twentieth century. If an increase of power makes an increase of evil – as well as good – inevitable, then we cannot

---

[38]Catherine Keller, *Apocalypse Now and Then: A Feminist Guide to the End of the World* (Minneapolis: Fortress, 2004).
[39]Metz, *Faith,* esp. 73, 169–77.
[40]Niebuhr, *Nature* II, 316–21.

merely think our way out of the horrors of history but will have to devise social structures capable of mitigating the unavoidable dangers of human power.

Before leaving this discussion of apocalypticism, mention should be made of the debates about millennialism that recur in Christian history and have been especially influential in the United States since the nineteenth century. Millennialism stems from the depiction in Revelation 20 of a thousand-year reign of Jesus Christ and the martyrs before the final judgement and end of history. In the early church period, this millennial reign was understood non-literally by official church authorities, who interpreted the millennium as a prediction of the dominance of the church after Jesus' death until the Second Coming. More literalist Christians, however, have developed a variety of scenarios to reconcile into one coherent series of events the various and conflicting biblical descriptions of the coming end of history. Pre-millennialism, with its view that Jesus will come first to defeat evil and establish the millennial reign of peace before ending history, tends to support a political quietism that rejects public life as the arena of the anti-Christ, whom only Jesus can defeat. Post-millennialism, with its expectation that Christians will institute the reign of peace before Jesus returns to end history, is more inclined to strive to perfect society. If Niebuhr is right about evil and good growing simultaneously in history, there is some (non-literal) truth on both sides. In any case, as Moltmann argued, these millennialist views are significant as efforts to account for the meaning of history in relation to the ultimate reign of God. Moltmann has further suggested that some form of millennialism is necessary for Christianity to honour the biblical and Jewish hope for the land of Israel.[41]

Spirited debate about the proper interpretation and application of not only the Parousia but each of these four eschatological symbols will no doubt persist. Yet some consensus has been achieved among mainstream Christian denominations. There is broad agreement that an otherworldly hope for a disembodied soul in heaven is inadequate to the conditions of human flourishing as well as to the authoritative traditions of Christianity. A more authentic Christian hope recognizes that human beings are constituted by their relations and so looks for history's fulfilment in a communion that establishes justice for all and includes physical reality and even non-human nature. Such a hope has obvious implications for the crises of climate change, economic disempowerment and migration (especially as this latter provides an opportunity for the greater unity-in-diversity that reflects the communion of God's reign).

The study of Christian eschatology further cautions against expecting humanity to build the reign of God on earth. Instead, Christians should place

---

[41] Jürgen Moltmann, *The Coming of God*, trans. Margaret Kohl (Minneapolis, MN: Fortress, 1996), 192–9; see also Webb, 'Eschatology', 500–6.

their ultimate hope in God even as they continue to do whatever they can to make the world better. At the other extreme, however, pre-millennialists may take this dependence on God to the point of deeming sociopolitical projects to be worthless, a stance that is too negative about human action. Mainstream Christian traditions today generally affirm some version of the Vatican II position that what we achieve here matters as we will find there (in the eschaton) the accomplishments of our lives and history, but perfected.[42]

As the above conversation suggests, theological eschatology has been deeply concerned to clarify and strengthen the public praxis of Christians in service of God's reign. Important as this is, I would like to suggest that Christian eschatology also has much to contribute directly to public discourse. It may seem implausible that the theological study of specifically religious beliefs could inform the thinking of people who cannot accept belief in God, an afterlife or any divine redemption of history. Yet the issues raised in theological eschatology about what constitutes a meaningful hope for history are issues for non-Christians too. Would not all hopes for history be improved by considering how broad the hope is, and whether non-human nature is included? Is not the question of how to give meaning to history without absolutizing contingent human projects a question everyone ought to consider? Certainly, the recognition that human knowledge is increasing the capacity for evil as well as good is something that demands greater attention in contemporary life than it has yet received, and the same can be said of the problem of what happens to the meaning of human life when we relinquish any hope for the dead, especially those who were the victims of history. These are issues fundamental to the articulation of any adequate historical hope, and public life is impoverished when such questions are sidelined as theological matters of interest only to religious people.

18.3 PUBLIC ESCHATOLOGY AND RELIGIOUS HUMILITY

The common assumption that religious beliefs are irrelevant to non-believers is not the only reason for resistance to the inclusion of religion in the conversations of a secular society. The more serious reason for excluding religion is that religious views can be (and have been) asserted as the final truth with nothing to learn from others, a stance that is destructive of public discourse. Furthermore, the insertion of religion into politics risks inflaming passions and heightening tribal divisions, particularly if people reject reasoned debate over their most deeply held beliefs and identity-forming commitments.

There are, however, solid theological grounds for refusing to treat religious beliefs about the ultimate as though these beliefs themselves are absolute and

---

[42]*Gaudium et spes*, 39.

unalterable. After all, the Abrahamic faiths believe in an infinite Creator who cannot be fully comprehended by conditional human thought or language. Other religious traditions may use different language, but most likewise affirm that the mystery of the ultimate transcends what humans can understand or describe. To insist, then, that one has the complete truth about God is more than an error: it is idolatry, as Espín has adeptly argued, because it treats finite concepts as if they were the infinite God.[43]

Niebuhr has similarly noted that belief in a transcendent God ought to be the source of a proper humility about the adequacy of human beliefs about God. He has further warned that if religious perspectives are not proffered with a humility that is open to other views, then a pluralistic society has no choice but to exclude religion from public debates. In such circumstances, the removal of religion is necessary but highly unfortunate, as politics loses the depth of meaning that religion provides. However, when religious views are presented with the appropriate humility, recognizing that beliefs about the ultimate can never be more than partially true, a public discussion of the meaning of politics from the perspectives of a variety of religions is possible.[44] Public theology then has an important role to play in defending religious humility and thus establishing the space for a more capacious conversation about the goals of public life.

18.4 CONCLUSION

The three contributions of theological eschatology developed here are intended to outline ways in which public theology can assist in the crucial task of confronting the crises of our time. First, contemporary public life seldom considers its need for a sense of purpose and generally fails to interrogate the hidden myths and metanarratives that hamper effective political action. Eschatological theology can and should bring these assumptions into question. Second, theological study of particular religious beliefs about the ends of human life and history not only serves to clarify the belief and praxis of the religious community but also to provide traditional religious wisdom that challenges naive expectations about the importance – and limits – of what can be accomplished in any society. Finally, when theologians and religious believers enter public life with a humility appropriate to any speech about the ultimate, they contribute and invite forms of reasoning that refuse the constraints of empirical and instrumental rationality.

---

[43]Espín, *Idol*, 80–2.
[44]Niebuhr, *The Children*, 134–8.

PART IV
Challenges for public theology

CHAPTER 19

Politics

AMY DAUGHTON

Public theology is fundamentally a political theology. It is understanding public theology as a political task that helps to explain how it may frame, assess and respond to the challenges posed by contemporary politics. This means beginning with how public theologians have identified 'the political' and how that is located within wider patterns of theological thinking about politics. Public theology is still partly formed by the challenges of communal life which its early contributors initially identified and those trajectories continue, but the character of politics today poses new challenges, which may shape the work of public theology anew.

19.1 PUBLIC THEOLOGY ON THE 'POLITICAL'

As a distinct theological approach, public theology has been primarily concerned with questions about the role of religion in public life. For those theologians who contributed to its emergence in the 1980s, the early questions were to do with the plurality of contemporary society and what this meant for how Christianity specifically, and religion more generally, could and should speak meaningfully. The continued development of public theology has remained largely focused on the topic of the role of religion in the public sphere; however, 'religion', 'public' and 'sphere' might be variously conceived. The interplay of religion and the public sphere therefore reveals the continuing motivation behind public theological scholarship: to argue for the role of religion as a commentator on and contributor to the fabric of the social order.

Arguing that point also involved resistance to the conflation of an emphasis on public, social life with the concerns of political theology as it arose in the immediate post-war period. Max Stackhouse made the case when he located the 'deepest roots' of political theology in Aristotle, arguing that that antecedent established 'the political order as the comprehending and ordering institution of all of society'.[1] Consequently, public theologians tend to read the political theology that emerged from the 1950s onwards in Europe as understanding the state as the decisive institution for assessing and shaping social and moral concerns. Political theology so conceived is concerned first with the concrete institutions of government and the execution of state power as the structures by which to critique and renew the political community. It is an assessment that has carried beyond the first generation of thinkers, as more recently Nicholas Wolterstorff has similarly suggested that 'Political theology is not theology with a political cast; it is theology of or about the political, more specifically, theology of or about the State'.[2]

Simple opposition of public and state will prove ultimately insufficient, but certainly, by contrast, public theology is suspicious of the state as the overarching category for considering collective ways of living. Instead, the public is ultimately prior to those settlements and so is a category distinct from discrete political institutions. Given its concerns over the narrowing down of collective life to the state, an important first task is therefore to offer the more complex picture of politics that public theology makes possible. Doing so also strengthens current understandings of public theology in two ways. First, it helps to locate public theology in relation to current debates on political thought and practice. Political theology has increasingly been used to refer not only to that first post-war generation of thinkers, newly re-situating political questions into the theological academy within a broader gathering of different approaches to political and social life. Second, public theology has something to say precisely about what 'theology of or about the political' consists in, and so is positioned to disrupt the rigidity of the state–public binary. This distinguishes what public theology may be able to offer in response to new and ongoing challenges of politics.

As an academic discipline political theology has come to encompass multiple different approaches to topics of political community. Rather than representing two ways of thinking that are fundamentally incompatible and therefore opposed, political theology and public theology are instead framed as different

---

[1] Max Stackhouse, 'Civil Religion, Political Theology and Public Theology: What's the Difference?', *Political Theology* 5, no. 3 (2004): 275–93 (281).
[2] Nicholas Wolterstorff, *The Mighty and The Almighty: An Essay in Political Theology* (Cambridge: Cambridge University Press, 2012), 2n2.

perspectives within a set of broader questions. This is perhaps especially well illustrated by what has increasingly become the ubiquitous definition of political theology as a disciplinary home for various approaches, articulated by Peter Manley Scott and William Cavanaugh:

> The political is broadly understood as the use of structural power to organize a society or community of people. Under this spacious rubric, politics may be understood for the purpose of a political theology in terms of the self-governance of communities and individuals. . . . Political theology is, then, the analysis and criticism of political arrangements (including cultural-psychological, social and economic aspects) from the perspective of differing interpretations of God's way with the world.[3]

Within this more expansive outline public theology takes a distinctive stance on what terms like 'self-governance' and 'political arrangements' might include – specifically, that they go well beyond the state. To be sure, politics as the task of statecraft is a core part of the political ordering of the community, but public theology instead calls on public discourse in the wider sense of civil society. In the public theological analysis, the cultural ideas, narratives, forms and activities of all areas and levels of society are cultural and moral resources, which can contribute to the self-understanding and collective practices of communities. It is in all these public contributions of civil society as well as statecraft that opportunities arise to uncover, develop and renew self-understandings of societies and their values.

Nevertheless, public theologians have long held to a distinction between the public, and politics as an activity that outworks from it, by distinguishing the public level of cultural meaning-making as 'pre-political'. Crucially, pre-political is not the same as *non-political*; the resources and renewals of the wider public are constitutive of the political community: they come to bear on the kind of collective, political life that a society values and pursues, shaping how and why civic and political institutions try to operate as they do. The public is a complex set of interweaving identities, associations and practices, which can form the work of politics, and indeed, be formed by it. This definitively locates public theological consideration of the political in the practices, relationships and communities found in concrete everyday life, in collective associations of all kinds, rather than solely at the state level.

---

[3] Peter Manley Scott and William T. Cavanaugh, 'Introduction', in *The Blackwell Companion to Political Theology*, ed. Peter Manley Scott and William T. Cavanaugh (Malden, MA: Blackwell Publishing, 2004), 1–3 (2).

When public theology concerns itself with politics then it is with discrete, concrete political institutions, but also political 'institutions' in the wider sense of collective practices, discourses and values. To say that public theology is a political theology is not to collapse all forms of collective activity into the political but, rather, to suggest that public theology's defining preoccupations are with how a given community orders itself, how it understands that ordering and what that means for the kind of life we can seek to live together. It is in the public and through public theology that we work out collectively what we think politics is *for*.

19.1.1 What is at stake?

Having located public theology in relation to other forms of thinking about politics, it is easier to see what role public theology is trying to play. Public theology summons our attention to politics, including its interaction with the character of the wider public sphere as politically formative. As Hak Joon Lee puts it, this is where public theology 'aims at gradual transformation of social order through the reinvigoration of society's moral fabric and the vocations of institutions and individuals'.[4] At the same time it seeks to engage in this transformation not through a theological saturation of the political but by attending to what diverse plural practices mean for the nature of the political community. While it may seek to change practices, albeit dialogically, the underlying purpose in discussing the political is as a contribution to the renewal of our commitment to living together, in all levels and spheres.

In its origins in the 1980s, that task of renewal was framed in response to the challenges to that commitment to life together. In her introduction to the broader discipline of political theology, Elizabeth Phillips distinguishes public theology from other two approaches, post-war political theologies and liberation theologies, by way of what they sought to resolve:

> If the enemy of Political Theology was impotent, bourgeois Christianity and the enemies of Liberation Theology were poverty and oppression, the enemies of Public Theology were sectarian Christianity and the loss of societal moral consensus.[5]

Specifically, public theologians began to work from the premise that in a context of increasing global proximity to each other, new forms of civilization, including those beyond nation states, were in view. As Stackhouse put it, 'the whole world

---

[4]Hak Joon Lee, 'Public Theology', in *The Cambridge Companion to Christian Political Theology*, ed. Craig Hovey and Elizabeth Phillips (New York: Cambridge University Press, 2015), 44–66 (54).
[5]Elizabeth Phillips, *Political Theology: A Guide for the Perplexed* (London: T&T Clark, 2012), 48.

is becoming one place'⁶. The concern was that there was a potentially widening gap between the understandings of life in cultures, religions, communities and the concrete forms of these new political, economic exchanges. New forms of political economy were developing globally, representing a new hegemonic order, detached from a moral vision that motivates and shapes collective ways of living. While public theologians sought to argue that such systems should be shaped by cultural, religious and moral resources of the public, they were also recognizing the increasing plurality of those resources and therefore of the moral and political visions that could be in play.

This dual commitment to the need for a shared commitment to living well together but also to the diversity of reasons for doing so shaped the public theological response. As Phillips's analysis discussed earlier identifies, the option of retreating into particular Christian communities in response was seen as sectarian, while the reality of plurality cast a possible shadow of relativism or assimilation. Public theologians concluded that to respond effectively, they would need to attend to the plural context into which they must make their case, and indeed, to the plural reasons those from other traditions and approaches would have for committing to the political community. What Lee characterizes as 'a dialogical openness to everybody in pursuing the common good of a society'⁷ became the driving shape and purpose for taking up public reason as a task of mutual reflection for the good of the political community.

Jürgen Habermas, that great advocate for the public sphere as a secular, or shared, space of discourse, has increasingly turned to religion as a potential actor in nourishing the idea of the common good as a shared responsibility. It is also Habermas who has named the threat to that quest, in the weakening of practical reason:

> practical reason fails to fulfil its own vocation when it no longer has sufficient strength to awaken, and keep awake, in the minds of secular subjects, an awareness of the violations of solidarity throughout the world, an awareness of what is missing, of what cries out to heaven.⁸

That challenge is not wholly different today. Yet it takes on a new urgency, confronted as we are with political needs that go beyond the bounds of any

---

⁶Max Stackhouse, 'Public Theology and Political Economy in a Globalizing Era', in *Public Theology for the 21ˢᵗ Century: Essays in Honour of Duncan B. Forrester*, ed. William Storrar and Andrew Mortan (Edinburgh: T&T Clark, 2004), 179–94 (179).
⁷Lee, 'Public Theology', 44.
⁸Jürgen Habermas, 'An Awareness of What Is Missing', in *An Awareness of What Is Missing: Faith and Reason in a Postsecular Age*, ed. Jürgen Habermas et al., trans. Ciarin Cronin (Cambridge: Polity Press, 2010), 15–23 (19).

individual political community, such as the supranational crises of refugee migration and climate justice, and the rise in populism. Again, this reinforces the commitment to the pre-political needed to nourish our commitments to live together, seeking just politics in relationships, practices and institutions. It is a newly intense summons to give attention to the mutual shaping and practices of politics and public thinking. What is at stake then remains the same for public theology as it was at its emergence, heightened in the face of rising political challenges: the survival of ways of life that are rooted in more than pragmatism, and hope for more than mere existence, negotiated in the context of a plural public.

To frame those new challenges, it is helpful to begin with the critical issues that public theology has been facing, and the ways those have shifted over the last generation of thinking and are shaping thinking today. This will be a crucial moment to review how public theology may need renewal in the face of the current challenges of politics.

19.2 POSTLIBERALISM, OR THE LIMITS OF LIBERALISM

The relationship between public theology and liberalism has always been important for understanding public theology itself. Its focus on plural visions of the good life, on the public as made up by various kinds of interplaying communities, was framed early as a critique of liberal political institutions. This stance has been made more complicated, however, by the rise of a collection of political-theological approaches that are, broadly, postliberal. Although their solutions vary, they are in agreement that the philosophical foundations of liberalism are fundamentally incompatible with Christian theological reasoning and do not offer a viable political settlement. Public theologians would also make similar philosophical objections to certain features of liberalism and to concrete liberal political outcomes. Yet its approach by way of public reason and civic society has, to an extent, placed it in a constructive relationship with liberalism. Consequently, postliberal thinkers' concerns do implicate the work public theology has undertaken. Lee puts this more strongly when he suggests that 'It would not be much of an exaggeration to say that postliberal theology is the nemesis of public theology, as it is critical of almost everything that public theology stands for'.[9] Not a promising beginning.

It may be worth first establishing the concerns that public theology itself raises in response to features of liberalism and liberal politics. Of particular concern for the public theologian are the strands of liberalism that owe most to

---

[9] Lee, 'Public Theology', 58.

the work of Thomas Hobbes. Liberalism is not monolithic, and the Hobbesian mode begins with certain expectations of human behaviour as self-interested. You have your interest and I have mine, and inevitably therefore there will be conflict and, if unchecked, violence. The state performs that check, by mediating interests into the greater need for peace, which is understood as the absence of violence between citizens, with violence retained as the tool of the state, its only legitimate wielder. Here we find one of the roots of public theological suspicion of state as the definitive category for the meaning of collective life. In this mode, key liberal norms are reduced: peace to an absence of violence; autonomy to mere individualism; and thus rights to an individualistic framework leaving the person atomistic and remote from community, context and convictions. Norms here appear in isolation from their ethical foundations as merely the requirements of pragmatism and so are worked out in practice without ethical reference points.

Yet, as Lee has also proposed, there may still be value in the norms themselves; 'for public theologians, the demise of a philosophical foundation of liberal values (such as democracy, human rights, tolerance, fairness) does not mean the loss of their practical values in a global, pluralistic society'.[10] Nevertheless, the response of public theologians has continued to focus on discovering and articulating plural foundations for these values.

One of the public theologian's tasks then has been to retrieve the intersubjective philosophical foundation that ground such norms, from within liberal traditions. Autonomy in the Kantian understanding, for example, is always oriented towards the dignity of the other person, in the face of which one places moral obligations upon oneself. Rights are necessarily coupled with responsibilities in this intersubjective framing. Another approach has been turn to the distinctive resources that constitute the origins of the interpreting Christian community, where an example might be the scriptural emphases on the vulnerable other – the widow, the orphan, the stranger and our mutual obligations to each other, but especially to the poor and the outcast.[11] This is a translative task, from the particular scriptural kernels of the Christian tradition to the normative commitments the theologian is calling on all to support. In this way, public theology seeks to offer dialogical engagement from theological resources with and into other ways of reasoning, as part of the plural public debate. These are the traditional methods of public theology: correlation and translation, understood as the means of offering critique aimed at the potential lack of ethical foundation to liberalism and its consequences.

---

[10] Ibid., 59.
[11] These examples helpfully illustrate the plurality of valuing that also crosses traditions, as this trajectory of Christian thinking has its origins in the Hebrew Bible.

In fact, this critique is not entirely different from that offered by postliberal theology. However, while the public theologian will seek to transform politics that has become individualistic by nourishing underlying commitments, the postliberal theologian diagnoses such politics as the inevitable outworking of the liberal state. There have been some influential analyses along these lines, but for assessing public theology's entanglement with liberalism, perhaps the most striking is William Cavanaugh's 'Killing for the Telephone Company'. In this article, Cavanaugh argues that the 'public' that is possible under liberalism is not the complex, plural space of various kinds of communal association but merely a space of contracts between individuals who each relate to the state. The state in turn, which should be treated as a public utility, is instead being deployed as if it is the foundation of communal identity, to the point where it becomes the symbol of patriotic loyalty. The consequence is that what is 'public', even in this impoverished sense, is conceived of as founded by and made possible by the state, rather than being foundational to it. This Cavanaugh frames as the consequence of the individualization in much liberal theory. Relying on the historical analysis of Robert Nisbet of the origins of the United States, Cavanaugh concludes:

> The history of the state is the creation of an increasingly direct relationship between state and individual by the state's absorption of powers from the groups that comprise what has come to be called 'civil society'. In other words, the state is not simply local government writ large. The state is qualitatively different; it is precisely that type of government that does not grow organically out of the self-government of social groups.[12]

This directly upends the hopes and expectations of public theologians. The liberal state in Cavanaugh's evaluation overwhelms the meaningfulness of other commitments and erases opportunities for those convictions to be publically treated.

Cavanaugh's analysis here is focused on the United States, but he argues that this historical pattern is the inevitable consequence of a politics rooted in liberalism. One should not underestimate the influence of this argument, which has come to dominate English-speaking debates about how theologians should reason about politics. Indeed, Phillips has described such analyses as the

---

[12] William Cavanaugh, 'Killing for the Telephone Company: Why the Nation-State Is Not the Keeper of the Common Good', *Modern Theology* 20, no. 2 (2004): 243–74 (256). In this quotation, Cavanaugh is referring to Robert Nisbet, *The Quest for Community* (Oxford: Oxford University Press, 1996), 104.

potential 'death knell'[13] of public theology, though noting the ubiquity of the term 'public' continues. The question this poses is whether public theology has, by translating into the 'public', thereby conformed to a system of secular liberal thinking, which devalues and erases precisely those communal identities, and cultural and religious ways of reasoning which public theologians prioritize.

One can acknowledge some resonances between the character of liberalism, albeit hard to pin down, and the expectations of public theology. For example, Stackhouse offered an explanation of the motivating thrust of public theology in terms that Robert Song would take up in his family resemblances of liberalism.[14] Public theology is

> rooted in the interaction of biblical insight, philosophical analysis, and the responsibility of the ecclesial community to engage in historical discernment of and constant reformation of the social order because it believed that certain kinds of *progress* could be made in human affairs.[15]

Public theologians would, by and large, resist the idea that public theology has *assimilated* to liberalism in this shared commitment. The 'liberal core' that Stackhouse is willing to claim is characterized by questioning given authority, including both liberal settlements and the Christian heritage:

> Not only can we critically reflect on the faith and morals handed down to us, but we can convert or transform what we inherit – and offer a reasonable account of why we do so. . . . Further, we can, in some measure, talk across boundaries and more or less discern what is valid and not valid in what others say. And we expect others to understand us and to challenge us where we do not make sense.[16]

Public theology expects the possibility of encountering truth and good reason in systems other than its own. That includes varieties of secular political liberalism, but also other religious, cultural and political forms of reasoning and practising.

Yet the postliberal counter is that these kinds of exchanges are simply not possible, both philosophically and practically. Elaine Graham articulates it: 'the need

---

[13] Elizabeth Phillips, 'The Church and The Elusive "Public"', in *Grace, Governance and Globalization*, ed. Martin G. Poulsom, Stephan van Erp, and Lieven Boeve (London: Bloomsbury, 2017), 238–47 (239).
[14] Robert Song, *Christianity and Liberal Society* (Oxford: Oxford University Press, 2006), 40–3. His final family resemblance is that of faith in a doctrine of progress.
[15] Stackhouse, 'Civil Religion, Political Theology and Public Theology', 284. Emphasis mine.
[16] Max Stackhouse, 'Liberalism Dispatched vs. Liberalism Engaged', in *Shaping Public Theology: Selections from the Writings of Max L. Stackhouse*, ed. Scott R. Paeth, Harold Breitenberg Jr. and Hak Joon Lee (Grand Rapids, MI: Eerdmans Press, 2014), 82–91 (84).

for any kind of "public" theology that engaged with non-theological disciplines is obviated since there is no autonomous or common space to which all forms of discourse contribute freely and equally.'[17] Too thoroughly undermined by the secular liberal settlement, there is no longer a neutral public sphere into which the church can speak as one among others, but instead an ideologically secular space that is already politically charged by materialist, individualistic values, and is resistant to alternative ways of thinking and acting and of meaning beyond the material.

Yet when one looks at postliberal alternatives, they respond in similar binary ways. With some diversity, they may be broadly construed as turning to the church as the definitive political community, and its thinking as a political confrontation to the atomistic liberal framework. For thinkers like Stanley Hauerwas,[18] it is a renewal of the church itself; for Cavanaugh, a sacramental transformation of political horizons; for Radical Orthodoxy, the task is metaphysical first, to once again recognize creation as participative in God, and in John Milbank's strand of that work, to refuse the vitality of any logic situated otherwise. Read superficially, the outworking of these various responses can smack of a reactionary retreat back into the institution of the church, albeit with very different readings of what 'church' here really indicates. In fact the outworking of these ideas is ongoing, and it is fair to note that the intention of Cavanaugh and Milbank at least is to aim at concrete, political engagement, and certainly Hauerwas has not ceased offering ethical, political commentary.

What these alternatives do clarify is the difference that remains between the public theology and postliberal critiques, which lies in their epistemological assumptions and the resulting divergence of what meaningful exchanges are possible across traditions. The consequence of the postliberal epistemological emphasis on truth living in the church is that engagement outside it could not be on equal terms. As Elaine Graham has argued, the concern is that 'the countercultural element, the refusal to play by the rules of the secular State, means that the church loses any foothold whatsoever in the public realm'.[19]

---

[17]Elaine Graham, *Between a Rock and a Hard Place: Public Theology in a Post-Secular Age* (London: SCM Press, 2013), 118–19.

[18]For a short introductory argument from Milbank, see, for example, John Milbank, 'Liberality versus Liberalism', *Telos* 134 (2006): 6–21. For Stanley Hauerwas, see Stanley Hauerwas, *A Community of Character: Toward a Constructive Christian Social Ethic* (London: University of Notre Dame Press, 1981).

[19]Graham, *Between a Rock and a Hard Place*, 116. See chapter four 'Public Speaking: Secular Reason and the Voice of the Church' in particular for Graham's assessment of some of the outworkings from these approaches.

19.2.1 Responding

Other than naming these philosophical divergent starting points, how might public theology respond to postliberal critiques? Perhaps of most importance is arguing that public theology does not rely on a somehow organically occurring neutral public space, which is now being degraded by liberalism. Rather, opportunities for dialogue and debate need to be created. One implication of this is the value of those features of liberal thinking and practice that support the generation of civic society and the possibilities for public discourse: freedoms of speech, assembly, association; commitments to the rule of law, public accountability, political representation. For those whose political recognition has been hard-won under liberalism (and not under Christendom), these forms of participation are not to be thrown out with the liberal bathwater.

A second implication is that, as we shall see when we turn to the burning challenges of contemporary politics, liberalism cannot be romanticized. It can be corrupt in its partnerships, violent in its apparatus and inhuman in its failures; public theology too must and does confront this. Public theologians are called to consider the public not only as a level of exchange but as something which must be built between people and groups. There is a political imperative to create it ourselves. Public theology obliges us not only to participate by sharing from our particular traditions and listening to others but also in creating the opportunities for conversation and collective actions. Such practices themselves represent the political outworking of the theological expectation that God is present in the material and that good may be met with in the world, not enclosed within the church. This is a timely reminder, as we consider plurality today, more than a generation on from public theology's establishment.

19.3 POST-SECULARITY AND PLURALITY

Implicit in the postliberal critiques discussed earlier is concern over what has been a growing consensus around the secularization of society. Public theologians have wished to understand secularization in terms of the political establishment of secularity as a shareable framework allowing for diverse, plural contributions to public discourse. However, two other layers of meaning in the use of secularization have been a challenge to such a reading.

One layer considers that by secularization societies are becoming 'less religious' – this might involve such empirically verifiable features as the weakening of the power of religious institutions, in comparison with 'dominant secular institutions of modern societies, such as nation-states and democratic politics, economic markets, science and technology, mass media, the entertainment industry and consumer culture';[20] shrinking numbers of religious practitioners; the decline in belief more generally.[21] José Casanova suggests that a second layer adds a theoretical evaluation of these more or less measurable features of contemporary life: that these changes are occurring as a consequence of modernization of various kinds, part of a broader assessment of religion as something happily being overcome by scientific, enlightened thinking, including the logic of a secular state. One of the strengths of both public theological and post-liberal critiques has been the excavation of this implicit value judgement; both have therefore framed their arguments as a response to an ideological secularity.

More recent work, however, has begun to disrupt the prevailing consensus with the suspicion that the theory of secularization may have spoken too soon. Taking a global perspective, Casanova suggests that the expected decline in religion has not proven to be the case outside Europe, even while the conception of the secular state has spread. Simultaneously, other patterns of globalization – economic, cultural, migratory – have had different consequences. The result is that religious identities and practices have become more scattered, connected and established in new communities, consequently becoming more varied across the world. The result is a more intricate picture than 'secularization' can really account for:

> global humanity is becoming simultaneously more religious and more secular, but in significantly different ways, in different types of secular regimes, in different religious traditions and in different civilizations. The adoption of a global perspective switches the focus from methodological nationalism and the dynamics of state secularization it entails to the paradigm of religious pluralism which accompanies processes of globalization.[22]

The landscape of religious pluralization can be seen even with local 'secularized' examples, such as the UK. Recent work on religion in the UK has revealed that while overall religious practice has waned, this is largely the consequence of specifically Christian practice sharply declining yet the diversity of practitioners

---

[20]José Casanova, *Global Religious and Secular Dynamics: The Modern System of Classification* (Leiden: Brill, 2019). Published simultaneously as issue 1, no. 1 (2019) of the *Brill Research Perspectives on Religion and Politics* (1–74).

[21]This is a tricky distinction to map – one helpful local example are the surveys brought together under the work of the Commission for Religion and Belief in British Public Life, which observe that even those who identify as Christian do not necessarily commit to specific religious doctrines, such as the resurrection. See the Commission for Religion and Belief in British Public Life, 'Living with Difference: Community, Diversity, and the Common Good' (Cambridge: Woolf Institute, 2015), §2.17, 18.

[22]Casanova, *Global Religious and Secular Dynamics*, 65.

is increasing as 'faith traditions other than Christian have younger age profiles and are therefore growing faster'.[23] Linda Woodhead's collaborative project has identified that there are other kinds of religious activity that cannot be captured in traditional ways:

> new entrants to the spiritual marketplace are more focused on supporting individuals in their everyday lives, fostering new kinds of identity and lifestyle, and linking the like-minded and like-hearted to one another in vast plurality of different forms of religious alliance . . . looser forms of association including small groups, occasional gatherings and festivals, and real and virtual networks.[24]

Although initially sounding more fragmented than simply diverse, Woodhead identifies political implications for these looser connections:

> activist forms of religiosity take new forms outside traditional politics, becoming rooted in electronically mediated sources of knowledge and campaigning, direct political action, international gathering and transnational communities of interest. The 'minoritization' of religion gives it a natural opportunity to serve as a natural support for a wide variety of identities and claims-making.[25]

Here the reality of pluralization, including outside church institutions, is itself changing the work of political activism from civil society, generating new associations aimed at community and well-being, or political causes such as the environment.[26]

Casanova's conclusion is that secularization has not proven accurate, and these new patterns of religious pluralization reset the stage for post-secularity. He suggests that these patterns of post-secularity are not only reflections of current demographics but are also prompting fundamental changes in the value judgements around religion and politics. Thinkers like Jürgen Habermas are 'abandoning or at least questioning the modern secularist stadial consciousness

---

[23] Commission for Religion and Belief in British Public Life, *Living with Difference*, 6.
[24] Linda Woodhead, 'Introduction', in *Religion and Change in Modern Britain*, ed. Linda Woodhead and Rebecca Catto (London: Routledge, 2013), 1–32 (27).
[25] Woodhead, 'Introduction', 26.
[26] See, for example, Graham Harvey and Giselle Vincett, 'Alternative Spiritualities: Mainstream and Marginal', in *Religion and Change*, ed. Woodhead, 156–71; and the collated work of Robert Bluck, Sophie Gilliat-Ray, David J. Graham, Gurharpal Singh and John Zavos, 'Judaism, Islam, Sikhism, Hinduism and Buddhism: Post-war Settlements', in *Religion and Change*, ed. Linda Woodhead in Woodhead, 85–149.

which relegates "religion" to a more primitive, more traditional, now surpassed stage of human and societal development'.[27]

19.3.1 Responding

Graham reminds us that 'elements of secularism and the logic of secularization still condition the conduct of public discourse',[28] yet the reality of diversifying plural religious convictions reaffirms the starting point of public theology. The commitment to recognizing plural forms of life and engaging with the consequent development of different forms of political conviction and action is revivified as communities and groups become differently rooted. At the same time, this also gives ground to disrupt the binary logic of political state, pre-political public in potentially more fruitful ways that public theology has hitherto often managed.

That challenge is well expressed in a critique offered by Elizabeth Phillips of specifically public theology, and its terms of engagement:

> I cannot imagine a definition of 'public' in relation to the common life of peoples, societies and states, in which the churches are something other than 'public'. It is specifically how our unexamined use of 'public' allows us to continue to frame it in binary relation to 'church' which concerns me.[29]

Phillips's intent here is to avoid an opposition of church and public that erases the church's character not only as a particular tradition of thinking and doing but its specifically *political* self-understanding. This is a danger if one prioritizes the 'public' as the only location for meaningful collective life. This, of course, is the same concern that public theologians level at the more ecclesially enclosed solutions of political theology, though from the other direction. In a situation of increasing religious pluralism, this assessment prompts public theology to think in more deliberately complex ways about all these terms: 'state', 'public' and 'church'.

The theological commitment to the public is to the good life that may be variously defined by normative, practical visions of living which inform distinct communities within the boundaries of the political whole and which contribute to forming and negotiating political norms and practices within that whole. The diverse groups and communities are already doing the work of transforming

---

[27]José Casanova, 'Exploring the Postsecular: Three Meanings of "The Secular" and Their Possible Transcendence', in *Habermas and Religion*, ed. Craig Calhoun, Eduardo Mendieta and Jonathan VanAntwerpen (Cambridge: Polity Press, 2013), 27–48 (33).
[28]Graham, *Between a Rock and a Hard Place*, 52.
[29]Phillips, 'The Church and the Elusive "Public"', 240.

their pre-political commitments to shared life together into political practices. In a sense, then, this is a plurality of publics that are in interplay with each other, and that are seeking to come together politically in a further shared commitment to living together well. This continues to underline what was established earlier, that the public is not a naturally occurring shared space, not a static space of discourse but a task to be built among groups, shaped by the political contributions they bring.

At the same time, the term 'church', which as the perennially invoked agent of public theology has always meant more than the institutional leadership, is having to loosen its boundaries further, to attend to the complexity of religious identity and how that identity interplays with other values. This first means recognition that engagement with other approaches will mean valuing reasoning drawn from more fragmented practices and movements of valuing, as well as systems of thought. Yet it also recognizes complexity within a theologian's own tradition, turning a critique back in to churches as well, as a reminder of their political responsibilities and of the diversity of critical viewpoints within and outside their communities. As ever, public theology must frame the work of correlation not only in terms of the church's contribution but also in terms of what it may – or must – learn, from what Graham calls the 'occasions of grace'[30] by which God is revealed throughout the world.

The navigation between sectarianism and fragmentation reveals an ongoing concern with the relevance and meaningfulness of specifically Christian understandings of how to live for each other, in the context of global political formations. Yet it is both a challenge and an opportunity, which acts as reaffirmation of public theology's underlying commitments and reminder of the changing political face of the world. That face turns to us ever more urgently, when we consider the character of contemporary politics.

19.4 POPULISM

Just as the secularization analysis is being disrupted by post-secularity, so too may the presumption of liberalism may be being disrupted by the increasing presence and significance of populist politics. The term 'populist' has increasingly been deployed in recent years to describe political movements both new and old, on the right and left, to the point where the meaningfulness of the term itself is debatable. Yet its increasingly pervasive use is not merely a fashionable shift in vocabulary among political commentators but reflects a demonstrable, measurable alteration of some electoral patterns. The PopuList project, the collaborative work of scholars who have been attending to

---

[30] Graham, *Between a Rock and a Hard Place*, 223.

populism as a phenomenon for some time, has mapped the election results of parties within thirty-one European countries, by the (sometimes overlapping) categories of populist, far right, far left and other, from 1989 to the present time.[31] It offers important evidence that populist politics is on the rise across the region. The pattern shown in the data is a striking demonstration of the increasing vote share of far-right populist parties, in particular, and of populist parties overall. For those considering the nature of contemporary politics, the publically accessible collation and analysis represented by PopuList is a gift. That these scholars have made it available freely may be in itself a marker of the severity of the dangers posed by populist politics.

The definition relied on by the PopuList team was established by Cas Mudde, and emphasizes an oppositional character, proposing that populist parties are

> parties that endorse the set of ideas that society is ultimately separated into two homogeneous and antagonistic groups, 'the pure people' versus 'the corrupt elite,' and which argues that politics should be an expression of the *volonté générale* (general will) of the people.[32]

From this definition the character of the community as oppositional is rooted in disagreement and identity, but there is more that might be added to clarify the risks that these features represent. Michael Freeden has rearticulated his definition following the 2016 UK EU membership referendum. For Freeden, populism is characterized by

> an insistent monism: that is, an inclination to conceive of society as a singular unitary body, as Paul Taggart and others have noted; an appeal to the origination and integrity of a defining founding moment or natality, even if not articulated as such; and a visceral fear of imported change in law, customs and people[33].

Taken together with Mudde's definition, populism is rendered as reductive in both its own commitments and in how it characterizes its opponents. That has consequences both in terms of the resources of thinking about the

---

[31]Matthijs Rooduijn, Stijn van Kessel, Caterina Froio, Andrea Pirro, Sarah de Lange, Daphne Halikiopoulou, Paul Lewis, Cas Mudde and Paul Taggart, 'The PopuList: An Overview of Populist, Far Right, Far Left and Eurosceptic Parties in Europe' (2019), www.popu-list.org (last accessed 13 February 2021).
[32]Cas Mudde, 'The Populist Zeitgeist', *Government and Opposition* 39, no. 4 (2004): 541–63.
[33]Michael Freeden, 'After the Brexit Referendum: Revisiting Populism as an Ideology', *Journal of Political Ideologies* 22, no. 1 (2017): 1–11 (4).

political community itself and in terms of how such accounts and their political outworking can be discussed.

First is the erasure of the plurality of accounts of the community itself, the narratives that feed the self-understanding of the political community's origins and boundaries. Consequently, there is the rejection of the need for public scrutiny of the single 'legitimate' account. Pauline Johnson has explored this feature of recent forms of populism, arguing that, by its stereotyping of opponents as divorced from the political will of the people, populist politics has neatly made the requirement to justify its claims publically an insult to 'the people'. Any public scrutiny by those who disagree is by definition the scrutiny of the enemy. In this way populist politics 'sidesteps the normative investment of the public use of reason'.[34] What this consists of is 'dispensing with the constraints of principled convictions, abstract modes of thinking, thoughtful discussion and reasoned argumentation, populism lends itself to an authoritarian rewriting of the ideal of an active civil society'.[35] Indeed, following Freeden's assessment mentioned earlier, the separability of such discourses where this kind of reflexive and reflective work might be done is already excised from within the political whole – society is a single entity, and the political exchanges between state and public activities, whether national or local, no longer operate.

Worrying in themselves, these features come to bear in various significant ways for the public theologian. First, the rejection of plural narratives about the political community itself, which has the further corollary of delegitimizing the plurality of reasons for which people may be committed to the political community and undermines exactly what public theology prizes. Second, there are concrete threats, such as the fracturing of commitments to judicial and democratic accountability seen in Poland and Hungary,[36] and damaging accounts of citizenship found in the UK.[37] Such examples no longer recognize members of the political community as participants in a shared endeavour and questions of national origins and boundaries come to bear in destructive ways. Third, this all builds to the weakening of the significance and meaningfulness of supranational horizons by the naturally nationalist emphasis of populisms,

---

[34] Pauline Johnson, 'In Search of a Leftist Democratic Imaginary: What Can Theories of Populism Tell Us?', *Journal of Political Ideologies* 22, no. 1 (2017): 74–91 (83).
[35] Ibid., 87.
[36] European Parliament Resolution of 16 January 2020 on ongoing hearings under Article 7(1) of the Treaty of European Union regarding Poland and Hungary 2020/2513(RSP), Approved text found at: https://www.europarl.europa.eu/doceo/document/TA-9-2020-0014_EN.html (last accessed 13 February 2021). This resolution pre-dates Victor Orban's open-ended extension to emergency executive powers, passed in Hungary on 30 March 2020.
[37] In the UK, an example is the withdrawal of citizenship from British-born people, who have joined Islamist forces abroad, where they have a nominal claim on another nationality.

eroding commitments to multilateral forms of politics such as the European Union, and arresting the urgent responses that are needed to ongoing supranational crises such as migration and climate change.

19.4.1 Responding

Populism represents a photo-negative image of public theology. Public theology insists on the plurality of narratives and consequent commitments to the political community, on the provisionality of that community and the need to negotiate, debate and participate, pushing constantly for a richer vision of the good life and its political outworking. In this insistence its theoretical opposition to the monist character of populist politics is clear; public theology begins from the position that the work of forming the political community is unfinished. There is agreement on this point from other strands of contemporary political theology, such as Luke Bretherton's observation that the

> political process may eventuate in a sense of shared identity, and any such identity will draw on prior cultures and traditions but is itself unstable and open-ended. The open-ended nature of a people's identity is masked by conflating it with nationality.[38]

Public theology represents important conceptual resources to refuse this closure of who a community is, in its own value for plurality, both in terms of cultural foundations for life lived together in political community and in the spheres of community activities and practices. Engaging as public theologians with all of this is a task of both imagination and practical reason, which populism eschews: to think our society anew and to engage concretely in negotiation, compromise, solidarity. There is an inseparability of thought and practice.

The resources of both imagination and practical reason have received particular attention in recent work on populism. Tim Stacey has suggested that populist politics and its reductive myth of the nation require a similarly 'mythic' response: 'The way to move beyond the divisive myths that fuel populist politics is not to transcend myth altogether, but to effectively include ordinary people in developing alternative myths of solidarity.'[39] Stacey suggests that some such stories can cut across the divisions of tradition and indeed are part of the seeking of the shared good undertaken politically, proposing that 'the collective search

---

[38]Luke Bretherton, *Christ and the Common Life: Political Theology and the Case for Democracy* (Grand Rapids, MI: Eerdmans, 2019), 425.
[39]Timothy Stacey, 'Beyond Populist Politics: Why Conventional Politics Needs to Conjure Myths of Its Own and Why It Struggles to Do So', *Global Discourse* 8, no. 4 (2018): 573–88 (586).

for shared beliefs and practices [take] a central place in the shaping of policy'.[40] Crucially, that search is conducted through community activism allowing the 'myths' that Stacey has in mind to be enacted. It is in sharing needs, desires, challenges that diverse partners articulate what politics is for, and name the vulnerabilities and suffering to which politics should respond: 'what cries out to heaven'.

In her reply to Stacey, Anna Rowlands has observed that this need for myths and practices of community finds an anthropological root in the heritage of liberalism, with which I have argued that public theology needs critical conversation.

> [W]e are simultaneously and without inherent contradiction self-determining, interdependent, vulnerable, failing, perfectible creatures who seek as an intrinsic part of our own good the good of others and of the whole – and who seek narratives that affirm and interpret this nature.[41]

In this way, Rowlands's response represents a balancing of imaginative practice and thought as she argues for both 'the fine texture of the political as it exists within communities and also . . . the full breadth of theoretical resources which exist to ground a call for something beyond the now-crumbling consensus'.[42] Public theology is summoned to attend to that plurality in political exchanges as well as the reasoning behind them. In her approach on this point, Rowlands is prompted by thinkers such as Simone Weil and Hannah Arendt, who emphasize the coincidence and obligation of sheer proximity. Needs and desires are shared and contrasted within the place in which we live, and so uncover disagreement, conflict, as well as the possibility of solidarity and consensus. Such exchanges are a sufficient beginning for a shared political enterprise, even in compromise. Paul Ricoeur had argued that 'We can take compromise, then, to be the form that clothes mutual recognition in situations of conflict and dispute resulting from the plurality of economies of standing'.[43] Although political exchange may be between plural ways of valuing and may be incommensurable, the only possibility of resolving the conflict is in the moral recognition of the other.

In this way, the mythic resources and local politics that both Stacey and Rowlands are evoking embody a challenge to the concrete threats of

---

[40] Ibid., 574.
[41] Anna Rowlands, 'Between Radical Orthodoxy and the Turn to the Empirical: A Reply to Stacey', *Global Discourse* 8, no. 4 (2018): 589–91 (589). Rowlands is here drawing on the legacy of T. H. Green.
[42] Ibid., 590.
[43] Paul Ricoeur, *The Course of Recognition*, trans. David Pellauer, Institute for Human Sciences Vienna Lecture Series (Cambridge, MA: Harvard University Press, 2005), 210.

populism: they represent the possibility that politics need not exclude ideas, narratives, reasoning or people, in order to establish community or negotiate within it. Nor is that limited to the local example. Hille Haker, in her work on migration and political polity, has argued, also along that Arendtian trajectory:

> What legitimizes the norms of institutional power is not an imaginary social contract of the past that *constrains* the power of individuals in the present and future, but exactly the opposite: power is institutionalized ethical and moral agency oriented towards *creating something new*.[44]

While none of this immediately offers us a concrete tool that brings populist political harms to account, it is a reminder that there is a political alternative in the 'creative power of public action'.[45] Haker argues that moral agency is found in intersubjectivity, where one recognizes responsibility for the needs and desires of the other and where one who is suffering is also a capable actor. The global calamities of environment and migration represent the ground for such new relationships of interpretation. This calls to public theology to revivify its own engagement with the move from pre-political convictions to political outworking.

That insight recalls an earlier piece of Elaine Graham's work where she advocated for a liberative foundation for public theology. Graham proposes that public theologians need to take on a particular posture for liberation, to 'regard part of their work as enabling the dispossessed to take a more active role in secular decision-making'.[46] Political exclusion is transformed into the summons for political engagement: 'the task is not so much one of translating or disseminating the results of their scholarship to a wider (possibly popular) audience, but one of aligning themselves as advocates and interpreters of the stories of struggle and survival from the grassroots'.[47] Here is the channel for advocacy and accountability in the face of populism, linking real experiences with political hopes and seeing all those entangled in a given issue as contributors to the political community, prioritizing the voices of those otherwise excluded.

---

[44]Hille Haker, 'No Space: Nowhere. Refugees and the Problem of Human Rights in Arendt and Ricoeur', *Études Ricoeuriennes / Ricoeur Studies* 8, no. 2 (2018): 22–45 (34).
[45]Ibid., 33.
[46]Elaine Graham, 'Power, Knowledge, Authority in Public Theology', *International Journal of Public Theology* 1, no. 1 (2007): 42–62 (43).
[47]Ibid., 47.

19.5 CONCLUSION

Populism impoverishes political thinking, at the levels of imagination, reasoned public exchange and concrete policy whether one considers the local or international stage. Yet while the work of politics can include the confrontation of incommensurable aims, that is not its defining nature. Actors throughout our communities have visions for our political life that transcend the traps of zero-sum thinking, and the reductive, excluding binaries of populist thinking.

What public theology is called to attend to then is the possibilities of politics, by replanting public theology in its original vision of plurality and public reasoning as sources for a renewal of our commitment to each other. This is a logic that reframes politics not solely as the outworking of relationships of conflict represented by populism and certain strands of liberalism. It is a logic that can also go further in refining and enriching the work of public theology itself by rejecting old binaries of state and church that only foreclose opportunities for exchange, and attending to the meaningful possibilities of what political practices reveal about our desires and convictions.

In this way public theologians need to consider what solidarity with each other really means. It is in sharing the imaginative visions and narratives of living well, in the concrete work of recognizing each other, in agreeing and disagreeing well together in the local work of communities. This ultimately is the work of solidarity: to commit to the other and to enable those opportunities for each other to be heard: to truly listen to voices that cry out – not only to heaven but to each other.

CHAPTER 20

Race, gender and public theology

BRIAN BANTUM

At the centre of Christian faith is the riddle of the body. The flesh is often feared, derided or seen as an encumbrance to salvation and life with God. But at the same time the body is the peculiar, singular point of experiencing God, love, transcendence, beauty, pleasure and welcome. The body is the icon of the very dirt from which it was formed – carbon, oxygen and hydrogen – shaped into organs and comprised of processes of metabolism, respiration, circulation, electrical synapses, sex, reproduction, consumption and excretion. We are animals in no uncertain terms.

And even in its animality the flesh bears witness to an aspect of the divine – Spirit – the ineffable, inarticulable presence of something more than chemical processes or organic attempts to survive: love, beauty, creation for creation's sake, ecstasy, grief and, in the midst of it all, mystery. Weaving in and out of our biological processes, our psychology, our social systems and our daily activity runs the constant presence of what we do not know, about ourselves, our motivations, the seemingly infinite universe that is our body, much less the fellow animals of all kinds, the systems of trees and air and rock, the cosmos that exists around us. And in the midst of it all, human beings, along with all that is, share in God's life, share in the miracle of difference – difference of species, difference of looks, of likes, of ways we experience, taste, smell, enjoy and order our worlds. But what do human beings make of these differences? How do we account for them?

Perhaps it is the perception of a thin membrane between creatures, animal and human, that the classification between humans carried such high stakes. Describing differences between human beings has a long and violent history, a history that begins as humans wrestle with how they are so different from the animals they raise and slaughter or fear or demonize. Christianity may not be unique in its patriarchy, but its contribution to the gendered violence of the ancient and modern world cannot be ignored. Who are the creatures that are closer to the animals? Who are the creatures that ought to be submissive and who are the ones that ought to exercise authority? These questions persisted in Christian communities. The Bible gives stories of women whose cleverness or wisdom or courage or faithfulness saved Israel and brought liberation. But somehow these stories were not read as normative for what a woman's body meant. In the face of the patriarchal obfuscations of women's lives in Scripture, they could not be written out of the stories of God with us, or the nascent moments of the church, or the lives of faithfulness that persisted in the midst of violence and empire. God continued to work in and through women, even if men tried desperately to hide the evidence.

But the story of gender would become more complicated after the fifteenth century and the era of colonial expansion, where the idea of race was cultivated, harvested and then woven together with patriarchal logics of gender. The notions of racial and gendered descriptions of the body can be understood as particular attempts to solve the riddle of flesh through what Hortense Spillers suggests is the creation of a body. She writes, 'before the "body" there is the "flesh," that zero degree of social conceptualization that does not escape concealment under the brush of discourse or the reflexes of iconography'.[1] The riddle of the flesh is resolved through a calculus of the body, measures of what seemingly is or is not animal, what is ideal, what is truly 'like' God and whose bodies can never measure up.

The riddle of the body and its inflections in racialized and gendered social systems is not unique to Christianity. But understanding race and gender in the twenty-first century in theological terms necessitates understanding Christianity itself as a religion of identity: identity that is not fixed or essential, but identity as a dynamic and ongoing process of what theorist Stuart Hall describes as negotiation. For Hall identity is not an essentialist phenomenon. Identity is a process. He writes,

> I use 'identity' to refer to the meeting point, the point of suture, between on the one hand the discourses and practices which attempt to 'interpellate',

---

[1] Hortense J. Spillers, 'Mama's Baby, Papa's Maybe: An American Grammar Book', in *Black, White, and in Color: Essays on American Literature and Culture* (Chicago: University of Chicago Press, 2003), 206.

speak to us or hail us into place as the social subjects of particular discourses, and on the other hand, the processes which produce subjectivities, which construct us as subjects which can be 'spoken'.[2]

From its earliest moments Christianity began as a group of Jewish women and men began to follow a man whose teachings broke open new ways to imagine their Jewishness, their manhood and womanhood, and their relationship to the Roman Empire. These answers were not fixed but constantly navigated as they had to look backwards to interpret what had happened to them, to consider and reconsider the words and life of Jesus, the life of his mother, Mary, and the teachings of the Torah and the prophets. This process would be a constant of Christian life and thought. The locus of this process was inevitably the problem of the body and the problems its particularities created for a movement trying to understand its connections to Jewishness, to gentiles, to Empire, to men and women and sex and eating and life in community.

The ancient world of Christianity's beginnings, whether its Jewish roots or the philosophical and pagan beliefs that swirled among one another, the question of the body was always a central problem. Is the flesh the centre of our most awful desires? Is its limitations and weakness something to be escaped? Is spirit what we truly are? The problems and challenges of Jesus' life and teachings, and the subsequent claims about his personhood, his death and resurrection would all press the question of our bodies, of what it means to say the Word became flesh, into deeper significance in Christian thought and life.

And while we are pressed by the larger transcendent questions of what our bodies mean and how they correspond to God's life, bodies do work in the world. They speak. They perform. They are worked upon, inscribed and etched with meanings and histories that are alien to them. Human beings are caught within this discourse, this current of what we say about ourselves and what is being said about us. But this discourse has not been even or equitable or just. Whether descriptions of people as property or dangers or overly emotional or unnatural leaders or alien or illegal – whose bodies matter and whose do not is a central tension in the history of human civilizations. These contested and contesting descriptions of who we are and who God is are theological productions.

For the earliest Christians the question of the body took on various forms: debates and controversies concerning Christ's person, baptism, communion, the relationship between Christ and his Jewishness, to Christianity's own Jewish beginnings, and Jewish neighbours, to women's roles in these new communities, to the shifting dynamics of class or nation or even the empire itself. But in each of these aspects of bodily life there are also the riddles of

---

[2]Stuart Hall, 'Introduction: Who Needs Identity?', in *Questions of Cultural Identity*, ed. Stuart Hall and Paul Du Gay (London: Sage, 1996), 5–6.

difference and the difficult entanglements and complications of existing as particular, limited fleshly beings.

While each of these aspects of Christian life has its own history and particular valence, one thing is clear: Christian identity complicates identities and lays bare both the culturally created aspects of identity and the ways all persons live into identities through the particularities of their flesh, the body they walk this world in. From the very beginning of the accounts of Jesus' birth there is the complication of gender, of Mary's yes to God and the inversion this means for Joseph's household. As Jesus walks through the first towns of his ministry, there is a destabilizing of Jewish identity and fidelity, and eventually even the confusion of Jewish and gentile identities, with kinship becoming a possibility that extended beyond blood or genealogy. Christianity is a faith that exists in the confusion of what bodies are and what they might be, dripping into the crevices of cultural expectation and calcification and gently or not so gently expanding and contracting until the moulds no longer hold.

But this is one way of reading Christian faith, a possible Pentecostal 'speaking in tongues' where the particularity of language is continually set ablaze by the Spirit such that one's words become heard in new ways, with capacity to hold and be heard in ways that outstrip their grammar. Another way of reading Christian history is through the lens of stabilities it sought to maintain, orthodoxy as measure of control, the divinization of maleness and the erasure of Jesus' Jewishness. In truth, perhaps, this is the Christianity that created the modern world, that accompanied ships that would traverse the seas and set boots on 'New Worlds', and eventually cultivate its most vicious crops – sexism and racism.

To contend with the complication of race and gender in the modern world, as theological phenomenon, they must be considered within the context of Christianity's constant struggle with its deconstruction of identity and the re-imagination of bodies. Gender and race have unique histories. In many ways, gender can be considered the older, the original violent differentiation. But differences of region, nation and ethnicity would eventually become the story of race. And in the modern world, race would come to be intertwined with gender and each would come to amplify one another, deepening the violence and complicating what redemption and salvation might look like. But the violence at the heart of sexist and racist imaginaries reflects a theological distortion rooted in the problem and possibility of the body, and the problem and possibility of difference at the heart of Christian faith.

20.1 THE PROBLEM OF THE BODY

The problem of the body was always a subtext of the question of who Jesus was. Some of the earliest Christian writings that reflect on Christ's person and work wrestle with Jesus' body, the possibility of his divinity or the reality of his humanity and the seeming impossibility that he could be both. The earliest Christian writers struggled to account for the claim 'The Word became flesh' because of how that flesh was imagined.³ The question of the body, whether Christ's body or our body were also questions about community.

Within generations Jewish identity and sensibilities are not simply forgotten but excised and used as a violent foil to claim Christian supremacy and suppression becoming disassociated from the earliest Jewish followers and their theological sensibilities, and in time defined over and against its very beginnings with a Jewish rabbi and his Jewish disciples. Christian identity is always a suturing, a negotiation, a fractured process of remembering, forgetting and, too often, creating new purities to resist the transformations that are just around the corner. From its very inception Christianity has been a public theology, entangled in questions of culture, power, politics, oppression and freedom. One way of understanding this is to say that Christianity is a religion that constructs bodies. It began as a religion pressing and reconfiguring itself in the earliest Jewish followers of a Jewish rabbi. But then these followers had to account for Jesus' interaction with gentiles, and eventually the scandalous inclusion of those gentiles into their numbers, and the eventual, definitive distinction from a sect of Judaism to its own faith, with predominately non-Jewish adherents.⁴ The distinction between Jews and Christians became a violent differentiation, with Christian identity being built upon notions of faithfulness and unfaithfulness, law and grace that legitimized Jewish exclusion and oppression. Then this religion moved from a persecuted sect to an alignment with empire, and theologians sought to align Christian faith with dominant philosophies or revive a distinction of church and world through ascetic practices or monastic vows.

Ignatius of Antioch, on his way to face lions and martyrdom, wrote to the churches under his care calling them to remember that Jesus 'really ate, really suffered, really died' and was really resurrected.⁵ Ignatius' belief was no mere doctrinal controversy. Jesus' bodily identity as God and human was tied to Ignatius' identity and hope for his own body and his people.

But whose bodies, and what form of life reflects faithfulness? The seeming transgressive claim that God became flesh did not seem to overturn dominant

---

³The significance of the invocation of flesh as the point of incarnation cannot be overstated. Whether in the distinction between body and flesh described by Spillers previously or in works on the distinction and relationship of humans and non-human animals in works such as David Clough's *On Animals*. The claim that the Word became flesh opens the possibility of God's identification with all that has flesh, as opposed to God became human, or a human body. See David Clough, *On Animals, Volume One: Systematic Theology* (London: Bloomsbury, 2012).
⁴See Willie James Jennings, *The Christian Imagination: Theology and the Origins of Race* (New Haven CT: Yale University Press, 2010).
⁵Ignatius of Antioch, 'Letter to the Trallians', in *Early Christian Fathers*, ed. Cyril Richardson, 1st Touchstone edn. (New York: Simon & Schuster, 1996), 100.

narratives of patriarchy in the nascent Christian movement even while the new communities and their theologies depended on women and the reimagining of women's lives as participants in divine action in the world.[6] While arguments concerning Jesus' divinity, the identity of Jesus, the nature of baptism and sacraments persisted, the women who led and funded movements, followed Jesus and supported his ministry and trained disciples were left out of the formal letters, accounts and histories of the developing church. Arguments for the full inclusion and recognition of women in the church have persisted in varying forms throughout the church's history and culminated in the feminist deconstructions of masculinity and patriarchy in the mid-twentieth century. But the question of the gendered body has been with Christianity from its very beginning, lurking beneath every Christological or eucharistic controversy. For every claim concerning the body of Christ, there is a seemingly silent question that is still being fleshed out – whose body?

While race as a formal category did not exist in the ancient world, there were ideas of nation, empire, ethnicity shaping ideas of identity and personhood. These boundaries and loci of identity were critical to the significance of Jesus' ministry and teaching. That is, this significance of Jesus' encounter with the Samaritan or Syrophoenician woman, his interaction with the centurion's daughter, all of these were significant because of the constructions of identity that created patterns of exclusion and difference. They were scandalous and powerful because of the ethnic and religious lines that Jesus crossed in his encounters with them, and the ways later interpreters and followers would reinterpret or inscribe new lines of faithfulness. And for early Christian writers, we see a wrestling, a struggle to account for the particularity of Jesus' life and ministry as a Jewish rabbi.

The earliest followers of Jesus were adapting, containing or breaking from the larger cultural and political formations of gender and racialized life, even while reinscribing the logics of gender and race in their nascent communities. These ebbs and floods are not neat genealogies but constant movement, pushes and pulls of power and dispossession and freedom and resistance. The same Christian faith that created justifications for enslavement or silence or death also served to illumine different ways of imagining life and cultivating human flourishing. Christian conceptualizations of human life do not escape the organic and constantly changing adaptations communities make as they attempt to make sense of themselves. Whether the earliest antecedents to

---

[6]See Elisabeth Schüssler-Fiorenza's essay 'Women in the Early Christian Movement' and Eleanor L. McLauglin's essay 'The Christian Past: Does It Hold a Future for Women?', in *Womanspirit Rising: A Feminist Reader in Religion*, ed. Carol P. Christ and Judith Plaskow (New York: HarperCollins, 1992), 84–92, 93–106.

racialized descriptions of ethnic and national difference or in descriptions of gendered personhood, Christianity's earliest practices, claims and histories, at various times, reinforced or subverted gendered and ethnic boundaries. So too, the birth of the modern world was created in the reciprocating representations of race and gender in order to reinforce and uphold white, male, patriarchal power.

20.2 BODIES, IDENTITY AND THE STORIES WE TELL OURSELVES

Christianity and its theological reflections are cultural productions. The ways that Ignatius or Justin Martyr or Augustine or any of the writers who shaped Christian traditions all did so working within processes of culture. To consider a theology of race, gender and theology it would certainly make sense to consider theological understandings of gender, problematic ways patriarchy shaped the writers of Christian Scriptures and theologies that those Scriptures were steeped and served in. But to move too quickly to the historical understandings of race and gender in theology would be to consider theological reflection to be an ahistorical or acontextual practice. This is slightly different from saying every theology is contextual. Yes, every theology is contextual. It arises from a particular people and seeks to address certain questions or ways of seeing the world and others. The so-called contextual theologies such as feminist theology, Black theology and so on are explicitly about the historical locations and challenges that give rise to their theological speech. The theologies that presuppose their own universality do not recognize that descriptions of God or Jesus or personhood have local beginnings and histories and cannot be universally applied to all people or to God or the Christian life.

But cultural production points to another aspect of theology's contextuality, the interrelationship between language, identity, power and representation. Culture is the particular patterns, practices, images and symbols that are shared by a people, that provide shared meaning, as Stuart Hall suggests. These meanings are not universal but rather processes of formation and negotiation, forming and being formed as people account for the difference in their own community and the differences outside of their community that require them to account for their symbols, their language, their identities. Hall writes,

> Though they seem to invoke an origin in a historical past with which they continue to correspond, actually identities are about questions of using the resources of history, language and culture in the process of becoming rather than being; not 'who we are' or 'where we came from', so much as what we might become, how we have been represented and how that bears on how

we might represent ourselves. Identities are therefore constituted within, not outside representation. They relate to the invention of tradition as much as to tradition itself.[7]

At the core of any theological speech or claim are ideas about who God is, what is a person, who is made in the image of God. These claims are productions of our language and cultural presumptions, not simply descriptions of what is.

Prior to Hall, the feminist theorist and novelist Simone De Beauvoir suggested a similarly constructed dynamic of gender with her famous saying 'a woman is not born, she is made'. But this construction was a production of language, small movements of daily life or legal barriers but one that always narrated femaleness in relationship to maleness. Beauvoir suggested the relationship 'male and female stand opposed within a primordial Mitsein [being with], and woman has not yet broken it'.[8] Beauvoir's observation highlights how domination and patterns of subjugation between men and women are expressed within necessary relations. Where the opposition of maleness and femaleness is articulated within an irrevocable nearness, man over woman, but always man with woman in either household patterns or normative narrations of vocation and place where women's lives and behaviours are perpetually bound to male-centric norms and modes of being. Beauvoir's lament concerning the seeming inevitable suffering within a relationship of being only further reiterates the fallen state of humanity, whose ultimate aim is an illusory autonomy.

In both Hall and Beauvoir race and gender are cultural productions made possible by very particular configurations of language about certain bodies, their possibilities and their limitations, and the legal, economic or social power to enforce those claims, creating a veneer of seeming divine or natural order. Theology is a cultural production that creates these bodies as much as it describes them. By correlating certain bodies closer to the image of God and others as closer to animals, or their characteristics being more animalistic, theology participates in the production of knowledges, of ways of understanding and shaping the world. Race and gender are only two of the ways bodies become aspects of this cultural production, signifying and being signified upon as societies move through time. To begin to consider the phenomena of race and gender theologically, we must always attune ourselves to the ways these ideas are inflections of a cultural production, attempts to create bodies (recalling Hortense Spiller's notion of body).

---

[7]Stuart Hall, *The Fateful Triangle: Race, Ethnicity, Nation* (Cambridge, MA: Harvard University Press, 2017), 4.
[8]Simone de Beauvoir, *The Second Sex* (New York: Vintage Books, 1989), xxv.

20.3 GENDER

Feminist theologians have suggested this pattern of domination has taken place not only within social constructions of the 'feminine' similar to what we see in Augustine but also in how women's lives have been narrated within particular modes of relationship with men and especially Jesus. Feminist theologian Elizabeth Schüssler-Fiorenza suggests,

> Women who read the Jesus story or have a 'personal' relationship to Christ take up the position that romance novels or films offer to women in relationship with men . . . men are to be education for themselves whereas women are to be socialized for men. The tendency to conceptualize as intimate live relationship between a believing woman and the exceptional man and singular hero . . . has a long theological tradition.[9]

The subjugation of women in relationship to men takes place within the orientation of women's lives (and hopes) inside of male certainty, the presuppositions of male knowledge or power that continue to permeate all facets of human society and continually circumscribe the lives of women. The structural realities of domination present in gender are iterated through radically interpersonal relationships between men and women on a daily basis that repeatedly order these relationships in radical connection to one another. These patterns of relation become reverberated through perpetual distortions of intimacy such as pornography, strip clubs and, on a more daily basis, in the magazine and fashion industry. These iterations occur in job interviews and office politics, on street corners and through subtle or not so subtle eye contact, leering, 'shouts of admiration' or the social systems that implicitly or explicitly penalize women for caring for children or elderly parents or spouses (while never asking why women are the people who inevitably juggle and sacrifice in these moments).

The question in these constructions is not what women's bodies mean intrinsically but how are they represented, what do they symbolize within the grammar and social structures mediated by the presumption of male superiority? And as recent articulations of LGBTQIA+ people have begun to press, what represents gender? What signifies belonging? Sutures once tied and divided maleness and femaleness in discreet, but inseparable categories. But these sutures are loosening, and the binaries are being folded and twisted until we cannot be quite sure which end is which, even while the violent legacies of misogyny and patriarchy march on.

---

[9]Elizabeth Schüssler-Fiorenza, *Jesus: Miriam's Child, Sophia's Prophet: Critical Issues in Feminist Christology* (New York: Continuum, 1994), 55.

20.4 RACE

But what do we mean by race? By ethnicity? By culture? The idea of race as a 'natural' category is a fairly new concept in human history. While differences between peoples and cultures have been prevalent throughout human history, the notion of race as a biological and theological category has its beginnings with European encounters with the world. In these encounters they sought to first theologically account for the physical differences that confronted them and the varying ways of life that seemed to accompany these physical differences.

Theologian Willie Jennings describes how the theological interpretations of the world's people would be articulated within 'great chain of being' wherein all the varieties of human life could be classified and understood in relationship to a transcendent ideal of the imago dei, an ideal that looked curiously like the European Christian male.

Returning again to Spillers's distinction between body and flesh, we see bodies being created in colonial encounter after colonial encounter. Jennings describes one such moment of description in the priest Zurara's exclamation of pity at the sight of the earliest slaves being unloaded from a Spanish ship in the early fifteenth century. He is at once attempting to understand what he is looking at and its seeming correspondence to his own body even while he attempts to understand a fundamental and unbridgeable difference. Ultimately this difference will be understood in terms of mastery where the Spaniards exhibit power over language, the power of perception and auctions (what are bodies for) – all taking place within a deep theological sensibility of God's order and mediation through the Spanish body.

This power serves to fundamentally re-create the world inside of a racial scale. Jennings writes,

> Through comparison, he describes aesthetically and thereby fundamentally identifies his subjects. There are those who are in between – almost white like mulattoes; and there are those who are black as Ethiopians, whose existence is deformed. Their existence suggests bodies come from the farthest reaches of hell itself. Zurara invokes, in this passage a scale of existence, with white at one end and black at the other end and all others placed in between.[10]

But this is done alongside and in conjunction with the creation of whiteness itself. The two are bound to one another and make one another intelligible.

---

[10] Jennings, *The Christian Imagination*, 23.

While the Spanish exhibited a profound mastery over language, over bodies and the power of perception to classify and 'locate' the meaning of these various bodies, they are doing so not as a distortion of their faith (or at least in their minds) but as an exercise of their faith.

But within several hundred years these theological interpretations of non-European bodies became solidified through the emerging scientific and rational lens of Enlightenment Europe. Theological categories were buttressed by scientific methods of classification. These scientific classifications became the basis of understanding certain people's purposes, limitations and possibilities. The study and comparison of skulls and body types were correlated to one's capacity to reason, to one's spirituality, to one's abilities and purposes in society. The American slave trade was built upon these twin foundations of theological and scientific classification, attributing to particular physical characteristics essential and fundamental meaning about their humanity (or inhumanity). The organizing poles of these classifications were an emerging self-understanding of European 'whiteness' and its corollary, African 'blackness'. While national, cultural, 'ethnic' and tribal identities had so long served as the locus of identity, in the shadow of a global colonial project race, whiteness, blackness and one's approximation to one or the other became fundamental aspects of human life in the colonized world.

Race in this emerging modernity was understood as having an essentialist construction. That is, certain physical attributes were signifiers of a deeper essential nature that was established by God and confirmed through rational scientific observation. This essentialist view of human difference served to justify the slave trade and the various racial differentiations in American (and colonial) society.

And yet, race is not as stable as we might have thought. To look at the notion of 'whiteness' in American society is to see the evolution and instability of these seemingly 'natural' categories.

Europe's African slave trade had become well established by the sixteenth century, bringing slaves to countries such as Spain and Portugal, and became increasingly common in the 'New World' by the seventeenth century. But it should be noted that Africans were not solely slaves upon these new ships, some came as slaves, and some came as indentured servants.

In this new land these identities were not entirely fixed, however. Notions of race, of whiteness and blackness, were constantly shifting. These shifts occurred increasingly in the New World as settlers began to ask the question of belonging, of servanthood, of calling. In the midst of this, the rhetoric regarding the African's 'place' in the world, their capacity for religion, for self-governance, became perpetual questions that served to not only justify African enslavement but also establish the criteria of American belonging and citizenship in terms of a nebulous category, whiteness. Historian Matthew Jacobson observes,

Although there were some exceptions, most laws of this kind delineated the populace along lines of color, and the word 'white' was commonly used in conferring rights, never abridging them. Scholars like Leon Higginbotham, Jr., have suggested, in practice the idea of citizenship had become thoroughly entwined with the idea of 'whiteness' (and maleness) because what a citizen really was, at bottom, was someone who could put down a slave rebellion or participate in Indian wars.[11]

Jacobson's observation regarding the racialized shape of citizenship must also be understood within the theological self-understanding of the American project (as an extension of the European colonial project). Understood within this light, American racial imagination is a theological claim of belonging, of who participates in the possibilities and promises of God's work.[12]

But in the midst of these articulations of belonging, something strange began to occur as the American project continued to develop. New people arrived. Chinese, Irish, Italians, Polish. And with their arrival a new set of 'what about' questions began to emerge. Who were these people and to whom did they belong? What constituted 'white'?

The Irish, the Italians, the Polish would begin to change their names, their food, their language and accents in the hopes of attaining the promise of citizenship. The Chinese had a more difficult task, for their faces betrayed a difference that could not be covered over with a change in name or dress (although some surely tried). And all along African Americans' bodies would be the measure against which these new peoples established their white credentials. The Black body would remain indelibly marked by difference. These questions would continue to evolve and adapt as waves of new immigrants came to America, causing long-time and recent immigrants alike to re-negotiate the terms of identity and belonging. For Asian Americans, whether fourth- or fifth-generation Chinese or Japanese or second-generation Korean or Vietnamese, citizenship would remain elusive, the 'perpetual foreigner' lingering on their faces as white and Black Americans repeatedly ask them, 'Where are you from? No, where are you really from?'

The patterns of exclusion and inclusion, of belonging and foreignness are not a spectrum but a vast web that entangles all of us, in various ways. For some of us the danger is perpetual and visceral. For others the estrangement comes in

---

[11]Matthew Frye Jacobson, *Whiteness of a Different Color: European Immigrants and the Alchemy of Race* (Cambridge, MA: Harvard University Press, 1998), 25.
[12]Jennings's *Christian Imagination* highlights the development of this modulation in the earliest encounters between Europe and the non-European world.

slow drips, pin-pricks that remind you on a daily basis that you do not belong. Race as well as ethnicity is a descriptive process, a negotiation.

The development of race as a means of description, as a set of ideas that can shift who is described and who can be classified by which terms, and what the inherent qualities certain features indicate are all aspects of what theorists describe as the constructed nature of race and identity. The notions of race and ethnicity, and even of gender are not inherent truths in themselves but are rather the accumulated ways of describing and giving meaning to particular visual signifiers. Race is a social construction and has no meaning in itself. What we must attend to, in this view, is dismantling the structures of oppression that have been built upon these falsehoods to create a more equitable society.

20.5 RACE AND GENDER

In the colonial creation of bodies it is the body of the Black woman that signifies how entangled the concepts of race and gender become in the birth of the New World. Womanist and Black feminist scholars have described how race and gender become violently intertwined in the experience of Black women in the Americas. Theologians and theorists such as Emilie Townes describes the 'cultural production of evil' that circulated around Black women's lives. Images such as the mammy, the benevolent servant who always appears with a smile and ready to cook a delicious meal, or the mulatta, whose light skin approximates whiteness even while their brown skin signals an underlying nature reduced only to sex.[13] These are only two of the stereotypes that inflected themselves on the lives of Black women, but in them there is the confluence of the gendered violence of reducing women to caretaking, to sexual fantasy, to a personhood stripped down only to utility. But upon these gendered patterns, race and blackness in particular signify a social order and whose bodies are meant to be used.[14]

These tropes are not mere images or stereotypes but are worked out in the emerging capitalist logics of the American project. Theologian Shawn Copeland describes how these stereotypes are intimately tied to economic and social systems. When the importation of slaves was made illegal in the United States enslaved Black women became crucial as reproductive capital. Whether through forced breeding or rape or simply tearing children from their mothers, the slave system in the United States continued to thrive. And in that violent

---

[13]See Emilie Maureen Townes, *Womanist Ethics and the Cultural Production of Evil* (New York: Palgrave Macmillan, 2006) and Spillers, 'Mama's Baby, Papa's Maybe'.
[14]For a deeper discussion of how these tropes continue in contemporary culture see Tamura Lomax, *Jezebel Unhinged: Loosing the Black Female Body in Religion and Culture* (Duke University Press, 2018).

practice the tropes of mammy and of sexualized body became paradoxically intertwined.[15] Black women's bodies were layered with significations of sexual deviance, even as they were layered with meanings of undesirability. But these reproductive capacities were not relegated only to slaves. Slave masters were frequent visitors to the quarters of their female slaves, often bringing friends or sons. To quote Langston Hughes the Southern sky was full of 'yellow stars'.[16] Black bodies were thus the objects of violent desire while also loathed as the very negation of white womanhood.

The Black female body thus constituted a point that was not outside of white life but penetrated white consciousness, creating a boundary of what was not pure even when the mixed child, this impurity, moved within white life, confronting its male and female inhabitants. In a similar manner the Black male body, in the years following the Civil War, would be seen as a severe threat against the purity of white womanhood. Accusations of rape and ill-intent were the common (though duplicitous) reasons for the lynch mobs that sprung up throughout the United States between 1870 and 1920.

While race and gender follow particular and distinct patterns of negotiation, subjugation and resistance in cultures, the modern world has nonetheless seen these two distinct ways of describing human difference coalesce in frightening and violent ways. But how does theology begin to contend with its own legacies of violent differentiation? How does it begin to embody a transgressive and freeing community, a true life in God in this world?

20.6 THE HOPE OF DIFFERENCE

The questions of race and gender are never simply questions about biological facts. Race and gender are questions of culture and identity. How does a society interpret particular bodies? And how do those interpretations indict? Render invisible? Privilege? Authorize? Put differently, what bodies are produced in a society? And conversely, how do the bodies that are born into this world, that are made by these worlds, begin to navigate who they are and what their bodies mean in the world?

Jesus' life and ministry participate in these dynamics of cultural production. Even as he walks in a world that finds the claims he seems to make about himself impossible, he seems to produce a cultural space where the bodies of

---

[15] See Shawn Copeland, *Enfleshing Freedom: Body, Race, Being* (Minneapolis: Fortress, 2010), 25–7. See also Saidiya V. Hartman, *Scenes of Subjection: Terror, Slavery, and Self-Making in Nineteenth Century America* (New York: Oxford University Press, 1997).
[16] Langston Hughes, 'Mulatto', in *The Collected Poems of Langston Hughes*, ed. Arnold Rampersad (New York: Vintage Books, 1994), 100–1.

those he meets might come to mean and exist in new ways. 'The Kingdom of God is here', he tells people again and again.

In this new Kingdom, his Jewishness is refracted into new ethnic and religious possibilities. In this new Kingdom, his mother comes to signify new possibilities of priestly existence and those seemingly reduced to their biological functions or sexual indiscretions are named for their faithfulness, are presented to their communities as those whose sins are no greater than any man's.

Jesus, the God man, is now not merely present in the flesh but actively working in the every day. God's 'vocation' is enacted within human life. To return again to the theological description of Shawn Copeland,

> In his relationships with women and men, Jesus embodied openness, equality, and mutuality. In his suffering and death on the cross, Jesus showed us the cost of integrity, when we live in freedom, in love, and in solidarity with others. In his resurrection, Jesus became the One in whom 'God's erotic power' releases bodily desire from the tomb of fear and loathing, the One who fructifies all loving exchange, the One who, in his risen body, quiets the restless yearning of our hearts.[17]

Copeland looks at the narratives of Jesus' life and does not see a man reinforcing patriarchal or ethnic binaries and norms. He enters into the rhythms of cultural production and disrupts them.

The incarnation is an entrance into Stuart Hall's conception of identity: 'identity is a process of articulation'. Theology as a public act is to negotiate the meanings written upon our bodies even as we write new meanings on our bodies. This 'writing' is always enacted. To write we mark lines, dots and curves and create letters, and placing those marks in a particular order, we create words, marks that bear meaning. Jesus' life, the descriptions of his life, the early disruptions of ethnicity, faith, law and gender of those early communities were a kind of writing, etching new meaning onto our bodies and the bodies of those we choose to live with. The incarnation was the most radical of these etchings as the Word became flesh: God written into flesh communicates new meaning to our flesh, to the animals we are.

Consequently, individuals and communities alike had to live into these ideals or articulate themselves within these norms seeking to show how they belonged, how their various attributes could be understood in light of the assertions the nation or community made about itself. History, in many ways, is the tracing of these various movements of groups and individuals into and out of one another

---

[17]Copeland, *Enfleshing Freedom*, 81.

– of the ways in which identities, individual and national, become articulated in relationship to one another in dynamic, ever-changing ways.

Such a claim then draws us to reflect upon not only Jesus' birth or Jesus' death on the cross as salvific moments but upon his very life through a new lens. His miracles, his feeding the poor and his eating with sinners are truly human acts and truly acts of God. When Jesus mourns, when Jesus asks for this cup to be passed from him, when he prays and when he eats, forgives, feels betrayal, in all of these moments we do not see the cessation of God. His life, even in its animality, is speaking to the ways that we do not need to leave off flesh in order to be like God, but in our flesh we might discover the deepest possibilities of our divinity.

If the body is the riddle of the Christian faith, Christ's flesh does not give us an easy answer. While much of Christian history has sought to reduce the meaning of the body to a series of easily interpreted signs of what a body is, the accounts of Christ provided in the lives of his followers and even in the Scriptures paint a much more complicated picture. While some might read Mary simply as the mother of Jesus, another way of reading her life is to see one whom God wanted to be like, to see a woman become a priest, a prophet and the holy of holies all in one body. Read this way we might begin to see new possibilities of what our bodies mean and how God both subverts and transfigures our flesh.

Seeing our flesh as icon, as transfigured animal, as bound up in dirt and dust and organic processes and beauty and love might allow us to resist the violent reductions that animate racialized and gendered violence. The riddle of the flesh is not eased in simplification but in the embrace of the complicated interrelationships and the dynamic ways we all seek to suture ourselves in the midst of a fragmented world.

In our flesh we must discover the beautiful and wondrous meanings of our manifold difference and the unfolding differences that our lives uncover from the womb to the tomb. Race and gender were ideas grounded in the presupposition that we knew what our bodies meant and we knew which bodies bore the greatest resemblance to God. But perhaps theology might begin to describe a new possibility, a possibility where the differences of our flesh are not occasions to consider who is closest to the image of God and who ought to live like animals. The incarnation, Jesus' life of disruption and new creation point to the possibility that every difference holds within the possibility of divine revelation. And the God who is revealed is manifold, infinite difference – multiplicity that cannot be conceived. Every difference we see is but one glimmer of God's glory and life. Perhaps we can live to see that all flesh might live freely.

CHAPTER 21

Public theology and culture

GRAEME SMITH

Public theologians are struggling to write originally and creatively about culture. Most public theologians are clear that culture matters, that it is important and should be studied, whether it is 'high culture', 'folk culture' or 'popular culture', to use Gordon Lynch's helpful delineation.[1] When theologians, including public theologians, talk about culture, they tend to have something comprehensive and significant in mind. Kathryn Tanner offers a definition which is not untypical. She distinguishes between a characterization of culture which refers to 'great works of art, philosophy, or literature' and the more comprehensive notion of culture as 'the whole social practice of meaningful action and more specifically to the "meaning dimension" of such action – the beliefs, values, and orientating symbols that suffuse a whole way of life'.[2] Tanner notes that the word 'culture' is one of the 'most widely used terms in the English language' and this is because it incorporates 'within its range of associations such notions as context, community, convention, and norm'.[3] As she goes on to say, 'To talk

---

[1] Gordon Lynch, *Understanding Theology and Popular Culture* (Oxford: Blackwell Publishing, 2005), 1–19.
[2] Kathryn Tanner, 'Cultural Theory', in *The Oxford Handbook of Systematic Theology*, ed. John Webster, Kathryn Tanner and Iain Torrance (Oxford: Oxford University Press, 2007), 527–42 (527).
[3] Ibid., 529.

about any human activity, with a recognition of its self-fashioning capacities and its historically and socially conditioned character, is inevitably to talk of culture.'[4] This can mean that public theology is itself a cultural activity, subject to the same analytical examination as the latest popular film, TV show, novel or art instillation, although theologians tend to resist this reduction of their discipline to a potentially minor tributary of cultural studies. More usually, for theologians, cultures are understood as vehicles for communicating significant social and political beliefs and values which can be identified, analysed and evaluated. It is the very comprehensive nature of culture which makes it a discourse with which theologians want to engage.

Not only does culture matter, culture is also fun, especially popular culture. When theologians write about culture, they are clearly not only writing about something that is important, with social and political consequences. They are also frequently pursuing their hobbies. Theologians are like other people, that is, they are amused, engaged, inspired and moved by cultural texts. Unlike early members of the Frankfurt School, most theologians who write about popular culture tend to do so with an appreciation of its capacity to entertain and engross as well as its political seriousness. This can include the seemingly trivial, as, with all due respect to his childhood, Chris Deacy illustrates with his reflections on 'Christmas Junior Choice'.[5] Deacy argues that his childhood memories of the radio programme, and then its place in his own children's upbringing, is something more significant than mere nostalgia. It led him to construct the thesis that Christmas can be understood as a religion. And my suspicion, although I have no inside information, is that Deacy is by no means alone in this engagement with personal preferences. Clive Marsh writing on *Breaking Bad*, Gordon Lynch on *Eminem* and Elaine Graham on *Star Trek* may well be other illustrations of the overlap between enjoyment and theological seriousness.[6] This is not to say that theologians are irresponsibly amusing themselves at the expense of their proper and expected engagement with the patristic doctrine of the atonement, or that popular culture is trivial, but that there is a sense in which, as Deacy notes, the study of culture by theologians can combine work and pleasure.

The question, in the relationship between public theology and culture, is how can theologians speak about culture with insight and with theological

---

[4]Ibid.
[5]Chris Deacy, *Christmas as Religion: Rethinking Santa, the Secular, and the Sacred* (Oxford: Oxford University Press, 2016), 87–102.
[6]Clive Marsh, *A Cultural Theology of Salvation* (Oxford: Oxford University Press, 2018), 95–105; Lynch, *Understanding Theology and Popular Culture*, 121–33; Elaine Graham, *Representations of the Post/Human: Monsters, Aliens and Others in Popular Culture* (Manchester: Manchester University Press, 2002), 132–53.

integrity? Before we look at that question, which is the main question of the chapter, there are some nomenclature issues which need sorting. The study of public theology and culture is a new discipline, as is illustrated by the diversity of terminology used. My argument has very specific points of reference about which it is important to be clear. In the paragraphs above I have fluctuated between the terms 'theologians' and 'public theologians'. Further, some mentioned earlier, like Deacy and Lynch, also talk about religious studies. I have also spoken about culture and popular culture. In the rest of what follows I shall be focusing primarily on popular culture for the simple expedients of space, that this is where I have undertaken most of my reading, and because this is the area most relevant to public theologians. Most of the theologians who write about popular culture do describe themselves as theologians but probably also would not reject terms like 'practical theologian' and 'public theologian'. This is also the case for those I mention who use the language of religious studies, although of course it would not be the case for many religious studies scholars. For the first part of the chapter I shall refer to these scholars as theologians because this is predominantly how they describe themselves and I am not aware of a distinctive discourse of public theology and culture. In the second part of the chapter I will use the phrase 'public theologians' for a very specific purpose as part of my argument.

My argument is that theologians have not yet discovered a way of speaking about popular culture well. By this I mean they have struggled, with only the rarest of exceptions, to pass Stephen Pattison's test of saying things that have captured the attention and imagination of those outside of the theological community.[7] Theologians tend to talk to each other about their work, but their theology hardly ever attracts the attention of non-theologians. The reason for this relative obscurity is that they conceive of the public theologian's task as being one of relating something called theology, which can lead to something called theological reflection, to something called culture, which is critically examined in cultural studies. In this schema theology tends to refer to either doctrine or biblical studies. Theological reflection then refers to the discourse produced when this doctrinal or biblical theology is related to context, in this case popular culture. As we shall see in the first part of the chapter, the attempt to relate theology and cultural studies, to produce theological reflection, means that a lot of theologians' engagement with culture is taken up with questions of methodology. This, in and of itself, need not be problematic, although it is not often interesting, except that in the interaction of theology and cultural studies, it is theology that is the perennial loser. In the work of theologians, it is cultural studies that produces

---

[7]Stephen Pattison, 'Public Theology: A Polemical Epilogue', *Political Theology* 2 (May 2000): 57–75 (63–4).

the important, original and exciting insights, which theological reflection then tends to confirm or reject. One reason for this is that theologians rarely actually conceive of their task as one of being analytically novel, imaginative and exciting. Rather they tend to think they need to be truthful, orthodox (in the broadest sense) and justice oriented. These are things which, of themselves, are not bad things but which are not always, or even often, the same as being unique, original and thereby interesting to non-theologians. Another reason is that it is the cultural theorists who tend to be the ones who do all the hard graft of analysis and evaluation. Cultural theorists are focused on the question of how we can analyse cultural texts, and what is their importance and significance. There is then little left for theologians to say except they approve or disapprove of what has been previously suggested by cultural theorists; and anyway other cultural theorists can also engage in such a critical task. Theology is thereby left as a non-analytical, but evaluative, veneer feeding off the scraps of cultural studies. Not surprisingly scholars, often including theologians, prefer to eat at the table.

Underpinning these problems is the issue of how theologians construct secularism. One of the reasons theology and culture are discussed as separate entities, to be related in some way methodologically, is that culture has, as a consequence of the acceptance that there are non-theological spaces, been treated by theologians as something different from theology. As we shall see this is done explicitly. It is theologians' presupposition that there is a secular space. This creates the methodological dilemma of how to relate theology to culture, a dilemma that does not affect cultural studies because it has only to ask what can be usefully said about either culture generally or specific cultural texts. In other words my argument is that the problem for public theology and culture is that it conceives of itself as public theology *and* culture, with culture being something that is prima facie non-theological. My main aim in the chapter is to analyse and discuss the problems caused by this separation of theology and culture. However, in the final section an alternative will be suggested, which, in part, helps illustrate the critique. In this alternate approach I am heavily influenced by the North American pragmatist philosopher Richard Rorty and his thinking about the future of philosophy. My first proposal is that we should stop thinking about 'theology' or 'public theology' as an essentialist discourse that can be identified, defined and known. There is no theology or public theology in some way 'out there', Truthful and waiting to be discovered and then related to cultural studies. Instead, we should think solely of 'public theologians' who are free to read what they want, watch and listen to what they want and write what they want, only becoming public theologians as and when they decide to describe themselves as such. These self-creating public theologians can interpret cultural texts as they wish, in the sense of, without reference back to a discipline called theology which will evaluate their 'orthodoxy'. Second, those who want to self-describe as public theologians, and who want to say they are doing public theology, as they have chosen to construct and define it, would be well served not to think of cultural texts as secular or cultural, by which is meant not theological. They should think of culture as itself a theological text, with theological agency and as, in fact, a very important public theology. The culture they read can be thought of as theological in and of itself, and so can be described and evaluated employing concepts and theories that are original, academically unique and theological in the sense of being most likely to be produced by people who read lots of public theology. In this sense we could say that a better title for this chapter would be 'Culture as Public Theology', albeit we would have to be clear this was not an essentialist claim about public theology but a way of recognizing that culture can be read by people who call themselves public theologians and described by these public theologians as public theology. The key point is that for public theologians who read culture as not secular, then the most important theological agent is culture. It is not the church or the academy who are the primary producers of a theology which then in some way interacts with culture. For their own reasons the church and the academy produce a theology which is doctrinal or biblical. Rather culture is the theologian, and the theology that it produces is very public. There are of course many objections theologians will want to raise to these proposals, as there are to Rorty's proposals for philosophy, and some of these will be discussed. The most regular objection is around questions of identity, that is, can public theologians write about anything they want? However, space will also be left at the end for an attempt to illustrate in more detail what public theologians reading cultural texts can achieve; and here the work of Robert Bellah will be mentioned. However, before that discussion we need to explore in detail the first question, namely, why it is that theologians struggle to speak well about culture?

21.1 WHAT IS WRONG WITH THE NOTION OF PUBLIC THEOLOGY AND CULTURE?

Theologians struggle to write creatively and originally about culture because they conceive of theology and culture as separate entities which need to be related methodologically. There are many illustrations of this problem and we only have space to examine a few, starting with Gordon Lynch's lucid and influential book *Understanding Theology and Popular Culture*.[8] Lynch is clear from the outset that a significant issue to be discussed is methodology. He writes, a 'major part of this book is therefore concerned with clarifying methodological issues in the theological evaluation of popular culture'.[9] Lynch conceives of culture and theology as two distinct discourses which need defining and then

---

[8] Lynch, *Understanding Theology and Popular Culture*.
[9] Ibid., x.

need to interact with each other. So his first chapter sets out to define popular culture, first by contrasting it with 'high culture' and 'folk culture', and then by recommending a way of conceiving of popular culture via a 'culturalist approach'. This is an approach 'proposed by (Raymond) Williams that studies (popular) culture more as a "way of life" for particular people in particular contexts'.[10] In effect Lynch is agreeing with Tanner that popular culture should be thought of more widely than the 'documentary' style analysis of particular cultural texts. Lynch argues that the culturalist approach involves 'looking at the wider structures, relationships, patterns and meanings of everyday life within which popular texts are produced and "consumed"'.[11] Like many theologians who write about culture, there is no doubting Lynch is very well informed about contemporary cultural theory and this shapes his definition. He is equally informed about theology, the second discourse he needs to define. In the second chapter of his book Lynch asks why it is that theologians and scholars of religion should study popular culture. This entails offering a brief definition of theology. The definition is then expanded in chapter 5, which is devoted to methodological questions. Lynch defines theology as *'the process of seeking normative answers to questions of truth / meaning, goodness / practice, evil, suffering, redemption, and beauty in specific contexts'*.[12] Lynch's definition is broad and inclusive, and, in light of the criticism offered above, one which he believes is dynamic and fluid, and not fixed and essentialist. In a manner that is indebted to Paul Tillich, Lynch argues that theology is not a 'static body of knowledge' but a process of 'exploring traditional theological resources in the light of contemporary questions, beliefs, values, practices, and experiences'.[13] This fluidity is seemingly reinforced when Lynch explains his theological methodology. This he describes as a 'revised correlational approach', building on the work of Don Browning.[14] In particular, 'rather than seeing theology as a process of correlating questions raised by culture to answers offered by religious tradition, a revised correlational approach envisages a more complex conversation involving questions and answers from both culture and tradition'.[15] For Lynch the most important aspect of the methodology is that it is conversational; no one perspective or tradition has an exclusive truth, all may contribute to the task of discerning what is truthful. At first sight this looks far from an essentialist definition of theology. However, there is a difficulty in Lynch's discussion, namely, how does Lynch distinguish between, on the one

---

[10] Ibid., 3–11, 15.
[11] Ibid., 15–16.
[12] Ibid., 94. Italics in the original.
[13] Ibid., 96.
[14] Ibid., 105.
[15] Ibid., 103.

hand, theology and, on the other hand, theological reflection, understood as the product of the conversation between theology and culture? At times Lynch appears to elide the two so that theology can be viewed as fluid because what is actually meant is the process of theological reflection. But in Lynch's schema the process of theological reflection assumes a body of knowledge known as theology which can participate in the conversational, reflection process. This body of knowledge might change as a result of the reflection process, but ultimately the process needs a body of knowledge called theology, even if the process then changes the content of that body of the knowledge. In other words Lynch is working with a methodology that requires two distinct and static discourses. This point is reinforced when we return to Lynch's definition of theology cited above and the list of topics to which theology seeks normative answers. These are not exclusively theological topics, but they are very familiar to theologians. Their choice is not random; they refer back to issues and questions which have historically taxed theologians, like the problem of evil, questions of ethics, suffering, redemption and aesthetics. In one sense Lynch's list seeks to be comprehensive, and in another sense we can see its theological provenance. Of course Lynch would be justified in his methodology if the results of the process were valuable and important. Lynch offers three case studies to illustrate his methodology in the final part of the book and, what we can note at this stage, is that this is the least substantial part of his work. However, before we get to this question of what theology offers in the study of culture, we need to show that Lynch is by no means alone in thinking of the relationship between theology and culture in this way.

The most important contemporary British public theologian is Elaine Graham. She, like Lynch, conceives of public theology and popular culture as two separate discourses, which need to be related. Her influential book, *Between a Rock and a Hard Place*, culminates in proposals for a new public theology methodology called Christian apologetics.[16] Like Lynch, whom she references, Graham believes that 'popular culture and media' are 'some of the most innovative and creative arenas within which people explore questions of truth and meaning: what it means to be human, the beginning and endings of life, the nature of difference, the future of the planet'.[17] Graham also has a far from traditional conception of what might be meant by theology. She resists notions that theology should be rationalist and propositional, arguing for something more performative, imaginative and narrative oriented.[18] However, she is also

---

[16]Elaine Graham, *Between a Rock and a Hard Place: Public Theology in a Post-Secular Age* (London: SCM Press, 2013), esp. Part 3, 177–233. See also Chapter 6 of this volume.
[17]Ibid., 208.
[18]Ibid., 203.

clear that there is a distinction to be made between the theological and the non-theological, identified as the secular. This means public theologians need to be 'bilingual'.[19] Graham is speaking of a non-theological space that is wider than culture, incorporating the social and political; however, the principle remains the same. Theology is a distinct discourse which needs translating so it can be understood in this different sphere. Public theology 'needs to be grounded in biblical and theological tradition but capable of being understood by those outside its own boundaries, appealing to reason and experience to show that the values of faith make good sense and better practice. This may involve a process of "translation" from confessional or dogmatic language into commonly understood concepts and values'.[20] The notions of bilingualism and translation are very helpful in allowing me to make my point because if culture is already a theological agent, if there is no secular in this sense, then we do not need to learn another language, nor do we need translators. We only need translation when there are distinct discourses.

Lynch and Graham are helpful contemporary illustrations of my argument, however, in the discussion of the relationship between theology and culture neither are (yet) treated as having written classic, foundational texts. This status belongs to Richard H. Niebuhr's book *Christ and Culture* and Paul Tillich's article 'On the Idea of a Theology of Culture', one or both of which are usually cited by scholars writing on the relationship between theology and culture.[21] Both of these texts illustrate the argument I am making, that theology and culture are analysed as distinct, identifiable discourses which need bringing into relationship with each other. The distinction is obvious in Niebuhr's work especially if we substitute the word 'theology' for the word 'Christ'. The first chapter of the book defines 'Christ' and then later 'Culture'.[22] As Lynch notes, Niebuhr does not propose a methodology for the interaction of theology and culture; rather, he offers a typology for understanding how they have been related historically. The typology is a spectrum ranging from 'Christ Against Culture', in which the distinction between the two discourses is obvious, via 'Christ Above Culture', 'Christ and Culture in Paradox', 'Christ the Transformer of Culture' to 'The Christ of Culture'. Of these it might be thought that Niebuhr's analysis of those theologians who speak about the 'Christ of culture' would significantly

---

[19]Ibid., 183, 232.
[20]Ibid., 232.
[21]Paul Tillich, 'On the Idea of a Theology of Culture', in *Paul Tillich: Theologian of the Boundaries*, ed. Mark Kline Taylor (The Making of Modern Theology. 19th and 20th Century Theological Texts, London: Collins Liturgical Publications, 1987, repr. [1919]), 35–54; H. Richard Niebuhr, *Christ and Culture* (New York: Harper & Row Publishers, 1951).
[22]Niebuhr, H. Richard, *Christ and Culture*, 11–29, 29–39.

challenge my argument. However, even in this category Niebuhr clearly has in mind a distinction between theology and culture, expressed this time as the separation of church and world. He describes the Christ of culture theologians as feeling 'no great tension between church and world, the social laws and the Gospel, the workings of divine grace and human effort, the ethics of salvation and the ethics of social conservation or progress'.[23] In other words it is not that culture is a theological agent with a theological voice, but rather that theologians and church people find much overlap in their theological and non-theological perceptions and views.

If Niebuhr is a relatively straightforward illustration of the argument, then Paul Tillich's lecture to the Berlin Kant Society in 1919 is far less clear, not least because of the unfamiliar terminology he employs. Tillich is outlining his argument for a 'theonomy' or 'theology of culture'. This has at its heart a distinction between 'form' and 'import or substance'.[24] Tillich writes, 'the autonomy of cultural functions is grounded in their form, in the laws governing their application, whereas theonomy is grounded in their substance or import, that is, in the reality which by these laws receives its expression or accomplishment'.[25] The form is to be analysed and evaluated by 'cultural science'. The 'import' or 'substance' is then the preserve of theologians because it is concerned with 'the meaning, the spiritual substantiality, which alone gives form its significance'.[26] At this point it might look like Tillich is proposing something akin to my argument, namely that culture is a theological agent. Tillich seems to be suggesting that there are two aspects to the analysis of culture and that one of these is theological, that is the analysis of import or substance. However, it soon becomes clear that Tillich more clearly resembles those theologians who distinguish between theology and theological reflection. He argues, and it is worth quoting at length to be clear, that there is an important distinction,

> The concrete religious experiences embedded in all great cultural phenomena must be brought into relief and a mode of expression found for them. It follows from this that in addition to theology as a normative science of religion, a theological method must be found to stand beside it in the same way that a psychological and a sociological method, etc., exist alongside systematic psychology. These methods are universal; they are suited to any object; and yet they have native soil, the particular branch of knowledge in

---

[23]Ibid., 83.
[24]Tillich, 'On the Idea of a Theology of Culture', 42.
[25]Ibid.
[26]Ibid., 43.

which they originated. This is equally true of the theological method, which is a universal application of theological questioning to all cultural values.²⁷

This theological method was described earlier, in relation to Lynch, as theological reflection. Tillich clearly has in mind a notion of theology that is separate from culture, and which he has in fact defined earlier as *'the concrete and normative science of religion'* which is to be 'based on the categories of philosophy of religion, with the individual standpoint being related to the standpoint of the respective confession, the universal history of religion, and the cultural-historical standpoint in general'.²⁸ While this could be more simply expressed, the point is clear. There is a distinction between the subject area of theology, the subject area of culture (meaning high culture), and then the theological methodology which Tillich calls 'a theology of culture'. The point is reiterated when Tillich discusses the ideal theologian. Tillich distinguishes between the 'church theologian', who is a specialist in systematic theology in the traditional sense, and the 'theologian of culture' who employs the new methodology devised by Tillich. Tillich's argument is that 'the only relationship possible is one in which each is the complement of the other; and the best way of achieving this is through personal union', something which has a whiff of autobiography about it.²⁹

21.2 CAN THEOLOGY ADD VALUE?

It is not my intention to go through a long list of theologians who write about culture to reiterate the point. There are plenty of other examples, not least of whom are Kelton Cobb in his important book *The Blackwell Guide to Theology and Popular Culture*, and also Clive Marsh, who has written influentially about theology and film and intriguingly about *A Cultural Theology of Salvation*, both of which will be discussed later.³⁰ Cobb is explicit that he continues Tillich's project, writing that he is convinced 'that it is worthwhile to resume Paul Tillich's efforts to interpret cultural artifacts for the religious substance that rumbles in deeper regions'.³¹ It is perhaps therefore not a surprise if the critique of Tillich applies equally to Cobb. However, the intention now is to ask

---

²⁷Ibid., 42.
²⁸Ibid., 37.
²⁹Ibid., 52.
³⁰Kelton Cobb, *The Blackwell Guide to Theology and Popular Culture* (Oxford: Blackwell Publishing, 2005); Marsh, *A Cultural Theology of Salvation* and see also Clive Marsh, *Theology Goes to the Movies: An Introduction to Christian Critical Thinking* (Abingdon: Routledge, 2007) inter al.
³¹Cobb, *The Blackwell Guide to Theology and Popular Culture*, 5.

whether this separation of theology and culture, and then the methodological efforts to relate them in some way, is fruitful. The focus on methodology would be entirely legitimate and valuable if theologians produced insights which were unavailable to other scholars, and which inspired, stimulated and excited these scholars. In other words, do all the efforts by theologians to construct new methodologies result in analyses which are original, insightful and can contribute to things like increased justice in society or greater peacefulness? My argument is that it is far from clear that they do and that this is largely because the theology in the pairing is understood in a very static, traditional and essentialist manner. Further the culture that is discussed is understood as entirely secular; that is, culture is not understood to be the main, or even only, theological agent.

Kelton Cobb has written a book on theology and culture which is one of the best contemporary examples of a theologian discussing popular culture. In the book initially he appears to contradict my analysis thus far because he suggests that 'the media' is a vehicle of theological insight, helping people think about things like love, pain, hope, sacrifice and grace, as well as being able to illustrate shared symbols, 'icons, myths and rituals'.[32] Cobb goes further and proposes that 'it is not off-limits to speak of culture, and of diverse cultures, in terms of divine providence or as embodiments of God's ideas – at least cautiously'.[33] In the book Cobb provides a helpful historical overview of how theologians have interacted with culture, concluding with Tillich, who inspires his methodology. Cobb also has a chapter on 'Theological Tools' which is a type of methodology chapter although we already know we are following Tillich's approach.[34] Cobb identifies and discusses several 'key concepts' from Tillich's theology of culture which are listed at the end of the chapter, including 'ultimate concern; the holy; ontological and moral faith; revelation and ecstasy; religious symbols; myth; liminality; and religion'.[35] What is odd is that Cobb almost immediately changes direction and states that part II of the book, entitled 'A Theology of Popular Culture', will 'be organized loosely along the lines of a traditional "systematic theology" with sections on God, human nature, sin, salvation, and eschatology'. In many ways both approaches look very promising, but it would seem that Cobb should choose one or the other. What follows, at the beginning of part II, is the first chapter of this theology of popular culture based on systematic theology, namely a chapter on God. Cobb is discussing some of the ways in which contemporary Western popular culture talks about

---

[32] Ibid., 72.
[33] Ibid.
[34] Ibid., 101–32.
[35] Ibid., 131–2.

God, exploring a number of films which mention God, before moving on to fiction which does the same. He then discusses topics such as commodities, marketing, technology and postmodernity before concluding with the key question, namely, what is 'popular culture telling itself about God?' His answer is as follows:

> Some take the view that God is more like us than theology has typically allowed. Among these, a new cluster of divine attributes is emerging. God can be evasive, temperamental, playful, vengeful, adventurous, overwhelmed, irresponsible, on a journey of self-discovery, loving like we are loving (in a fickle way), distracted, a sensualist, weary, demoralized, sad, and, most of all, lonely.[36]

In one sense this is very helpful because it is clear that something cultural has theological agency. However, the question, which Cobb does not discuss, is how do we distinguish between a 'theology of culture' and the theologies of people who produce cultural texts? In other words, is not the danger that his list of God's attributes is no more a summary list of the views of a variety of people who have spoken about God through cultural texts? The list does demonstrate that God is not dead, as far as popular culture is concerned, but this does not mean that this summary description of God is interesting or helpful. It might well be hoped that the theological process adds more than a mere repetition of the attributes of God which cultural producers have created. What is missing is any sense in which there are theological categories, or a theory which links these categories, which tells us something about our society beyond the fact that it still talks about God. In other words what is missing is a contribution from the theologian beyond identifying things in culture that might be considered theological. Ultimately, it is difficult to say who God is as a result of Cobb's analysis, or why such a picture might matter to others, because the picture is so diverse and multifaceted. This sense that there is little coherent to be said is reinforced by Cobb's final conclusion in which, after similar chapters on the other aspects of systematic theology, he states that of 'the myriad religious messages that are being asserted in popular culture, there is one that, for me, stands out', namely that, there is 'a yearning for a reality beyond all simulations'.[37] This does sound like a theologians' response to secularism, but it does not look like a systematic theology of culture.[38] And

---

[36]Ibid., 175.
[37]Ibid., 292.
[38]There is a sense from the start of the book that resisting secularism was Cobb's intention. Ibid., 3–8.

it is difficult to know what useful insights are added by this theology to our understanding of society and its workings. The originality comes from the cultural texts, but the diversity of their theologies leads to a lack of coherence when it comes to talking about a theology of culture or its implications. Cobb is aware of the eclectic nature of popular culture's image of God when he states that 'American popular culture' has a skill at *'bricolage'*, a cultural studies methodology he had discussed earlier in the book.[39] But the problem is that the cultural bricolage Cobb analyses detracts from any value that comes from identifying the theologies. This does raise the question, however, of whether a more coherent analysis of what popular culture states theologically might provide more helpful insights.

If the problem with Cobb is the diverse and eclectic scope of his cultural and theological analysis, then it may be that a more valuable theological critique of culture, and thereby of society, can be achieved by focusing on one theological topic. This is what Marsh undertakes in his *A Cultural Theology of Salvation*.[40] Marsh's work has a missionary intent. He wants to explore how salvation might be discussed in contemporary Western society given an assumed, predominant, theological illiteracy. In this sense the book can be understood as another response to the problem of secularism.[41] Marsh connects the social and cultural discourse about 'happiness', which he argues is a central topic for discussion in the West, with theology by suggesting that happiness is 'a key agenda item for theology'.[42] Marsh has a methodology for relating happiness to theology, which he calls the 'critically dialogical approach' and which he argues can employ non-Christian cultural resources to inform Christian thinking.[43] However, the question here is not about his methodology but the results of the focus on one doctrinal topic, salvation and its discussion partner, happiness, in the theological study of popular culture. After the first part of the book, which covers the methodological discussion, the second part looks at the idea of 'Salvation within Western Culture'. This entails chapters discussing a series of films, TV shows, books, paintings, music and then less obviously developments in psychology and the social, economic and political impact of capitalism. What is clearly demonstrated is that the topics which Marsh designates as theological are discussed in cultural texts.[44] In this Marsh mirrors Cobb, Lynch, Graham and many others. It is then in part III of the book that the theological contribution should come to the fore. The first of the two chapters in this

---

[39]Ibid., 137.
[40]Marsh, *A Cultural Theology of Salvation*.
[41]Ibid., 2–3.
[42]Ibid., 21.
[43]Ibid., 30. See also note 41 for a more detailed definition of the methodology.
[44]Ibid., 107.

part lays the foundation for the chapter to follow, which is the presentation of salvation in the 'contemporary understanding'. In this chapter Marsh discusses human sinfulness, personal and social, the Christian doctrine of salvation, and the notion of church. He states, for instance:

> We can see that salvation, understood as present participation in Christ, is a multidimensional experience, affecting body, mind, and heart. It comes into play as we seek to be loving people, whilst we also interact with all of the cultural stimuli in and through which we expand our grasp of what it means to be free and loving. More precisely, we are being expanded by God in our understanding of what it means to be free and loving, the more we open ourselves up to learning what it means to live 'in Christ'.[45]

Two points can be made here. First it is not clear that Marsh's detailed analysis of culture has added much, if anything, to our theological understanding of doctrine, let alone a theological understanding of society. This theology looks very much like the orthodox Christian theology which predates the cultural texts Marsh has studied. Second, there is a danger that it appears, from the second sentence, that in fact the role of cultural texts is to enable us to be good Christians. This might be what Marsh means by his missionary intent. But from our perspective it means little has changed theologically. The same difficulties appear in a further summary quotation in which we try to discern what Marsh's project has produced that might be of value to non-theologians.[46] He writes,

> More narrowly, salvation is about how created beings deal with the limitations of their creatureliness, especially with how to deal with imperfections, with flaws and frailty, and with wilful wickedness. Freedom brings both risk and responsibility. God's 'letting be' of creation means that so much is not as it should be. How, then, God works with those creatures who, in freedom, choose to work with God and accept the way in which God enables frailties to be faced, burdens to be lifted, and evil to be overcome forms the core of the doctrine of salvation more narrowly construed.[47]

Again my point, and the justification for the long quotation, is that Marsh has added little, if anything, that is new or original with this understanding of salvation. To be fair to Marsh, he does avoid the trap many theologians

---

[45]Ibid., 210.
[46]It should be clear that this question of value to the non-theologian is my question and Marsh might well respond by stating that this was not his purpose in the study.
[47]Ibid., 211.

who write about culture fall into, namely referencing little or no contemporary theology. Marsh's credentials as a doctrinal theologian shine through in the chapter, just as his standing as a cultural theorist is apparent in the previous part of the book. But what is not clear is what is added when he seeks to combine the theology and cultural theory. What seems to be produced looks to all intents and purposes like orthodox Christian doctrine. This is further demonstrated in the 'Conclusion' to the book where Marsh addresses the question 'What, then, *Is* Salvation?'[48] In the first section he repeats a salvation template he has previously discussed, namely that salvation is 'From', 'For', 'By', and/or 'Into' something. He then lists ten headings which are expressions of salvation in everyday life. They are: 'ultimate well-being', 'health', 'acceptance', 'being forgiven', 'forgiving', 'safety', 'celebration', 'happiness', 'contentment' and 'blessedness'.[49] Again, it is possible to see how these notions arise from the cultural texts Marsh has discussed, and it is possible to see how they relate to Christian ideas about salvation. But they offer little that changes how we think about society. In many ways what my argument amounts to is that Marsh would have been better off not including part III in his book, thereby removing the methodological contortions, and focused instead on developing part II into a more systematic analysis of society. Despite exploring only one doctrinal topic, Marsh ends up with a list, a type of bricolage, which does not offer systematic insights into the nature of society from a theological perspective as a result of the study of culture. In fact, like those discussed earlier, Marsh works with a model of theology as a discourse that is essentialist and which thereby limits what he thinks the theologian can do when confronted with popular culture.

21.3 POPULAR CULTURE AS PUBLIC THEOLOGY

The main purpose of this chapter has been to analyse and critique the relationship between public theology and popular culture. However, the inevitable question emerges of what alternative is available if we are to avoid the traps described earlier. There is not much space left to discuss this, but I want to highlight two priorities that hopefully might lead public theologians to sidestep the dangers I am describing and which might help with further understanding the nature of my critique. In essence what I want to argue is that we need to stop thinking about public theology *and* popular culture, and instead, think of popular culture *as* public theology. Thinking in this way has two core elements.

The first element is to keep thinking of the big picture. In his book *The Broken Covenant* Robert Bellah makes the following assertion:

---

[48]Ibid., 213–28.
[49]Ibid., 219–28.

It is one of the oldest of sociological generalizations that any coherent and viable society rests on a common set of moral understandings about good and bad, right and wrong, in the realm of individual and social action. It is almost as widely held that these common moral understandings must also in turn rest upon a common set of religious understandings that provide a picture of the universe in terms of which the moral understandings make sense. Such moral and religious understandings produce both a cultural legitimization for a society which is viewed as at least approximately in accord with them and a standard of judgment for the criticism of a society that is seen as deviating too far from them.[50]

In some ways Bellah's book, and also the work by Philip Gorski which builds on it, is an attempt to understand historically the nature of these moral foundations and their relationship to religious belief.[51] The point here is not to discuss this approach in detail but instead to suggest that a theological evaluation of popular culture could have as its aim the analysis of the ethico-religious undercurrents informing social and political debates and expressed in popular culture. A theological evaluation of popular culture will develop theological analytical categories which it then seeks to relate theoretically with a view to saying something significant about society, especially its moral assumptions. In this sense public theologians can move beyond the secularism debate to discuss what it means that cultural producers are being theological other than the fact that seemingly non-theological people still find theology relevant. The point has been proven, by the likes of Lynch, Graham, Marsh and Cobb, that popular culture has theological agency. The question now is what does that mean for society?

Second, it is time to liberate the public theologian from the tyranny of 'theology'. An end should be brought to the presumption that there is something called 'theology' which is 'out there', waiting to be discovered, usually under the guise of ideas about revelation, and in some way related to cultural studies. In a version of Richard Rorty's notion that philosophy should no longer be concerned with a 'Truth' which is in some ways 'out there', so I want to argue that a 'theology' does not exist in any way independently of the theologian who constructs it. There is no definitely definable body of knowledge called theology to which other discourses can relate. My suspicion is that in claiming to be theological there is a danger that some theologians are using 'theology' as

---

[50] Robert Bellah, *The Broken Covenant. American Civil Religion in a Time of Trial* (Chicago: The University of Chicago Press, 2nd edn. [1975], 1992), xvi.
[51] Philip Gorski, *American Covenant. A History of Civil Religion from the Puritans to the Present* (Princeton, NJ: Princeton University Press, 2017).

a substitute term for truth and so behaving in the 'philosopher-king' type ways described by Rorty.[52] Analogously to Rorty, we would be better off thinking of the self-creating theologian who constructs and invents a theology for particular purposes. Theology is no more than what the self-identifying theologian says it is.

The question will certainly be asked about identity: what makes a public theology actually 'theology' if we follow Rorty's approach? There are two possible answers to this question. Rorty's answer, if we read it across from philosophy, would be that nothing makes theology 'theology'; but that does not matter. The naming game, this desire for identification, is a trap to be avoided whenever it raises its ugly head. What matters for writers who might call themselves theologians is not whether they are conforming to some pre-existing notion of what theology is, and so have the right to call themselves theologians, but that they write things that are interesting to others, engaging, therefore probably original and unique, and which help to make society more just and equal. In other words theologians should worry more about being read, about writing things other people want to think about and discuss, than about being authentically and identifiably theological. The second answer would be to say that theology is what theologians say it is. Again the priority here is to avoid anything essentialist. But someone who wants to say they read theology, that they can identify topics that they call theological, and that they produce theology, is thereby a theologian. It can be assumed that it would be very rare to find such a person who did not look like what is traditionally called a theologian. But, in much the same way that an artist can claim for their work that it is art, so it is not necessary to say much more than if someone wants to call their work theology, then it can be so named. The judgement to be made is not whether it really is theology, but will it engage people, will it change hearts and minds, will it make society better. If the answer to these questions is 'yes', then public theologians should be pleased to call it theology. And this produces a change of emphasis on what is meant by theological education. Theological education is no longer about learning the truths that constitute the body of knowledge called 'theology', but instead the process of learning how to form and create oneself as an original, innovative and imaginative producer of valuable theology. At the end of *Philosophy and the Mirror of Nature* Rorty refers to this process for the philosopher as 'edification'.[53] The question is not what theology do you know but what can you do to form and create yourself as a theological producer so that you generate material which is of interest

---

[52]Richard Rorty, *Philosophy and the Mirror of Nature* (Princeton, NJ: Princeton University Press, 1979), 317.
[53]Ibid., 360.

to and importance for society, a society which of course includes churches. The personal journey of the theologian becomes the significant part of the theological education because the theology produced is personal, as opposed to truthful. It could be both, of course, but that it is the latter does not really matter.

My argument has been that there is a series of phenomena, bound up under the term 'popular culture', which can be read theologically in a way that has implications for our understanding of social and political life. Popular culture has theological agency, like the church and the academy. This means we need to think of the relationship between theology and popular culture differently. What is important is how public theologians speak of culture in ways that are imaginative, creative, valuable, original and thereby of importance to others. That is, how can public theologians read culture theologically with a view to understanding society more deeply.

CHAPTER 22

Economics

DEVIN SINGH

22.1 INTRODUCTION

This chapter establishes a conversation between public theology and matters of economics. I argue that public theology is characterized by attempts to make intelligible, practical and useful contributions to public efforts to tackle specific issues or challenges. As such, the claims and interventions of public theology should be accessible and ultimately beneficial and relevant to extra-theological or extra-ecclesial audiences being addressed. I claim, furthermore, that public theology's distinct contributions are best manifested in concrete cases and highly contextual interventions, including at the mundane level of policy, institutional changes and community organizing. In demonstrating these values while addressing the economic realm, I do not cover all matters of economics more broadly or economic theory itself but, instead, focus concretely on the problem of debt and, even more narrowly, on the case of payday lending. I provide a description of such practices as well as the theological and ethical challenges they raise and seek to bring theological reflection and practice to bear on proposals to resist dehumanizing and exploitative dynamics in

---

This research was conducted while in residence at the Center of Theological Inquiry, Princeton, and I gratefully acknowledge its support and the benefits of conversation with its staff and other resident fellows. Research support was also provided in part by the Luce Foundation's 'Public Theologies of Technology and Presence' project, which I gratefully acknowledge. I have benefitted from research assistance from Alexander Zureick, and I am much obliged for comments on this manuscript from Marcia Pally and Joshua Mauldin.

predatory lending. Ultimately, I demonstrate the capacious and flexible nature of theological responses to such economic challenges, underscoring the importance of contextual and relational commitment by public theologians to their chosen public audience and community, in order to align their pragmatic interventions in solidarity with the concerns of those addressed.

22.2 THE AIMS OF PUBLIC THEOLOGY

While a relatively recent development within theology, public theology has a venerable pedigree and has generated vigorous discussion and debate for decades.[1] Some definitions of public theology link it to Christianity's long apologetic tradition, one typically concerned with vindicating the truth or relevance of the Christian faith before non-believers. In this sense, one might be doing public theology when giving a public defence of the plausibility or merit of Christian claims. As one summary puts it, public theology seeks 'to communicate the Christian message to non-Christian audiences in many different contexts so that it can be understood and either appropriated or rejected'.[2] These approaches of making Christian truth 'intelligible' to the world or of providing a reasonable 'defence' of Christian faith strike me as already well covered by evangelism and traditional apologetics and as such do not justify a need to create a new category called 'public theology'.

In contrast to such approaches, my entry into public theology seeks to foster a conversation over what resources from Christian theology might be of relevance and use to broader publics, those with little to no stake in Christian identity or community. If there is an apologetic burden of public theology, it is highly pragmatic, demonstrating the value of Christian theological and ethical resources to address public concerns in ways that are agreeable to and compelling for said publics. If there is a persuasive task for the public theologian, it is not to convince others of the truth and viability of the undergirding Christian message or world view; it is to convince others of the value and merit of the theologically informed proposal(s) to address whatever problem or challenge is under consideration.

Here, then, one possible outcome to be anticipated by the public theologian is the public's use of a particular public theological proposal while jettisoning

---

[1] Paul Tillich, *Theology of Culture* (New York: Oxford University Press, 1959); David Tracy, *The Analogical Imagination: Christian Theology and the Culture of Pluralism* (New York: Crossroad, 1981); Jürgen Moltmann, *God for a Secular Society: The Public Relevance of Theology* (London: SCM Press, 1999); Martin Marty, 'Reinhold Niebuhr: Public Theology and the American Experience', *Journal of Religion* 54, no. 4 (1974): 332–59.
[2] Joshua Furnal, 'Going Beyond Faith: Kierkegaard's Critical Contribution to Public Theology', *Studies in Christian Ethics* 32, no. 4 (2019): 527–40 (538).

or ignoring whatever scriptural or theological claims upon which the proposal is based. The public theologian should accept such application as in no way incoherent or incomplete and should not insist on the public's acceptance of all theological and potentially transcendent premises upon which a given proposal might draw. This is not accommodationist and need not be seen as an abdication of Christian truth or some sort of 'watered-down' version of theology. In fact, a compelling case can be made that Christian public theology has nothing of interest or value to offer unless it maintains some links to Christian tradition and its vast theological inheritance. Otherwise, it remains unclear what difference *theology* makes here.

Yet, recognizing that different forms of speech and different conversations can have various aims, public theology is one mode of speaking theologically, one whose validity criterion is the plausibility of its proposals for whatever public it addresses. The church may maintain its practice of calling non-believers to faith and repentance, for instance, but this evangelical orientation can coexist alongside and not supplant public theology. Otherwise, by insisting that the public accept a scriptural or theological basis for a project rather than the project itself, the church continues a long and troubling tradition of offering social aid at the price of conversion.[3]

If we are to claim a critically distinct category of communication moving from theological and ecclesial contexts out into spaces of unbelief or alternative belief, it strikes me that the 'public' qualifier makes openness crucial. As Chul Ho Youn writes, 'If theology wishes to take part in public discourse, it ought to defend its claim in a way understandable to non-believers as well and demonstrate its truth through its transforming power for the common good of a society.'[4] Simply using theology to speak to pressing issues in the broader public sphere, therefore, on its own, does not make something public theology. This is not to say that theology should not continue to articulate itself comprehensively in the public sphere; this is to say that what makes a particular set of proposals *public* theology is their capacity to be assessed and implemented by a diverse set of publics who need not hold to the undergirding set of theological or revelational premises.

In this sense, I agree with Christoph Hübenthal's assessment that the secular should be taken seriously on its own terms and that 'the basic rationale of the secular itself must serve as a principle when public theology undertakes its critical,

---

[3]One such result in missionary history was the creation of the so-called rice Christians, those who professed faith for the sake of access to food and other resources provided by missionaries. Typically, theological critique of this phenomenon is based on concern over the insincerity of conversion. My concern, rather, is based on the cruelty of such an approach to aid programmes.
[4]Chul Ho Youn, 'The Points and Tasks of Public Theology', *International Journal of Public Theology* 11 (2017): 64–87 (75).

ethical and orientating functions'.⁵ At the same time, as Hübenthal shows, this does not mean excluding theology from the analysis. Part of public theology's role is to highlight the theological justifications for the secular and to reveal to the secular its theological dimensions. Such an approach also disrupts easy binaries between the religious and secular to show their mutual imbrications.⁶ Public theology might avoid repeating such simplistic bifurcations, and, rather than presenting itself as a dispatch from sacred to profane, it can locate itself within a messy context that always already contains both.

Beyond this, I am also sympathetic to even more radical visions where public theology is conceived as a theological offering and self-giving, where theological commitments might relinquish themselves to a secular *telos*.⁷ In this sense, public theology's ends are immanent and can even be supportive of a secular sphere.⁸ Such support and self-relinquishing by theology mean that public theology can commit itself to what might be seen as arguably secular or pluralistic ends, ones that do not necessitate some form of praise or recognition of God or vindication of Christian identity but ends that include human flourishing broadly construed.⁹

In its engagement with the so-called public sphere, public theology need not be more accommodationist as opposed to prophetic or reformist as opposed to revolutionary, as it is sometimes characterized in various typologies.¹⁰ A public theology might advocate prophetic intervention and revolutionary change with regard to a particular issue. The test will be whether a public exists for which such claims and tactics are legible and deployable. To take models of deliberative democracy and public reason as only allowing for discursive procedures that make no significant changes to the system is to accept the worst caricatures of liberalism and the potentially entrenched structural violence of the status quo. To be sure, when one's audience includes those in power, protectors of the

---

⁵Christoph Hübenthal, 'The Theological Significance of the Secular', *Studies in Christian Ethics* 32, no. 4 (2019): 455–69 (468).
⁶Talal Asad, *Formations of the Secular: Christianity, Islam, Modernity* (Stanford: Stanford University Press, 2003).
⁷This is one way to interpret the direction taken by Bonhoeffer's speculations on 'worldly theology'. See Dietrich Bonhoeffer, *Letters and Papers from Prison*, trans. Eberhard Bethge (London: SCM Press, 1953). See also Philip Goodchild's invocation of Vanstone and Koyama in Philip Goodchild, 'Culture and Machine: Reframing Theology and Economics', *Modern Theology* 36, no. 2 (2020): 391–402, and my response in Devin Singh, 'Lamentable Theology: A Response', *Modern Theology* 36, no. 2 (2020): 409–19.
⁸I gesture towards principles for this in Devin Singh, 'Decolonial Options for a Fragile Secular', in *In the Image of Man: Race, Coloniality, and Philosophy of Religion*, ed. Yountae An and Eleanor Craig (Durham, NC: Duke University Press, 2021).
⁹Obviously, I would part ways with critics who might insist here that human flourishing must include recognition of the divine as defined by Christianity or other 'world religions'.
¹⁰Contra, for example, Sebastian C. H. Kim, *Theology in the Public Sphere* (London: SCM Press, 2011), 22–5.

status quo, the proposal may appear more reformist in nature. But one may also construct public theologies with those who are marginalized or whose social agency is otherwise limited and who may be opting for a dramatic change to their sociopolitical and economic context. Ultimately, there is nothing intrinsic within the commitment to publicness that demands reform over revolution.

Another critical element of public theology is its calling to address concrete concerns and offer specific solutions that can be implemented. Public theology bears the task of digging into the weeds of practical and policy matters, to show in detail how theological and ethical claims and criteria might have a bearing on a particular challenge. Public theology may certainly invoke doctrinally sophisticated, transcendent and abstract metaphysical notions, but remaining at such levels undercuts its responsibility for ensuring that non-theological publics can grasp the implications of its vision. This call for specificity and contextual responsiveness means that any given public theology need not be beholden to all publics at all times. The aspirations of some public theologies 'to engage in public discussions to shape universal values and ideas that may be generally accepted by all peoples' strikes me as a recipe for blandness and irrelevance.[11] Rather, articulations of public theology should not feel overburdened to address all possible audiences and scenarios.

While public theology has taken the form of general prescriptions, I am calling for the move to greater specificity, to wade into the risky world of making concrete recommendations. This means that public theologies assume the risks of more definite proposals. These include risks of error or of appearing wrong or foolish, or of quickly becoming irrelevant as history moves on and situations change. These are the risks of politics and policy, of making actual decisions and supporting certain directives and paths over others. These are the beautiful and noble risks of concrete life with actual people who have specific needs and discrete challenges. At the same time, public theology's attention to theological claims, principles and traditions should help resist captivity to the politics *de jour*.

Public theology can remain selective about which publics it seeks to address, departing from blanket proclamations in the proverbial 'marketplace of ideas' and instead seeking attentive consideration of the other(s) in question.[12] This partially addresses concerns raised by Joshua Furnal regarding the undue burden placed on public theologians to become 'geniuses', mastering the terms and knowledge necessary to dialogue with multiple publics in the quest for

---

[11]Youn, 'The Points and Tasks of Public Theology', 82. Youn is paraphrasing Max L. Stackhouse, *God and Globalization Volume 4: Globalization and Grace* (New York: Continuum, 2007), 78–9, 90.

[12]See the basis for this in Amy Daughton, '*Rerum Novarum*: Theological Reasoning for the Public Sphere?', *Studies in Christian Ethics* 32, no. 4 (2019): 513–26 (517).

universalism. As he rightly warns, 'it is impossible for the public theologian (or a talented set of theologically informed polyglots) to achieve the basic universalising aim of public theology'.[13] I would submit that it is not an unreasonable burden to require of the would-be public theologian the capacity to speak to at least some non-theological public(s). If a theologian is not able to establish dialogue with any other public besides fellow academic theologians, this theologian has fallen into a pitiable position. Yet, while the public theologian should be sufficiently conversant in some other non-theological context, this does not call for mastery of many, let alone all, publics. This is one trap of the universalizing thrust.

In the case of economics, where social challenges often reflect class conflicts and competing interests, public theologies may opt not to address all players involved, but be selective in their audiences for the sake of a particular programme of action. In this chapter's specific consideration of payday lending, I address the context of underserved and precarious communities who use payday lending services and those involved in policy and community intervention in terms of such services. I do not address bankers or lending organizations, although one might plausibly develop a public theology directed towards them as well. This does not mean, however, that other implicated players are wholly excluded from the analysis. A commitment to theological principles such as the common good means that the impact of a proposal on others must remain part of the consideration. Yet, while public theology writ large might eventually engage all conceivable publics, specific attempts to persuade a particular audience towards implementation need not include all potentially related parties.

22.3 PUBLIC THEOLOGY AND ECONOMICS

David Tracy famously contributed a tripartite analysis of the publics of theology: church, academy and society. He further differentiated the broad category of society into three subcategories: polity, culture and 'technoeconomic structure'.[14] Max Stackhouse, among others, has extended this analysis towards a special focus on the economy as a realm for ethical engagement in the public sphere.[15] In my view, economics and the economy are significant enough to deserve categorization as a major kind of public and a substantial assemblage of public concerns. It strikes me that the global experience of the economy today makes such a claim rather uncontroversial and in need of no defence. While the

---

[13] Furnal, 'Going Beyond Faith', 529.
[14] Tracy, *The Analogical Imagination*, 7.
[15] Stackhouse, *God and Globalization*.

ways one engages economic concerns certainly vary, it is rare to claim that the economy is not a primary public concern.

Such economic centrality is certainly due to globalization, which is Stackhouse's primary focus, but is also due to an earlier history of colonization. It is also a result of the longer historical process of economic 'disembedding', famously described by the economic historian Karl Polanyi.[16] In other words, one of the reasons why economic issues are pertinent to the lives of everyone is that the market has come to be construed as an abstract entity, conceptually distinct from the social relationships in which exchange functions. The irony of course is that despite its global reach, the market itself as an entity remains an abstraction and cannot be located in time and space. Around this market abstraction, discourses on analysing and managing the market have arisen, signalled by the early modern birth of political economy and economic science as fields of inquiry. Therefore, public theology's capacity to address something called the 'economy' and to dialogue with a field called 'economics' is bound up with the processes of disembedding and abstraction as much as with globalization.

This process of disembedding and creating an abstract, enclosed entity known as a private yet (somehow and paradoxically) free market is also the history of the enclosure movement and what has been termed primitive accumulation. Along with the genocidal pillage of native and enslaved peoples and of the earth and soil during colonization, the seventeenth and eighteenth centuries saw the decline of public and common lands in Europe, accessible to and useable by all, the erection of boundaries and walls to demarcate private property, the expulsion of serfs and peasantry from land access and the creation of exploited wage labourers who could return to work the land at a loss to themselves and gain to their employer.[17] Such privatizations also included new layers of policing and control of women's bodies as sites of reproductive power, as Silvia Federici's important work has shown.[18] Thus, when we enter into discussions about engaging something called the modern economy or market system, we must also bear in mind its very recent historical creation, a process and history that, as Marx put it, 'is written in the annals of [hu]mankind in letters of blood and fire'.[19] Public theologians' desires to address matters of 'the economy' as such do well to keep in mind the fraught political history of the construction of this public.

---

[16]Karl Polanyi, *The Great Transformation* (New York: Rinehart, 1944).
[17]Ibid.; Randal Joy Thompson, *Proleptic Leadership on the Commons: Ushering in a New Global Order* (Bingley, UK: Emerald, 2020).
[18]Silvia Federici, *Caliban and the Witch: Women, the Body, and Primitive Accumulation* (Brooklyn, NY: Autonomedia, 2004).
[19]Karl Marx, *Capital: A Critique of Political Economy*, trans. Ben Fowkes, vol. 1 (London: Penguin Books, 1976), 875.

Responsible public theology also requires genealogical awareness of the public role theology has played in the history of Western societies and of societies influenced by Western political and economic arrangements due to colonization and globalization. This role includes the centuries of direct influence by the church during Christendom, the presence of missionaries alongside colonial administrators during the age of global conquest and the continued implicit operation of theological assumptions and values in aspects of secular modernity. Public theology should also remain cognizant of the basic sociological fact that the church and theological reflection take place within society and culture and so remain affected by them. This means that public theology should not naively imagine itself communicating across a stark secular-sacred divide or position itself as speaking from a pure ecclesial space. It speaks from a theological location influenced by various publics, and it speaks to publics already to some extent influenced by theology.

In terms of economic matters, this means that the rich and complex history of development in economic attitudes, values and institutions in the West is implicated in and through Christian history as well. The West has long been shaped by diverse Christian preaching about the dangers of wealth, the responsibility towards the poor and vulnerable, the value of almsgiving, the evils of usury, the importance of work, the possibility that riches signal God's blessings, the virtues of capitalism or socialism and the like. Such societies have also been affected, more indirectly, by Christian theologizing about God's redemptive payment through Christ, humanity's ransom from death, indulgences to remit sin debt, monastic vows of poverty and other ecclesial practices that shaped public opinion on economics even without direct ethical exhortation on such topics. To enter the fray in the present and speak on economic issues in the mode of public theology is to enter a complex and fraught arena, where many theological voices and traces have long been at work. Such a baseline awareness calls for humility that proposals might offer micro-level suggestions on matters long discussed rather than groundbreaking visions of theological novelty and originality. While this might be seen as a minor point, issues of tone and the mode by which proposals are presented matter greatly for the sake of dialogue and intervention.

A variety of themes and doctrines from Christian scripture and tradition present themselves as potential sources for such reflection, so many that I refrain from any attempt to summarize them. Naturally, one's selection of themes and of scriptural and theological sources is conditioned by other factors. One's political affiliations and predilection towards particular economic arrangements shape how one might use scripture and tradition to engage the public. Rather than pretending otherwise, as if one could be 'purely biblical or theological', whatever that might mean, public theologians – as contextual theologians – should demonstrate self-reflexivity and transparency in terms of their social locations and commitments as they bear on the matter at hand.

22.4 THE CASE OF PAYDAY LENDING

Of the many potential economic themes or sectors for engagement, here I focus on one particular case: payday lending in a US context. My aims in these final sections are to provide a brief description of payday lending, explain some ethical concerns it raises and what socio-economic, political and theological problems it signals, reflect on possible theological topics as sources for engagement and advance a preliminary set of proposals to address the situation. While I attempt here the rudiments of a public theology applied concretely to a circumscribed issue and set of publics, the moves here will be preliminary and insufficient. I can only sketch a course for what a more in-depth analysis, proposal and project roadmap for engagement might look like. These brief sections, then, in no way live up to the demands I have placed on public theology.

Payday lending is a practice that has emerged to address the need for immediate cash among those living in financially precarious circumstances. In the United States, the practice emerged during the Great Depression, although may have been taking place informally long before this period.[20] Forms of short-term, high-cost lending have existed in every society for millennia. As the name suggests, payday lending allows an individual access to cash immediately, receiving a loan plus a fee to be paid off with a forthcoming paycheck. Borrowers most often use these payday loans to cover short-term living expenses such as food, rent, utilities and childcare. In exchange, they write a check to the lending agency for the full amount lent plus a fee, which amounts to interest on the loan. The payday lender will later cash the check on a specified date, presumably after the borrower has deposited their actual, forthcoming paycheck. The lender thus receives back the amount lent plus a premium. Such fees can vary and often range from 15 to 30 per cent and higher.

Payday lending is targeted at those who receive some form of wage, and who thus participate in the wage labour system to some degree. In other words, payday lending is not geared towards the fully precarious who have no source of predictable income – although informal lenders and loan sharks exist for such populations, to be sure. It is also geared towards those who have checking accounts, and therefore is not a service aimed at the unbanked, although payday lending storefronts are often combined with check cashing services for the unbanked.[21]

---

[20]See Jean Ann Fox, 'Unsafe and Unsound: Payday Lenders Hide Behind FDIC Bank Charters to Peddle Usury', *Consumer Federation of America (CFA)*. 30 March 2004. Cited in Michael A. Stegman, 'Payday Lending', *Journal of Economic Perspectives* 21, no. 1 (2007): 169–90.

[21]One study indicates the average and median income for families who utilized payday loans was $32,614 and $30,892, respectively. See Amanda Logan and Christian Weller, *Who Borrows From Payday Lenders?: An Analysis of Newly Available Data* (Center for American Progress, 2009), cdn.americanprogress.org/wp-content/uploads/issues/2009/03/pdf/payday_lending.pdf.

Public ethical concerns around payday lending centre on the high fees charged, which appear usurious and predatory. Long-term loans at such rates would be crippling. 'When the fee for a short-term payday loan is translated into an annual percentage rate (APR), the implied annual interest rate ranges between 400 and 1000 percent.'[22] The fact that they are small-scale fees and short-term loans renders them repayable, although analysts note that it is common for borrowers to roll previous loans into future ones, demonstrating their inability fully to repay an initial loan and their ongoing obligation to the lender, with mounting fees. Indeed, there are concerted marketing efforts within payday loan companies to persuade customers to roll their loans forward and perpetuate indebtedness. Sales agents are incentivized via commissions and bonuses to re-enroll borrowers. Always seeking to increase their profit margin, payday lenders have a financial stake in extending the indebtedness of those in need.

Another concern around payday lending is its racialization. Most payday lending takes place within African American communities, and Black families are disproportionately implicated in and affected by such short-term loans.[23] This raises questions about intentional predation on vulnerable communities in the form of economic racial profiling and raises concerns about underlying inequities that render such communities vulnerable to these practices. There is also evidence of a gender gap in lending, where women are targeted and responsible for a majority of loan requests.[24] Intersectional analysis reveals that it is women of colour who appear the most vulnerable to such lending practices and who reflect a disproportionate percentage of borrowers.

Many states have long had anti-usury laws on their books. One of the primary means of intervention has been to invoke such laws, which have been rarely enforced historically, to argue that payday lending is predatory and usurious. States have set limits on the fees lenders can charge, effectively reducing interest rates and capping the number of times borrowers can renew in order to limit the long-term compounding effects of such debts. Lenders are shrewd innovators, however, devising new lending schemes and terms that appear to abide by the letter of the law yet offer workarounds. Incorporated

---

[22]Stegman, 'Payday Lending', 170.
[23]See James R. Barth, Jitka Hilliard, and John S. Jahera Jr., 'Banks and Payday Lenders: Friends or Foes?', *International Advances in Economic Research* 21 (2015): 139–53. One study suggests that African Americans are 105 per cent more likely to use payday loans than are people of other ethnicities and races. See S. Ilan Guedj, 'Report Reviewing Research on Payday, Vehicle Title, and High-Cost Installment Loans', *Bates White Economic Consulting White Paper*, 14 May 2019, https://lawyerscommittee.org/wp-content/uploads/2019/05/Report-reviewing-research-on-payday-vehicle-title-and-high-cost-installment-loans.pdf.
[24]Amy Schmitz, 'The Gender Divide in Payday Lending', *Credit Slips*, 15 October 2012, https://www.creditslips.org/creditslips/2012/10/the-gender-divide-in-payday-lending.html

national chains have also thus far been allowed to abide by the rules of the state in which they are incorporated even while doing business in other states. The popular practice of incorporating in Delaware or North Dakota reflects such states' lax lending laws, enabling banks and payday lenders to extend such practices elsewhere in the United States.

Furthermore, much payday lending is now transcending various state regulations against usurious rates through the internet. Here, technologically mediated distance allows further buffer from regulations of predatory lending, allowing lenders to seek harbour in the complexity of laws governing internet marketing and taking advantage of needy borrowers despite local regulations. Regulating payday lending on the internet is new territory to which states have been slow to respond. Any analysis of this and other pressing economic problems cannot neglect the central role that digital technologies have come to play in complicating the power of economic technologies. While coins were a radical technological innovation 2,500 years ago that we are still struggling to comprehend, the recent innovations in digital currencies and cryptocurrencies add new layers of complexity that require analysis. Fin-tech innovations include peer-to-peer lending and other digital cash applications that make contracting loans much easier. While this reduces the barriers to entry and thus increases the likelihood of borrowing, it may also introduce competition and drive down the cost of such loans.

Despite the understandable concerns around the high fees associated with payday lending, some observers claim a high repayment and low default rate among borrowers, as well as the apparently low negative economic impact of such borrowing. One study suggests a strong correlation between usage of payday lending and barriers to other forms of credit, indicating a real role played by such lenders in providing liquidity to cash-strapped borrows. The same study shows little negative impact on borrowers' already low credit scores through the use of payday loans.[25] Other studies appear to corroborate the low detrimental impact of such lending by showing little improvement in credit scores in states that banned or severely limited payday lending.[26]

My current interpretation of such studies showing the low negative impact of payday lending is not that payday lending is necessarily good or harmless, but that it is not much worse than the already bad options available in the United States for the economically vulnerable. While states, policymakers and community organizations should make every effort to prevent predatory rates,

---

[25]Neil Bhutta, Paige Marta Skiba, and Jeremy Tobacman, 'Payday Loan Choices and Consequences', *Journal of Money, Credit and Banking* 47, no. 2–3 (2015): 223–60.
[26]Chintal A. Desaia and Gregory Elliehausen, 'The Effect of State Bans of Payday Lending on Consumer Credit Delinquencies', *The Quarterly Review of Economics and Finance* 74 (2017): 94–117.

it is clear that underlying conditions that create the need for such short-term lending need to be addressed. Banning or remediating payday lending rates appears to address symptoms, and even risks harming the vulnerable who may have no other recourse to cash or credit in precarious situations. Rather than eliminating access to such funds, efforts should be made both to ensure such funding is fair and non-exploitative and to reduce the need for the vulnerable to depend on such resources. Theological and ethical interventions might address ways to provide cheaper and more supportive cash and credit to the needy but must also take on more fundamental social inequities that create the need for lending and borrowing for the basics of life in the first place.

One of the structural inequities and gaps into which payday lending steps is the delay and deferral of payment that is built into most wage systems. When a labourer begins working for an employer, the labourer must weather a span of time before he or she is paid. Aside from day labourers who are (hopefully) paid at the end of the workday, for many employees a pay period is two weeks or a month. The labourer begins in a state of deficit and remains so until payment. As labour historian Michael Denning notes, labour power 'is one of the few commodities that is consumed before it is paid for. With most commodities, one pays and then enjoys'.[27] This means that a labourer offers labour value to the employer and the employer is in debt to the labourer until the labour is paid for. Yet the employer enjoys an interest-free loan of labour from the worker, and it is the worker who suffers the debt. Such a relation is always masked and never acknowledged.

To add to this subtle exploitation of delayed payment for labour time, it is typically understood (even if often forgotten) that the wage provided by the employer is not simply recompense for labour. It is directed towards the reproduction of the labouring class, to the activities of rest and recuperation outside of work that enable the labourer to return the next day. The employer is paying not only for labour time but for the energy and effort required to restore and renew living labour. Without the wage, a worker gives his or her labour power freely and must find other means to subsist until payday. As Denning observes, tellingly, 'Everyday we make an interest-free loan of our labor power to our employers. And, short of cash, we are forced to take out interest-bearing loans to cover the "revolving" costs of eating and dressing and living, as well as the long-term costs of housing, commuting, procreating and schooling.'[28]

Payday lending can be seen as a stop-gap measure, cropping up to address a real need, but doing so in a way that exploits and often exacerbates that need.

---

[27]Michael Denning, 'The Fetishism of Debt', *Social Text: Online*, 2011, https://socialtextjournal.org/periscope_article/the_fetishism_of_debt/.
[28]Ibid.

Lending emerges as a possibility in conditions of inequality. Whereas lending could conceivably be ameliorative, seeking to provide actual help and employ generous rates and terms of repayment that allow a debtor to get back on their feet and thereby reduce inequality, lending typically takes forms of extraction and expropriation where additional capital or labour power are drawn out of the worker to attempt to repay the loan. Predatory lending serves to increase rather than close the gap between creditor and debtor classes.

22.5 PUBLIC THEOLOGY AND PAYDAY LENDING

When addressing matters of debt theologically, it is important to note the long history of interaction between debt economies and Christian thought. Such interaction includes both the ways debt has shaped theological claims and influenced the theological imagination, and the ways ethical reflection has centred on debt as a consistent problematic and has shaped social practice in response. Christianity's ancient roots in Judaism make use of debt metaphors for sin and spiritual guilt in the Hebrew scriptures, part of the heritage of Persian exile as well as broader ancient Near Eastern reflection on debt relations.[29] Such contexts also convey the language of debt cancellation, a practice of ancient Near Eastern emperors to rebalance economic inequality. Imperial language of debt remission was ascribed in early Israelite thought to God as the regent who required that the covenantal people carry out such traditions to benefit the needy and vulnerable among them.[30] Christian theological heritage includes the influence of Greco-Roman legal institutions around property and restitution, which came to shape assumptions of debt slavery and release, for instance, terms also incorporated into scripture. Debt bondage becomes inscribed into Christian thought to portray a state of bondage to sin, death and the devil, out of which Christ provides redemption.[31] Such logic arguably informs soteriological notions of satisfaction as well, where release from the sin debt humanity owed to God is paid by the perfectly obedient Christ.[32]

In addition to these significant but understudied economic logics to many doctrinal formulations in Christianity, we have the more well-known history of

---

[29]Gary A. Anderson, *Sin: A History* (New Haven: Yale University Press, 2009).
[30]Gregory Chirichigno, *Debt-Slavery in Israel and the Ancient Near East* (Sheffield: JSOT Press, 1993); Devin Singh, 'Debt Cancellation as Sovereign Crisis Management', *Cosmologics*, 18 Jan 2016.
[31]Devin Singh, *Divine Currency: The Theological Power of Money in the West* (Stanford: Stanford University Press, 2018); Devin Singh, 'Sovereign Debt', *Journal of Religious Ethics* 46, no. 2 (2018): 239–66.
[32]Bruce Marshall, 'Debt, Punishment, and Payment: A Meditation on the Cross, in Light of St. Anselm', *Nova et Vetera* 9, no. 1 (2011): 163–81; Hollis Phelps, 'Overcoming Redemption: Neoliberalism, Atonement, and the Logic of Debt', *Political Theology* 17, no. 3 (2016): 264–82.

explicit ethical reflection on and exhortation concerning the ethics of lending. Patristic authors warned of the dangers of wealth and greed and called for generosity towards the needy. Basil the Great and Gregory of Nyssa challenged wealthy lenders in their congregations to convert their loans into gifts, with the understanding that they were either to be repaid interest-free or at times not repaid at all.[33] The justification here was that one's loan would be repaid by God in eternity.[34]

The Middle Ages saw much innovation around usury prohibitions, including scholastic parsing of the variations on loans, the time value of money and nature of financial labour. Beyond the moral condemnation of usury as harming the poor as found in earlier patristic texts, medieval churchmen invoked usury as a theft of time, which belongs to God, as well as a form of sloth, since money was gained without direct labour. Aristotelian condemnations of the unnaturalness of money reproducing itself also informed scholastic reflection on the perversities of interest.[35] Such condemnations also converged with the problematic treatment of Jews within Europe and antisemitic codes that excluded Jews from many professions while opening up financial trades as permissible. Jewish moneylenders occupied a marginal and liminal position in society, at once scorned and vilified for their dealings while preserved as necessary for a society always in need of liquid capital.

To tell the story of debt in the Middle Ages as simply one of prohibition is incorrect, however. Lending relations were rethought on a variety of lines: accommodations for the labour of lending – and, hence, charging a fee that was defined not as interest but as wage; provisions for a natural rate of interest that was determined to be socially and morally acceptable by natural law; joint venture agreements for profit sharing and shared risk between lender and borrower and so on. Beyond redefining relations, scholastics contributed to new forms of lending, including the category of public borrowing by the prince that prepared the way for the modern, debt-funded nation state.[36] Monastic

---

[33]Brenda Llewellyn Ihssen, 'Basil and Gregory's Sermons on Usury: Credit Where Credit Is Due', *Journal of Early Christian Studies* 16, no. 3 (2008): 403–30.
[34]Gary A. Anderson, *Charity: The Place of the Poor in the Biblical Tradition* (New Haven: Yale University Press, 2013); Peter Brown, *The Ransom of the Soul: Afterlife and Wealth in Early Eastern Christianity* (Cambridge: Harvard University Press, 2015).
[35]Jacques Le Goff, *Your Money or Your Life: Economy and Religion in the Middle Ages*, trans. Patricia Ranum (New York: Zone Books, 1998); Joel Kaye, *A History of Balance, 1250–1375: The Emergence of a New Model of Equilibrium and its Impact on Medieval Thought* (New York: Cambridge University Press, 2014).
[36]Odd Langholm, *Economics in the Medieval Schools: Wealth, Exchange, Value, Money and Usury according to the Paris Theological Tradition, 1200–1350* (Leiden: Brill, 1992); Giacomo Todeschini, 'Usury in Christian Middle Ages. A Reconsideration of the Historiographical Tradition (1949–2010)', in *Religione e instituzioni religiose nell'economia Europea. 1000–1800*, ed. Francesco Ammannati (Firenze: Firenze University Press, 2012); Berndt Hamm, '"Buying Heaven": The

thinkers also invented the concept of the mortgage. The church engaged in moneylending as well, in ways that masked interest or sought compensation through the price of the loan.

Protestant Reformers provided further innovations, making new allowances for reasonable rates of interest, and sometimes following or explicitly rejecting the example of their Catholic forebears. Eventual secular defences of usury, such as, most famously, Jeremy Bentham's, take as one of their starting points a theologically determined notion of just price or natural rate of interest.[37] Even while Bentham rejects such scholastic claims, in such oppositions he encodes theology as his dialectical counterpoint, meaning theological traces bear examination even in secular arenas of economic reflection.

While space precludes a detailed exposition, any number of directions might be taken for a public theology of payday lending: reflection on ancient usury restrictions to retrieve the spirit of the law and not simply its letter, which is easily circumvented; ecclesiologically informed models of lending communities prioritizing care and the preferential option for the poor and vulnerable; theologically informed political organizing to increase public benefits and spending to eliminate the need for private borrowing; wage and labour reform drawing on vast Christian social teaching that reduces the need for borrowing; and total denouncement of debt or more pragmatic and realistic distinctions between safer and more predatory loans.[38] Such initiatives would be deployed at a local level through policy interventions, organizational charters, protests and teach-ins, election campaigns and various other moves to make concrete institutional progress and transform the economic environment.

Coupled with rich theological resources is an ethical commitment to connection, presence and observation of a particular context where payday lending appears to be a community concern. A key theme that emerges in scriptural reflection on debt and appears relevant is the issue of relational distance and the communal impact of lending. One is more prone to lend to and exploit an other who appears relationally distant, and one feels more

---

Prospects of Commercialized Salvation in the Fourteenth to Sixteenth Centuries', in *Money as God? The Monetization of the Market and its Impact on Religion, Politics, Law, and Ethics*, ed. Jürgen von Hagen and Michael Welker (Cambridge, UK: Cambridge University Press, 2014).

[37]Jeremy Bentham, 'Defence of Usury', http://www.econlib.org/library/Bentham/bnthUs1.html (Library of Economics and Liberty, 1818). See the discussion in Ilsup Ahn, *Just Debt: Theology, Ethics, and Neoliberalism* (Waco, TX: Baylor University Press, 2017).

[38]Examples of this latter tension are seen in Kathryn Tanner's depiction of the total incompatibility of debt relations with Christian identity, on the one hand, and Ilsup Ahn's provisions for less destructive forms of lending which stem from necessity, on the other. See Kathryn Tanner, *Christianity and the New Spirit of Capitalism* (New Haven: Yale University Press, 2019); Ahn, *Just Debt*.

accountable to one's own, however defined.[39] Such proximities were reflected in ancient Near Eastern prohibitions about lending within one's community.[40] Such exchanges, if made at all, were to be offered as gifts or as interest-free loans. One of the themes here pertains to lenders and borrowers directly knowing each other. Relational bonds should be maintained; debt should not corrode connection to neighbour; and agreements should be made between persons and not faceless organizations.

The importance of maintaining community bonds and avoiding relational distance reveals why racialization and segregated communities amplify the exploitative power of debt. Predatory lending occurs across racial lines because perceived racial others are not seen as part of the community. More favourable rates are offered to those from within one's community akin to preferential treatment for one's family members. While the dichotomy is overplayed, the contrast between gifts within the family and monetary relations outside the domestic sphere is at least a template to engage, to consider whether generous familial gift relations can be extended to one's community inclusively, such that forms of lending remain flexible, generous and open to various types of reciprocal return beyond extraction of interest.

Policies or organizational criteria for lending might include attention to the details of one's neighbours' existence and needs. Money is to be lent within the community, for the good of the community. This prevents capital flight and ensures reinvestment and sustainability.[41] There is a broader return one receives if the money lent stays close by and helps elevate those nearby. Even if a lender is not recouping as much back through interest or fees, or even if they incur periodic losses, ideally the money is spent in ways that aid community members, meaning it returns to build up the community. The benefits of lending to others within the community come back to the lender in myriad ways beyond extractive interest or the return of principal. Such proposals can be informed by theological concerns of neighbourliness, community care, notions of value that exceed the balance sheet and senses of profit that go beyond financials.

---

[39] Such concerns relate to covenantal relations that respect the freedom and independence of the other with whom one enters into communally supported agreements of mutual care. See Marcia Pally, *Commonwealth and Covenant: Economics, Politics, and Theologies of Relationality* (Grand Rapids, MI: Eerdmans, 2016); Timothy Gorringe, 'Can Bankers be Saved?', *Studies in Christian Ethics* 14, no. 1 (2001): 17–33.

[40] Roland Boer, 'Reconsidering Debt Remission in Light of the Ancient World', *Continental Thought and Theory* 1, no. 2 (2017): 292–305; Chirichigno, *Debt Slavery*.

[41] The Community Reinvestment Act (1977) attempted to address capital flight by requiring banks to lend a proportion of their funds to underserved communities, but it has been far from perfect. There are numerous loopholes and negative incentives, and it applies to banks but excludes other potential lending institutions. The law could be refined, improved and expanded, however, to address some of the concerns raised here.

In addition to credit unions as obvious alternatives to predatory lenders as well as to corporate banks that appear unconcerned for the needy individual, alternative forms of lending pools might be established within community lending groups, churches and other non-profit organizations to steward funds and mediate lending and borrowing. It is known that subprime lenders exploited pastoral relations with at-risk communities in order to offer predatory loans in the run-up to the 2008 financial crisis.[42] These same communal networks could be used to offer helpful and supportive financing.

Additionally, the emergence of technological platforms that enable peer-to-peer lending creates possibilities as well as new perils to navigate. Recalling Tracy's subcategory of 'technoeconomic structure' as a relevant public for theology to engage, we are reminded of the ways technology and economy remain integrated.[43] Economic innovations are typically also technological innovations, just as technological innovations are for the sake of economy, broadly construed. In the case of community lending, technology must be used to facilitate local connection rather than enable exploitation at a distance. There are a variety of ways that one might find access to cash and credit at competitive rates that are below the exorbitant fees charged by corporate lenders. Again, proximity and personalization are assets here and lending organizations that are located within and accountable to these communities in need should be prioritized.

The widespread practice of granting easy or low-interest credit to low-risk borrowers who already demonstrate financial strength, while applying punitively high interest rates to risky borrowers who are in need, is precisely the opposite of what should be the case. It makes little sense ethically to extract more from already precarious borrowers and force a higher payback from them when they are already at higher risk for default. Why not offer lower interest rates to at-risk borrowers to ensure a higher likelihood of repayment and save the higher rates for speculative investments offered to financially strong borrowers looking for capital to fund new ventures?

Indeed, the dichotomy between consumptive loans to address life needs and productive loans to generate further capital through entrepreneurial adventures should be maintained and should impact the terms of lending. In the case of payday lending, with its consumptive loans to help precarious borrowers get by, the terms should be favourable and aimed to maximize the chances of repayment and not entrap them in further obligations through high rates and rollovers. A theologically informed ethic of care and preference for the poor

---

[42] Hanna Rosin, 'Did Christianity Cause the Crash?', *The Atlantic*, Dec 2009, https://www.theatlantic.com/magazine/archive/2009/12/did-christianity-cause-the-crash/307764/
[43] Tracy, *The Analogical Imagination*.

could merge well here and support a proposal that would also serve the public good.

The steps that remain to actualize this chapter's insights into an actual public theology of payday lending require selection of a particular community or set of communities with a common set of concerns. It would entail a close study of the policy and infrastructural dynamics involved, as well as direct interface, interviews and relationship building with the various agents, from borrowers to lenders to community leaders and activists. It would include involvement in church or other spiritually informed groups that might have relational ties and a relative bearing on the challenges at hand. It would involve extensive dialogue, humble listening and reflecting back to the community the needs and concerns being heard. Finally, of course, it would involve dialogical examination of the theological resources that might shed light on and offer practical solutions. Such solutions would be accessible and understandable to the community and able to be considered, appropriated or rejected, and concretely enacted. In such ways the actual publicness of the theology would manifest.

CHAPTER 23

Ecological theology as a public theology

HILDA P. KOSTER

23.1 INTRODUCTION

In an age of climate disaster ecological and environmental concerns are among the most pressing public issues facing humankind. Indeed, the very possibility of planetary flourishing depends on whether we, as a global community, will be able to respond adequately to the challenge anthropogenic climate change poses to our life together on this fragile planet. Ecological theologians, church leaders and ecumenical ecclesial bodies such as the World Council of Churches have urged Christians, politicians and all people of good will to take the ecological limits of our planet with utmost seriousness. They persistently advocate a sustainable energy policy that does justice to those who are least responsible but are carrying the burden of climate change. Pope Francis's encyclical *Laudato si': On Care for our Common Home* (2015) has been the most prominent ecclesial voice to date and, one could argue, a primary example of an effective public theology.[1]

This chapter argues that as a form of public theology, ecological theology stands to gain from public theology's understanding of the task of theology as a *public* discourse. Whereas public theology and ecological theology are

---

[1] Pope Francis, *Laudato si': On Care for Our Common Home* (Huntington, IN: Our Sunday Visitor, 2015).

two different movements within contemporary theology that historically originated in different concerns, their trajectories overlap in some interesting ways. Both theologies emerged in the 1970s as a corrective response to what they identified as fundamental deficiencies in (modern) Christianity. Public theology sought to correct the inward-focused nature of much modern theology, which made theology a parochial discourse accessible only to those in the church or the discipline of academic theology.[2] Ecological theology, on the other hand, was a critique of Christian theology's anthropocentric, individualistic and otherworldly orientation. Both movements are deeply concerned with issues related to the common good, that is, the well-being of the society at large, and seek to offer a Christian critique of cultural patterns and habits that undermine the conditions for our shared life. Furthermore, public theology and ecological theology have grown into global movements and, hence, reflect a growing global awareness while sensitive to context and differences. And whereas both movements received their originating impulse from within North Atlantic liberal Protestant theology, they have become richly ecumenical and increasingly multi-religious in outlook.

In addition to these common features, public and ecological theology share connections to a wide variety of theological approaches and schools, including political and liberation theology, Catholic social thought, intersectional feminist and Black theology, and process theology. Hence, they are not easily defined as distinct schools of theology. Ecological theology especially is far too diverse methodologically to be properly called a theological school. The South African eco-theologian Ernst Conradie, who has made a significant contribution to mapping the terrain of ecological theology, therefore prefers to speak of 'the journey of doing eco-theology'.[3] Similarly, as the movement of public theology has accelerated over the past decades, it too has seen the definitions of what counts as public theology proliferate. The most generally agreed-upon definition of public theology to date has been articulated by E. Harold Brietenberg Jr., who, in a much-quoted essay 'To Tell the Truth: Will the Real Public Theology Please Stand Up?', defines public theology as 'theological informed public discourse about public issues, addressed to the church, synagogue, mosque, temple or other religious body, as well as the

---

[2]Linell E. Cady, 'Public Theology and the Postsecular Turn', *International Journal of Public Theology* 8 (2014): 292–312 (294).
[3]Ernst M. Conradie, 'The Journey of Doing Christian Ecotheology: A Collective Mapping of the Terrain', *Theology* 116, no. 1 (2013): 4–17 (11). See also, Ernst M. Conradie, Sigurd Bergmann, Celia Deane-Drummond, and Denis Edwards, eds, *Christian Faith and the Earth: Current Paths and Emergent Horizons in Ecotheology* (London: Bloomsbury, 2014). This publication resulted from the five year-long international research project 'Christian Faith and the Earth' (2007–12), which was coordinated by Ernst M. Conradie.

larger public or publics, argued in ways that can be evaluated and judged by publicly available warrants and criteria'.[4] Arguably, this definition sketches more of an umbrella for various ways of doing theology publicly than it demarcates a detailed methodology. Yet it is precisely because public theology ultimately is a nomenclature for a broad range of theologies concerned with the common good that it allows for ecological theology to be interpreted as a public theology of sorts.

In what follows I will first sketch part of the 'journey' of ecological theology. My sketch is not meant as a comprehensive overview of the development of ecological theology but rather brings into focus what I call 'the public turn' in ecological theology. I argue that ecological theology becomes public discourse, and, hence, can be described as a form of public theology, when it takes up a concern with ecological and climate justice.[5] The second part of this chapter further fleshes out this reading of ecological theology as public theology by putting it in conversation with South Africa's *Kairos* theology. Itself an example of public theology, *Kairos* theology developed in resisting South Africa's state theology that supported the South African apartheid ideology.[6] I argue that this makes it an important resource for an eco-justice theology as it confronts deep divisions within Christianity's response to climate change – divisions that became especially pronounced during the years of the Trump administration in the United States. As environmental theologian Willis Jenkins observes, '[w]hereas only a decade before WUSE (White US Evangelical) leaders supported some action on climate change, by 2016 the WUSE faction had turned hostile towards any form of political attention to climate change and began enlisting theology to depict the very idea of climate relations as inimical to Christianity'.[7] An eco-justice theology wants to be articulate about its task as a public theology vis-à-vis these 'wrong kinds' of public theological discourse, especially in the North Atlantic context.

---

[4]E. Harold Brietenberg Jr., 'To Tell the Truth: Will the Real Public Theology Please Stand Up', *Journal of the Society of Christian Ethics* 23, no. 2 (2003): 55–96 (66).
[5]For my analysis of the shift towards eco-justice I rely on the excellent analysis of the early development of ecological theology by Roger S. Gottlieb. Cf. Roger S. Gottlieb, *A Greener Faith: Religious Environmentalism and Our Planet's Future* (Oxford: Oxford University Press, 2006), Chapter 1.
[6]For the insight that public theology was shaped in part by resisting the so-called 'wrong kinds of public theologies', such as the theologies supporting the Nazi ideology in Germany in the 1930s and South African apartheid theology in the mid-twentieth century, see Cady, 'Public Theology and the Postsecular Turn', 292–312 (295).
[7]Willis Jenkins, 'Working with Politics', in *T&T Clark Handbook of Christian Theology and Climate Change*, ed. Ernst M. Conradie and Hilda P. Koster (London: Bloomsbury, 2020), 70–82 (71).

23.2 THE PUBLIC TURN IN ECOLOGICAL THEOLOGY

From the outset the aim of ecological theology has been twofold: to articulate an adequate theological response to the growing ecological crisis and to redress the anthropocentric, individualistic and otherworldly orientation of most (modern) Christian theology. The latter critique has been famously levelled at Christianity by historian Lynn White Jr., who in his 1967 article 'The Historical Roots of Our Ecological Crisis' blamed Western Christianity for the utilitarian posture towards the non-human world that, in tandem with technological prowess, has led to our current predicament.[8] Most notably, White accused Judaism and Christianity for 'descacralizing nature'. Once the world is viewed as the product of a transcendent sky God, White wrote, once holiness is removed from our surroundings and transferred without residue to their source, the way is paved for using those surroundings any way we wish. God's command to Adam in Gen. 1.28 – fill and subdue the earth – becomes a religious licence for humans to dominate, to exploit and (whether this was intended or not) to ruin.[9] White did insist that 'more science and more technology are not going to get us out of the present ecological crisis until we find a new religion or rethink our old one'.[10]

Whereas ecological theology should not be reduced to a response to White's thesis, White's essay played an important catalysing role in the 'greening' of theology. Another originating moment was John B. Cobb's Jr. publication *Is It Too Late? A Theology of Ecology* (1971). Drawing on the process thought of Alfred North Whitehead (1861–1947), Cobb criticized Christian theology's narrow concern with human salvation and its emphasis on God's transcendence at the expense of divine immanence.[11] Cobb argued that Christian theology should take nature, or the more-than-human world, as the context for doing theology. Whereas Cobb's little book marked the start of ecological theology as a theological movement, ecological theology

---

[8] Lynn White, Jr., 'The Historical Roots of Our Ecological Crisis', *Science* 155, no. 3767 (1967): 1203–7.
[9] Ibid., 8–9.
[10] Ibid., 10. White went on to propose we retrieve the life and work of St. Francis of Assisi, who he called 'the greatest radical in Christian history, since Christ'. While this is may be an overstatement, it is without doubt very significant that the current Pope took on the name of Pope Francis after St. Francis of Assisi.
[11] John B. Cobb Jr., *Is It Too Late? A Theology of Ecology* (Minneapolis: Fortress Press, 2021, original edition 1971). Cobb initiated many interdisciplinary conversations in theology and ecology. For his work on biological sciences see Charles Birch and John B. Cobb Jr., *The Liberation of Life: From the Cell to the Community* (Cambridge: Cambridge University Press, 1982). For his visionary work on economics see John B. Cobb Jr. and Herman E. Daly, *For the Common Good: Redirecting the Economy toward Community, the Environment, and a Sustainable Future* (Beacon Press, 1994; original edition 1989).

became much more prominent in the 1980s with Jürgen Moltmann's *God in Creation* (1985), Sallie McFague's *Models of God* (1987) and Thomas Berry's *The Dream of the Earth* (1988).[12] Building on these trailblazing publications, ecological theology accelerated in the 1990s with the work of theologians such as Calvin DeWitt, Jay McDaniel, Leonardo Boff, Ivone Gebara, Denis Edwards, Catherine Keller and many others.[13]

It is important to note that not all ecological theology has been equally amenable to White's assessment of Christianity's role vis-à-vis the environmental crisis. Moltmann, for instance, rejected the idea that Christianity is to blame for our ecological predicament. While Moltmann conceded that modern theology detached God from the natural world and was narrowly concerned with human salvation, he feels that Christianity, and especially biblical creation theology, offers significant resources to correct these tendencies and could become a resource for countering the utilitarian attitude towards the more-than-human world. To this end, Moltmann's *God in Creation* proposed a *panentheistic* theology of creation that envisions God's creative and sustaining presence in creation as Spirit. In her book *Models of God*, Sallie McFague (1933–2019) offered a feminist analysis of the connection between patriarchal language for God and the abuse of the earth and the oppression of women. Yet while her work was fiercely critical of Christianity's hierarchal dualism that detaches the divine from embodied, physical existence, she, too, set out to green Christian theology by retrieving 'older' notions for God's relationship to the world. Her seminal book *The Body of God: An Ecological Theology* (1993) went back to the long-lost 'organic' tradition in Christianity, which saw the church as the body of Christ. Extending the scope of this tradition, McFague proposed that we envision the world as God's body and think of God as the Spirit animating this body. And while she argued in favour of the holiness of the earth, this notion was derived from the doctrine of the incarnation: if God can become

---

[12]Jürgen Moltmann, *God in Creation: A New Theology of Creation and The Spirit of God*, trans. Margaret Kohl (Minneapolis: Fortress Press, 1993, original edition 1985); Sallie McFague, *Models of God: Theology for a Nuclear Age* (Minneapolis: Fortress Press, 1987); Sallie McFague, *The Body of God: An Ecological Theology* (Minneapolis: Fortress Press, 1993); Thomas Berry, *The Dream of the Earth* (Berkeley: Counter Point, 2015; original edition 1988).
[13]Calvin DeWitt, *Earth-Wise: A Biblical Response to Environmental Issues* (Grand Rapids: CRC Publications, 1994); Jay McDaniel, *With Roots and Wings: Christianity in an Age of Ecology and Dialogue* (Maryknoll: Orbis Books, 1995), Denis Edwards, *Jesus the Wisdom of God* (Maryknoll: Orbis Books, 1995); McFague, *The Body of God*; Leonardo Boff, *Cry of the Earth; Cry of the Poor* (Ecology & Justice) (Maryknoll: Orbis Books, 1997; original edition 1995); Ivone Gebara, *Longing for Running Water: Ecofeminism and Liberation*, trans. David Molineaux (Minneapolis: Fortress Press, 1999); Catherine Keller, *Apocalypse: Now and Then: A Feminist Guide to the End of the World* (Minneapolis: Fortress Press, 1996) and *Face of the Deep: A Theology of Becoming* (London: Routledge, 2003).

flesh, there is no reason that flesh – and by extension all of life – cannot become Godly.[14]

Finally, the distinct contribution of the Catholic priest and scholar of religion Thomas Berry (1914–2009) needs mentioning. Influenced by the work of the palaeontologist and theologian Teilhard de Chardin, Berry argued in favour of a new universe story for theology, a story primarily rooted not in the poetry of Genesis but in the reigning scientific account of cosmic and biological evolution.[15] This story, Berry believed, reveals that the universe *itself* is the primary mode of God's presence. Yet whereas Berry sought to engender awe and wonder for the mystery of nature and the cosmos by investing theology with a scientific understanding of nature, he agreed with White that from the perspective of the ecological crisis, science was as much in need of religion as religion was in need of science. The reigning scientific mode of knowing too often objectifies the world, losing the ability not only to express awe and wonder but also to see and 'be concerned with the integral functioning of the earth community'.[16] Berry's work also originated the field of religion and ecology, which is associated with the work of Yale scholars of religion John Grimm and Mary Evelyn Tucker, who are the founding directors of the Yale Forum of Religion and Ecology.[17] Tucker and Grimm organized a series of conferences at the Harvard Center for the Study of World Religions (1996–8), which led to the subsequent publication of the multi-volume book series *Religions of the World and Ecology* (Harvard University Press). Whereas the Harvard conferences and the subsequent book series agreed that religions have often been ambiguous when it comes to valuing the more-than-human-world, the overriding premise was a positive one, namely that the world religions are tremendous resources for addressing the ecological crisis.[18]

---

[14]McFague, *The Body of God*, 191–3. See also Anne M. Clifford, *Introducing Feminist Theology* (Maryknoll: Orbis Books, 2001), 235–8.
[15]For an account of Thomas Berry's life and work see Mary Evelyn Tucker, John Grimm and Andrew Angyal, *Thomas Berry: A Biography* (New York: Columbia University Press, 2019); Heather Eaton, ed., *The Intellectual Journey of Thomas Berry; Imagining the Earth Community* (Lanham, MD: Lexington Books, 2014).
[16]Berry, *The Dream of the Earth*, 13.
[17]For an overview of the field of Religion and Ecology, see John Grim and Mary Evelyn Tucker, *Ecology and Religion* (Island Press, 2014). Other institutes and networks inspired by the work of Thomas Berry are the Elliott Allen Institute for Theology and Ecology (EAITE) at the University of St. Michael's College in the University of Toronto (Canada), the Thomas Berry Forum for Ecological Dialogue at Iona College (New Rochelle, NY) and the Thomas Berry foundation (thomasberry.org).
[18]The Harvard project identified 'seven common values that the world religions hold in relation to the natural world: reverence, respect, reciprocity, restraint, redistribution, responsibility and restoration'. According to Tucker and Grimm, the task at hand is to retrieve and expand on these values, including the various ways they are interpreted within and between religious traditions.

23.2.1 The public turn to eco-justice

In tandem with the burgeoning field of religion and ecology, ecological theology in the 1990s continued the efforts of the eco-theological pioneers to green Christian theology. This period also saw a turn away from retrieving creation theology and cosmology towards a concern with the way ecological degradation disproportionally affects poor and marginalized communities, and especially communities of colour.[19] Rosemary Ruether's *Gaia and God: An Eco-Feminist Theology of Liberation* (1992) illustrates this turn to ecological justice. Her eco-feminist analysis insists that a healed relation with the earth 'demands that we must speak of eco-justice, and not simply of domination of the earth as though that happened unrelated to social domination'.[20] Indeed, Ruether recommends nothing less than a social reordering to bring about 'just and loving interrelationship between men and women, between races and nations, between groups presently stratified into social classes, manifest in great disparities of access to the means of life'.[21] Additional publications marking the turn towards ecological justice were Leonardo Boff's *Cry of the Earth, Cry of the Poor* (1997) and eco-feminist theologian Ivone Gebara's *Longing for Running Water* (1999). Both these Latin American liberation theologians adopted the new cosmology of Thomas Berry yet proposed a more integrative approach to ecology, namely, one that addressed both the plight of the earth and the struggle of the poor for survival and a dignified life. Their work thus shifted the attention of ecological theology from a concern with the protection of wilderness and biodiversity to a concern with toxic waste, lack of clean drinking water and environmental health. More recently, Catholic eco-theologian Daniel Castillo has pushed the analyses of Boff and Gebara even further away from the field of ecological cosmology by adopting the discourse of political ecology, which focuses on the myriad ways social-political and economic interests 'remake and often degrade the eco-social context of poor and marginalized communities'.[22]

Of the many social issues eco-theologians focus on, three hold particular importance: economic, racial and gender justice. John Cobb's book *For the*

---

[19]As a social justice movement, eco-justice protests the placement of toxic landfills and incinerators in poor and marginalized communities and the outsourcing of polluting industry or toxic waste to countries with less economic capital and weak democratic infrastructures. Eco-justice thus expands the scope of ecological concern to the health and environmental protection of vulnerable communities.

[20]Rosemary Radford Ruether, *Gaia and God: An Eco-Feminist Theology of Earth Healing* (San Francisco: Harper SanFrancisco, 1992), 3. Ruether first drew the connection between environmental destruction, patriarchy and sexism in her book *New Woman, New Earth: Sexist Ideologies and Human Liberation* (Boston: Beacon Press, 1995; original edition 1975).

[21]Ruether, *Gaia and God*, 1. See also Chapter 10.

[22]Daniel Castillo, *An Ecological Theology of Liberation: Salvation and Political Ecology* (Maryknoll: Orbis Books, 2019), 8.

Common Good: Redirecting the Economy toward Community, the Environment, and a Sustainable Future (1989), co-authored with the economist Herman E. Daly, was an example of a reflection on economics. Critical of economic globalization and the pervasive influence of multinational corporations, Cobb and Daly proposed a rich combination of policy and value changes, arguing in favour of bioregionalism.[23] Typically, eco-justice theologians are highly critical of market capitalism. For instance, Sallie McFague's *Life Abundant: Rethinking Theology and Economy for a Planet in Peril* (2001) is a critique of capitalism's veneration of endless economic growth and its relentless drive to create a world of compulsive consumers.[24] Like other eco-justice theologians McFague draws on biblical and theological images for re-imaging the good life in just and sustainable ways.

Whereas Ruether and others had attended to racial inequity, it was not till James Cone's seminal essay 'Whose Earth Is It Anyway?' that ecological theology started thematizing environmental racism.[25] Cone argued that the mechanistic and instrumental logic that leads to 'the exploitation of animals and the ravaging of nature' is the same logic that 'led to slavery . . . and the rule of white-supremacy throughout the world'.[26] According to Cone, in other words, ecological destruction is fuelled by the very same objectifying and domineering rationality that serves white supremacy and (settler) colonialism. Environmental ethicist Larry Rasmussen, in a recent essay on climate injustice, adds that this logic is the logic of extractive capitalism: 'Bodies, together with labor and land, were possessed and commodified. Their status as sacred and their value as ends were lost. They were means and means only.'[27] Similarly, eco-womanist theologian Melanie Harris demonstrates that African American women parallel a female-gendered concept of earth: both are subject to the racist project of colonization that commodifies and devalues the earth and poor women of colour.[28] Harris's work is an example therefore of the intersectional analysis of race, gender and ecology within eco-justice theology.

---

[23] John Cobb Jr. and Herman E. Daly, *For the Common Good: Redirecting the Economy toward Community, the Environment, and a Sustainable Future* (Boston: Beacon Press, 1989). See also John Cobb Jr., *Sustainability: Economics, Ecology & Justice* (Maryknoll: Orbis Books, 1992).
[24] Sallie McFague, *Life Abundant: Rethinking Theology and Economy For a Planet in Peril* (Minneapolis: Fortress Press, 2001).
[25] James H. Cone, 'Whose Earth Is It Anyway?', in *Earth-Habitat: Eco-Injustice and the Church's Response*, ed. Dieter Hessel and Larry Rasmussen (Minneapolis: Fortress Press, 2001), 23–32.
[26] Ibid., 23.
[27] Larry Rasmussen, 'Climate Injustice', in *Companion to Public Theology*, ed. Katie Day and Sebastian Kim (Leiden: Brill, 2017), 349–69 (355).
[28] Melanie Harris, *Eco-Womanism: African-American Women and Earth-Honoring Faits* (Maryknoll: Orbis Book, 2017). Harris's analysis builds on a trailblazing article by Delores Williams, who drew a connection between the rape and forced impregnation African enslaved women by slave owners and the predatory logic of strip-mining in the Appalachian Mountains. Delores Williams, 'Sin,

The climate change crisis has brought a new urgency and focus to eco-theological reflection on eco-justice. Poor and Indigenous communities, especially in the Global South, have contributed very little to the climate crisis. Yet they are disproportionally affected by the consequences of climate change, such as rising sea levels, drought and melting polar ice. In the words of Lutheran environmental ethicist Cynthia Moe-Lobeda, climate change and resource extraction 'screams white privilege, class privilege, and environmental racism'.[29] Climate justice therefore has become an important focus of ecological theology. And because poor women and girls in the majority world and marginalized communities in minority world are especially affected by climate change, climate justice takes the form of gender justice. Responding to this reality, though admittedly less so to issues of gender, Pope Francis in *Laudato si'* insists that we approach ecological concerns through the framework of an 'integral ecology'. He writes, 'We are faced with one complex crisis which is both social and environmental. Strategies for a solution demand an integrated approach to combating poverty, restoring dignity to the excluded, and at the same time protecting nature.'[30] As intimated in the introduction to this chapter, this vision is widely shared by other churches and ecumenical bodies. The World Council of Churches (WCC) in its statement on climate change stresses that care for creation and justice go hand in hand: 'Care for creation and justice are at the centre of the WCC work on climate change. The Bible teaches the wholeness of creation and calls human beings to take care of the garden of Eden (Gen 2.15). The God of the Bible is a God of justice who protects, loves, and cares for the most vulnerable among his creatures.'[31]

Nature, and Black Women's Bodies', in *Ecofeminism ad the Sacred*, ed. Carol J. Adams (New York: Continuum, 1993), 24–9.

[29]Cynthia Moe-Lobeda, 'The Spirit as Moral-Spiritual Power for Earth-Honoring, Justice Seeking Ways of Shaping Our Life in Common', in *Planetary Solidarity: Global's Women's Voices on Christian Doctrine and Climate Justice*, ed. Grace-Ji-Sun Kim and Hilda P. Koster (Minneapolis: Fortress Press, 2017), 249–73 (251).

[30]Pope Francis, *Laudato si'*, 139. While Pope Francis's emphasis on ecological justice by way of 'integral ecology' flows rather organically from Catholic Social Teaching, it also was shaped by the writings of Leonardo Boff. Whereas the Pope does not reference Boff directly, Boff's influence is palpable in Francis's much-quoted exhortation that 'A true ecological approach always becomes a social approach; it must integrate questions of justice in debates on the environment, so as to hear both *the cry of the earth and the cry of the poor*'. *Laudato si'*, 45. Italics in the original.

[31]Cf., https://www.oikoumene.org/what-we-do/care-for-creation-and-climate-justice (last accessed 14 December 2020). The World Council of Churches formerly connected a concern for the integrity of creation with social justice in its 1990 convocation *Justice, Peace, and Integrity of Creation*, which was held in Seoul, South Korea. This convocation was the outcome of the Justice, Peace, and the Integrity of Creation (JPIC) conciliar process that began in 1983 at the WCC Assembly in Vancouver and continued past 1990 with various study programmes. Of special significance is the *Theology of Life* study, which grounded the work of JPIC within the lived experience of local communities around the globe. For a helpful overview of the work of the WCC, see Wesley

Whereas this sketch of the turn to eco-justice is far from exhaustive, it demonstrates that the concern for ecological justice emerged in ecological theology under influence of eco-feminist, Black and liberation theologies. On the one hand, these theologies expanded their own focus on human justice to include a concern for ecology; on the other hand, however, these theologies also pushed ecological theologies to theologize the intersection of ecology and social justice. Roger Gottlieb describes the latter development as a shift from a theological concern with 'reforming religious traditions' to being focused on 'challenging beliefs and institutions throughout society as a whole'.[32] Interestingly, he insists that when eco-theology takes the form of eco-justice, it overlaps with secular environmentalism and progressive political movements. Gottlieb observes that while 'eco-justice is ultimately *rooted* in a vision of the Sermon on the Mount or God's command "Justice, justice shall you pursue" (Deut. 16.20; also Qur'an 16.90), many of its *goals* are indistinguishable from those of the Sierra Club, neighborhood activists, or anti-globalization protestors at the World Social Forum'.[33] According to Gottlieb, then, it is by way of its emphasis on eco-justice and climate justice that ecological theology expresses a commitment to move to the public arena. And while this move is not an uncommon one for socially engaged theologies, ecological justice requires that ecological theologians develop 'a comprehensive vision of collective, structural change that extends far beyond religion's usual subject matter'.[34]

In short, then, when ecological theology concerns itself with ecological justice, it becomes theologically informed public discourse about the common good, and, hence, a public theology. Recalling Brietenberg's definition of public theology, public theology seeks to engage public issues related to the common good in a public manner, that is 'by adopting forms of reasoning that are compelling, at least potentially, to those who stand beyond the border of the religious community'.[35] Eco-justice theologies engage with publics beyond institutional religion, such as policymakers, environmental activists and economists, on issues that are not strictly speaking the domain of church teaching or theology. They typically develop a comprehensive social, political and economic vision in dialogue with and by listening to non-theological disciplines. They further use conceptual language that is accessible to these disciplines. Eco-justice theologies are moreover not primarily interested in defending the legitimacy of theology over and against other discourses on issues such as climate change. Instead, they

---

Granberg-Michaelson, 'Climate Change and the Ecumenical Movement', in Conradie and Koster, *T&T Clark Handbook of Christian Theology and Climate Change*, 340–50.
[32]Gottlieb, *A Greener Faith*, 45.
[33]Ibid.
[34]Ibid., 46.
[35]Breitenberg Jr., 'To Tell the Truth: Will the Real Public Theology Please Stand Up', 66.

want to be in dialogue with and learn from these discourses, while making a theologically informed constructive contribution of their own.[36]

As an eco-justice theology, ecological theology thus is a form of public theology. As such it stands to benefit from an engagement with public theology, or such is the claim of this chapter. Whereas the story of public theology is usually told chronologically – as I have done with ecological theology – the South African theologian Dirk J. Smit has argued that there are in fact several narratives of the origin and development of public theology, depending on the perspective and subject location of diverse publics.[37] Each of these narratives offer their own account of the nature and task of public theology. I will draw here on one such account, namely the public theology that emerged in the *Kairos* document. I argue that this account of public theology clarifies the task of eco-justice theology as public theology in a time like this, that is, a time in which the world is running *out* of time when it comes to acting on climate change.

23.3 A PUBLIC ECOLOGICAL THEOLOGY: INSIGHTS FROM *KAIROS* THEOLOGY

The *Kairos* document emerged as a biblically and theologically founded protest of the oppressive apartheid theology developed in service of South Africa's racist political regime.[38] Appropriated by the Dutch Reformed Church in South Africa, apartheid theology was in essence *state* theology, 'based on self-serving understandings of the "order of creation," supporting the status quo and justifying unjust social structures'.[39] Anti-apartheid theology, on the other hand,

---

[36]Not all ecological theologians and ethicists would see their work as a form of public theology. Michael Northcott, for instance, judges that most public theologies risk watering down the gospel message and thus tend to weaken the gospel's proposal for an altogether different social–economic order. Influenced by the communitarian ethics of John Howard Yoder and Stanley Hauerwas, Northcott proposes that instead of contributing aspects or 'fragments' of Christian teaching to the public conversation, ecologically minded Christians should instead bear witness to the alternative social order made visible through Jesus' life and ministry. For instance, instead of translating Christian ideas about industrial food production for secular consumption, Christians should *model* sustainable and just food practices that flow from the Eucharist. Cf., Michael S. Northcott, 'Farmed Salmon and the Sacramental Fest: How Christian Worship Resists Global Capitalism', in *Public Theology for the 21st Century*, ed. William F. Storrar and Andrew R. Morton (London: T&T Clark, 2004), 213–30.
[37]Dirk J. Smit, 'The Paradigms of Public Theology – Origins and Development', in *Contextuality and Inter-contextuality in Public Theology*, ed. Heinrich Bedford-Strohm, Florian Höhne and Tobias Reitmeiter (Zürich: LIT Verlag GmbH & Co, 2013), 11–23.
[38]The Kairos document is a biblical and theological founded critique of the oppressive apartheid theology that had been appropriated by the Dutch Reformed Church in South Africa. It was issued by a group of mainly Black South African theologians. Cf. https://kairossouthernafrica.wordpress.com/2011/05/08/the-south-africa-kairos-document-1985/ (last accessed 22 March 2021).
[39]Ibid., 7.

arose out of a context of struggle and resistance against state repression and racism.[40] Contrary to state theologies, then, anti-apartheid theology was done from a perspective of below, that is, from the perspective of South Africa's Black majority victimized by the apartheid regime. The anti-apartheid theology of the *Kairos* document, therefore, was not a 'reified statement' but saw theology itself as 'an ongoing part of the struggle against apartheid', and in service of 'the construction of a non-racial democracy'.[41] Moreover, whereas *Kairos* theology was first and foremost a critique of the state theology legitimizing apartheid, it was critical also of theologies put forward by the English-speaking churches that rejected apartheid but did not go far enough 'in their social analysis and advocacy for justice' and ultimately were 'satisfied with a superficial, individualistic reconciliation'.[42]

The prophetic urgency that is implied by the *Kairos* document rings true also in our current moment of climate change-related disasters. The Greek term *Kairos* implies the right or opportune moment. From a theological perspective *Kairos* acquires a sense of providence: '[t]ime is no longer simply linear time: it can become the 'right time' in terms of reading the divine will'.[43] The Ecumenical 'green' Patriarch Bartholomew has called the climate crisis a *Kairos* moment for our churches and the world: 'For the human race as a whole there is now a *Kairos*, a decisive time in our relationship with God's creation. We will either act in time to protect life on earth from the worst consequence of human folly, or we will fail to act.'[44] And, indeed, climate scientists tell us that we are reaching dangerous thresholds of carbon dioxide levels past which it will be impossible to reverse runaway catastrophic changes, such as melting the Greenland and West Antarctic ice sheets, or the melting of methane-rich Arctic permafrost. The 2018 special report by the Intergovernmental Panel on Climate Change (IPCC), the leading world body for assessing the science related to climate change, its impacts and potential future risks, states loud and clear that at the current rate the world could be 1.5° Celsius hotter than it was prior to the industrial revolution as soon as 2030,[45] which would be an increase of 0.5° from current temperatures. Limiting global warming to 1.5°C will mean that the world needs to zero out emissions

---

[40] Ibid.
[41] Ibid.
[42] Day and Kim, 'Introduction', 7.
[43] Ibid., 363.
[44] His All Holiness Patriarch Bartholomew, Symposium on the Arctic, 7–12 September 2007, Greenland: 'The Mirror of Life: Part 3, Symposium Closing Address', http://orth-trasfiguration.org/library/orthodoxy/mirros (last accessed 15 April 2021). Quoted in Barbara Rossing 'God Laments with Us: Climate Change, Apocalypse and the Urgent *Kairos* Moment', *The Ecumenical Review* 62, no. 2 (2010): 119–30 (126).
[45] Cf., https://www.ipcc.ch/2018/10/08/summary-for-policymakers-of-ipcc-special-report-on-global-warming-of-1-5c-approved-by-governments/ (last accessed 15 April 2021).

from fossil fuels and deforestation by mid-century. While this may sound that we have a window of hope, it is equally important to realize that the global average temperature is already 1°C above pre-industrial levels, and, hence, that many of the disasters related to climate change are already happening. Over 1 million people living near coasts have been forced from their homes due to rising seas and stronger storms. In the United States, for instance, the Biloxi-Chitimacha-Choctaw tribe of Isle de Jean Charles in the Gulf of Mexico and the Inupiat of the Alaskan village of Shishmaref on the Chuckchi Sea have seen their ancestral land destroyed by rising sea levels and catastrophic storms. Together with many other climate-vulnerable people around the world, these tribes lost not just their homes and livelihoods but also their culture. The Covid-19 pandemic, itself caused by the increasing encroachment of humans on vulnerable ecosystems, has only intensified the suffering of climate-vulnerable people, even as it has temporarily reduced greenhouse gas emissions.[46]

In addition to naming our current climate moment as a *Kairos* moment, *Kairos* theology also helps clarify the task and nature of eco-justice theology as a public theology in three important ways. First, it makes clear that eco-justice theology is a *prophetic* theology; that is, it is critical of the status quo and the economic and political powers that keep us hooked on life-endangering fossil fuels. Yet, it also is fiercely critical of churches and academic theologies that are still proceeding as if the world is not on edge. *Kairos* theology named the struggle against apartheid a matter of *status confessionis*, that is, an issue with which the very essence of the faith is at stake. The analogy with climate change is quite clear. As Jenkins observes, this is a time for Christian theology to explain the basic incompatibility of certain positions on climate change with the Christian faith. He states, 'perhaps it is nearing time for the church catholic to explain why, at least for those living in high polluting societies, integrating climate-mediated relations into responsibilities of the faith has become a *status confessionis* – a matter on which the Christian faith stands or falls'.[47] According to Jenkins, then, calling action on climate change a *status confessionis* means not

---

[46]After rising steadily for decades, global carbon dioxide emissions fell by 6.4 per cent, or 2.3 billion tonnes, in 2020, as the Covid-19 pandemic squelched economic and social activities worldwide, according to new data on daily fossil fuel emissions. The decline is significant – roughly double Japan's yearly emissions – but smaller than many climate researchers expected given the scale of the pandemic and is not expected to last once the virus is brought under control. The United States contributed the most to the global dip, with a nearly 13 per cent decrease in its emissions, due mostly to a sharp decline in vehicle transportation that began with lockdowns in March 2020 and continued as the pandemic escalated at the end of the year. Globally, the energy sector most affected by pandemic lockdowns and restrictions was aviation, where emissions fell 48 per cent from their 2019 total. Cf., https://www.nature.com/articles/s41558-020-0797-x (last accessed 15 April 2021).

[47]Jenkins, 'Working with Politics', 70.

only that complacency on climate change is not an option, it also clarifies that factions of Christianity that willfully refuse to acknowledge their responsibility for climate change are losing 'their plausible claim to belong to the body of faith'.[48] In other words, while there are times to respond to conflict within the Christian community by finding commonality, this might be a time to intensify the dogmatic significance of conflicting positions. A public ecological theology taking its lead from the public theology that emerged in the *Kairos* document will need to push the churches to press upon the faithful that this is an issue that touches the very core of the Christian witness.

Kairos theology further brings into focus eco-justice theology's commitment to an epistemological preference for the poor and marginalized. Whereas church statements and official letters, including *Laudato si'*, speak on *behalf of* the poor, they typically do not speak *with* the voice of poor people experiencing climate change first-hand. *Jenkin* theology urges eco-justice theology to practice a gaze from below, that is, to give voice to those people, especially women and Indigenous people, who are directly suffering climate change-related disasters, and who are fighting for acknowledgement by and compensation from their governments and the international community. When it comes to the theological contribution to public debates on climate justice, eco-justice theologians typically align themselves therefore with grassroot religious environmental movements representing minority voices. Eco-justice theologies do want to collaborate with the Catholic Church, the WCC and other ecclesial institutions. Indeed, many of the statements and studies issued by ecclesial bodies are themselves examples of a public ecological theology committed to ecological justice. *Kairos* theology clarifies, however, that the first commitment of eco justice theologies is to grassroot communities experiencing ecological-related suffering. As a public theology, then, eco-justice theology is located neither in the church nor in the academy, but rather occupies an 'in and between space', identifying itself with grassroot environmental movements, including religious movements, resisting ecological and climate injustice. And because religious environmentalism is increasingly an interfaith movement, eco-justice theology is not just ecumenical but also multi-religious.[49]

A final way, then, in which eco-justice theology aligns with *Kairos* theology is that it stresses the importance of being actively involved with societal

---

[48]Ibid., 72.
[49]A well-known example of such interfaith work in the United States is Interfaith Power and Light, which grew out of an interfaith initiative by the Episcopal Church in California and has grown into an organization with chapters all over North America. Cf., https://www.interfaithpowerandlight.org/about/mission-history/ (last accessed 15 April 2021). For a helpful overview of interfaith work on climate change in the United States, see Paul O. Ingram, 'Working with Climate Activists in Other Traditions', in *T&T Clark Handbook on Christian Theology and Climate Change*, 136–46.

transformation. Thus, whereas the *Kairos* document saw theology as 'an ongoing part of the struggle against apartheid', eco-justice theology wants to be part of the struggle for a just and sustainable society.[50] Eco-justice theology therefore does not just identify with grassroots movements but actively joins forces with, for instance, the struggle of Indigenous peoples resisting multinational fossil fuel corporations and pipeline construction. The latter was the case when churches, faith groups and religious organizations joined the Sioux tribe's water protectors during the months-long protest against the Dakota Access Pipeline at Standing Rock (North Dakota) in the fall of 2016.[51] Yet becoming part of the struggle can also take the form of working together with non-governmental organizations and other stakeholders. For instance, the South Africa Faith Communities Environmental Institute (SAFCEI) partnered with Earthlife, an African environmental and anti-nuclear organization, and successfully fought the government's plan to sign a nuclear procurement agreement with a Russian state-owned nuclear energy corporation, a plan that would have tied the country into unnecessary debt and would do little in terms of providing affordable, clean and sustainable energy to poor South Africans.[52] Eco-justice theology emerges from these struggles. Yet it is not simply a form of activism. It is more accurate to say that its theological reflection springs from and is informed by its involvement with these grassroots movements. There are many examples of this type of eco-justice theology. One example is *Planetary Solidarity: Global Women's Voices on Christian Doctrine and Climate Justice* (2017), which is a collection of theological essays emerging from the concrete struggles for survival by women experiencing serious threats to their livelihood, health and dignity due to climate change-related destruction.[53]

---

[50]Kim and Day, 'Introduction', 7.
[51]Cf., https://www.npr.org/2016/12/11/505147166/in-their-own-words-the-water-protectors-of-standing-rock (last accessed 15 April 2021).
[52]Cf., https://safcei.org/nuclear-deal-blocked/ (last accessed 15 April 2021). Yet another example of eco-justice work partnering with NGOs such is the Institute of Ecological Civilization, which emerged out of the vision of John B. Cobb, Jr.
The EcoCiv institute originated in the 2015 international conference 'Seizing and Alternative: Toward an Ecological Civilization', which was organized by the Center for Process Studies at the Campus of Pomona College in Claremont (CA). The EcoCiv Institute has actively partnered with organizations such as Forum 21, People for Earth Forum, the Land Institute, the Parliament of the World's Religions and the Center for Earth Ethics on issues such as water justice and energy. While based in California, it works internationally, regularly holding conferences and convenings in South Korea, China, the United States and (in 2019) South Africa. Cf. https://ecociv.org/ (last accessed 15 April 2021).
[53]Grace Ji-Sun Kim and Hilda P. Koster, eds, *Planetary Solidarity: Global Women's Voice and Christian Doctrine on Climate Justice* (Minneapolis: Fortress Press, 2017).

23.4 IN CONCLUSION

This chapter has sought to demonstrate that ecological theology, as an eco-justice theology, is a public theology that stands to benefit from an engagement with South African *Kairos* theology and the understanding of public theology that has emerged from it. Yet notwithstanding the many ways *Kairos* theology clarifies the task and role of a public ecological theology for a time of climate disaster, it is in closing equally important to observe also that ecological theology challenges public theology to extend its scope. Whereas, as we saw, eco-justice theologies typically tend to focus on the ways vulnerable human communities are affected by climate change and destruction of ecosystems, the approach always is a holistic one. Human life is understood in the context of the flourishing of ecosystems. In other words, eco-justice theologies start with an awareness of and appreciation for the interdependence of all of life. Eco-justice theologies thus push back against the overtly human-centred focus of much public theology. This means that we are charged to attend to ways in which the more-than-human realm is 'the ontological grounding for all other publics'.[54] For as the public ecological theologian Clive Pearson observes, 'in a time of climate change the Earth sets the terms by which the conversation is framed'.[55] Thus, whereas ecological theology is a public theology, there is no public theology that in today's climate must not also be an ecological theology of sorts.

---

[54] Timothy Harvie, 'A Politics of Connected Flesh: Public Theology, Ecology, and Merleau-Ponty', *International Journal of Public Theology* 13 (2019): 494–512 (497).
[55] Clive Pearson, 'The Purpose and Practice of a Public Theology in a Time of Climate Change', *International Journal of Public Theology* 4, no. 3 (2010): 356–72 (360).

CHAPTER 24

Challenges for public theology

Sports

DRIES VANYSACKER

Like politics, religion, culture, economics and ecology, sports can be considered as one of the most important challenges for public theology. The ubiquity and eminent position of sports in our contemporary society cannot be denied. Even the least athletically inclined person is confronted on a daily basis with sports, whether in the media or in her or his immediate surroundings. Professional sports is an immense business, and inasmuch as sports as a leisure activity contributes to public health, it is now often considered to be part of the mission of governments.[1] The questions before us, then, are why public theology should address itself to sports as such and, furthermore, how it can or should do this. These are the questions to which this chapter addresses itself.

---

[1] See, for example, the mission and the year report of 'Sport Vlaanderen', the sport administration of the Flemish government, https://www.sport.vlaanderen/over-sport-vlaanderen/ (last accessed 22 July 2020); for the 'Nederlandse Rijksinstituut voor Volksgezondheid en Milieu (RIVM)' in the Netherlands, see https://www.sportenbewegenincijfers.nl/ (last accessed 22 July 2020).

24.1 THE CHURCH AND CATHOLIC THEOLOGY: SILENT ON SPORTS?

Church and theology could certainly ignore sports since sports, at least in some circles, is perceived as having more to do with physicality than spirituality. In that way the myth is continued that Thomas Hughes's philosophy of 'muscular Christianity', characterized by a belief in patriotic duty, discipline, self-sacrifice, masculinity and the moral and physical beauty of athletics, with which the English and American Protestant denominations gushed about in the mid-nineteenth century, is still the monopoly of the latter, while Catholicism should be seen as a pure spiritual religion that considers the body – and especially sports – as troublesome or even a necessary evil.[2]

The fact is that there is a wide gap between Protestant and Catholic scholarship on the topic of sport. Compared with the multiple scientific publications and academic conferences concerning church, theology and sports that the Protestant world produces, Catholic attention to is meagre.[3] One of the leading international research groups devoted to the study of Christian faith within the world of sports, the Sport and Christianity Group, is Protestant and Anglican in origin. It was created in 2013 by American and British academics and athletes who were active in the disciplines of kinesiology, recreation, physical education, wellness, sport management, sport and social justice, and (pastoral) theology. Sports ministers and coaches are also involved in the group.[4] Since 2016 the group has organized a Global Conference on Sports and Christianity, which meets every three years. The first such meeting (2016) saw St John University at York as the hosting institution; in 2019 Calvin University (Grand Rapids, Michigan, USA) and Hope College (Holland, Michigan, USA) co-organized the conference. These large conferences welcome academics from the human and positive sciences and also ministers active within all kinds of Protestant denominations. Via blogs and mailings, the group distributes a current bibliography of literature in English on sports and Christianity. In 2017 the group decided to launch a *Declaration on Sport and the Christian Life*, a twelve-point document detailing how to fit sports within a Christian framework. These twelve points can be summarized thus:

---

[2] D. Stanley Eitzen and George H. Sage, 'Religion and Sport', in *Religion and Sport: The Meeting of Sacred and Profane*, ed. Charles S. Prebish (Westport, CT: Greenwood Press, 1993), 80–117; Clifford Putney, *Muscular Christianity: Manhood and Sports in Protestant America, 1880–1920* (Cambridge, MA: Harvard University Press, 2001); Nick J. Watson, Stuart Weir and Stephen Friend, 'The Development of Muscular Christianity in Victorian Britain and Beyond', *Journal of Religion & Society* 7 (2005): 1–18.
[3] Cf. Nick J. Watson and Andrew Parker, *Sport and the Christian Religion: A Systematic Review of Literature* (New Castle, Cambridge: Scholars Publishing, 2014), xiv–224.
[4] https://sportandchristianity.com/founders/ (last accessed 22 July 2020).

1. Sports has a legitimate place in the Christian life.
2. Sports touches all dimensions of human life.
3. The true value of sports is inherent in the experience itself.
4. Sports has many benefits but they are conditional.
5. Sports programmes can be a vital component of Christian education.
6. Well played, sports can glorify God.
7. Competition is an essential element of sports.
8. God does not favour one player or team over another.
9. In sports, the Christian virtues are manifested most clearly in behaviours that go beyond obeying the rules of games.
10. We are created to move, enjoy and exercise care over our bodies.
11. Watching sports can be a way to celebrate God's goodness.
12. Sports can be a means of spiritual formation.[5]

Given this organization's focus on sport and faith, it is no coincidence that most academic initiatives concerning the public theology of sports have taken place with reference to it. Of these recent initiatives, we mention in the following only the most recent and well known.

Lincoln Harvey shows in his *A Brief Theology of Sport* (2014) how the autotelicity of sports mirrors the autotelicity of creation. Autotelicity is the quality of being an end in itself. According to Harvey, God created as an act of autotelic play – play that was rooted in the incarnation of Christ. Humankind and the world were unnecessary. Though God did not need to create, God did create, and humankind is meaningful. From this view of creation, Harvey argues that when we play – unnecessary but meaningfully – we are living out our deepest identity as unnecessary but meaningful creatures. Sports, he argues, has remained popular throughout history precisely because it resonates with our very being and mirrors who we are as the creation of God. In Harvey's argument, sports is about humanity – it is about who we are as the creation, not about God.[6]

Robert Ellis takes a different perspective. In his *The Games People Play: Theology, Religion and Sport* (2014), Ellis makes space for a transcendent experience in sports and play. He writes,

---

[5] Cf. Nick J. Watson and Andrew Parker, *Sport and the Christian Religion*, 125–30; https://sportandchristianity.com/declaration/ (last accessed 22 July 2020).
[6] Lincoln Harvey, *A Brief Theology of Sport* (London: SCM Press, 2014), See, for example, 76–87.

> We might speak of sport as a kind of dramatization, a ritual form, of play. If so, and thinking as we have been of sport as a possible vehicle for an encounter with the Ultimate Player, it might also be possible to speak of participation in such sport as being a participation in God's playful creativity, or creative play, and so even a participation in God's self. . . . But if play and sport can be (though are not necessarily) a participation in God's playful creativity and even in God's self, then one might expect such goods to follow.[7]

According to Ellis, humankind's practice of sports presents to the participant a real possibility of growing closer to God, indeed, of having godly goods flow from sports. Here he makes play and sports like aesthetic experience. Unlike Harvey, however, he does not see this as a separate realm where humanity celebrates itself but rather a realm where one might encounter God.

Erik W. Dailey argues in his article 'Sport and Transcendence through the Body' (2016) that

> if sports is a form of play that is embodied, that our bodies are unified in body and soul/mind, and that our bodies are what we have for encountering God, then sports is, like religion, a route for transcendence mediated through utilization of our created selves.[8]

In their article 'Sport, Christianity and Social Justice? Considering a Theological Foundation' (2019), Gregg Twietmeyer, Nick J. Watson and Andrew Parker write 'that given that the sport–theology field has grown exponentially over the last decade, one could argue that this area of academic enquiry and ecclesiological practice has "arrived"'. According to them,

> Scholars, activists, and representatives of the global Church, who operate in the sport–theology–social justice realm now have the opportunity to expand the field by: (a) engaging and collaborating with scholarly groups, such as The Global Network of Public Theology[9] to heighten awareness of the field and enhance its credibility within the discipline of theology; (b) further integrating the study of theological/social justice issues on sports into school, university, and theology/religious curricula . . . / . . .; and (c) undertaking interdisciplinary and multi-method research and Church programs that examine (and address) a wide range of social justice issues in, and through, sports.[10]

---

[7] Robert Ellis, *The Games People Play: Theology, Religion and Sport* (Wipf & Stock, 2014), 147.
[8] Published in *International Journal of Public Theology* 10 (2016) 486–506.
[9] See https://gnpublictheology.wordpress.com/ (last accessed 22 July 2020).
[10] Published in *Quest* 71, no. 2 (2019): 121–37 (132–3).

Only a few Catholic faculties of theology are involved with sports as a field of study. Christoph Hübenthal is an exception to the rule in Germany and the Netherlands. He focuses both on moral issues in sports such as doping, manipulation, corruption and violence but also on the question of how sports can be understood as to be part of a good life. He actively collaborated with Kevin Lixey, Dietmar Mieth and Norbert Müller on a more systematic-theological approach of sports in the light of a Vatican research group.[11] In his contribution 'Morality and Beauty: Sport at the Service of the Human Person' (2012), Hübenthal states that

> Sport eventually serves the human being by creating a feeling of comprehensive gratitude and a cognition of the need for ultimate meaning. This is what sports actually can evoke in every human being. It cannot, however, answer the questions whether there is an addressee of gratitude and whether the ultimate meaning is really given.[12]

Another member of this group, Mgr Carlo Mazza, Emeritus bishop of Fidenza and consultor of the Dicastery for Laity during the years 2008/16, relates sports to human development:

---

[11]See, for example, 'Sportethik: Misserfolg und Amoral. Was die Erfolgsgeschichten im Profifußball verschweigen – "Goal – Lebe deinen Traum"', in *Angewandte Ethik und Film*, ed. Thomas Bohrmann and Matthias Reichelt (Wiesbaden: Springer VS, 2018), 259–82; Joris Delporte, 'Supporters vieren het toeval, Koning Contingentie, dossier "Religie, sport en ethiek: Sportief voorsmaakje toont honger naar God"', *Tertio* 978 (2018): 9–10; 'Sport als ondramatische enscenering van het levensdrama', *Speling. Tijdschrift voor Bezinning* 66 (2014): 2, 24–30; 'Mehr als nur dabei sein – Inklusiver Sport als moralische Aufforderung', in *Sport im Spiegel der UN-Behindertenrechtskonvention. Interdisziplinäre Zugänge und politische Positionen*, ed. Florian Kiuppis and Stefan Kurzke-Maasmeier (Stuttgart: Kohlhammer, 2012), 273–87; 'Immerhin schön und gut. Zur vermeintlich religiösen Dimension des Sports', in *Es lebe der Sport. Gesellschaftliche und ethische Aspekte eines Massenphänomens*, ed. Thomas Sternberg and Ludger Schulte-Roling (Münster: Dialogverlag, 2012), 127–45; 'Sportethik', in *Handbuch Angewandte Ethik*, ed. Ralf Stoecker, Christian Neuhäuser and Marie-Luise Raters (Stuttgart, Weimar: Metzler, 2011), 197–201; 'Sport im Dienst der menschlichen Person. Prolegomena zu einer christlichen Sicht des Sports', in *Sport und Christentum. Eine anthropologische, theologische und pastorale Herausforderung*, ed. Dietmar Mieth, Norbert Müller and Christoph Hübenthal (Ostfildern: Matthias-Grünewald-Verlag, 2008), 59–74; Christoph Hübenthal, 'Der menschliche und religiöse Sinn des Sports', *Diakonia - Internationale Zeitschrift für die Praxis der Kirche* 34 (2005): 235–41; Christoph Hübenthal, 'Normen und Werte im Sport', *Ethik Kontrovers* 9 (2001): 14–23; Ommo Grupe, Dietmar Mieth and Christoph Hübenthal, eds, *Lexikon der Ethik im Sport* (Schorndorf: Hofmann, 1998); Andreas Lienkamp and Claus Weingärtner, eds, 'Wodurch der Sport zu Werten kommt', in *Was ist des Sportes Wert?* (Mühlheim: Katholische Akademie, 1997), 56–68.

[12]Published in *Sport & Christianity: A Sign of the Times in the Light of Faith*, ed. Kevin Lixey, Christoph Hübenthal, Dietmar Mieth and Norbert Müller (Washington: The Catholic University of America Press, 2012), 61–78 (78).

the Church asks sport not only to respect the identity of the person, but also to allow the individual to develop his or her full potential with regard to God's plan for his or her life.[13]

24.2 HISTORICAL ECCLESIASTICAL AND THEOLOGICAL ATTENTION ON BODY CULTURE AND SPORTS

Despite the fact that the majority of recent theological attention that has been placed on body culture and sports has come from within Protestant-oriented sources, church and Catholic theologians have for centuries addressed themselves to questions of sport.[14] Indeed, from its very start, the church has dialogued on sports and related topics. We know, for instance, that St Paul used sports metaphors to explain the Christian life to the pagans.[15]

Some Church Fathers continued to utilize this method; even so, these authorities tended to maintain a distance from what they considered to be a pagan body culture.[16] During the Middle Ages, laity and clergy, secular as well as regular, organized plays and sports on holidays and Sundays. During the thirteenth century in the region of what is now northern France, a kind of handball game (*jeu de paume*) was introduced on the European continent. This activity, considered to be the precursor of tennis, was practised in many monasteries and abbeys.[17] Such games were lent theological support by the writings of Thomas Aquinas, who argued that there can be 'a virtue about games' because virtue has to do with moderation. A virtuous person, by this account, should not be working all the time; he or she also needs time for play and recreation. The Renaissance humanists and the early Jesuits made use of Aquinas' understanding of virtue when they decided that students needed time for play and recreation during the course of the school day. This was the

---

[13]Carlo Mazza, 'Sport as Viewed from the Church's Magisterium', in *The World of Sport Today: A Field of Christian Mission* (Vatican City: Libreria Editrice Vaticana, 2006), 55–73 (63).

[14]Dries Vanysacker, 'The Catholic Church and Sport. A Burgeoning Territory within Historical Research!', *Revue d'histoire ecclésiastique. Louvain Journal for Church History* 108, no. 1 (2013): 342–54.

[15]Victor Pfitzner, 'Was St. Paul a Sport Enthusiast? Realism and Rhetoric in Pauline Athletic Metaphors', in *Sport and Christianity. Historical and Contemporary Perspectives*, ed. Nick Watson and Andrew Parker (Abington: Routledge, 2013), 88–111.

[16]Alois Koch, 'Biblical and Patristic Foundations for Sport', in *Sport and Christianity*, ed. Lixey, 139–55.

[17]Ferdinand Antonin Vuillermet, *Les Jeunes Gens et les Sports* (Paris: Lethielleux, 1925), 15–26 ('L'Église et les sports').

original rationale for the inclusion of play and sports in educational institutions in the Western world.[18]

From the beginning of the nineteenth century through the middle of the twentieth, schools, boarding schools and after-school recreation programmes, exercised in annex gymnastics and sports associations, would contribute to a major network of sports for the Catholic youth. Within the Catholic European colleges, secular priests, but especially regular orders, played a major role in sports activities. These orders included the Jesuits, Josephites, Benedictines, Dominicans, Salesians of Don Bosco, Xaverian Brothers and Brothers of the Christian Schools. From these Catholic education environments, modern sports imported from the Anglo-Saxon world, such as football, rugby, lawn tennis and hockey, were spread throughout European society, providing the impetus for the formation of various teams and competitions.[19] This education method was also transferred to the overseas mission territories.[20] In France, the Dominican order, led by Henri Dominique Lacordaire (1802–61), restarted the Catholic education system and, in collaboration with Henri Didon (1840–1900), introduced gymnastics, body culture and competition sports on the curriculum. The slogan the latter used for his college sports – *'Citius, Altius, Fortius'* (faster, higher, stronger) – eventually became the motto of the modern Olympic Games.[21]

At the end of the nineteenth century and at the beginning of the twentieth century, the popes were very open towards gymnastics and the modern sports. The involvement of Pius X (1903/14) with the Baron de Coubertin – himself a product of Jesuit education – and with the restarted Olympic Games is mirrored in his strong support to the candidacy of Rome to organize the Games of 1908.[22] Even after

---

[18]Patrick Kelly, *Catholic Perspectives on Sports: From Medieval to Modern Times* (New York: Paulist Press, 2012).

[19]Roland Renson, 'Corpus Alienum: Naschoolse Sport in Het Katholiek Onderwijs', in *Voor lichaam & geest. Katholieken, lichamelijke opvoeding en sport in de 19de en 20ste eeuw*, ed. Mark D'hoker, Roland Renson and Jan Tolleneer (Leuven, 1994), 99–121; Jan Tolleneer, 'De Belgische Katholieke Turnbond (1892–1992)', ibid., 123–47.

[20]Dries Vanysacker, '"Sport with a Mission": Sport as a Means of Renewed Catholic Apostolate among Indigenous People in former Belgian Congo (1919–59)', in *Gods, Games, and Globalization. New Perspectives on Religion and Sports*, ed. Rebecca Alpert and Arthur Remillard (Macon: Mercer University Press, 2019), 41–57.

[21]Jean-Jacques Bruxelle, 'Le Père Didon (1840–1900) et la pratique régulière d'une activité physique', in *Les cultures du corps et les pédagogies chrétiennes XIX-XXe*, ed. Guy Avanzi and François Hochepied (Paris, 2010), 47–64; Norbert Müller, 'Die olympische Devise 'citius, altius, fortius' und ihr Urheber Henri Didon', in *Forum Kirche und Sport*, band 2, Wissenschaftliche Kommission des Arbeitskreises Kirche und Sport (Düsseldorf, 1996), 7–27.

[22]Antonella Stelitano, Quirino Bortolato and Alejandro Mario Dieguez, *Pio X, le Olimpiadi e lo sport*, Treviso, 2012; Dries Vanysacker, 'Les rapports entre l'Église catholique et les Jeux olympiques modernes (1896–1920)', in *Revue générale. Réflexion et culture*, ed. Vincent Dujardin and Frédéric Saenen, vol. 3 (Louvain-la-Neuve: Presses Universitaires de Louvain, 2020), 59–69.

the failure of the project, Pius X continued his interest in sports and endorsed the International Catholic Federation of Physical Education (FICEP), which was launched in 1911.[23]

At the same time one notices within the Catholic theology after the First World War a fierce criticism towards the ever stronger professionalism and competitive passion that was emerging within the world of sports. According to the adherents of the so-called Catholic anti-sport movement, the body was totally subordinate to the soul and the spirit. The fact that the body cult was promoted by ideologies such as national socialism and fascism was for them the proof of where excesses in sport could lead. According to them, sports competitions for women also threatened the ideal of motherhood and the Catholic ideal of marriage, since such activities seemed to them to lead to women's masculinization. The public gymnastic parties and sports competitions in Germany and Italy, featuring women and girls in swimsuits, were strictly disapproved and considered as immoral by church authorities. Hence, during the interwar period, one preferred in some Catholic milieus asceticism, sober entertainment and games without any form of competition. In sum, this period saw the value of the body, body culture and sports called into question.[24]

In many countries, for instance Belgium, the Netherlands and Italy, recreation and sports activities were, as many social–cultural activities, organized within a subdivided society. The role of the Catholic Action and the influence of the diocesan bishops became more and more influential.[25] Codewords were: keeping control and self-organization within the Catholic pillar. In the Netherlands, for example, the Episcopal Mandate of 15 July 1933 emphasized the very disadvantageous consequences for faith and morals to which Catholics exposed themselves by sporting in neutral milieus. In Italy, the bishops fiercely defended

---

[23]Laurence Munoz and Jan Tolleneer, eds, *L'Église, le sport et l'Europe. La Fédération International Catholique d'Éducation Physique (FICEP) à l'épreuve du temps (1911–2011)* (Paris: L'Harmattan, 2011).

[24]Antonius Gerardus Weiler, *Tussen jeugdzorg en jeugdemancipatie. Een halve eeuw jeugd en samenleving in de spiegel van het katholieke maandblad dux 1927–1970*, Bronnen en studies Katholiek Documentatie Centrum Nijmegen, 9, (Baarn: 1979); Dries Vanysacker, 'Wielerapostolaat, een evidentie in de katholieke Lage Landen? Een blik op de houding van de kerk en gezaghebbende geestelijken tegenover de professionele wielersport (1900–1971)', *Trajecta* 23 (2014): 91–119 (97–9).

[25]Marjet Derks and Marc Budel, *Sportief en katholiek. Geschiedenis van de katholieke sportbeweging in Nederland in de twintigste eeuw* (Nijmegen: Katholiek Documentatie Centrum, 1990); Jacques Hoorens, *Monseigneur P.J. Boymans (1914–1984). De priester in de sport* ('s-Hertogenbosch: NKS Boymansfonds, 2002); Luc Schokkaert, 'De Vlaamse katholieke jeugdbewegingen en lichamelijke opvoeding en sport', in D'hoker, *Voor lichaam & geest*, 149–77; Laurence Munoz, *Une histoire du sport catholique. La fédération sportive et culturelle de France, 1898–2000* (Paris: L'Harmattan, 2003); Ernesto Preziosi, *Gedda e lo sport. Il Centro Sportivo Italiano: un contributo alla storia dell'educazione in Italia* (Molfetta: Edizioni la meridiana, 2011).

the privilege of the 'Azione Cattolica' within Mussolini's regime to continue the organization of the youth and sports movements within the Catholic pillar.

The increasing popularity of body culture and sports, together with their abuse by European totalitarian regimes during the interwar period, constituted a huge challenge for the Catholic Church and Pius XI (1922/39).[26] The pope did not long remain silent. In his encyclical *Divini illius Magistri*, issued on the last day of 1929, the pope decided among other things that the church and Catholics themselves should totally separate the physical education of boys from that of girls. He further stipulated that this separation could not be left in the hands of the state and the families alone.[27]

Pius XII (1939/58), who as a papal nuncio in Germany previously had experienced the excesses of sports, underlined the positive power of sports as a relaxing factor, but warned at the same time of idolizing the body. Sports was not a purpose on its own, he maintained, but could be a tool to train the body to serve important duties in life, namely family life, studies, work and religious activities. It was the task of the church to remediate the world of sports by means of the Catholic Action, and Gino Bartali (1914–2000), a pious contemporary cycling star from Italy, fitted wonderfully in that approach.[28]

It is obvious that the Church Institute and the theologians were forced to take a stance towards this modern approach to sport. According to Catholic theology, there was a hierarchical relation between body and soul in which the body stood at the service of the soul. Depending on the accentuation of the role of the body, a theologian could have a rather negative or positive vision on body culture and sports.[29]

This anthropology gradually changed under the influence of existentialist philosophy, according to which the human person was rather approached in a holistic way and was considered as an incarnated soul. Moreover, by the 1960s the position of sports became ever more important in popular culture, as

---

[26]Dries Vanysacker, 'The Attitude of the Holy See toward Sport during the Interwar Period (1919–39)', *The Catholic Historical Review* 101 (2015): 794–808; Dries Vanysacker, 'La position du Saint-Siège sur la gymnastique féminine dans l'Allemagne de l'entre-deux-guerres (1927–1928) à partir de quelques témoignages tirés des archives des nonciatures de Munich et Berlin', in *Incorrupta monumenta ecclesiam defendunt. Studi offerti a mons. Sergio Pagano, prefetto dell'Archivio Segreto Vaticano. Vol.1: La Chiesa nella storia. Religione, cultura, costume*, ed. Andreas Gottsmann, Pierantonio Piatti, Andreas E. Rehberg (Città del Vaticano: Archivio Segreto Vaticano, 2018), 1663–75.

[27]http://www.vatican.va/content/pius-xi/en/encyclicals/documents/hf_p-xi_enc_31121929_divini-illius-magistri.html (last accessed 22 July 2020).

[28]Lixey, 'Sport in the Magisterium of Pius XII', in *Sport & Christianity*, 104–20.

[29]Derks and Budel, *Sportief en katholiek*, 65–92; Marjet Derks, '"Harten Warm, Hoofden Koel". Katholieken en lichaamscultuur: dans en sport, 1910-1940', *Jaarboek van het Katholiek Documentatiecentrum* 12 (1982): 100–32; Leo Kenis, '"Wat gij ook doet, doet alles ter ere Gods". Kerkelijke en theologische opvattingen over sport', in *Voor lichaam & geest*, ed. D'hoker, 13–41.

demonstrated on the one hand by the fact that more and more people actively participated in sports and on the other hand by the fact that the new medium of television permitted supporters to follow competitions and games 'de visu'.

From the 1960s, the popes of the Vatican II Council, John XXIII (1958/63) and Paul VI (1963/78) vigorously fostered dialogue between the church and the world of sports. The Pastoral Constitution on the Church in the Modern World, *Gaudium et Spes*, began with the thesis that 'nothing genuinely human fails to raise an echo in their hearts' (Preface, 1). In Article 61, it is stated concerning culture that modern society, due especially to the increased circulation of books and to the new means of cultural and social communication, has been able to foster a universal culture. Further, by a more or less generalized reduction of working hours, the leisure time of most men had increased.

> May this leisure be used properly to relax, to fortify the health of soul and body through spontaneous study and activity, through tourism which refines man's character and enriches him with understanding of others, through sports activity which helps to preserve equilibrium of spirit even in the community, and to establish fraternal relations among men of all conditions, nations and races. Let Christians cooperate so that the cultural manifestations and collective activity characteristic of our time may be imbued with a human and a Christian spirit.[30]

Paul VI articulated the common features between sports and Christian life and connected the ideals of the Olympic movement with those of the Catholics:

> Physical efforts, moral qualities, love for peace: on the basis of these three points the dialogue which the Church is maintaining with the world of sports is genuine and friendly. It is our wish to make the latter wider and more fertile.[31]

Without any doubt, John Paul II (1978/2005) was the pope who elevated engagement and dialogue with sports to its highest level, certainly as regards the hierarchy of the Catholic Church.[32] After the Great Jubilee of 2000, during

---

[30] http://www.vatican.va/archive/hist_councils/ii_vatican_council/documents/vat-ii_const_19651207_gaudium-et-spes_en.html (last accessed 22 July 2020).

[31] Paulus VI, address to members of the International Olympic Committee, 28 April 1966, http://www.vatican.va/content/paul-vi/fr/speeches/1966/documents/hf_p-vi_spe_19660428_comitato-olimpico.html (last accessed 22 July 2020).

[32] See, for example, Pontificium Consilium pro Laicis, *The World of Sport Today. A Field of Christian Mission. International Seminar. Vatican, 11–12 November 2005*, Vatican City, 2006; Carlo Mazza, 'Sport in the Magisterium of John Paul II', in *Sport & Christianity*, ed. Lixey, 121–38.

which he addressed 80,000 young athletes at the Olympic Stadium of Rome,[33] he decided upon the establishment of a 'Section Church and Sports' within the 'Papal Council for the Laity' in 2004. This institute, also during the successive Pontificate of Benedict XVI (2005/13), engaged in several academic studies on sports and promoted a Christian perspective on sports, insisting on the importance of sports both for a more humane, peaceful and just society and for a new evangelization.[34] Francis, the current pope, has for his part been far from silent on sports. In 2013 he established within the 'Pontifical Council for Culture' a 'Department Culture & Sports' for three stated reasons. First, it was designed to bring together the saving message of the gospel and the world of sports, in order to open it up further to the Christian faith, which creates culture. Second, it was established to encourage the use of sports as an educational resource and tool for the cultural development of peoples. Third, along with other offices of the Holy See in this sector, it was intended to establish relationships with international sports bodies, and with Catholic sports associations. Fourth and finally, it was meant to facilitate dialogue at the Church University with sportspeople, sports centres and organizations, and to promote meaningful encounters between these cultural worlds.[35]

24.3 GIVING THE BEST OF YOURSELF (2018)

On 1 June 2018 the Holy See promulgated for the first time ever an official perspective on sports. The document *Giving the Best of Yourself*, prepared and edited by the Dicastery for Laity, Family and Life, in collaboration with specialists from all over the world, stresses its essence in the subtitle: it is a 'document on the Christian perspective on sport and the human person'.[36]

In this document, sports is defined as

> bodily motions of individual or collective agents who, in accordance with particular rules of the game, effect ludic performances which, on the condition of equal opportunity, are compared to similar performances of others in a competition. (2.2. What is sport?)

---

[33]http://www.vatican.va/content/john-paul-ii/en/homilies/2000/documents/hf_jp-ii_hom_20001029_jubilee-sport.html (last accessed 22 July 2020).

[34]Dicastery for Laity Family and Life, 'Documents on sport', http://www.laityfamilylife.va/content/laityfamilylife/en/sezione-laici/i-papi-e-lo-sport.html (last accessed 22 July 2020).

[35]Pontifical Council for Culture, 'Department of Culture and Sport', http://www.cultura.va/content/cultura/en/dipartimenti/sport.html (last accessed 22 July 2020).

[36]https://press.vatican.va/content/salastampa/en/bollettino/pubblico/2018/06/01/180601b.html (last accessed 22 July 2020). See also in print: *Giving the Best of Yourself. A Document about the Christian Perspective on Sport and the Human Person*, Vatican City, Dicasterium pro Laicis, Familia et Vita, 2018 (52). We stick here very close to chapter 1, on the pages 9–14 of the printed text.

It is very interesting to have a close look at the motive and the purpose of the document (chapter 1). In this paragraph I will stay very close to the text of the document, which I really want to use as a primary source to demonstrate its importance as an expression and exercise of public theology by the Holy See.

The document underlines that

> giving one's very best is a fundamental theme in sports, as athletes both individually and collectively strive to achieve their goals in the game. When a person gives his very best, he experiences satisfaction and the joy of accomplishment. The same is true in human life in general and in living out the Christian faith. We all want to be able to say one day, with St. Paul, 'I have fought to the end the good fight, finished my course, I have kept the faith.' (2 Tim 4:7). The document attempts to help the reader understand the relationship between giving our very best in sports and in living the Christian faith in every aspect of our lives.

The answer to the question why the church issues such a document – or why public theology should be interested in sports – is

> that the Church from its rich and deep experience of humanity very humbly wants to deal this experience with sports and wants to raise its voice in the service of sports. The Church values sports in itself, as an arena of human activity where the virtues of temperance, humility, courage, patience can be fostered and encounters with beauty, goodness, truth and joy can be witnessed. These kinds of experiences can be had by people of all nations and communities from across the world irrespective of the standard or level of sports. It is this dimension that makes sports such a truly modern global phenomenon and therefore something the Church is passionately interested in.

The document argues that the church has been a sponsor of the beautiful in art, music and other areas of human activity throughout its history.

> This is ultimately because beauty comes from God, and therefore its appreciation is built into us as his beloved creatures. Sports can offer us a chance to take part in beautiful moments, or to see these take place. In this way, sports has the potential to remind us that beauty is one of the ways we can encounter God. The universality of the sports experience, its communicative and symbolic strength, and its great educational and training potential are very evident today. Sports is now a phenomenon of civilization that fully resides in contemporary culture and permeates the styles and choices of many people's lives so we could question ourselves as Pius XII

did on 20 May 1945: 'How can the Church therefore not be interested in sports?'.[37]

Thus, the church as the people of God is connected to and is genuinely interested in sport as a contemporary human reality. Naturally, the church feels called to do everything possible within its immediate sphere of influence to ensure that sports is carried out in a humane and reasonable manner.

The church feels co-responsible for sports and for safeguarding it from the lapses that threaten it every day, particularly those of dishonesty, manipulations and commercial abuse. In addition, the document warns of the political–ideological use and abuse of sports and of the potential of sports to serve the interests of blind nationalism. As John Paul II put it on 12 April 1984,

> Sport is the *joy of life, a game, a celebration*, and as such it must be properly used [. . .] and freed from excess technical perfection and professionalism through a recovery of its free nature, its ability to strengthen bonds of friendship, to foster dialogue and openness to others, as an expression of the richness of being, much more valid and to be prized than having, and hence far above the harsh laws of production and consumption and all other purely utilitarian and hedonistic considerations in life.[38]

The church desires to be of service to all who work in sports, whether such individuals work in paid roles or, as the vast majority of cases, they are involved as volunteers, officials, coaches, teachers, administrators, parents or as athletes themselves.

The church approaches the world of sports because it desires to contribute to the construction of an increasingly authentic, humane sports. Sports is human universal and has taken on a new level of importance in our time and so it too finds an echo in the heart of the people of God. The church understands the human person as a unit of body, soul and spirit, and seeks to avoid any kind of reductionism in sports that debases human dignity.[39] Moreover, according to John Paul II:

---

[37]Pius XII, Address to Italian Sportsmen, 20 May 1945, http://www.vatican.va/content/pius-xii/it/speeches/1945/documents/hf_p-xii_spe_19450525_sport.html (last accessed 22 July 2020).
[38]John Paul II, Homily, 12 April 1984, http://www.vatican.va/content/john-paul-ii/it/homilies/1984/documents/hf_jp-ii_hom_19840412_messa-sportivi.html (last accessed 22 July 2020).
[39]Francis, Address to the Italian Tennis Federation, 8 May 2015, http://www.vatican.va/content/francesco/it/speeches/2015/may/documents/papa-francesco_20150508_federazione-italiana-tennis.html (last accessed 22 July 2020).

The Christian attitude towards sport as towards the other expressions of the person's natural faculties such as science, learning, work, art, love, and social and political commitment is not an attitude of rejection or flight, but one of respect, esteem, even though correcting and elevating them: in a word, an attitude of redemption.[40]

An attitude of redemption is present in sports when the primacy of the dignity of the person is respected and sports serves the human person in his or her integral development. As Pope Francis put it:

The bond between the Church and the world of sports is a beautiful reality that has strengthened over time, for the Ecclesial Community sees in sports a powerful instrument for the integral growth of the human person. Engaging in sports, in fact, rouses us to go beyond ourselves and our own self interests in a healthy way; it trains the spirit in sacrifice and, if it is organized well, it fosters loyalty in interpersonal relations, friendship, and respect for rules.[41]

Having articulated the motivations and purpose for the dialogue between the church and sports in chapter 1, the document explores in chapter 2 the reality of sports from its origins to its modern contexts. In doing so, it reflects on a definition of sports and the relevance of sports in and for the world. The document then in chapter 3 dives deeper into an anthropological understanding of sports and its importance specifically for the human person as a unity of body, soul and spirit. *Giving the Best of Yourself* then discusses how sports speaks to our greater search for ultimate meaning and promotes human freedom and creativity. The experience of sports is one that involves justice, sacrifice, joy, harmony, courage, equality, respect and solidarity along this search for meaning. Ultimate meaning from a Christian understanding is the ultimate happiness that is found in the experience of the all-encompassing love and mercy of God as realized in a relationship with Jesus Christ in the Spirit, an experience which takes place in and is lived out in the community of faith. In chapter 4, the document proceeds to explore specific challenges to the promotion of a humane and just sport, including the debasement of the body, doping, corruption and the sometimes negative influence of spectators. The church recognizes her shared responsibility with sports leaders to point out wrong directions taken and unethical behaviour and to steer sports in a way that

---

[40] John Paul II, Homily, 12 April 1984, http://www.vatican.va/content/john-paul-ii/it/homilies/1984/documents/hf_jp-ii_hom_19840412_messa-sportivi.html (last accessed 22 July 2020).
[41] Francis, Address to members of the European Olympic Committee, 23 November 2013, http://www.laityfamilylife.va/content/dam/laityfamilylife/Documenti/sport/eng/magisterium/Francis/ai-delegati-comitati-olimpici-europei-eng.pdf (last accessed 22 July 2020).

promotes human development. Finally, in chapter 5 the document presents 'an overview of the Church's ongoing efforts to contribute to the humanization of sports in the modern world. Sports in its various contexts, such as amateur and professional arenas, can and does serve as an effective tool for education and the formation of human values'. The editors of the document stress that there are still more topics related to the possibilities and challenges of sports that are not discussed in the document. The text is therefore not meant to serve as an exhaustive summary of the theories and realities pertaining to sports; rather, it seeks to articulate the church's understanding of the sports phenomenon and its relationship to faith.

24.4 A NEW POTENTIALITY FOR PUBLIC THEOLOGY?

One could and should ask oneself how, based on *Giving the Best of Yourself*, church and theology, and especially public theology, can continue to search for a new dialogue with the sports phenomenon. In other words, is there something new to be found in the document of 2018 which opens up new potentiality for public theology?

The past teaches us that the church since the pontificate of Leo XIII (1878–1903) regularly makes statements on extra-ecclesial social phenomena. A look at the official website of the Vatican reveals that the popes, on at least 200 occasions since the beginning of the twentieth century, whether in audiences or addresses, have touched the themes of physical culture and sports.[42] A certain evolution can be determined in these documents and texts from ecclesiastical recuperation and engagement towards an ecclesiastical perspective on these phenomena as a service to the world. The latter attitude is certainly to be found in *Giving the Best of Yourself*, which has to be situated in the line of Vatican II. It is no coincidence that the document refers a couple of times to *Gaudium et Spes*.

But the document seems to take a step further. Not only does it aim to adjust the world of sports and protect it from excesses through a Christian perspective on sports but it also wants to learn from sports as a phenomenon. This is actually in line with *Gaudium et Spes*, section 44:

> Just as it is in the world's interest to acknowledge the Church as an historical reality, and to recognize her good influence, so the Church herself knows how richly she has profited by the history and development of humanity.

This means that the church can learn from the world and the contemporary history. For ecclesiastical documents, this position is rather exceptional. Even

---

[42]Addresses and speeches per Pope: Pius X (3), Benedict XV (1), Pius XI (5), Pius XII (20), John XXIII (9), Paul VI (35), John Paul II (120), Benedict XVI (11) and Francis (33).

more remarkable is the fact that what can be learnt from sports is strongly connected with what can be called the almost religious aspect of sports: sacrifice for a higher purpose and entity, empathy for the game as game and the gratuitous character of sports. Sports and play in themselves are no purpose, but by being merged in them, our human person changes. The document is innovative in that sports is considered to be a form of grace. Sports are an occasion of joy for those who engage in them and even for its passionate followers and supporters. Play thus creates its own disinterested reality to which all are asked to subordinate themselves.

In an accompanying 'Message to the Prefect of the Dicastery for Laity, Family and Life', Pope Francis stresses, among others, that

> Sports is a *meeting place* where people of all levels and social conditions come together to reach a common aim. In a culture dominated by individualism and the gap between the younger generations and the elderly, sports is a privileged area around which people meet without any distinction of race, sex, religion, or ideology, and where we can experience the joy of competing to reach a goal together, participating in a team, where success or defeat is shared and overcome; this helps us to reject the idea of conquering an objective by focusing only on ourselves. The need for others includes not only teammates but also managers, coaches, supporters, the family; in short, all those people, who, with commitment and dedication, make it possible to 'give the best of oneself'. All this makes sports a catalyst for experiences of community, of the human family.

And especially for the Christian athlete:

> holiness will, therefore, consist in living sports as a means of encounter, personality formation, witnessing, and proclaiming the joy of being Christian with the people around oneself.[43]

In the aforementioned definition the document gives to sports, there is also the element 'ludic performances'. Sports is ideally conceived as an activity which pursues no external purposes but has its purpose in itself: it is autotelic – it has an end only in itself. Such internal purposes can be, for instance, the perfection of a particular motion, the surpassing of one's former achievements or those of others or the act of playing well together as a team to win a competition.

---

[43] 'Message of Pope Francis to the Prefect of the Dicastery for the Laity, Family and Life in occasion of the publication of the document "Giving the best of yourself" on the Christian perspective of sports and the human person', in *Giving the Best of Yourself: A Document about the Christian Perspective on Sport and the Human Person* (Vatican City: Dicasterium pro Laicis, Familia et Vita, 2018), 5–6.

Of course, the document does not deny that modern sports, particularly professional sports, also serve such external purposes as the attainment of glory for the nation, the demonstration of the supremacy of a political system or the making of money. If, however, an external purpose dominates or even nullifies the intrinsic purpose, the nature of the activity changes, as the document states, from play to labour. Moreover, according to *Giving the Best of Yourself*, the performances of professional athletes can never reach the ideal of sport if they conduct their labour without a ludic attitude (2.2. What is sport?).

In addition, in line with *Gaudium et Spes*, the document connects play with joy. Play, in an atmosphere of fair play, elevates sports to a joyful activity not only for the athletes themselves but for the passionate followers as well. Through sports human beings can experience beauty. Together with Pope Francis, *Giving the Best of Yourself*, inspired by Hans Urs von Balthasar, understands sports as a potential aesthetic faculty of the human being in the quest for ultimate meaning: the deepest truth of who we are in God's image and likeness (3.10. Sport Reveals the Quest for Ultimate Meaning).

This vision differs from that of the Jesuits and also from John Paul II's and Benedict XVI's vision in that it maintains that sports teaches us sacrificial spirit, or perseverance, which one can implement in other areas of life. This is the approach of the virtues, which the popes mentioned earlier suggest:

> You are administrators certainly; *but you are educators as well*, since sport can effectively inculcate many higher values, such as loyalty, friendship and team-spirit. It is especially important to keep this in mind at a time when football has also become as it were a global industry. It is true that football's financial success can help to sustain praiseworthy new initiatives, such as FIFA's 'Charity Project'. But it can also contribute to a culture of selfishness and greed. That is why the finer values of sport must be emphasized and passed on through the bodies represented in your Federation.[44]
>
> . . ./. . .
>
> You, dear athletes, shoulder the responsibility – not less significant – of bearing witness to these attitudes and convictions and of incarnating them beyond your sporting activity into the fabric of the family, culture, and religion. In doing so, you will be of great help for others, especially the youth, who are immersed in rapidly developing society where there is a widespread loss of values and growing disorientation.[45]

---

[44]John Paul II, Address to members of the FIFA, 11 December 2000, http://www.vatican.va/content/john-paul-ii/en/speeches/2000/oct-dec/documents/hf_jp-ii_spe_20001211_fifa.html (last accessed 22 July 2020).

[45]Benedict XVI, Address to the members of the Austrian Alpine Ski team, 6 October 2007, http://www.laityfamilylife.va/content/dam/laityfamilylife/Documenti/sport/eng/magisterium/BenedictXVI

The document studies this aspect of sports without profound elaboration and opts, by giving several perspectives, to leave space for different interpretations of sports and play. Per the wishes of Pope Francis, the original text was made less theological with a view to it being understandable to athletes and spectators, who may not be theologically well versed. In an earlier phase of the editorial preparation of *Giving the Best of Yourself*, one that started during the Pontificate of Benedict XVI, the role of theologians was more prominent. In that sense, there is still work to be done in the field of public theology on the themes touched only superficially by the document.

As mentioned in the introduction of the document itself, *Giving the Best of Yourself* did not exhaust all possible areas in the dialogue between church, public theology and sports. Neither did the document resolve the ongoing problems. One can ask oneself if the vision of sports as a gratuitous experience or grace sufficiently prepares the reader and athlete to recognize – and arms them to counter – all potential threats. In other words, does the church really commit itself to engage, together with other institutions, the dangers and excesses within the world of sports? And what about emerging research areas as theological analysis of disability sports. The potential areas for analysis are myriad: prayer in sports; sports and exercise psychology; the theory and practice of sport chaplaincy; theological reflection on exercise, health and well-being; women, sports and the Christian faith; global perspectives on sports and Catholicism and Christianity; sports, religion and popular culture; beauty and aesthetics in traditional and alternative/extreme sports; theological examination of child and youth sports; fatherlessness, fatherhood and sports; interpersonal relationships in sporting contexts. And, of course, many more.[46]

In any case, the vision elaborated in the Vatican document offers new potentialities for public theology: in the core of contemporary culture, especially in sports, a possibility is present where gratuitousness of life is embodied. This means that there are challenges enough with which the two existing Sports Sections within the Vatican, as well as for the academic Catholic (public) theologians, can engage vis-à-vis the phenomenon of sports. But the opportunity is even greater still. The fact that *Giving the Best of Yourself* is presented as a *Christian* perspective on sport and the human person – and indeed, that the document is written in an easily comprehensible way – opens the doors to an ecumenical dialogue on sports.

/2007-10-6%20SPEECH%20to%20Austrian%20ski%20team%20ENG.pdf (last accessed 22 July 2020).
[46]Watson and Parker, *Sport and the Christian Religion*, 100–18: 'Emerging Research Areas'.

PART V
The international scope of public theology

CHAPTER 25

Africa

DION A. FORSTER

Africa and its varied peoples remain deeply religious.¹ However, religion plays an ambivalent role in both public life and the private lives of Africans. In some instances, faith is constructive, orientating, allowing for meaning-making that contributes towards flourishing, resilience and resonance.² In other instances it has proven to be destructive, harmful and life-negating.³ In part this has to do with dominating social imaginaries that shape how reality and history are constituted in the variety of contexts that make up present-day Africa.⁴ Naturally, to understand this, one will have to consider the current situation of Africa and Africans in relation to forces of globalization. Some attention must also be given to the historical relationships among peoples and nations within the variety of African contexts. Moreover, it is important to remember the

---

¹Sunday Bobai Agang, H. Jurgens Hendriks and Dion A. Forster, eds, *African Public Theology* (Carlisle, Cumbria: Langham Partnership: Hippo Books, 2020), xiii, 1; Luis Lugo and Alan Cooperman, *Tolerance and Tension: Islam and Christianity in Sub-Saharan Africa* (Washington, DC: Pew Research Center, 2010), 1; Hennie Kotze, 'Religiosity in South Africa and Sweden: A Comparison', in *Freedom of Religion at Stake: Competing Claims among Faith Traditions, Sates and Persons*, ed. Dion A. Forster, Elisabeth Gerle, and Göran Gunner, Church of Sweden Research Series 18 (Eugene, OR: Pickwick Publications, 2019), 3–4.
²Samuel Waje Kunhiyop in Agang, Hendriks, and Forster, *African Public Theology*, xiii–ix.
³Sunday Bobai Agang, *The Impact of Ethnic; Political; and Religious Violence on Northern Nigeria; and a Theological Reflection on Its Healing* (Carlisle: Langham Monographs, 2011); Dion A. Forster, 'New Directions in Evangelical Christianities', *Theology* 122, no. 4 (1 July 2019): 267–75.
⁴Achille Mbembe, *On the Postcolony* (Berkeley; Los Angeles; London: University of California Press, 2001), 1–3.

tensions that exist between certain dominant religious traditions (particularly Christianity, Islam and African Traditional Religions), and the contemporary political, economic and cultural aspirations of Africans. Postcolonial and decolonial discourses must feature in any discussion of faith and public life in the variety of African contexts. The histories of conquest and colonial occupation by Arabic, Belgian, Dutch, English, French, German, Portuguese, Spanish and more recently American and Chinese groupings have left certain indelible 'marks' on African societies and African identities.[5]

As a result of this, it is important to spend some time critically considering the subjects of this chapter – Africans who bear their faith in a variety of publics across this vast continent.

First, it is important to demystify the notion of 'Africa' or 'the African'. Second, we shall need to pay attention to the complex interplay between the sacred and the secular in various African contexts. The configuration of the role, contribution and identity of faith and theology differs significantly from some Western contexts. In order to make this task manageable, this chapter will focus primarily on relatively contemporary expressions of Christianity in a variety of African contexts. Then, some attention will need to be given to what we mean when we speak of 'public theology' in this context. In particular, the discussion of African public theologies will be largely framed in relation to the development of public theology as an academic enterprise with particular ties to the Global Network for Public Theology (GNPT) and the *International Journal for Public Theology* (*IJPT*) in recent decades.

The structure of this chapter will thus be as follows. We shall begin with a critical conceptual discussion of the notions of Africa and Africans. Having established some ways in which we can reasonably think about, and talk about, Africa, we shall move on to a consideration of the relationship between faith and life in various African contexts. In this section, we would like to show how religion and the religious are configured within the constellations of meaning that make up the social, ethical and pragmatic boundaries for structuring life in various African societies. Next, we can rightly ask the question, 'Isn't all theology ultimately public theology?'[6] This section will provide some conceptual frameworks within which we can talk about the public role of faith

---

[5]Ibid., 1–3; Nokuzula Mndende, 'African Traditional Religion and Freedom of Religion in South Africa', in *Freedom of Religion at Stake: Competing Claims among Faith Traditions, Sates and Persons*, ed. Dion A. Forster, Göran Gunner, and Elisabeth Gerle (Eugene, OR: Wipf & Stock Publishers, 2019), 157–74.

[6]Nico Koopman, 'Some Contours for Public Theology in South Africa', *International Journal of Practical Theology* 14, no. 1 (April 2010): 123–38 (124); Jürgen Moltmann, Nicholas Wolterstorff and Ellen T. Charry, *A Passion for God's Reign: Theology, Christian Learning and the Christian Self*, ed. Miroslav Volf (Grand Rapids, MI: Wm. B. Eerdmans Publishing, 1998), 24.

in general terms, and public theology as a specific contemporary approach to theological sensemaking, in particular. Using these concepts, we will be able to trace the development, understandings and contributions of public theologies, and public theologians, in various African contexts. Naturally, such a discussion cannot be exhaustive. However, it will outline major trends, characteristics and understandings in public theologies in some African contexts. Finally, the chapter will conclude with a discussion of some challenges, critiques and opportunities that can be considered by contemporary African public theologians and public theologies.

25.1 DEMYSTIFYING AFRICA AND AFRICANS FROM THE WESTERN GAZE

This chapter focuses on public theologies in Africa. However, what do we mean when we speak of 'Africa'?[7] Of course, one could answer that question in many ways. In the popular imagination, Africa is both a place and a people. But of course, the more one considers this answer, the more one comes to realize that Africa is many different places and many different people. Moreover, even a cursory study of the subject of Africa shows us that Africa (and Africans) is viewed very differently by outside observers, than by Africans themselves. The histories of colonialism, slavery, apartheid and ongoing exploitation of the human and natural resources of the continent expose the gaze to which Africa and Africans are subject. Racism, Afro-pessimism and Afro-phobia continue to loom large in the global cultural imagination. Achille Mbembe rightly notes that speaking 'rationally about Africa is not something that has ever come naturally'.[8] It is important that we face this fact, if we are to understand both the conception of African public theologies and what possible contribution might emerge from among African public theologies for the rest of the world.

For the outside observer, we cannot speak in any meaningful sense of 'Africa as a country'.[9] I remember some years ago, while teaching at a leading American University, being asked by one of the senior staff members if I would be willing to sing the 'African National Anthem' at a public gathering. As with all large land masses, there are significant differences in vegetation, topography and climate. From the tropical regions at the equator to the vast deserts of the Sahara. Yes, the continent is one land mass, but it is varied and differentiated.

---

[7]cf. Vy Mudimbe, *The Invention of Africa: Gnosis, Philosophy, and the Order of Knowledge* (Lulu Press, Inc, 2020).
[8]Mbembe, *On the Postcolony*, 1.
[9]Marcus Mosiah Garvey, 'Hail! United States of Africa Poem by Marcus Mosiah Garvey', https://www.poemhunter.com/poem/hail-united-states-of-africa/?utm_source=facebook&utm_campaign=tavsiye_et&utm_medium=tavsiye_et (last accessed 1 May 2020).

This variety has significantly shaped the peoples and cultures of Africa. Among them are nomadic subsistence communities and settled farmers. There are traders, craftspeople and intellectuals. There are the very rich and the very poor. There are light-skinned persons and dark-skinned persons. Moreover, there are significant differences in language, culture, ethnicity and religion, among the peoples of Africa.[10] From Muslims of Arabic and European descent in the North to the Bantu and Khoi peoples of the Christianized South. Many contemporary differences come from the role that European, and more recently American and Chinese, powers have exercised upon particular people groups, in specific regions, at certain times in history. The reality of the existence of these persons, these places and these experiences denotes what Mbembe terms African *facticity*.[11] For Mbembe, this means that Africa, and Africans, need not justify their identity or existence to external observers, 'since things and institutions have always been there, there is no need to seek any other ground for them than the *fact of their being there*'.[12] Why do I make this point? Well, there is a tendency that whenever Africans write or speak about Africa we have to contend with myths, untruths, half-truths and prejudices about our peoples and places. The dominance of Western intellectual systems in the academy, or political systems in geo-politics, or economic systems in globalized markets, does not necessarily mean that they are more sophisticated, advanced, moral or desirable. These systems dominate by virtue of a complex set of historical events that have led to the current configuration of our global (and localized) social, political and economic lives.[13]

Christianity in Africa is itself an object lesson on how fortunes can change over history.

The African theologian and philosopher, John Mbiti notes that 'Christianity in Africa is so old that it [Christianity] can rightly be described as an indigenous, traditional, and African religion'.[14] Many of Christianity's early doctrines, and early theologians (Tertullian, Origen, Cyprian, Athanasius, Augustine of Hippo, Cyril of Alexandria), and early heretics (Sabellius and Arius are notable examples) come from locations such as Carthage, Alexandria and Hippo in North Africa.[15] Indeed, some forms of early African Christianity continue to this day in parts of Ethiopia and certain parts of Northern and Eastern Africa

---

[10]Mudimbe, *The Invention of Africa*, 1–9.
[11]Mbembe, *On the Postcolony*, 3.
[12]Ibid., 3–4.
[13]Dion A. Forster, 'Editorial: Democracy and Social Justice in Glocal Contexts', *International Journal of Public Theology* 12, no. 1 (23 April 2018): 1–4.
[14]John S. Mbiti, *African Religions & Philosophy* (Oxford; Portsmouth, NH: Heinemann, 1990), 229.
[15]Sebastian Kim and Kirsteen Kim, *Christianity as a World Religion: An Introduction* (London: Bloomsbury Academic, 2016), sec. 1768 of 10074.

– much like they did in the first seven centuries of the faith. However, the same cannot be reasonably claimed for the countries and Christianities, in sub-Saharan Africa, which largely arrived via missionaries and colonists to the subcontinent. As Mbiti says in *Concepts of God in Africa*, 'African peoples are not religiously illiterate.'[16] Regardless of how Christianity, and other indigenous, and imported, religious traditions came to be established on the continent, Africans were religious people long before the dawn of Christianity.

Without wanting to stretch this point too far, there are a few things that are worth noting as we begin to consider public theologies in Africa. First, Africa is vast and varied, and so are the Africans who inhabit the continent. Second, the Western gaze has sometimes been harsh and misguided. At times this has been because of notions of Western supremacism (based on Western cultural exceptionalism, and unconscious readings of global histories). At other times it is because of the inability to understand how Western economic, political and cultural privilege came to be established in relation to African (Asian and Latin American) subjugation. Third, if we are to honestly learn from public theologies from Africa and Africans, we will have to accept that even the 'dominated have a rich and complex consciousness; that they are capable of challenging their oppression; and that power, far from being total, is endlessly contested, deflated, and reappropriated but its "targets"'.[17] Indeed, we are seeing signs of this as African Christians, and African Christianities, establish themselves in the West, or challenge and transform traditionally Western Christian traditions.[18]

This reality has both opportunities and challenges for the dominance of Western theologies and polity in some global Christianities. First, there are opportunities to re-imagine Christianity in relation to postcolonial theological discourses emerging from Africa. As the weaknesses, inadequacies and immorality of some Western economic, political and social systems begin to be exposed, and Western Christians and Christianities seek to re-establish their identities outside of the hegemony of unchecked capitalism, rampant individualism and certain forms of political order that silence disagreement, a great deal can be learnt from the various expressions of Christianity that are forming in many African countries and communities.[19] As the African public theologian John de Gruchy notes, notions such as decolonization and Africanization are not only renewing African Christianities; they also offer some hope and opportunity in relation to the vacuum that is being left by the exhaustion of Western secularism,

---

[16] John S. Mbiti, *Concepts of God in Africa* (Santa Barbara, CA: Praeger Publishers, 1970), xiii.
[17] Mbembe, *On the Postcolony*.
[18] See some pertinent examples in Forster, 'New Directions in Evangelical Christianities', 267–75.
[19] See, for example, Dion A. Forster, 'Revival, Revolution and Reform in Global Methodism: An Understanding of Christian Perfection as African Christian Humanism in the Methodist Church of Southern Africa', *Black Theology an International Journal* 16, no. 1 (3 December 2018): 1–18.

individualism and capitalism.[20] In many Western contexts, as in Africa, the search for truer identity, and deeper meaning, has created an opening for the resurgence of frameworks of meaning, some of which are positive and life giving, others which are challenging and even destructive (such as forms of religious fundamentalism, nationalisms and consumerism).[21] This leads us to the second important point that needs to be noted. African Christian identities are varied, and they are also *facticit* – as we discussed earlier. We should not romanticize or idealize Africa, Africans or African Christianities. While Christianity seems to be growing numerically at a rapid rate on the African continent,[22] not all expressions of the Christian faith that come from Africa, which are now spreading to America, Europe and Asia, are constructive or responsible. Two clear contemporary examples are the split of the Anglican Communion, and the impending split of the United Methodist Church (a global Methodist denomination), because of differing views on human sexuality and the Christian faith among American and European Christians on the one hand and African Christians on the other.[23] The polity (Church Law) of these denominations have proven incapable of resolving complex theological issues in which African numerical dominance can 'out-vote' the American and European constituencies from which these Christian traditions first spread to Africa. Radical cultural differences are finding their way into complex theological engagements, and the politics of numbers is proving as unhelpful in the church as it has in many older democracies. Then there are the unanticipated consequences of Western values being filtered through Africa, back to the West with dire and destructive consequences. In West Africa, in particular, the uncritical intersection of contemporary neoliberal capitalism and neo-Pentecostal Christianities has led to massive growth in what are known as 'prosperity' churches.[24] These churches often count their membership in the hundreds of thousands, even millions, of adherents. As a result of global migration, they have spread to countries such as the UK, the Ukraine and France, where they not only attract African

---

[20]John W. De Gruchy, 'Humanism, Religion and the Renewal of Culture: A Review', *Modern Theology* 31, no. 1 (January 2015): 195–200 (196).

[21]Jens Zimmermann, *Incarnational Humanism: A Philosophy of Culture for the Church in the World* (Downers Grove, IL: Inter-Varsity Press, 2012), 9–10.

[22]Kim and Kim, *Christianity as a World Religion*, sec. 2463 of 10074; Philip Jenkins, *The Next Christendom: The Coming of Global Christianity* (Oxford: Oxford University Press, 2011), 1–2.

[23]See, David N. Field, *Bid Our Jarring Conflicts Cease: A Wesleyan Theology and Praxis of Church Unity* (Nashville, TN: Global Board of Higher Education for Ministry, 2017); Forster, 'New Directions in Evangelical Christianities', 267–75.

[24]Jenkins, *The Next Christendom*, xiii, 4, 82–6; Kim and Kim, *Christianity as a World Religion*, secs. 2444, 2480, 2494 of 10074.

migrants but also impact the indigenous populations and historical churches.[25] Some of the largest churches in the UK and parts of Eastern Europe are neo-Pentecostal 'prosperity' churches who have uncritically adopted some of the most destructive elements of contemporary Western social imaginaries, mixed in with very conservative African cultural practices and values.[26]

Hence, it would be wise for the reader to critically reconsider her or his conception of Africa and Africans. In order for us to 'think rationally about Africa', we shall need to understand the complex history that has shaped the diverse contexts and people living on this content. Moreover, we shall need to engage any prejudices we may have against Africa and Africans, or any proclivities we may hold for our own cultural, political, economic and religious sensibilities. Finally, as we consider the contribution of African public theologies to the rest of the world, we need to do so with a measure of critical appreciation. We should appreciate that the people of Africa have a great deal to offer by virtue of their history, lived experience and the diversity and richness of their cultures, languages, philosophies and religious expressions. However, we must also do so critically, acknowledging that some of the worst of our contemporary social imagination[27] has taken root in African Christianity and, by sheer numbers, is being transplanted uncritically, and harmfully, to communities across the globe.

In the section that follows we shall delve a little deeper into religion and life in African contexts, and we shall do so by paying attention to the myths, beliefs, philosophies and convictions that have shaped African Christianities in relation to public life.

25.2 ON RELIGION AND LIFE IN CONTEMPORARY AFRICAN CONTEXTS

In early 2020 a significant scholarly monograph entitled *African Public Theology* was published.[28] This 450-page book contains twenty-nine chapters written by authors from all over the African continent that discuss the ways in which contemporary African Christians are engaging in a variety of issues of public concern. Among the topics that are addressed are some 'soft' issues, such as identity, gender, democracy, civil society and citizenship. Then there are also some more 'concrete' issues under consideration, such as theology

---

[25] Forster, 'New Directions in Evangelical Christianities', 270; Jenkins, *The Next Christendom*, 120–35; Kim and Kim, *Christianity as a World Religion*, sec. 2511 or 10074.
[26] Kim and Kim, *Christianity as a World Religion*, sec. 2463 of 10074; Forster, 'New Directions in Evangelical Christianities', 267–75.
[27] Charles Taylor, *Modern Social Imaginaries* (Durham, NC: Duke University Press, 2004), 23.
[28] cf. Agang, Hendriks, and Forster, *African Public Theology*.

and work, the environment, corruption, poverty, ecology, interfaith relations and intergenerational issues. A recurring theme throughout the book is the importance of religion in the social, political and religious consciousness of Africans across the continent. The book itself enters into a dialogue with an important policy document from the African Union, *Agenda 2063: The Africa We Want*. This document notes that 'Africa is a continent of people with religious and spiritual beliefs, which play a profound role in the construction of the African identity and social interaction'.[29] Africa pushed back against the scholarly and popular notions of religious decline made popular in the late nineteenth and early twentieth centuries, by persons such as Auguste Comte, Herbert Spencer, Emile Durkheim, Max Weber and Karl Marx. They contended that religion would weaken and eventually vanish in both public and private life.[30] It has not done so in Africa. What is worth noting is the social and geographic location of many of these commentators. Hennie Kotze rightly points out that one of the most important critiques of the misrecognition of religious decline and religious growth around the world was due to the fact most research of that nature 'generally emphasized trends in church attendance by Protestants and Catholics in Europe'.[31] In large measure, these studies did not include data from Africa, Asia and Latin America.[32] Norris and Inglehart's research shows, however, that religious sentiments, and adherence to formalized religion, 'persist most strongly among vulnerable populations, especially those living in poorer nations, facing personal survival-threatening risks'.[33]

This is an important observation in relation to the prevalence and importance of African public theologies. Instead of merely engaging in a quantitative study of church attendance, or religious adherence, Norris and Inglehart's research focused on the qualitative measure of 'existential security' that religion provides.[34] In order to qualitatively evaluate the importance of religion in persons lives one needs to adopt an axiomatic approach that engages two primary realities: (1) the 'security axiom' and (2) the 'cultural traditions' axiom.[35]

Since very many Africans remain vulnerable because of poverty, war, natural disasters, inadequate state structures and globalized exploitation of both natural

---

[29]African Union, 'Agenda 2063: The Africa We Want' (2015), 2, https://au.int/en/Agenda2063/popular_version (last accessed 9 December 2020).
[30]Kotze, 'Religiosity in South Africa and Sweden: A Comparison', 3.
[31]Ibid., 4; cf. Pippa Norris and Ronald Inglehart, *Sacred and Secular: Religion and Politics Worldwide* (Cambridge: Cambridge University Press, 2011), 7; Charles Taylor, *A Secular Age* (Cambridge, MA: Harvard University Press, 2009), 1.
[32]Kotze, 'Religiosity in South Africa and Sweden: A Comparison', 4.
[33]Norris and Inglehart, *Sacred and Secular*, 4.
[34]Ibid.
[35]Kotze, 'Religiosity in South Africa and Sweden: A Comparison', 4–6.

and human resources, they would score much lower on the 'security axiom' than their counterparts in the West. This reality is borne out in many global indices, such as GDP per capita, GINI coefficient and the Human Development Index, to name but a few such metrics. One of the clearest illustrations of vulnerability is to be found in measuring where different African nations sit on the pre-materialist/materialist/post-materialist continuum. In Inglehart's important book, *The Silent Revolution*,[36] he charts the move from materialist to post-materialist values in various Western societies. Materialist societies are those in which survival and the maintaining of physical safety are a primary concern, whereas post-materialist societies tend to emphasize issues related to self-expression and quality of life. A materialist society will be concerned about economic and social security. Whereas a post-materialist society will be dominated by concerns over issues such as work satisfaction, personal fulfilment and so on, Kotze argues that because of the extreme vulnerabilities that many Africans experience, they could be classified as existing on the 'pre-materialist' end of the continuum.[37] Pre-materialist measurements include working towards providing shelter for all people, providing clean water for all people, making sure that everyone is adequately clothed, making sure that everyone can go to school, providing land for all people and providing everyone with enough food to eat.[38] It is not yet dealing with the quality of these items (as in a materialist society) or the experience evoked in relation to choices between quality options (as in the post-materialist society). A pre-materialist society is simply working to achieve the basic minimum for survival. Many Africans, and African societies, subsist on this side of the continuum. They are extremely vulnerable.

The next axiom is the role 'cultural traditions' play in the shaping of identity, values and beliefs. Traditional secularization theories rest upon understandings of a decline in 'religious participation'.[39] Such measurement is based upon the presupposition that there is a separation between religion and everyday life. As has already been mentioned, this is inadequate to describe lived religion, pre-cognate theologies, cultural and social beliefs, and everyday spiritualties of most Africans. The 'cultural traditions' axiom assumes 'that the distinctive world views that were originally linked with religious traditions have shaped the cultures of each nation in an enduring fashion'.[40] Indeed, as noted earlier, John Mbiti rightly claims that Africans are not religiously illiterate, and they never have

---

[36] Ronald Inglehart, *The Silent Revolution: Changing Values and Political Styles Among Western Publics* (Princeton, NJ: Princeton University Press, 2015).
[37] Kotze, 'Religiosity in South Africa and Sweden: A Comparison', 7.
[38] Ibid., 7.
[39] Ibid., 9; Taylor, *A Secular Age*, 1–3.
[40] Norris and Inglehart, *Sacred and Secular*, 17.

been.[41] Religion did not arrive on the African continent with the missionaries. African Traditional Religions, African cultures and African philosophies play a very significant role in the shaping of African identities, African theologies and African religious beliefs and practices.[42] One identifiable characteristic in many African philosophies and religions is the continuum of connectedness between the 'sacred' and the 'secular'. Cornel du Toit writes that for Africans in general, 'there are no ontological gaps between existing entities. The Western natural-supernatural dualism is foreign. . . . God, humankind, extra-humans and sub-humans are all regarded as integral parts of a single totality of existence. God's actions are not experienced as extra-ordinary. African metaphysical thinking is holistic'.[43] Of course, we should not be idealistic about this notion, as some have done. In many African contexts individualism, secularism and materialism are increasingly evident, as they are in other parts of the globalized world. However, in large measure, all of reality, and indeed all of life in Africa, is still subject to what Charles Taylor would call 'enchantment'.[44] The concept is best explained as the opposite of Max Weber's term 'disenchantment'.[45] The 'enchanted world', then, 'is the world of spirits, demons, and moral forces which our ancestors lived in'.[46] This enchanted view of the world significantly influences 'cultural traditions'. Whereas in some Western societies, religion and the religious are viewed with suspicion, distrust and even scorn, that is not the case in most African contexts.[47] Religion plays a central role in what may be called the 'cultural imagination' and the 'social imaginary' of most African societies and the persons that constitute them.

Many contemporary ethicists and philosophers agree that all persons shape their lives according to a sort of 'cultural imagination'. Graham Ward, a professor at Oxford University, says that the cultural imagination is a set of inherited, unquestioned, beliefs, values and social commitments that a

---

[41]Mbiti, *Concepts of God in Africa*, xiii.
[42]Ibid., 1; Mbiti, *African Religions & Philosophy*, 3–4; Mndende, 'African Traditional Religion and Freedom of Religion in South Africa', 157–74; Dion A. Forster, 'Translation and a Politics of Forgiveness in South Africa? What Black Christians Believe, and White Christians Do Not Seem to Understand', *Stellenbosch Theological Journal* 14, no. 2 (2018): 77–94; Dion A. Forster, *The (Im)Possibility of Forgiveness: An Empirical Intercultural Bible Reading of Matthew 18.15–35* (Eugene, OR: Wipf and Stock Publishers, 2019), 21–57.
[43]C. W Du Toit, ed., *The Integrity of the Human Person in an African Context: Perspectives from Science and Religion* (Pretoria: Research Institute for Theology and Religion, 2004), 30.
[44]Taylor, *A Secular Age*, 25.
[45]N. Gane, *Max Weber and Postmodern Theory: Rationalization versus Re-Enchantment* (New Jersey: Springer, 2002), 20–7, 40.
[46]Taylor, *A Secular Age*, 25–6.
[47]Agang, Hendriks, and Forster, *African Public Theology*, xiii, 1–2.

society adopts over time.⁴⁸ The 'cultural imagination' shapes what we think is possible, and impossible. It informs how we believe we should live, act and engage socially. It informs what we find attractive and unattractive, what we believe is morally and ethically right, or wrong, and even what we believe to be true and good. These are all aspects of our cultural imagination at work. Charles Taylor uses a slightly different term to describe this phenomenon. He calls it the modern 'social imaginary'.⁴⁹ The 'social imaginary' constitutes those sets of beliefs, ideas and values that shape the ways in which people 'imagine' their 'social existence' functions or should function. The 'social imaginaries' are not set in concrete, and they are not universal. Neither do they remain static throughout history. What is acceptable in one context may be completely unacceptable in another, and what was considered necessary at one point in history may be considered barbaric in another. Social imaginaries are, thus, the imaginative boundaries of our social and moral lives. Religion figures prominently in the cultural imagination and social imaginary of many African societies. Indeed, as Elisabeth Gerle notes, '[r]eligion has always played an important role in [African] society. Its pervasive presence has often shaped shared world views. As a result, it is often almost impossible to differentiate between culture and religion'.⁵⁰ Thus, Africa and Africans tend to feature in a qualitatively significant manner on both the 'security axiom' and 'cultural traditions' axiom as religious individuals and religiously predisposed societies. As a result, it is not strange to see religion playing an overt role in the shaping of political life, economic systems, cultural values and societal norms.⁵¹ In this sense one could reasonably assert that in Africa the distinction between private faith and public faith does not operate, or need to operate, in the same way as it does in many secularized Western societies.

There are at least two, broad, ways in which this can be understood. First, and most easily identifiable, are those approaches that come from the field of religious studies. These approaches draw upon history, sociology and anthropology to offer descriptive and analytical insights into the various religions, their adherents, practices and presence in various forms of public life. Second are the approaches that come from theology and philosophy. This second grouping seeks to understand what persons believe, why they hold their beliefs, what the intentions of their beliefs are, what consequences these

---

⁴⁸Graham Ward, *Unimaginable: What We Imagine and What We Can't* (London: I.B.Tauris, 2018), 10–11.
⁴⁹Taylor, *Modern Social Imaginaries*, 23; Taylor, *A Secular Age*, 159–211.
⁵⁰Dion A. Forster, Göran Gunner, and Elisabeth Gerle, eds, *Freedom of Religion at Stake: Competing Claims among Faith Traditions, Sates and Persons*, Church of Sweden Research Series 18 (Eugene, OR: Wipf & Stock Publishers, 2019), xvii.
⁵¹Lugo and Cooperman, 'Tolerance and Tension'.

beliefs might hold and at times they make judgements on the moral and ethical appropriateness of such beliefs in relation to historical values and doctrines.

In concluding this section, we can thus reasonably argue that religion is prevalent in African societies. It plays an important role in shaping public life, both positively and negatively. It is for this reason that academic theologians across the varying African contexts have sought to engage in public theological research while entering into conversation with the various publics of society in which theological contributions are formulated and propagated (the church, society at large and the academy).[52] At times, such research is undertaken formally as a form of 'public theology'. This is done by persons who identify themselves, and their work with some general characteristics of public theology,[53] or with guilds, centres or institutes of public theology on the continent and internationally.[54] At other times, the work of theologians or groups is recognized as being identifiable as a form of public theological engagement.[55] In the section that follows we shall delve a little deeper into these aspects.

---

[52]David Tracy, 'Three Kinds of Publicness in Public Theology', *International Journal of Public Theology* 8, no. 3 (26 August 2014): 330–4; D. J. Smit, 'What Does 'Public' Mean? Questions with a View to Public Theology', in *Christian in Public Aims, Methodologies, and Issues in Public Theology*, ed. Len Hansen (Stellenbosch: SUN Press, 2007), 11–47.

[53]For some discussion on the characteristics and nature of public theologies please see, Dirkie J. Smit, 'Does It Matter? On Whether There Is Method in the Madness', in *A Companion to Public Theology*, ed. Sebastian C. H. Kim and Katie Day (Leiden: Brill, 2017), 67–94; Dion A. Forster, 'The Nature of Public Theology', in *African Public Theology*, ed. Sunday Bobai Agang, H. Jurgens Hendriks, and Dion A. Forster (Carlisle, Cumbria: Langham Partnership: Hippo Books, 2020), 15–26.

[54]Koopman, 'Some Contours for Public Theology in South Africa', 123–38; Abraham A. Berinyuu, 'Doing Public Theology in Africa: Trends and Challenges', in *International Academy of Practical Theology, Pathways to the Public Square*, ed. Elaine Graham and A. Rowlands (Münster: LIT Verlag, 2005), 147–56; John W. de Gruchy, 'Public Theology as Christian Witness: Exploring the Genre', *International Journal of Public Theology* 1, no. 1 (2007): 26–41; Agang, Hendriks, and Forster, *African Public Theology*.

[55]G. M. H. Loubser, 'A Public Theologian: A Critical Study of J. Wentzel van Huyssteen's Postfoundationalist Facilitation of Interdisciplinarity' (Thesis (DTh), Stellenbosch University, 2012), https://scholar.sun.ac.za/handle/10019.1/20169 (last accessed 7 December 2020); Dion A. Forster, 'Worship as 'Protest': Johan Cilliers as a Public Theologian?', *STJ | Stellenbosch Theological Journal, Johan Cilliers Festschrift* 5, no. 2 (November 2019): 155–74; Philomena Njeri Mwaura, 'The Circle of Concerned African Women Theologians and Their Engagement in Public Theology: A Pathway to Development', *Pathways to African Feminism and Development, Journal of African Women's Studies Centre* 1, no. 1 (2015): 90–104; Vuyani S. Vellem, 'The Reformed Tradition as Public Theology', *HTS Teologiese Studies / Theological Studies* 69, no. 1 (2013): 1–5; Bastienne Klein, 'On Becoming and Being a Woman Theologian in South Africa: In Conversation with Denise Ackermann', *Journal of Theology for Southern Africa* 118 (2004): 40–52 (40).

25.3 ON PUBLIC THEOLOGIES IN AFRICAN CONTEXTS

As was already hinted at, public theology and public theologians are identified in at least two ways in the varying African contexts. First, there are those institutions, and persons, who claim to be engaged in public theological research. In 2016 the GNPT was hosted on the African continent for the first time since it was founded in 2007. The GNPT had been invited by Prof Nico Koopman, one of (south) Africa's best-known public theologians. The author of this chapter, Dion A. Forster, served as the hosting chair for the GNPT, and the Centre he directs, the Beyers Naudé Centre for Public Theology at the University of Stellenbosch, served as the institutional host for the meeting.[56] The continent, however, already had a longstanding and rich association with GNPT since Nico Koopman, Russel Botman and Dirkie Smit were among the founder members of the Network in 2007. Throughout the rest of Africa there was also already a rich, vibrant and even critical engagement with public theologies. Persons such as Sunday Agang (the primary editor of *African Public Theology*), Tersur Aben, John de Gruchy, Godwin Akper, Sarojini Nadar, Isabel Phiri, Julie Claassens, Andries van Aarde, Tinyiko Maluleke, Mercy Amba Oduyoye, Etienne de Villiers, Musa Dube, Vuyani Vellem, Christina Landman and Rothney Tshaka (to name just a few) were all writing, supervising students and participating in regional, continental and international public theological events. Among the very first articles published in the *IJPT* are contributions by African public theologians such as John de Gruchy[57] and Dirkie Smit.[58]

However, there is also a more general sense in which public theology had been operating, and was identifiable, on the African continent. In the second sense, African theologians throughout history have been engaging theologically with issues of public concern. There are far too many African theologians, and particular issues, to mention by name in this category. However, a retrospective consideration easily identifies contributions from African theologians on issues such as justice, ethics, economics, politics, science, culture and gender. These persons, and their contributions, are understood as public theologies in the sense that Koopman claims that since all Christian theology 'reflects on the love of the triune God for the world. . . . At its heart, therefore, [all] Christian theology is public theology'.[59]

---

[56]Forster, 'Editorial', 1–4.
[57]De Gruchy, 'Public Theology as Christian Witness', 26–41.
[58]Dirkie Smit, 'Notions of the Public and Doing Theology', *International Journal of Public Theology* 1, no. 3 (2007): 431–54.
[59]Koopman, 'Some Contours for Public Theology in South Africa', 123.

In this sense, faith and the theologies that inform it have had, and continue to have, a profound influence on public life in a variety of African contexts. However, as Samuel Waje Kunhiyop notes, the purpose of theology is not only to study the nature, intention and will of God; rather, 'it also involves the study of how God interacts with his creation'.[60] In particular, Sunday Agang contends that the task of an African public theology is to enliven responsible and faithful Christian faith among African Christians in all three publics (the church, the academy and society at large) for the glory of the God who is just, merciful, gracious and loving and for the common good of human and non-human creation.[61] He says,

> What Africa needs is not just a Christian theology but a Christian theology that is concerned with how all aspects of human knowledge, understanding and faith in God can translate into a deep moral commitment to building a better society, one which is strong in faith, love, justice and wisdom. Such a theology can be called a public theology.[62]

The first thorough survey of African public theologies was conducted by H. Russel Botman in 2000 in a book chapter entitled 'Theology after Apartheid: Paradigms and Progress in South African Public Theologies'.[63] Botman surveyed African theologies and identified the emergence of a series of paradigmatic theological shifts in Africa at the turn of the millennium. This comes after the end of Apartheid in South Africa, the horrors of the Rwandan Genocide and after some decades of postcolonial independence for many countries on the continent. He viewed this period as constituting a paradigm shift in African theologies. According to Dirk J. Smit, the paradigmatic shift that Botman identified involved a renewed theological focus on the 'political, cultural and economic realities of the time . . . following different images, pursuing different metaphors, making different proposals, holding conflicting viewpoints, and raising new questions'.[64] Smit developed Botman's notion and identified what he considered the paradigmatic shifts which contributed towards what we call 'public theology' in contemporary theological scholarship:[65]

---

[60]Agang, Hendriks, and Forster, *African Public Theology*, xiii.
[61]Ibid., 3–5.
[62]Ibid., 8.
[63]H. Russel Botman, 'Theology after Apartheid: Paradigms and Progress in South African Public Theologies', in *Theology in the Service of the Church: Essays in Honor of Thomas W. Gillespie*, ed. Wallace M. Alston, Jr. (Grand Rapids, MI: W.B. Eerdmans Pub., 2000), 36–51.
[64]Smit, 'Does It Matter? On Whether There Is Method in the Madness', 67.
[65]Dirk J. Smit, 'The Paradigm of Public Theology – Origins and Development', in *Contextuality and Intercontextuality in Public Theology*, ed. Heinrich Bedford-Strohm, Florian Höhne and Tobias Reitmeier (Theology in the Public Square, 4; Munster: LIT Verlag, 2013), 11–23.

- The increasingly visible role of religion in public life. This includes forms of civil religion, the politicization of religion and the religionization of politics.
- How religion and theology affect and are affected by public reasoning in society, the academy and the church.
- The contextualization of theologies in vastly different social, religious and political contexts such as Africa, Europe, Asia, Australia and the Americas.
- The relationship between theologies and public struggles in contexts of injustice and conflict. For example, the role that the churches played in dismantling Apartheid in South Africa.
- The role that theology and the church have played in contributing towards knowledge in fields such as service delivery, gender debates and issues of environmental concern. Of course, not all contributions were positive or constructive. However, some were.
- Theology and the public return of the religious (e.g. religious fundamentalisms, religious violence and extremism, as well as the resurgence of interest in religion and spirituality as making a positive and constructive contribution to the lives of persons and communities across the world).

Each of these paradigmatic shifts emerged within, or in response to, changing contexts (political, social and religious). The mutual engagement between faith and life, increasingly reasonable and meaningful exchanges between theology and other academic disciplines, and the critical reflection on history and context are identifiably important aspects of public theology as a new paradigm in African theology. Smit's view of public theology coheres with those of Kunhiyop and Agang. Smit suggests that public theology is 'a visionary and normative project, seeking to take a position, to make a difference, to serve what matters . . . it is the urge to show the world what theology looks like. It is concerned with issues of common interest and of the common good, whatever that might mean. It is about discipleship as transformation'.[66] A few years later, Koopman further narrowed the focus of public theology in Africa by framing his understanding of the concept in terms of three primary questions:

- What is the inherent public nature of God's love for Africa (and our world)?

---

[66]Smit, 'Does It Matter? On Whether There Is Method in the Madness', 89.

- How can we understand and articulate the rationality of God's love for Africans and Africa (and the rest of the world)?
- What are the meaning and implications of God's love for every facet of life (not only the overtly religious or religious institutions or functions)?[67]

For Koopman these three framing questions help us rethink, and re-imagine, the 'contents of our faith', that is, what it means to be authentically and responsibly Christian; the 'rationality of our Christian faith', that is, what our faith and beliefs may mean for, and in, our contexts and our lives within those contexts; and the 'implications of Christian faith for all facets of life', that is, how our theology moves us from belief to action, from doctrine to ethics, from worship to mission.[68] Hence, Koopman moves from theology and public presence (in its broadest sense) towards a clearer expression of how and why theology is to be present in public life. It is to be a rational engagement with the various publics of society for the sake of honouring the implications of Christian faith for all facets of life, including the economic, political and social systems of our continent and its people. In Africa, a theological contribution is viewed as one 'public' contribution among many others (such as political thought and economic theory). In this regard public theology constitutes the 'bridge' that meaningfully translates the contributions from 'society at large' to the theological academy and the church, and from the church and theological academy to other disciplines and public discourses in society at large – it is interdisciplinary, transdisciplinary and multilungual in nature.[69]

25.4 SOME PROBLEMS AND PROMISES IN AFRICAN PUBLIC THEOLOGIES

It would be irresponsible if we did not focus on some of the critiques and identifiable challenges in African public theologies. We shall begin by highlighting and considering some of the major objections to African public theologies, and then conclude this section by considering some ways in which African public theologies might hold value for discussions of public theology in other contexts, and among a broader audience.

The most robust, and widely recognized, critique of public theology in the African context has come from liberation theologians and Black African theologians, such as Tinyiko Maluleke and Rothney Tshaka. Maluleke and

---

[67]Koopman, 'Some Contours for Public Theology in South Africa', 124.
[68]Ibid., 124.
[69]Forster, 'The Nature of Public Theology', 15–26; Smit, 'Does It Matter? On Whether There Is Method in the Madness', 85–7.

Tshaka express the concerns of these theological traditions by questioning whether a public theological approach can ever be contextual enough to engage the complexities and uniqueness of Black and African socio-religious contexts and experiences.[70] Both Maluleke and Tshaka ask whether an approach to theology that does not focus primarily on social analysis (as liberation theologies do)[71] or existential experience (as Black theologies do) would have value in the broader African social context. Maluleke and Tshaka, and more recently Urbaniak,[72] have critiqued the approaches, and methods, associated with the persons and places that are identified as offering a public theological contribution in Africa as being too Western and non-contextual in nature. Maluleke's primary concern is that,

> public theology is trapped in an attempt to universalize concepts, similar to earlier forms of [colonial] theology, and does not take developing world theologies seriously. It is post-coloniality, rather than postmodernity, that... is of importance to [South] African society.[73]

Maluleke's primary concern is that public theologians, and their theologies, are incapable of addressing the ongoing 'anger' in African societies since they tend to employ theological language and objectives, such as reconciliation and forgiveness, which are much more closely aligned to both universal theological ideals and the intentions of Western theologies that seek to maintain the status quo of Black and African subjugation.[74] For this reason, primarily, he contends that 'a theory of resistance as found in liberation theologies' is crucial for addressing the concerns of contemporary African life.[75]

---

[70] Rothney Stok Tshaka, 'African, You Are on Your Own! The Need for African Reformed Christians to Seriously Engage Their Africanity in Their Reformed Theological Reflections', *Scriptura: International Journal of Bible, Religion and Theology in Southern Africa* 96 (2007): 533–48; Rothney S. Tshaka, 'On Being African and Reformed? Towards an African Reformed Theology Enthused by an Interlocution of Those on the Margins of Society', *HTS Theological Studies* 70, no. 1 (2014): 1–7; Tinyiko Sam Maluleke, 'Reflections and Resources The Elusive Public of Public Theology: A Response to William Storrar', *International Journal of Public Theology* 5, no. 1 (2011): 79–89.
[71] Cf., Maluleke, 'Reflections and Resources The Elusive Public of Public Theology', 79–89.
[72] Jakub Urbaniak, 'Elitist, Populist or Prophetic? A Critique of Public Theologizing in Democratic South Africa', *International Journal of Public Theology* 12, no. 3-4 (2018): 332–52; Jakub Urbaniak, 'What Makes Christology in a Post-Apartheid South Africa Engaged and Prophetic? Comparative Study of Koopman and Maluleke', *Theology and the (Post) Apartheid Condition: Genealogies and Future Directions* 1 (2016): 125–45; Jakub Urbaniak, 'Theologians and Anger in the Age of Fallism: Towards a Revolution of African Love', *Black Theology* 12, no. 2 (2017): 87–111; Jakub Urbaniak, 'Probing the 'Global Reformed Christ' of Nico Koopman: An African-Kairos Perspective', *Stellenbosch Theological Journal* 2, no. 2 (2016): 495–538.
[73] Maluleke, 'Reflections and Resources The Elusive Public of Public Theology', 79.
[74] Ibid.
[75] Ibid.

There is a great deal of merit in this critique. The particular must always be held in tension with the universal – in this case, the history, and current reality, of Africans must surely be engaged in a careful and robust manner if a particular theology is to have value for the context. However, one could also ask whether this task is only to be achieved through a liberation theology. Or perhaps, a liberative theological approach should be prioritized in certain contexts and settings, while other theological approaches can be of value in different settings. As stated earlier, it would be a mistake to treat Africa, and all Africans, as sharing one history, and one current existential experience. Moreover, there is a logical disjuncture in this argument – if what is required is a sensitivity to the uniqueness of each context, then to universalize Black theology, or liberation theology, would undermine the contextual uniqueness of each situation, and the kind of theology that is required to adequately engage that context. A careful reading of Maluleke and Tshaka's arguments shows that they are aware that their privileging of liberation theology, and Black African theologies, in Africa is meant to be held in tension with other universal theological claims. As such, it would be fair to conclude that they are not dismissing public theologies outright but, rather, seeking to aggregate and critique particular approaches to faith and public life in Africa that are inadequate to address specific concerns and needs of Africans. This does not mean that a carefully constructed engagement between faith and contextual issues of public concern – perhaps a liberative, Black, African engagement with faith and public life – would be entirely inappropriate or unwelcome.

A final significant critique that I will highlight against African public theologies is a critique that is brought by feminist public theologians. To date the most constructive African contribution has come from Professor Julie Claassens in an article entitled 'Towards a Feminist Public Theology'.[76] Given the historically patriarchal nature of African academic theologies, the absence of extensively developed feminist public theologies in the African context is a critique within itself. Professor Esther McIntosh has been outspoken about the patriarchal nature and character of public theologies around the world.[77] In particular she rightly shows that public theological research is dominated by male theologians and approaches to theology that can function in ways that

---

[76] L. Juliana Claassens, 'Towards a Feminist Public Theology: On Wounds, Scars and Healing in the Book of Jeremiah and Beyond', *International Journal of Public Theology* 13, no. 2 (2019): 185–202.

[77] Esther McIntosh, 'Public Theology, Populism and Sexism: The Hidden Crisis in Public Theology', in *Resisting Exclusion: Global Theological Responses to Populism*, vol. 1, LWF Series 2019 (Geneva, Switzerland: Lutheran World Federation, 2019), 215–28, https://www.lutheranworld.org/sites/default/files/2019/documents/studies_2019_resisting_exclusion_en_full.pdf.

exclude women and women's perspectives.[78] This is certainly a critique that we are subject to in African theologies in general and African public theologies in particular. While there are a number of significant women public theologians on the continent (such as Musa Dube, Isebel Phiri, Denise Ackermann, Mercy Amba Oduyoye, Julie Claassens, Sarojini Nadar, to name just a few), the reality is that public theological research is largely occupied by men and men's world views and concerns. Moreover, if one were to look at the chosen conversation partners that are highlighted in published books and articles on public theologies around the world, they are largely dominated by men. This is also true of African public theologies. This critique is valid and it is taken seriously. It requires concerted attention and a choice for critical self-reflection and corrective action. The only answer to this critique is to encourage African public theologians to be intentional about how we do our theology, with whom we undertake the theological task, and what issues we choose to address in our public theological research.

This section of the article has sought to highlight, and give attention to, some of the necessary and important critiques, against African public theologies. However, having considered the content of the critiques, it can be concluded that the intention of the various critiques is not to dismiss, or invalidate, the importance of engaging faith and public life in a mutual and dynamic interchange, but rather for the quality, intention and location of this interchange to be undertaken with particular attention to the context, concerns and lived experiences of Africans.

As was mentioned earlier, the challenges that Africa, and African Christians, face are specific to our context, but they are not entirely unique. The contribution of African Christianities to global theological discourses will increase as the numerical dominance of African Christianities increases globally in years to come. It will be necessary to maintain both an appreciative and a critical regard for African public theological contributions. Moreover, it will be necessary for theologians from around the world, including African theologians, to maintain a measure of self-critical humility. At times we may need to discern what aspects of our own cultural imaginations and social imaginaries have adulterated, misinformed or misshapen our theological convictions and contributions. What is certain is that there is the possibility for mutual enrichment, and growing in faithfulness, through discerning the gifts and contributions that each context,

---

[78]Esther McIntosh, 'Special Issue – Hearing the Other: Feminist Theology and Ethics', *International Journal of Public Theology* 4, no. 1 (2009): 1–4; Esther McIntosh, 'Issues in Feminist Public Theology', in *Public Theology and the Challenge of Feminism*, ed. Stephen Burns and Anita Monro (London: Routledge, Taylor and Francis Group, 2015), 63–74.

and the theologies from those contexts, has to offer global public theological discourses.

25.5 CONCLUSION

This chapter sought to offer some insights into the complexities, and realities, of contemporary public theologies in Africa. In the process we were encouraged to recognize the diversity of people, places and experiences that make up Africa and the persons who live on the continent. Next we considered the role that religion plays in a variety of African contexts. A primary conclusion of this section is that religion, in its many ambivalent forms, holds great importance for both private and public life in Africa. Next we traced the nature and character of what we call 'public theology' in Africa. In particular, we focused on contemporary Christian theologies on the continent in relation to the GNPT and the *IJPT*. Finally, we considered some of the problems and promises of African public theologies.

What we can conclude is that there is a vibrant, and contested, engagement with public theologies on the African continent. This takes on both formal and informal guises. Moreover, there is promise in African theologies, but there are also some problems to be aware of. We should recognize that African public theologies cannot be ignored or disregarded since they play a significant role in the global academy, through migration and globalization in churches all over the world and in shaping values and religious perceptions in society at large.

CHAPTER 26

Public theology in Asia

ALEXANDER CHOW

The term 'public theology' automatically presumes there is such a thing as 'private theology'. It also suggests that there is a difference between public and private religion, and public and private spheres. As such, public theology is often a discourse which attempts to negotiate the 'secular' and the 'post-secular'. However, as Talal Asad has rightly pointed out, 'Secularism as political doctrine arose in modern Euro-America.'[1] It is therefore foreign to most other contexts. Likewise, public theology arose as a way of articulating Christianity's contribution in societies where it once reigned as the dominant ideology – Christendom, if you will – but has since shrunk in size and in strength and finds itself clamouring to reclaim its lost voice.

Christian public theology in Asia has a very different starting point.[2] There are only two Asian countries which have a Christian majority: the Philippines and East Timor. Both have over 90 per cent of their population who identify as Christians, the vast majority of whom are associated with Catholicism. Many presume South Korea, home to the largest single congregation of the world – Yoido Full Gospel Church in Seoul with over 800,000 members – to also have a Christian majority. But Catholicism and Protestantism combined in

---

[1] Talal Asad, *Formations of the Secular: Christianity, Islam, Modernity* (Stanford, CA: Stanford University Press, 2003), 1.
[2] Although there may be other forms of public theology that can be discussed, this chapter will focus on Christian public theology as it has been expressed in continental Asia, and 'public theology' will presume a Christian expression.

South Korea has never exceeded 30 per cent of its population and has recently witnessed declining numbers.

Generally speaking, public theology in Asia has needed to contend with Christianity's existence as a minority and, often, marginal religion. Other ideologies – Hindu, Buddhist, Muslim, Confucian and Communist – have been given preference.[3] Part of this is due to the historic and contemporary prevalence of these ideologies in Asia. However, many of them have also offered rationale for political power – from Asian forms of the divine right of kings to a variety of forms of nationalism. Christians have needed to negotiate their own understandings of responsibility and duty in the world, with Asian societies which rarely have been welcoming to their public existence. As we shall see, public theology in Asia is a deeply contextual enterprise, which has critically negotiated Christian and non-Christian resources in situ for public engagement. Given the vast and diverse span of Asia, this chapter will necessarily be selective.[4] It will highlight case studies from three major expressions of public theology in Asia – liberation, dialogue and subversion – in order to demonstrate the determination of Christians to live out their faiths *publicly* despite the often unsympathetic environments.

26.1 LIBERATION

The Indian theologian Felix Wilfred identifies the agency of the subalterns as the starting point of his book *Asian Public Theology*. He explains that public theology needs 'to overcome various forms of exclusion in the global world which are experienced . . . in terms of caste, class, gender, ethnicity, physical disabilities and so on'.[5] Wilfred continues to explain that his reflections are shaped by the two most affected subalterns – *dalits* and women. As such, Wilfred sees the primary expression of public theology in Asia as one framed

---

[3] It is worth noting that, in many Asian contexts, 'religion' and 'philosophy' were terms that needed to be invented only when interacting with foreign (mainly Western) powers. While I will follow the practice of authors being cited, this chapter will tend to use the term 'ideology' as a more encompassing description. See Jason Ānanda Josephson, *The Invention of Religion in Japan* (Chicago, IL: University of Chicago Press, 2012); Robert Eric Frykenberg, 'Constructions of Hinduism at the Nexus of History and Religion', *Journal of Interdisciplinary History* 23, no. 3 (Winter 1993): 523–50.

[4] Asia is a vast and populous continent, encompassing two-thirds of the world's population. For a glimpse into the complexity of any discussion about the pluriform expressions of 'Asian Christianity' (let alone Asian Christianity outside the Asian continent), see Peter C. Phan, 'Introduction: Asian Christianity/Christianities', in *Christianities in Asia*, ed. Peter C. Phan (Malden, MA: Wiley-Blackwell, 2011), 1–6.

[5] Felix Wilfred, *Asian Public Theology: Critical Concerns in Challenging Times* (Delhi: ISPCK, 2010), xxiv.

in postcolonial and liberation theological discourses.⁶ This makes sense, given that postcolonial criticism is best known through its Asian theorists – in literary studies (e.g. Edward Said, Gayatri Spivak and Homi Bhabha) and in biblical and theological studies (e.g. R. S. Sugirtharajah, Kwok Pui-lan, Angela Wai-Ching Wong and Felix Wilfred).⁷ Furthermore, while postcolonial theologies are heavily shaped by literary theories and, therefore, tend to be focused on the Bible as literature, liberation theologies in Asia have often been informed by the developments within Catholic liberation theology in Latin American.⁸ While their starting points are different, postcolonial and liberation theologies are, according to Sugirtharajah, 'companions in arms, fighting the good fight' with a 'commitment to liberation'.⁹

Regardless of the theoretical bases, public engagement often means fighting against a dictatorial or imperial force – liberation or *revolution* – as opposed to public theologies of *reform* often found in Western liberal democracies. Early expressions of 'liberation' can be seen in the Philippines, one of the few Christian-majority contexts of Asia. During the Philippine Revolution (1896–8), Spanish friars often sided with Spanish colonial powers, while Filipino clergy tended to support nationalist and revolutionary forces.¹⁰ Although the teachings of Spanish friars tended to underscore an otherworldly version of Christianity, this was transformed by Filipino epics, values and practices. Popular Catholic spirituality brought together Christological imagery in forms such as the Passion Play to critique

---

⁶As discussed in Gaspar Martinez, 'The distinction of public theology from political and liberation theologies' (chapter 5 of this volume), there is often a debate around the relationship between public and political and liberation theologies. But in Asia, these lines are much more blurred. See also Sebastian C. H. Kim, *Theology in the Public Sphere: Public Theology as a Catalyst for Open Debate* (London: SCM Press, 2011), 20–5.
Elsewhere, Wilfred explains that public theology in Asia must exist in service of liberation – liberation is the goal of public theology. Felix Wilfred, 'Public Theology in Service of Liberation', *Vidyajyoti Journal of Theological Reflection* 83, no. 7 (July 2019): 485–504.
⁷Ironically, while all of these individuals are originally from Asia, most of them were trained and now working and living outside of Asia and, therefore, have privileged positions.
For a critique of postcolonial theory in Asian public theology, see Vinoth Ramachandra, *Subverting Global Myths: Theology and the Public Issues Shaping Our World* (Downers Grove, IL: IVP Academic, 2008), 245–61.
⁸In the twentieth century, Latin America witnessed the growth of theologies of liberation coming from Catholic and Evangelical Christians. For convenience, herein, 'Latin American liberation theology' will refer to the broad Catholic expressions. For a recent work on the Evangelical expression of *misión integral*, see David C. Kirkpatrick, *A Gospel for the Poor: Global Social Christianity and the Latin American Evangelical Left* (Philadelphia: University of Pennsylvania Press, 2019).
⁹R. S. Sugirtharajah, *Postcolonial Criticism and Biblical Interpretation* (Oxford: Oxford University Press, 2002), 117.
¹⁰John N. Schumacher, *Revolutionary Clergy: The Filipino Clergy and the Nationalist Movement, 1850–1903* (Quezon City: Ateneo de Manila University Press, 1981).

the colonial situation and to call for change and revolution.[11] In many ways, these early developments, alongside the growth of peasant unionization during American sovereignty, formed the basis for the 'theology of struggle' – liberation theology in the Philippines under the Ferdinand Marcos regime.[12]

In the Philippines, as in Latin America, theologies of liberation often brought together Marxist analysis with Christianity.[13] Yet, for some Asians, Marxism's framing of the oppressed in terms of the proletariat is limited in its applicability across different contexts. For instance, the Dalit theologian Arvind Nirmal argues that Marxism is problematic because it 'neglects the caste factor which adds to the complexity of Indian socio-economic realities'.[14] Caste is not merely a form of socio-economic stratification. It is also a division of ethnic groups into the fourfold hierarchy of the *varna* system – a system which excludes *dalits*, described as *avarna*, who are among the most repressed peoples in Indian society. According to Nirmal, Dalit theology challenges Indian Christian theology's obsession with the Hindu Brahminic tradition, which legitimizes caste. Instead, Dalit theology seeks to empower theological reflections about, for and from *dalits* who constitute the majority of Christians in India.[15]

A similar contention with the Marxist roots of Latin American liberation theology exists within Minjung theology in South Korea.[16] Like Nirmal, Kim Yong-bock critiques Marxist analysis, explaining:

> Philosophically speaking, the proletariat is 'confined' to socio-economic (materialistic) determination, so that it is bound to historical possibilities and the internal logic of history. The minjung suffers these limitations in reality; yet the minjung as historical subjects transcends the socio-economic determination of history, and unfolds its stories beyond mere historical possibilities to historical novelty – a new drama beyond the present history to a new and transformed history.[17]

---

[11]Reynaldo Clemeña Ileto, *Pasyon and Revolution: Popular Movements in the Philippines, 1840–1910* (Quezon City: Ateneo de Manila University Press, 1979).
[12]Kathleen M. Nadeau, *Liberation Theology in the Philippines: Faith in a Revolution* (Westport, CT: Praeger, 2002).
[13]See Victor Aguilan, 'Theology of Struggle: A Convergence of Christianity and Marxism in The Philippines', *Asia Journal of Theology* 27, no. 2 (October 2013): 153–71.
[14]Arvind P. Nirmal, 'Towards a Christian Dalit Theology', in *An Eerdmans Reader in Contemporary Political Theology*, ed. William T. Cavanaugh, Jeffrey W. Bailey, and Craig Hovey (Grand Rapids, MI: Eerdmans, 2012), 537–52 (539).
[15]Ibid., 541–2.
[16]See Suh Kwang-sun David, 'A Biographical Sketch of an Asian Theological Consultation', in *Minjung Theology: People as Subjects of History*, ed. Commission on Theological Concerns of the Christian Conference of Asia (Maryknoll, NY: Orbis, 1983), 15–37 (15–17).
[17]Kim Yong-bock, 'Messiah and Minjung: Discerning Messianic Politics over against Political Messianism', in *Minjung Theology*, 183–93 (184).

Therefore, *minjung* was a term articulated to highlight the subjectivity of the oppressed, regardless of the form of power relations – economic, racial, gendered, educational and so on. Minjung theology arose as a movement for the oppressed working class in the midst of the staunchly anti-communist military regime of Park Chung-hee. Hence, while critiquing the injustices of the regime, it needed to protect itself from being identified with communism. Furthermore, it was articulated against the dominant conservative Protestantism of the day, which was seen as complicit with the powerful elites and focusing on spiritual liberation and church growth.

After the eventual end of authoritarian rule in 1987, younger generations of Minjung theologians searched for new incarnations of the *minjung*.[18] For instance, Park Soon-kyung regards the first generation of Minjung theologians as having been far too antagonistic towards communism.[19] She sees the insistence on the difference between the *minjung* and the proletariat as a product of an anti-communist political discourse. This resulted in a theology which is insufficient for bringing about reconciliation and unification across North and South Koreas. She sees the divide on the Korean peninsula as caused by foreign powers – first by Japan, then by the Soviet Union and the United States – and across a common *minjok* ('people' or 'ethnicity') with a common *minjung* in its midst.

Park Soon-kyung's analysis reminds us that public theology, when taking up the goal of liberation, underscores *who* does the liberating and the *whom* one is liberated from. In the case of Palestinian liberation theology, greater emphasis is placed on the question of *what* is liberation for. Naim Ateek, like some of the earlier examples, draws inspiration from Latin American liberation theology. However, instead of challenging its Marxist underpinnings, Ateek critiques the use of the Exodus motif:

> The Exodus and the conquest of Canaan are . . . a unified and inseparable theme. For to need an exodus, one must have a promised land. To choose the motif of conquest of the promised land is to invite the need for the oppression, assimilation, control, or dispossession of the indigenous population. . . . Instead of the wars and bloodshed of the biblical account, it is my hope that Palestinians will return to *share* the land of Israel-Palestine.[20]

---

[18]See Volker Küster, *A Protestant Theology of Passion: Korean Minjung Theology Revisited* (Leiden: Brill, 2010), 131–49.
[19]Park Soon-kyung, 'The Unification of Korea and the Task of Feminist Theology', *In God's Image* (June 1988): 17–23.
[20]Naim Stifan Ateek, *Justice and Only Justice: A Palestinian Theology of Liberation* (Maryknoll, NY: Orbis, 1989), 87 (emphasis in original). For the origins of the Exodus motif, see Brian Stanley,

As Rosemary Ruether explains in the foreword to Ateek's book:

> Palestinian are victims of a Zionist liberation theology and ideology. The Jewish exodus from oppression in Europe is the rationale for their conquest. . . . Jewish redemption is Palestinian oppression.[21]

In other words, the liberated can very easily become the new oppressor. Christians are found both on the side of liberation and in collusion with the oppressor. This ascribes to public theology a double task: liberating the oppressed and liberating fellow Christians from their oppressive mindsets.

26.2 DIALOGUE

Public theology insists on Christian public voices. Given Christianity's minority existence in much of Asia, outspoken calls for liberation may not be tenable. Christian public theologians often recognize the importance of public engagement alongside non-Christians, using dialogue with the ideological other as a basis for working towards the common good. But a prerequisite for dialogue is the recognition that there is something different parties can dialogue about. The Sri Lankan Jesuit Aloysius Pieris explains this poignantly: 'A small minority church claims to offer "liberation" to Asia without first entering into liberative streams of Asian religion, which has its own antidotes against mammon.'[22] For Pieris, too many Christians have spoken of liberation as though it is unheard of in Asia; instead, Christians must recognize and work with Asian religionists who have long fought for spiritual and social emancipation. Christians must partner with non-Christians in speaking into the common concerns of society. This is echoed in the Federation of Asian Bishops' Conferences, which, since its first assembly in 1974, has argued that the Roman Catholic Church in Asia must be involved in a triple dialogue with the cultures, the religions and the poor of Asia, in order to realize an integral preaching of the gospel that combines the search for holiness and the search for justice.[23]

Christianity in the Twentieth Century: A World History (Princeton, NJ: Princeton University Press, 2018), 216–38.

[21]Rosemary Radford Ruether, 'Foreword', in Ateek, *Justice and Only Justice*, xii. For similar discussions in other contexts, see Robert Allen Warrior, 'Canaanites, Cowboys, and Indians: Deliverance, Conquest, and Liberation Theology', *Christianity and Crisis* 49, no. 12 (September 1989): 261–5; Musa W. Dube, *Postcolonial Feminist Interpretation of the Bible* (St. Louis, MO: Chalice Press, 2000), 58–70.

[22]Aloysius Pieris, *An Asian Theology of Liberation* (Edinburgh: T&T Clark, 1988), 50.

[23]See Gaudencio B. Rosales and C. G. Arévalo, eds, *For all the Peoples of Asia: Federation of Asian Bishops' Conferences Documents from 1970 to 1991* (Maryknoll, NY: Orbis, 1992), xxiv–xxvii, 14–16, 22–3.

The model for dialogue is Jesus' earthly ministry. Kosuke Koyama, as a Japanese missionary to Thailand, has argued that Christian work must underscore an incarnational approach of 'neighbourology', whereby the Christian does not engage the non-Christian simply as an object of evangelism but with a deep sense of solidarity as neighbours.[24] Sadayandy Batumalai builds on Koyama's views in the midst of Christian–Muslim relations in Malaysia, in which most Christians are ethnic Chinese, Indian or Iban, and the ethnic Malay majority are constitutionally defined as being Muslim – to leave Islam would be to become non-Malay. Batumalai contends that Christians need to uphold a Christology of neighbourology:

> Christian understanding is that God took the initiative for God-man and an inter-human relationship in Jesus Christ. This understanding needs to be spelt out . . . in an Islamic framework. . . . Islam emphasizes only the prophecy and not the personhood, while Christianity underlines both the message and the messenger, especially the words and deeds of Christ. Their emphasis is on the Quran as a means for human solidarity; our emphasis is on the living Christ through his Spirit, for both God and human solidarity.[25]

Irrespective of ethnic and religious divides, Christians and Muslims can 'co-operate for national solidarity, peace and prosperity. In our loving struggle with others for the good of the community, we both learn and communicate God's love for all'.[26] Batumalai asserts that this is how Christians can offer both a prophetic voice and an experience of neighbourly hospitality with their Muslim neighbours.

Another prominent example of dialogue can be found in China. Uniquely, the propaganda system of the one-party political state manages freedom of religious belief and civil society in a 'directed public sphere'.[27] For instance, we may consider the main national state-sanctioned Protestant organization in China, the Three-Self Patriotic Movement (TSPM), and its long-term leader, K. H. Ting (also known as Ding Guangxun).[28] In the years immediately after the

---

[24] Kosuke Koyama, *Water Buffalo Theology*, rev. and exp. edn. (Maryknoll, NY: Orbis, 1999), 64–7.
[25] Sadayandy Batumalai, *A Prophetic Christology of Neighbourology: A Theology for a Prophetic Living* (Kuala Lumpur: Seminari Theoloji Malaysia, 1986), 248.
[26] Ibid., 249.
[27] See Timothy Cheek, *The Intellectual in Modern Chinese History* (Cambridge: Cambridge University Press, 2015), 129. For a useful comparison, see Peter C. Phan, 'Church and State Relations in Vietnam, 1975–2015', in *Asian Christianities: History, Theology, Practice* (Maryknoll, NY: Orbis, 2018), 62–86.
[28] For a broader discussion of the TSPM's public theological engagement, see Alexander Chow, *Chinese Public Theology: Generational Shifts and Confucian Imagination in Chinese Christianity* (Oxford: Oxford University Press, 2018), 48–69.

Cultural Revolution (1966–76), Ting contributed to the two most important religious policy documents of the period: Document 19[29] and the clauses on religion in the 1982 revision of the Constitution. As such, he helped provide the framework for religious believers – inside and outside the TSPM – to have legal existence and a public voice. In 1985, Ting established the Amity Foundation, the first faith-based non-government organization, to encourage the participation of local TSPM-affiliated congregations in the Chinese civil society through rural development programmes, HIV/AIDS prevention clinics and care for orphans and the elderly.[30]

Theologically, though Ting appreciated many aspects of Latin American liberation theology, he argues in a 1985 speech that 'many Chinese Christians believe that the eternal theme for Christianity and its theology should not be political liberation . . . but should rather be reconciliation of humanity with God'.[31] Ting recognized the strengths of Latin American liberation theology in what it says about God's partiality to the poor and the need for theological praxis. However, he continues in this speech to explain that political liberation is not needed because 'we in China have already been liberated for over thirty years'[32] – that is, by the Communist Party in 1949. While some may dispute this claim and still clamour for liberation in China, such overtness has historically been met with opposition, imprisonment and death. For K. H. Ting, holding dual roles as a churchman and as a statesman, his public theology has been framed in terms of dialogue between the church and the state. Some of this may be seen as a reflection of his Anglican upbringing and consecration in 1955 as an Anglican bishop of Zhejiang,[33] given that the Church of England has

---

[29]Produced in 1982, Document 19 is also known by its longer name, 'The Basic Viewpoint and Policy on the Religious Question during Our Country's Socialist Period'. A translation can be found in Donald MacInnis, ed., *Religion in China Today: Policy and Practice* (Maryknoll, NY: Orbis Books, 1989), 8–26.

[30]Birgitta Larsson, 'Amity and Civil Society', in *Growing in Partnership: The Amity Foundation 1985–2005*, ed. Katrin Fiedler and Zhang Liwei (Hong Kong: The Amity Foundation, 2005), 218–20.

[31]K. H. Ting, 'Inspirations from Liberation Theology, Process Theology and Teilhard de Chardin', in *Love Never Ends: Papers by K. H. Ting*, ed. Janice Wickeri (Nanjing: Yilin Press, 2000), 199. Whatever one thinks about Ting's dismissal of Latin American liberation theology in China, it is useful to recognize the growing interest of this form of theology in Hong Kong in the wake of the 2014 Umbrella Movement, as well as the 2019–20 protests around the extradition bill. See Justin K. H. Tse and Jonathan Y. Tan, eds, *Theological Reflections on the Hong Kong Umbrella Movement* (New York: Palgrave Macmillan, 2016); Kwok Pui-lan and Francis Ching-wah Yip, eds, *The Hong Kong Protests and Political Theology* (Lanham, MD: Rowman and Littlefield, 2021).

[32]Ting, 'Inspirations from Liberation Theology', 199.

[33]Ting is said to have been greatly influenced by the writings of William Temple, and has even been called a 'Chinese William Temple' by his biographer. Philip L. Wickeri, *Reconstructing Christianity in China: K. H. Ting and the Chinese Church* (Maryknoll, NY: Orbis Books, 2007), xxv. See Alexander Chow, 'Revisit Asian Christian Public Witness: K. H. Ting', in *Resurgent Asia: Renewal*

manifested a particular form of church–state relations which differ greatly from the free church tradition dominant in the United States. However, Christian dialogue with the ideological other often risks the perception that one is in collusion with the other. This is one of the main reasons why there is a de facto division in China between state-sanctioned religious entities such as the TSPM and the Catholic Patriotic Association, and unregistered 'house churches' or 'underground churches'.

Since China's move towards rapid urbanization in the 1990s, a new form of Protestantism has been developing in China within its urban centres, often drawing from a renewed interest in Calvinism.[34] Some argued for China to uphold a stronger sense of the rule of law and constitutionalism. Wang Yi, for instance, was a law professor and human rights lawyer, who later became the Reformed senior pastor of the Chengdu Early Rain Church. Wang went as far as to claim that the best model for constitutionalism can be found in the covenantal theology of the Puritan faith tradition.[35] Others, such as those associated with the 1,000-member Beijing Shouwang Church, drew from Dutch Neo-Calvinism and argued that the church needs to be a vehicle for constructive dialogue with the state as a 'third church' or 'third way' – as opposed to the deadlock between the 'illegal' house churches and the 'adulterous' TSPM.[36] While the earlier generation of house churches maintained a clandestine existence, leadership within Shouwang argue that urban churches now must pursue a goal of openness and integrity; they should seek legal status as an NGO, yet outside of the TSPM system, in order to more actively participate in and transform the civil society.[37] As one Shouwang leader argues, 'God's word or biblical truth must enter into a culture and, expressing itself in every domain of this culture, become God's common grace in human society. This is the church's cultural mandate.'[38]

---

and *Christian Public Witness in Asia*, eds. Jooseup Keum and Atola Longkumer (New Delhi: ISPCK, forthcoming).
[34]See Chow, *Chinese Public Theology*, 92–114.
[35]Wang Yi, 'The Possibility of Political Theology: Christianity and Liberalism', *Chinese Law and Religion Monitor* 8, no. 1 (2012): 96–118.
[36]Jin Tianming, 'Tuidong jiaohui dengji dao jintian' (The Promotion of Church Registration), *Xinghua* (Almond Flowers) (Spring 2008): 40–2.
This reflects Abraham Kuyper's teachings on sphere sovereignty, whereby the church and the government are seen as independent, sovereign entities that can and should engage one another in constructive dialogue. Abraham Kuyper, 'Sphere Sovereignty', in *Abraham Kuyper: A Centennial Reader*, ed. James D. Bratt (Grand Rapids, MI: Eerdmans, 1998), 461–90; Abraham Kuyper, 'Calvinism and Politics', in *Lectures on Calvinism* (Grand Rapids, MI: Eerdmans, 1931), 78–109.
[37]Sun Yi, 'Jidujiao jiuguo qingjie dui jiaohui guan de yingxiang' (The Influence of Christian National Salvation Complex upon Ecclesiology), *Xinghua* (Almond Flowers) (Winter 2012): 37–40.
[38]Sun Mingyi, 'Zhongguo jiaohui chengsheng guan ji wenhua shiming lianxiang' (The Relationship between Sanctification and the Cultural Mandate in the Chinese Church), *Xinghua* (Almond

However, these attempts at a dialogical public theology in China no longer seem tenable. While K. H. Ting had success in navigating church–state relations, after his death, the TSPM has not been able to maintain a strong public voice. In 2014–16, when the TSPM leader Joseph Gu (also known as Gu Yuese) issued a public statement against the removal of crosses and the razing of church buildings – registered and unregistered – throughout Zhejiang province, he was removed from his post and arrested on embezzlement charges. In terms of the urban churches, by 2018, both Shouwang and Early Rain have been shuttered by the government; Wang Yi was arrested and given a nine-year prison sentence for 'inciting subversion of state power and illegal business operations'.

In contrast to liberation, dialogue has offered Christians one option to seek a peaceful *modus vivendi* in Asia. However, as we have seen, these expressions of public theology in Asia are often subject to the impulses of the current regime.

26.3 SUBVERSION

If outspoken protest and dialogue are untenable, any public engagement must find an alternative route and an alternative public voice. As Elaine Graham puts it, 'Public theology is not only concerned to do theology *about* public issues, but called to do its theology *in* public, with a sense of transparency to those of other faiths and none.'[39] In this manner, public theology is articulated not through the vocalization of the faith but through the living of the faith – an expression of the living God animating humanity.

Let us revisit the case of the Korean peninsula with this in mind. While Minjung theology was first articulated in the 1970s–1980s, Minjung theologians readily trace the origins of their movement to the rise of Protestantism in Korea, especially in the early 1900s.[40] For instance, during the height of Japanese colonialism, Korean reformers embraced Woodrow Wilson's 'Fourteen Points' about self-determination at the Paris Peace Conference and initiated the March First Movement of 1919. Of the thirty-three signatories of the Declaration of Independence against the Japanese colonial state, sixteen were Korean Protestants. The March First Movement was also the first major social

---

Flowers) (Winter 2008): 31 (my translation).
[39]Elaine Graham, *Between a Rock and a Hard Place: Public Theology in a Post-Secular Age* (London: SCM Press, 2013), 232–3.
[40]See Choo Chai-Yong, 'A Brief Sketch of a Korean Christian History from the Minjung Perspective' and Kim Yong-Bock, 'Korean Christianity as a Messianic Movement of the People', in *Minjung Theology*, 73–9, 80–119.

movement that Korean women were involved in. Of the 471 women arrested by Japanese forces, 60 per cent were Korean Protestants.[41]

One of the leading signatories of the Declaration of Independence was the revivalist Gil Seon-ju (also known as Kil Sŏn-ju), described by some as the 'father of Korean Protestantism'. However, due to his political involvement in March First, Gil was imprisoned for two and a half years. While in jail, Gil became preoccupied with the book of Revelation. Upon his release, he no longer spoke about political activism but of millennialist hope found in the Second Coming of Christ.[42] Interestingly, in 1929, the Japanese police arrested him again – this time for being a 'disturber of the minds of the people' because of his millennialist message.[43] What is important here is that the Japanese authorities recognized the *subversive* power of Gil's message. As we know from the early church, those who confessed that Jesus is Lord and embraced a heavenly kingdom subverted the claim that Caesar is Lord and denied his earthly kingdom.[44]

Likewise in China in the 1920s–1930s, many of the most famous revivalists – Watchman Nee (also known as Ni Tuosheng), John Sung (also known as Song Shangjie), Paul Wei (also known as Wei Enbo) – preached a message of spiritual salvation and eternal hope.[45] This was remarkable given that many of them had physical ailments such as tuberculosis, and the sociopolitical realities of their day included Western and Japanese imperialism, the decline of Confucian values and the rise of various forms of Chinese nationalism. Their messages seemed completely ignorant of their own physical impediments and the sociopolitical challenges of their day, yet saw remarkable appeal.

Returning to South Korea in the 1970s, Minjung theologians often critiqued conservative Protestants as upholding an apolitical position and simply emphasizing *kibock sinang* ('faith of seeking this-worldly blessings'). However, Sebastian Kim has argued that *kibock sinang* is not entirely apolitical, given that it offered a means to uplift the poor and met people's needs of material blessing and physical healing.[46] One of the most prominent exemplars of

---

[41] Sebastian C. H. Kim and Kirsteen Kim, *A History of Korean Christianity* (Cambridge: Cambridge University Press, 2014), 119–21.
[42] Kim Chong Bum, 'Preaching the Apocalypse in Colonial Korea', in *Christianity in Korea*, ed. Robert E. Buswell, Jr. and Timothy S. Lee (Honolulu: University of Hawai'i Press, 2006), 149–66 (152).
[43] Charles F. Bernheisel, 'Rev. Kil Sunju', *The Korea Mission Field* 32, no. 2 (February 1936): 30.
[44] This is why passages like Rom. 10.9, 1 Cor. 12.3 and Phil. 2.9-10 were so radical in their day. See Craig A. Evans, 'King Jesus and His Ambassadors: Empire and Luke-Acts' and Gordon L. Heath, 'The Church Fathers and the Roman Empire', in *Empire in the New Testament*, ed. Stanley E. Porter and Cynthia Long Westfall (Eugene, OR: Wipf and Stock, 2011), 120–39, 259–79.
[45] See Lian Xi, *Redeemed by Fire: The Rise of Popular Christianity in Modern China* (New Haven, CT: Yale University Press, 2010).
[46] Kim, *Theology in the Public Sphere*, 110–16.

this approach is David Yonggi Cho, the founding senior pastor of the Yoido Full Gospel Church mentioned at the outset of this chapter. For Cho, central to the gospel is a threefold blessing of salvation – encompassing spiritual, circumstantial and physical dimensions – and often described as part of the advent of the prosperity gospel in South Korea.[47] Perhaps another example of this can be found in Cho's mother-in-law, Choi Ja-shil, who cofounded Yoido with Cho in 1958. While Cho is known for his speaking ministry, Choi was known for her healing ministry, visiting and caring for the poor and the infirmed.[48] As Sebastian Kim explains, 'Pastor Cho and others certainly have succeeded in exploring the Korean traditional religiosity of seeking blessings and expanded the meaning of blessing in the context of poverty.'[49] What we see in *kibock sinang* is a subversive expression of public theology. It addresses the material and the physical needs of the masses, in a time when the dominant regime has overlooked its responsibilities to its citizens.

In other parts of Asia, we likewise see Christianity as offering an alternative paradigm to the dominant ideology of the central state. This is demonstrated in the present-day national border between Myanmar (formerly known as Burma) and India.[50] Today, the Chin people in Myanmar[51] and the Naga people in Northeast India are both around 90 per cent Christian.[52] While Christianity reached these peoples during the British colonial period, mainly through Baptist missions, it made limited headway. The greatest growth occurred during indigenous Christian revival movements in the region, in the 1950s–1960s among the Naga and in the 1970s among the Chin. While there are a number of factors involved in these developments, it is quite clear that both these groups, as ethnic minorities, associated conversion to Christianity with a social and political upliftment when juxtaposed against the often oppressive forces of Buddhist nationalism (within Burma/Myanmar) and Hindu nationalism

---

[47]Wonsuk Ma, 'David Yonggi Cho's Theology of Blessing: Basis, Legitimacy, and Limitations', *Evangelical Review of Theology* 35, no. 2 (April 2011): 140–59.

[48]Julie C. Ma, 'Korean Pentecostal Spirituality: A Case Study of Jashil Choi', *Asian Journal of Pentecostal Studies* 5, no. 2 (July 2002): 235–54.

[49]Kim, *Theology in the Public Sphere*, 113.

[50]This geopolitical border arose as a result of a series of political decisions and the creation of nation states, from British colonialism to independence. Prior to such a border, many of the peoples in this region shared a common history.

[51]There is considerable debate about whether to address this group as the 'Chin' or the 'Zomi'. I will use 'Chin' for this chapter given that my focus is on the group in Chin state. See David Vumlallian Zou, 'A Historical Study of the "Zo" Struggle', *Economic & Political Weekly* 45, no. 14 (3 April 2010): 56–63.

[52]The Chin/Zomi peoples are found primarily in Myanmar's Chin state and in many of the states in Northeast India. Likewise, Naga peoples are today in Nagaland and other states of Northeast India, but also parts of Myanmar, like Kachin state.

(within India).⁵³ Christianity has become central to these constructed identities – a subversive public theology or, as Elaine Graham puts it, a theology in the public.

26.4 CONCLUSION

As stated in the outset of this chapter, Christian public theology in the vast land of Asia has arisen with Christianity as primarily a minority ideology. As such, Christianity has searched for a voice in a public sphere that has not always been supportive of – indeed, sometimes incredibly hostile towards Christians. Just as Christianity is generally considered a 'Western' or 'foreign' religion in Asia, it is unmistakable that Asian public theologies draw resources from the outside. Some are Christian resources such as Latin American liberation theology, Catholic social teaching or Protestant magisterial (primarily Anglican and Calvinist) understandings of public theology. Others are non-Christian resources such as Marxism or postcolonialism. These external resources are hardly adopted naïvely but are scrutinized in relation to their contexts, as has been seen in the cases of Dalit and Minjung theologians in their critiques against Marxism. We also have paradoxical developments, such as Baptists who come from Anabaptist and English separatist traditions, yet who underscore a strong sense of nationalism. Christians in Asia need to grapple with the tension between an inherited or adopted Christianity and the sociopolitical realities they face on the ground.

In the translation of Christianity into the Asian context, the grammars of historic Asian ideologies also shape the new utterances of Christian public speech. The Chinese public theologies of K. H. Ting and of the newer urban churches reflect a millennia-old Chinese notion of Confucian literati – 'public intellectuals', if you will – scholar-officials trained in the Chinese classics for the purposes of running the imperial bureaucratic system.⁵⁴ As Tu Weiming explains, 'Confucian followers were primarily action intellectuals, deeply immersed in "managing the world" (*jingshi*) of economics, politics, and society.'⁵⁵ However, Confucianism in China and Korea – like Hinduism in India – gave preference to the intellectual elites. In China and Korea, popular movements drawn from Daoism and Muism have historically led to a tradition

---

⁵³See Pum Za Mang, 'Buddhist Nationalism and Burmese Christianity', *Studies in World Christianity* 22, no. 2 (August 2016): 148–67; John Thomas, *Evangelising the Nation: Religion and the Formation of Naga Political Identity* (Abingdon: Routledge, 2016).
⁵⁴For a fuller discussion, see Chow, *Chinese Public Theology*, 27–47.
⁵⁵Tu Weiming, 'Intellectuals in a World Made of Knowledge', *The Canadian Journal of Sociology* 30, no. 2 (Spring 2005): 219–26 (220).

of subverting the state orthodoxy dominated by Confucianism.[56] Ironically, while Minjung theology and *kibock sinang* appear to be on opposite poles of both theological and political spectrums, the two theologies are said to be inspired by Korean Muism. Likewise in India, some theologies of liberation are said to come from the *Shakti* devotional tradition, which draws from a pre-Aryan understanding that subverts the hegemony of Vedic Hinduism.[57] These reconfigurations of Christianity vis-à-vis historic Asian ideologies have produced rich ways of articulating Christian public theology in Asia.

Whether public theology in Asia is expressed liberatively, dialogically, subversively or in some other form, it has manifested itself in a much stronger public voice than is represented by its numbers. Public theology in Asia should not simply be admired from afar from other societies as simply a novel and idiosyncratic development. Perhaps the greatest contribution of public theology in Asia to the broader discourse of public theology concerns the ways by which Christianity has struggled for a public voice in a hostile environment – whether this be in Asia, other parts of the majority world or the post-secular West.

---

[56]See Ralph R. Covell, *Confucius, the Buddha, and Christ: A History of the Gospel in Chinese* (Eugene, OR: Wipf and Stock, 1986), 182–205; Kirsteen Kim, *The Holy Spirit in the World: A Global Conversation* (Maryknoll, NY: Orbis Books, 2007), 112–32.

[57]Robin H. S. Boyd, *An Introduction to Indian Christian Theology*, rev. edn. (Delhi: ISPCK, 1975), 241–3; Kim, *The Holy Spirit in the World*, 69–71.

CHAPTER 27

Public theology in Australia

ROBERT GASCOIGNE

27.1 INTRODUCTION

Public theology in Australia can be helpfully considered in two periods: before and after the 1960s. Before the 1960s, Australian society can be understood in terms of a Christian secularity, marred by sectarianism. During this period, successful public theology, expressed from specific denominational contexts, sought to sustain and communicate the key beliefs and values of Christian faith in Australian society while restraining or minimizing sectarian reaction. From the mid-1960s, Australian secularity can no longer be considered specifically Christian but rather as a pluralist ethical, religious and philosophical space. During this period, successful public theology seeks to speak within Australian secularity as a dialogic space, resisting those tendencies that seek to reduce secularity to ideological secularism or practical materialism.

27.2 PRE-1960S: A CHRISTIAN SECULARITY, MARRED BY SECTARIANISM

The Australian colonies, which federated to form the Commonwealth of Australia in 1901, had not known an established church, except for a limited form of establishment of the Anglican church in the first colony, New South Wales, from its foundation in 1788 to 1836, when Governor Bourke initiated the Church Act, providing government support to all major denominations.[1] However, 'By the late nineteenth century, and beginning with South Australia in 1851, all colonies had achieved what was universally called a "separation of church and state", that is, the severance of the financial support for the churches originally enshrined in Governor Bourke's 1836 New South Wales Church Act'.[2]

The Australian Constitution came into force with the federation of the six Australian colonies in January 1901. Section 116 of the Constitution lays down that 'The Commonwealth shall not make any law for establishing any religion, or for imposing any religious observance, or for prohibiting the free exercise of any religion, and no religious test shall be required as a qualification for any office or public trust under the Commonwealth'. This has not meant, however, that the churches play no role in Australian public life or that the Australian state does not cooperate with or assist the churches in certain ways. As Bruce Kaye argues:

> At Federation the constitution set out in Clause 116 some apparently clear guidelines while retaining in the preamble a clear reference to God – as indeed did the oath of the current governor-general. The High Court interpretation of clause 116 has taken Australia in a different direction from the USA. Whereas the US tradition has moved to a doctrine of separation of church and state and a doctrine of non-entanglement, the Australian version has moved to a position of non-separation of church and state and a doctrine of equitable entanglement. The broader and social institutional effect of this has been to assert that religion has a recognized place in public life and in public institutions in a way that is quite different from the USA. Australia may not be a religious state, but it is a state that incorporates religion in the statutory view of public life.[3]

This 'recognized place in public life' for the Christian churches, prior to the 1960s, can be understood as a 'Christian secularity'.[4] Although no colony had

---

[1] 'The 1820s and 1830s saw significant and rapid shifts in the church's relationships with government. . . . In the 1820s, when Tory conservatism was on the ascendant, the wealth and power of Australian Anglicanism increased to the point of "quasi-establishment"; ten years later the mounting pressures of liberal reform led to the removal of the formal precedence of the Anglican Church.' Anne O'Brien, 'Religion', in *The Cambridge History of Australia, Volume 1: Indigenous and Colonial Australia*, ed. Alison Bashford and Stuart Macintyre (Melbourne: Cambridge University Press, 2013), 419.
[2] Stephen Chavura, John Gascoigne and Ian Tregenza, *Reason, Religion and the Australian Polity: A Secular State?* (Abingdon, OX: Routledge, 2019), 2.
[3] Bruce Kaye, 'From Anglican Gaol to Religious Pluralism: Re-Casting Anglican Views of Church and State in Australia', in *Church and State in Old and New Worlds*, ed. Hilary M. Carey and John Gascoigne, Brill's Series in Church History, vol. 51 (Leiden: Brill, 2011), 289–90.
[4] In *Reason, Religion and the Australian Polity: A Secular State?*, Chavura, Gascoigne and Tregenza argue that the dominant use of the term 'secular', 'throughout most of Australian history, possibly

an established church, the life and teaching of the Christian churches were the background for both faith and ethics for Australian society. One crucial aspect of this was the support of the Christian churches for Australian democracy, expressed in different ways by the major denominations. The Catholic Church began to support the Australian Labor Party (ALP) soon after its foundation in 1891. Cardinal Patrick Moran, the Irish archbishop of Sydney (in office 1884–1911), expressed his support for the ALP on a number of occasions, in part because of the compatibility of its policies with the teaching of Leo XIII's *Rerum Novarum* (On the Condition of the Working Classes).[5] For many Protestant Australians, notably Alfred Deakin, second prime minister of Australia and a man deeply engaged with religious and philosophical questions, membership of the ALP was unacceptable for reasons related to Protestant emphasis on the freedom of individual conscience, since it required ALP members of Parliament to sign a pledge that they would vote according to party policy.[6]

Brian Fletcher emphasizes how prominent Anglicans valued individual rights, social justice and the rule of law:

> these principles, together with a strong belief in the virtue of democratic government, form core values often described as central to what it means to 'be Australian'. They originated in the period when the British influence on Australia was at its height and they did much to ensure that the transition to the present-day multicultural society proceeded smoothly and without the tensions that erupted elsewhere in the world. The Anglican church could not

---

up to the Second World War and even slightly beyond, saw no mutually exclusive relationship between it and confessional religion, Christianity in particular' (10).

[5] In his 'Catholicism and Socialism: The 1905 Controversy in Australia', A. E. Cahill notes Moran's awareness that the 'majority of Irish-Australian Catholics were supporters of the Labor Party' and rejected a campaign against 'socialism' in the name of the church. Moran emphasized the applicability of Leo XIII's *Rerum Novarum* to Australian conditions and the importance of the social apostolate. A. E. Cahill, 'Catholicism and Socialism: The 1905 Controversy in Australia', *Journal of Religious History* 1, no. 2 (December 1960): 88–101, (94–5). See also Philip Ayres, *Prince of the Church: Patrick Francis Moran 1830–1911* (Carlton, VIC: Miegunyah Press, 2007): Chapter 13 'Constructing a Catholic-Labor Entente 1901–05'.

[6] Judith Brett, in her *Australian Liberals and the Moral Middle Class: From Alfred Deakin to John Howard* (Cambridge: Cambridge University Press, 2003), notes that 'to sign the pledge was, in Deakin's words, to ask a man to give up what made him a man, "his judgement and his conscience", and this they could not do' (40). For one period of his life Deakin was a member of the 'Australian Church', a non-dogmatic Christian denomination which abandoned creeds and legislated ecclesiastical forms, formed in 1885 with Charles Strong as its leader, a former Presbyterian minister expelled from his pulpit at Scots Church in Melbourne. Deakin's multifarious philosophical and religious experimentation also included theosophy and spiritualism. Judith Brett, *The Enigmatic Mr Deakin* (Melbourne: The Text Publishing Company, 2017), 208–9.

claim to have been solely responsible for such values, but it did play a major part in ensuring that they were embedded in the national consciousness.[7]

Fletcher notes that the Anglican church 'suffered from being burdened by its image as a predominantly middle-class institution', yet 'reality did not fully equate with image. There is evidence to indicate that the church was more inclusive of the different social groups in Australia than was any other denomination'.[8] Bishop Ernest Burgmann (1885–1967), Anglican bishop of Goulburn, was a prominent example of an Australian Anglican church leader committed to social justice. Stephen Pickard emphasizes Burgmann's debt to the English Christian socialist tradition, particularly S. T. Coleridge and F. D. Maurice: 'Foundational to this tradition in which Burgmann stood was a theological conviction about the presence and action of God in the world. This arose out of twin co-ordinates of incarnation and redemption in Christ.' For Pickard, Burgmann's 'incarnational sacramental socialism . . . meant that there was no part of society that the light of the gospel of God could not shine into, illuminate, and renew'.[9]

The sociocultural background of 'Christian secularity' is also evident in the use of the Bible by prominent Australian politicians of this period. Robert Menzies, a Presbyterian, was, initially, prime minister from 1939 to 1941. After losing office, he gave a number of radio addresses, including the very influential 'The Forgotten People' in May 1942, in which he spoke of the middle class as those who have

> responsibility for homes – homes material, homes human, homes spiritual. I do not believe that the real life of this nation is to be found either in great luxury hotels and the petty gossip of so-called fashionable suburbs, or in the officialdom of organized masses. It is to be found in the homes of people who are nameless and unadvertised, and who, whatever their individual religious conviction or dogma, see in their children their greatest contribution to the immortality of their race.[10]

To illustrate what he meant by 'homes spiritual', Menzies cited Robert Burns's poem 'The Cotter's Saturday Night', in which a frugal Scottish householder reads to his children from the Bible. In her *The Bible in Australia: A Cultural History*,

---

[7]Brian H. Fletcher, *The Place of Anglicanism in Australia: Church, Society and Nation* (Mulgrave: Broughton Publishing, 2008), 254.
[8]Ibid., 246–7.
[9]Stephen Pickard, '"A Most Meddlesome God": A Christian Future for the Church.' *St Mark's Review* 240 (2017): 161–2.
[10]Robert Menzies, 'The Forgotten People', http://www.liberals.net/theforgottenpeople.htm (last accessed 3 February, 2020).

Meredith Lake notes that, during his time at Melbourne University, Menzies 'attended Bible classes, joined the campus Christian union and adopted what became a lifelong habit of daily Bible reading.'[11] For Lake, 'the Bible informed *and* tempered his view of individuality. When it came to the nation, he thought in the terms of civic Protestantism – imagining a Christian community, with a Christian calling that shaped its conduct in the world.'[12] In 1944, Menzies founded the Liberal Party of Australia, re-conceiving the conservative side of Australian politics, and went on to become the longest-serving prime minister of Australia, 1949–66. In 1960 he was the guest of honour at the opening of Bible House, Canberra.[13]

Another influential example of the use of the Bible in a secular context was Labor prime minister J. B. 'Ben' Chifley's 'Light on the Hill' speech, which was made to a party conference in 1949, and owed some of its resonances to Matt. 5.14-16:

> I try to think of the Labor movement, not as putting an extra sixpence into somebody's pocket, or making somebody Prime Minister, or Premier, but as a movement bringing something better to the people, better standards of living, greater happiness to the mass of the people. We have a great objective – the light on the hill – which we aim to reach by working for the betterment of mankind not only here but anywhere we may give a helping hand. If it were not for that, the Labor movement would not be worth fighting for.[14]

Both Protestant and Catholic communities supported Australian patriotism and the British crown, although this was nuanced in different ways, with Australian rather than imperial patriotism being more pronounced in the Catholic community.[15] This consensus came under great pressure during the anti-conscription campaigns in the First World War, since the Irish archbishop of Melbourne, Daniel Mannix, was one of the most prominent public figures on the anti-conscription side.[16] Partly because of the conflict over conscription, the post-war period was marred by bitter sectarian tension.

---

[11]Meredith Lake, *The Bible in Australia: A Cultural History* (Sydney: NewSouth Publishing, 2018), 247.
[12]Ibid., 248.
[13]Ibid., 281.
[14]David Day, *Chifley* (Sydney: HarperCollins, 2001), 488.
[15]Edmund Campion, *Australian Catholics: The Contribution of Catholics to the Development of Australian Society* (Ringwood, VIC: Viking, 1987): Chapter 2, 'Finding an Australian Identity'. This was partly due to the Irish patriotism of Cardinal Moran and other Irish bishops. See Ayres, *Prince of the Church*, for example, 250, 273–6.
[16]See B. A. Santamaria, *Daniel Mannix: A Biography* (Melbourne: Melbourne University Press, 1984). Chapter 6, 'Mannix and Conscription'.

In general terms, the Catholic hierarchy attempted to encourage political integration with wider Australian society, while providing for, and enforcing, sociocultural separation. It resisted calls for a distinctly Catholic political party, but at the same time devoted great energy and resources to a separate Australian Catholic school system and to enforcing the Vatican's ban on 'mixed marriages', promulgated in Pope Pius X's *Ne Temere* decree of 1907. The implications of this decree – and of the sectarian context – are poignantly illustrated in Prime Minister Ben Chifley's personal life. Chifley's future wife, Lizzie,

> made clear, perhaps under pressure from her parents, that she was not willing to convert to Catholicism to marry Chifley. At the same time, he was under pressure from his devout parents to follow the church into which he had been born. It was an impossible position that left him distraught and divided in his emotions until finally his course was set. He would marry in a Presbyterian church and incur whatever penalties had to be paid. As he explained to a friend, 'One of us has to take the knock. It'd better be me.'[17]

The political integration of the Catholic community, largely through the ALP, met its greatest challenge with the increasing strength and prestige of Communism in Australia after the Second World War. Communist domination of a number of trade unions led to counter-organization of Catholic trade unionists led by B. A. ('Bob') Santamaria, a layman who founded the 'Catholic Social Studies Movement', which clandestinely – and successfully – turned back communist influence. Santamaria and other leaders of 'The Movement' were very critical of the leadership of the ALP as compromised by their perceived lack of a firm stance against any kind of communist influence. 'The Movement' had been founded as part of official 'Catholic Action' and led by the Catholic bishops, but its activities led to a decision by Cardinal Norman Thomas Gilroy, archbishop of Sydney, and his deputy, Bishop James Carroll, to petition the Vatican to restrict 'The Movement's' political activities. In Melbourne, Santamaria was vigorously defended by the elderly Archbishop Mannix. The Vatican ruled in Gilroy's favour, and Santamaria's organization became a purely lay group, dissociated from official Catholic Action. In the meantime, however, he and others had founded the Democratic Labor Party (DLP), as a protest against the ALP leadership. The DLP subsequently gave its political preferences (which play an important part in the Australian electoral system) to the conservative parties, which kept the ALP out of office until 1972. The formation of the DLP became a kind of political bridge which many Catholics crossed to eventually vote directly for the conservative parties. The DLP ceased to have any political

---

[17]David Day, *Chifley*, 92–3. They were married in June 1914.

influence after the 1974 Federal election, but its formation was, in the first place, a break with the earlier Catholic practice of avoiding a political party with denominational associations and, in the second place, led to the breaking of the historical link between the ALP and the Catholic community, so that by the 1980s Australian politics was free of any substantive links between denominational and political allegiance.[18]

In his *Australian Religious Thought*, Wayne Hudson argues that 'sacral secularity' played an important role in Australian society in this period: 'by "sacral secularity" I mean the tendency to associate the secular with sacral characteristics, while acknowledging its relative autonomy from ecclesiastical control'.[19] This tendency is an example of how 'in nineteenth- and early twentieth-century Australia the nature of the secular was what was being worked out, and, in many cases, the need to delimit ecclesiastical interference was balanced by concern to promote religion and morality'.[20] One of the most prominent examples of this 'sacral secularity' was the honouring of Anzac Day, an annual ritual held on April 25th, on the anniversary of the landing of ANZAC (Australian and New Zealand Army Corps) forces on the Gallipoli Peninsula in 1915, as part of the unsuccessful campaign (initiated by Winston Churchill) to weaken the Ottoman Empire by a landing near Istanbul. Hudson notes that Anzac Day and its associated ritual 'had Anglo-Catholic beginnings in Brisbane, where Canon D. J. Garland developed most of the features of Anzac Day celebrations in an attempt to sacralise the new nation'.[21]

However, for some time the 'sacral secularity' of Anzac Day also fell victim to sectarian divisions, since Catholic clergy were forbidden by canon law to take part in the dawn service led by a Protestant clergyman. In view of this, leaders of the Returned Services League (RSL), the principal Australian war veterans' association, approached the Anglican archbishop of Sydney, Hugh Gough,

> about revising the service to a form acceptable to the Catholics. They suggested a service in which all the prayers would be led and conducted by leaders of the RSL or armed services. A clergyman from one denomination would give the Anzac Address which would be patriotic and not religious.

---

[18]Bruce Duncan's *Crusade or Conspiracy: Catholics and the Anti-Communist Struggle in Australia* (Sydney: UNSW Press, 2001) is a comprehensive and judicious study of this complex of events, including its background in the Vatican's conception of Catholic Action.
[19]Wayne Hudson, *Australian Religious Thought* (Clayton: Monash University Publishing, 2016), 61.
[20]Ibid., 66.
[21]Ibid., 67.

Gough took the suggestion to Gilroy and seven other denominations. All agreed.²²

In 1963, Cardinal Gilroy, who had been a junior wireless operator on a naval vessel close to the landing zone at Gallipoli, gave the Commemoration Address: 'the initiative had come from the RSL and Archbishop Gough, but it certainly furthered Gilroy's ambition for the Catholic Church to be recognised as contributing in a loyal way to Australian life, but without compromising its doctrines'.²³

The 1950s were the high noon of Australian Christianity. There is much evidence of the powerful influence of Christian evangelists during this decade, culminating in Billy Graham's 1959 crusades. In their *Attending to the National Soul: Evangelical Christians in Australian History 1914-2014*, Stuart Piggin and Robert D. Lindner argue that

> the unprecedented and incomparable success of the '59 crusades is probably evidence that Australia in reality if not by reputation was one of the most evangelical of the world's nations. . . . What has become clear in retrospect, however, was that the 1959 Billy Graham crusade was a peak achievement of the evangelical movement in Australia, rather than the harbinger of a brilliant new period of achievement for it.²⁴

For both Catholic and Protestant denominations, the 1960s brought radical change and, by some measures, decline. Vatican II encouraged Catholics to ecumenical endeavours, introduced a vernacular liturgy and gave the Bible greater prominence in Catholic life. However, in 1968 the encyclical *Humanae vitae*, prohibiting the use of artificial contraception by married couples, led to widespread non-compliance and criticism of this expression of Papal authority. The decades after Vatican II have shown a marked decline in participation in the Sunday eucharist and of vocations to the priesthood and religious life.

Protestant communities also experienced a decline in the Sunday School system that had been such an important part of Protestant parish life. Knowledge and confident use of the Bible was also to decline:

> Given the broad social trends evident since at least the 1960s, it is likely that overall biblical literacy is lower in Australia now than at any other time

---

²²John Luttrell, *Norman Thomas Gilroy: An Obedient Life* (Strathfield, NSW: St Pauls Publications, 2017), 221–2.
²³Ibid., 223.
²⁴Stuart Piggin and Robert D. Lindner, *Attending to the National Soul: Evangelical Christians in Australian History 1914–2014* (Victoria: Monash University Publishing, 2020), 285, 289.

since colonization by the British. The public conversation with the Bible goes on, but fewer Australians are familiar with the text and its interpretation in a way that enables them to participate in the conversation critically and effectively.[25]

In the light of all these changes, public theology in Australia must now be conducted on a markedly different basis to the 'Christian secularity' characteristic of the period before the 1960s.

27.3 POST-1960S SECULARITY AS A PLURALIST AND DIALOGIC SPACE

Since the 1960s, Australian society can be conceived of as a pluralist and dialogical space.[26] Rather than being a shared background of faith and ethics, Christian faith and the Christian churches are now one presence among others. In the light of its Constitution, and its social history, Australian society is a secular space, in the sense that no church or religion enjoys particular political privileges. This secular space has the potential to be a dialogic space, a space of cross-cultural engagement for the sake of the common good. Australian secularity can be interpreted and realized as a space which enables and encourages all communities of faith to live in fruitful coexistence and to contribute to public life, on the basis of a commitment to shared values and to civil discourse, exercising the religious freedom enshrined in the Constitution. In more classical language, it can be a space of dialogue between faith and reason, expressing a contemporary sense of natural law as an ethical consensus grounded in civil discourse.

These shared values can characterize a common humanity: a commitment to the dignity of the human person, the common good and the flourishing of community through peace and justice. Although different communities of faith and belief draw this commitment from different sources, they can all engage with each other in this shared space for the sake of a common witness to our human fragility, preciousness and capacity to give and receive a self-sacrificial love sustained by hope, whether that hope be inchoate or inspired by religious

---

[25] Lake, *The Bible in Australia*, 350.
[26] Some material in this part of the chapter has been adapted and incorporated, with permission, from my essay: Robert Gascoigne, 'Secularity as Cross-Cultural and Dialogic Space: The Australian Example', in *Doing Asian Theological Ethics in a Cross-Cultural and Interreligious Context*, ed. Y. S. L. Chan, J. F. Keenan, S. G. Kochuthara (Bengaluru, India: Dharmaram Publications, 2016), 47–58.

narratives and symbols.[27] In this context, the Christian churches proclaim their hope in the risen Christ, in his forgiveness of sins and overcoming of death, as a public truth offered to their fellow citizens with love and respect.

This understanding of secularity is informed by an understanding of secularization as differentiation: that is, that secularization does not mean the disappearance of religion from political and social life but rather the differentiation of different aspects of society and culture leading to the independence of a range of social institutions and practices, for example, politics, the market and science, from religion.[28] It is important to emphasize that the dialogic and cross-cultural character of this secular space is not simply a given but a process of engagement, often with a dialectical character. Communities of faith and belief must constantly strive to maintain and enhance this space. Much of this engagement will be to resolve what our common humanity means, in terms of the great questions of public ethical life. The Australian government's 'Apology to the Stolen Generation of Aboriginal Australians', for example, was made in February 2008 by the then prime minister Kevin Rudd, after a long and contentious political and public debate about the significance and appropriateness of such an apology, a debate that wrestled with the meaning of apology and forgiveness for grievous wrongs done in the past which had scarred the lives of many living indigenous Australians.[29] The dialectical character of this engagement means that it can affect different communities of faith and belief in reciprocal ways, enabling – and sometimes provoking – them to expand or examine their own consciousness in particular areas of ethical life.

The pluralism of contemporary Australian life includes many different Christian denominations, a number of world faiths and a spectrum of agnostic and atheist philosophical world views. There has been a Jewish community

---

[27]In his *Australian Soul: Religion and Spirituality in the Twenty-First Century* (Melbourne: Cambridge University Press, 2006), Gary Bouma characterizes Australian religious belief as marked by a 'shy hope' (27) and argues that 'while in the twentieth century religion and spirituality often provided an identity and meaning for people, in the twenty-first century the core is the production and maintenance of hope' (30).

[28]An interpretation of secularization as differentiation is an important feature of José Casanova's *Public Religions in the Modern World* (Chicago: University of Chicago Press, 1994), and of David Martin's *The Future of Christianity: Reflections on Violence and Democracy, Religion and Secularization* (Farnham: Ashgate, 2011).

[29]'Apology to Australia's Indigenous peoples', https://www.australia.gov.au/about-australia/our-country/our-people/apology-to-australias-indigenous-peoples (last accessed 3 February, 2020). Rudd was one of Australia's most theologically well-informed and sophisticated prime ministers, as exemplified by his essay 'Faith in Politics', *The Monthly*, October 2006, 22–30, which pays particular attention to Dietrich Bonhoeffer's legacy. In his *In God They Trust? The Religious Beliefs of Australia's Prime Ministers 1901–2013* (Sydney: Bible Society Australia, 2013), Roy Williams offers an account of Rudd's religious beliefs in their relationship to his personal life and political career, as well as those of many other prime ministers.

in Australia since the beginnings of the Australian colonies, which greatly increased in size during the 1930s and after the Holocaust. Jews play a distinguished part in many sectors of Australian life, especially in Sydney and Melbourne. The Muslim community has grown considerably in size since the 1970s, particularly through immigration from Lebanon and Turkey, and is now about 2 per cent of the Australian population. The Buddhist community, deriving in particular from refugee immigration since the wars in Indo-China, is of similar size. There are also Hindu and Sikh communities.[30] Most Aboriginal Australians are Christians; however, their Christian faith coexists with, and is inflected by, sensibilities and practices deriving from the ancient spirituality of Australian indigenous communities. In recent decades, many Aboriginal Australian Christians have sought to more explicitly embody their traditional beliefs and practices in their Christian life, sometimes with the encouragement of church leadership.[31]

There have been strands of atheistic thought in Australia since the nineteenth century, expressed in various forms of liberal individualism, utilitarianism and Marxism. Since the 1960s, libertarian atheism has had considerable influence in the academic and media communities. Since the 1970s, conceptions of human rights have become important in Australian social and political debates. In many respects, the churches have supported and contributed to the discourse of human rights. However, in recent years, the question of the meaning and scope of human rights has become strongly contested in Australian public debate, in particular the relationship between the right to religious freedom (including the rights of the churches and church schools in employment and related matters) and the rights of LGBTQI+ citizens. Different Christian communities have different stances on aspects of this complex of questions, which has shown that human rights discourse is not as straightforward as it was in the 1970s, when it first came into prominence as a protest against totalitarian regimes in the name of human dignity.[32]

---

[30] For studies of the different religious communities in Australia, see James Jupp, ed., *The Encyclopedia of Religion in Australia* (Melbourne: Cambridge University Press, 2009).

[31] Since the 1980s there has been a number of initiatives in developing Christian theology in ways informed by Australian Aboriginal spirituality, practices and art. See, for example, Rainbow Spirit Elders, *Rainbow Spirit Theology: Towards an Australian Aboriginal Theology*, 2nd edn. (Hindmarsh, SA: ATF Press, 2007); Miriam Rose Ungunmerr-Baumann, *Australian Stations of the Cross* (Blackburn, VIC: Collins Dove, 1984).

[32] In his *The Last Utopia: Human Rights in History* (Cambridge, MA: Belknap Press, Harvard University Press, 2010), Samuel Moyn reflects on the transition in human rights discourse from anti-totalitarian protest to 'an exploding variety of rival political schemes' (227). Amartya Sen's *The Idea of Justice* (Cambridge, MA: Belknap Press, Harvard University Press, 2009) recognizes the appeal of human rights discourse but argues that claims to specific rights need to be carefully argued in public debate. See in particular 'Human Rights and Global Imperatives', 356–65.

The crucial value of this shared secular space is threatened by a range of political, commercial and ideological influences, which lessen the capacity for civil discourse and mutual understanding by various modes of exploitation of fear or by reductions of meaning which marginalize the contribution that religious traditions can make to public life. Because of this, there is a constant danger that a shared secular space can cease to be dialogic and become merely a space held together by formal political and legal norms and economic processes. Although Australia has generally enjoyed social peace, it would be, to say the least, foolish complacency to think that this peace could be maintained only with such minimal resources.

Politically, there are a number of voices that seek to exploit fear of difference, especially in relation to asylum seekers and to Islam. Many political leaders realize that the most peaceful and effective way to reduce Islamist militancy is by fostering respectful engagement and dialogue with the Muslim community. There have also been sustained attempts by church and academic agencies to foster dialogue and mutual understanding.[33] However, some politicians and media figures seek instead to exploit fear of Islamist militancy in ways that marginalize and alienate the mainstream Muslim community. This not only deprives the Australian community of the best defence against such militancy but also undermines attempts by Muslim community leaders to maintain peaceful dialogue with the government and with other communities of faith. It also displays a lack of respect for Islam as a world faith which bears witness to an almighty and compassionate God.

Powerful commercial interests undermine the commitment to the common good in favour of economic individualism in as much of Australian life as possible. Through a multifarious media presence which exacerbates a perspective on life made up of material desires, superficial celebrity, acquisitiveness, envy and competitiveness, these commercial interests challenge and subvert conceptions of the common good which seek to put material needs in their proper place in the order of humane priorities. This has been particularly clear in the refusal of many influential figures in business, media and political circles to accept the facts of climate change, because to do so would imply renunciation of the

---

[33]For example, the work of the Centre for Christian-Muslim Relations, an agency of the St Columban's Mission Society, https://www.columban.org.au/about-us/mission-offices/columban-centre-for-christian-muslim-relations/ (last accessed 3 February, 2020), and of the Public and Contextual Theology Research Centre (PACT), https://www.csu.edu.au/pact (last accessed 3 February, 2020). There have been two major reports on Islamophobia in Australia, edited by Derya Iner, based at the Centre for Islamic Studies and Civilizations, Charles Sturt University: *Islamophobia in Australia 2014–16* (Sydney 2017) and *Islamophobia in Australia Report II, 2017–18* (Sydney 2019), both published jointly by Charles Sturt University and ISRA (Islamic Sciences and Research Academy Australia).

economic freedom to exploit the natural environment as much as commercial prerogatives and preferences allow.

Ideological secularism seeks to redefine public secular space not as a space where different faiths can meet and engage but as a space stripped bare of religion altogether, based in an ideology of secular humanism, which is an attempt to impose one world view on public life. This world view is now usually expressed as libertarian individualism, which in all key areas of ethics decries and denies the insights into human existence which the world faiths can bring to the public forum. This was sometimes evident in the debate over same-sex marriage in Australia, which was construed by many purely as a matter of equality and personal commitment, rather than taking into account the other goods of marriage.[34] While many secular humanists are actively committed to projects for the common good,[35] secularism as an ideology is easily manipulable by commercial interests which recast autonomy in terms of individual desire and acquisitiveness.

One of the most important and controversial areas of public theology concerns its scope and emphasis in relation to the different spheres of personal and social life. The Christian gospel concerns all aspects of human existence, but different Christian communities at different times and places have emphasized some more than others, to the point of exclusivity or neglect. Broadly speaking, Christian communities may or may not emphasize the following areas as key to their life and mission: personal life, especially sex and sexuality; family life and bonds; life issues, especially beginning and end of life; medical and bioethics; social justice, including economic, communal, racial and cultural justice; ecological issues; political ethics, in particular questions of war and peace. Many debates and tensions in the field of public theology, and the life of the Christian churches, concern the relative emphasis to be given to these areas.

Notoriously, some of the greatest tensions within and between Christian communities have to do with the relative emphasis given to the ethics of personal and family life and to economic ethics, especially the critique of market capitalism. As noted earlier, before the 1960s the Catholic community had stronger links to the Labor movement and to social democracy, while the conservative parties were more often linked to members of Protestant communities. However, these denominational alliances ceased to have any significant relevance after the 1970s. Within both Protestant and Catholic

---

[34]Same-sex marriage has been legal in Australia since December 2017, after an act of the Australian Parliament confirmed the result of a postal plebiscite which supported this measure by a clear majority (62 per cent to 38 per cent).

[35]Peter Singer, the distinguished Australian philosopher (now professor of bioethics at Princeton University), is a prominent example of a committed secular humanist and utilitarian who has made important contributions to animal welfare and philanthropy; he is strongly critical of traditional Christian beginning and end of life ethics, in ways that respect the canons of civil discourse.

communities 'culture wars' have broken out in recent decades in relation to the respective emphasis to be given to different dimensions of ethics, including the reality of climate change and its relationship to market capitalism.[36] Clive Pearson sums up the challenging implications for public theology:

> There is an issue embedded here which has to do with the inner integrity of the Christian faith as well as its capacity to speak into a public forum that is likely to be bemused by the plurality of Christian witness. The otherworldly and eschatological natures of a Christian profession can look for a new heaven and a new earth, where there is no connection with this present age. There is no theological need to be bothered with climate change or the common good at all. The letter columns in denominational newspapers are often littered with a mixture of scientific scepticism concerning climate change and theological suspicion. One of the audiences for a public theology is to talk back into the churches and handle the internal debate as well.[37]

The relationship between personal conversion, family ethics and social justice has been particularly controversial in evangelical communities in Australia. Stuart Piggin and Robert Lindner identify three branches of Australian evangelicalism in recent decades: Conservatives, Progressives and Charismatics/Pentecostalists, with their most influential leaders, respectively, Peter Jensen (former Anglican archbishop of Sydney) and his brother Phillip (former dean of St Andrew's Anglican Cathedral Sydney); Tim Costello, former head of World Vision Australia; and Brian Houston, founder and senior pastor of Hillsong Church, founded in Sydney, now with an extensive international presence.[38] Commitment to social justice has been central to the progressive strand, exemplified by World Vision, Australia's largest charitable agency. Both the Sydney Anglicans and the Hillsong Pentecostals 'are now committed to social welfare as integral to their ministries, after some conservatives fought against that understanding for decades and the Pentecostals largely ignored that responsibility until it became essential to their image as a caring community'.[39]

---

[36] In her *God under Howard: The Rise of the Religious Right in Australian Politics* (Sydney: Allen and Unwin, 2005), Marion Maddox develops a critique of the government of John Howard (Prime Minister 1996–2007) as deploying a blend of neoliberalism and social conservatism imported 'from an arena where it was already well-developed, namely, the further fringes of the American religious right. Howard's skill was in stripping this fundamentalist melange of its overtly theological trappings' (198).
[37] Clive Pearson, 'The Purpose and Practice of a Public Theology in a Time of Climate Change', *International Journal of Public Theology* 4, no. 3 (2010): 356–72 (360).
[38] Piggin and Lindner, 'Tensions and Initiatives within the Evangelical Movement in the 1990s', in *Attending to the National Soul*, Chapter 16, 480–502.
[39] Ibid., 532.

In recent years 'the leaders of all three streams acknowledge the desirability of bringing a prophetic ministry to bear on social issues in order to achieve a greater engagement with the wider society'.[40]

In his 'Public Theology and Political Ethics', Bishop Heinrich Bedford-Strohm emphasizes that a public church must speak both prophetically and constructively: prophetic speech cannot be opposed to wisdom speech.[41] The importance of balancing prophetic and wisdom speech has been particularly clear in the tensions between some church leaders and representatives of the LGBTQI+ community, where fidelity to Christian tradition on the nature of marriage has needed to be balanced with respect for the personal dignity of LGBTQI+ citizens and church members. A more straightforwardly prophetic response has been evident in some criticisms of government policy in a number of areas, including the treatment of refugees and asylum seekers. David Hilliard notes that a 'number of Anglican leaders, and the heads of some Anglican welfare agencies, established a strong public presence so that their statements challenging government policies were widely reported'.[42] In 1977 the Congregational, Methodist and Presbyterian churches in Australia came together to form the Uniting Church of Australia. Its inaugural assembly issued a 'Statement to the Nation' in June 1977, strongly emphasizing prophetic themes of justice and human rights in fidelity to the God of Jesus Christ, 'under whose judgement the policies and actions of all nations must pass'.[43]

Since Christian tradition itself is comprehensive, embracing the whole range of moral challenges, then the expression of that tradition in Australia should be equally comprehensive. Australian Christian identity should avoid being formed as a counterthrust to some recent socio-ethical developments in Australian society. The lamentable frequency of abortion, the advocacy of euthanasia by many voices and the range of social forces that seek to deprive sex of its deepest meanings are all opposed to the meaning of humanity in a Christian perspective. Yet this does

---

[40]Ibid., 561.
[41]Heinrich Bedford-Strohm, *Liberation Theology for a Democratic Society: Essays in Public Theology*, collected by M. Maedler and A. Wagner-Pinggéra (Zürich: LIT Verlag, 2018), here at 19. In Robert Gascoigne, 'The Meaning of Christian Prophecy in a Liberal Secular Culture', *Political Theology* 17, no. 6, 540–54, I have argued that authentic Christian prophecy is characterized by witness, courage, discernment and a concrete, contextual focus. One task of discernment is to judge the appropriateness of denunciation or dialogue in specific contexts.
[42]David Hilliard, 'Pluralism and New Alignments in Society and Church, 1967 to the Present', in *Anglicanism in Australia: A History*, ed. Bruce Kaye (Melbourne: Melbourne University Press, 2002), 128. Maddox, in *God under Howard*, 240–2, notes that in particular Archbishop Peter Carnley, Anglican archbishop of Perth and a distinguished systematic theologian, was taken to task by Howard government ministers Peter Costello and Alexander Downer for his criticism of government policies.
[43]https://assembly.uca.org.au/resources/introduction/item/134-statement-to-the-nation-inaugural-assembly-june-1977 (last accessed 3 February 2020).

not mean that Australian Christianity should understand its own identity as being essentially about opposing such voices and forces, since to do so would be to mirror an individualist society's preoccupation with the ethics of individual life and with sex. Rather, Australian Christianity should communicate a genuinely comprehensive response to the challenges to our humanity that we experience today, which will certainly include life ethics and sexual ethics, but also social, political and ecological ethics. In this way, the churches' ethical communication is shaped not by reaction to some recent social developments but rather by the comprehensiveness of the Christian church's moral teaching itself, based in the dignity of the human person as created in the image of God and redeemed by Jesus Christ. This more comprehensive response has the potential to express the church's evangelizing mission through dialogue. It can engage with a range of voices within public space, on the basis of mutual respect and good will, and an acknowledgement of difference. On this basis, Australian Christianity can make a discerning and differentiated response to the moral changes that are taking place, affirming the key markers of Christian ethical tradition while seeking to communicate that tradition in a way that is open to development.

The churches' engagement in the field of sexual ethics has been gravely compromised by the recent evidence of culpable neglect on the part of some officeholders in the churches in terms of the sexual abuse of children by members of the clergy and of religious congregations, most frequently in the Catholic Church.[44] The severe humiliation that this has caused is an opportunity for examination of conscience and for listening, especially to the voices of the victims of abuse. Needless to say, this nefarious history of abuse and concealment has made it much more difficult for Australian Christian churches, the Catholic Church in particular, to communicate the meaning of Christian faith for faithful, respectful and fruitful sexual relationships, but it remains, as always, its mission and calling to do so.

27.3 CENTRES AND AGENCIES OF PUBLIC THEOLOGY IN AUSTRALIA

There are a number of centres and agencies engaged in public theology in Australia. In the Catholic Church, the principal agency devoted to public theology is the Australian Catholic Social Justice Council, which advises the

---

[44]The Royal Commission into Institutional Responses to Child Sexual Abuse was announced by the government of Prime Minister Julia Gillard in 2012, and was in session from 2013 to 2017, submitting a final report in December 2017. For a detailed study of the Commission and the Australian Catholic Church, see Neil Ormerod, 'Sexual Abuse, A Royal Commission and the Australian Church', *Theological Studies* 80, no. 4 (2019): 950–66.

Office for Social Justice of the Australian Catholic Bishops' Conference.[45] The Social Justice Council publishes an annual 'Social Justice Statement' on a range of topics. The statements have been published annually since 1940 on Social Justice Sunday (from 2020 the last Sunday in August).[46] The Anglican Board of Mission,[47] the national mission agency of the Anglican Church of Australia, engages in a number of projects and publishes a range of resources relevant to public theology and social justice concerns. Uniting Justice Australia is 'the justice unit of the National Assembly of the Uniting Church in Australia, pursuing national matters of social and economic justice, human rights, peace and the environment'.[48] Like the Catholic and Anglican agencies, it publishes a range of resources related to matters of public theology. In particular the Uniting Church of Australia, together with The Salvation Army, published an e-book, *Holiness and Social Justice*, in 2018 after a process of dialogue and reflection, and offered this to the Australian public.[49]

The Public and Contextual Theology Research Centre (PACT), based at Charles Sturt University's Canberra campus, is a major academic centre of public theology[50] having members drawn from a number of Christian denominations and world faiths. PACT is a founding member of the Global Network for Public Theology and 'is committed to becoming the lead centre in the Asia-Pacific region for research at the interface of theology and public issues'. Its current director is the Right Reverend Professor Stephen Pickard, a bishop of the Anglican Church of Australia. Strategic research priorities for 2017–21 include Christian–Muslim Relations in Australia, Religious Social Service Agencies and Religion, Ethics and the Anthropocene. Associate Professor Clive Pearson, a founding member of PACT and of the Global Network of Public Theology, is the current editor of the *International Journal of Public Theology*.

The Centre for Public Christianity,[51] based in Sydney, is a 'not-for-profit media company that offers a Christian perspective on contemporary life'. It seeks 'to promote the public understanding of the Christian faith by engaging mainstream media and the general public with high quality and well-researched print, video, and audio material about the relevance of Christianity in the 21st century'. The Ethos Centre,[52] the Evangelical Alliance's Centre for Christianity

---

[45] https://socialjustice.catholic.org.au.
[46] For a collection of more recent statements, see *Building Bridges: Social Justice Statements from Australia's Catholic Bishops, 1988–2013*, edited with an introduction by Sandie Cornish (Alexandria, NSW: Australian Catholic Social Justice Council, 2014).
[47] https://www.abmission.org.
[48] https://www.unitingjustice.org.au (last accessed 3 February 2020).
[49] https://assembly.uca.org.au/hsj (last accessed 3 February 2020).
[50] https://www.csu.edu.au/pact/welcome.
[51] https://www.publicchristianity.org.
[52] http://www.ethos.org.au.

and Society, based in Melbourne, whose current director is Rev Dr Gordon Preece, combines the activities, publications and personnel of two centres: the Zadok Institute for Christianity and Society and the Evangelical Alliance's Department of Public Theology. The Australian Theological Forum (ATF), initiated and led by Hilary Regan, has been an important contributor to public theology in Australia since the 1990s. Its activities include the ATF press[53] and the journal *Interface*, which focuses on a wide range of questions in public theology.

---

[53] https://atfpress.com.

CHAPTER 28

Public theology in Europe

Towards a performative-political approach

MARTIN KIRSCHNER

In this chapter, I understand public theology not as a label or clearly defined theological approach but as an articulation of the public responsibility that any theology has to bear. In this sense, the basis and starting point of public theology are not shared theoretical assumptions but the challenges and opportunities, the threats and fears, the visions and hopes which characterize a specific situation and which concern believers as well as non-believers. This starting point has also a spiritual dimension, as it needs trust, hope and courage to face reality and to take up responsibilities precisely where no ready-made answers are available. In this light, it is necessary to reflect on the current situation in the specific context of Europe, taking Europe as a particular part of the world, but also as a cultural idea or even a (spiritual or secular) ideal. Europe's particularity as well as its universal responsibility must be recognized. The identity of Europe does not simply exist as a fact, as a timeless idea or essence, but is (re-)constituted and transformed in an ongoing public process of deliberation and shared memories, narrations and counter-narrations, of crossing borders and (re-)defining boundaries, developing visions of what Europe is and what it ought (not) to be. In that respect the idea of Europe itself is neither neutral nor innocent. Europe must be critically de- and reconstructed in an ongoing process of reform and renewal. After the fall of the iron curtain, and in view of the dangers of a mere economical, technocratic and functional integration of Europe, Jacques Delors coined the much-quoted term to 'give a soul to Europe'.[1] The metaphor has been widely received and controversially discussed.[2] Although it is not per se religious, but aims at a broad cultural debate in civil society, this phrase marks in a certain way the place of a public theology in Europe.

Starting from the global crisis as a challenge of Western modernity and of political liberalism (28.1), I will discuss the quest for a cultural identity of Europe as challenge for a European Public Theology (28.2). With reference to J. Derrida and Pope Francis, I will argue for an open, performative understanding of European identity. In consequence, the place of religion in the European public sphere will be reconsidered, taking up the debate on 'post-secularity' (28.3). I will propose a *performative-political* approach (28.4), which, finally, I will relate to recent challenges and crises (28.5).

28.1 THE GLOBAL CRISIS OF MODERNITY AS EUROPE'S HERITAGE AND CHALLENGE

It can hardly be denied that we are currently experiencing a multi-layered crisis of global reach. The Covid-19 pandemic makes this crisis more visible and acute, but the pandemic is more the symptom than the cause. It reveals the vulnerability of our civilization, the fundamental inequality we produce and our ongoing dependence on ecological conditions of life, which we are not able to control or to guarantee, but which we are able to destroy. The strategies against Covid-19 follow the classical path of trying to regain control: measures of restriction and control over the population to ensure *security*; an unprecedented expansion of national debt to compensate for the consequences of the measures (in those countries that can afford it), focusing on *systemically relevant* areas; large-scale, scientifically proven ways of combating epidemics that are to be applied globally, but which reproduce and aggravate structural inequalities; further digitalization of communication and trade which strengthen the power of digital corporations; and so on. While the public focuses on the daily case numbers and emergency measures, the socio-economic and ecological crises

---

[1] Quoted from Commission of the European Communities (ed.), 'Summary of Addresses by President Delors to the Churches', 14 May 1992 (No. 704E/92), cf. https://austria-forum.org/af/Wissenssammlungen/Symbole/Europasymbole/Seele_Europas (last accessed 15 September 2021).
[2] Cf., for example, Thomas Meyer, *Die Identität Europas. Der EU eine Seele?* (Frankfurt am Main: Suhrkamp, 2004); Sylvia Losansky, *Öffentliche Kirche für Europa. Eine Studie zum Beitrag der christlichen Kirchen zum gesellschaftlichen Zusammenhalt in Europa*, Öffentliche Theologie Bd. 25 (Leipzig: Evangelischen Verlagsanstalt, 2010), esp. 17–19; Gijsbert van den Brink and Gerard den Hertog, eds, *Protestant Traditions and the Soul of Europe* (Leipzig: Evangelische Verlagsanstalt, 2017). Werner Weidenfeld places his assessment of European integration as a whole under the heading of the search for the 'soul of Europe': Werner Weidenfeld, *Europas Seele suchen. Eine Bilanz der europäischen Integration* (Baden-Baden: Nomos Verlagsgesellschaft mbH & Co, 2017).

are becoming more acute. Climate change and mass extinction have become threats, whose catastrophic consequences are already being experienced in very concrete terms, with regional variations in severity. The ecological crisis puts humanity under enormous pressure to act, especially since significant ecosystems such as the rainforests, coral reefs and polar regions are reaching the tipping points at which development becomes irreversible. The necessity to respond to these crises collectively by changing the system and the way of life deepens the political conflicts and the polarization of societies. These problems meet the crisis of liberal democracy, of the rule of law and of multilateralism. The trend seems to go towards anarchy, organized crime and failing states on the one hand, and towards authoritarian politics and new forms of economic colonialism on the other.

Although history as a state of permanent crisis forms part of the modern world view,[3] the ongoing escalation and acceleration of these crises is not just another form of alarmism. It results from the dynamics of modernity and the 'dialectics of enlightenment'[4] itself: the capitalist globalization, the reductionist and technocratic access to reality, and the culture of dominion, extractivism and waste destroy the ecological balance of the planet and the social bonds of humanity. In this way, the crisis challenges the Western concepts of modernity, enlightenment, liberalism and the idea of universal application of human rights.

In this global situation, Europe plays an important and highly ambivalent role: It is part of the crisis, as a cause, as affected by it, but also as a possible answer. It contains and experiences the conflicts between centre and periphery, between the different cultures and religious traditions within its own borders. For numerous migrants and refugees Europe is a destination of desperate hope, but, betraying its core principles, it has turned its borders to zones of exception and the Mediterranean Sea to a hidden mass grave. Still, if Europe takes its responsibility and participates in joint action and international cooperation, it might become a source of hope and inspiration for the world. The process of European integration and the European Union as its most significant political result contains such hopes: it is a unique model for cooperation, rule of law and for a post-national, multi-level form of democratic governance. On the other hand, it is de facto also an important driver of a technocratic and bureaucratic

---

[3]Cf. Reinhart Koselleck, Nelly Tsouyopoulos and Ute Schönpflug, 'Krise', in *Historisches Wörterbuch der Philosophie*, ed. Joachim Ritter, Karlfried Gründer and Gottfried Gabriel (Basel: Schwabe Verlag, 1976).

[4]Cf. Adorno and Horkheimer. The recent report to the Club of Rome also draws attention to the situation of a 'full earth', whose limits to growth have long been exceeded by humanity and call for an 'Enlightenment 2.0', which also refers to the wisdom of spiritual and religious traditions: cf. Ernst Ulrich von Weizsäcker and Anders Wijkman, *Come on! Capitalism, Short-Termism, Population and the Destruction of the Planet: A Report to the Club of Rome* (New York: Springer, 2018).

form of politics with weak democratic legitimization, which pushes forward neoliberal globalization, tightens social disparities and applies human rights only selectively.

To appreciate the role of Europe in the current global crisis, the events of 1989/91 and their interpretation are of key importance. They have changed not only the political map of Europe but also the global geopolitical constellation and the ideological mapping of the world. The overcoming of Europe's division and the fall of the Berlin Wall, the largely peaceful revolution by civil movements and the newfound freedom were a moment of immense renewal for Europe. At the same time, however, politics after 1989/91 are at the root of the crises, which then became increasingly manifest in the twenty-first century and led to the current challenge of Western liberalism. Recent analyses offer conclusive interpretations of why the hopes of 1989 were disappointed.[5] They place the events in the context of a wider neoliberal framework that dominated politics since the 1980s and succeeded in establishing itself as the only remaining ideology with a worldwide impact after 1989. The studies agree on the thesis that Western liberalism won the Cold War, but it failed to maintain the peace that followed. Liberalism not only failed to build a new world order but led to a social disembedding of economy, to a dominance of organized private interests and to a hegemonic globalization that fuelled cultural and religious conflicts all over the world. It produced the antagonisms and polarization that led to a turn towards fundamentalist, authoritarian and illiberal options and to a social disintegration even at the core of Western democracies.

> What we witness in the West today is not a temporary setback in a progressive development, not a 'pause', but a reversal. It is the unmaking of the post-1989 world, and the most dramatic feature of this ongoing transformation is not the rise of authoritarian regimes, but the changing nature of democratic ones in many Western countries.[6]

Together with Steven Holmes, Krastev interprets the development after 1989 as a worldwide project of imitating Western liberalism, which presents itself without alternatives while becoming increasingly unstable. In the East-

---

[5]Cf. Philipp Ther, *Die neue Ordnung auf dem alten Kontinent. Eine Geschichte des neoliberalen Europa*, 3rd edn. (Berlin: Suhrkamp Verlag, 2014); Philipp Ther, *Das andere Ende der Geschichte. Über die Große Transformation* (Berlin: Suhrkamp, 2019); Ivan Krastev and Stephen Holmes, *Light That Failed: A Reckoning* (New York/London: Pegasus Books, 2019); Ivan Krastev, *After Europe* (Philadelphia: Penn University Press, 2017); Andreas Reckwitz, *Das Ende der Illusionen. Politik, Ökonomie und Kultur in der Spätmoderne*, 3rd edn. (Berlin: Suhrkamp, 2019); Andreas Reckwitz, *Society of Singularities* (Cambridge, MA: Polity, 2020).
[6]Ivan Krastev, 'Majoritarian Futures', in *The Great Regression*, ed. Heinrich Geiselberger (Cambridge, UK: Polity Press, 2017), 65–77 (66).

Central European countries, he recognizes the model of imitating the West with the perspective of integration into the EU, the price of which is the acceptance of the cultural hegemony of the West. In view of the internal social and cultural tensions and the crisis of the West, as it became visible with the financial crisis of 2007/08, this imitation turned into an authoritarian-populist counter-politics, now being imitated in the Western democracies.

Following the interpretation of Krastev and Holmes, the current crisis exposes the blind spot of Western modernity: while presenting itself as the morally and technologically superior path of enlightenment and autonomous self-determination, it has been interwoven from the beginning with conquest, colonial exploitation and imperial hegemony. This ambiguity characterizes Europe. The challenge of decolonization affects Europe's internal structures, both in the East and the West.

28.2 THE SEARCH FOR A (CULTURAL) IDENTITY OF EUROPE AS A CHALLENGE FOR PUBLIC THEOLOGY

The need to define Europe (anew) on a cultural level accompanies Europe from the very beginning. Europe cannot be identified with a territory but is rather a changing space of interaction whose borders and centres shift throughout history, whose identity is fought over. This changeability of Europe becomes particularly evident in countries like Britain, Russia, Georgia and Turkey, where questions of geographic and cultural affiliation and identity arise repeatedly. A Mediterranean, Atlantic and Eurasian orientation compete with each other. At the same time, Europe has reached out to the whole world with the age of 'discoveries', with colonialism and the progressing globalization. By this, Europe itself was transformed, it has absorbed influences from all over the world and it contains the diversity of the world within.[7] As an internally diverse space of interaction without clear boundaries, Europe must be brought forth over again on a cultural and political level. In this process, historical, cultural and normative moments intertwine – religions playing a crucial part.

How can one speak of a European identity at all in this given diversity? On a first level, one could search the foundation for a European identity in a consensus, which would serve as a common ground in the resolution of political conflicts and in the integration of Europe. But is such a consensus more than a solemnly staged insinuation? Who would define such a consensus (and against whom)? The relative homogeneity that it presupposes does not exist (anymore?), even on the national level. Accordingly, the attempts to establish a

---

[7] Cf. François, Etienne and Serrier, Thomas, eds, *Europa. Notre Histoire* (Paris: Les Arènes, 2017), part 3: Mémoires – monde.

kind of 'civil religion' at the European level – the symbolic staging of a common history, the offers of identification with the institutions and unifying values – remain artificial.[8] The debates about a European constitution and constitutional patriotism, about the significance of Christianity and of the Enlightenment, about the place of Islam and Turkey's possible membership in the EU indicate this difficulty. Every appeal to a basic consensus meets dissent; the formulation of a principal culture excludes other perspectives; the position of the majority must be gauged morally as well as in terms of democratic theory by its treatment of minorities. While cultural-essentialist strategies will emphasize national identities and claim the *Europe of nations* at best geo-strategically or as a *bulwark against Islam*, a cosmopolitan culture and universalist principles point beyond Europe to the one world and humanity, struggling to acknowledge the value of the particular and concrete.

Accordingly, normative models of a European identity must prove their efficiency precisely by being able to mediate between unity and diversity, particularity and universalism, identity and difference. This raises the question of which instance can provide such mediation and on what normative basis. Here, religious and secular approaches to Europe come into play. Pope John Paul II, for example, in his efforts to overcome the East–West conflict, relied on the unifying and reconciling power of the Christian faith.[9] In his post-synodal letter 'Ecclesia in Europa' (EE) of 2003, he emphasizes (in n. 19) on a normative level the 'subordination of political power to the law and to respect for the rights of the person and of nations', which he traces to a variety of roots in Europe: he recalls 'the spirit of ancient Greece and the Roman world, the contributions of the Celtic, Germanic, Slavic, Finno-Ugric peoples, Jewish culture and the Islamic world'. However, he says, one must 'recognize that these inspirations have historically found in the Judeo-Christian tradition a force capable of reconciling them, consolidating them, and promoting them' (EE 19). He thus combines a normative, human rights foundation with the recognition of a diversity of cultural and religious roots, which in turn are mediated by the Judeo-Christian tradition. In this way, however, he assigns a

---

[8]Cf., for example, Dieter Grimm, *Europa ja – aber welches? Zur Verfassung der europäischen Demokratie*, 2nd edn. (München: C.H. Beck, 2016); Jürgen Habermas, 'Braucht Europa eine Verfassung?' in *Zeit der Übergänge. Kleine politische Schriften IX*, ed. Jürgen Habermas (Frankfurt am Main: Suhrkamp, 2001), 85–103; Ernst-Wolfgang Böckenförde, *Staat, Nation, Europa. Studien zur Staatslehre, Verfassungstheorie und Rechtsphilosophie*, 2nd edn. (Frankfurt am Main: Suhrkamp, 2000).

[9]Cf. Sylvia Losansky, *Öffentliche Kirche für Europa. Eine Studie zum Beitrag der christlichen Kirchen zum gesellschaftlichen Zusammenhalt in Europa* (Leipzig: Evangelische Verlagsanstalt, 2010), 62–96; Joachim Rabanus, *Europa in der Sicht Papst Johannes Pauls II. Eine Herausforderung für die Kirche und die europäische Gesellschaft* (Paderborn: Schöningh, 2004).

central role for European culture to the Catholic Church as a mediating force between particular cultures and universally valid norms.

Joseph Ratzinger/Pope Benedict XVI identifies as the decisive mediating instance the encounter of biblical faith with Greek philosophy relating faith and reason to each other: 'Christianity is the synthesis, mediated in Jesus Christ, between the faith of Israel and the Greek spirit. [. . .] In my opinion, Europe in the narrower sense emerges from this synthesis and rests on it.'[10] The distinction of faith and reason, which has significantly shaped European cultural history, is taken up. The Hellenization Process of Christianity does not appear as a historical and time-conditioned process of enculturation alongside others but as a standard against which other ways to relate faith and reason are measured.[11] The recourse to such a binding synthesis further sharpens the conflicts in relation to the modern and postmodern critiques of reason, to religious pluralism and to overcoming Eurocentrism, especially as Ratzinger presents his position not only in the mode of religious confession but with the claim of universal reason.

In recent years, Jürgen Habermas, whose understanding of a post-secular society and a post-metaphysical philosophy is closely linked to his understanding of European culture and its Greek and Hebrew roots, has developed a more critical definition of the relationship between faith and reason. Here too the 'constellation of faith and knowledge' is structure-forming for European philosophy. However, he arrives at clearly different results than Ratzinger. At least to a certain extent, he reflects on his own contextuality in a multicultural, globalized, postcolonial world, which would make an intercultural and critical discourse necessary. He conceives his 'genealogy of post-metaphysical thinking' as a reconstruction of a rationally comprehensible history of learning, claiming normative validity through this figure of justification.[12] The different and often conflicting approaches to reality and concepts of good life cannot be integrated into one world view but have to be mediated by a public discourse based on a

---

[10]Cf. Joseph Ratzinger, 'Europa – verpflichtendes Erbe für die Christen', in *Europa. Horizonte der Hoffnung*, ed. Franz König and Karl Rahner (Graz u.a.: Verl. Styria, 1983), 61–74 (68); Joseph Ratzinger, *Der Gott des Glaubens und der Gott der Philosophen* (Freiburg; Basel; Wien: Herder, 2020); Siegfried Wiedenhofer, 'Die Frage der europäischen Identität in der Theologie von Joseph Ratzinger/Benedikt XVII', in *Die Seele Europas. Papst Benedikt XVI. und die europäische Identität*, ed. Clemens Sedmak and Stephan Otto Horn (Regensburg: Pustet, 2011), 249–88; Georg Essen, '"Hellenisierung des Christentums" als kulturhermeneutische Deutungskategorie der Moderne', in *Christliches Europa? Religiöser Pluralismus als theologische Herausforderung*, ed. Klaus Viertbauer and Florian Wegscheider (Freiburg, Basel, Wien: Herder, 2017), 81–103.

[11]The religious–theological explosiveness of this position was ignited by the statements on Islam in his Regensburg speech. Cf. Knut Wenzel, ed., *Die Religionen und die Vernunft. Die Debatte um die Regensburger Vorlesung des Papstes* (Freiburg im Breisgau: Herder, 2007).

[12]Cf. Habermas, *Auch eine Geschichte*, I, 69.

formal and procedural concept of reason. The history of European philosophy, in dealing with the difference between faith and knowledge, leads to the unfinished project of Enlightenment as self-reflection and rational freedom. Again, the question arises of how such a position relates to that which remains excluded by rational discourse.

Through his own learning processes, Habermas increasingly broadens his understanding of communicative reason and public discourse, discerning different claims to validity and opening them for convictions anchored in the lifeworld, for religion, as well as for an intercultural dialogue between the different paths through modernity. The orientation towards discourse and autonomous reason in the sense of Kant leads via Hegel, Feuerbach, Marx, Kierkegaard to Peirce and Mead into a turn towards the performativity of life forms.[13] Still, Habermas does not enter into a discussion with contemporary, postmodern and post-structuralist approaches of a performative constitution of embodied, socially embedded subjectivity.

Such a turn towards the performative, which replaces a consensus or mediation of diversity with an open understanding of European identity to be carried out anew in the present, is what I would like to outline briefly with references to Jacques Derrida and Pope Francis.

In his essay 'The Other Heading', which goes back to a lecture at a colloquium on 'The Cultural Identity of Europe' shortly after the fall of the Berlin Wall,[14] Jacques Derrida turns to the problematic of how the 'very old subject [sujet] of cultural identity' (5), can be addressed at all. Thereby, he not just takes 'Europe' as an exemplary case of this question but traces in his essay the close linkage between the notion of identity, the name of 'Europe' and its 'exemplarity'. From the beginning, Derrida hints at the performative character of European identity: he locates the question for a European identity, always threatened by exhaustion and calling for renewal, in the 'Today', which requires a response: 'If this meeting had any chance of escaping repetition, it would be only insofar as some *imminence*, at once a chance and a danger, exerted pressure on us' (5). Statements on European identity respond to and intervene in a certain situation. The identity they aim at is not available as something to be detected but is brought

---

[13]Cf. Habermas, *Auch eine Geschichte*, II, 557–766.
[14]Cf. Jacques Derrida, 'The Other Heading: Memories, Responses, and Responsibilities', in *The Other Heading: Reflections on Today's Europe* (Bloomington, IN: Indiana University Press, 1992), 4–83. As a background for my reading of the text, cf. Michael B. Naas 'Introduction: For Example', in Derrida, *The Other Heading: Reflections*, vii–lix; and the interpretation of Peter Zeillinger in 'Europa als ob nicht Europa. Jacques Derrida über Identität, Verantwortung und Vertrauen (zum 90. Geburtstag Jacques Derridas am 15. Juli 2020', https://www.feinschwarz.net/europa-als-ob-nicht-europa-jacques-derrida (last accesed 22 September 2021); Peter Zeillinger, 'Kriterien für Recht und Gerechtigkeit. Europa und die politischen Konsequenzen des Denkens von Jacques Derrida', in *Ethica. Jahrbuch des Instituts für Religion und Frieden* (2003): 61–9.

forth. The quest for identity confronts with the experience of time. Derrida links this with a first 'axiom of finitude', associated with 'a swarm . . . of questions' whether the search for identity should 'return to a Europe of origins' or 'depart from Europe'. This quest for Europe ('a certain Europe does not yet exist. Has it ever existed?' [7f]) leads to a paradox in the notion of identity itself. The claim for identity is bound to a non-identity: 'what is proper to a culture is to not be identical to itself' (9). This does not mean 'to not have an identity, but not to be able to identify itself' or, in other words: to take the form of a subject, saying 'me' or 'we', is only possible 'in the non-identity to itself or . . . in the difference with itself' (9). Identity, as a relation to oneself and to the other, cannot be stated but needs the cultivation of this relation, a 'culture of oneself as the culture of the other' (10). European identity is then nothing given to be regained or defended, but it is a relation to be cultivated in its openness and exposure to the other, constituting identity as a responsibility heading to the other and to the future.

With the title 'The Other Heading', Derrida opens a broad field of meanings and associations ranging from the title/head of a chapter to the end of an outer limb to the temporal end/goal/telos, referring to navigation, the course and the captain, linking Europe as the geographical western end of Eurasia to the idea of Europe, which always reaches out into the world and towards the other, being confronted with the fact that there are other headings, and other than a heading. Europe tends to confuse its location 'with that of an advanced point, [. . .] with a heading for world civilization or human culture in general. The idea of an advanced point of *exemplarity* is the *idea of the* European *idea*, its *eidos*, at once as *arché* [. . .] and as *telos*' (24). This constitutes a tension between the particular/regional and the universal/global, in which the hegemonic position of one's particular identity is claimed in the name of its responsibility for the whole.

By deconstructing the discourses on Europe, Derrida reveals their paradoxical structure. The focus shifts to *how* to speak of Europe: 'Or indeed in attempting to *invent another gesture*, an epic *gesture* in truth, that presupposes memory precisely in order to determine identity from alterity, from the other heading and the other of the heading, from a completely other shore?' (29f.). By understanding cultural identity not as 'the opaque body of an untranslatable idiom' but 'as the irreplaceable inscription of the universal in the singular' that moves into 'the responsibility of testifying for universality' (73), it cannot justify the claims of a European identity, but it establishes a responsibility for others and an obligation to the future to come.

In the style of Pope Francis and in the form of his statements on Europe,[15] I recognize such a different gesture in public theology, which translates the

---

[15] Cf. http://www.comece.eu/speeches-of-pope-francis-on-europe-60457 (last accesed 22 September 2021); for an interpretation see Martin Kirschner, 'Die öffentliche Aufgabe der Theologie in der

doctrinal proclamation of his predecessors into an open, procedural, pluralistic and dialogical communication of European identity, which corresponds to the outlined performativity of identity in its unescapable relation to alterity.

Pope Francis develops his understanding of Europe not from a *central* idea but focuses on the pluralism of regions, cultures and religions, which requires dealing with tensions and disparities in power and public recognition (*centre–periphery*). A renewal of European identity demands a broad dialogue that cuts across groups, denominations, milieus, and that aims not only and primarily at consensus but at the common construction of a liveable future. The pope proposes the polyhedron as a model of a unity in which the whole is more than the sum of the parts, but at the same time the parts can preserve their individuality without being determined by an organizing centre that dominates the whole (EG 236f., FT 215). In this model, there is no centre which could be claimed for one's own position. Thus, the church, too, is understood eccentrically and kenotically, as a church on the move ('going forth', 'Iglesia en salida', Evangelii Gaudium 20). The church finds its identity by turning towards those to whom it most owes active solidarity. Pope Francis calls for initiating open processes rather than owning or occupying spaces (cf. *Evangelii Gaudium* 222–5). Open processes cannot be controlled by individuals; they emerge through interaction and dialogue between different people. Correspondingly, this requires the development of a synodal church and an ecumenical synodality that initiates and allows such processes of learning and maturation within Christianity.

Such a future-oriented, processual understanding of European identity corresponds to a certain form of memory that turns to the past in order to gain orientation and hope from its struggles, sufferings and promises.[16] The return to Europe's roots in Jerusalem, Athens and Rome must prove itself on Lampedusa and Lesbos. The moral integrity of Europe depends on the turning towards those who are excluded, marginalized and have no voice. Giving a soul to Europe essentially depends on the *re-membrance* of those excluded or even annihilated as *members* of society. They cannot participate in any discourse. In his disputes with Joseph Ratzinger and Jürgen Habermas, Johann Baptist Metz has called for such an anamnetic understanding of reason, which is rooted in the historical thinking of Israel.[17] This opening to history and memory, to alterity and

---

Krise Europas: Überlegungen im Anschluss an Papst Franziskus', in *Die gegenwärtige Krise Europas. Theologische Antwortversuche*, ed. Martin Kirschner and Karlheinz Ruhstorfer (Freiburg: Herder Verlag, 2018), 29–66.

[16]Cf. the address of Pope Francis at the sixtieth anniversary of the treaty of Rome, 24 March 2017: https://www.vatican.va/content/francesco/en/speeches/2017/march/documents/papa-francesco_20170324_capi-unione-europea.html (last accessed 22 September 2021).

[17]Cf. inter alia Johannes Baptist Metz and Johann Reikerstorfer, *Memoria passionis. Ein provozierendes Gedächtnis in pluralistischer Gesellschaft* (Freiburg: Herder, 2017). The limits of formal reason and discursivity have been disputed between Enrique Dusserl, Karl-Otto Apel and

difference goes beyond Eurocentric concepts of faith and reason and opens up for the 'Epistemologies of the South'[18] and a polycentric world which will reshape Christianity. In view of the crises scenarios mentioned at the beginning, it is time to give up the claim to superiority of European culture and to enter into new learning processes, which testify the 'inscription of the universal into the singular' (Derrida) understanding universalism as a responsibility and hospitality for the other, acknowledging one's own limitations and transcending boundaries.[19]

28.3 RELIGION IN THE EUROPEAN PUBLIC: SECULAR RESTRICTIONS AND POST-SECULAR PLURALIZATION, REMEMBRANCE AND TESTIMONY, OPTIONALITY AND SELF-TRANSCENDENCE

The place of religion in the public is closely linked to the conflicting understandings of Europe. Conceiving Europe as a vanguard of universal modernization often goes hand in hand with a normative concept of secularization, which takes the Western European decline of religious practice and affiliation as standard for a global development. Conversely, identitarian reconstructions of a Europe of nations within a Christian occident or as a bulwark against Western decadence rely on religion as an identity-forming factor, supporting fundamentalist movements or new forms of the 'symphony' of state and church. The model of a culturally and religiously heterogeneous Europe with global responsibility, to the contrary, questions the clear distinctions between religious and secular.

The term 'post-secular' society was introduced into the debate by Jürgen Habermas.[20] Post-secularity does not indicate a sociological reversal in religiosity, nor the negation of secularization processes, but reflects the lasting

---

others in the intercultural Dialogue North-South: Raúl Fornet-Betancourt, ed., *Konvergenz oder Divergenz? Eine Bilanz des Gesprächs zwischen Diskursethik und Befreiungsethik* (Aachen: Verlag der Augustinus-Buch, 1994).

[18] Cf. Boaventura de Sousa Santos and Maria Paula Meneses, eds, *Knowledges Born in the Struggle. Constructing the Epistemologies of the Global South* (New York: Routledge 2020); Carlos Mendoza-Álvarez, *La resurrección como anticipación mesiánica. Duelo, memoria y esperanza desde los sobrevivientes* (Ciudad de México: Universidad Iberoamericana, 2020); Juan José Tamayo-Acosta, *Theologien des Südens,* Theologien der Welt, Vol. 1 (Freiburg; Basel; Wien: Herder, 2020).

[19] In *Fratelli tutti* Pope Francis develops this movement of a 'political love' that transcends boundaries from the parable of 'a stranger on the road' in Lk. 10.25-37, which turns the power to define who is my neighbour from the self to the other: caring for the other I become his or her neighbour.

[20] Jürgen Habermas, *Glauben und Wissen. Friedenspreis des deutschen Buchhandels 2001* (Frankfurt a.M.: Suhrkamp, 2001). For an overview of the debate on post-secularity, see William A. Barbieri, ed., *At the Limits of the Secular: Reflections on Faith and Public Life* (Grand Rapids, MI: William B. Eerdmans Publishing Company, 2014); Matthias Lutz-Bachmann, ed., *Postsäkularismus. Zur Diskussion eines umstrittenen Begriffs* (Frankfurt am Main: Campus-Verl., 2015).

public significance of religion and faith, even in the most secularized societies. William A. Barbieri in his overview on the debate distinguishes six 'Faces of Post-Secularity'.[21] He relates them to Charles Taylor's three dimensions of the secular: public secularity as an emptying of autonomous public spheres from religion, secularization as the decline of religious practice and affiliation, and secularity as an 'immanent frame' that changes the conditions of faith. To the latter Barbieri adds secularity as 'a specifically temporal conception rooted in the experience of ordinary, as opposed to higher time'. This framing of temporality and space leads to the centre of Taylor's narrative of the 'secular age'[22] and is crucial for the discussion of post-secularity.

I focus on this aspect, because the (often implicit) understanding of space and time shapes experience and language, subjectivity and action, sociality and world. The demarcation and opposition of a secular and a religious realm correspond to two conceptions of space and time: on the one hand, the plannable-available time of an immanently conceived world as a space of human action, on the other hand, a transcendent and unavailable 'higher' time, which is assigned to the sphere of the divine. Transcendence remains opposed to immanence and is at best externally connected with it in a special realm of the *sacred* or *religious*, which can be linked to heteronomous claims to power in the name of God. The resulting competition between the two areas not only leads to struggles for political power and public influence but also shapes theology and the church. Self-determination and ecclesiastical authority, human and divine nature, freedom and grace, time and eternity are opposed, one side constantly threatening to overwhelm the other.

Thus, the fundamental challenge for theology is to think the relationship between immanence and transcendence in such a way that both sides interpenetrate and enable each other, without one side being dissolved into the other, mixed with it or, conversely, separated from it. In the theological tradition, the formula of the Council of Chalcedon provides a kind of 'grammar' for this, which concerns not only Christology but the relationship between creature and Creator in general. The greater closeness to God is not at the expense of creaturely freedom but makes it possible. The divine and the human interact 'unseparated' and 'unmixed' in the living process of existence, constituting a dynamic unity which lives from the difference and confirms

---

[21]William A. Barbieri, 'The Post-Secular Problematic', in *At the Limits of the Secular: Reflections on Faith and Public Life*, ed. William A. Barbieri (Grand Rapids, MI: William B. Eerdmans Publishing Company, 2014), 129–61.
[22]Charles Taylor, *A Secular Age* (Cambridge, MA: The Belknap Press of Harvard University Press, 2007); see also: Florian Zemmin, Colin Jager and Guido Vanheeswijck, eds, *Working with a Secular Age: Interdisciplinary Perspectives on Charles Taylor's Master Narrative* (Berlin, Boston: de Gruyter, 2016).

it.[23] In the immediacy of the event, God and human being come into contact without remaining separate or being confused. This interrupts the ecclesiastical and political forms of mediation, their structure of 'exception' as inclusive exclusion.[24] The Second Vatican Council takes up this Chalcedonian grammar in its sacramental understanding of the church, opening it for a messianic understanding of history: the event of revelation cannot be conceived without the free response of human faith and conversely. The sign-like mediation in word, sacrament and ecclesial communion refers to this interplay of divine and human freedom; it occurs only in the concrete, limited consummation, which is related to the whole of history in the hope of the coming Kingdom of God.[25]

The philosophical preconditions for thinking such entanglement relation of transcendence and immanence historically have been developed in critical confrontation with classical metaphysics and transcendental philosophy in an increasingly radical turn to history, language and concrete existence. On the one hand, the immanent frame of an onto-theological concept or of different world views is opened up, realizing the unassailable precedence (diachrony, différance, anarchy) of the event, of alterity and difference, without in turn positivizing or identifying such transcendence that breaks into immanence.[26] In his outline of a practical fundamental theology, Johann Baptist Metz reduced such a figure to the concise formula: 'Shortest definition of religion; interruption.'[27] On the other hand, the figure of a 'transcendence from within' is explored in numerous

---

[23]Cf. Gregor Maria Hoff, 'Wer ist Christus? Das Symbolon von Chalkedon als Grammatik des Glaubens?', *Salzburger Theologische Zeitschrift* 8 (2004): 17–29; Josef Wohlmuth, 'Chalkedonische Christologie und Metaphysik', in *Religion, Metaphysik(kritik), Theologie im Kontext der Moderne, Postmoderne*, ed. Markus Knapp and Theo Kobusch (Berlin, NY: de Gruyter, 2001), 333–54. Erwin Dirscherl, *Das menschliche Wort Gottes und seine Präsenz in der Zeit. Reflexionen zur Grundorientierung der Kirche* (Paderborn: Verlag Ferdinand Schöningh, 2014), 26–35, 46–85.

[24]In his Homo Sacer project, Giorgio Agamben elaborates this ontological basic structure of the political, which cannot be eliminated or replaced, but which can be uncovered and which must be dealt with in such a way that it is opened up to what is excluded in each case, transferred into a non-possessive use and therein interrupted in its violence. Cf. in particular the epilogue: Giorgio Agamben, *The Omnibus Homo Sacer* (Stanford, CA: Stanford University Press, 2017); as well as the interpretations by Peter Zeillinger and myself in Martin Kirschner, ed., *Subversiver Messianismus. Interdisziplinäre Agamben-Lektüren* (Baden-Baden: Academia Verlag Richarz, 2020), 245–304, 305–64.

[25]Cf. Martin Kirschner, 'Catholicity as Witness and Dialogue: The Council´s Foundation of Faith in Dei Verbum as Hermeneutical key', in *Revisiting Vatican II. 50 Years of Renewal. Vol II: Selected Papers of the DVK International Conference*, ed. Shaji George Kochutara (Bangalore: Dharmaram Publications, 2015), 329–45; Martin Kirschner, 'Kirche der Armen und Zeichen messianischer Hoffnung', *Theologische Quartalschrift* 193, no. 3 (2013): 220–9.

[26]See, for example, Emmanuel Lévinas, *Jenseits des Seins, oder, anders als Sein geschieht*, 2nd edn. (Freiburg - München: Karl Alber, 1998).

[27]Johann Baptist Metz, *Faith in History and Society. Toward a Practical Fundamental Theology*, ed. James Matthew Ashley (New York: Crossroad Publishing Company, 2016), 157; see also Lieven Boeve, *God Interrupts History. Theology in a Time of Upheaval* (New York: Continuum, 2007).

philosophical and theological approaches, which trace the dynamisms of a self-transgression in the immanent (in matter, in language etc.), which does not come to rest in any finite formation. The (inter-)relation of faith and reason, of aesthetical perception, theoretical insight and practical responsibility cannot be objectified in different world views anymore, but they shape different forms of life and a use of bodies in which subjectivity, objectivity and communality are constituted in a performative way.

In this context, religious and secular convictions have the character of options that have to be affirmed, lived and ventured in the awareness of their contingency. As an option, faith does not exist in a supra-temporal way; rather, it must become accessible and be carried out, dared and proven anew in every generation and situation, responding to present challenges and historical 'contrast experiences' (Schillebeeckx), turning back to the sources and looking forward to the coming Kingdom. The optionality of faith corresponds to an open dialogue of convictions, which does not aim at domination and superiority but assumes common responsibility for the future by turning to the other and listening to the 'cry of the poor and the earth'.[28]

28.4 A PERFORMATIVE-POLITICAL APPROACH TO PUBLIC THEOLOGY

In view of the crises mentioned at the beginning and the erosion of existing (political, epistemic, ecclesiastical etc.) orders, a performative approach addresses the underlying cultural–ontological dimension of 'the political', in which these orders and structures are grounded.[29] The concept of performativity does not only aim at specific speech acts (such as an oath or a promise) or at a dimension of communicative action but refers to an understanding of embodied practice and historical forms of life, in which the processes of subjectivation, socialization and normativization are intertwined and cannot be separated. In conversation with post-structuralist, deconstructive and decolonial approaches, the paradoxes and contingencies, power relations and mechanisms of exclusion that are effective in language, culture and discourses are exposed. The public sphere, its standards of rationality and the rules of discourse cannot be presupposed as a neutral framework but are part and result of the struggle for visibility, recognition and liveability. The political comes into view from

---

[28]Cf. Pope Francis, Encyclical Laudato si' 49, in the background: Leonardo Boff, *Cry of the Earth, Cry of The Poor* (Maryknoll, NY: Orbis Books, 1997).
[29]Cf. Oliver Marchart, *Die politische Differenz. Zum Denken des Politischen bei Nancy, Lefort, Badiou, Laclau und Agamben*, 4th edn. (Berlin: Suhrkamp, 2019); Thomas Bedorf - Kurt Röttgers, ed., *Das Politische und die Politik* (Frankfurt am Main: Suhrkamp, 2010).

its processual dimension: in the demarcation of public/private, political/non-political, rational/irrational, 'us' and 'they', the arena of the public, the rules of discourse, belonging and participation are defined, in which the institutions, processes and contents of the political are then located. In this context, the place, the bodies and the manner of staging have a special weight.[30]

In recent years, different and opposing movements have shown how a public sphere is created and changed, how discourses on Europe have shifted and political systems have been questioned through physical presence and collective performances. The 'colour revolutions' in Eastern Europe as now in Belarus, the movements against refugees and against an imagined Islamization of Europe, the mass mobilization of the 'Brexiteers' and the 'Remainers' in Britain, 'Fridays for Future' and 'Extinction Rebellion', the protests against Corona politics and the demonstrations for Nawalny point in very different directions, in part opposing each other. Not only the content but the form of the protests and the political performances make the difference. The distinctions between legitimate and illegitimate, nonviolent and violent forms of protest, between an articulation of the popular will and its manipulation or populist appropriation are themselves highly political and refer to subtle distinctions in the performance of the political.

A key theo-political criterion in the performance of the political is whether the place of the absolute is identified, occupied and claimed implicitly for one's own position – often connected with a demonization of the other, or whether, conversely, the performance of the political in all its decisiveness and radicality responds and testifies to the absolute in such a way that it can at the same time relativize and correct itself, out of responsibility before others and without confusing itself with the absolute, staying open to the greater truth and justice that theologically point to the eschatological God.

The public and the private, the political and the theological intersect in the performativity of testimony, in which cognition and recognition, the expression of life and the commitment to truth are linked, and which is thus epistemically as well as ethically fundamental.[31] Witnessing or giving testimony goes deeper than a communicative action that aims to convince someone of something. It is interwoven with the life and survival of the witness, with his or her form of life that calls for recognition, with a concrete situation that must not be evaded, with a place that has to be occupied and cannot be abandoned. In testimony,

---

[30]Cf. Judith Butler, *The Force of Nonviolence: An Ethico-Political Bind* (London/New York: Verso, 2020); Judith Butler, *Notes Toward a Performative Theory of Assembly* (Cambridge, MA: Harvard University Press, 2018).
[31]Cf. Sibylle Schmidt, 'Ethik und Episteme der Zeugenschaft', dissertation (Konstanz: Konstanz University Press, 2015); Sibylle Schmidt, Sybille Krämer and Ramon Voges, eds, *Politik der Zeugenschaft. Zur Kritik einer Wissenspraxis* (Bielefeld: Transcript. 2011).

responsibility before the other, personal authenticity and propositional contents, concrete situation and the unconditionally valid, subjective experience and objective truth go together 'without separation or confusion'. The testimony even refers to that, which cannot be (sufficiently) remembered, translated or represented – as in the witness of survivors of trauma, violence and atrocities.[32]

In the case of religious convictions, the testimonial structure of human acts becomes particularly clear. The testimony of God as a basis of faith, church life and theology oscillates between *genitivus subiectivus* and *obiectivus*: Does human testimony give witness to God, or does God testify to Godself in human witness? It is decisive that the one cannot be stated without the other.[33] The event of God's revelation in history cannot be recorded, objectified or reassured; it can only be witnessed (afterwards, with delay). It demands a free response from the human being in the present taking responsibility towards the future to come.[34] But this also means that the testimony is itself an event, even if it refers to an original event with which it may not be confused. Thus, tradition cannot be conceived as mere repetition or perseverance of events in the past, but it has itself the character of a series of events: the testimony of faith can never be mechanically reproduced; rather, every 'repetition'/'iteration' makes at the same time new appropriations, innovations, permanently shifting the meaning of concepts and dogma. Living tradition happens as ongoing transformation. This refers to the *tradentes*, to the *traditum*, to its language and to the forms of expression, but also to history as such, which in Christian faith is to be transformed by the event of salvation, becoming 'messianically' reoriented and recapitulated in Christ-Messiah.

28.5 'A SOUL FOR EUROPE' – IN THE MIDST OF CRISIS?

As outlined in this chapter, Europe is currently confronted with serious global challenges and crises that call the modern model of the political into question and are closely linked to it. There are approaches that understand Europe as the outpost of a rational politics with a universal claim, linked to the promises

---

[32]Cf. Giorgio Agamben, *Remnants of Auschwitz. The Witness and the Archive* (New York: Zone Books, 1999).
[33]Emmanuel Levinas has brought this paradox to the short formula: 'Revelation happens through the one who receives it.' Cf. Erwin Dirscherl, *Das menschliche Wort*, 29–35. Or in the words of Hans Urs von Balthasar, *Verbum caro*, Skizzen zur Theologie 1 (Einsiedeln: Johannes Verlag, 1960), 98: 'Nur in der Antwort haben wir das Wort'.
[34]Cf. Peter Zeillinger, 'Offenbarung als Ereignis. Zeitgenössische Philosophie, die Rede von Gott und das Sprechen der Bibel', *Salzburger Theologische Zeitschrift* 21 (2017): 25–101. Peter Zeillinger, 'Geschichtliche Erinnerung und textuelle Autorität. Beantwortung der Frage "Was ist gute Theologie?"', in *Dialog und Konflikt. Erkundungen zu Orten theologischer Erkenntnis*, ed. Martin Kirschner (Ostfildern: Matthias Grünewald-Verlag, 2017), 149–74.

of development and progress, enlightenment and reason, human rights and freedom. Other approaches, conversely, retreat to particular identities and fall back on Europe for their self-assertion and defence. In contrast, I had argued for an open, performative understanding of Europe's cultural identity, understood as universal responsibility before others in the awareness of its own particularity and limitedness, committed to the open process of building a liveable future together. In doing so, I have turned the focus from religion and politics as opposing institutionally anchored spheres towards the political and the theological as distinguishable but interrelated dimensions of living (together). In the performativity of testimony this interweaving of the political and the theological becomes particularly evident. In such a perspective, transcendence and immanence, divine grace and human freedom cannot be separated or juxtaposed. The framing of a homogeneous, linear time and a delimitable and controllable space proves to be questionable, fragile and secondary when the kairological time of the event comes into view, to which the testimony responds that has to be ventured towards the coming future. Reception and gift, unavailability of the other and spontaneity of the self, responsibility and freedom intertwine and constitute a (co-)responding and (co-)responsible political agency that is not founded in sovereignty or autonomy but in the shared vulnerability, interdependence and responsibility that constitute the political. In such a performative perspective, how can a public theology contribute to dealing with the current challenges and crises?

I can just make a few indications, turning the theological focus on structures and processes in which political and ecclesial action take place. Wherever these structures and actions present themselves as if they were without alternative or absolute, legitimized by a sovereign instance which cannot be questioned and called to account, theological objection and the deconstruction of such structures and claims will be necessary. Likewise, wherever memory and remembrance, the voice of past generations and the cry of victims are silenced, the witness and vicarious advocacy of the community of believers are needed, whose hope in God also grants a future to the dead and the victims of history. Facing the structures of inclusion and exclusion effective in the present, the way in which the life and interests of some (in the *centre*) matter and are represented, while others (struggling for survival on the *peripheries*) are neglected, made invisible or even are annihilated, the truth of faith must prove itself in its force to lead to a conversion and change of perspective, which turns towards those excluded and overseen. Finally, faith and the testimony of God prove their political relevance by keeping the future open as a space for new events to come. In this, they testify to a hope that is neither optimism nor mere reassurance of the afterlife but corresponds to the assumption of responsibility in life here and now.

Theology cannot solve the problems and crises, but it can contribute to recognize them and to encourage the dialogue and cooperation which is needed to deal with them.

CHAPTER 29

Public theology in North America

Commonality amid plurality

NICHOLAS HAYES-MOTA

29.1 INTRODUCTION: TWO TRANSFORMATIONS IN NORTH AMERICAN PUBLIC THEOLOGY

'Public theology', as both a term and a distinct academic field, originated within the United States in the mid-1970s. In the last two decades, it has expanded well beyond its formative context in North America, to emerge as a truly global phenomenon. Yet in its birthplace, some have perceived signs of decline. As of the early 2010s, Sebastian Kim observed, public theology publications within the United States had diminished, and the field's initiative appeared to have shifted elsewhere, as other regions quickly outstripped the United States in establishing institutional centres for public theology.[1] One might also observe that, globally, North American public theology still remains most associated with its founding figures, like Martin Marty, David Tracy and Max Stackhouse. Meanwhile, within the United States itself, it no longer commands the same breadth of academic interest that it did from the 1980s through the

---

[1] Sebastian Kim, *Theology in the Public Sphere: Public Theology as a Catalyst for Open Debate* (London: SCM Press, 2011), 6.

early 2000s, when debates over the place of religion in 'public life' galvanized many leading intellectuals beyond academic theology proper.[2]

Nevertheless, a simple decline narrative for North American public theology would be quite premature.[3] Since 2000, North American public theology has not so much declined as transformed, and this in two critical respects.[4] First, the field has *pluralized*, along several dimensions: It is now substantially (though perhaps not yet sufficiently) less white, male and US-centric than it was in its formative years, thanks to the efforts of many more recent public theologians. As it has pluralized, it has also *hybridized*, as feminist, Black and Latine theologians, among others, have intentionally blended the discourse of public theology with other theological – often, liberationist – streams. Second, and not unrelatedly, North American public theology has taken a 'practical turn', shifting from the narrower preoccupation with public *discourse* characteristic of its early decades towards a much more expansive concern with diverse *practices* of public action. In addition to academic texts or individual theologians, practical 'performances' of public theology like the US Movement for Black Lives and faith-based community organizing have now become critical loci for theological reflection.[5]

To fully appreciate the extent to which these two trends have transformed North American public theology, it will be necessary in each case to briefly revisit its formative decades and then trace the course of its development since. Doing so will enable me to highlight not only the vectors of change but also the lines of continuity. Simultaneously, it will allow me to present a somewhat

---

[2] Kristin Heyer provides a helpful overview of these debates, spanning theology, philosophy and social science literature, in Kristin E. Heyer, *Prophetic & Public: The Social Witness of U.S. Catholicism* (Washington, DC: Georgetown University Press, 2006), 1–25. Though conversations about religion's place in political society have by no means stopped, the primary terms of debate – as well as, of course, the *dramatis personae* – have changed. It is rarely religion's *public* (versus private) character that is now at issue, as it was in the classic US debates over public theology. As Linell Cady observes, it is now broadly recognized that '[r]eligion is clearly public, political, and often dangerous and divisive'; contemporary debate more frequently concerns the nature of secularity and 'postsecularity', and the specific respects in which religions are 'political'. Linell E. Cady, 'Public Theology and the Postsecular Turn', *International Journal of Public Theology* 8, no. 3 (2014): 292–312 (297).

[3] Here is worth noting that, as of 2014, the United States was still the second-largest contributor (after the UK) to the *International Journal of Public Theology*. Sebastian Kim, 'Editorial', *International Journal of Public Theology* 8, no. 2 (2014): 121–9 (121).

[4] In a survey of this scale, my focus cannot but be selective. Though in my judgement these two trends are the most far-reaching in their implications, one could certainly highlight others, such as, for example, 'the postsecular turn', which Linell Cady discusses in Cady, 'Public Theology and the Postsecular Turn'.

[5] Katie Day and Sebastian Kim open their recent *Companion to Public Theology* with an example from the Movement for Black Lives, and later identify the 'performed' character of public theology as one of its distinguishing marks. Katie Day and Sebastian Kim, 'Introduction', in *A Companion to Public Theology*, ed. Sebastian Kim and Katie Day (Leiden: Brill, 2017), 1–21 (1, 17).

different narrative of the identity and trajectory of North American public theology than the widely familiar 'founding story', which tends to prioritize only the figures and texts in the field from 1974 through roughly 2000.[6] My aim here is not to replace that narrative but to expand and enrich it. In fact, as I will try to show, the two developments I trace have genuinely enabled North American public theology to better become what it was always intended to be: *a vehicle for finding common identity in the midst of the plural and particular*. At the same time, the new plurality of voices and methods within North American public theology itself has raised fresh questions about what common identity holds *it* together as a field. In my conclusion, I turn to these questions and offer my own response to them.

29.2 FINDING THE COMMON, THROUGH THE PARTICULAR: THE PLURALIZATION OF PUBLIC THEOLOGY

The project of finding common identity in the midst of plurality and particularity has defined 'public theology' since its very beginnings. Public theology's founding figures were primarily concerned to articulate a common US identity amid the country's religious pluralism. When religious historian Martin Marty first coined the term 'public theology' (and unwittingly launched the field) in 1974, it was to introduce a category for figures, like Reinhold Niebuhr, who were able to give voice to the nation's identity in a uniquely compelling way while speaking in the language of their own religious tradition.[7] As sociologist Robert Bellah (who quickly appropriated the term) observed, 'public theologians' succeeded in this task not by abandoning their theological particularity but by convincingly interpreting the American religious experience 'through their own theological concepts'.[8] It was this characteristic that distinguished 'public theology' from Bellah's related concept of 'civil religion', the broadly shared 'religious dimension of American political life'.[9] Civil religion was general and 'symbolically open or empty', embodying no one religious tradition in

---

[6] Kim and Day rehearse the 'common historical narrative' that public theologians worldwide tell about the field's US origins in Ibid., 3–5.

[7] Marty introduced the terms 'public theologian' and 'public theology' in two seminal works from 1974, the latter of which was an analysis of Niebuhr. See Martin E. Marty, 'Two Kinds of Two Kinds of Civil Religion', in *American Civil Religion*, ed. Russell E. Richey and Donald G. Jones (New York: Harper & Row, 1974), 139–57; Martin E. Marty, 'Reinhold Niebuhr: Public Theology and the American Experience', *The Journal of Religion* 54, no. 4 (1974): 332–59.

[8] Robert N. Bellah, 'American Civil Religion in the 1970s', in *American Civil Religion*, ed. Rusell E. Richey and Douglas G. Jones (New York, 1974), 255–71 (258).

[9] Ibid., 255.

particular, whereas public theology represented an articulation of the country's common identity from the vantage point of a particular religious tradition.[10]

The first constructive theologians to appropriate Marty's term, Catholic theologians John Coleman and David Hollenbach, understood the project of public theology in an analogous sense. Both advocated it specifically as a revision to the 'public philosophy' promoted by John Courtney Murray (whose larger project of reconciling Catholic and American identity they otherwise wished to continue).[11] Murray had maintained that in its 'public arguments' about the nation's common good, the church should only employ the language of 'natural law', which was morally universal and so accessible (in principle) to all rational persons. Coleman and Hollenbach, by contrast, argued that the church should address the American public in a theologically explicit voice. Speaking in the richer symbolic languages of biblical and Christian tradition, they argued, would enhance, rather than compromise, the church's capacity to articulate a common national identity, and better move US citizens to action for the common good.[12]

A few years later, David Tracy, in *The Analogical Imagination*, would carry this project still further.[13] Seeking to provide a 'route from a chaotic pluralism to a responsible one', Tracy constructed a philosophical foundation for public theology's premise that discourse rooted in a specific religious tradition could nevertheless convey meaning and truth to those beyond it – and so qualify as 'public'.[14] With his famous account of theology's multiple 'publics' (society, academy, church), Tracy aimed to equip theologians with the theoretical tools to speak intelligibly not merely to those outside their discipline and faith traditions but also to each other, across the intradisciplinary divides that prevailed among fundamental, systematic and 'practical theologians' (Tracy's term for liberation, political and other theologians who made *praxis* a theological source) during the 1970s. By offering a comprehensive account of 'the major differences and

---

[10]Ibid., 258.
[11]The relevant articles are, in order of appearance, John A. Coleman, 'Vision and Praxis in American Theology: Orestes Brownson, John A. Ryan, and John Courtney Murray', *Theological Studies* 37 (1976): 3–40; David Hollenbach, 'Public Theology in America: Some Questions for Catholicism after John Courtney Murray', *Theological Studies* 37, no. 2 (1976): 290–303; and David Hollenbach et al., 'Theology and Philosophy in Public: A Symposium on John Courtney Murray's Unfinished Agenda', *Theological Studies* 40 no. 4 (1979): 700–15.
[12]As Coleman put it, 'The tradition of biblical religion seems the most potent symbolic resource we possess to address the sense of drift in American identity and purpose'. Hollenbach et al., 'Theology and Philosophy in Public', 706.
[13]David Tracy, *The Analogical Imagination: Christian Theology and the Culture of Pluralism* (New York: Crosrroad, 1981).
[14]Tracy's theory of the classic, in particular, served this purpose. See Ibid., 14, 58.

the major similarities among all existing theologies', he hoped 'the possibilities of collaboration . . . might become real again'.[15]

Nonetheless, if from the first US public theology sought commonality in pluralism, the field itself reflected only a limited pluralism during its early decades. On the one hand, as Benjamin Valentin observed, by 2002 US public theology had emerged as a genuinely ecumenical (Catholic and Protestant) field and encompassed projects that ranged theologically from 'neortholdox' to 'liberal constructivist' and politically from 'conservative' to 'leftist'.[16] The following year, in an influential article that remains the best survey of the field at that time, E. Harold Breitenberg also identified three distinct kinds of literature (historical-interpretive, methodological and constructive) within it, each organized around different construals of 'public theology' itself.[17] On the other hand, in certain other respects, early US public theology was quite homogenous, as Breitenberg's article also illustrates. Among the exhaustive number of scholars cited, nearly all are white and male – and those few who are not, with the singular exception of Linell Cady, are confined to the footnotes.[18] Likewise, apart from Duncan Forrester, Breitenberg's survey focuses almost exclusively on the United States, as does the work of most scholars he references. Rather than a fault in Breitenberg's study, these limitations reflect the field as it was, both in self-conception and in fact.

Already by the time Breitenberg wrote, however, public theology was starting to change, thanks first to the initiative of Black and Latine theologians. An early pioneer was Victor Anderson, who by 1998 had emerged as an incisive internal critic of Black theology and a proponent of 'African American public theology'.[19] Anderson criticized Black theology for 'ontologizing blackness', by which he meant defining a certain set of essentialized characteristics as constitutive of Black identity and then constructing both Black theology and Black politics entirely around them. A fixation on ontological Blackness, he argued, made Black theology insensitive to the many kinds of plurality within

---

[15]Ibid., 79.

[16]Benjamin Valentin, *Mapping Public Theology: Beyond Culture, Identity, and Difference* (Harrisburg: Trinity Press International, 2002), 85.

[17]E. Harold Breitenberg, 'To Tell the Truth: Will the Real Public Theology Please Stand Up?', *Journal of the Society of Christian Ethics* 23, no. 2 (2003): 55–96.

[18]Cady's important work from 1993 established her as the first influential woman public theologian. See Linell E. Cady, *Religion, Theology, and American Public Life* (Albany: State University of New York Press, 1993).

[19]Victor Anderson, *Beyond Ontological Blackness: An Essay on African-American Religious and Cultural Criticism* (New York: Continuum, 1995); Victor Anderson, 'The Wrestle of Christ and Culture in Pragmatic Public Theology', *American Journal of Theology & Philosophy* 19 no. 2 (1998): 135–50; Victor Anderson, *Pragmatic Theology: Negotiating the Intersections of an American Philosophy of Religion and Public Theology* (Albany: State University of New York Press, 1998).

the African American community and focused it too narrowly on a politics of Black 'revolution' or, short of that, radical protest.[20] Though Anderson recognized a place for the latter, he advocated that Black theology become more oriented to both internal and external pluralism and take up the project of finding commonality on both fronts, identifying Howard Thurman and Cornel West as models.[21] What was needed was a theology that could 'explicate the content of liberation not only in terms of positive self-consciousness at the various levels in which African American life is lived: class, ethnicity, gender, and sexual orientation', but also in 'the often compromising realm of public policy'.[22] Black radical politics needed to become *coalition* politics, and Black theology *public* theology.

By 2002, Anderson's arguments found an echo within Latine theology, in the complementary work of Benjamin Valentin.[23] Like Anderson, Valentin began with an internal critique of Latine theology.[24] Whereas the latter had focused on interpreting, celebrating and defending Latine culture, Valentin argued it needed to articulate a broader 'public agenda' around which Latine people could find common cause with other marginalized communities.[25] At the same time, Valentin recognized the legitimacy of 'postmodern suspicion' of 'the common' and criticized public theology for 'often neglecting the consideration of cultural specificity, race, gender, and inequality when it comes to interpreting the conditions for and possibilities of public arenas of citizen discourse and association'.[26] Drawing on Nancy Fraser's feminist critical theory, he argued for the necessity of multiple 'subaltern counterpublics': spaces in which specific communities marginalized from the national (white) 'public sphere' could develop their own solidarity and form their own political consciousness prior to entering the public sphere.[27] Latine public theology, Valentin maintained, should therefore by no means abandon its commitment to building up a specific Latine Christian 'counterpublic'; rather, it should complement it with an outward-facing orientation towards the wider 'public'. A Latine public theology would be an explicitly hybrid theology, befitting the hybrid character of *Latinidad* itself.[28]

---

[20] Anderson, *Beyond Ontological Blackness*, 103, 144.
[21] Ibid., 49.
[22] Ibid., 161.
[23] Valentin, *Mapping Public Theology*.
[24] While Valentin's study used the term 'Latino/a', as was conventional in academia in the early 2000s, I use the more current and inclusive term 'Latine' here to reflect evolving linguistic norms.
[25] Ibid., 68.
[26] Ibid., 76, 120.
[27] Ibid., 118–29.
[28] Ibid., 68–72.

Anderson and Valentin were not alone in their turn to public theology. Both belonged to a group of Black and Latine theologians, first organized by Valentin and Anthony Pinn, who collaborated to initiate dialogue between their two theological traditions, which until then had remained largely independent of each other.[29] All further recognized dialogue was needed as much within as across their traditions, since distinct streams of Womanist and *Mujerista* theology had emerged as counterpoints to the male and heterosexual perspectives predominant in Black and Latine theology.[30] Valentin and Pinn hoped that through dialogue, Black and Latine theologians could find commonality at multiple levels, from the systematic-theological, to the experiential, to the practical and political. In Valentin's words, what was needed was a 'broad public perspective in our theologies', one which could 'connect the sociopolitical and economic struggles of our Latino/a communities to the similar struggles of other marginalized groups and the progressive sensibilities of other constituencies in the United States'.[31] Importantly, none of the theologians engaged in these dialogues saw public theology as a replacement either for their own (broadly shared) liberationist commitments or for theological reflection on the specific experience of their own communities. Instead, like Valentin, they hybridized, approaching public theology as a complement to Black and Latine theology, and a shared framework for bringing them together. In subsequent years, the dialogue continued to expand, such that by 2011, Harold Recinos was able to convoke Black, Latine, indigenous American and Asian American theologians to present the first truly 'multiethnic perspective on U.S. public theology'.[32]

Meanwhile, throughout the 2000s, women theologians were also entering public theology and similarly adopting its discourse while hybridizing it with other theological currents. Mary Doak, Lisa Cahill, Kristin Heyer, Rosemary Carbine, Katie Day and Helene Slessarev-Jamir were all key figures in this process. Though only Carbine developed an explicitly 'feminist public theology', most of these theologians drew on feminist theory; simultaneously,

---

[29]For the first work of this group, see Anthony B. Pinn and Benjamin Valentin, eds, *The Ties That Bind: African American and Hispanic American: Latino Theologies in Dialogue* (New York: Continuum, 2001).

[30]Parts IV and V of *The Ties That Bind* were specifically dedicated to the work of Womanist and Latina theologians.

[31]Benjamin Valentin, 'Strangers No More: An Introduction to, and an Interpretation of, U.S. Hispanic/Latino/a Theology', in *The Ties That Bind: African American and Hispanic American/Latino/a Theologies in Dialogue*, ed. Anthony B. Pinn and Benjamin Valentin (New York: Continuum, 2001), 38–53 (53).

[32]Harold J. Recinos, 'Introduction', in *Wading through Many Voices: Toward a Theology of Public Conversation*, ed. Harold J. Recinos (Lanham, MD: Rowman & Littlefield, 2011), 1–13 (13).

they opened dialogue on other fronts.³³ Both Doak and Heyer built bridges between public theology and theological movements often framed in opposition to it, in Doak's case narrative theology (e.g. Stanley Hauerwas), in Heyer's the Catholic radical tradition (e.g. Michael Baxter).³⁴ Cahill developed a public theological bioethics, deeply informed both by feminist ethics and Catholic Social Teaching.³⁵ Day and Slessarev-Jamir turned public theology towards practical efforts for social change at the urban grassroots.³⁶ In fact, all of these theologians played a critical role in reorienting public theology from rational discourse to a broader conception of practice, as I discuss in the next section.

The expansion of public theology beyond the United States constitutes a final way in which the field pluralized and hybridized during the 2000s. Though scholars abroad had already begun to adopt the discourse of public theology, it was in 2007 that the global field's 'kairos moment' (in William Storrar's apt phrase) arrived, with the simultaneous launch of the Global Network for Public Theology (GNPT) and the *International Journal of Public Theology (IJPT)*.³⁷ Both developments opened US public theologians to a much wider field of interlocutors and concerns, such that many began to expressly identify a 'global' orientation as a constitutive feature of public theology.³⁸ Simultaneously, public theologians not originally from the United States, such as Storrar and (more recently) Sebastian Kim, moved to and became leaders of the field within the United States, serving as local anchors for the global conversation. Kim, Hak Joon Lee and Paul Chung also exemplify the leading role public theologians of Asian – and specifically, Korean – Protestant backgrounds now play as bridge-builders across racial, national, religious and disciplinary borders; Chung, for example, is a pioneer of both postcolonial and inter-religious public theology.³⁹

The globalization of public theology has also broadened the scope of 'North American' public theology beyond the United States to other parts of

---

³³See especially Rosemary P. Carbine, 'Ekklesial Work: Toward a Feminist Public Theology', *The Harvard Theological Review* 99, no. 4 (2006): 433–55.
³⁴Mary Doak, *Reclaiming Narrative for Public Theology* (Albany: State University of New York Press, 2004); Heyer, *Prophetic & Public: The Social Witness of U.S. Catholicism*.
³⁵Lisa Sowle Cahill, *Theological Bioethics: Participation, Justice, Change* (Washington, DC: Georgetown University Press, 2005).
³⁶See Helene Slessarev-Jamir, 'The Mission of Public Theology in an Age of Empire', *Missiology: An International Review* 34, no. 1 (2006): 31–40; Katie Day, 'The Construction of Public Theology: An Ethnographic Study of the Relationship between the Theological Academy and Local Clergy in South Africa', *International Journal of Public Theology* 2, no. 3 (2008): 354–78.
³⁷William Storrar, '2007: A Kairos Moment for Public Theology', *International Journal of Public Theology* 1, no. 1 (2007): 5–25.
³⁸See Day and Kim, 'Introduction', 16.
³⁹See, for example, Hak Joon Lee, *The Great World House: Martin Luther King Jr. and Global Ethics* (Cleveland, OH: Pilgrim Press, 2011); Paul S. Chung, *Postcolonial Public Theology: Faith, Scientific Rationality, and Prophetic Dialogue* (Eugene, OR: Cascade Books, 2016).

the region. During the last decade especially, public theologians from Canada and the Caribbean have entered the field.[40] Caribbean public theology presents many parallels with US Black and Latine theology, since it too is rooted within the liberationist tradition of particular historically oppressed (and internally plural) communities, and so represents a hybrid of public and liberation theologies.[41] In fact, since many Black and Latine theologians within the United States trace their roots to the Caribbean or Central America, these theological streams cannot be neatly kept apart. Though there is as yet no explicitly 'North American' – or pan-American – public theology, such criss-crossing lines of identity and history raise the question of whether there ought to be.

In sum, since the 2000s, North American public theology has expanded well beyond its origins as a white, male discourse about the common identity that held the United States together across its religious divides. It has become, instead, a far more multi-dimensionally pluralistic dialogue among scholars of diverse identities, communities, geographies and theological commitments. At the same time, what has carried through across all these transformations is the same basic orientation: a commitment to finding and articulating *the common*, in the midst of the plural and particular, alongside a refusal to accept any 'commonality' that sacrifices the plural and particular. In effect, both the term and the discourse of 'public theology' have actually provided a vehicle for creating the common – and for bringing a new and more expansive 'public' into being.

29.3 FROM PUBLIC DISCOURSE TO PUBLIC ACTION: THE PRACTICAL TURN IN PUBLIC THEOLOGY

If public theologians have always prioritized finding the common in the plural and particular, for its first three decades, the field's conception of *how* to do this was relatively narrow. Until the 2000s, US public theology was overwhelmingly focused on *public discourse* – and often a fairly specific conception of the latter – as the medium for creating commonality. Throughout the 1980s and 1990s, it was quite common for public theologians, in speaking of 'the public realm' (which was almost always implicitly national in scope), to conceptualize

---

[40]To the best of my knowledge, Mexican theologians have yet to appropriate the discourse of public theology. For contextualizing Canadian public theology, see the helpful comparative analysis by Mark G. Toulouse, 'Two Nations under God: Religion and Public in Canada and the United States', *International Journal of Public Theology* 8, no. 3 (2014): 267–91.

[41]The *IJPT*'s 2013 special issue on Caribbean public theology provides an excellent introduction to the field and some of its leading voices, as well as to the political geography of the Caribbean. For an overview, see Garnett Roper and Esther D. Reed, 'Editorial: Special Issue--Matters of the Caribbean', *International Journal of Public Theology* 7, no. 4 (2013): 345–54.

it not only as a 'sphere' distinct from 'the state' and 'the market' but also as a kind of deliberative 'public conversation' or 'public debate' among plural parties with differing moral and religious perspectives.[42] Within this context, the public theologian's role was one of framing compelling 'public arguments' to influence the conversation, and move 'the public' (i.e. the American people) as a whole towards collective agreement on their common good. In effect, what many public theologians understood themselves to be doing was shaping, through argument, a national moral and/or cultural consensus, so as to ultimately influence public policy. Thus, in 1996, Victor Anderson could define public theology as 'the deliberate use of distinctively theological languages and commitments to influence substantive debate on public discourse, including public policy'.[43] Anderson's definition was not idiosyncratic; to the contrary, it reflected the consensus of the field.

Public theology's preoccupation with 'public discourse' had multiple roots. Though founding figures Marty and Bellah were as concerned with culture and symbolic experience as with discourse per se, both prioritized language as the vehicle by which these were 'articulated'; by the 1980s, Bellah's focus had accordingly shifted from Americans' 'civil religion' to their 'moral languages'.[44] Likewise, though Coleman and Hollenbach advocated 'public theology' in distinction to John Courtney Murray's 'public philosophy', they took from Murray a conception of political society as itself a kind of 'dialogue' and were explicitly concerned to defend the public use of theological discourse.[45] David Tracy argued that *all* theology was a form of 'public discourse', and went on to theorize the 'plausibility structures' of its three distinct 'publics'.[46] Meanwhile, during the 1980s and 1990s, theories of the 'public sphere', Rawlsian 'public reason', Habermasian 'discourse ethics', 'deliberative democracy' and 'communitarianism' (with which Bellah was sometimes identified) all became highly influential across the US academy and within public theology itself.[47] All these intellectual currents conceptualized 'the public' as an arena constituted by discourse, and in most cases argumentative, rational (i.e. 'reason-giving')

---

[42]For a classic, and influential, example, see Michael J. Himes and Kenneth R. Himes, *Fullness of Faith: The Public Significance of Theology* (New York/Mahwah, NJ: Paulist Press, 1993), especially 1–25.
[43]Anderson, 'The Wrestle of Christ and Culture in Pragmatic Public Theology', 136.
[44]See Robert N. Bellah et al., *Habits of the Heart: Individualism and Commitment in American Life* (Berkeley, CA: University of California Press, 1985), 20–6.
[45]See fn. 11, *supra*. See also John Courtney Murray, *We Hold These Truths: Catholic Reflections on the American Proposition* (Kansas City, MO: Sheed & Ward, 1960), 6.
[46]Tracy, *The Analogical Imagination*, 5, 22.
[47]For an illuminating historical contextualization of these trends, see Katrina Forrester, *In the Shadow of Justice: Postwar Liberalism and the Remaking of Political Philosophy* (Princeton: Princeton University Press, 2019), especially 231–8, 252–62.

discourse. Hence the most prominent controversy over 'public theology' during these years concerned the place of 'religious reasons' and 'religious discourse' in 'public debate'.[48]

Beginning in the 2000s, however, North American public theologians, especially women, began to challenge the field's fixation on rational public discourse, and to advocate a broader focus on public *practices*. One of the first to do so was Mary Doak. In her *Reclaiming Narrative for Public Theology* (2004), Doak drew upon figures as diverse as Johann Baptist Metz, Stanley Hauerwas and Ronald Thiemann to pursue a 'project of developing and debating national narratives'.[49] Narratives, she claimed, were often more important than argumentative, rational discourse for articulating and consolidating political identity. Doak also commended the intentional use of public theological narratives to advance a more self-critical and genuinely pluralistic vision of the United States than typically prevailed in the nation's dominant white culture. Alongside Abraham Lincoln, she looked to Latino theologian Virgilio Elizondo and Womanist theologian Delores Williams as exemplary 'narrative public theologians'.[50]

Not long after Doak, Rosemary Carbine drew on feminist theology to further expand public theology's orientation. Carbine criticized accounts of the 'public church' and 'public theology' that focused on 'public argument' for implicitly equating 'the Church' in its capacity as a political actor with 'institutional church leaders alongside (often male and ordained) church spokespersons'.[51] Such accounts both ignored the political role of 'everyday church members, particularly women' and placed far too much confidence in the power of the church's public statements to actually influence society. By contrast, Carbine contends, '[e]ffective public theology has less to do with influencing debate in a not-quite-shared community of rational discourse and more to do with fostering an array of democratic practices that aim to remake the public itself, to create a more inclusive and just common life'.[52] Carbine's 'feminist public theology' consequently prioritizes three 'practices of public

---

[48]For an influential example that frames the debate, see Robert Audi and Nicholas Wolterstorff, *Religion in the Public Square: The Place of Religious Convictions in Political Debate* (Lanham, MD: Rowman & Littlefield, 1997). See also fn. 2, *supra*.
[49]Doak, *Reclaiming Narrative for Public Theology*, 20.
[50]Ibid., 173–206.
[51]Rosemary P. Carbine, 'Claiming and Imagining: Practices of Public Engagement', in *Prophetic Witness: Catholic Women's Strategies for Reform*, ed. Colleen M. Griffith (New York: Crosrroad, 2009), 176–85 (176).
[52]Rosemary P. Carbine, 'Public Theology: A Feminist View of Political Subjectivity and Praxis', in *Questioning the Human: Toward a Theological Anthropology for the Twenty-First Century*, ed. Lieven Boeve, Yves De Maeseneer, and Ellen Van Stichel (New York: Fordham University Press, 2014), 148–63 (151).

engagement' beyond public argument. These comprise rhetorical practices, which present public theological claims in multiple genres of expression (e.g. poetry, music, speech); symbolic practices, which reinterpret religious symbols for their sociopolitical meaning; and prophetic practices, which criticize the social order and theologically envision a more hopeful alternative.[53]

Katie Day's public theology has carried the turn from public discourse to practice further still. Day criticizes the often monological character of public theology: 'Much academic public theology presupposes its project to be expressive; that is, a one-way communication of the church speaking to the public.'[54] What is missing, she contends, is any sociologically grounded account of the individual and institutional actors who actually construct 'public theology' and the processes they employ. Likewise, Day maintains, public theologians frequently fail to consider whether and how public theology is actually 'engaging and impacting social realities', or 'which institutional structures are facilitating' its formulation, transmission and impact.[55] Rather than envisioning public theology as a form of *public address* on the part of 'the church', Day therefore proposes it be reconceptualized as a participatory *social process* through which diverse religious actors communicate and act together for the purpose of 'remaking the public'.

Day's proposal naturally leads in the direction of ethnography (which she herself employs) as a methodological means for investigating how specific religious social actors, from local congregations to national advocacy groups and social movements, actually create and 'perform' public theology in practice. It likewise highlights questions of efficacy: Do public theological actors actually succeed in promoting the common good in their social context? Day is not alone in her concern for these questions. In the last fifteen years, several other theologians have shifted public theology towards ethnography, including Kristin Heyer, Helene Slessarev-Jamir, Rosemary Carbine (in more recent work) and Luke Bretherton.[56] For Day, Slessarev-Jamir, and especially

---

[53] Ibid., 178–82.
[54] Day, 'The Construction of Public Theology', 357.
[55] Ibid., 358.
[56] See, for example, Heyer, *Prophetic & Public: The Social Witness of U.S. Catholicism*; Helene Slessarev-Jamir, *Prophetic Activism: Progressive Religious Justice Movements in Contemporary America* (New York: New York University, 2011); Rosemary P. Carbine, 'Placards, Icons, and Protests: Insights into Antiracist Activism from Feminist Public Theology', in *The Gift of Theology: The Contribution of Kathryn Tanner*, ed. Rosemary P. Carbine and Hilda P. Koster (Minneapolis, MN: Fortress Press, 2015), 313–43; Luke Bretherton, *Resurrecting Democracy: Faith, Citizenship, and the Politics of a Common Life* (Cambridge: Cambridge University Press, 2015). Though Bretherton, originally from the UK, identifies as a 'political' theologian rather than a public theologian, both his work on ethnographic method and his studies of community organizing have been influential in North American public theology.

Bretherton, a particular locus of interest has been the tradition of community organizing founded by Saul Alinsky in 1930s Chicago.

Alinsky organizing, which William Storrar has called 'one of the most significant developments in public theology today', first came to wider attention in 2008, when the presidential election of one-time community organizer Barack Obama raised its profile.[57] Also called 'faith-based', 'institution-based' or 'broad-based' community organizing, Alinsky organizing works by drawing together institutions – predominantly congregations – within a given geography (most often a neighbourhood, city or metro area) to collaborate in promoting their own shared interests. One of its most distinctive characteristics is its multi-constituency and multi-issue character. Alinsky organizing intentionally brings communities together across differences of race, class, religion and political ideology, not to promote any single issue, group, or cause but to collectively discern and pursue a common agenda through ongoing democratic processes. Over the last several decades, it has proved a successful vehicle for low-income communities, working alongside middle-class communities, to secure social goods like better housing, education, employment and healthcare – and sometimes more far-reaching political reforms – while cultivating their own political agency and building lasting relationships across potentially isolating or polarizing lines of difference.[58]

In several respects, Alinsky organizing appears to align uniquely with the defining commitments of public theology, as Mary McClintock Fulkerson observes.[59] For one, organizing quite literally puts theology 'in public': it not only engages congregations in taking various kinds of political action but encourages the use of overtly religious language, symbolism, ritual and prayer, from specific traditions, in its public actions. As Fulkerson also notes, organizing's pluralist, reformist, non-ideological and non-revolutionary approach to 'common good' politics more resembles the orientation of public theology than it does traditional liberation theology (though hybrid public-liberationist theologies complicate this generalization).[60] In my judgement, however, the most fundamental

---

[57]William Storrar, 'Preface', in *Yours the Power: Faith-Based Organizing in the USA*, ed. Katie Day, Esther McIntosh, and William Storrar (Leiden: Brill, 2013), vii–xii (viii).

[58]Brad Fulton and Richard Wood offer an overview of Alinsky organizing and survey the contemporary landscape, in Brad Fulton and Richard L. Wood, 'Interfaith Community Organizing: Emerging Theological and Organizational Challenges', in *Yours the Power: Faith-Based Organizing in the USA*, ed. Katie Day, Esther McIntosh, and William Storrar (Leiden: Brill, 2013), 17–40. Bretherton's *Resurrecting Democracy* offers the most extensive theological study of the history and practice of Alinsky organizing, anchored in his ethnographic study of a UK-based group called London Citizens.

[59]Mary McClintock Fulkerson, 'Receiving from the Other: Theology and Grass-Roots Organizing', in *Yours the Power: Faith-Based Organizing in the USA*, ed. Day, McIntosh and Storrar, 41–54 (47).

[60]Ibid., 46–7.

analogy between organizing and public theology is that both are defined by what Rosemary Carbine has compellingly named a *convocative* orientation: a commitment to 'conjoin disparate groups . . . into an "ultimate public"' and 'to theologically envision and enliven a common political order that is designed to counter a potentially excessive individualism and a potentially divisive identity politics in U.S. public life'.[61] Alinsky organizing's whole purpose, like public theology's, is to 'convoke' commonality across plurality and particularity. And like public theology, it does so not by suppressing the particular but by acknowledging and honouring it. From diverse traditions and communities, organizing weaves together a kaleidoscopic solidarity.

At the same time, the very analogy between Alinsky organizing and public theology also brings into relief some important differences. Organizing 'convokes' not primarily through dialogue aimed at mutual understanding, much less argumentative rational discourse, but through complex processes of relationship-building and public action oriented towards decidedly concrete and practical ends. Dialogue and deliberation certainly comprise a dimension of this process, but only one among others. Second, as its practitioners understand it, organizing is above all a practice for building collective *power* ('people power') and for wielding that power effectively, at times in highly conflictual ways.[62] It is not principally through 'public argument', 'prophetic critique' or even through 'protest' that organizing promotes the common good of its members but through the consolidation and strategic exercise of political power, if need be against other 'power holders' (politicians, corporate leaders, landlords etc.) Moreover, its convocative capacity cannot be extricated from its power-building orientation: the two are constitutively intertwined. It is the desire for shared power to effect shared ends which, in the case of organizing, creates 'political community'.

In the turn to practices like Alinsky organizing, we can observe just how far some within North American public theology have travelled from the field's earlier focus on 'public discourse' and 'public policy'. It is by no means the case that all in the field have followed this course; other public theologians still hew closer to public theology's original orientation, such that one might identify methodology as another key dimension in which the field has pluralized. Nevertheless, both the turn to practice, in general, and the turn to organizing, in particular, pose a challenging question to academic public theologians: How does our own 'practice' relate to, and perhaps stand to learn from, public theological practices like organizing? And, if (as Day contends) *doing* 'public

---

[61] Carbine, 'Ekklesial Work: Toward a Feminist Public Theology', 436.
[62] Aaron Schutz and Mike Miller, eds, *People Power: The Community Organizing Tradition of Saul Alinsky* (Nashville: Vanderbilt University Press, 2015), 2.

theology' means more than simply 'addressing the public' or analysing public discourse, just what more does it mean for us?

29.4 CONCLUSION: PUBLIC THEOLOGY AS POLITICAL PROJECT

Evidently, North American public theology has transformed dramatically over the past twenty years. Taken together, the field's pluralization and 'practical turn' have effected a sizeable shift in the practitioners, scope, methods and self-conception of North American public theology, as compared to its formative decades. Nevertheless, a deeper continuity persists throughout these transformations: North American public theology's constitutively 'convocative' orientation, its commitment to finding the common in and through the plural and the particular. Arguably, contemporary public theology embodies its own aspiration better than it ever has before. On the other hand, given the far greater plurality (including the methodological plurality) that now characterizes the field, it may well be asked, What is the 'common' identity, if any, that now holds public theology itself together?

The concept of 'the public' might seem to afford the natural answer to this question. After all, defining the 'public' (or 'publics') has been a primary concern of public theologians since Tracy, and Sebastian Kim is only one among several public theologians to suggest that a more robust theoretical (and theological) account of the public is a necessary first step for securing public theology a viable disciplinary identity.[63] However, contemporary conceptions of 'the public' often remain closely linked to sociological theories of the 'public sphere', as Kim's own (which draws on Habermas) does, and so tend to persist in conceptualizing it discursively.[64] Consequently, it is not clear how well they can accommodate the turn to practice, or answer the associated critiques, made by other public theologians. My own belief is that public theology would be better served by defining 'the "public" with which it is concerned in a much broader sense, precisely as *the common* or *'res publica'*, while leaving this term intentionally indefinite. Correlatively, I would resist equating the 'public' with 'the public sphere', which has overly specific, and contestable, sociological connotations. Though there remains a pressing need to examine which social theories are most fruitful for conceptualizing 'the public' – I myself favour those which employ 'civil society' rather than 'the public sphere' as their operative category

---

[63]e.g. Sebastian Kim, 'Editorial', *International Journal of Public Theology* 11, no. 2 (2017): 135–9 (136). For a contrasting opinion, see Cady, 'Public Theology and the Postsecular Turn', 300.

[64]Kim, *Theology in the Public Sphere: Public Theology as a Catalyst for Open Debate*, 10–14.

– I doubt a consensus at the level of social theory is a plausible prospect, or a likely means for grounding the identity of public theology.[65]

For similar reasons, I think it is important to resist the tendency to define 'public theology' as a substantive theological 'paradigm'. Especially among North American theologians influenced by Max Stackhouse, it is common to frame 'public theology' in contrast to 'political theology' and 'liberation theology', understanding all three as substantive (and to some degree opposing) paradigms for understanding the political order and the church's right relation thereto.[66] Yet the prevalence of hybrid public theologies in contemporary North America, many of which are both liberationist and public, reveals such contrasts to be contentious and premised on overly simplistic ideal-types. Conversely, such substantive conceptions of 'public theology' also invite its wholesale rejection by scholars working in other theological frameworks who nevertheless share much in common with public theology more broadly construed. For example, Luke Bretherton, a political theologian, explicitly rejects public theology on the grounds that it 'assumes it is necessary to translate theological concepts into the idioms and frameworks of liberalism'.[67] Yet Bretherton's own theology of 'common life politics', informed by his engagement with Alinsky organizing, closely resembles certain strands of public theology and indeed has been influential within the field.

Both of these strategies for defining public theology thus ultimately prove too narrow, defining the field as a whole in a way that applies only to some of the particular approaches within it. By contrast, I would argue, the longer trajectory of North American public theology suggests the field is best understood neither as a substantive theological paradigm nor a 'theology of the public sphere' but as an open-ended *collective project*. It is nothing more, and nothing less, than the convocative project itself: the theological project of forging a common life – a 'public' – and achieving a common good in and through deep plurality, without sacrificing the particularity of specific differences to any hegemonic 'generality'.[68] What drove Black, Latine, feminist, Caribbean and other North American theologians to first embrace 'public theology' as a frame for their own projects was precisely their commitment to this wider horizon. They often

---

[65]Michael Edwards provides an excellent account of the concept of 'civil society', and argues that it can incorporate, but should not be reduced to, a concept of 'the public sphere'. See Michael Edwards, *Civil Society*, 3rd edn. (Cambridge, UK: Polity, 2014).

[66]See, for example, Max L. Stackhouse, 'Civil Religion, Political Theology and Public Theology: What's the Difference?', *Political Theology* 5, no. 3 (2004): 275–93; Hak Joon Lee, 'Public Theology', in *The Cambridge Companion to Political Theology*, ed. Craig Hovey and Elizabeth Phillips (Cambridge: Cambridge University Press, 2015), 44–65 (53–7).

[67]Luke Bretherton, *Christ and the Common Life: Political Theology and the Case for Democracy* (Grand Rapids, MI: Eerdmans, 2019), 33.

[68]This formulation is itself inspired by Bretherton's work, as is much in this conclusion.

found it necessary to revise the field's operative concepts of 'the public' and of 'public theology' itself; what they found essential to preserve was its core commitment to discerning commonality amid plurality.

At the same time, if understood in these terms, one cannot evade the conclusion that public theology is as much a *political* as a theological project. Its 'identity' is always premised on a political question: With whom, in particular, do we seek to create a common life, and how? North American public theology began by presupposing a specific answer to this question: the citizens of the United States, whose collective identity it strove to articulate in theological terms. As its subsequent trajectory shows, however, this answer was both too narrow and too broad. Too narrow, because it neglected to consider how US identity relates to global identity, as later public theologians have found it necessary to do. Too broad, because it presumed a common 'American' identity too easily, while failing to grapple with the full depth of the 'pluralism' that actually characterizes the United States. That pluralism comprises differences of race, class, gender, sexuality, geography and citizenship status as much as religion; it also involves not only 'disagreement' but social conflict, across entrenched inequalities of power.

Hence the task of convoking commonality is never so simple as articulating a shared identity and persuading others to embrace it – as public theology was originally conceived to do. It is also necessary to make judgements about the relative priority, and 'ordering', of the various communities to which one belongs, acknowledging that their very real conflicts often cannot be quickly resolved by appeals to a common good. US Black and Latine theologians chose to prioritize finding common ground among themselves, because they recognized the 'American' public *de facto* meant the white public, which was neither interested nor prepared to receive them as coequal members. Hence, though still seeking to engage the national community, they looked first to each other, and to others who might be allies, to create a new 'public' (or 'counterpublic') within it. In other words, informed by their theological reflection upon the experience of their communities, they made a political judgement.

In contemporary North America, these issues are not merely 'theoretical'. As the United States passes through what Robert Jones has called the 'end of white Christian America'– the demographic and cultural collapse of a previously hegemonic vision of American identity – the stakes of articulating and convoking 'our' political community could not be higher.[69] It seems no exaggeration to say that, within the last decade, the United States has experienced the resurgence of an idolatrous form of 'civil religion', one founded upon an ethno-nationalist and isolationist vision of 'America' and baptized by distorted forms of white

---

[69] Robert P. Jones, *The End of White Christian America* (New York: Simon & Schuster, 2016).

Christianity. This American civil religion is literally death-dealing, both for the millions of people within the country's borders whom it writes out of 'American' identity and for the millions at or beyond its borders whom it turns away, imprisons or shuts out, with little sense of the United States' own responsibility for the economic and ecological catastrophes that drive migrants to its borders in the first place. We on the North American continent – and, perhaps, well beyond it – urgently need new articulations of what is common among us, amid our many differences. Simultaneously, we need new political practices, of the kind that can actually bring a greater community, and common good, into being. And informing both, we need new theologies: public theologies that can help us discern how God is at work in our midst, convoking us to practice and to order our common life, across all the walls that divide us.

CHAPTER 30

Public theology in Latin America

ENEIDA JACOBSEN

Latin America is a context economically placed within a global capitalist mode of production, and under threat of extinction because of climate change. The orientation towards the accumulation of capital fuels the devastation of our forests worldwide. Neoliberalism is capitalism's political face. Its aim is to privatize goods in society – seeds, water, lands, medical care – rather than to make them public goods. Public theology in Latin America is on the alert against the devastating effects of neoliberalism. The means of reproduction of lives are controlled by a small percentage of humans. Wildlife loses kilometres of territory each day that human dominion goes on. In 2019, motivated by the massive Amazon rainforest fires that year, Roman Catholic bishops representing the Pan-Amazon Synod – which covers nine countries of the region – held an assembly to discuss the vulnerable situation of the Amazon rainforest and the biodiversity the forest sustains. The document is an expression of how public theology may take place by means of engaging theologians, ecclesial leaders and lay leaders from various cultural contexts aimed at the urgent task of making human life sustainable on the planet. I read in the Final Document of the Amazon Synod the call for society to turn away from neoliberalism, opting for modest and nature-caring ways of living. Public theology takes the shape of a critical discourse against our current economic system. The privatization of lands and knowledge has not benefitted the elderly, the sick or the poor. Latin America ought to be made public for the sake of nurturing all of its peoples and animals.

30.1 LATIN AMERICA UNDER NEOLIBERALISM

International food companies such as Nestlé, Pepsico, Coca-Cola, Kellogg's, Unilever and Mars produce a large part of the food we eat. These companies are among the top plastic polluters of the world. They are also known for using ingredients derived from genetically modified crops. Everything comes from somewhere. Who grows these plants? Bayer, who recently merged with Monsanto, is the world's largest producer of genetically modified seeds. There are several Bayer branches in Latin America,[1] where farming families have become largely dependent on the company's seeds and pesticides.[2] Despite the opposition of environmentalists, the German company is building in Chile the largest seed factory in Latin America.[3] Room for GMO-fed cattle and plantations is for decades being cleared in the Amazon region. Cattle ranching and soy cultivation are the leading causes of deforestation in the region.[4]

Bulk carriers leave Latin American shores loaded with heavy amounts of raw materials such as minerals, grains, meat, lumber and oil. Operating through busy shipping lines and on polluting rods of deforested lines across forests, the world industry buys raw materials with the purpose of reselling finished goods. Among the most profitable industrialized goods on the market are pharmaceuticals, agrochemicals, electronics, war technologies, cars and plastic. Cattle ranching, soybean cultivation, lumber extraction, mining, road-building and infrastructure constructions are activities that lead to deforestation, yet are also, under the current economic conditions, necessary for the process

---

[1] There are Bayer branches in Argentina, Bolivia, Brazil, Chile, Colombia, Cuba, El Salvador, Guatemala, Honduras, Mexico, Nicaragua, Panama, Paraguay, Peru, Uruguay and Venezuela. According to Bayer's website: http://www.bayer.com (last accessed 25 January 2021).

[2] See Laura Gutiérrez Escobar and German Vélez, 'The Struggle for Peoples' Free Seeds in Latin America: Experiences from Brazil, Ecuador, Colombia, Honduras and Guatemala', *Right to Food and Nutrition Watch: Keeping Seeds in Peoples' Hands* 08 (2016): 68–76. Brazil is the second largest producer of transgenic cultures in the world, after the United States. A large part of the world's diet can be traced to transgenic crops. Gerardo Otero and Pablo Lapegna speak of a 'neoliberal food regime'. Neo-regulations authorize the people's expropriation of lands and the accumulation by elites. Gerardo Otero and Pablo Lapegna, 'Transgenic Crops in Latin America: Expropriation, Negative Value and the State', *Journal of Agrarian Change* 16 (2016): 665–74.

[3] See: 'Environmentalists Alarmed as Bayer Builds Latin America's Largest Seed Factory in Chile', *GMWatch*, January 2020, https://www.gmwatch.org/en/news/latest-news/19289-bayer-builds-latin-america-s-largest-seed-factory-in-chile-environmental-groups-alarmed (last accessed 25 January 2021).

[4] Petterson Valea et al., 'The Expansion of Intensive Beef Farming to the Brazilian Amazon', *Global Environmental Change* 57 (2019): 1–11; Sérgio Sauer, 'Soy Expansion into the Agricultural Frontiers of the Brazilian Amazon: The Agribusiness Economy and Its Social and Environmental Conflicts', *Land Use Policy* 79 (2018): 326–38; Sergio Rivero et al., 'Pecuária e desmatamento: uma análise das principais causas diretas do desmatamento na Amazônia', *Nova Economia* 19, no. 1 (2009): 41–66.

of production of many of the goods that humans and domesticated animals consume daily.

Neoliberal governments in Latin America have been supporting the expansion of capitalist activities in the Amazonian region over the rights of traditional populations. The neoliberal agenda is characterized by the absence of regulations over relations of exchange, the right of private ownership and a minimal state. Low-paid labour ensures high profits. The whole scheme serves the maximization of profits. The more money, the greater the power to influence political decisions. The circle is complete. Politics becomes a commodity alongside others. The legal apparatus works for gains, not for people and the continuation of life on earth. When governments do not promote the neoliberal agenda of deregulation and privatization and, instead, favour democratic participation and the socialization of public goods, they must 'get out of the way', as Noam Chomsky writes in *Profits over People*.[5] The neoliberal order does not favour democratic participation because it is not profitable to afford housing for the elderly, and good education and food for the young ones. In neoliberalism, social expenses are taken to belong to private initiatives. States are assigned the role of supporting the private sector by actions such as insuring banks and financially rescuing corporations in times of crisis.

Several blood-shedding, military-led regime changes in Latin America in the second half of the nineteenth century took place when there was a political turn opposing business-controlled politics. Being home country to many powerful international companies, the United States supported coups d'état in Guatemala (1954), Dominican Republic (1963), Brazil (1964), Chile (1973), Argentina (1976), Grenada (1983), Venezuela (unsuccessful in 2002) and Bolivia (2019), among other countries in Latin America and worldwide. Acting on behalf of business interests, the Central Intelligence Agency (CIA) of the United States became known for acts opposing agrarian reforms and the nationalization of industries. History demands scepticism over the genuine status of democracy in our post-dictatorial states, as the influence of global economic elites remains overwhelming.[6]

---

[5]Noam Chomsky, *Profit over People: Neoliberalism and Global Order* (New York/Toronto: Seven Stories Press, 1999), 20.

[6]See Alan L. Mcpherson, *A Short History of U.S. Interventions in Latin America and the Caribbean* (Chichester, West Sussex: Wiley-Blackwell, 2016). Eduardo Galeano speaks of 'open veins' of gold, cacao, rubber, cotton, petroleum, iron, copper and other items that run though the Latin American continent and that have been exploited since the beginning of European colonization. The book has become a classic of Latin American history: Eduardo Galeano, *Open Veins of Latin America: Five Centuries of the Pillage of a Continent* (New York: Monthly Review Press, 1997). The case of Guatemala is paradigmatic: by 1950, the US Corporation United Fruit Company was earning twice as much as Guatemala's national yearly revenue. United Fruit Company was the largest landowner in Guatemala, and in control of the country's only port to the Atlantic Ocean. The

In the volume *Public Theology: A Debate from Latin America*, Claudio Carvalhaes problematizes the relation between the globe's wealthy North and the poor South. Under hegemonic economic interests, the Latin American context remains a colony of richer countries. Subaltern populations and their movements continue to be repressed by political and economic powers. Expressing suspicion towards public theologies that may ignore the economic inequality between the very rich and the poor, Carvalhaes writes, 'to not put oneself on the side of the poor is to do a toothless theology that is dominated by whom controls power'.[7] Political neutrality is not something that public theology can achieve, nor is it desirable. Néstor Míguez, in the same volume, explains that neoliberalism is kept in place by local elites who give their support to global elites. The military is the elites' physical power. Consumers' desires are produced within market expectations. The gains of the economy feed the empire, which tends to privatization and neutralization of democratic initiatives. Míguez's reading of the Latin American situation leads to a materialistic conception of the public in a society:

> The public is not only the space of discussion, the open activity: there are also physical spaces, territories, and resources, services and public goods, elements and activities necessary for life in society that constitute, necessarily, as public, because without them life is impossible. But the imperial ideology every now and then insists on privatizing them, and convert them into property and merchandise. The more private there is, the less public.[8]

Latin American populations resist the privatization of their lands in favour of public access of people to basic goods. In the year 2019 a wave of mass demonstrations has been seen in several Latin American countries, demanding

---

largest portion of the company's lands were neither cultivated nor ecologically preserved, thus falling under the scope of the land reform law proposed by Guatemala's first democratically elected president Jacobo Árbenz. Political lobbying in the United States led to Árbenz's removal from office in Guatemala in the year of 1954. Stephen Schlesinger and Stephen Kinzer, *Bitter Fruit: The Story of an American Coup in Guatemala* (Cambridge, MA: Harvard University, David Rockefeller Center for Latin American Studies, 2005).
[7]Claudio Carvalhaes, 'Teologia pública e pós-colonialismo', in *Teología pública: un debate desde América Latina*, ed. Rudolf Von Sinner and Nicolas Panotto (São Leopoldo: EST, 2016), 27–35, 33: '[. . .] não assumir o lado dos pobres é fazer teologia banguela e dominada por quem controla o poder.'
[8]Néstor Míguez, 'Teología pública e Imperio', in *Teología pública: un debate desde América Latina*, ed. Rudolf Von Sinner and Nicolas Panotto (São Leopoldo: EST, 2016), 37–45 (41): 'Lo público no es solo el espacio de discusión, la actividad abierta: también hay espacios físicos, territorios y recursos, servicios y bienes comunes, elementos y actividades necesarios para la vida en sociedad que se constituyen, necesariamente, como públicos, pues sin ellos la vida es imposible. Pero la ideología imperial una y otra vez insiste en privatizarlos, en convertirlos en propiedad y mercancía. Mientras más sea lo privado, menos será lo público.'

the improvement of basic living conditions threatened under the current neoliberal order. People demonstrated for the preservation and expansion of indigenous lands, the redistribution of uncultivated land, the socialization of education and medical services, the nationalization of industries and the occupation of politics by the people.[9] The 2019–20 protests in Chile were triggered by the price rise of public transportation, whereas the payment to the labouring population remained the same. The working class has been paid not even the necessary for its reproduction. The neoliberal order disfavours the well-being of the people and is cruel towards those who cannot sell their labouring force, such as the elderly and the ill. Worldwide there is a growing movement of people who have become acquainted with the way the global economy works for the benefit of billionaires, indifferent to people's needs for housing, health and transportation. People want a different model of economy. As the resistance against neoliberalism grew, so did actions to silence the voices of protest. The 2019–20 Latin American protests have counted dozens of protestors killed, hundreds of people injured and thousands arrested. The brutal police repression in Chile left hundreds with eye injuries by robber bullets. Massive police repression has met protestors in Bolivia, Ecuador, Colombia and Haiti. The Amazonian region has reported a dramatic increase in the assassination of indigenous leaders in recent years.[10] What purpose does the killing of our social leaders and guardians of our forests serve?

Because life is exploited for profits, saving the Amazon becomes an unattainable aim within the paradigm of neoliberalism. Miners and loggers are paid pennies for their labour time, and yet they find no safer alternative to make a living. There is no compensation for the pollution of our rivers and the lives they support. Most indigenous populations receive no payment for their service of conservation of our forests and their waters. In the likeness of a heartless machine, the economic system drags humans and other living beings into sacrificing their finitudes to serve the lifeless purpose of money-making

---

[9]See: Enrique Crespo Peñaherrera; and David Morales Olalla, 'Inequality Triggered Protests across Latin America', *World Economic Forum*, Jan. 2020, https://www.weforum.org/agenda/2020/01/inequality-triggered-protests-latin-america-2019 (last accessed 25 January 2021); Emilia Rokas-Sasse, 'South America's Protests Fueled By "Extreme" Social Inequality', *Deutsche Welle*, Oct. 2019, https://www.dw.com/en/south-americas-protests-fueled-by-extreme-social-inequality/a-50977566 (last accessed 25 January 2021).

[10]See: Gabriel Leão, 'Killing the Messengers: Rising Violence Against Journalists and Indigenous Leaders Defending the Amazon', *CounterPunch*, October 2019, https://www.counterpunch.org/2019/10/11/killing-the-messengers-rising-violence-against-journalists-and-indigenous-leaders-defending-the-amazon (last accessed 25 January 2021); 'In Memoriam: 28 Indigenous Rights Defenders Murdered in Latin America in 2019', *Cultural Survival*, January 2020, https://www.culturalsurvival.org/news/memoriam-28-indigenous-rights-defenders-murdered-latin-america-2019 (last accessed 25 January 2021).

even by means of deforesting and as a consequence making lands inhabitable for most species. The poor are left with minimal state welfare provisions, as anything that does not maximize corporations' profits has no political incentive. Meanwhile, the rich only get richer: 1 per cent of the world population holds as much wealth as all the remaining 99 per cent.[11] Neoliberalism finds ways to profit even from the ecological crisis it creates.[12] What does theology have to say?

30.2 PUBLIC THEOLOGY AND THE AMAZON SYNOD

The neoliberal order and its devastating consequences for the poor and nature are a central concern for public theology in Latin America. In this section, I read the proposals advanced by the Synod of Bishops for the Pan-Amazon Region after its meeting in Rome in October 2019 as a theological critique against the effects of neoliberalism on the Amazon rainforest. The document may be taken as an example of public theology insofar as it is a critical theology voiced in the public space with the involvement of many people concerned for the vulnerability to which the lives sustained by the Amazon forest have been exposed. The Final Document of the Amazon Synod criticizes our current economic model for the devastating consequences it has brought upon the Amazon rainforest and its populations.[13] Landowners and business interests lead the exploitation of natural resources and the expropriation of indigenous lands. Against 'dominant economic and political interests',[14] the document calls for 'sustainable economic activities'.[15] Because of the Amazon's vital role in maintaining life on earth, the preservation and decolonization of the Amazon are of the greatest urgency.

---

[11] According to data from the Oxford Committee for Famine Relief (Oxfam), in 2010, a total of 388 individuals had the same amount of wealth as the bottom half of the human population. In 2015, the number went down to 62 individuals. In 2019, the 26 richest people owned as much as the poorest 50 per cent. Oxfam's 2020 report found that 'the 22 richest men in the world have more wealth than all the women in Africa'. A small taxation on the billionaires' wealth would be sufficient to maintain every child on the planet in school. Cf. OXFAM, *Time to Care: Unpaid and Underpaid Care Work and the Global Inequality Crisis* (Oxford: Oxfam International, 2020), 10, https://oxfamilibrary.openrepository.com/bitstream/handle/10546/620928/bp-time-to-care-inequality-200120-en.pdf (last accessed 25 January 2021).
[12] See Naomi Klein, *The Shock Doctrine: The Rise of Disaster Capitalism* (New York: Metropolitan Books/Henry Holt, 2007).
[13] Synod of Bishops special assembly for the Pan-Amazonian Region, *The Amazon: New Paths for the Church and for an Integral Ecology: Final Document* (Vatican: 2019), http://www.vatican.va/roman_curia/synod/documents/rc_synod_doc_20191026_sinodo-amazzonia_en.html (last accessed 25 January 2021).
[14] Ibid., 10.
[15] Ibid., 11.

According to information provided in the document, 'the Amazon plays a critical role as a buffer against climate change and provides invaluable and fundamental life support systems related to air, water, soils, forests and biomass'.[16] Deforestation not only ceases the process of carbon absorption but also releases stored carbon dioxide into the atmosphere, which contributes to global warming. Condensation from the forest creates flying rivers responsible for precipitation cycles far beyond the Amazon region. Despite the Amazon rainforest's role as the 'biological heart' of earth, 'the territory and its inhabitants are disappearing, especially the indigenous peoples'.[17] White humans' treatment of the Amazon has transformed the region into 'a wounded and deformed beauty, a place of suffering and violence'.[18] Languages, cultures, animals and plants die under the rule of neoliberalism.

The crisis in our time is at once social, economic and environmental. The economic factors that lead to the destruction of the Amazon forest and to climatic imbalance are the same that create poverty and inequality among people in society. Accordingly, 'ecology and social justice are intrinsically united'.[19] Human intervention in the region has 'assumed a voracious and predatory attitude that tends to squeeze reality until all available natural resources are exhausted'.[20] The 'unlimited exploitation' of natural resources in the Amazon 'responds to the logic of greed' that is 'typical of the dominant technocratic paradigm'.[21] In response to the current 'socio-environmental crisis', people are called for an 'ecological conversion'.[22] A 'profound personal, social and structural conversion'[23] which will uphold 'a model of development in which commercial criteria are not above environmental and human rights criteria'.[24]

The encyclical *Laudato si*'s notion of 'integral ecology'[25] inspires the church to pay attention to the ways in which humans and nature live in relation.

---

[16]Ibid., 11.
[17]Ibid., 2. The following 'threats to life' are enumerated in the document: 'appropriation and privatization of natural goods, such as water itself; legal logging concessions and illegal logging; predatory hunting and fishing; unsustainable mega-projects (hydroelectric and forest concessions, massive logging, monocultivation, highways, waterways, railways, and mining and oil projects); pollution caused by extractive industries and city garbage dumps; and, above all, climate change. [. . .] Behind all this are dominant economic and political interests, with the complicity of some government officials and some indigenous authorities. The victims are the most vulnerable: children, youth, women and our sister mother earth'. Ibid., 10.
[18]Ibid., 10.
[19]Ibid., 66.
[20]Ibid., 71.
[21]Ibid., 66.
[22]Ibid., 65.
[23]Ibid., 81.
[24]Ibid., 73.
[25]Cf. Francis, *Encyclical Letter Laudato si' of the Holy Father Francis: On Care of Our Common Home* (Vatican City, 2015), http://www.vatican.va/content/francesco/en/encyclicals/documents/

'Everything in the world is connected.'[26] A paradigm of justice inspired by the conception of integral ecology listens to *'both the cry of the earth and the cry of the poor'*.[27] Time will not hold much longer: 'it is urgent to face the unlimited exploitation of our common home and its inhabitants'.[28] Recognizing 'the central role of the Amazon biome for the equilibrium of the planet's climate', the church ought to encourage the international community to 'provide new economic resources for its protection and for the promotion of a model of just and solidary development'.[29] The Amazon Document admits that people might not 'modify the destructive model of extractivist development immediately'. However, that is no reason for not making clear 'whose side we are on': (1) denouncing 'the violation of human rights and extractive destruction'; (2) supporting 'campaigns of divestment from extractive companies responsible for the socio-ecological damage of the Amazon'; (3) and calling 'for a radical energy transition and the search for alternatives'.[30] People must act so as to rely less on fossil fuels, reduce waste, recycle, plant trees, consume less, live more modestly and support sustainable transportation, electricity and agriculture.[31]

Greed in human hearts has systemic consequences. According to the Amazon Document, 'greed for land is at the root of the conflicts that lead to ethnocide'.[32] The situation makes the demarcation and protection of indigenous territories an urgent task. Lands are being invaded through extractive activities such as mining, logging, extensive monocultures and cattle ranching. The Amazon Document affirms the church's commitment to being a voice of protest for the lives of indigenous communities threatened by the delay of territory demarcation, huge projects that impact the environment, and 'the economic model of predatory and ecocidal development'.[33] Indigenous leaders who speak out for their communities' rights are often silenced either through physical violence or through public policies. Government norms and supported practices tend to favour 'the expansion of areas of natural resource extraction and infrastructural mega-project developments, which exert pressure on ancestral

---

papa-francesco_20150524_enciclica-laudato-si.html.
[26] *The Amazon*, 66; *Laudato si'*, 16. 'Integral Ecology' is taken as a perspective for public theology in Jefferson Zeferino; Raquel de Fátima Colet; Alex Villas Boas, 'Religião, educação e direitos: a contribuição da ecologia integral na perspectiva da teologia pública', *Caminhos: Revista de Ciências da Religião* 17 (2019): 14–26.
[27] *The Amazon*, 66.
[28] Ibid., 67.
[29] Ibid., 68.
[30] Ibid., 70.
[31] Ibid., 81–4.
[32] Ibid., 45.
[33] Ibid., 46.

indigenous territories'.³⁴ To counteract the dominant economic paradigm we must 'seek alternative economic models, more sustainable, friendly to nature, and with solid spiritual support'. The economic system must be transformed so as to no longer harm nature and concentrate 'economic and political power in the hands of a few'.³⁵ The presence of the person who represents Christianity in the Amazon region as pictured in the Amazon Document must at once oppose neoliberal logics and respect indigenous people's beliefs.

The church is called to respect indigenous peoples' habits, traditions and wisdom in the spirit of intercultural theology. Unlike dominant currents of Western thought that tend to fragmentation, indigenous peoples of the Amazon offer 'an integrated vision of reality'.³⁶ Evangelization must not destroy indigenous peoples' cultures but contribute to strengthening their values.³⁷ Evangelization is regarded as 'a gift of Providence that calls everyone to salvation in Christ'.³⁸ Yet, the historical processes of Christianization and colonization cannot be distinguished easily in history as neither of them took place apart from the other. The document insists that 'despite military, political and cultural colonization, and beyond the greed and ambition of the colonizers, there were many missionaries who gave their lives to transmit the Gospel'.³⁹ There are examples of missionaries who opposed colonial powers. Nonetheless, on a broad scale, teaching indigenous peoples about the Christian God has been a practice benefiting colonization and greed. Slaves have been encouraged to remain slaves; lords, to accumulate riches; women, to be submissive to men. The Synod's plea for ministries conferred for men and women 'in an equitable manner'⁴⁰ still represents a long path for the Catholic Church. How radically anti-capitalist and anti-patriarchy would the new evangelization have to be if it indeed ought to 'reject a colonial style of evangelization'?⁴¹ Is a non-colonial style of evangelization something possible within a hierarchical, largely masculine as the structure of authority goes up, and by dominant Western traditions influenced organization? To what extent is evangelization without colonization ever possible?

A trace of death has been left by the European colonizer, who came to Latin American territory accompanied by the Christian church. Languages, communities of humans, animals and plants have been consistently held under

---

³⁴Ibid., 69.
³⁵Ibid., 72.
³⁶Ibid., 44.
³⁷Cf. Ibid., 54.
³⁸Ibid., 15.
³⁹Ibid., 15.
⁴⁰Ibid., 95.
⁴¹Ibid., 55.

death sentence since Christian Europeans' arrival on Latin American soil. With an eye on history, an attitude of suspicion must characterize any theology that reflects on the public presence of religion in society: Where does religion start, and where does capitalism end?[42] The warning of the Amazon Document is thus of the greatest social relevance: the church must 'distance itself from the new colonizing powers' and live in the example of those who were so brave as to collide with 'the powers that exploited the resources and oppressed the local populations'.[43] There might not be much time left for the church to make amendments for the destruction that it has helped bring upon the Amazon region.

30.3 LET LATIN AMERICA BE PUBLIC!

Our Latin American lands have been expropriated from plants and animals, from their indigenous populations and from the hungry poor in order for the fruits of the lands to be distributed among a small percentage of humans. Private ownership expands as our forests shrink. Forests, lands and cities have become private goods. Even public spaces are forbidden to homeless people and free-money travellers, who with difficulty find places where they can rest, eat and use the restroom. Tents are not permitted in most parks, as even the public is private in our lands. Families that occupy abandoned lands are taken as criminals. Why do not animals and plants hold rights over lands, instead? When will our churches open their doors for tired travellers to spend the night? When will our streets and trails finally be safe for women at night? When will our parks carry fruit-giving trees for the hungry and have public fountains of clean water for the thirsty? When will our lands produce food to feed everyone, and not to enrich investors of the food industry? When will the diversity of indigenous populations, as well as the many lives of animals and plants of the forests, take priority over mining, logging and the agri-business? When will our planet be saved?

Public theology stands for considering land, water and forests as public goods. The preservation of God's works of creation is threatened under private ownership. Hospitals, universities and markets: To whom should they belong?

---

[42] The idea of capitalism as a religious phenomenon, and many religious expressions as capitalism can be read in Walter Benjamin, 'Capitalism as Religion [Fragment 74]', *The Frankfurt School on Religion: Key Writings by the Major Thinkers*, trans. C. Kautzer, ed. E. Mendieta (New York: Routledge, 2005), 259–62.

[43] Ibid., 15. 'Colonialism is the imposition of some people's ways of life on others, whether economically, culturally or religiously. We reject a colonial style of evangelization. Proclaiming the Good News of Jesus implies recognizing the seeds of the Word already present in cultures.' Ibid., 55.

When we speak of theology as public, I understand that theology also is a good that we would like to belong to everyone: public libraries and universities will be places that people can freely attend for their theological investigations. Theology does not pertain to churches only. The thought of the divine is a very public one. It speaks to something deep in our beings. 'God' might be the word of meaning that we look for and might or not be able to name in moments of despair and need for hope beyond the present. 'Why have you abandoned me?'[44] – are the Psalmist's words of despair attributed to Jesus in his final hour during the public display of his pain. Even in negation and doubt, there we find the affirmation of the thought of God. The thought is given to us, and not created. We think God in communities and in dialogue with ourselves – selves that are also born out of communities.[45]

Besides its existential dimension, the thought of the divine is also public for coming to us through a certain religious tradition, which itself lives through ideas and images of each society, in conformity, as well as in rejection. Christianity arose as a revolutionary movement under the 'shadow of Empire'.[46] Jesus was a victim of the empire, executed under its laws. The first meetings of Christians, hosted by women in their homes, were held in secret, away from the view of Roman authorities. Several nations lived under Roman occupation during the first centuries of the Christian era. The apostle Paul understood himself as 'apostle to the nations'[47] defeated by the Romans. According to Davina Lopez, in the public art of the time, the conquered nations are represented as weak, acquiescent and feminine.[48] In his transformation through Christ, Paul confronts the hierarchical ideal of the victorious male soldier, as he himself is

---

[44]Mk 15.34: 'Ελωϊ Ελωϊ λαμὰ σαβαχθανεί' (Eberhard Nestle, *Bible: N.T. Greek Text with Critical Apparatus* (London: British and Foreign Bible Society, 1904)).

[45]For the notion that thoughts are public, see Charles Taylor, *Sources of the Self: The Making of the Modern Identity* (Cambridge, MA: Harvard University, 1989).

[46]Neil Elliot, *The Arrogance of Nations: Reading Roman in the Shadow of Empire* (Minneapolis, MN: Fortress Press, 2008).

[47]Paul describes himself as 'apostle to the nations' (Cf. Rom. 11.13; 15.16; Acts 9.15). Nations, τα ἔθνη, signify foreignness: but foreign to whom? In a sense, the Gentiles stand in a binary opposition with the Jews, but they are also, together with the Jews, the others to the Romans. Following Davina Lopez, the nations are by no means an apolitical category: by affirming himself as apostle to the nations, and announcing a message that in many ways went against the empire ideology of the time, Paul stood in subversive solidarity with the colonized peoples under the emperor's ever-expanding dominance. For Lopez, we may assume that Paul was familiar with the Roman representation of *ta ethne*, and that, as apostle to the nations, he knew that his mission was directed to the same peoples that the Romans portrayed as female, inferior, conquered and nonresistant. Davina C. Lopez, *Apostle to the Conquered: Reimagining Paul's Mission* (Minneapolis: Fortress Press, 2010).

[48]The art of Roman imperial ideology, according to Lopez's study, persistently communicates the hierarchical construct: 'Roman is to nation as male is to female.' Lopez, *Apostle to the Conquered*, 26–55.

on the side of the weakness and feminineness of the defeated, chosen by God to shame the strong.[49] The divine is no longer to be found in the higher position of the conqueror but with the bodies of the subdued, in suffering, persecution and distress. Because the divine is to be encountered in weakness, Paul comes to the paradoxical conclusion: 'when I am weak, then am I strong'.[50]

We learn from Paul's message that God does not choose the manliness of the conquering soldier. God does not choose the whiteness of the world's biggest companies' shareholders or the safety of the upper classes. God chooses the weaker side of imperial practice and ideology. The God of life stands on the side of the victims of neoliberalism: landless families, the homeless, children with malnutrition, life-risking miners, women who daily carry heavy water on their shoulders, refugees fleeing from war, victims of patriarchy and racism, people filling profit-oriented prisons, also animals in industrial confinement, animals dying in forest fires and from pollution, all biodiversity under threat of extinction. Animals are embraced by God's love, as God did not make herself human: God made herself animal so she could undergo suffering, and die.[51]

Paul's theology of power in weakness is consistent with the prevalent biblical message of liberation from oppression and what liberation theology calls God's 'option for the poor'. In political terms, a choice for the poor means, as Jon Sobrino puts it, that the poor become the centre of political concern.[52] Only when all political endeavours are centred on the poor, oriented to assist and stand in solidarity with those who need most, may we speak of a just society. The market exists to serve the ends of food, clothing and shelter. An economy oriented to infinite progress, consumption and profit has lost its purpose, has lost its Spirit and lives under the letter of the law that kills.[53] Laws that privilege the interests of the few, interests of corporations, pharmaceutical companies and the war industry – furthermore, laws that institutionalize hatred and xenophobia towards the weaker parts of our global order – have no commitment with the suffering poor.

---

[49] 1 Cor. 1.27: 'And the Weak Things in the World Chose God to Shame the Strong' ('καὶ τὰ ἀσθενῆ τοῦ κόσμου ἐξελέξατο ὁ Θεός ἵνα καταισχύνῃ τὰ ἰσχυρά').
[50] 2 Cor. 12.10: 'ὅταν γὰρ ἀσθενῶ, τότε δυνατός εἰμι.'
[51] On suffering at the historical condition of God's revelation, see Miriam Leidinger, *Verletzbarkeit gestalten: Eine Auseinandersetzung mit 'Verletzbarkeit' anhand der Christologien von Jürgen Moltmann, Jon Sobrino und Graham Ward* (Regensburg: Friedrich Pustet, 2018).
[52] Jon Sobrino, *No Salvation Outside the Poor: Prophetic-Utopian Essays* (Maryknoll, NY: Orbis Books, 2008).
[53] See Franz J. Hinkelammert, *La maldición que pesa sobre la ley: las raíces del pensamiento crítico en Pablo de Tarso* (San José: Editorial Arlekín, 2010). Paul was aware of the curse that weighs on the law. According to Hinkelammert, this curse becomes manifest when we treat the observance of the law as path for salvation. The law is violent, and when misused, sin easily imposes its deathful power through it. For the law not to kill, we must go beyond the law, transgress it in faith so that love and trust in the God of life may be at its source. The 'source of discernment and reflexivity' for the law is that of the 'life of the body'.

The power of empire is masculine: it relates to land as men are taught to relate to women: through strength, aggressiveness, intimidation. The power of empire is the institutional face of everyday masculine domination. The power of conquering empires has existed in Latin America before European colonizers arrived, although, since that time, it has undergone systematic expansion towards a global order. The world-system that came about after 1492, according to Enrique Dussel, organizes countries between centre and periphery. The centre controls the system. Any thinking that is critical and aims at liberation 'judges as perverse the system that causes negative effects, even if they are unintentional, massive, and destructive from an ecological and social point of view'.[54] Public theology in Latin America, if on the side of the poor, will advocate for the overcoming of an economic system based on private property because it has excluded a large part of human and non-human populations from access to basic means of survival.[55] Latin America and God's works of creation ought to be made public, less private. Once society becomes itself a public good, the same will happen to theology. Public theology will no longer be an ideological instrument of the elites but a mode of expression by the common people in their struggles for justice and care for nature.

What a linguistic heresy to speak of a region with hundreds of languages, millions of species of animals and plants under generalizing names! The name Latin America is revealing of international relations of oppression. Neoliberal regions lie within a money-oriented order, oppressive against non-profiting lives. It takes an entire world to feed the 1 per cent. The capitalist order made its way to Latin America under Latin languages. Since then, all lands on the planet have been divided through illusory human lines. The lines exclude from ownership: animals, plants as well as the majority of the world's human population. National states and landowners exist within a juridical and legislative system historically raised to protect private property. Because resources are used without concern for the continuity of life, each day our biodiversity, languages and cultural modes of exchange and of being human are brought closer to extinction. Foreign and national money-holders look at the Amazon forest as starving vultures over an already dead body. Nature is no longer sacred but something to be exploited.

Who sells the cures for our diseases? From where do pharmaceutical companies buy the knowledge for their power? Where do we eat the meat that

---

[54]Enrique Dussel, *Hacia una filosofía política crítica* (Bilbao: Desclée, 2011), 142: 'La ética crítica [. . .] juzga como perverso el sistema que causa efectos negativos, aunque sean no-intencionales, masivos, destructores desde un punto de vista ecológico y social.'

[55]On the centrality of private property in capitalism, see Ulrich Duchrow and Franz Hinkelammert, *Property for People, Not for Profit: Alternatives to the Global Tyranny of Capital* (London: Zed Books, 2004).

causes the deforestation of the Amazon? Products of labour can be accessed for as long as we are in possession of the form in which the exchange of commodities takes place: money. That was characteristic of early capitalism as it is of its complexly politicized form of neoliberalism. Is the destruction of our forests equivalent to the wealth capitalism has produced? Is there any 'real value', as the Amazon Document asks, that economic and extractive activities can return to the land and to society, 'considering the wealth that it extracts from them and the socio-ecological consequences'?[56] What reparation will the top-polluting companies offer to counteract our planetary ecological crisis? For how much longer will money be the commodity that pays for life?

30.4 CONCLUSION

A 'public Latin America' is a calling to create spaces where humans and animals can live, eat, sleep and have access to health and education. Public theology condemns the satisfaction of universal needs by means of money and affirms the right of all to be nourished by our life-giving earth. I looked at the Amazon Synod as an example of public theology insofar as the initiative has been a public theological voice against the economic oppression of the Amazon region. The final document of the Synod acknowledges the need for an economic model that is not dependent on fossil fuels, not geared towards consumerism and not harmful towards nature and peoples. The entirety of the Latin American context has been impacted by neoliberalism. A perceptually small yet powerful elite inside and outside of our countries controls the production and exchange of goods, the mass media as well as policymaking processes so as to expand its control and profits. The Amazon is being killed in the hands of neoliberalism.

Actions of hope and resistance are being carried out by the working class, the marginalized, feminist and Black movements, indigenous leaders and their communities. Public theology has the task of supporting history in its course for human and animal liberation, opposing the dictatorship of money and private ownership. May Latin America become public, so life may flourish! The idea has been around for quite some time. I only help teach it to the younger generation. Look around and judge for yourself: Where do the seeds of your eating come from? Where can you buy a Coca-Cola drink? If your water is not clean for drinking, who has been polluting it? What can we do to counteract neoliberalism from our different contexts? What are our economic alternatives? Can our world's forests, waters and living creatures still be saved?

---

[56] *The Amazon*, 72. Large-scale mining is taken as an example of an economic practice responsible for 'substantially diminish[ing] the value of life in the Amazon'.

INDEX

Aarde, Andries van 481
Abduh, Muhammad 237
Abelard, Peter 291, 297
Aben, Tersur 481
Ackerman, Denise 487
Adenauer, Konrad 95
Adorno, Theodor W. 92
Africa 469–88
Agamben, Giorgio 329
Agang, Sunday 481, 483
Akper, Godwin 481
Alexander, Valentina 313
Ali, Ausaf 236–7
Alinsky, Saul 228, 550
Alinsky organizing 550, 551, 553
Althusius, Johannes 261
Amazon Synod 556, 561–5, 569
Anderson, Victor 542–4, 547
Anglicanism 311–12, 316, 474, 503–6, 516–19
Anselm of Canterbury 291
apartheid 286, 442–6, 471, 482–5
apologetics 64, 68, 76–7, 97, 109–12, 180–5, 251–3, 316–17
  dialogical 120
  origins of 114–19
  performative 122
  positivist 119–20
Arendt, Hannah 305, 377–8
Aristides of Athens 118
Aristotelism 51–2, 54, 325

Aristotle 33, 35, 322, 328, 333, 360
Arius 472
Asad, Talal 74, 489
Asia 489–502
Ateck, Naim 493
Athanasius of Alexandria 472
Athenagoras of Athens 117
atonement 291–2, 297, 397
Audard, Catherine 25
Augustine of Hippo 4, 87, 89–90, 99, 102, 116, 175, 269, 279, 307, 309, 332–3, 386, 388, 472
Australia 483, 503–20
authority 28, 30, 52–3, 70, 116, 238, 254–5

Bach, Johann Sebastian 218
Bacote, Vincent E. 210
Balthasar, Hans Urs von 464
Barbieri, William 532
Barrera, Albino 157
Bartali, Gino 456
Barth, Karl 182, 198, 212, 230–1
Bartholomew I (Ecumenical Patriarch) 81
Basil the Great 427
Bauckham, Richard 344, 346–7
Bauhn, Per 60–1
Bavinck, Herman 258
Baxter, Michael 545
Beauvoir, Simone de 387
Beckford, Robert 314–15, 319

Bedford-Strohm, Heinrich   207, 219, 517
Bell, Daniel   30, 308
Bellah, Robert   128, 133–9, 141, 145,
   204, 400, 410–11, 540, 547
Benedict XVI   82, 156, 458, 464, 527
Benne, Robert   205, 211–12
Bentham, Jeremy   428
Berger, Peter   112
Berry, Thomas   436–8
Beyers Naudé, Christiaan Frederick   287
bilingualism   22–3, 108–9, 118–19, 409
Blackness   313, 390, 392, 542–3
Black theology   283–300, 312–17, 386,
   433, 486, 539, 542–6, 553
Black women   291–3, 392–3
Bloch, Ernst   102
Bloechl, Jeffrey   320
Blondel, Maurice   89
Blumenberg, Hans   49
body   175, 307–9, 317–21, 333–7,
   380–5, 393–5, 453–8
body politic   113, 124, 317
Boesak, Allan   284, 286, 290
Boff, Leonardo   104, 436, 438
Bonaventure   328
Bonhoeffer, Dietrich   5, 92, 201, 231,
   247, 259, 295
Borgman, Erik   280–2
Botman, Russel   481–3
Bourke, Richard   503–4
Breitenberg, E. Harold   201–2, 223, 433,
   441, 542
Bretherton, Luke   308, 376, 549–50, 553
Brown, Wendy   128, 145–6
Browning, Don   401
Buc, Philippe   326–7
Buchanan, Pat   169
Buddhism   226, 230–1
Bultmann, Rudolf   131
Burgmann, Ernest   506
Burns, Robert   506
Burns, Stephen   305, 307
Butumalai, Sadayandy   495
Byung-mu, Ahn   233

Cady, Linell   151, 542
Cahill, Lisa   544
Calhoun, Craig   20
Calvin, John   87

capabilities approach   158–60
capitalism   339, 344–6, 475, 556–61
Carbine, Rosemary   307, 544, 548–9, 551
Carroll, James   508
Carvalhaes, Claudio   559
Casanova, José   73, 166–8, 170, 370–1
Castillo, Daniel   438
Catholicism   44, 147–63, 489
Catholic Social Teaching   38, 82, 94,
   147–58, 433, 501, 545
Cavanaugh, William   59, 269, 274, 361,
   366, 368
Chifley, Ben   507–8
Cho, David Yonggi   500
Choi, Ja-shil   500
Chomsky, Noam   558
Chung, Paul   230–3, 545
Chung-hee, Park   493
Churchill, Winston   509
Cicero, Marcus Tullius   44
citizenship   78, 124, 226–7, 390–1
Claessens, Juliana   481, 486–7
climate change   81–4, 339–40, 346–7,
   440–7, 523, 556
Clooney, Francis   231, 233
Cobb, John   435, 438–9
Cobb, Kelton   405–8, 411
Cohen, Aryeh   234
Coleman, John   541, 547
Coleridge, Samuel Taylor   506
colonialism/colonization   74, 92–3, 103,
   204, 252, 287–8, 314, 341, 344,
   389–92, 420–1, 471, 498–504, 525,
   564–8
common good   4, 6, 8, 34–6, 44, 78–9,
   82, 154–8, 511, 541
*Compendium of the Social Doctrine of the
   Church*   155
comprehensive doctrines   23–6, 29
Comte, Auguste   476
Cone, James   285–93, 297–8, 439
Confucianism   501–2
Connolly, William   73
Connor, Bull   259
Conradie, Ernst   433
contractualism   13, 20, 23–7, 234, 378
Copeland, Shawn   392, 394
Copernicus, Nicolaus   51
Coppola, Sofia   3

cosmopolitanism   16–17, 25, 27, 29, 526
Costello, Tim   516
Coubertin, Pierre de   454
Coulanges, Fustel de   328
covenant   234–5, 259–64, 426, 497
Covid-19   289, 444, 522
Crétien, Jean-Louis   320, 332–3, 335
cross   95, 103–4, 144, 285–300, 394–5
culture   9, 159–61, 187, 191–3, 389,
    396–413, 456–9, 462–5, 526–31
Cutcheon, Russel   129–30, 133, 143–4
Cyprian of Carthage   472

Dailey, Erik W.   451
Dalai Lama   81
Dalit theology   89, 492, 501
Daly, Herman E.   439
Darwall, Stephen   58
Darwin, Charles   340
Day, Dorothy   94
Day, Kathie   212, 227, 544–5, 549, 551
Deacay, Chris   397–8
Deakin, Alfred   505
debt   426–31
Declaration on Sport and the Christian Life   449
decolonization   288, 470, 473, 525, 534, 561
deforestation   444, 557, 561–2, 569
Deleuze, Gilles   336
Delores, Jacques   521
democracy   19–20, 24, 26, 33–7, 39–46,
    77–9, 166–72, 176–8, 207–8,
    226–7, 234–41, 524–5, 558–9
Deneulin, Séverine   161
Denning, Michael   425
Derrida, Jacques   522, 528–9, 531
Descartes, René   51–2, 55
DeWitt, Calvin   436
Didon, Henri   454
discrimination   93, 158–9, 311
Doak, Mary   304, 544–5, 548
doctrine of God   265–82
Don Bosco, Giovanni Melchiorre   454
Dooyeweerd, Herman   261
Dube, Musa   481, 487
Dulles, Avery   114
Duns Scotus, John   54–7
Durkheim, Emile   476

Dussel, Enrique   568

Eaton, Matthew   235
Ecclesia in Europa   526
ecclesial political theology   307–10, 317–19
ecclesiology   301–19
eco-feminism   438, 441
ecology   82–4, 432–47, 562–3
economics/economy   93–4, 150–6, 345–6, 414–31, 438–9, 555–64
eco-theology   84, 232, 435–42
ecumenism   200–20
Edwards, Denis   436
Elizondo, Virgilio   548
Ellis, Robert   450
Engineer, Asghar Ali   237
environment   81–4, 438–41, 445–6, 562
Erp, Stephan van   266
eschatology   102, 160, 189–90, 277–8, 307–10, 339–55
Espín, Orlando   342, 351, 355
ethnicity   383, 385, 387, 389, 392, 394
Eucharistic ecclesiology   172–6
Europe   521–37
Evangelicalism   112, 119, 169, 210, 269, 510, 516
Evangelii Gaudium   530

faith   83–8, 100–3, 107–24, 131–3, 224–30, 273–8, 304, 383–5, 415–16, 444–6, 469–70, 482–6, 511–19, 534
Faith in the City   302–4, 311–12
Fanon, Frantz   92
feminist theology   248, 385–8, 436–8, 486–7, 539, 544–8
Fenton, Allison   317
Feuerbach, Ludwig   528
Fichte, Johann Gottlieb   58–9
Fletcher, Brian   505
Floyd, George   316
Ford, David   224
Forrester, Duncan   209, 223, 305, 307, 542
Fracer, Nancy   543
France-Williams, Azariah   312, 318
Francis (Pope)   82–3, 345–6, 351, 440, 522, 528–30
Frankfurt School   26, 92, 397

Frederici, Silvia 420
Freeden, Michael 374–5
freedom 14–16, 35–6, 44–6, 54–67, 98–9, 159, 171–2, 176, 255, 279, 281, 342, 409, 505, 537
Frei, Hans 180–3, 185, 188–92, 195–9
Freire, Paulo 315
Fried, Johannes 53
Fukuyama, Francis 344
Fulton, Brad 228–30
fundamentalism 31, 79, 289, 531
Furnal, Joshua 418

Galilei, Galileo 51
Gandhi, Mohandas 233
Garland, Canon 509
Gascoigne, Robert 32
Gaudium et Spes 153–4, 157, 348, 457, 462
gay marriage 164, 170–2, 176–8
Gebara, Ivone 436, 438
Geertz, Clifford 183
gender 76, 380–95, 440
gender justice 215, 438, 440
Gerle, Elisabeth 479
Gewirth, Alan 61
Gillespie, Michael Allen 50
Gilroy, Norman Thomas 508, 510
Giving the Best of Yourself 458–62, 464–5
globalization 78, 108, 112–13, 150–2, 219, 267–8, 370, 420, 469, 523
Global Network for Public Theology (GNPT) 1, 213, 223–5, 287, 451, 470, 481, 488, 519 545
Gogarten, Friedrich 49
Gorski, Philip 411
Gottlieb, Roger 441
Gough, Hugh 509–10
grace 89, 270, 278–82, 309, 404
Graham, Billy 510
Graham, Elaine 76, 123, 268–70, 272, 279, 304, 310, 316, 367–8, 372–3, 378, 397, 402–3, 408, 411, 498
Grand, Jacqueline 290
Gregory of Nyssa 427
Grimm, John 437
Grimshaw, Mike 76–7
Gruchy, John de 207, 224–5, 473, 481

Gu, Joseph (Gu Yuese) 498
Gutiérrez, Gustavo 96, 104, 349

Habermas, Jürgen 13, 23–30, 50, 54–5, 57–8, 60, 71–2, 113, 206, 227, 252, 363, 371, 527–8, 530–1, 547, 552
Hadrian (Roman Emperor) 118
Haker, Hille 378
Hall, Stuart 381, 386, 394
Hanafi, Hassan 237
happiness 33–9, 44–7, 408
Hardiman, Fransisco Brandi 227
Harris, Melanie 439
Hart, David Bentley 121
Harvey, Lincoln 450
Hauerwas, Stanley 31, 180–2, 185–8, 191, 193–5, 197, 199, 368, 545, 548
Healy, Nicholas 187, 317–18
Hegel, Georg Wilhelm Friedrich 92, 105, 528
Heidegger, Martin 331
Held, David 150
Hendrickse, Canon Clarence 312
hermeneutics 27–30, 79–82, 101, 181–5, 233, 252, 324–5
Heyer, Christa 544–5, 549
Higginbotham, Leon 391
Higton, Mike 183
Himes, Kenneth R. 211
Himes, Michael J. 211
Hinduism 112, 233, 492, 500–2
Hitler, Adolf 259
Hobbes, Thomas 16, 365
Höffe, Otfried 23
Höhne, Florian 141
Holiness and Social Justice 519
Hollenbach, David 541, 547
Holmes, Steven 524–5
hope 101–4, 273, 340–3, 347–54
Horace (Quintus Horacius Flaccus) 92
Horkheimer Max 92
Hosen, Nadirsyah 237
Houston, Brian 516
Hübenthal, Christoph 281, 416–17, 452
Huber, Wolfgang 206–7, 214
Hudson, Wayne 509
Hughes, Thomas 449
Humanae Vitae 510

human dignity 150, 161–2, 241, 460, 513
human rights 40, 171, 222, 233, 236, 241, 249, 513, 563
Hume, David 91, 105
Huntington, Samuel 127, 144, 176

identity 386–7, 525–6, 529–30, 540
Ignatius of Antioch 386
incarnation 110–11, 182, 185, 309, 328–34, 394–5, 506
indigenous peoples 445–6, 472–5, 512–13, 562–5
individualism 186, 473–4, 513–15
inequality 177, 339–40, 424, 522, 559–62
Ingelhart, Ronald 476–7
injustice 78, 81, 83–4, 102–6, 150, 155–6, 161–2, 302, 317, 350, 439, 455
Islam 128, 176, 236–9, 495, 514, 526

Jacobsen, Eneida 266
Jacobson, Matthew 390
Jaggesar, Michael 313
Jefferson, Thomas 91
Jenkins, Willis 434, 444
Jennings, Willie 312, 389
Jensen, Peter 516
Jensen, Philipp 516
Jesus of Nazareth/Jesus Christ 2–3, 6, 63, 88, 98, 101, 103–4, 106, 115, 144, 182, 184–5, 188–9, 192, 195–6, 198, 229, 249, 251, 260, 272, 284–6, 288, 290–9, 348, 350–1, 353, 382–6, 388, 392–5, 461, 495, 499, 517–18, 527, 566
Joas, Hans 49, 171
John Paul II 82, 105, 155, 242, 457, 460, 464, 526
John XXIII 153, 156, 457
Johnson, Pauline 375
Jones, Robert 554
Jonker, Willie 287–8, 293–8
Joseph of Nazareth 383
Judaism 75, 88, 224, 233–5, 384
Julian of Norwich 320
justice 23–6, 79–84, 103, 118–19, 148–50, 155–62, 215–19, 231–5, 249–50, 253–6, 258–63, 271–80, 434, 438–51, 481–3, 515–19
justification 294–5
Justin Martyr 87, 115–16, 118, 386
Justitia in Mundo 156

Kairos document 442–7
Kant, Immanuel 13–18, 20–1, 25–6, 29–30, 55–60, 92, 100, 105, 181, 294, 365, 528
Kataliko, Emmanuel 299–300
Katongole, Emmanuel 298–9
Kaye, Bruce 504
Keller, Catherine 352, 436
Kennedy, John F. 134–5
Kepler, Johannes 51
Khorchide, Mouhanad 237–8
Kierkegaard, Søren 528
Kim, Sebastian 212, 305, 500, 538, 545, 552
King, Martin Luther 5, 259
Kingdom of God/reign of God 106, 212, 292, 348–54, 394, 533
Kirwan, Michael 349
Koopman, Nico 286–8, 481, 483–4
Körtner, Ulrich H. J. 203
Kotze, Hennie 476–7
Koyama, Kosuke 495
Krastev, Ivan 524–5
Krings, Hermann 58–9
Küng, Hans 296
Kunhiyop, Samuel Waye 482–3
Kuyper, Abraham 5, 210, 261

Lacordaire, Henri Dominique 454
Lake, Meredith 507
Landman, Christa 481
Langston, Hughes 393
Las Casas, Bartholomé de 104
Latin America 73, 89–93, 105–6, 491–3, 496, 556–69
Latin theology 539, 542–6, 553
Laudato si' 82–4, 351, 432, 440, 445, 562
Lee, Hak Joon 362–5, 545
Lefort, Claude 73
Leibniz, Gottfried Wilhelm 52, 55
Leo XIII 152, 462, 505
Lewis, Bernard 144

LGBTQ people   97, 388, 513, 517
liberal democracy   33–47, 171, 523
liberalism   37–46, 127–46, 171–6, 268–9, 345–7, 364–9, 522–4
liberation   490–4
liberation theology   86–107, 284–5, 484–6, 491–6
Lincoln, Abraham   91, 201, 205, 548
Lindbeck, Georg   130–1, 180–2, 190–5, 197–9
Lindner, Robert   510, 516
liturgy   269, 320–38, 510
Lixey, Kevin   452
Locke, John   25, 91
Lopez, Davina   566
Lovat, Terry   236
Löwith, Karl   49
Lubac, Henri de   89
Luther, Martin   231
Lynch, Gordon   396–8, 400–3, 405, 408, 411
Lyotard, Jean-François   344

McBride, Jennifer   318
McClintock Fulkerson, Mary   318, 550
McDaniel, Jay   436
McElroy, Robert W.   211
McFague, Sally   436, 439
McGrew, Anthony   150
McIntosh, Esther   486
MacIntyre, Alasdair   79, 236
Magnis-Suseno, Franz   227
Maid, Nurcholish   237
Mandry, Christof   24
Mannion, Gerard   266
Mannix, Daniel   507
Marcos, Ferdinand   492
Maréchal, Joseph   89
market(s)   19, 96, 345–6, 420
Marsh, Clive   397, 408–11
Marsilius of Padua   52–3
Martin Alcoff, Linda   306
Marty, François   14
Marty, Martin   1, 90, 128–9, 133, 137–43, 145, 204–6, 538, 540–1, 547
Marx, Karl   420, 476, 528
Marxism   343, 345, 492–3, 501, 513
Mary (mother of Jesus)   382–3, 395

Mary Magdalene   334
Mater et Magistra   156
Mauleleke, Tinyiko   284–5, 288, 481, 484–6
Maurice, Frederick Denison   506
Mazza, Carlo   452
Mbembe, Achille   471–2
Mbiti, John   472–3, 477
Mead, George Herbert   528
Meireis, Torsten   201
Menzies, Robert   506
metaphysics   54–7, 268, 277–80, 321–5, 478
Methodism   474, 517
Metz, Johann Baptist   20, 91, 95, 102–3, 206, 308, 350, 352, 530, 533, 548
Mieth, Dietmar   452
migration   378
Míguez, Néstor   559
Milbank, John   31, 59, 64, 326, 368
Minjung theology   89, 492–3, 498–502
missio Dei   123, 249
Mittleman, Alan   234
modernity   43–5, 49–50, 93–6, 522–5
Moe-Lobeda, Cynthia   440
Mofokeng, Takatso   290
Moltmann, Jürgen   49, 91, 95, 102–3, 206, 349, 353, 436
Monro, Anita   305, 307
Moore, Andrew   275–6
Moran, Patrick   505
Moses (Biblical Prophet)   258
Moughtin-Mumby, Andrew   315
Mudde, Cas   374
Muhammad (Prophet)   237–8
Mujerista theology   544
Müller, Norbert   452
Murray, John Courtney   5, 94, 98–100, 106, 149, 211, 236, 541, 547
Mussolini, Benito   456

Nadar, Sarojini   481, 487
Nagel, Thomas   57
Nagl-Docekal, Herta   26
natural law   34–9, 44–5, 99–100, 150, 163, 211, 541
Naudé, Piet   287
Nee, Watchman (Ti Tuosheng)   499
neoliberalism   344–6, 556–61, 569

Neoplatonism 51–2, 54, 356
Ne Temere 508
Newton, Isaac 52
Ng, Peter Tze Ming 224
Nicholas of Cusa 326
Niebuhr, H. Richard 5, 93, 106, 403–4
Niebuhr, Reinhold 93–4, 98–100, 106, 140–1, 201, 205, 247, 259, 342, 349, 352–3, 355, 540
Niles, D. Preman 233, 241
Nirmal, Arvind 492
Nisbet, Robert 366
Noah (Biblical Patriarch) 258
Norris, Pippa 476
North America 538–55
Novak, David 234
Nussbaum, Martha 149, 158–60, 162
Nyirumbe, Rosemary 299–300

Obama, Barack 550
Ockham, William of 50–3
O'Donovan, Oliver 39
Oduyoye, Merci Amba 481, 487
Oeldemann, Johannes 218
Oldham, J. H. 110
Olympic Games 454–8
Oorschot, Frederike van 201
Origen of Alexandria 87, 291, 322, 328, 330–2, 472
Ormerod, Neil 271–2, 276
Orthodox churches 81, 167–78, 216
Orthodoxy 164–78
Osthövener, Claus-Dieter 32
Overeem, Patrick 122

Pacem in Terris 153
Pannenberg, Wolfhart 49
Parker, Andrew 451
Pascal, Blaise 52, 89, 330
Paul (Apostle) 88–9, 115, 335–6, 352, 453, 459, 566–7
Paul VI 156, 457
payday lending 422–30
peace 82, 152, 185–6, 194, 207–9, 215–16, 219, 249–50, 353, 498, 514–15
Pearson, Clive 66, 447, 516, 519
Peirce, Charles Sanders 528
Pelikan, Jaroslav 87

Penner, Myron 120
Pentecostalism 210, 314, 474–5, 516
Perkinson, Jim 319
Peter Lombard 88
Peterson, Erik 349
Peukert, Helmut 20
Phillips, Elizabeth 362–3, 366, 372
Phiri, Isabel 481, 486
Pickard, Stephen 506, 519
Pieris, Aloysius 494
Piggin, Stuart 510, 516
Pinn, Anthony 313, 544
Pius X 454–5, 508
Pius XII 456, 459
Plato 88, 323, 335
pluralism/pluralization 71–4, 112–14, 369–73, 531–4
Polanyi, Karl 420
political theology 39–47, 73, 86–107, 359–62
politics 308–10, 359–79, 523–5
populism 34, 41–6, 373–9
Populorum Progressio 156
postcolonial theology 89, 106, 230–1, 233, 240–1, 470–3, 491, 501, 545
postliberalism 43–5, 130, 179–99, 269, 364–9
postmodernism 344–7
post-secularity 69–85, 112–14, 167, 369–73, 531–4
poverty 103–4, 559
Preece, Gordon 520
preferential option for the poor 88, 98, 103, 106, 428, 567
pre-materialist society 477
privatization 559, 565
Protestantism 91, 201, 203, 205–9, 213–19, 428, 449, 493–9, 509–10
Pro Veritate 287
public discourse 60–5, 94, 205–6, 262, 354, 369, 546–8
public/private distinction 15, 19–21, 25, 43, 55, 70–1, 77–8, 90–1, 99–100, 165–6, 248
public reason 14–24, 79, 100–1, 241
public sphere 13–32, 59–61, 165–70, 359–62, 552
public theology
    aims of 415–19

bilingualism 22–3, 108–9, 118–19, 409
as Black theology 283–300
and capabilities 160
charisms of 304–5
coining of the term 137–42
concept of 201
critique on 267–70
denominational origins 204–10
in dialogue with others 90–1
distinct from other theologies 55, 86–106
feminist 544, 548
functions of 109–12
hybridization of 539–46
inter-religious 240–3
non-Christian 146
and other religions 221–43
performative-political 534–6
pluralization of 539–46
and *polis* 97–101
as political project 552–5
as political theology 359–62
popular culture as p.th. 410–13
postliberal 185–90
and post-secularity 74–81
practical turn of 546–52
praxis of 214–18
as public discourse 201–2, 249–53
as public good 566
scope of 1–10
and the secular 63–8
Pui-lan, Kwok 491
Putin, Vladimir 169
Putten, Robert van 122

Quadragesimo Anno 153

race 311–12, 380–95
racism 311–17, 383, 439–40, 471
Radford Ruether, Rosemary 438–9, 494
Radical Orthodoxy 72, 269–70, 277, 368
Rahner, Karl 87, 89
Rasmussen, Lara 84
Rasmussen, Larry 439
Ratzinger, Joseph 527, 530
Rawls, John 13, 23–7, 72, 165, 167, 227, 241, 547
Recinos, Harold 544
Reddie, Anthony 313–15

Reformed Churches 216–17, 287, 442
Regan, Hillary 520
religion(s)
civil 134–7
as community 17
as comprehensive doctrine 26
and globalization 113
intelligibility of 190–2
as language 191
pluralization of 74–7
privatization of 96, 105, 165, 250, 252
as resource for motivation 23–4
as symbols 131–2
traditional 477–8
truth of 192–8
Rerum Novarum 152, 505
resurrection 350
Ricoeur, Paul 13, 27–30, 60, 62, 327, 377
Riordan, Patrick 155
Ritschel, Albrecht 294
Roosevelt, Theodore 38
Rorty, Richard 167, 399–400, 411–12
Rössler, Dietrich 214, 217
Rousseau, Jean-Jacques 91, 134
Rowlands, Anna 377
Rudd, Kevin 512
Rupert of Deutz 334

Sabellius 472
Sacks, Jonathan 235
Sagovsky, Nicholas 150
Said, Edward 491
salvation 6, 102, 273–4, 281–2, 292–6, 349–50, 408–10
Sandel, Michael 154
Santamaria, Bob 508
scepticism 112–14
Schieder, Rolf 31
Schillebeeckx, Edward 273, 280, 348–50, 534
Schlag, Thomas 146
Schleiermacher, Friedrich 32, 87, 89, 105, 129–31, 198, 293–4
Schmitt, Carl 49, 73
Schüssler-Fiorenza, Elisabeth 388
sciences 50–2, 83, 346–7
Scott, Peter Manley 361

Second Vatican Council 153–4, 510, 533
secular 48–68, 70–6, 150, 167–8, 281, 403, 416–17, 531–4
secularism 72–3, 113, 167–8, 407–11, 515
secularity 70–2, 167–8, 512
secularization 38, 49–57, 70–3, 112–13, 369–73, 512, 531–2
Segundo, Juan Luis 104
sensus communis 322–3
Seon-ju, Gil 499
Shin, Daniel 183
Shoa 89, 92, 95, 102, 106, 343, 350
Singgih, Emanuel Gerrit 227
slavery 312–14, 471
Slessarev-Jamir, Helene 544–5, 549
Smit, Dirk J. 147, 204–10, 287, 442, 481–3
Smith, James K. A. 269–70, 272, 277–80
Sobrino, Jon 104, 567
social ethics 216, 247–64
social evolution 52–3
social justice 93, 119, 148–50, 157–62, 215–19, 253–4, 262, 451, 505–6, 515–19
solidarity 106, 156, 376–9
Sölle, Dorothee 91, 95, 103, 296
Song, Robert 367
Soon-kyung, Park 493
soteriology 54, 283–300, 426
Spencer, Herbert 476
Spillers, Hortense 381, 387, 389
Spinoza, Baruch 52, 55
sports 448–65
Spufford, Francis 121
Stackhouse, Max 46–7, 107, 111, 119, 211, 250, 261, 267–8, 272–3, 278, 360, 362, 367, 419–20, 538, 553
Stacy, Tim 376–7
Steden, Ronald van 122
Storrar, William 76, 223–5, 240, 304, 307, 545, 550
Stout, Jeffrey 167
Strange, Daniel 270, 275
Strauss, Leo 49
Sugirtharajah Rasiah S. 491
Sunarko, Adrianus 227
Sung, John (Song Shangjie) 499
synaesthesia 320–2, 328–33

Taggart, Paul 374
Tanner, Kathryn 187, 274, 396, 401
Taylor, Charles 59, 60, 70, 72, 113, 165, 167, 478–9, 532
Tebartz-van Elst, Franz-Peter 218
Tertullian 87, 117–18, 472
Thatcher, Margaret 311
Thiemann, Ronald 187–8, 211, 548
Thodosius I (Roman Emperor) 108
Thomas Aquinas 87–8, 276, 322, 328, 330–2, 453
Thurman, Howard 543
Tillich, Paul 87, 94, 106, 109, 129–33, 135–9, 141–5, 401, 403–6
Ting, K. H. (Ding Guangxun) 495–6, 498, 501
Tippett, Krista 120–1
Toit, Colonel du 478
Towens, Emilie 392
Tracy, David 2, 77, 94, 98, 100–1, 106, 109–10, 149, 182–5, 190, 197, 201, 205, 230, 251–3, 257, 260, 262–3, 304–5, 419, 430, 538, 541, 547, 552
tradition 27–32, 34–9, 109–11, 120–1, 204–5, 207, 211–14, 342, 401, 477, 541
Troeltsch, Ernst 231
Trump, Donald 127–8, 143–4, 146, 434
Tshaka, Rothney 481, 484–6
Tucker, Mary Evelyn 437
Turner, Denys 276
Tutu, Desmond 233
Twietmeyer, Gregg 451
two-kingdoms doctrine 211

Unger, Abraham 235
Urbaniak, Jakub 485

Valentin, Benjamin 542–4
Vallem, Vuyani 284–6, 481
Vermeule, Adrian 43, 44
Verstraeten, Johan 163
Villiers, Etienne de 481
Voegelin, Eric 49

Walker Grimes, Katie 317
Ward, Graham 277–8, 280, 307–10, 317, 478

Ware, Kallistos   172
Warner, Michael   78
Watson, Nick J.   451
Weber, Max   27, 59, 476, 478
Wei, Francis C. M.   224
Wei, Paul (Wei Enbo)   499
Weil, Simone   377
Weiming, Tu   501
Welby, Justin   316
West, Cornel   543
West, Thomas G.   36
White, Lynn   435
whiteness   305–7, 390
Wickremesinghe, Lakshman   233
Wilfred, Felix   232–3, 490
Williams, Delores   290–2, 297–8, 548
Williams, Raymond   401
Williams, Rowan   59, 276, 324–5
Wilson, Woodrow   38, 498
Windrush Scandal   315–16
Winter, Gibson   254–5
Wolterstorff, Nicholas   360
Wong, Angela Wai-Ching   491
Wood, Richard L.   228–30
Woodhead, Linda   371
Worch, Sabrina   233
World Council of Churches   78, 208–9, 432, 440, 445
Wyngaard, Cobus van   306–8, 310, 319

Yi, Weng   497–8
Yong-bock, Kim   492, 499
Youn, Chul Ho   416

Zizioulas, John   173–5
Zurara, Gomes Eanes de   389

www.ingramcontent.com/pod-product-compliance
Lightning Source LLC
Chambersburg PA
CBHW080932300426
44115CB00017B/2788